Target C#

Simple Hands-On Programming with Visual Studio 2022

Gerard Byrne

Apress®

Target C#: Simple Hands-On Programming with Visual Studio 2022

Gerard Byrne
Belfast, Ireland

ISBN-13 (pbk): 978-1-4842-8618-0   ISBN-13 (electronic): 978-1-4842-8619-7
https://doi.org/10.1007/978-1-4842-8619-7

Managing Director, Apress Media LLC: Welmoed Spahr
Acquisitions Editor: Joan Murray
Development Editor: Laura Berendson
Coordinating Editor: Jill Balzano

Cover designed by eStudioCalamar

Cover image designed by Freepik (www.freepik.com)

Distributed to the book trade worldwide by Springer Science+Business Media New York, 1 New York Plaza, Suite 4600, New York, NY 10004-1562, USA. Phone 1-800-SPRINGER, fax (201) 348-4505, e-mail orders-ny@springer-sbm.com, or visit www.springeronline.com. Apress Media, LLC is a California LLC and the sole member (owner) is Springer Science + Business Media Finance Inc (SSBM Finance Inc). SSBM Finance Inc is a **Delaware** corporation.

For information on translations, please e-mail booktranslations@springernature.com; for reprint, paperback, or audio rights, please e-mail bookpermissions@springernature.com.

Apress titles may be purchased in bulk for academic, corporate, or promotional use. eBook versions and licenses are also available for most titles. For more information, reference our Print and eBook Bulk Sales web page at http://www.apress.com/bulk-sales.

Any source code or other supplementary material referenced by the author in this book is available to readers on GitHub (https://github.com/Apress). For more detailed information, please visit http://www.apress.com/source-code.

Printed on acid-free paper

My book is dedicated to Maura, Ryan, and Peter.

Table of Contents

About the Author ....**xv**

Acknowledgments ....**xvii**

Introduction ....**xix**

Chapter 1: .NET 1
    .NET: What Is It? 1
    .NET Core: What Is It?.. 2
    C# Language Versioning... 3
    .NET and C# Compilation Process... 5
    Compile Time and Runtime 6
    Framework and Library.. 7
        Library 7
        Framework 8
    Managed and Unmanaged Code 10
    Chapter Summary 10

Chapter 2: Software Installation.. 13
    About the .NET Framework 13
        Installing the .NET Framework 14
        Installing Visual Studio 21
    Chapter Summary 25

Chapter 3: Introduction... 27
    Computer Program... 27
        Programming Languages 28
        A Computer Program: A Recipe 29

Type in C#..32

The Basic Operations of a Computer 37

C# Program Application Formats 37

Format 1: Console Application 37

Format 2: .NET MAUI...39

Format 3: ASP.NET Web Applications 40

The Structure of a C# Program 40

Namespaces...46

Classes 47

Chapter Summary 50

Chapter 4: Input and Output **53**

Write to and Read from the Console 53

Change Console Display Settings 69

Chapter Summary 75

Chapter 5: Commenting Code **77**

C# Single-Line Comments...79

New .NET 6 Templates 84

C# Multiple-Line Comments..89

Chapter Summary 91

Chapter 6: Data Types..**93**

Data Types, Variables, and Conversion..93

Data Types 93

Conversion from One Data Type to Another 96

C# 8 Nullable Reference Types 126

Chapter Summary 140

Chapter 7: Casting and Parsing **143**

Data Types, Casting, and Parsing 143

Chapter Summary 157

Chapter 8: Arithmetic **159**

   Arithmetic Operations 159

      Common Arithmetic Operators 161

      Integer Division 162

      Solution Explorer and Project Analysis 166

   Chapter Summary 192

Chapter 9: Selection **195**

   Arithmetic Operations 195

      Selection 195

      Comparison Operators 196

      The switch Construct 217

      The switch Construct Using when 225

      switch with Strings 231

      switch with Strings 239

      Logical Operators 247

      Using the AND Operator 249

      Using the OR Operator 255

      Using the NOT Operator 260

      Conditional Operator (Ternary Operator) 264

      Nested Ternary Conditional Operator 268

   Chapter Summary 273

Chapter 10: Iteration **275**

   Iteration and Loops 275

      Introduction to Iteration 275

      For Loop 276

      While Loop 298

      Do (While) Loop 313

   Chapter Summary 327

Chapter 11: Arrays 329

Arrays: A Data Structure 329

    Single-Dimensional Arrays 332

    foreach Loop 348

    Ranges and Indices: C# 8 and Above 362

Chapter Summary 372

Chapter 12: Methods 375

Methods: Modularization 375

    Methods: Concepts of Methods and Functions 375

    Some Points Regarding Methods 377

    Three Types of Methods 381

    Void Methods 382

    Value Methods 397

    Parameter Methods 407

    Method Overloading 425

    C# 7 Local Function 429

    C# 8 Static Local Function 434

    C# 10 Null Parameter Checking 437

    C# 10 Null Parameter Checking Approach 441

Chapter Summary 443

Chapter 13: Classes 447

Classes and Objects in OOP 447

    A Class Is a Data Structure 448

    Constructor 490

    Additional Example for Classes and Objects 503

Chapter Summary 521

Chapter 14: Interfaces 523

Interfaces and Abstract Classes 523

    The Interface or Abstract Class as a Manager 525

    Instantiate the Abstract Class? 533

Static Members of the Abstract Class 539

Concept of an Interface 552

Implementing Multiple Interfaces... 562

Concept of Default Method in an Interface.. 582

Concept of Static Methods and Fields in an Interface... 590

Chapter Summary 592

Chapter 15: String Handling 595

String Handling and Manipulation.. 595

String Literals 597

Substring 601

Length 604

StartsWith() 605

Split()... 607

CompareTo()... 611

ToUpper() and ToLower().. 615

Concat().. 616

Trim()... 617

Replace()... 619

Contains()... 621

IndexOf()... 622

Insert()... 624

String.Format()... 627

What About $@ or @$? 637

Chapter Summary 644

Chapter 16: File Handling 647

File Handling 647

An Overview of File Handling 648

File Class 649

Writing to a File 658

Reading from a File 665

Copy a File.. 671

Delete a File...674

StreamReader Class...677

StreamWriter Class..679

Reading from a Stream 680

Writing to a Stream 682

Async Methods and Asynchronous Programming 685

FileStream...687

Chapter Summary 691

Chapter 17: Exception Handling 693

Exceptions..693

What Is an Exception? 693

try 696

catch..697

finally...699

throw 699

Multiple Exceptions 704

FileNotFoundException..707

finally...710

StackTrace...713

throw 714

rethrow 716

Chapter Summary 725

Chapter 18: Serialization 727

Serialization and Deserialization..727

Deserialization..728

Attribute [NonSerialized] 728

Serializing the Object 738

Deserializing the Serialized File to a Class..743

Access Modifier [NonSerialized]..749

Serialization Using XML.. 751

Serialization Using JSON 762

Chapter Summary 770

Chapter 19: Structs.. **773**

Concept of a Struct as a Structure Type.. 773

Difference Between Struct and Class 774

Struct with a Default Constructor Only... 776

Struct with a User Constructor 779

Struct Instantiation Without the New Keyword... 780

Struct Instantiation with the New Keyword 781

Creating a Constructor... 783

Creating Member Properties (Get and Set Accessors).................................. 784

Encapsulation 788

Readonly Struct 788

Creating a Readonly Struct.. 789

C# 8 readonly Members 793

C# 8 Nullable Reference Types 797

Chapter Summary 802

Chapter 20: Enumerations **803**

Concept of Enumerations.. 803

Defining an Enumeration 804

Enumerated Values: Use and Scope 806

Enumeration Methods 809

Using the foreach Iteration 811

Enumeration Values: GetValues() 814

Assigning Our Own Values to the Enumeration 815

Use the GetName() and GetValues() Methods... 817

Sample Application Using Enumerations.. 818

Chapter Summary 830

Chapter 21: Delegates 831

Concept of Delegates 831

Single Delegate 835

Multicast Delegates 838

More Complex Example 842

Chapter Summary 852

Chapter 22: Events 853

Concept of Events 853

Publisher and Subscriber 853

Declare an Event 856

Raise an Event 857

Handle an Event 857

Add a Method to an Event Using += 864

Refer the Event to a Second Method Using += 865

Refer the Event to a Third Method Using += 867

Remove a Method from an Event Using -= 869

Chapter Summary 870

Chapter 23: Generics 873

Concept of Generics 873

Generic Class, Generic Method, Generic Parameters 877

Generic Class, Generic Method, Mixed Parameter Types 883

Generic Method Only 885

Chapter Summary 891

Chapter 24: Common Routines 893

Common Programming Routines with C# 893

Linear Search 893

Binary Search (Iterative Binary Search) 900

Bubble Sort 908

Insertion Sort 914

Chapter Summary 922

Chapter 25: Programming Labs 923

C# Practice Exercises 923

Chapter 4 Labs: WriteLine() 924

Chapter 6 Labs: Data Types 928

Chapter 7 Labs: Data Conversion and Arithmetic 936

Chapter 8 Labs: Arithmetic 940

Chapter 9 Labs: Selection 942

Chapter 10 Labs: Iteration 947

Chapter 11 Labs: Arrays 953

Chapter 12 Labs: Methods 959

Chapter 13 Labs: Classes 966

Chapter 14 Labs: Interfaces 974

Chapter 15 Labs: String Handling 977

Chapter 16 Labs: File Handling 982

Chapter 17 Labs: Exceptions 986

Chapter 18 Labs: Serialization of a Class 989

Chapter 19 Labs: Structs 996

Chapter 20 Labs: Enumerations 1002

Chapter 21 Labs: Delegates 1011

Chapter 22 Labs: Events 1017

Chapter 23 Labs: Generics 1026

Chapter Summary 1031

Chapter 26: C# 11 1033

C# New Features 1033

Raw String Literals 1034

New Lines in String Interpolations 1042

List Patterns 1044

Auto Default Struct 1050

Warning Wave 7 1055

Chapter Summary 1057

Index 1059

Chapter 26: Programming Labs 923

06 Practice Exercises 923

Chapter 5 Labs: Data Types 928

Chapter 7 Labs: Data Conversion and Arithmetic 930

Chapter 8 Labs: Modules 940

Chapter 9 Labs: Selection 942

Chapter 10 Labs: Iteration 947

Chapter 11 Labs: Arrays 952

Chapter 12 Labs: Methods 964

Chapter 13 Labs: Classes 969

Chapter 14 Labs: Interfaces 972

Chapter 15 Labs: Error Handling 977

Chapter 16 Labs: File Reading 982

Chapter 17 Labs: Exceptions 986

Chapter 18 Labs: Serialization of a Class 991

Chapter 19 Labs: Structs 996

Chapter 20 Labs: Enumerations 1002

Chapter 21 Labs: Delegates 1011

Chapter 22 Labs: Events 1017

Chapter 23 Labs: Generics 1020

Chapter Summary 1021

Chapter 26: C# 11 1023

C# New Features 1023

Raw String Literals 1024

New Lines in String Interpolations 1042

List Patterns 1044

Auto-Default Struct 1050

Warning Wave 7 1055

Chapter Summary 1057

Index 1059

About the Author

Gerard Byrne is a senior technical trainer for a US-based Forbes 100 company. He works to upskill and reskill software engineers who develop business-critical software applications. He also helps refine the programming skills of "returners" to the workforce and introduces new graduates to the application of software development within the commercial environment.

Gerard's subject expertise has been developed over a multidecade career as a teacher, lecturer, and technical trainer in a corporate technology environment. He has delivered a range of courses across computer languages and frameworks and understands how to teach skills and impart knowledge to a range of learners. He has taught people in the use of legacy technologies such as COBOL and JCL and more "modern" technologies and frameworks such as C#, Java, Spring, Android, JavaScript, Node, HTML, CSS, Bootstrap, React, Python, and Test-Driven Development (TDD).

Gerard has mastered how to teach difficult concepts in a simple way that makes learning accessible and enjoyable. The content of his notes, labs, and other materials follows the simple philosophy of keeping it simple while making the instructions detailed. He is passionate about software development and believes we can all learn to write code if we are patient and understand the basic coding concepts.

Acknowledgments

Writing a book is a rewarding undertaking, but it requires time, effort, and patience, patience from those around you in your life.

So I have to start by thanking my wife, Maura, and my sons, Ryan and Peter, for "facilitating" me as I worked over many hours, days, weeks, and months to write this programming book.

I also wish to thank my great friend David from whom I have learned so much and with whom I have had the pleasure of delivering many enjoyable programming courses. If I need coding inspiration and humor, I always know to talk to David.

Finally, I want to say thank you to Joan Murray from Apress for helping me get the book proposal approved and to the whole Apress team who have worked with me and worked behind the scenes to get the book published. I am grateful for your help and fully understand that this book has so much of your effort within it.

Introduction

The chapters in this book will cover coding in C# using the Visual Studio Integrated Development Environment (IDE) from Microsoft. Other Integrated Development Environments exist, such as Visual Studio Code, and the code from the applications in the chapters will work within any Integrated Development Environment capable of running C# code. While the step-by-step instructions and screenshots in the book are based around the Visual Studio Integrated Development Environment, they can still be used by those preferring a different Integrated Development Environment.

The first two chapters of the book introduce us to the .NET framework, the Visual Studio Integrated Development Environment, and how to complete the required software installation. With the necessary tools installed, we are then introduced to what a computer program is, before we start to write our own computer programs. We then begin to cover the core concepts needed when developing C# code and which can be applied to other programming languages. We cover a wide range of core programming concepts, including data types, selection, iteration, arrays, methods, classes and objects, serialization, file handling, string handling, and exception handling. Studying these chapters is more than enough to allow us to develop applications that emulate commercial application code.

All examples in the chapters are fully commented to ensure we can understand the code and to enhance our knowledge of the C# programming language. Reading the comments within the code examples is essential; they are an integral part of the book and will enhance our understanding of C# and will help explain why the code does something or what the code is doing.

After we have completed the core chapters, Chapters 1–13, we continue our C# journey by looking at more advanced topics starting with interfaces and abstract classes, which are essential concepts for all developers. In later chapters we work with classes and "lightweight" classes such as structs. We also look at more complex concepts when we study delegates in Chapter 21, and this leads us naturally into Chapter 22 on events and Chapter 23 on generics. We also study chapters involving the common concepts of string handling and file handling where we see the importance of exception handling, which we also study in Chapter 17. Having gained lots of coding experience and having read and applied the core and advanced C# concepts, we look at common programming routines and use C# to code them. The routines include linear search, binary search, bubble sort, and insertion sort.

The book then completes with labs, additional exercises, for the majority of the programming chapters we have covered. Each exercise in a lab is supported with a working solution just in case we have difficulty completing any of the lab exercises.

The book is ideal for beginners, those refreshing their C# skills, or those moving from another programming language. It is ideally suited for students studying programming at high school or at university and is an excellent resource for teachers who deliver programming lessons. The book offers detailed explanations and the code has excellent comments to support learning. By using clean code with proper naming, the code is intuitive to read and understand.

Reading the book is one thing, but actually coding the examples using an Integrated Development Environment is the most important thing if we wish to get the best understanding of the C# language. Hands-on experience while reading this book is the key to success.

We should think about two things before we begin our programming journey through this book:

"Life begins at the edge of our comfort zone" and
"Think about now, and believe."

Often the thought of getting started can make us "frightened" and "uncomfortable." We need to believe in ourselves and understand that while there will be "lows" during the learning, we will survive them and move to the inevitable "highs."

Programming can be rewarding and thankfully it is within our ability to write code. The chapters in this book will help us to learn about coding, teach us how to code, and make us realize that it is indeed realistic for us to program in the C# language.

As we start learning C#, it is important to realize that the target of being able to write computer applications in C# will seem large as there is a lot to learn, but we should take comfort in the fact that as we complete each chapter and gain experience in writing our applications, the target gets closer and the amount of learning gets smaller. In essence, as we move along our learning pathway, we gain competence in concepts that will be continually used in our application code.

CHAPTER 1

.NET

.NET: What Is It?

First, let us say that C# is a programming language, while .NET is the runtime that C# and other languages are built on. They are very different things, and when we program in C#, we need to be aware that we will intrinsically be using .NET. The version of .NET will be whatever version we download when we wish to start programming in C#. What .NET gives us as developers are libraries of code that save us from having to write our own code to perform particular tasks. For now, just think of a library as something where there are methods, small blocks of code, that perform a particular process.

A simple example would be a method in the library that allows us as developers to display text to a console window. This could be the `WriteLine()` method, and it is located in the `Console` class, which belongs inside a namespace called `System`. Our line of code could be

```
System.Console.WriteLine("------- Learn To Code With C# ------");
```

Or later as we become more familiar with the code, we will probably want to code it like this:

```
Console.WriteLine("------- Learn To Code With C# -------");
```

Either way, for now, we simply want to understand that if we add the text to be displayed between the open and close brackets () of the WriteLine() method, it will be displayed to the console. We do not have to write the code that makes it display in the console; we just accept that the C# language and .NET handle all this for us. So let us just think of .NET as giving us code in the form of methods that will save us lots of time when developing an application. Also, we should think **method** when we see the open and

1

© Gerard Byrne 2022
G. Byrne, *Target C#*, https://doi.org/10.1007/978-1-4842-8619-7_1

close brackets **()**. Other examples of methods that we will become very familiar with are Write() and ReadLine(), but there are many built-in methods from the libraries that we will use.

We should also be aware that we can program in languages other than C#, like F# and Visual Basic (VB), but .NET is underpinning all of the programming languages supported by it. The libraries in .NET are shared between all the languages, thereby avoiding duplication of libraries and their contained methods. This makes sense as "on the surface" the WriteLine() method for displaying to the console should be the same no matter what .NET-supported language we program in. We do not need to concern ourselves that the different languages "under the hood" use different compilers.

As well as supplying developers with invaluable functionality through its methods and constructs, .NET includes a **runtime environment** for applications. This runtime environment is called the Common Language Runtime (CLR), and it is the "engine" that produces the magic to allow us as developers to write code in any of the .NET-supported languages, and it will run on any device that has .NET installed. It is a "**virtual machine**" that lets .NET exist on a device and then it can manage .NET applications running within.

Finally, think of .NET this way: it is the environment and C# lives within it, as do other languages. Yes, it is like us: the earth is the environment, and we live within it alongside others. The environment supplies us with many useful facilities like sunshine, air, and rain, and we use these in our life as we wish to do. Our environment offers us many facilities, some we use and some we don't use. Well, the same goes when we program in C# and use .NET; we will use some of the facilities, and we will not use others.

.NET Core: What Is It?

We have just read about .NET being the runtime that C# and other languages are built on, but there is a history to .NET that can confuse us, so we will look at this history in order to help us better understand how we have reached the stage where we now just say .NET, as we have done in the preceding introductory paragraphs.

The evolution and progression of .NET implementations and their names has led to confusion around the .NET topic. The history has been as follows:

- **.NET Framework** was launched as .NET Framework 1 in 2002 and went on to have versions up to the last version of .NET Framework 4.8. It allowed only for the development of Windows applications.

- **.NET Core** was introduced in 2016 in an attempt to include cross-platform support, for example, for Linux and MacOS. .NET Core went from version 1 to the last version, 3.

- **.NET** was introduced as .NET 5 in 2020 with Microsoft dropping the name Core and naming it with 5 rather than 4, in an attempt to differentiate from the .NET Framework, which was version 4. .NET 6 then followed in 2021 and in 2022 .NET 7.

So we can see that .NET Core aimed, for the first time, to give developers the facilities to develop for non-Windows devices such as mobile phones and Linux and Mac operating systems, using a standard set of libraries, which we mentioned earlier as being methods that give us functionality without having to write the code. It was not created to allow for development of desktop applications.

.NET Core was aimed at making .NET more modern, faster, and more scalable, and we could say that the philosophy behind it was to allow developers to build code once and that would run on any platform. Nowadays, we will hear a lot of talk about micro-services, small units of code living independently in the ecosystem, but able to communicate with each other when required, and .NET Core offers developers the opportunity to build micro-services.

We can therefore see that Microsoft started by offering us the .NET Framework, which ran only on Windows, and then evolved to offering us .NET Core, which allowed for cross-platform development. And now we have .NET, which runs on any platform and is the future with new releases every November. .NET is therefore a replacement for the other two.

As we are interested in developing our C# programming skills, we do not need to concern ourselves with the underlying runtime.

C# Language Versioning

There are many versions of the C# programming language, and this can cause confusion when we wish to write code and are required to choose a language level. To make the situation more confusing, there are many versions of .NET, which the C# language must work with. To help us and take the "pain" out of making the C# language version choice, the C# compiler will make the decision as to which version of C# to use, based on the .NET version we have chosen to develop our application in. This is a feature aimed at ensuring that we, as developers, are using the latest C# version for the chosen .NET version. When we use the Visual Studio Integrated Development Environment, it will use the .NET version installed on our computers, and, consequently, we will be availing of the latest version of the C# language that can be used with this .NET version. By using the highest C# version, we get the latest language features, but we still have the choice to use a different version if this is required. Caution is required when manually choosing the language level as we may be trying to use language features not supported by the selected .NET version.

By looking on the Microsoft site docs.microsoft.com, we will get the latest information about versions of the .NET framework and the C# language. We can also download versions of .NET from the Microsoft site dotnet.microsoft.com. So information from the site and relevant to our discussion and learning is as follows:

- C# 10 is only supported on .NET 6 and newer versions.

- C# 9 is only supported on .NET 5 and newer versions.

- C# 8 is only supported on .NET Core version 3.x and newer versions.

- C# 7.3 is the latest supported version for the .NET Framework.

Once we start to write our code in the Visual Studio Integrated Development Environment, we will create a C# project, which will generate a .csproj file, and it is within this file that we are able to set the language level. Visual Studio does not supply us with a user interface (UI) to make changes to the .csproj file, but we can select the file and edit its contents to ensure that the language version is set. An example of the code contained in the .csproj is shown in Listing 1-1.

Listing 1-1. Language level within the .csproj file

```
<PropertyGroup>
    <LangVersion>10</LangVersion>
</PropertyGroup>
```

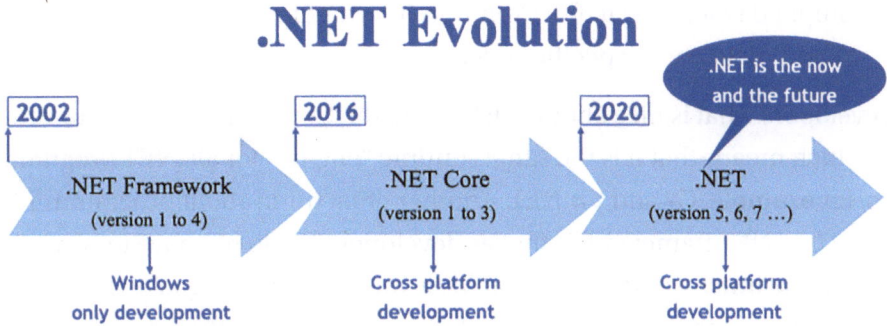

Figure 1-1. *.NET evolution – .NET Framework to .NET Core to .NET*

.NET and C# Compilation Process

Part of the .NET framework is based on giving developers the tools they require to convert their C# code into a format that can be understood by the operating system that will run the application. As developers we follow a process to make the code we have written in our chosen .NET programming language into machine-readable code. Here are the steps of the compile process:

- Write the code in C# or another .NET programming language.

- **Compile** the code using the compiler, which checks the code for errors such as in syntax. We can then make the required changes.

- The compiler produces **Common Intermediate Language (CIL)** files and these files for C# would be similar if we had written our code in another .NET programming language. That is the "beauty" of .NET – write in any language and it will compile to the same thing.

- The **Common Language Runtime** (CLR) takes control of the process, and we previously read that the Common Language Runtime is

  the "engine" that produces the magic to allow us as developers to write code in any of the .NET-supported languages, and it will run on any device that has .NET installed.

- Once the intermediate language has been generated, the Common Language Runtime process uses the **Just-In-Time (JIT) compiler** to create the code that the specific operating system running the application requires. This means our development code has been

compiled twice, first to the Common Intermediate Language and
second to machine-specific code.

For developers what is nice about .NET is that the Common Language Runtime is
common, which means that it is the same runtime "engine" for all .NET programming
languages, for example, C# and VB.NET. Another great thing about programming in
C# and using the .NET framework is that as developers we do not have to concern
ourselves with the inner workings of compiling, intermediate language, Just-In-Time
compiling, and machine code. It is all handled for us. We write the C# code and get it free
of compilation errors, and .NET takes over. We do not even have to concern ourselves
about different hardware and processors. As long as the .NET framework is available on
the device running the application, everything is handled. Figure 1-2 offers a way to look
at the compile process.

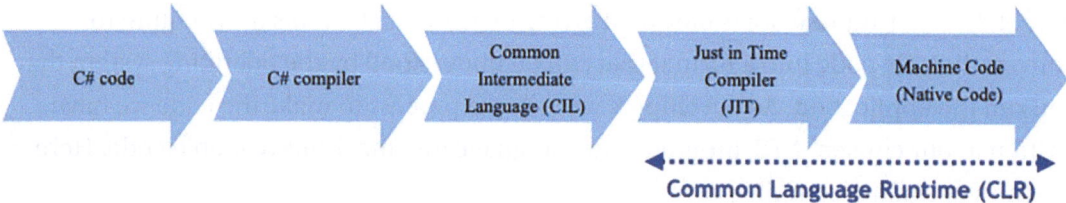

Figure 1-2. *The compile process*

Compile Time and Runtime

As we learn about programming, we hear the terms *compile time* and *runtime*, so it
is important to understand the difference and their role in the development process.
Figure 1-3 offers a way to look at which parts of the development process are compile
time and which are runtime.

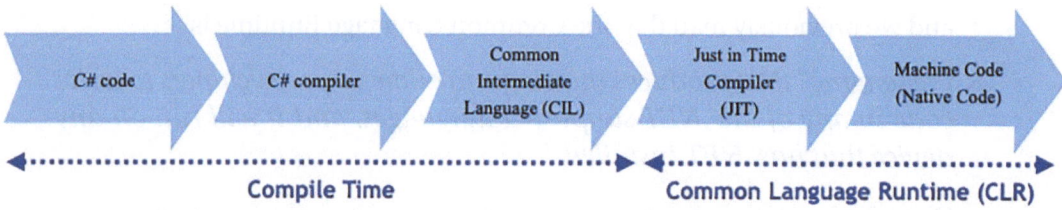

Figure 1-3. *Compile time and runtime*

When we choose to compile our code, the compiler takes the code and does some processing. Often the compile process finds errors in the code, for example, typographical errors, and we will be prompted to make changes to fix these **compilation errors**. So we are at compile time when we have written some code, and we choose to compile it in one of several different ways, for example, choosing Run from a menu, pressing a specified function key like F5, or typing a command at the command line. At compile time our code is still C#, but when the compiler finishes its processing, it will produce files in the form of an executable file, an .exe, or a dynamic link library, a .dll. These files are still not capable of being understood by the computer the code is to run on as the computer processor only understands machine code.

Now the second stage of the process is where we meet the runtime. When we want the application to run on a computer, this is the runtime, and it is the Common Language Runtime that handles this phase. At runtime the .exe or .dll files are converted to machine code capable of being read by the specific computer processor that the application is being run on. The conversion to machine code at runtime is handled by a specific part of the Common Language Runtime called the Just-In-Time compiler. Even though the compilation errors have been fixed and the code compiles, there is no guarantee that the code will run. If the code does not run at runtime, there will be **runtime errors,** and these are much more serious than compilation errors and present themselves where the end user can see them. This will not be a "happy" experience for the end user and should never happen, but things like this do happen. It is a rather unfortunate part of software development. A runtime error could occur because a file is not found or the memory is fully allocated, and often the consequence of a runtime error is the termination of the application.

Framework and Library

While learning to program, we will hear the terms *framework* and *library* being used widely, but it is easy to get confused about what each does and why they are different.

Library

At the start of this chapter, we read the following:

> *For now, just think of a library as something where there are methods, small blocks of code, that perform a particular process.*

This is a simple explanation, but we can go further and say that it is a collection of routines, blocks of code, that can be reused and have been thoroughly tried and tested. FinMath is a numerical library for the .NET platform that offers developers classes and methods for mathematical, scientific, and financial applications. As developers we use the libraries by calling the methods of the library whenever we require them in our code. We control the use of the libraries, and we should make use of libraries rather than writing our own code to perform the same functionality as library functions. All this fits in with the important concept of **reusing** software functionality when we can.

Think of a library in the context of building our own motor vehicle. We will choose the type of engine, the body shape, the number of seats, the wheel types, the color we will spray on the bodywork, etc. We are in control of what to include and what to leave out.

Framework

At the start of this chapter, we read the following:

> *So let us just think of .NET as giving us code in the form of methods that will save us lots of time when developing an application.*

This is also a simple explanation, but we can be more accurate by saying that the framework controls the calling of libraries rather than us as developers calling the libraries. Think of a framework like buying a limited-edition motor vehicle where have no choice in terms of the configuration. The vehicle is designed and built so we cannot customize it and we cannot pick the type of engine, the body shape, the number of seats, the wheel types, the color of the bodywork, etc. We are not in control of what to include. The special edition is a "constant," and all the vehicles are identical.

Throughout our lifetime as developers, we will use many frameworks and libraries, and they both help us through their tested and reusable code. The essential difference is that as developers we call the code from the library, but the frameworks will call our code, as in Figure 1-4. Put in technical speak, we say it is all about **inversion of control**.

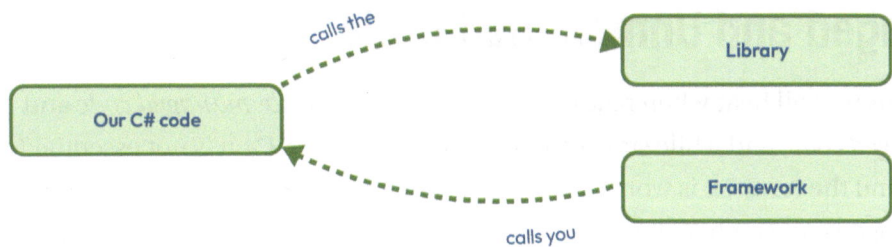

Figure 1-4. *Framework vs. library*

In terms of real-world business, we can see that there are many food franchise companies and they offer people the opportunity to invest their own money and become a franchisee. As a franchisee you follow the framework set up by the franchise company. You use their logo, their paper cups, their coffee, their burgers, or whatever. A franchisee cannot pick and choose and say, "I'll use the paper cups, but I want to sell different coffee or different burgers or use different fillings." The franchise company is like our coding framework, as shown in Figure 1-5.

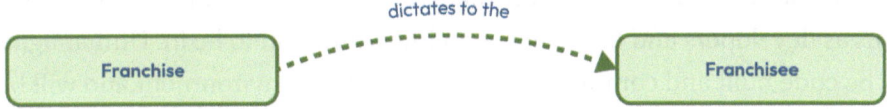

Figure 1-5. *Framework in business*

On the other hand, a public house might be "tied" to a particular beer company and as such they can only sell the beer from that company. However, they can sell what soft drinks they want, whatever food they like, etc. This is like a library in that the public house owner has selected this beer company but can use other non-libraries for their soft drinks, meaning that they could choose a different supplier every day or choose a different soft drink every day, as shown in Figure 1-6.

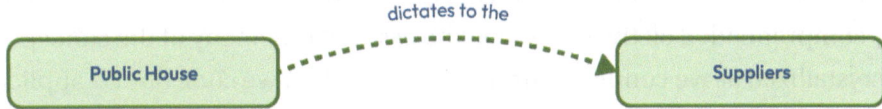

Figure 1-6. *Library in business*

Managed and Unmanaged Code

Two terms we will hear when reading about C# and .NET are *managed code* and *unmanaged code*, and while starting to learn to program in C# it is not essential to fully understand the terms, it is worth having at a conceptual overview.

Managed code is code that is managed by the Common Language Runtime, which we read about earlier where we stated that

> *At runtime the .exe or .dll files are converted to machine code capable of being read by the specific computer processor that the application is being run on.*

The Common Language Runtime also takes care of wider issues such as memory allocation and garbage collection. Therefore, we do not need to concern ourselves with these things; we just concentrate on coding the C#.

Unmanaged code is code that must be managed by us as developers. We take over the role of the Common Language Runtime, and we need to manage the wider issues such as memory allocation and garbage collection. This adds many additional tasks for us as developers and this is never an ideal situation to be in. Unmanaged code will be code built and compiled outside of the .NET environment and will be in machine-readable form, unlike managed code which will be in intermediate language. Unmanaged code is therefore read directly by the hardware operating system it is running on. The preference will always be that we are using managed code, and that is what we get when using C# and the .NET framework.

Chapter Summary

In this chapter we have learned so much about the .NET framework, but it has been theoretical. However, it is theory we need to know before we start coding. We may not have fully comprehended all the theory, but be assured that many of the concepts will become crystallized as we continue our reading and when we code our C# applications.

There should be many key takeaways from this chapter, but we should clearly understand that C# is a programming language, while .NET is the framework that the C# and other languages are built on. We should also understand the difference between compile time and runtime. We learned that after compiling, our code files in the form of an executable file, an .exe, or a dynamic link library, a .dll, are produced. At runtime the .exe or .dll files are converted to machine code capable of being read by the specific computer processor that the application is being run on. Very importantly, we also learned that a library is a collection of routines, blocks of code, that have been compiled, can be reused, and have been thoroughly tried and tested. And we will use them in coding our applications.

We have started reading this book with the aim of increasing our knowledge and understanding of C#. We are at the start of the learning journey and the final target can be thought of as being at the center of a set of concentric circles. As we progress through the chapters of this book, our knowledge, understanding, and ability to program in C# will gradually increase, while the amount we have to learn will decrease. The outer circles of the concentric circles will disappear as we move closer to the circle at the center, our target. Having completed this chapter, we are at the outer circle, but we are moving closer to our target.

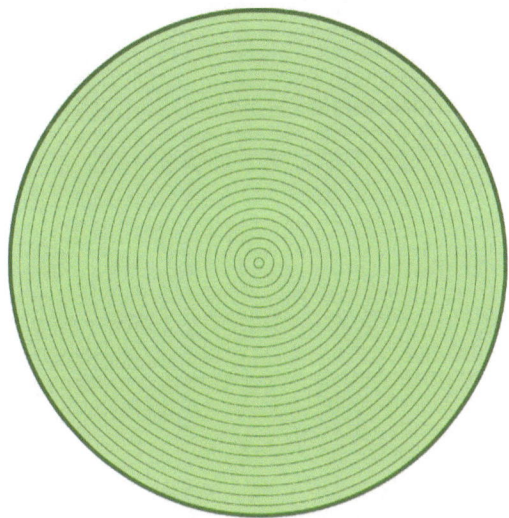

Our target is getting closer

CHAPTER 2

Software Installation

About the .NET Framework

Before we can write C# code, we will need to have the .NET framework installed on our computer. The .NET framework comes in two formats:

1. The Software Development Kit (SDK)

   The Software Development Kit is required when we wish to create .NET applications, and this is exactly what we will be doing as we complete the chapters in the book. Therefore, we will need to download the Software Development Kit to our computer.

2. .NET runtime

   The .NET runtime is used when we wish to run a .NET application. As we develop C# applications, we will use the Software Development Kit, but within it there will be the .NET runtime, so we can develop and run our applications using just the Software Development Kit. However, an end user of our application only needs the .NET runtime to run the application. If our application was to be run on a television, then the television would need to have the .NET runtime installed on it, or the developer would need to have included the .NET runtime with

© Gerard Byrne 2022
G. Byrne, *Target C#*, https://doi.org/10.1007/978-1-4842-8619-7_2

the application. Three different versions of the .NET runtime exist
as indicated in this list:

- .NET runtime, which is the most basic runtime but will be suffice
  for most .NET applications

- Desktop runtime, which also includes the basic .NET runtime

- ASP.NET Core runtime, which also includes the basic
  .NET runtime

As we will be installing the Software Development Kit, we do not need to worry
about the .NET runtime installation, as all three of the preceding .NET runtimes are
installed for us.

Installing the .NET Framework

The .NET framework installation can be performed using the Microsoft installer for
Windows, MacOS, or Linux. The process is very similar no matter what operating system
is being used.

1. Go to the Microsoft download page:

   https://dotnet.microsoft.com/en-us/download/dotnet

2. Click the .NET framework to be downloaded. We will be using
   .NET 6.0, but from Figure 2-1 we can see that there is a preview
   version of .NET 7.0. We can also see that .NET 6.0 is the latest
   version. The latest version will change over time so it will be
   acceptable to download whatever the latest version is and the
   code within this book should still run.

∧ Supported versions

Version	Release type	Support phase	Latest release	Latest release date	End of support
.NET 7.0	Preview ⓘ		7.0.0-preview.6	July 12, 2022	
.NET 6.0 (latest) ←	LTS ⓘ	Full ⓘ	6.0.7	July 12, 2022	November 12, 2024
.NET Core 3.1	LTS ⓘ	Maintenance ⓘ	3.1.27	July 12, 2022	December 13, 2022

Figure 2-1. .NET version on the Microsoft site

Figure 2-1 has two terms with rectangles around them and two terms circled. It will be useful for us to understand the terms and their importance when developing C# applications. When we look at the Microsoft website .NET and .NET Core official support policy (microsoft.com), we see that they say the following:

We'll publish new major releases of .NET every year in November, enabling developers, the community, and businesses to plan their roadmaps. Even numbered releases are LTS releases that get free support and patches for three years.

- Long Term Support (LTS)

  When we see that a .NET version, release, is annotated with LTS (Long Term Support), we are being told by Microsoft that the version will be supported by them for 3 years after its initial release. We can see from Figure 2-1 that .NET version 6.0 will be supported until November 12, 2024, and we could easily determine that .NET version 6.0 was released in November 2021.

  .NET version 7 according to Microsoft will be released in November 2022 with LTS to November 2025.)

- Preview

  When we see a .NET version annotated with Preview, we should, before we download and install, understand that such releases are typically not supported, but they are offered for public testing ahead of the final release. Once the preview goes live, the status changes and we can feel "safe" to download and install it.

  There is also a term called *Current* and this release or version will be supported for 6 months after a subsequent Current or Long Term Support release.

Current releases are supported for 6 months after a subsequent Current or LTS release. As stated, earlier releases happen every 12 months so the support period for Current will be 18 months.

- Full

  Full means full support, and during the support period, .NET will be updated to improve the functional capabilities and mitigate security vulnerabilities.

- Maintenance

  Maintenance means maintenance support, and during the support period, .NET will only be updated to mitigate security vulnerabilities. According to Microsoft the maintenance support period is the final 6 months of support for any release, Current or LTS. After the maintenance period ends, the release is out of support.

So, when we are choosing a download, it would seem appropriate to download the one annotated as latest and with Long Term Support.

Software Development Kit Version

The version of the Software Development Kit (SDK) to be downloaded will be dependent on the computer it is being installed on, for example, Windows, MacOS, or Linux. In our case it will be for a Windows platform as the chapters in the book use the instructions and screenshots from a Windows installation, but, if you choose to use a different installation, the instructions and screenshots will be very similar and little – if any – changes will be required. The Windows version, like the MacOS and Linux versions, has different architecture options, and by selecting the architecture, we are specifying the device we wish to use with the SDK. The types of architecture are

x86

This represents a 32-bit CPU and operating system.

x64

This refers to a 64-bit CPU and operating system.

ARM and ARM64

Traditionally we would have had the x86 32-bit CPU, then we had the x64 64-bit CPU, and now we have the ARM and ARM64, which are used on a range of devices such as mobile devices and even Internet of Things (IoT) devices.

ARM and x86 are for 32-bit processors, whereas ARM64 and x64 are for 64-bit processors.

Usually for Windows computers, it will be the x64 version, as shown in Figure 2-2, but we should click the required version for our hardware to start the download.

3. Click the version of the Software Development Kit required to start
    the download process.

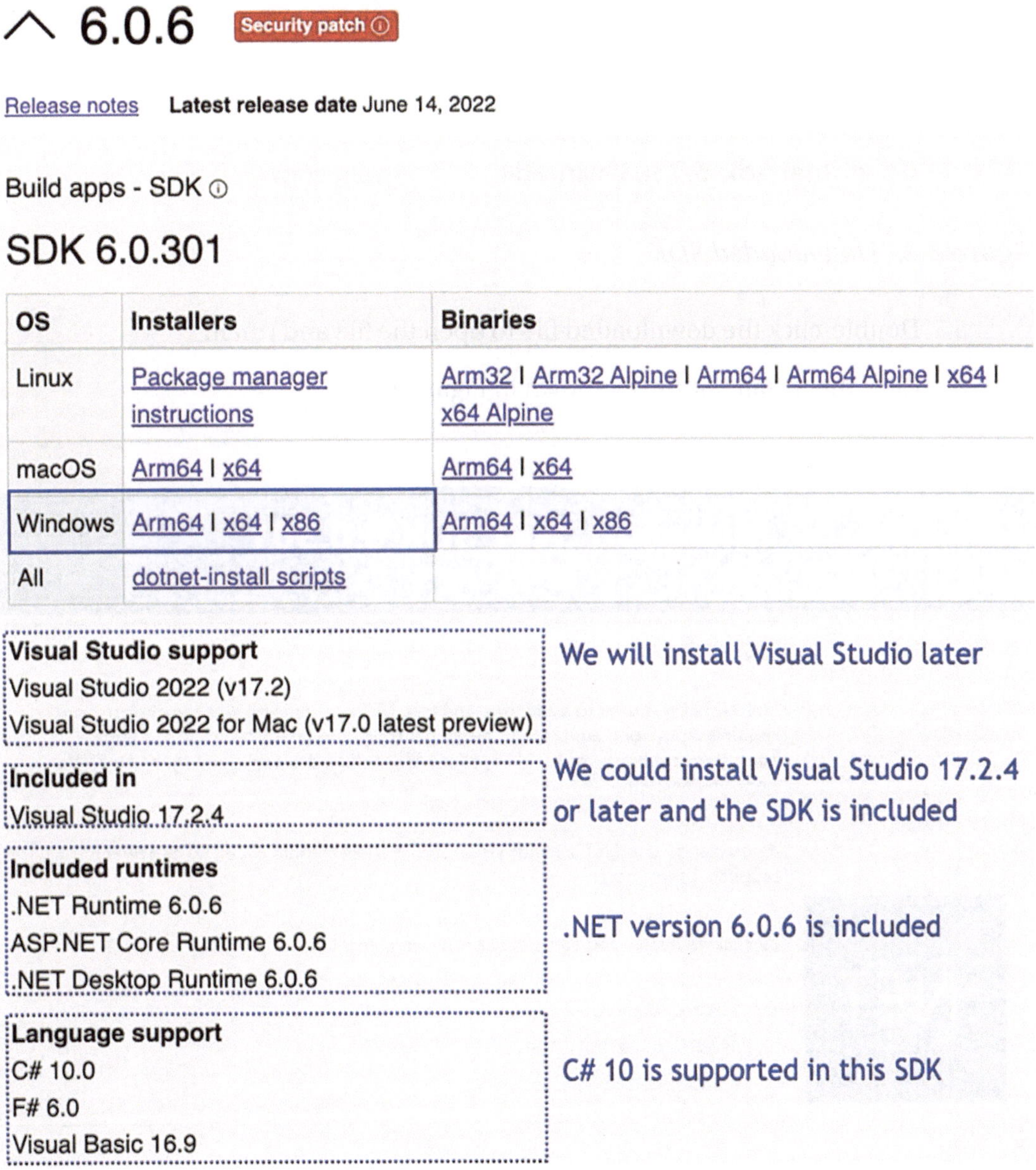

︿ **6.0.6** `Security patch ⓘ`

Release notes   **Latest release date** June 14, 2022

Build apps - SDK ⓘ

SDK 6.0.301

OS	Installers	Binaries
Linux	Package manager instructions	Arm32 ǀ Arm32 Alpine ǀ Arm64 ǀ Arm64 Alpine ǀ x64 ǀ x64 Alpine
macOS	Arm64 ǀ x64	Arm64 ǀ x64
Windows	Arm64 ǀ x64 ǀ x86	Arm64 ǀ x64 ǀ x86
All	dotnet-install scripts	

Visual Studio support
Visual Studio 2022 (v17.2)
Visual Studio 2022 for Mac (v17.0 latest preview)

We will install Visual Studio later

Included in
Visual Studio 17.2.4

We could install Visual Studio 17.2.4 or later and the SDK is included

Included runtimes
.NET Runtime 6.0.6
ASP.NET Core Runtime 6.0.6
.NET Desktop Runtime 6.0.6

.NET version 6.0.6 is included

Language support
C# 10.0
F# 6.0
Visual Basic 16.9

C# 10 is supported in this SDK

Figure 2-2. *SDK*

4. Locate the downloaded file in the Downloads folder, as shown in Figure 2-3, or wherever you downloaded the file to.

Figure 2-3. *Downloaded SDK*

5. Double-click the downloaded file to open the file and run it.

6. Click the Install button, as shown in Figure 2-4.

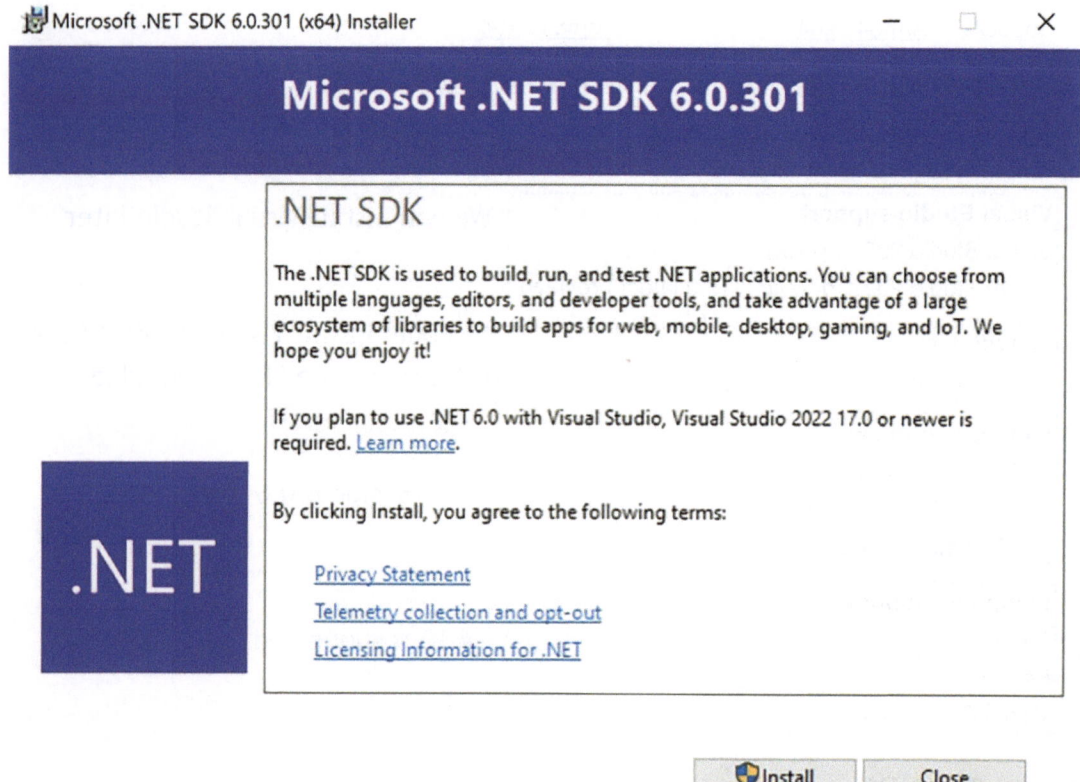

Figure 2-4. *Installation start screen*

7. If asked about permitting the installation, as shown in Figure 2-5, click the **Yes** button to grant permission.

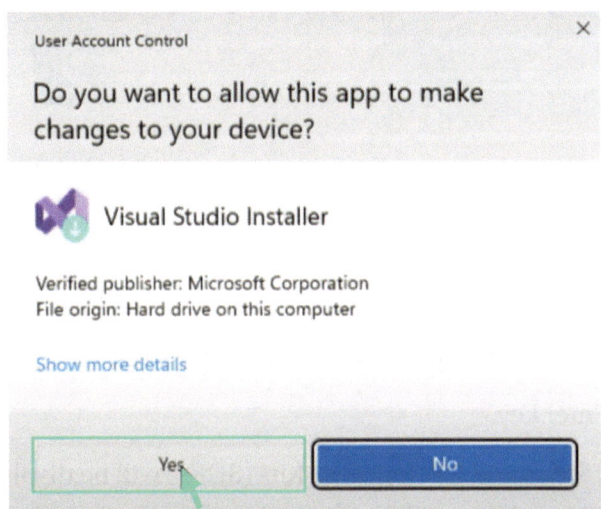

Figure 2-5. *Permitting the installation*

8. After the installation, click the Close button.

We can see from the final installation window what was installed and where.

Verify the .NET Framework Installation

We can now check that the .NET framework was successfully installed. To do this we will need to open the Command Prompt or PowerShell or the Terminal on a Mac operating system.

1. Open the Start menu on Windows.

2. Type cmd.

3. Press the Enter key.

4. A Command Prompt window should appear.

If the Command Prompt does not appear, we can use PowerShell, so click the Start menu and type PowerShell and press the Enter key, as in Figure 2-6.

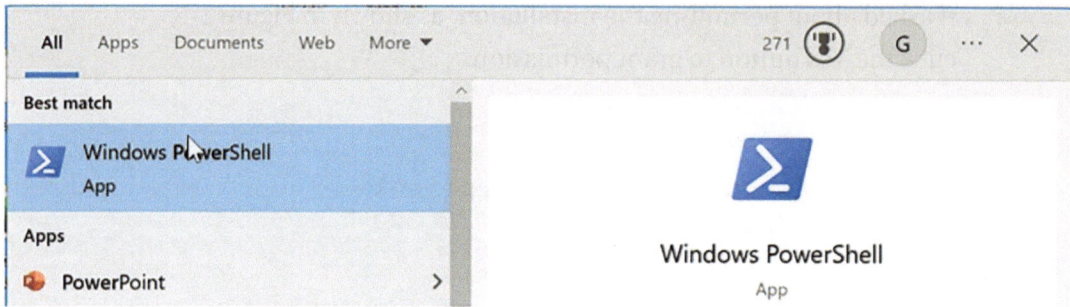

Figure 2-6. *Windows PowerShell*

5.   At the Command Prompt, >, type dotnet –list-sdks.

6.   Press the Enter key.

A list of the .NET Software Development Kits (SDKs) will be displayed as in Figure 2-7. There may only be one SDK, the 6.0.3 that we downloaded, and that is fine. Figure 2-7 shows a computer that has several SDKs installed.

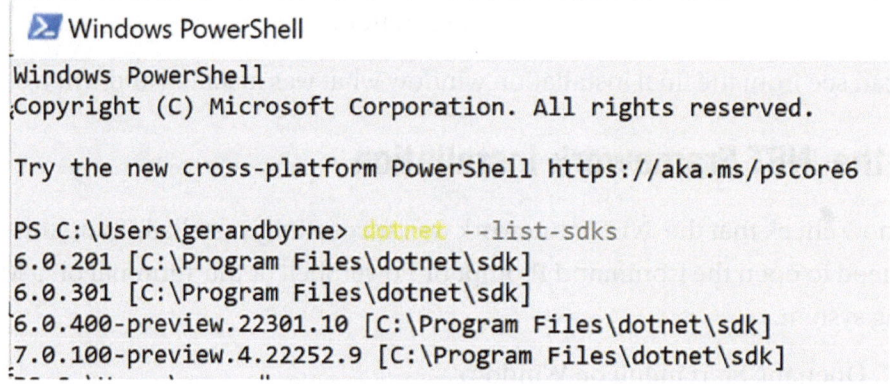

Figure 2-7. *Verification of the SDK installation*

7.   At the Command Prompt, >, type dotnet –list-runtimes.

8.   Press the Enter key.

The message will appear as shown in Figure 2-8 and this verifies that the .NET runtimes have been installed successfully.

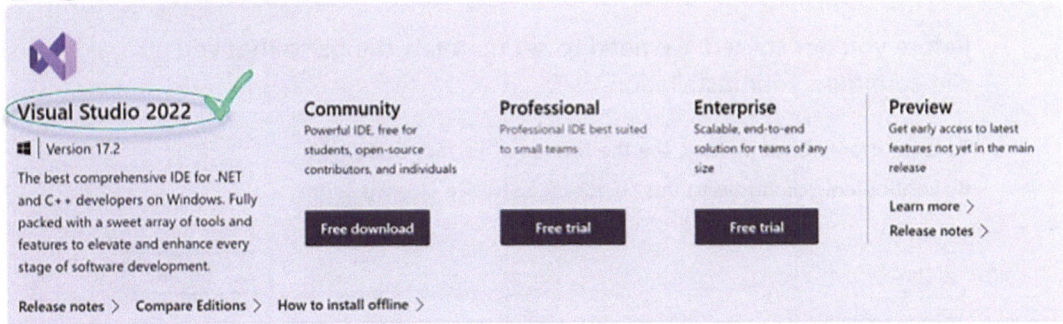

```
Windows PowerShell                                                          —    □
PS C:\Users\gerardbyrne> dotnet --list-runtimes
Microsoft.AspNetCore.App 3.1.26 [C:\Program Files\dotnet\shared\Microsoft.AspNetCore.App]
Microsoft.AspNetCore.App 6.0.3 [C:\Program Files\dotnet\shared\Microsoft.AspNetCore.App]
Microsoft.AspNetCore.App 6.0.5 [C:\Program Files\dotnet\shared\Microsoft.AspNetCore.App]
Microsoft.AspNetCore.App 6.0.6 [C:\Program Files\dotnet\shared\Microsoft.AspNetCore.App]
Microsoft.AspNetCore.App 7.0.0-preview.4.22251.1 [C:\Program Files\dotnet\shared\Microsoft.AspNetCore.App]
Microsoft.NETCore.App 3.1.22 [C:\Program Files\dotnet\shared\Microsoft.NETCore.App]
Microsoft.NETCore.App 3.1.26 [C:\Program Files\dotnet\shared\Microsoft.NETCore.App]      Included runtimes
Microsoft.NETCore.App 6.0.2 [C:\Program Files\dotnet\shared\Microsoft.NETCore.App]        .NET Runtime 6.0.6
Microsoft.NETCore.App 6.0.3 [C:\Program Files\dotnet\shared\Microsoft.NETCore.App]        ASP.NET Core Runtime 6.0.6
Microsoft.NETCore.App 6.0.5 [C:\Program Files\dotnet\shared\Microsoft.NETCore.App]        .NET Desktop Runtime 6.0.6
Microsoft.NETCore.App 6.0.6 [C:\Program Files\dotnet\shared\Microsoft.NETCore.App]
Microsoft.NETCore.App 7.0.0-preview.4.22229.4 [C:\Program Files\dotnet\shared\Microsoft.NETCore.App]
Microsoft.WindowsDesktop.App 3.1.26 [C:\Program Files\dotnet\shared\Microsoft.WindowsDesktop.App]
Microsoft.WindowsDesktop.App 6.0.2 [C:\Program Files\dotnet\shared\Microsoft.WindowsDesktop.App]
Microsoft.WindowsDesktop.App 6.0.3 [C:\Program Files\dotnet\shared\Microsoft.WindowsDesktop.App]
Microsoft.WindowsDesktop.App 6.0.5 [C:\Program Files\dotnet\shared\Microsoft.WindowsDesktop.App]
Microsoft.WindowsDesktop.App 6.0.6 [C:\Program Files\dotnet\shared\Microsoft.WindowsDesktop.App]
Microsoft.WindowsDesktop.App 7.0.0-preview.4.22229.2 [C:\Program Files\dotnet\shared\Microsoft.WindowsDesktop.App]
```

Figure 2-8. *Verification of the runtimes installed*

Installing Visual Studio

To be able to use .NET when following this book, we will use Visual Studio 2022 with a version of 17.0, or higher, installed on our computer.

1. Go to the Microsoft Visual Studio download page:

    `https://visualstudio.microsoft.com/downloads/`

2. Click Visual Studio 2022 when the web page opens, as in Figure 2-9.

Downloads

	Community	**Professional**	**Enterprise**	**Preview**
Visual Studio 2022 ✓	Powerful IDE, free for students, open-source contributors, and individuals	Professional IDE best suited to small teams	Scalable, end-to-end solution for teams of any size	Get early access to latest features not yet in the main release
⊞ Version 17.2				
The best comprehensive IDE for .NET and C++ developers on Windows. Fully packed with a sweet array of tools and features to elevate and enhance every stage of software development.	Free download	Free trial	Free trial	Learn more > Release notes >
Release notes > Compare Editions > How to install offline >				

Figure 2-9. *Visual Studio 2022*

3. When the next window appears, choose Community 2022 from the drop-down list of versions as in Figure 2-10. Visual Studio 2022 includes .NET and this is fine even though we downloaded .NET separately. The download should start.

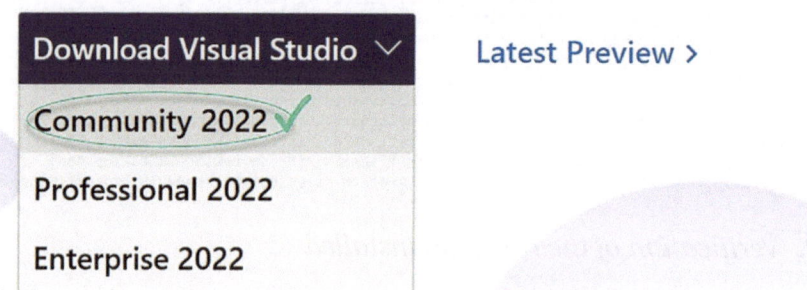

Figure 2-10. *Download of Visual Studio 2022 Community Edition*

4. Locate the downloaded file in the Downloads folder or wherever you downloaded it to.

5. Double-click the file to open the file and run it.

6. If asked about permitting the installation, click the Yes button to grant permission and then click the Continue button to allow the installer to continue its process, as in Figure 2-11.

Visual Studio Installer

Before you get started, we need to set up a few things so that you can configure your installation.

To learn more about privacy, see the Microsoft Privacy Statement.
By continuing, you agree to the Microsoft Software License Terms.

Figure 2-11. *Permitting the installer*

The installer will begin and the software will be installed, as in Figure 2-12.

Visual Studio Installer

Getting the Visual Studio Installer ready.

Downloaded

Installed

Figure 2-12. *Installation*

Now we need to decide on what workloads to download, and in the context of learning C# with this book and the coded applications, we will only need the .NET desktop development workload.

7. Click the .NET desktop development tile and make sure the checkbox becomes ticked.

There will be a drop-down menu, as shown in Figure 2-13, and we can leave it at the default of Install while downloading.

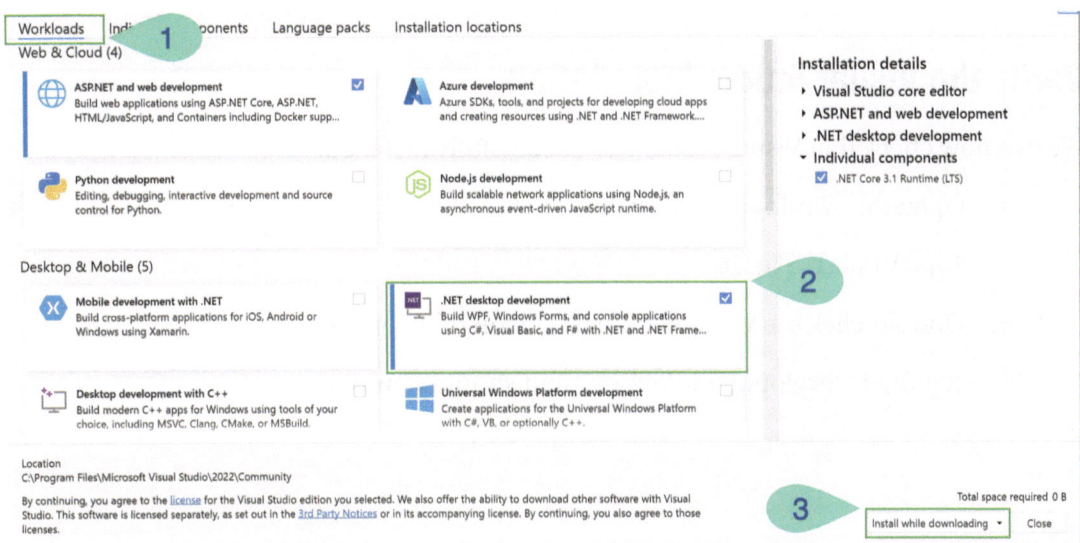

Figure 2-13. *Workload choices*

8. Click the Install button.

Visual Studio will download the relevant files based on the workloads we selected, just the .NET desktop development workload in our case.

9. Finally, click the Launch button.

10. Now we need to sign in with our Microsoft account so click the Sign in button, or if we need to create a new account, click the No account link to create a Microsoft account.

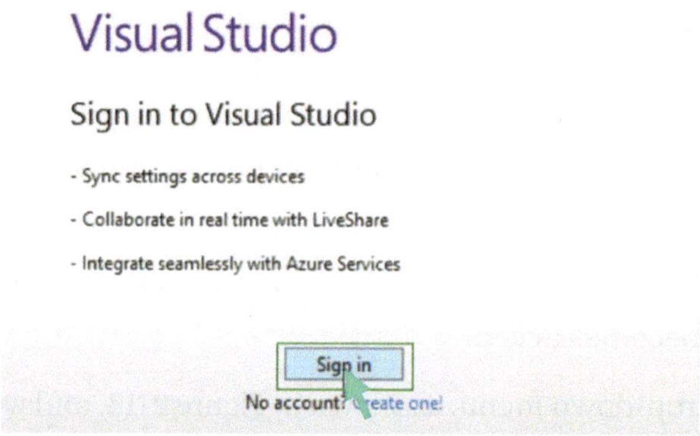

Figure 2-14. *Sign in*

Verify the Visual Studio Installation

We can now check that Visual Studio was successfully installed.

1. Open the Windows Start menu.

2. Type Visual Studio.

3. Double-click the Visual Studio 2022 icon that appears.

The Integrated Development Environment should now open.

Chapter Summary

In this chapter we have learned about downloading .NET and the Visual Studio Integrated Development Environment, both of which allow us to write C# applications. The setup is obviously crucial for developers and often it can be a "painful job" to get the setup right, but we saw that when we downloaded the Software Development Kit for .NET version 6, it supported Visual Studio 2022. Therefore, when we downloaded Visual Studio 2022, the two parts were compatible.

Finishing this chapter, we have increased our knowledge and we have advanced from the outer circle and are moving closer to the target.

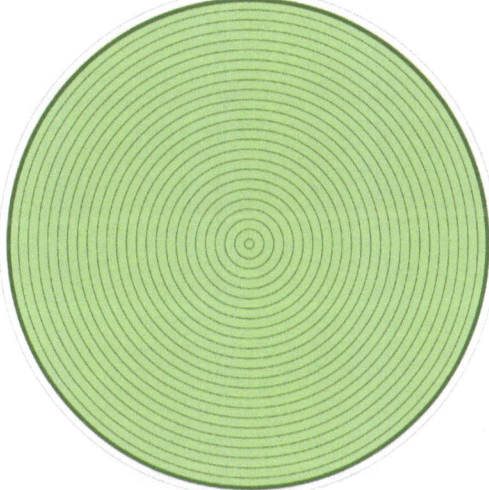

Our target is getting closer

Chapter Summary

In this chapter we'll be informed about downloading .NET and the Visual Studio integrated development environment, both of which allow us to write C# applications. The setup is obviously crucial for developers and often it can be a "painful job" to get the setup right, but we saw that when we downloaded the Software Development Kit for .NET we chose it as "proposed Visual Studio 2022." Therefore, when we downloaded Visual studio 2022, the two parts were compatible.

Finishing this chapter, we have the content just reviewed, and we have advanced from the outset, hand and are having closer to the target.

Don't mind it sipping, chapter.

CHAPTER 3

Introduction

Computer Program

We will be using C# to write computer programs, just like many programmers in companies around the world use C# to write programs in the commercial environment. So a very good starting point before writing code is to fully understand what a computer program is. We can think of a computer program as

- A sequence of data instructions created by a programmer

- Instructions that tell the computer what operations it should execute

- Instructions that tell the computer how it should execute an operation

- Instructions written in a special programming language, for example, C#, Java, C++, or COBOL

Besides C# there are a large number of programming languages available to developers. Each programming language will have particular advantages and disadvantages when compared with the other programming languages, but they will all be useful for writing software applications. It is important to understand that some programming languages are

- More powerful than others, for example, C#

- Better for developing applications requiring fast processing, for example, C

- Better for developing web-based software applications, for example, JavaScript

© Gerard Byrne 2022
G. Byrne, *Target C#*, https://doi.org/10.1007/978-1-4842-8619-7_3

- Better for developing computer games, for example, C++

- Better for data analytics, for example, Python

- Better for scripting, for example, Perl

The preceding points should help us understand that there are many programming languages available for software developers, but they all have concepts that can be applied across many of the languages. So, by the time we finish reading this book, entering and running all the example code, and doing all the exercises, we will be in a strong position to recognize and apply constructs in the Java programming language or the C++ language and indeed other programming languages, as well as our main focus, the C# language.

Programming Languages

It is certainly great to have a choice of programming languages but at times this makes it difficult to choose the correct one when writing a software application. In the following list, we can see some facts about programming languages:

- There are many different programming languages to choose from.

- Each language has its own set of very strict language rules.

- C# is one such programming language.

- Other languages include Java, C++, Visual Basic, Python, JavaScript, COBOL, Swift, Objective-C, Ruby, and Go.

- Programming languages such as C#, Java, C++, and Visual Basic are **high-level languages,** since they have a high correlation with a spoken and written language.

- Assembly language is a **low-level language**, as it has a low correlation with a spoken and written language and is more like the language the computer can understand.

- Every computer program will need to be **"translated"** into "**machine code**" that the computer can understand, for example, byte code, object code, and binary code.

- The process of "translation" is carried out by **compilers**, **interpreters,** or **assemblers.**

A Computer Program: A Recipe

Can we compare a computer program to a recipe used for baking or cooking? Let us think about a recipe that we might use in our kitchen to create the end product of **fifteens**, as in Figure 3-1.

Figure 3-1. *A fifteen, the output from my favorite recipe*

The information we need might be written in a book or on a website like that shown in Table 3-1.

Table 3-1. *A recipe for fifteens*

Ingredients	Instructions
15 digestive biscuits 15 marshmallows 15 glacé cherries, cut into halves or smaller About 150 ml of condensed milk 100 g of desiccated coconut	Add 15 digestive biscuits to a bag and "smash" the biscuits with a rolling pin until they are fine crumbs. Place the crumbs in a mixing bowl. Slice the 15 marshmallows into pieces; we decide how big the marshmallows should be. Slice the 15 cherries in half or smaller; we decide how big the cherries should be. Add the cherries and marshmallows to the digestive biscuit crumbs in the mixing bowl. Stir the mixture until the cherries and marshmallows are spread evenly around the biscuit crumbs. Pour the 150 ml of condensed milk on top of the biscuit, glacé cherry, and marshmallow mix. Mix the contents in the bowl and add more condensed milk if required, so that the mixture is not dry. Cut a large piece of tinfoil and spread half of the coconut onto the tinfoil. Scoop the wet biscuit, glacé cherry, and marshmallow mix onto the tinfoil and add the other half of the coconut to the mixture. Roll the tinfoil over the mixture to create a sausage shape. Move the rolled mixture to the fridge and leave in the fridge for 3 or 4 hours. Remove the roll from the fridge and cut it into 15 slices.

As we can see, the recipe contains

- A list of instructions, directions, written in a language – in this case it is English.

  Likewise, a computer program contains a list of statements, directions, written in a programming language such as C#.

- A list of ingredients. The ingredients are of various types, for example, biscuits, marshmallows, glacé cherries, condensed milk, and desiccated coconut.

  Likewise, a computer program contains a list of variables, ingredients. The variables will be of various types, for example, numbers, text, Customer, and Policy.

The following two code examples show the structure of code for C# and Python. Even at this early stage, by looking at the code examples, we should see some similarities between the two different programming languages, C# and Python. By completing the chapters in this book, we will become more familiar with C# programming, and other programming languages will be less "daunting" to look at and to program with.

Listing 3-1 shows C# code, which will ask the user to input two values and then totals the values. The program is like our recipe; it is a set of instructions.

Listing 3-1. Sample C# program code

```csharp
int counter = 0;
int totalofallclaims = 0;          variables (list of ingredients)
int inputnumber = 0;

while (counter < 2)                statements (list of instructions)
{
    //Input a number
    Console.WriteLine("What is the value of the claim: -- ");
    inputnumber = Convert.ToInt32(Console.ReadLine());

    //Add the number to the total
    totalofallclaims = totalofallclaims + inputnumber;

    // Add one to the value of count
    counter = counter + 1;
}
    // Print out the total of the claims that have been entered
    Console.WriteLine("The total of the claims that have been
                            input is " + totalofallclaims);
```

Listing 3-2 shows Python code, which will ask the user to input two values and then totals the values. The program is like our recipe; it is a set of instructions.

Listing 3-2. Sample Python program code

```python
counter = 0
totalofallclaims = 0          variables (list of ingredients)

while counter < 2:            statements (list of instructions)
    #Input a number
    inputnumber = int(input("What is the value of the claim:-- "))

    #Add the number to the total
    totalofallclaims = totalofallclaims + inputnumber

    #Add one to the value of count
    counter = counter + 1

# Print out the total of the claims that have been entered
print("The total of the claims that have been input is ",
totalofallclaims)
```

Type in C#

In C# we will often refer to the variables and their **types**. So, when we see the word *type* in relation to a variable, we need to say to ourselves type means a variable that has a particular **type**, for example, int, float, or char. A type indicates the data type of the variable, which will be stored, for example, bool, byte, sbyte, char, decimal, double, float, int, long, or short.

In C# all data is defined within a type. So we could have a type called Car and the data might include the odometer reading. The odometer reading might be of type int and we would say that the odometer type is int and it is contained within a Car type.

For now, we just need to understand we will have variables in our C# code and they will have a type. We will get more information and knowledge of types as we progress through the chapters and topics. C# is a strongly typed programming language and this means the type of a variable cannot be changed once it has been declared. This is not the same principle in some other programming languages.

Following up on the last point on types, it is important to understand that C# is a collection of types and these can be thought of as

- **Built-in types,** also called **predefined** or **primitive** data types, which include the ones we previously mentioned, for example, `bool`, `byte`, `sbyte`, `char`, `decimal`, `double`, `float`, `int`, `long`, and `short`.

- **User-defined types,** which we as developers create because we wish to have our own custom types. We said earlier that the odometer type could be int and it could be contained within a Car type. But we should think, *Where did the Car type come from?* Well, the answer is we would have to create it. C# does not provide us with a primitive or predefined type called Car. When building applications, we may wish to have types like Car, Customer, Policy, Agent, Claim, etc. This will be covered when we meet Chapter 13.

When we write a C# program, we are linked to .NET, and we can avail of what is called the **Common Type System (CTS)**. Think about professional programmers in companies throughout the world who use a variety of programming languages. Within a company there may be a team of developers building an application using Visual Studio, but some developers are writing their code using C#, while others are writing their code using VB.NET and each language has its own data types. So how will it work when they wish to put the application together and have the C# parts communicate with the VB.NET parts. Well, that is one of the benefits of .NET and its Common Type System as it takes control and ensures that the different types from the individual languages are compiled to a common data type.

The Common Type System defines types as being one of two kinds:

1. **Value type**

   Value type variables directly contain their values. The value types handled by the Common Type System are

   - **Primitives**, for example, `bool`, `byte`, `sbyte`, `char`, `decimal`, `double`, `float`, `int`, `long`, and `short`

   - **Enumerations**, which are used to assign constant names to a group of integer values, as in Listing 3-3

Listing 3-3. Example of an enumeration

```
enum PolicyStatus
{
  Live,
  Finished,
  Held
}
```

In this example, Listing 3-3, the compiler will assign the integer 0 to the constant value called Live, 1 to the constant value called Finished, and 2 to the constant value called Held.

Listing 3-4. Example of an enumeration with the default values overwritten

```
enum PolicyStatus
{
  Live = 1,       // We are assigning the value as 1 rather than a
                     default of 0
  Finished = 99,  // We are assigning the value as 99
  Held = 2        // We are assigning the value as 2
}
```

In this example, Listing 3-4, we as developers have assigned the integer value 1 to Live, 99 to Finished, and 2 to Held, thereby overriding the default values.

Listing 3-5. Example of an enumeration with default values assigned

```
enum WeekDays
{
    Monday,      // Monday is assigned a value of 0
    Tuesday,     // Tuesday is assigned a value 1
    Wednesday,   // Wednesday is assigned a value 2
    Thursday,    // Thursday is assigned a value 3
    Friday,      // Friday is assigned a value 4
    Saturday,    // Saturday is assigned a value 5
    Sunday       // Sunday is assigned a value 6
}
```

In this example, Listing 3-5, the compiler will assign the integer values 0–6 to the constant values held in the enum, the days of the week.

- **Structure (struct)**, which is used to store data

Listing 3-6. Example of a struct

```
struct Policy
{
  public int PolicyId;
  public string PolicyType;
  public double MonthlyPaymentAmount;
}
```

In this example, Listing 3-6, we as developers have created a structure that will be used to hold data about a policy.

Listing 3-7. Another example of a struct

```
struct Claim
{
  public int PolicyId;
  public double ClaimAmount;
}
```

In Listing 3-7, we as developers have created a structure that will be used to hold data about a claim. We will see more about enumerations and structs when we study them in their separate chapters.

2. **Reference type**

   When we talk about a reference type, we mean we are not dealing with the actual value, the real data, but we are dealing with a **reference** to the data held in memory. The reference types handled by the Common Type System are

   - **Root**, for example, Object

   - **String**, for example, string policyType;

- **Arrays**, for example, string[] repairShopClaims = new string[8];

- **Classes**

  Listing 3-8 shows an example of a class called Policy.

Listing 3-8. Example of a class

```
namespace insurances
{
    class Policy
    {
        public int PolicyId;
        public string PolicyType;
        public double BasePremiumAmount;

        public  void CalculateBasePremium()
        {
            if (policyType.Equals("Home"))
            {
                basePremiumAmount = 100;
            }
            else
            {
                basePremiumAmount = 200;
            }
        } // End of CalculateBasePremium() method
    } // End of Policy class
} // End of namespace
```

- **Interfaces**

- **Delegates**

We should not be concerned about these Common Type System types, for now. It is just important that we realize there are different types within C# and the Common Type System of .NET. As we progress through the chapters, we will gain more knowledge of the types, and more importantly we will consistently use them in all our coding examples.

The Basic Operations of a Computer

Under the direction of a program, written in a programming language and converted to machine-readable code, the computer can perform operations as shown in Table 3-2.

Table 3-2. *Basic operations of a computer*

Input	The computer can accept user input from the keyboard.
Process	The computer can perform arithmetic calculations and other types of processing.
Output	The computer can display a message or a result on the screen or some other output source.
Combination	The computer can combine these operations in three ways:
	Sequentially – A sequence of operations is performed one after the other.
	Repeatedly – A sequence of operations is performed a number of times.
	Selectively – One, two, or more sequences of operations are performed depending upon a condition, **for example**, is counter <2.
Subprograms	A program can contain a number of smaller programs. We can for now call a subprogram a method or a function.

C# Program Application Formats

Every programming language will have a structure that we need to understand and abide by if we wish to write code using that language. In the C# programming language, there are basic elements that all C# programs must have, and these basic elements depend on which format of application we are developing. In this book we will be concentrating on writing code for console applications, and as we go through the chapters in the book, we will gain more understanding of console applications. Using C#, we can write applications for different formats, three of which are discussed in the following.

Format 1: Console Application

In a console application, we use the Command Prompt, better known as the console, to accept **input** from the user and to display **output** data to the user. In the distant past, we only had console applications. There were no "windowed" applications and fancy graphics. Figure 3-2 shows what the console might look like.

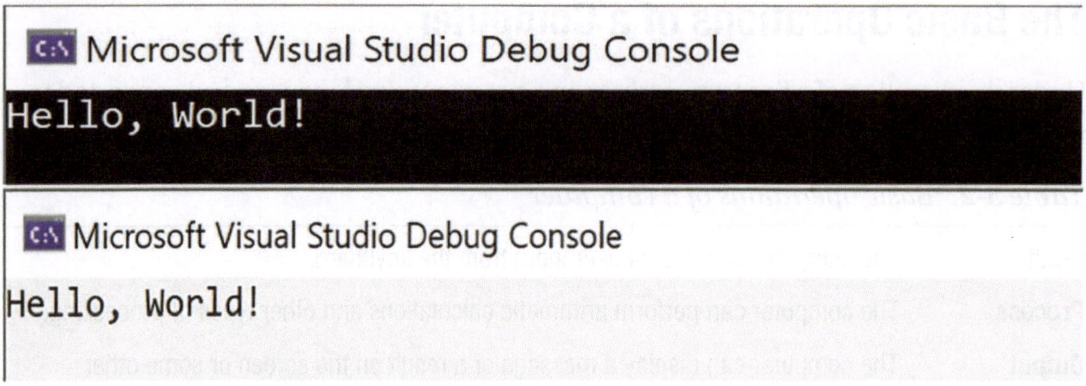

Figure 3-2. *Console application sample output*

We can think of the console as a two-tone screen like the black and white screen in the top section of Figure 3-2, although it can be changed, as shown in the lower section of Figure 3-2. The console is where input from the user is accepted and output from the computer program is displayed. Nowadays, while Windows and web-based applications are the predominant application formats for C#, console applications are still used to perform many tasks, which are not dependent on a "pretty" user interface (UI).

We will be using an Integrated Development Environment (IDE) called Visual Studio Community Edition, and when we write our C# code in the editor of Visual Studio, we will need to run it to make sure it works properly. Our C# console application will run in a console window, which may have a black background and white text or some other combination of colors.

In learning to program, it is very important that we understand the programming concepts and forget about user interface design. The interface design can be built into the applications that we create, after learning all the core programming concepts. In reality we need to concentrate on ensuring that our code is well designed, has no errors or bugs, and works as required. There would be no point in having code that did not work properly, and there would be absolutely no point in having a well-designed, "pretty" user interface that was not functioning as expected because the code behind it was not working correctly.

Figure 3-3 shows the console window for a very basic C# console application. It also shows the code that has been written to produce the console application. The code will be explained later in this chapter.

```
Program.cs  ⊡ ✕
C# Playground                                                    ▼  ⚙ ConsoleV1.Program
     1      using System;
     2
     3    ⊟namespace ConsoleV1
     4     {
              0 references
     5    ⊟    internal class Program
     6          {
                0 references
     7    ⊟        static void Main(string[] args)
     8             {
     9                Console.ReadLine();
    10             } // End of Main() method
    11         } // End of Program class
    12     } // End of ConsoleV1 namespace
    13
```

Figure 3-3. *Console application code and sample output*

Format 2: .NET MAUI

Using .NET MAUI, we can develop apps that run on Windows, Android, iOS, and MacOS, as in Figure 3-4. .NET MAUI is a shortened version of .NET Multi-platform App UI. So .NET MAUI is a cross-platform framework for creating mobile and desktop applications with C# and XAML.

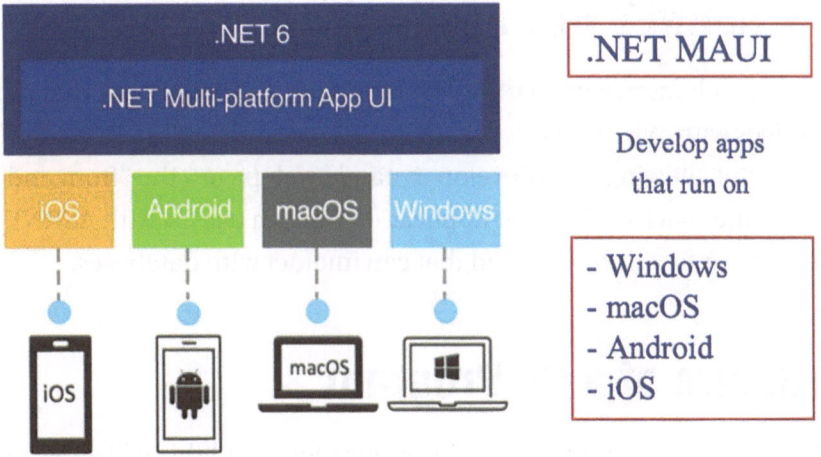

Figure 3-4. *Cross-platform development using .NET MAUI*

Figure 3-5 shows an example from the Microsoft website showing C# code and an Android emulator displaying an application.

```csharp
namespace MyFirstMauiApp;

public partial class MainPage : ContentPage
{
    int count = 0;

    public MainPage()
    {
        InitializeComponent();
    }

    private void OnCounterClicked(object sender, EventArgs e)
    {
        count++;

        if (count == 1)
            CounterBtn.Text = $"Clicked {count} time";
        else
            CounterBtn.Text = $"Clicked {count} times";

        SemanticScreenReader.Announce(CounterBtn.Text);
    }
}
```

Figure 3-5. *.NET MAUI sample code from the Microsoft website*

Format 3: ASP.NET Web Applications

ASP.NET is a free web framework, created by Microsoft, to allow us to build modern web apps and services with .NET and C#. With ASP.NET we can use C# alongside HTML, CSS, and JavaScript allowing us to develop dynamic web pages, the "front end" of our application. For the "back end" of our application, we can use C# with ASP.NET to develop code for our business logic and that can interact with databases.

The Structure of a C# Program

In this book we will concentrate on console applications, and this will allow us to focus on the C# programming language concepts rather than concerning ourselves about the design of a user interface. We saw in Figure 3-3 the general code of a C# console application, and the program code in Listing 3-9 shows similar "traditional" code so we can talk about a feature that can be used.

Listing 3-9. General syntax and format for a C# program

```
using System;

namespace ConsoleVersion1
{
    public class Program
    {
        public static void Main(string[] args)
        {
            Console.ReadLine();
        } // End of Main() method
    } // End of Program class
} // End of ConsoleVersion1 namespace
```

The 11 lines of code shown in Listing 3-9 represent what has been a "typical" starting point for a new console application when using Visual Studio. Interestingly, from all the lines of code, only one of them contains executable code, Console.ReadLine().

However, we can use a new feature called **top-level statements**, shown in Listing 3-10, that will allow us to simplify the code. We only need two lines of code. Really, one as the first line is a comment added by Microsoft.

Listing 3-10. Top-level statements, two lines

```
// See https://aka.ms/new-console-template for more information
Console.ReadLine();
```

With the C# templates for .NET version 6, we will be given top-level statements by default as a starter, which is very nice, but if we do not want to have them, we can either

- Delete them when the code appears and add our own code, which we will do throughout the chapters in the book.

- Switch them off when we are creating the project, as in Figure 3-6.

Additional information

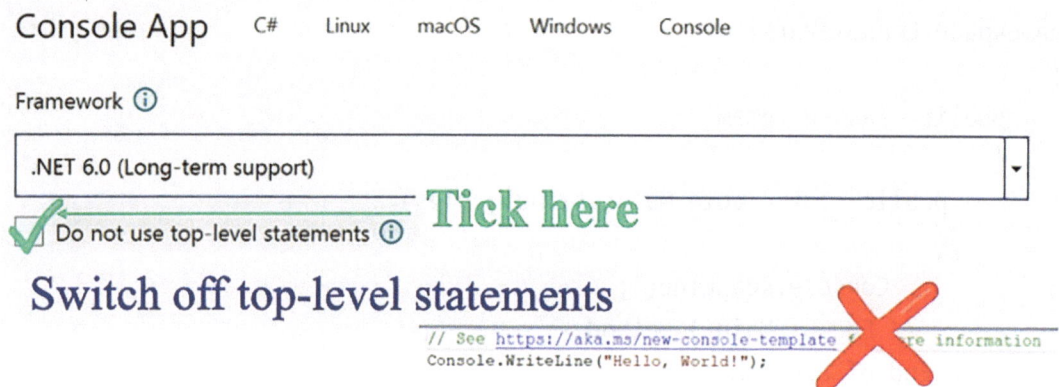

Figure 3-6. *Switching off top-level statements*

We will delete the top-level statements when they appear so we are reinforcing the fact that "under the hood" of these top-level statements there is code. When we are starting to learn C# code, it is good to see what the "real" code looks like, not the cut-down version. As we become experienced, it will be fine to use the top-level statements and indeed it would be expected that as developers we would do so. It is also important to understand that top-level statements can only be used in one source file in our project application, and we will be creating more than one file in our projects. If we tried to use top-level statements in more than one file in the project application, the compiler would give us an error.

Code Analysis

This analysis of the code in Listing 3-9 will help us fully understand the basic form of the C# console application code.

Namespace

- All code is enclosed within a namespace. In this example our namespace is called *ConsoleVersion1*. The name starts with the line

  ```
  namespace ConsoleVersion1
  ```

  Essentially, a namespace is like a folder, an area to store classes, the code. Namespaces provide us as developers with a way to keep one set of names separate from another. The class names declared in one namespace do not conflict with the same class names declared in another.

Think about a Microsoft Word document that we might create and save as CSharpNotes.docx:

- Understand that we cannot create a new Word document and save it with the same name in the same folder as the CSharpNotes.docx document, as this would cause the operating system to ask us if we wanted to replace, overwrite, the existing file.

- On the other hand, if we save the file with the same name but in a different folder, this will be fine.

  The reason for this is that the folders allow us to keep files separate from one another and the actual name of the file will include the folder name.

  Examples

  C:\Gerry\Documents\MyNotes\CSharpNotes.docx

  C:\Gerry\Documents\MyClassNotes\CSharpNotes.docx

  In the same way that we have different folders to separate our Word or other documents, we have namespaces in C# to separate our classes, code files. Just like every Word document will be in a folder, every class must be inside a namespace.

- Below the namespace name is the **opening curly brace,** which is matched by the **closing curly brace** at the end. Therefore, all code is wrapped within the namespace braces. So the namespace code looks like Listing 3-11.

Listing 3-11. Namespace syntax

```
namespace ConsoleVersion1
{
} // End of namespace
```

Opening and closing braces are widely used to contain blocks of code and segregate the blocks of code from each other.

Namespaces are therefore used in C# to avoid name conflicts and to control the access to classes and so on. With namespaces it makes it easier to locate related classes that hold our code, and they provide a structure for projects, which, in a commercial application, could contain hundreds of classes and other files. This is what we read earlier when we said .NET contains many libraries of code that are useful to us when we write our code.

Class

- The C# code is wrapped within the namespace but it must also then be written or contained within a class. In this example our class is called **Program**. So the class looks like Listing 3-12.

Listing 3-12. Class syntax

```
public class Program
{
} // End of Program class
```

- Below the class name is the **opening curly brace,** which is matched by the **closing curly brace,** just above the namespace closing brace. Therefore, our code is wrapped within the class braces.

Method

- The main entry point of our console application will be the **method** called Main. A method is simply a number of lines of code, a block of code. Later in this book, we will look at methods in detail.

- Our lines of code for the Main() method are enclosed between the **opening curly brace** and the **closing curly brace**. So the Main() method looks like Listing 3-13.

Listing 3-13. Main() method syntax

```
public static void Main(string[] args)
{
    Console.ReadLine();
} // End of Main() method
```

The Main method has two keywords before it:

- `static` – Later in the book when we look at classes and methods in detail, we will become familiar with the use of the keyword *static*. For now, just forget about static and simply accept its use in the code as shown.

- `void` – This means that when all the lines of code within a method are executed, no value will be returned from the method – it is a void return. We will see more about this later in the book when we look at methods in detail.

The Main method has some text within the brackets:

- `string[]` – We will see more about this later in the book when we look at arrays in detail. Essentially, it means that the Main() method can accept, be given, input values that are of type string. The **[]** means that it is an array of strings, one or more string values. So the Main() method can accept a number of values, variables, of type string.

- `args` – args is the name of the string array. If we change the name from args to something else, it will not affect the running of the program. In Figure 3-7, **args** has been amended to **gerry** and the program has been run. The result is the same as that shown earlier, the only difference being the name of the array.

```csharp
using System;
using System.Collections.Generic;
using System.Linq;
using System.Text;
using System.Threading.Tasks;

namespace ConsoleVersion1
{
    public class Program
    {
        public static void Main(string[] gerry)
        {
            Console.ReadLine();
        } // End of Main() method

    } // End of Program class
} // End of ConsoleVersion1 namespace
```

Figure 3-7. *Renaming the args array to gerry*

It should be noted that not all our code will be written inside the Main() method or indeed any method, but it will be written within a class, which is always contained within a namespace.

Namespaces

As we have read earlier, a console application is contained within a **namespace**. A namespace may be thought of as a storage area for some **classes,** which themselves contain **methods**. Microsoft has written thousands of base classes and stored them in namespaces. When we write our C# code, we will create many more classes and we must follow the same practices as Microsoft and store our classes within our own namespaces. Storing our classes in namespaces makes code more manageable and easier to maintain.

A namespace can be likened to the folders that we keep our files in. We create different folders to hold different files in a structure that best suits our system. Likewise, we can create namespaces to hold our classes, and we can use the namespaces created by Microsoft in our code to get access to the Microsoft base classes. The lines of code at the start of the program code usually have a format that starts with the keyword using. The keyword **using**, as shown in Listing 3-14, refers to the fact that we wish to use classes that are contained in the namespace that follows the word using. In our earlier code example, Listing 3-9, we used the Console class. Therefore, the compiler needs to know where to look for this class, and that is why we have the using System statement at the top of the code. Remember, namespaces contain classes that themselves contain methods and it will be these methods, blocks of code, that we will use.

Listing 3-14. The using keyword for importing namespaces

```
using System;
using System.Collections.Generic;
using System.Linq;
using System.Text;
using System.Threading.Tasks;

namespace ConsoleVersion1
{
    public class Program
    {
        public static void Main(string[] args)
        {
```

```
        Console.ReadLine(;
    } // End of Main() method
  } // End of class
} // End of namespace
```

Classes

As stated earlier a console application is contained within a namespace and within the namespace there will be a **class** or **classes.** A class is used to allow us to create **our own types** using C# code. A class is like an outline that will let us define the type we want, using other types, methods, and variables. In the example code, Listing 3-14, we have a class called Program. As we become more proficient in our C# coding, we will begin to develop our own more complex classes.

Here we will look at some examples that could be created in real applications:

- A class for the type **Pizza**, to define that all pizzas have

  - A pizza base

  - A pizza sauce

  - Toppings

Once we define the blueprint class for the pizza, we will be able to use the class to create specific **types** of pizza. For example, we can create a Hawaiian pizza or a vegetarian pizza. The two classes, Hawaiian pizza and vegetarian pizza, are called **instances** of the class, and each instance will contain a pizza base, a pizza sauce, and a topping(s).

- A class for the type **InsuranceQuote** to define that all quotes must have

  - An applicant's forename

  - An applicant's surname

  - An applicant's date of birth

  - A method to calculate the insurance premium

Once we define the blueprint class for InsuranceQuote, we will be able to use the class to create specific types of InsuranceQuote. For example, we can create a CarInsuranceQuote or a HomeInsuranceQuote. The two classes, CarInsuranceQuote and HomeInsuranceQuote, are called instances of the class, and each instance will contain an applicant's forename, an applicant's surname, an applicant's date of birth, and a method to calculate the insurance premium.

What we should be clear about is that by the time we start Chapter 13 on classes and objects, which is a complex topic, we will be well prepared and should find the complex topic more manageable.

The starting point, before we code, is to be clear about the following concepts:

- **A class exists inside a namespace.**

- **A class can contain variables, for example,** forename, surname, and dateofbirth.

- **A class can contain methods, for example,** CalculateInsurancePremium().

The term *instance* has been used to describe our **copy** of the class. More importantly it is possible to say our "copy" is an **object**. We will study **classes** and **objects** in more detail in a future chapter.

As we go through the course chapters, we will be reminded of the fact that **a class contains methods and variables**. This is a key concept and will be relevant when programming all the code examples. We will also see later that, instead of saying variable, we will say **property** or **field** or **member** when we talk about them in classes, but in our learning just think variables.

To expand this key concept of **variables** and **methods** within a **class**, take a closer look at the way they have been written:

> variable **forename**
>
> variable **surname**
>
> variable **dateofbirth**
>
> method **CalculateInsurancePremium()**

- Notice that a variable has a name that we give to it. It is one word.

- Notice that a method has a name that we give to it followed by the open bracket, followed by the close bracket, that is, **()**.

   So **() means a method**, like the Main() method as shown in Listing 3-15.

Listing 3-15. Main() method has open and close brackets ()

```
public static void Main(string[] args)
{
    Console.ReadLine();
} // End of Main() method
```

The Main() method is interesting because it accepts an input. As developers we can code any method to accept input. Alternatively, we can code a method so it does not accept a value or values.

Naming a Class: Class Identifiers

When using C#, we will notice that there are two naming conventions that are followed:

- **camelCase** – Where the first letter of the first word in an identifier is lowercase and the first letter of all other words are uppercase, for example, carInsurance

- **PascalCase** – Where the first letter of each word in an identifier is uppercase, for example, CarInsurance

In terms of clean code, some things should be considered as good practices:

- When naming a class, we should use a noun phrase.

- The class name should describe what the class does; make the name descriptive.

- Use the singular rather than the plural, **for example**, use Agent rather than Agents.

- Start the class name with a capital letter.

- Keep the class name and the filename the same. This is not always required, but it would be seen as the norm and makes for consistent naming across all classes.

- Use PascalCase, which means every word in the class name starts with a capital letter. This is better than using underscores, as in Table 3-3.

- The class name could begin with an @ symbol, which would also allow us to use C# keywords as the class name, but maybe not a good idea!

Table 3-3. *Valid and invalid class identifiers*

Valid class identifier	Invalid class identifier
Program	Program Version 1
Customer	1Customer
Student	%Student
Author	*Author
@double (but don't use it)	double
Bank_Account	Bank Account
Customer_Order	\Customer Order
Mailing-List-For-Customers	Mailing List For Customers
Student~Results~For~Test	Student Results For Test
Car_Insurance_Quote	-Car-Insurance-Quote

When we are learning to code, using naming conventions can be helpful, but do not obsess over them. The important thing is to get to understand and program in the C# language.

Chapter Summary

In this chapter we have learned about programming languages and some features that apply to C#. We have learned that

- A computer program is a set of instructions created by a programmer.

- A computer program is like a cooking or baking recipe.

- The computer can perform input, process, and output using the program.

- C# programs can be used in writing **console** applications, .NET MAUI mobile applications, ASP.NET **web** applications, and many other types.

- There is a structure to all C# programs, which includes the use of **namespaces**, **classes,** and **methods**, including the `Main()` method.

- The keyword `using` is used with a namespace to "import" another namespace.

- Classes contain **variables** (properties, fields, members) and **methods.**

- Methods always have the **()** after them, for example, Main().

In finishing this chapter and increasing our knowledge, we are advancing to our target.

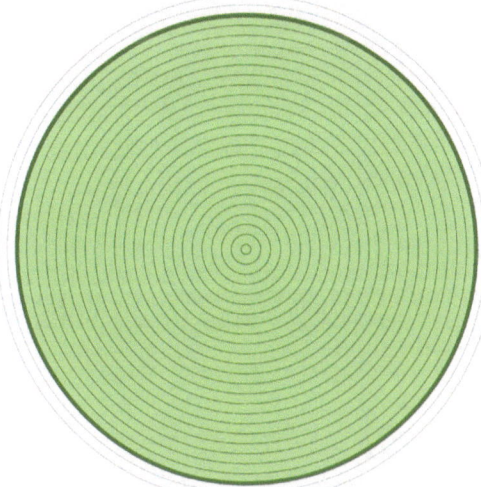

Our target is getting closer

CHAPTER 4

Input and Output

Write to and Read from the Console

We learned in Chapter 3 that under the direction of a program, written in a programming language and converted to machine-readable code, the computer can perform the following tasks, as shown in Table 4-1.

Table 4-1. *Input, output, and process*

Input	The computer can accept user input from the keyboard.
Process	The computer can perform arithmetic calculations and other types of processing.
Output	The computer can display a message or a result on the screen.

This chapter will concentrate on how to **output to the console**. We will also use a basic .NET method to **read from the console**, which is an example of **input**. It is very important to understand that what we learn by completing the examples in this chapter will

- Help us build more complex code examples in future chapters

- Show us commands that are used in real-world applications

- Get us started with two important aspects of any programming language – **input** and **output**

Looking back at Figure 3-2 from Chapter 3, we can think of the console as a black and white screen where input from the user is accepted and output from the computer program is displayed. The console colors can be changed as we can see from the lower part of Figure 4-1.

© Gerard Byrne 2022
G. Byrne, *Target C#*, https://doi.org/10.1007/978-1-4842-8619-7_4

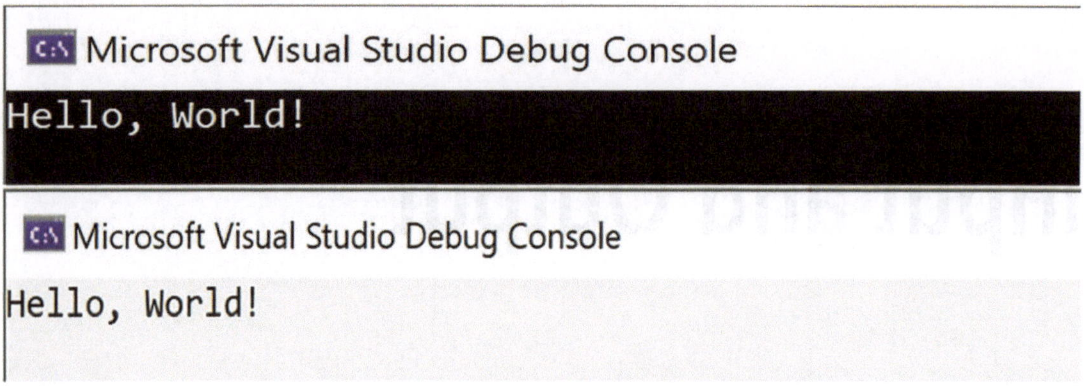

Figure 4-1. *Console in black and white and alternative color*

So our console will display data, and in the C# programming language, we could achieve this with the line of code shown in Listing 4-1.

Listing 4-1. The WriteLine() method to display data on the console

```
Console.WriteLine();
```

Code Analysis

- Fact 1

  First, we can see the keyword `Console`, so we might imagine this means something that interacts with the console, yes, the "screen," where input from the user is accepted and output from the computer program is displayed.

- Fact 2

  The second part is the full stop or period as it is also known. In programming languages like C#, the full stop means that we want to use a part or element of the **object** that appears to the left of the full stop, in this case Console. The object will generally be a class, and we talked a little about classes in the previous chapter, but we will also read a whole chapter on classes and objects. Now, let's look back to what we learned in the previous chapter:

*As we go through the course chapters, we will be reminded of the fact that **a class contains methods and variables**. This is a key concept and will be relevant when programming all the code examples.*

So, if Console is a class, it can contain methods and variables. When we add the full stop after the class name, we are saying we want to use either a method or a variable that is inside the class. Remember () indicates a method. It was also said in the previous chapter:

*Likewise, we can create namespaces to hold our classes, and we can use the namespaces created by Microsoft in our code to get access to the **Microsoft base classes**.*

Microsoft base classes will be like the classes we write; they contain methods and variables, which we can use without having to write them. Console is one such base class and it therefore contains methods and variables that we can use.

- Fact 3

  The third part is `WriteLine()`.

  Let's look back to what we learned in the previous chapter:

  So () means a method.

  We should now be able to recognize that WriteLine() is indeed a method, and as it has nothing between the brackets (), we should understand that this means the method accepts no value or values. We will see in Chapter 12 on methods that it is a parameterless method; it accepts no parameters, values.

- Fact 4

  Console belongs to a **namespace called System**. This is not obvious from the line of code, but it will become obvious as we start to write the code in our Integrated Development Environment (IDE). To explain this, we can think back to what we learned in the previous chapter:

The lines of code at the start of the program code usually have a format that starts with the keyword using.

The word `using` refers to the fact that we wish to use classes, and ultimately the methods and variables in the classes, that are contained in the namespace that follows it, for example, `using System;`.

So we can see a namespace called System being used in our C# code and this illustrates another important concept to get used to when programming:

We will use classes that already exist to help us build our own applications using C# code.

Always remember the key fact that **a class contains methods and variables**, so when we tell our code to use an existing class, which exists in a namespace, we are doing this to get access to methods and variables that already exist and will help us in building our application with C# code.

When we use an Integrated Development Environment like Microsoft Visual Studio, we will receive assistance when we type a class name followed by the dot or period. We call this **dot notation,** and it presents us with a list of methods and variables that exist in the class, very handy for us as developers. Figure 4-2 shows an example of what Visual Studio presents developers when the dot is entered after the keyword Console. We see the variables, also referred to as fields, members, or properties, and the methods that exist in the Console class.

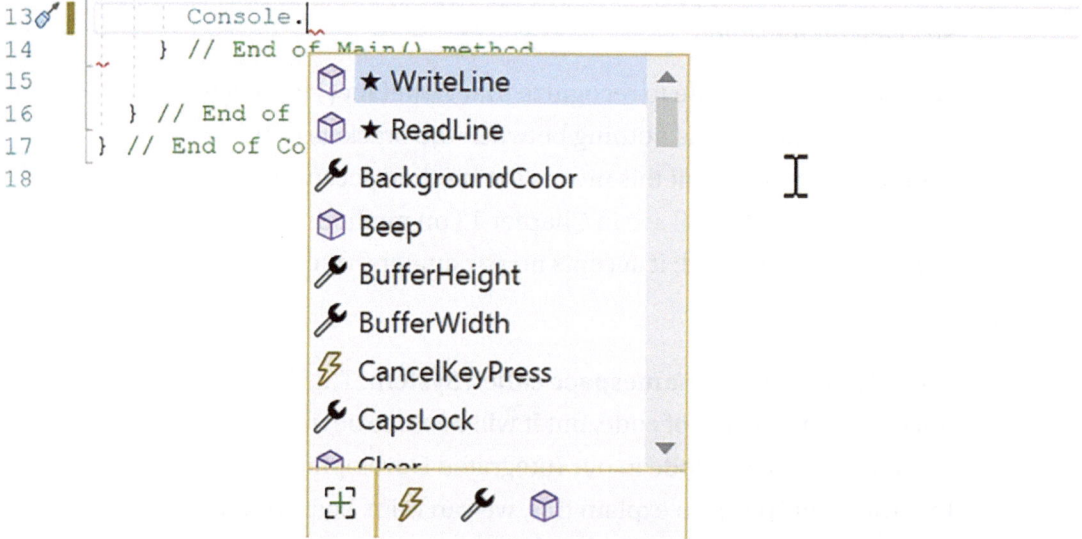

Figure 4-2. *Dot notation showing methods and properties of the Console class*

If we study the icons, this will help when we are coding our applications. There are three different icons representing three aspects of the class. For now, let's just get familiar with two of the icons that represent the variables and the methods:

The spanner

The spanner represents a **property** of the class. Let's look back to what we learned in the previous chapter:

We will also see later that, instead of saying variable, we will say property or field or member when we talk about them in classes.

So we use the word property when we are inside a class, but we may also see it called a member. Clicking the spanner icon at the bottom of the pop-up window will display only the properties of the class, as shown on the left-hand side in Figure 4-3.

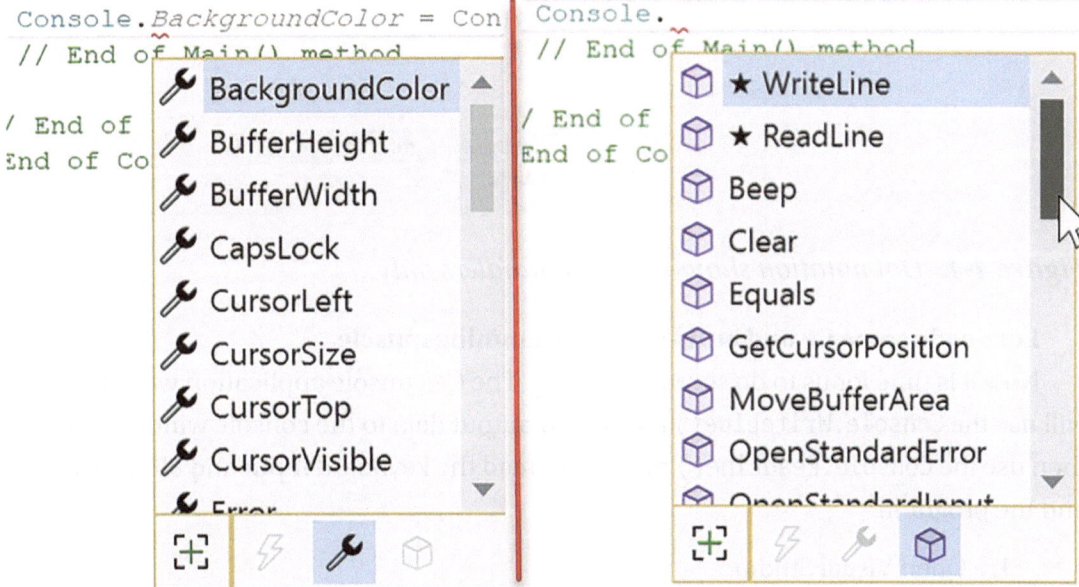

Figure 4-3. *Dot notation showing properties on the left and methods on the right*

The cube

The cubes, as shown on the right-hand side in Figure 4-3, represent the **methods** of the class. A method is a block of code.

The "lightning bolt" symbol

The "lightning bolt," as shown in Figure 4-4, represents an **event handler**. This is more related to actions from controls on a form, like clicking a button. Later in the book, we will study events within a console application, but events for form-based applications are not part of our book. We will be concentrating on console applications rather than form- or web-based applications. However, as we have read previously, once we get the core programming skills, the fundamentals, it will be possible to apply these to form- and web-based applications where events like clicking a button will be commonplace. Such programming can also be classified as **event-driven programming**.

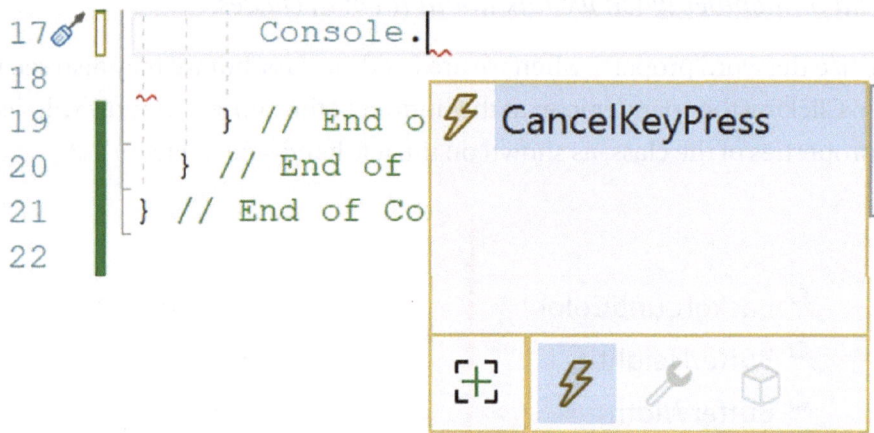

Figure 4-4. *Dot notation showing event handlers only*

Let's code some C# and build our programming muscle.

Now it is time for us to do some C# coding. The C# console application we will code will use the `Console.WriteLine()` method to output data to the console window and then use the `Console.ReadLine()` method to read the keyboard input and effectively end the program.

1. Open Visual Studio.

2. At the launch screen, choose Create a new project, as in Figure 4-5.

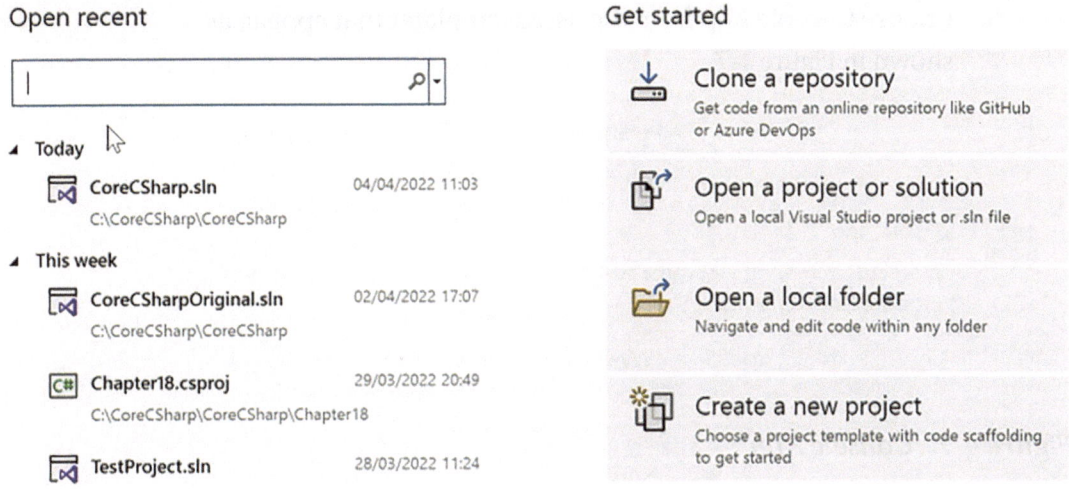

Figure 4-5. *Create a new project*

3. Choose C# as the programming language from the drop-down list, as shown on the left-hand side of Figure 4-6.

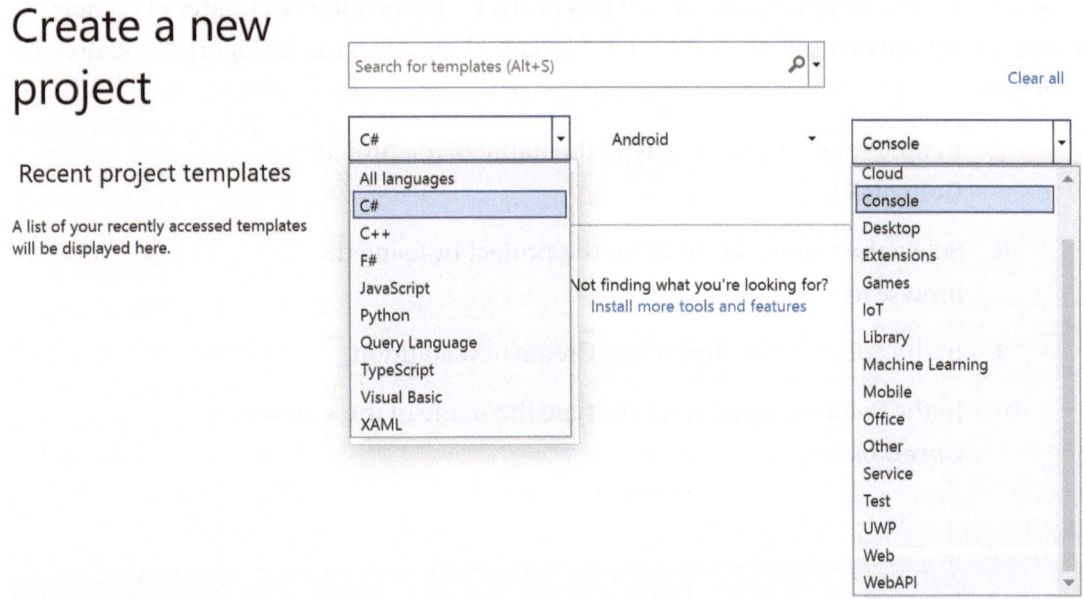

Figure 4-6. *Select the language as C#*

4. Choose Console in the project type section, as shown on the right-hand side of Figure 4-6.

5. Choose Console App from the listed templates that appear, as shown in Figure 4-7.

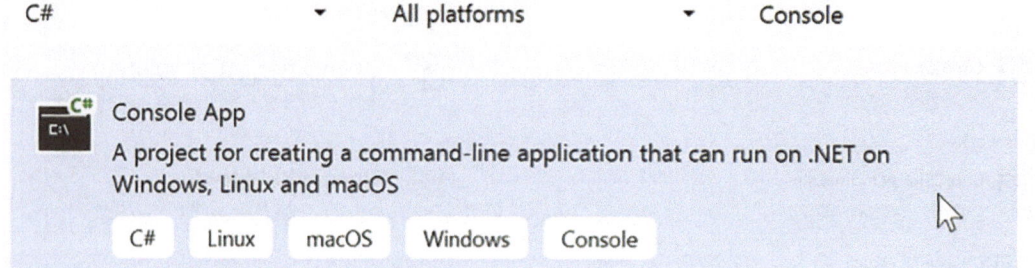

Figure 4-7. *Console App*

6. Click the Next button.

All our code can be saved in one location called a solution. The solution is really a folder on our computer. Once we create the solution, we will create projects within it, and these projects are really folders within the solution. So now we need to create a solution on our computer as we create this project. The location is a matter of choice; we decide where to locate the solution folder and the project folder. Figure 4-8 shows an example.

7. In the Project name area, type the name of the project – **ConsoleV1**.

8. Select the storage location for the project by using the … browse icon.

9. In the Solution box, leave it as Create new solution.

10. In the Solution name text box, type the name of the solution – *CoreCSharp*.

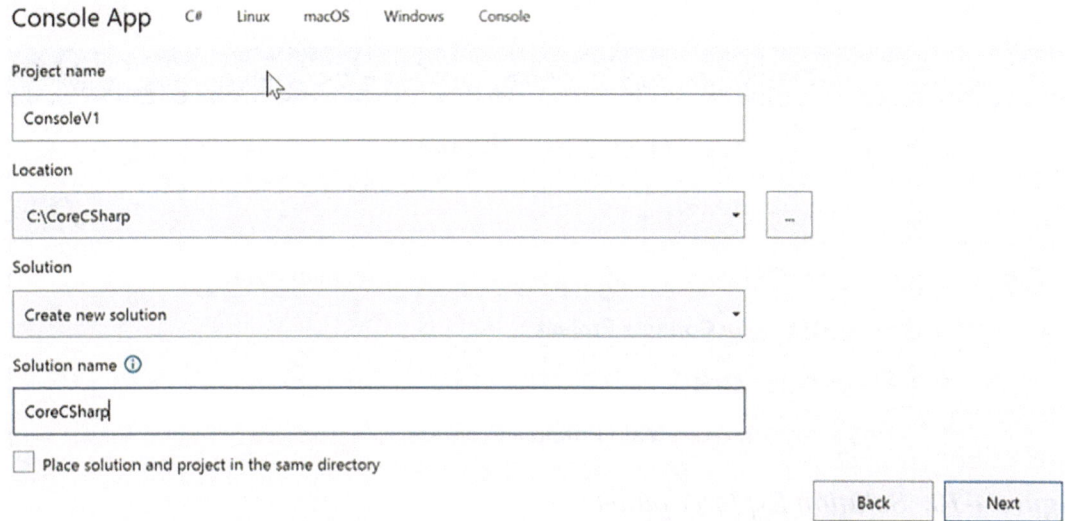

Figure 4-8. *Solution and project details*

11.   Click the Next button.

12.   Choose the framework to be used, which in our projects will be
.NET 6.0 or higher, as shown in Figure 4-9. Remember to switch off
top-level statements.

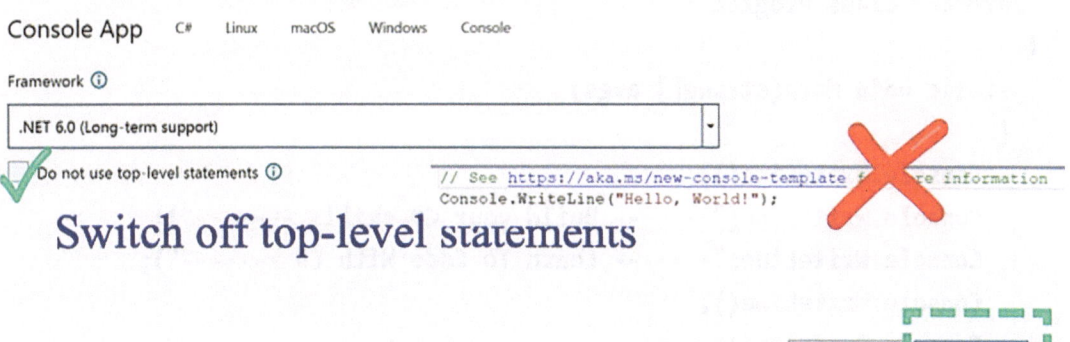

Figure 4-9. *Choose the framework version*

13.   Click the Create button.

The structure of the solution will be like that shown in Figure 4-10.

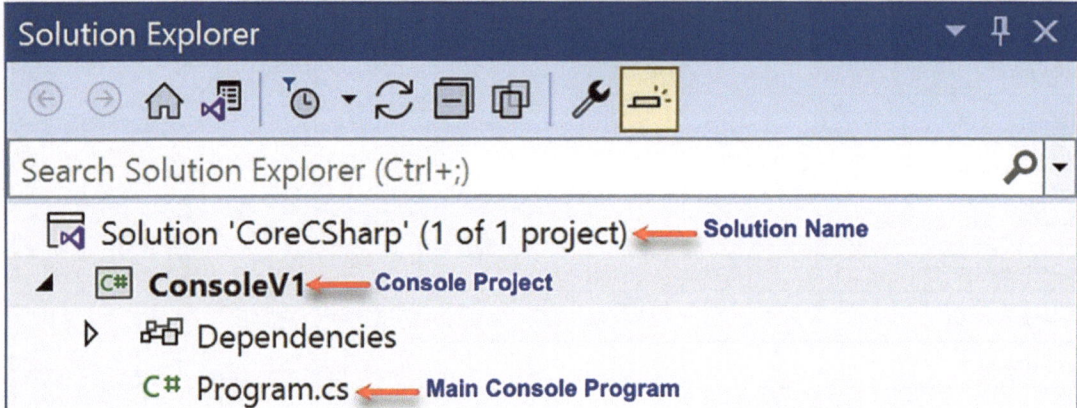

Figure 4-10. *Solution Explorer panel*

14.   Double-click the Program.cs file in the Solution Explorer window.

15.   Amend the code as shown in Listing 4-2.

Listing 4-2. ConsoleV1 code

```
using System;

namespace ConsoleV1
{
  internal class Program
  {
    static void Main(string[] args)
    {
      Console.WriteLine();
      Console.WriteLine("------- Build your C# skills -------");
      Console.WriteLine("------- Learn To Code With C# -------");
      Console.WriteLine();
      Console.ReadLine();
    } // End of Main() method
  } // End of Program class
} // End of ConsoleV1 namespace
```

Sometimes we will be given a template with some code existing within it, or we might copy code from a source such as the Internet, and we will have using statements at the top. When this happens, we need to be sure we will need all the using statements.

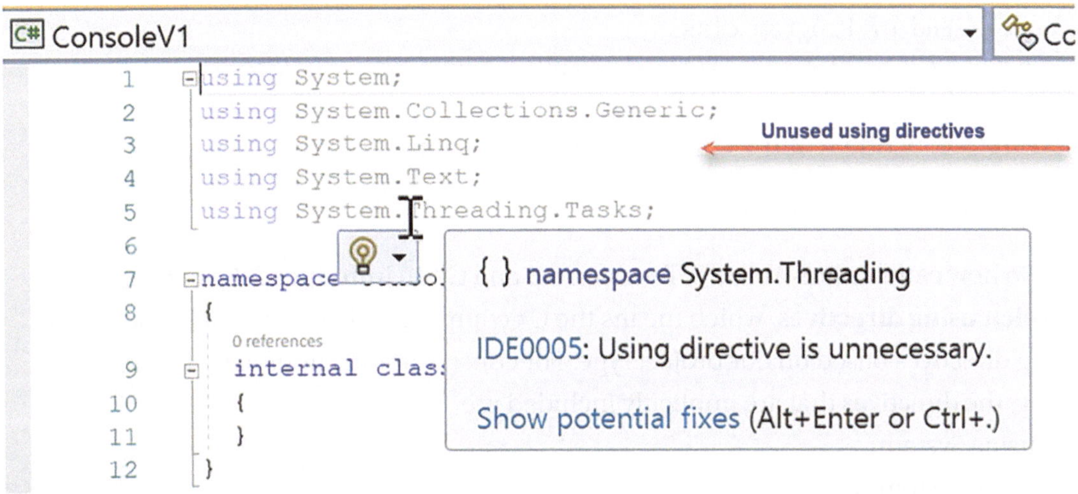

Figure 4-11. *Unused code – unused using statements*

We will see from Figure 4-11 that some of the using statements look different from those we typed in our code. We will see that those we did not enter in our code are being **"flagged"** by our Integrated Development Environment; the lines have gray text. This indicates that they are not being used in our code, and hovering over one of the unnecessary lines of code produces a pop-up message as shown in the Figure 4-11. Removing unused code is a basic principle for writing what is termed **"clean code."** We will now look at some ways in which we could "tidy" our code by removing using directives that are unnecessary.

We saw in the last chapter that the code as shown in Listing 4-3 could be shortened using top-level statements to the code shown in Listing 4-4.

Listing 4-3. "Traditional" code sample

```
using System;

namespace ConsoleVersion1
{
    public class Program
    {
```

```
    public static void Main(string[] args)
    {
        Console.ReadLine();
    } // End of Main() method
} // End of Program class
} // End of ConsoleVersion1 namespace
```

Listing 4-4. Code when we use top-level statements

```
    Console.ReadLine();
```

So how can this be? Well, .NET version 6.0 and C# 10 introduced the concept of **implicit using directives**, which means the C# compiler will automatically add a set of using directives based on our project type. For console applications, which we will be using, the directives that are implicitly included are

using System;

using System.IO;

using System.Collections.Generic;

using System.Linq;

using System.Net.Http;

using System.Threading;

using System.Threading.Tasks;

Therefore, this is why we do not have to include the using System; statement at the top of our code.

C# 10 also introduced the concept of a **global using directive**, which means we do not have to write the same using directives in each file in our project. It is now possible to convert an ordinary using directive into a global using directive by adding the global modifier: global using System;. If we add this at the top of any file in our project, it will be as if we added it to all the files in the project.

Another way to manage the using directives is to use the context menu, which can be displayed by right-clicking in the code. There will then be an option to Remove and Sort Usings, as shown in Figure 4-12, and if this is selected, the unnecessary using directives will be removed, while all other required using directives will be sorted.

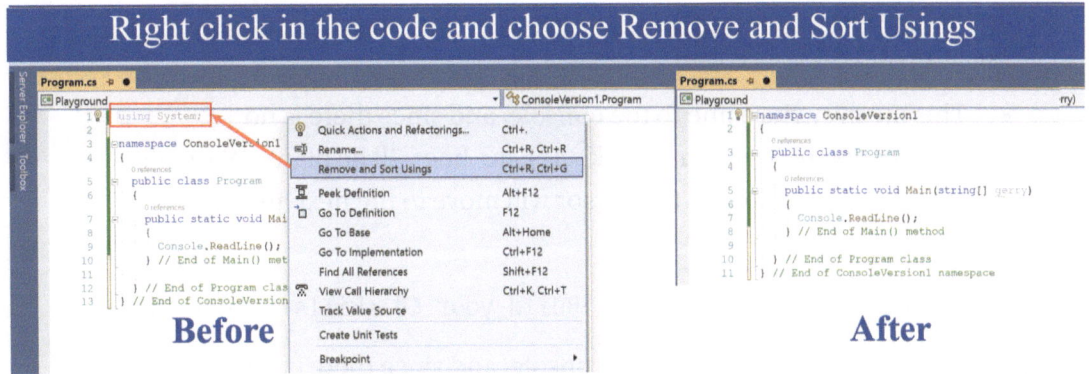

Figure 4-12. *Context menu with the Remove and Sort Usings option*

16. Click the Debug menu.

17. Choose Start Without Debugging.

Figure 4-13. *Console output in black and white*

18. Press the Enter key to continue the code execution as the code has paused on the Console.ReadLine() statement waiting for a key to be pressed on the keyboard, as shown in Figure 4-13.

19. Press the Enter key again to close the console window.

The console window will disappear, and the application will be terminated as there are no lines of code to be executed after the Console.ReadLine() line.

Code Analysis

```
Console.WriteLine()
```

- This means write a line to the console, and since there is no information between the brackets (), the line will be blank. With the WriteLine() command, the cursor will move to the next line as its final act.

```
Console.WriteLine("------- Build your C# skills -------");
```

- This means write a line to the console, and since there is information between the brackets (), the line displays the text exactly as shown between the **double quotes ""**. The double quotes indicate that the displayed text is always going to be whatever has been typed between the double quotes; it is a string. The text is therefore a `constant`; it will not change throughout the lifetime of the application. We could say it is *not a variable, so it is a constant*. With the WriteLine() command, the cursor will move to the next line as its final act.

```
Console.ReadLine()
```

This means read a line from the console. It is **input**.

- Fact 1

  Here again, first, we can see the keyword `Console` and, as stated previously, this refers to something that interacts with the console. In this case we will use Console to interact with the console in Visual Studio, where **input from the user will be accepted**. This is different from the output from the computer program in Listing 4-2 when we used the Console.WriteLine() method.

- Fact 2

  The second part is the **dot**, the full stop or period as it is also known. As we saw earlier, in C# code the full stop means that we want to use a part or element of the object that appears to the left of the full stop. The part or element will be a variable or a method.

- Fact 3

  The third part is `ReadLine()`.

  We should now be able to recognize that ReadLine() is indeed a method; it has the brackets () at the end. As this method has nothing between the brackets (), we should be aware that this means the method takes in no value. It is empty of input **parameters**.

- Fact 4

  Console belongs to a namespace called `System`. As stated previously, this is not obvious from the line of code. If we really wanted to make this fact obvious, we could have written the line of code as `System.Console.ReadLine();`

In our code we could

- Use the full naming convention `System.Console.ReadLine();` and **NOT** have the `using System` at the top of the code.

- Use the shortened version `Console.ReadLine();` and have the `using System` at the top of the code.

As developers it is our choice. The reality is that most developers in the technology world will probably use the shortened version. We will therefore see in nearly every commercial C# application code a lot of using statements at the top of the code, including `using System`, **but we must remember that this directive is one of the directives that are implicitly included in a console application and it can therefore be omitted.**

20.   Amend the code, as in Listing 4-5, to add a statement that requests the user to press a key on the keyboard.

Listing 4-5. WriteLine() to ask to press a keyboard key

```
Console.WriteLine("------- Learn To Code With C# -------");
Console.WriteLine();
Console.WriteLine("Press any keyboard letter to continue");
Console.ReadLine();
} // End of Main() method
```

```
} // End of class
} // End of namespace
```

21. Amend the code, as in Listing 4-6, to display a message saying Goodbye to the user. Then, as we see the message, add another read line statement.

Listing 4-6. WriteLine() to display a message and ReadLine() to read a key

```
    Console.ReadLine();
    Console.WriteLine("Goodbye");
    Console.ReadLine();
  } // End of Main() method
  } // End of class
} // End of namespace
```

22. Click the File menu.

23. Choose Save All.

24. Click the Debug menu.

25. Choose Start Without Debugging.

The console window will appear, as shown in Figure 4-14, with the message being displayed. The cursor will be flashing waiting for user input.

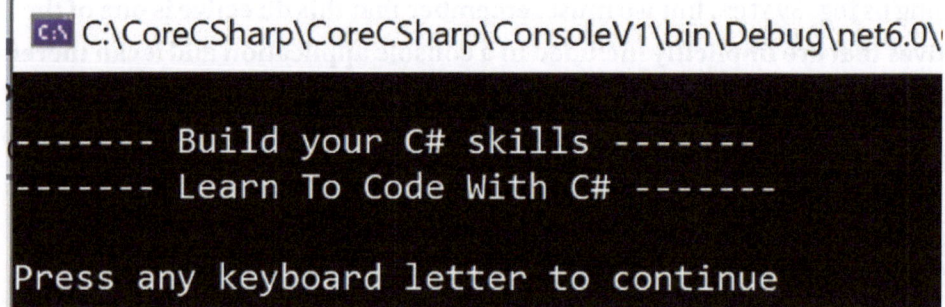

Figure 4-14. *Console waiting for a key press*

26.   Press any key on the keyboard.

The Goodbye message will appear, as shown in Figure 4-15, and the cursor will be flashing waiting for user input.

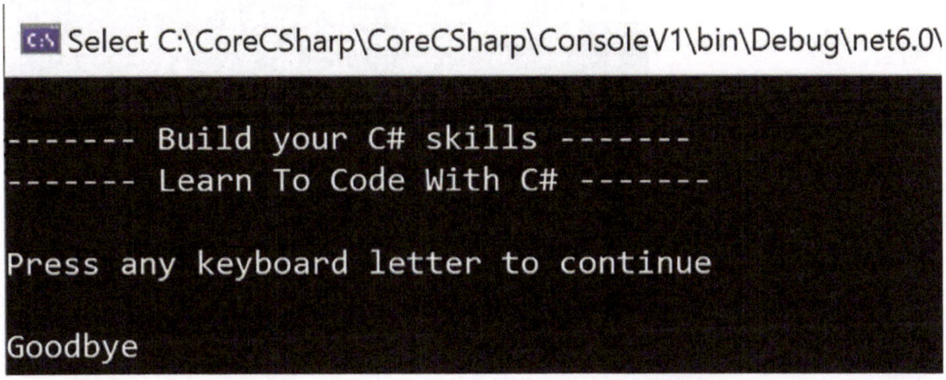

Figure 4-15. *Console accepts a key and displays the message*

27.   Press the Enter key on the keyboard.

28.   Press the Enter key again.

Now that we have the concept of input and output and we have started using lines of C# programming code that industry developers use, we can progress to using other programming concepts in our code.

Change Console Display Settings

When the console window is visible on the screen, we can amend the console window preferences, as shown in Figure 4-16.

1.   Click the Debug menu.

2.   Choose Start Without Debugging.

3.   Click the icon in the top left of the console window.

4.   Choose Properties from the drop-down list, as shown in Figure 4-16.

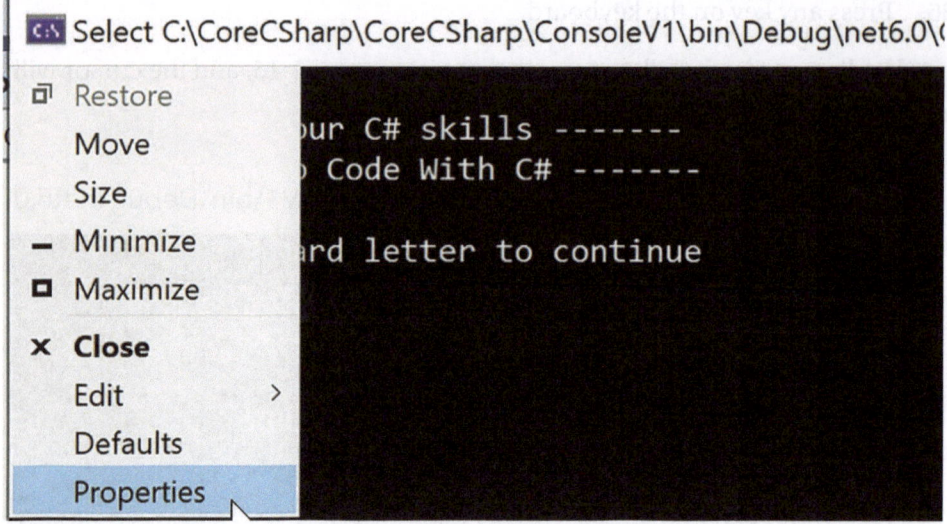

Figure 4-16. *Console display settings*

5. Click the Screen Text radio button, as shown in Figure 4-17.

6. Change the values for the Red, Green, and Blue to be 0, as shown in Figure 4-17.

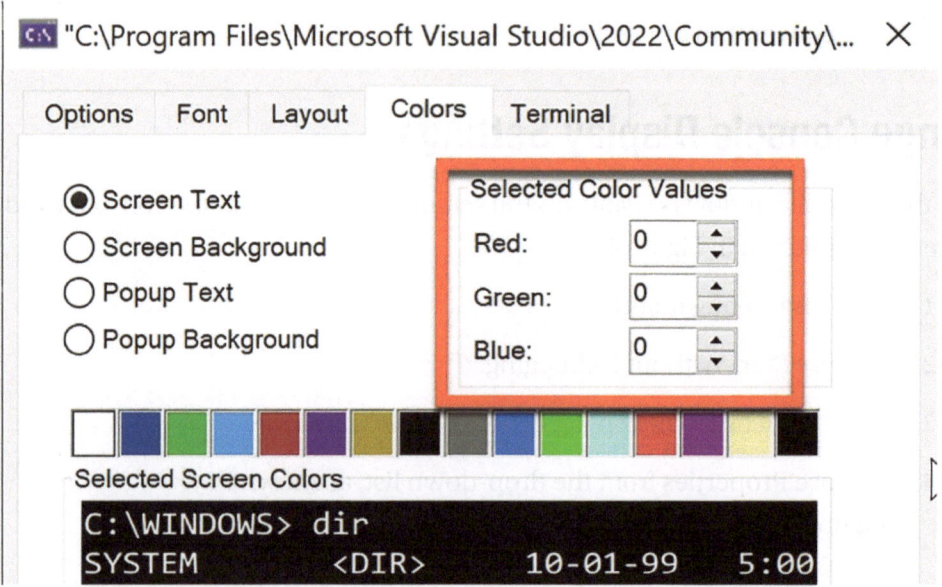

Figure 4-17. *Console display settings – text color*

7. Click the Screen Background radio button, as shown in
    Figure 4-18.

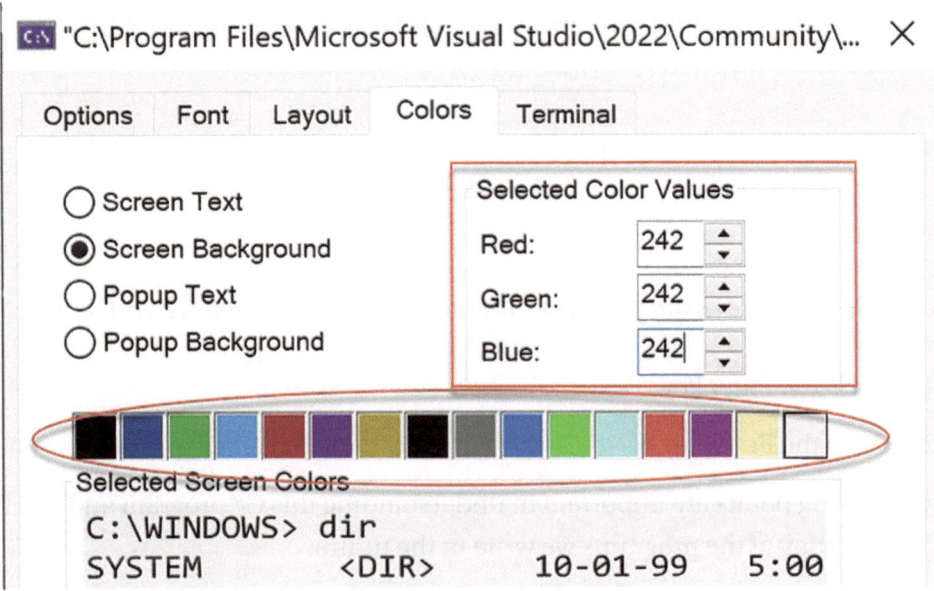

Figure 4-18. *Console display settings – background color*

8. Change the background color by picking from the row of
    displayed colors or entering values for the RGB colors, as shown in
    Figure 4-18.

9. Click the OK button.

10. Press the Enter key.

The console window will be as shown in Figure 4-19, with the message being
displayed. The cursor will be flashing and is waiting for user input.

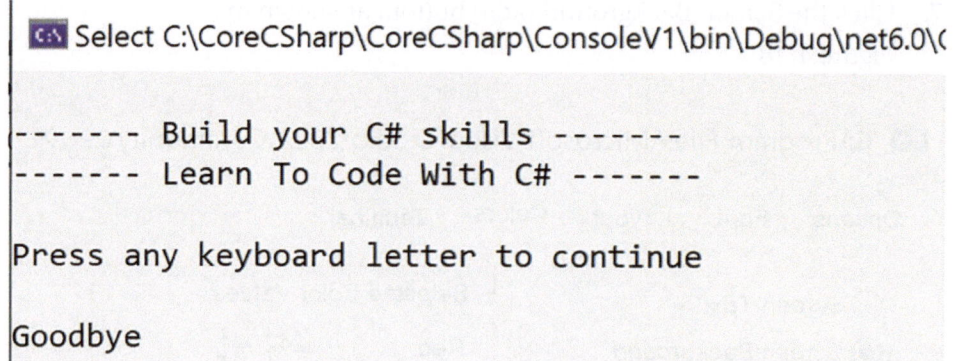

Figure 4-19. *Console display settings have changed background and text*

11. Press the Enter key.

12. Press the Enter key.

The following points are important in understanding this C# program and will be applicable to many of the programs we write in the future:

- The **using statements** at the top of the code represent namespaces that contain classes that we need to help our program work.

- Classes are program code that hold **properties** and **methods** that are made available to the programmer.

- We are developing a C# project and the project has a **Program.cs** class.

- It is in this Program class that we have written our code. In future projects we can rename the Program class or add a new class and give it a name of our choice.

- This class has what is called an **access modifier** in front of the word class. The access modifier is the **default access modifier** of **internal**. Having the default take control is never a good idea or good practice. We could, and should, add an access modifier instead of the default to help make the code more readable and understandable. It is our program, so we need to control what is going on. If we add the word **public** in front of the word class, as in Listing 4-7, we are telling the class that it is accessible by other code in the project; this is a simplified definition but sufficient for us at the moment.

- If we remove the keyword internal from in front of the word class,
  then the default will be used and the code will be the same whether
  or not the word internal is present.

Listing 4-7. The public keyword in front of the class

```
namespace ConsoleV1
{
   public class Program
  {
    static void Main(string[] args)
    {
```

- The curly left brace on the line following `internal class Program`
  matches the closing brace on the second last line of the example, as
  in Listing 4-8, with the comment `// End of class`. This is because
  the whole class definition is between the open and close braces.

Listing 4-8. The opening and closing curly braces to contain the code

```
namespace ConsoleV1
{
  internal class Program
  {
    static void Main(string[] args)
    {
    } // End of Main() method
  } // End of class
} // End of namespace
```

- The code in the class can be included within the method
  called **Main()**.

  As we read the chapters in the book, we will often see that when
  a method is referred to by name, it will also include the open and
  close parentheses, (). This technique is used to emphasize and

reinforce that () means a method, a block of code. The actual
name of the method is the name without the (), for example, Main
rather than Main().

- The method also has what is called an **access modifier** in front of the
  words `static void`. The access modifier may not be visible because
  we did not type it, and so the **default access modifier** of **private** is
  invisibly added. We could add a different access modifier. We could
  add the word public in front of the word static, as in Listing 4-9,
  and therefore we are telling the Main() method that it is accessible
  by other code in our project. Remember the idea of default is not
  helping us fully understand the code we are reading or writing.

Listing 4-9. The public keyword in front of the Main() method

```
namespace ConsoleV1
{
  internal class Program
  {
    public static void Main(string[] args)
    {
    } // End of Main() method
  } // End of class
} // End of namespace
```

- The **method signature**, `Main(string[] args)`, defines the name of
  the method, **Main**, which is followed by the method body, which is
  enclosed in braces.

- The words `static` and `void` will be explained later, but they are
  always used with a Main() method. The two words static and void are
  examples of C# keywords, words that have a special meaning in a C#
  program and that cannot be used for any other purpose.

- The other keywords in the preceding example are `public` and `class.`

- The Console.WriteLine() statement displays the text contained between the brackets () and inside the quotes in a console window.

- The Console.ReadLine() statement waits to read a line of text from the console. The line of text is determined when the Enter key has been pressed.

- These lines of code within the Main() method constitute C# statements, that is, commands to be carried out.

- Each C# statement is terminated by a semicolon ;

Chapter Summary

In this chapter we have seen and applied the concept of **input** and **output** and we have started using lines of C# programming code that industry developers use. We started using the Integrated Development Environment, Visual Studio, to maintain a solution that contains our first C# project. We will be adding other projects to this solution, but we have made a great start in developing a solution with a project, which helps with the concept of separation of concern, which means each of our projects can work independently. Within our project we met the Program.cs class where we added our code. In typing our code, we met the method, represented as a cube; the property, represented as a spanner; and the event, represented as a lightning bolt. And we saw that colors within the code editor, like the symbols, helped make our code easier to code, read, and eventually maintain. Finally, we looked at how to change the console appearance from a black background to another color using the Properties option.

As we progress, we will be using other programming concepts in our code, but we have made great progress in learning the essentials for writing a C# application using an Integrated Development Environment like Visual Studio. We have used C# statements, and if we refer to the recipe in Table 3-1 in Chapter 3, we will see that statements are like the ingredients of the recipe.

In finishing this chapter and increasing our knowledge, we are advancing to our target.

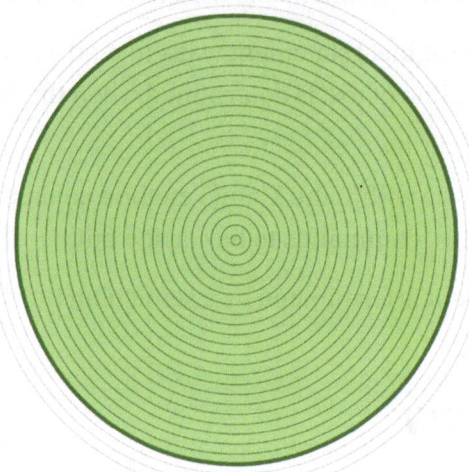

Our target is getting closer

CHAPTER 5

Commenting Code

We learned in Chapter 4 that our application code can involve input and output and that the input and output can be completed in the console window. The output from our application is the visible part for an end user and it is important they have a good experience when seeing the output. The user experience is often referred to as the UX and can involve the developer making use of colors, emphasis, layout, etc. to make the application readable and pleasing to look at.

This chapter will concentrate on how to create a **good user experience for the developer** rather than the end user, when they are creating, reading, and maintaining code. It is particularly important to understand that as developers we should be having a good user experience when we look at any application code, whether it is our code or someone else's.

As a starting point, we will state that one of the current themes in the domain of programming in the commercial environment is writing **self-documenting** code. This is a great idea and one that we can achieve by writing C# code statements that will be easily understood by other developers who will read, use, or maintain the code. In fact, it can even make the original writer of the code, us, understand it better when returning to it to make amendments. We should always keep the strategy of self-documenting code foremost in our thoughts. Writing self-documenting code can be easy to do and can involve simple steps and techniques, which will become "second nature" after a while. These include

- Adding **astutely placed comments** as explanations in our code.

- Not overusing comments. Not everything will need a comment if the code is written well, but comments can be a big help to the reader.

- Our **variable names** being such that they explain the variable purpose.

© Gerard Byrne 2022
G. Byrne, *Target C#*, https://doi.org/10.1007/978-1-4842-8619-7_5

- Our **method names** being such that they explain the method purpose.

- Our **class names** being such that they explain the purpose of the class.

Another strategy is to use colors in the coding statements. We should have already noticed that the Visual Studio Integrated Development Environment has colored parts of our code. Examples of code coloring are shown in Figure 5-1.

```csharp
using System;

namespace ConsoleV1
{
    0 references
    internal class Program
    {
        0 references
        static void Main(string[] args)
        {
            Console.WriteLine();
            Console.WriteLine("------- Build your C# skills -------");
            Console.WriteLine("------- Learn To Code With C# -------");
            Console.WriteLine();
            Console.WriteLine("Press any keyboard letter to continue");

            Console.ReadLine();
            Console.WriteLine("Goodbye");
            Console.ReadLine();

        } // End of Main() method
    } // End of Program class
} // End of ConsoleV1 namespace
```

Figure 5-1. *Visual Studio code coloring*

This code coloring within Visual Studio is one way in which Microsoft has attempted to help developers who write and read code.

Note

In the code examples we will use throughout the chapters in this book, there will be lots of comments used to help us understand the code, but if these were commercial applications, we would not have as many comments.

Make sure to read the code comments in the course code examples as they have invaluable information that adds to and supplements the text of this book. They are in the code to help clarify what we are doing and why we are doing certain things. So we should not ignore them. We should read them, but we do not necessarily have to type the comments into our code.

Comments can be used to give information such as

- A description indicating the purpose of the application

- Information about the developer or developers

- The date on which the program was first created

- The date when maintenance occurred, for example, when lines of code were amended, added, or deleted

- What a line of code or lines of code are doing

- The purpose of a method

- The purpose of a delegate that is linked to a method

- The purpose or intrinsic workings of a complicated formula

C# Single-Line Comments

Single-line comments in C#, and many other programming languages, are preceded by two forward slash symbols, //. The // indicates a single-line comment, which is generally used for brief comments. Some developers will write the comments above the code, while others will use the comment on the same line as the code. Both types are shown in Listings 5-1, 5-2, and 5-3.

Example 1

Listing 5-1 shows an example of three single-line comments, which could be used at the start of a program to give the user information about the program, the developer, and the creation date. The comments are at the start of the program code before any C# statements are entered.

Listing 5-1. Single-line comments

```
// Program:   A simple C# program to output text and read input
// Author:    Gerry Byrne
// Date of creation: 01/06/2021
```

Example 2

Listing 5-2 shows a single-line comment, which gives the user information about the class called Program that follows it. The single-line comment appears above the code statement.

Listing 5-2. Single-line comment above code

```
// This is our only class and it will contain the Main method
class Program
```

Example 3

Listing 5-3 shows a single-line comment, which gives the user information about the line of code. In this case the single-line comment appears on the same line as the code statement.

Listing 5-3. Inline comment

```
Console.ReadLine(); // This code line waits for the user input
```

Projects and Solutions

Before we start writing the code for this chapter, let us think about the project we created in Chapter 4. When we created it, we gave the project the name ConsoleV1, which was perfectly fine at the time, but definitely not very descriptive. We will talk more about naming later. Now, when we wish to code the example for this chapter, where will we put our code?

Well, we can do this in

- The existing project in the solution, where we can amend the existing class or create a new class to hold the new code

- A new folder within the existing project

- A new project that we can create

For this exercise we will create a new project in the existing solution, and we will rename the existing project to ensure its name fits in with the way we will name all the projects for the chapters in the book. But what should we call the old and new projects? If we think about what we have just talked about, self-documenting code, we should question the name of the project and folders within it. When we created the project in Chapter 4, we called it ConsoleV1, but maybe it should have been named better, for example:

- ConsoleApplications

- Coursecode

- Chapter4

If we decide that a name change would be appropriate, we can **rename** the project, but will the code in the class need to be changed? No, this will not affect the code in the project.

Rename the ConsoleV1 project:

1. Make sure the solution and project are open in Visual Studio.

2. Right-click the ConsoleV1 project name.

3. Choose Rename, as shown in Figure 5-2.

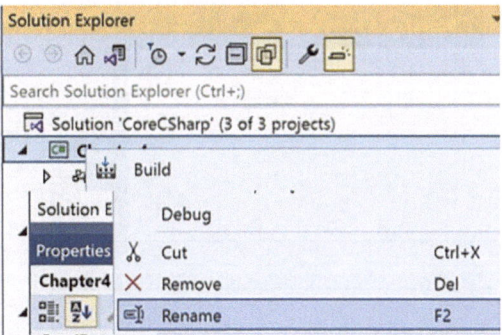

Figure 5-2. *Renaming a C# project*

4. Name the project Chapter4.

5. Press the Enter key.

The project within the solution is now displayed within the Solution Explorer panel with the new name as shown in Figure 5-3. We will not worry for now about the namespace name in the program code.

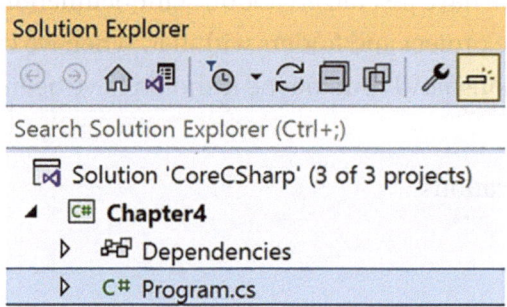

Figure 5-3. *Renamed C# project*

Add a new project to hold the code for this chapter:

6. Right-click the CoreCSharp solution name in the Solution Explorer panel.

7. Choose Add, as shown in Figure 5-4.

8. Choose New Project.

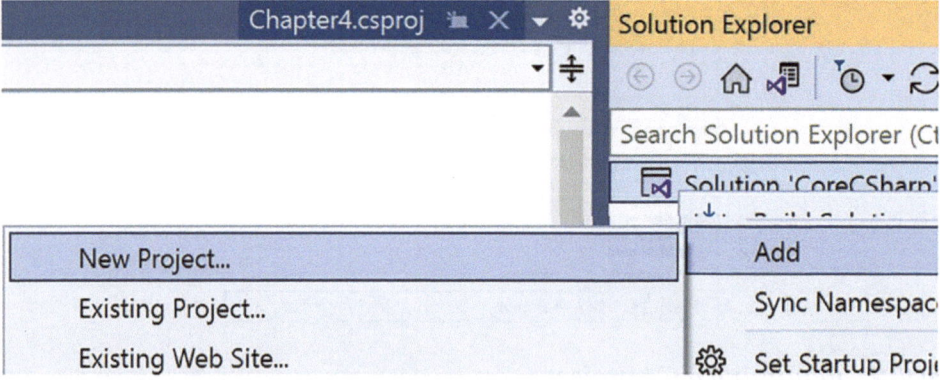

Figure 5-4. *Adding a new C# project*

9. Choose Console App from the listed templates that appear, as shown in Figure 5-5.

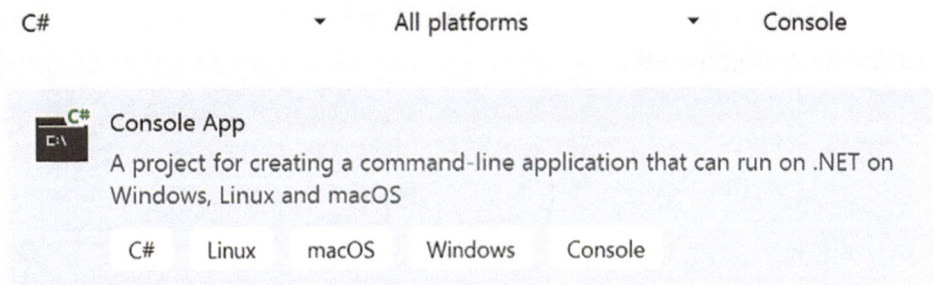

Figure 5-5. *Selecting a new C# console project*

10.   Click the Next button.

11.   Name the project Chapter5, leaving it in the same location, as shown in Figure 5-6.

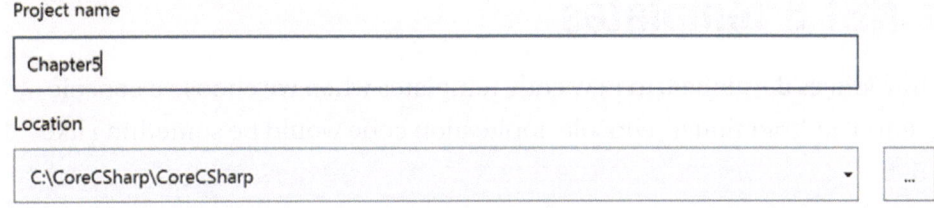

Figure 5-6. *Naming a new C# console project*

12.   Click the Next button.

13.   Choose the framework to be used, which in our projects will be .NET 6.0 or higher, as shown in Figure 5-7.

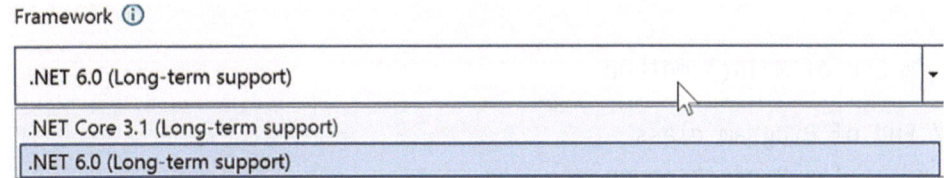

Figure 5-7. *Choosing the project framework*

14.   Click the Create button.

Now we should see the two projects, Chapter4 and Chapter5, within the solution called CoreCSharp (Figure 5-8).

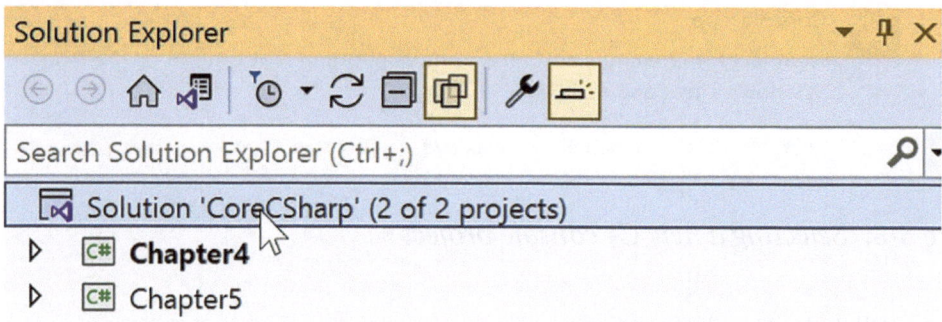

Figure 5-8. *Solution Explorer displaying all projects*

New .NET 6 Templates

.NET 6 introduces developers to new code templates when we choose a console application. The "traditional" console application code would be something like Listing 5-4.

Listing 5-4. A "traditional" code example

```
namespace TestProject
{
  internal class Program
  {
    static void Main(string[] args)
    {
    } // End of Main() method

  } // End of Program class
} // End of TestProject namespace
```

In .NET 6 the console application template code will be like Listing 5-5.

Listing 5-5. Code template in .NET 6

```
// See https://aka.ms/new-console-template for more information
Console.WriteLine("Hello, World!");
```

Remember we can switch off top-level statements when we create a new project, as in Figure 5-9.

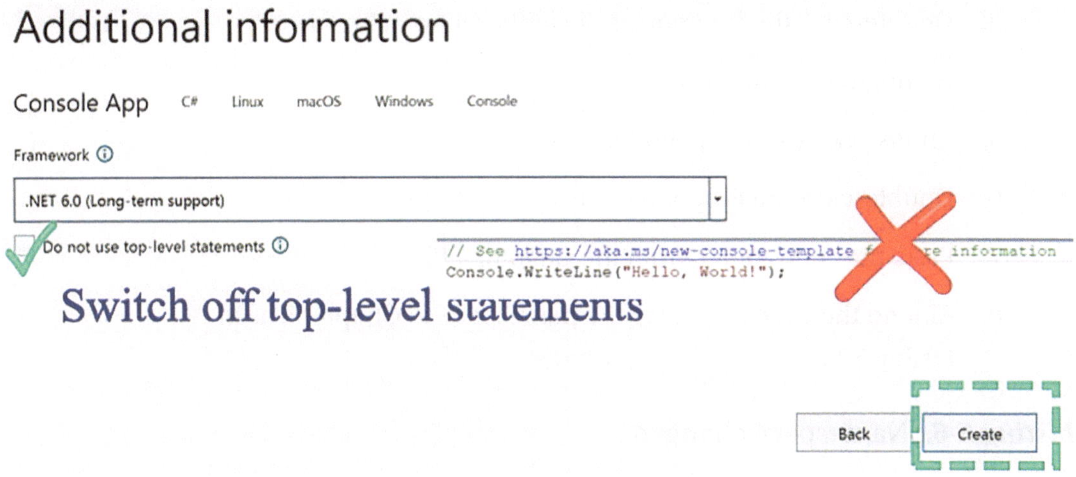

Figure 5-9. *Switching off top-level statements*

This new template code reflects new C# 10 features, which allow us to simplify our code. The two template codes, Listings 5-4 and 5-5, are effectively the same thing and will work in C# 10. C# 10 therefore allows us to

---

Write the code for the Main() method, leaving out the namespace, class, Main() method, and using statements.

This is very nice, when you know what you are doing and have a good understanding of the core C# programming fundamentals. For now, and throughout the chapters in this book, we will overwrite the code in the new template and work with the "older" format, where we will code the namespace name and the class name, include the Main() method when required, and display all the using statements. If we switch off the top-level statements by ticking the checkbox once on any project creation, the option will be remembered for future projects. All of this will become abundantly clear when we code the examples. By using our format in the chapter examples, it will allow us to understand C# code much better and be able to read code already written in this format, and we can then start using the "shortcut" style for future applications.

We will now copy the code from the Chapter4 Program.cs file and paste it into the Chapter5 Program.cs file.

1. Double-click the Program.cs file in the Chapter5 folder.

2. Delete the two lines of code in the Program.cs file.

3. Double-click the Program.cs file in the Chapter4 project.

4. Highlight all of the code.

5. Choose Copy from the Edit menu.

6. Double-click the Program.cs file in the Chapter 5 folder.

7. Paste the code copied from the Chapter 4 file.

8. Amend the code to change the namespace to Chapter5, as in Listing 5-6.

Listing 5-6. Namespace changed

```
namespace Chapter5
{
  public class Program
  {
    public static void Main(string[] args)
    {
      Console.WriteLine();
      Console.WriteLine("------- Build your C# skills -------");
      Console.WriteLine("------- Learn To Code With C# -------");
      Console.WriteLine();
      Console.WriteLine("Press any keyboard letter to continue");
      Console.ReadLine();
      Console.WriteLine("Goodbye");
      Console.ReadLine();
    } // End of Main() method
  } // End of Program class
} // End of Chapter5 namespace
```

We will now amend the code to include comments to demonstrate the use of single-line comments before a line of code and at the end of a code line.

9. Add comments to the program code, as in Listing 5-7.

Listing 5-7. Single-line comments

```
// Program:    A simple C# program to output text and read input
// Author:    Gerry Byrne
// Date of creation:    01/06/2021

namespace Chapter5
{
  // This is our only class and it will contain the Main method
  public class Program
  {
    public static void Main(string[] args)
    {
      Console.WriteLine();
      Console.WriteLine("------- Build your C# skills -------");
      Console.WriteLine("------- Learn To Code With C# -------");
      Console.WriteLine();
      Console.WriteLine("Press any keyboard letter to continue");
      Console.ReadLine();// This line waits for the user to input
      Console.WriteLine("Goodbye");
      Console.ReadLine();
    } // End of Main() method
  } // End of Program class
} // End of Chapter5 namespace
```

10. Right-click the Chapter5 project in the Solution Explorer panel.

11. Choose Set as Startup Project.

12. Click the File menu.

13. Choose Save All.

14. Click the Debug menu.

15. Choose Start Without Debugging.

The console window will appear as shown in Figure 5-10 and ask us to press any letter on the keyboard.

C:\ C:\CoreCSharp\CoreCSharp\Chapter5\bin\Debug\net6.0\Chapter5.exe

```
------- Build your C# skills -------
------- Learn To Code With C# -------

Press any keyboard letter to continue
```

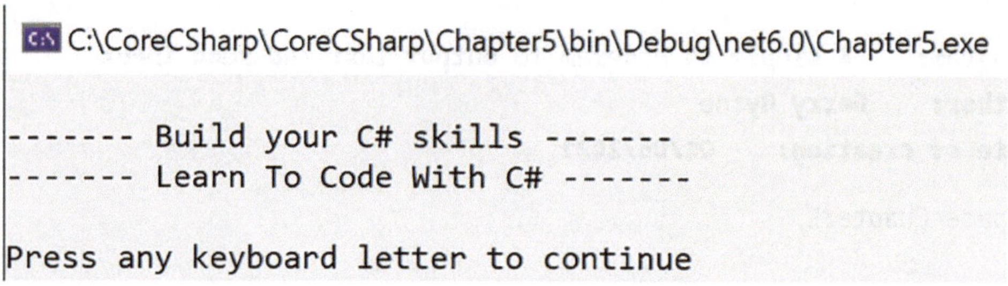

Figure 5-10. *Console output – waiting on keyboard input*

16.   Press any letter on the keyboard to continue, for example, **a**.

17.   Press the Enter key.

The Goodbye message is displayed as shown in Figure 5-11.

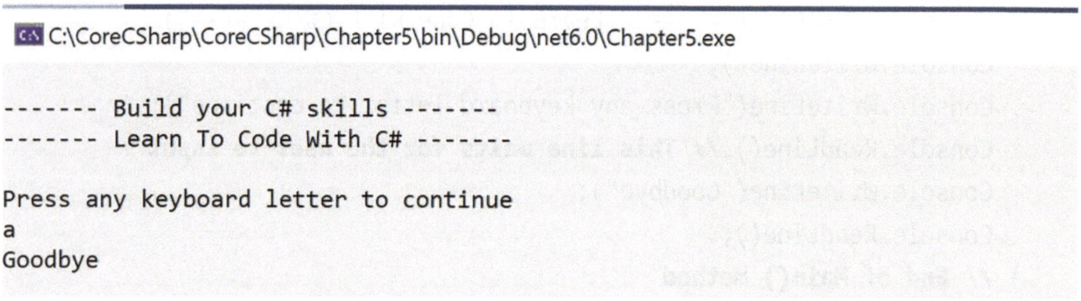

C:\ C:\CoreCSharp\CoreCSharp\Chapter5\bin\Debug\net6.0\Chapter5.exe

```
------- Build your C# skills -------
------- Learn To Code With C# -------

Press any keyboard letter to continue
a
Goodbye
```

Figure 5-11. *Console output*

18.   Press the Enter key.

19.   Press the Enter key.

The code has produced an application that performs exactly as it did before we added the comment lines. So **comments are for a reader of the code** and do not change what the application does. The **comments are ignored in the process of building and compiling** the program from the source code we have written.

C# Multiple-Line Comments

Multiple-line comments, also called **comment blocks,** are enclosed between the symbols /* and */ and are used for longer comments. The /* is the start and the */ is the end of the block comment, as in Listing 5-8. We can also enclose a single-line comment between /* and */ symbols and it is still a valid comment.

Listing 5-8. Multiple-line comment

```
/*
Longer comments in a C# program can easily extend over several lines so
long as they start with the proper characters. This is an example of
multiple line comments
*/
```

We will now add a multiple-line comment that will help explain what a C# namespace is used for and another to say a little about the Main() method. As stated earlier, throughout the chapters we will use comments, and it is important to read them as they act as reinforcement of our knowledge or as an explanation.

1. Add the multiple-line comments, as in Listing 5-9, to our program code.

Listing 5-9. Multiple-line comments

```
// Program: A simple C# program to output text and read input
// Author:  Gerry Byrne
// Date of creation: 01/06/2021

/*
C# programming namespaces are commonly used in two ways:

1. C#, or more precisely .NET, uses namespaces to organise the
many classes it contains (remember classes contain methods and
variables)
2. C# allows us as developers to create our own namespaces.
We can use the namespace keyword to declare a namespace
e.g. namespace Chapter5
```

```
A namespace can have the same name as the project but it can
also be any name we wish. The name is independent of the
Project name
*/
namespace Chapter5
{
  // This is our only class and it will contain the Main method
  public class Program
  {
    /*
    We now have our main method which will contain all our code.
    As we become a better developer, we will not have all our
    code contained within the main method.
    This would be seen as poor code and not fitting in with the
    design principle of modular code.
    */
    public static void Main(string[] args)
    {
```

2. Click the File menu.

3. Choose Save All.

4. Click the Debug menu.

5. Choose Start Debugging.

    The console window will appear and ask us to press any letter on
    the keyboard.

6. Press any letter on the keyboard to continue, for example, **a**.

7. Press the Enter key.

    The Goodbye message is displayed as shown in Figure 5-12.

```
C:\CoreCSharp\CoreCSharp\Chapter5\bin\Debug\net6.0\Chapter5.exe

------- Build your C# skills -------
------- Learn To Code With C# -------

Press any keyboard letter to continue
a
Goodbye
```

Figure 5-12. *Console output*

8. Press the Enter key.

9. Press the Enter key.

Chapter Summary

In this chapter we have added comments to our code to help us understand what the code is doing and to reinforce certain aspects of the C# programming language. We have used comments to give information about namespaces and the Main() method. Remember the golden rule: **only use comments when they are required and the code itself is not self-documenting.**

The code for the names of

- The namespace

- The project

- The class

- The variables

- The constants

should be self-documenting, which means that no comments should be necessary for them. Some people would say

> *If we cannot write legible code, then it is unlikely we will be able to write legible comments.*

Harsh? Maybe, but it reinforces the point that comments should not be a replacement for self-documenting code.

In finishing this chapter and increasing our knowledge, we are advancing to our target and making good progress.

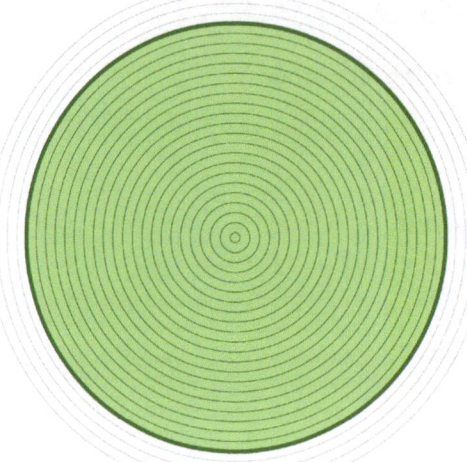

Our target is getting closer

CHAPTER 6

Data Types

Data Types, Variables, and Conversion

We learned in Chapter 5 that while we can use single- and multiple-line comments, they should not be a replacement for self-documenting code. Comments are added to help the reader of the code, but when the code is written expressively with proper namespace names, class names, variable names, etc., there is a limited need for comments. We should set an objective of zero need for comments.

In this chapter we will use code that is well documented for the purposes of helping us understand and read the code. It is not how we would do it in a real application, and if it was commercial code, we would be breaking the objective of zero need for comments.

We will learn from this chapter about the very important concepts of **data types and variables**. We will use data types and variables in all the C# programs in this book. That is how crucial they are to C# programming. We should also be aware that data types and variables exist in all programming languages and are a core building block for the code we will write.

Data Types

There are different data types in C#, and we will use **value types and reference types**. In C#, value types contain data, and we will use value types such as those shown in Table 6-1.

© Gerard Byrne 2022
G. Byrne, *Target C#*, https://doi.org/10.1007/978-1-4842-8619-7_6

Table 6-1. *Value types in C#*

Bool	byte	char	decimal
float	double	int	long
short	uint	ushort	

When we declare a data type, we are reserving memory to store a value. Each data type will have a particular size of memory that needs to be set aside. In C#, and indeed in other languages, these value types are referred to as **primitive types**. The primitive types are therefore predefined by the C# language and their names are reserved keywords.

When we use C# as our programming language, we will inherently be using .NET. .NET also allows us to use other programming languages such as Visual Basic .NET and F#, each of which has its own data types. This might seem strange that we can have an int data type in C#, an int data type in F#, and an int data type in Visual Basic .NET. So how do we ensure that the data types for each .NET programming language have the same meaning? Well, this is where the **Common Type System (CTS)** comes into play. The Common Type System has the overarching data types that all language data types are tied to. The concept is called **interoperability**, the ability to exchange and make use of information.

Data types in C# and Visual Basic (VB) are shown in Table 6-2, along with the equivalent data type in .NET. For now, **do not get too distracted by all this theory**. All will become clear as we code our examples. However, it is easy to see the connection between the language types and the .NET types.

Table 6-2. *C# and VB data types and correlation with the .NET framework types*

C# type	VB type	.NET type	Bytes	Description
bool	**Boolean**	**Boolean**	1	Contains either true or false
char	**Char**	**Char**	2	Contains any single Unicode character enclosed in single quotation marks such as 'c'

Integral types

C# type	VB type	.NET type	Bytes	Description
byte	**Byte**	**Byte**	1	May contain integers from 0 to 255
sbyte	**SByte**	**SByte**	1	Signed byte from −128 to 127
short	Short	**Int16**	2	Ranges from −32,768 to 32,767
ushort	**UShort**	**UInt16**	2	Unsigned, ranges from 0 to 65,535
int	**Integer**	**Int32**	4	Ranges from −2,147,483,648 to 2,147,483,647
uint	UInteger	**UInt32**	4	Unsigned, ranges from 0 to 4,294,967,295
long	**Long**	**Int64**	8	Ranges from −9,223,372,036,854,775,808 to 9,223,372,036,854,775,807
ulong	**ULong**	**UInt64**	8	Unsigned, ranges from 0 to 18,446,744,073,709,551,615

Floating-point types

C# type	VB type	.NET type	Bytes	Description
float	**Single**	**Single**	4	Ranges from $\pm 1.5 \times 10^{-45}$ to $\pm 3.4 \times 10^{38}$ with 7 digits of precision Requires the suffix "f" or "F"
double	**Double**	**Double**	8	Ranges from $\pm 5.0 \times 10^{-324}$ to $\pm 1.7 \times 10^{308}$ with 15–16 digits of precision
decimal	**Decimal**	**Decimal**	12 **16 in VB**	Ranges from 1.0×10^{-28} to 7.9×10^{28} with 28–29 digits of precision. Requires the suffix "m" or "M"

Note

- Data types are represented in the C# language using **keywords**, so each of the preceding data types – float, double, etc. – is a keyword in C#.

- Keywords are defined by the language and cannot be used as identifiers.

- **string** is also an acceptable data type in C#, so string is also a keyword, but string is not a value type – it is a reference type. Unlike value types, a reference type does not store its value directly; rather, it stores the address where the value is being stored. Reference types therefore contain a pointer to a memory location where the data is held.

Conversion from One Data Type to Another

Sometimes when we code, we will receive a message to the effect that data cannot be converted from one data type to another data type. This will become clearer as we go through the course chapters, but what we will learn is that when we want to convert from one data type to another data type, this can happen in one of two ways using either

- **Implicit** conversion

  This means that in our code we do not need to do anything, as the conversion is automatically handled by the compiler.

- **Explicit** conversion

  This means that we will need to code the data type conversion as the conversion cannot be done automatically. The compiler will complain, through an error message, if it cannot handle the conversion.

Figure 6-1 shows implicit and explicit conversion possibilities.

Figure 6-1. *Implicit and explicit or widening and narrowing conversions*

Converting

We will be able to perform data type conversions using methods from the System. Convert class. The class methods allow us to perform

- Widening conversions

  Widening occurs when a small primitive data type value is automatically accommodated in a bigger, wider, primitive data type.

  If we convert from an **int to a decimal,** this is an example of a widening conversion.

  Widening conversions that are acceptable include

  - byte – Which is convertible to short, int, long, float, or double

  - short – Which is convertible to int, long, float, or double

  - int – Which is convertible to long, float, or double

  - long – Which is convertible to float or double

  - float – Which is convertible to double

Automatic conversion will take place if the two data types are compatible and the destination data type is larger than the data type being converted. **Automatic conversion is therefore essentially a widening conversion.**

- Narrowing conversions

    Narrowing occurs when a larger primitive data type value is accommodated in a smaller, narrower, primitive data type.

    If we convert from a value that includes a fraction, decimal, float, etc. to an integer data type, the fractional part will be lost, and narrowing will occur.

    Narrowing conversions that are acceptable include

    - `short` – Is convertible to byte or char

    - `int` – Is convertible to byte or short

    - `long` – Is convertible to byte or short

    - `float` – Is convertible to byte, short, int, or long

    - `double` – Is convertible to byte, short, int, long, or float

When we use narrowing conversions in our code, we will see that we must explicitly do the conversion by placing the new data type in parentheses (), like the () we use in methods. The data type we are converting to sits in front of the object to be converted and within the parentheses (). We will see plenty of this as we code the examples in the book. Listing 6-1 shows an example of code that uses the conversions we have just talked about. We will not type this code.

Listing 6-1. Conversion using (byte)

```
class Program
{
  public static void Main(string[] args)
  {
    byte commissionFactor;
    byte commissionPremium;
    int commissionValue = 257;
```

```
    double monthlyInsurancePremium = 296.99;
    Console.WriteLine("Narrowing conversion from int to byte.");
    //(byte) means we wish to convert to byte the commissionvalue
    commissionFactor = (byte)commissionValue;
    Console.WriteLine("\nThe car commission value is: " +
    commissionValue + "\nbut when converted to a byte the car " +
    "commission factor is: " + commissionFactor);

    Console.WriteLine("\nConversion of double to byte.");

    /*
    (byte) means we wish to convert monthlyinsurancepremium to byte
     So, we will now have 296.99 minus 256 which is 40
    (forgetting the decimal places)
    */
    commissionPremium = (byte)monthlyInsurancePremium;
    Console.WriteLine("\nThe monthly insurance premium is: " +
        monthlyInsurancePremium + "\nand the car commission " +
        "premium is: " + commissionPremium );
    } // End of Main() method
} // End of Program
```

Now we will look at creating code to build an application that will simulate a car insurance quotation application. Firstly, we will create a string variable called vehicleManufacturer that will hold the value input by a user. Remember to read the comments carefully as they fully explain what we are doing.

Add a new project to hold the code for this chapter.

1. Right-click the solution CoreCSharp.

2. Choose Add.

3. Choose New Project, as shown in Figure 6-2.

Figure 6-2. *Add a new project*

4. Choose Console App from the listed templates that appear, as shown in Figure 6-3.

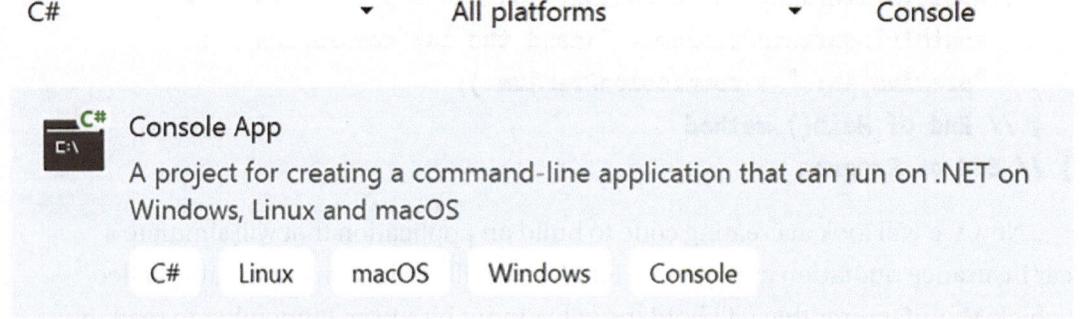

Figure 6-3. *Console App for .NET*

5. Click the Next button.

6. Name the project Chapter6 and leave it in the same location.

7. Click the Next button.

8. Choose the framework to be used, which in our projects will be .NET 6.0 or higher, as shown in Figure 6-4.

Framework ⓘ

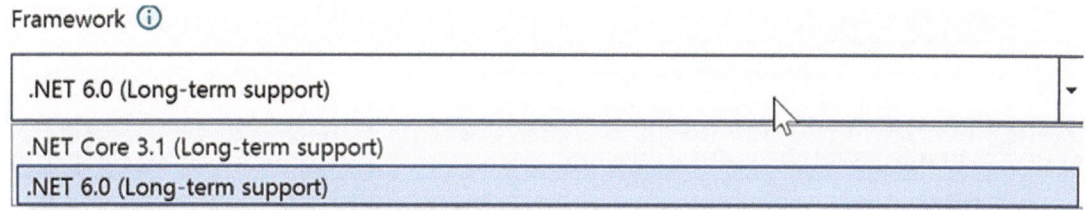

Figure 6-4. *Choosing the project framework*

9. Click the Create button.

    Now we should see the Chapter6 project within the solution called
    CoreCSharp, as shown in Figure 6-5.

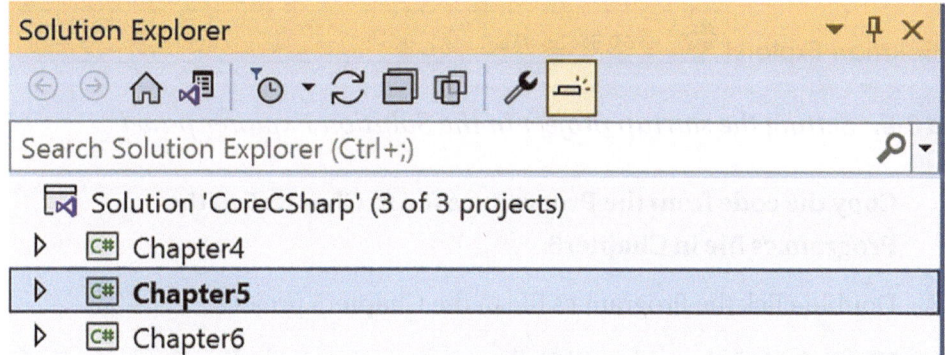

Figure 6-5. *Solution folder with project folders*

    Figure 6-5 shows that Chapter5 is in bold text and Chapter6 is not.
    But what does this mean? Well, it means that Chapter5 is the
    active project, the startup project.

10. Right-click the project Chapter6 in the Solution Explorer panel.

11. Click the Set as Startup Project option, as shown in Figure 6-6.

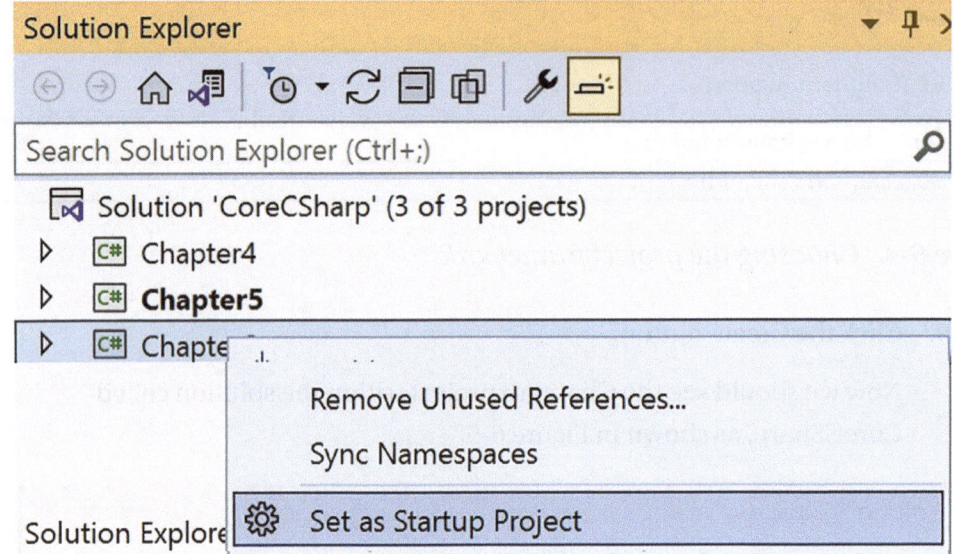

Figure 6-6. Setting the startup project in the Solution Explorer panel

Copy the code from the Program.cs file in Chapter5 to the Program.cs file in Chapter6.

12. Double-click the Program.cs file in the Chapter5 project.

13. Highlight ALL the code within the program, yes, including the namespace and Main() method.

14. Choose Copy.

15. Double-click the Program.cs file in the Chapter6 folder.

16. Highlight the existing code and delete it.

17. Right-click inside the blank editor window where we have just removed the code.

18. Choose Paste.

    Now, the namespace is called Chapter5 so we will rename it to Chapter6. We have a choice in how to rename the namespace to Chapter6, so select **one** of the following approaches to rename the namespace.

    We could

19. Right-click the word Chapter5.

20. Choose Quick Actions and Refactorings, as shown in Figure 6-7.

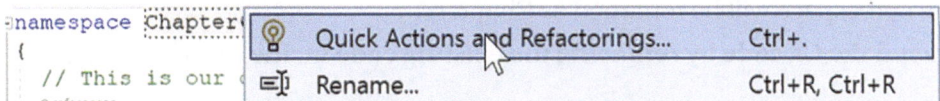

Figure 6-7. *Refactoring using Quick Actions and Refactorings*

21. Click the Change namespace to match folder structure, as shown
     in Figure 6-8.

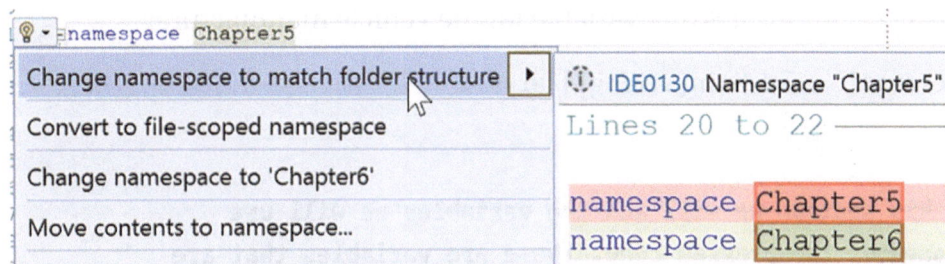

Figure 6-8. *Choosing a possible refactoring option*

22. Press the Enter key.

     The namespace will be renamed as Chapter6.

     Or we could

- Right-click the word Chapter5.

- Choose Change namespace to Chapter6, as shown in Figure 6-9.

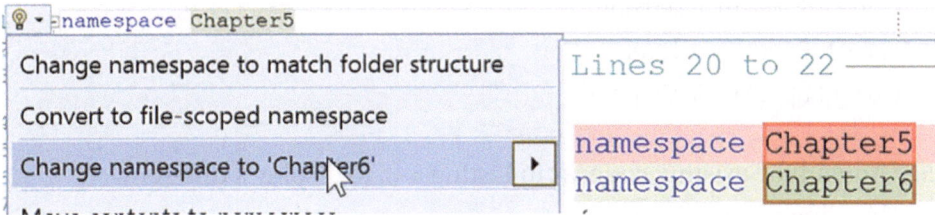

Figure 6-9. *Using rename to refactor*

- Type Chapter6, overwriting the word Chapter5.

- Press the Enter key.

The namespace will be renamed as Chapter6.

Amend the C# code by replacing the existing code inside the Main method.

23. Highlight the code inside the Main() method and delete the existing code.

24. Amend the existing code by adding the String variable called **vehicleManufacturer,** as in Listing 6-2.

Listing 6-2. Adding a String variable for the vehicle manufacturer

```
public static void Main(string[] args)
{
  /*
  In this section we will add the variables we will use
  throughout the program code. These are variables that are
  going to be of a specific data type. Once we declare a
  variable and have said what its data type is, we cannot
  change the variable's data type.

  The data type is immutable, it cannot be changed over time.
  First we will add a variable called vehicleManufacturer of
  data type string.
  */
  String vehicleManufacturer;

    } // End of Main() method
  } // End of Program class
} // End of Chapter6 namespace
```

25. Amend the existing code, as in Listing 6-3, to display a different heading and message.

Listing 6-3. Displaying a heading and message for the user

```
The data type is immutable, it cannot be changed over time.
First we will add a variable called vehicleManufacturer of
data type string.
*/
String vehicleManufacturer;

Console.WriteLine();
Console.WriteLine("---- Car Quotation Application ----");
Console.WriteLine();
Console.WriteLine("Type the vehicle manufacturer");
Console.WriteLine("and press the Enter key");
Console.WriteLine();

    } // End of Main() method
  } // End of Program class
} // End of Chapter6 namespace
```

Read the vehicle manufacturer.

26. Amend the existing code, as in Listing 6-4, to read the user input
     and assign it to the vehicleManufacturer variable.

Listing 6-4. Reading user input and assigning it to a variable

```
Console.WriteLine("Type the vehicle manufacturer");
Console.WriteLine("and press the Enter key");
Console.WriteLine();

/*
The next line of code tells the program to wait for the
user to input something. When the user presses the Enter
key this will indicate that the input has been completed.
We have also said that we want the data entered at the
console to be assigned to the variable vehicleManufacturer
which we set up earlier with a data type of String.
```

```
We can now see that the data entered through the console
is going to be held in the program as data type string.
*/
vehicleManufacturer = Console.ReadLine();

    } // End of Main() method
  } // End of Program class
} // End of Chapter6 namespace
```

27. Amend the existing code, as in Listing 6-5, to display a blank line.

Listing 6-5. Displaying a blank line

```
vehicleManufacturer = Console.ReadLine();

Console.WriteLine();

    } // End of Main() method
  } // End of Program class
} // End of Chapter6 namespace
```

We will now ask the user to press any key on the keyboard and then display a Goodbye message, and we will add a ReadLine() statement, so the console doesn't disappear, and we can see the Goodbye message. We will finally have to press any key to end the program and have the console window disappear.

28. Amend the existing code, as in Listing 6-6.

Listing 6-6. Displaying a message for the user

```
vehicleManufacturer = Console.ReadLine();

Console.WriteLine();

Console.WriteLine("Press any letter on the keyboard ");

// This code waits for the user to input form the keyboard
Console.ReadKey();

Console.WriteLine("Goodbye");
Console.ReadLine();
```

```
    } // End of Main() method
  } // End of Program class
} // End of Chapter6 namespace
```

29.   Click the File menu.

30.   Choose Save All.

31.   Click the Debug menu.

32.   Choose Start Debugging.

The console window will appear and display the message asking the user to enter the vehicle manufacturer. The cursor will be flashing, waiting for user input.

33.   Click in the console window.

34.   Type Ford as the manufacturer name.

35.   Press the Enter key on the keyboard.

The cursor moves to the next line and displays the message asking the user to press any letter on the keyboard.

36.   Press any key on the keyboard.

The Goodbye message appears, and the cursor will be flashing waiting for user input, as shown in Figure 6-10.

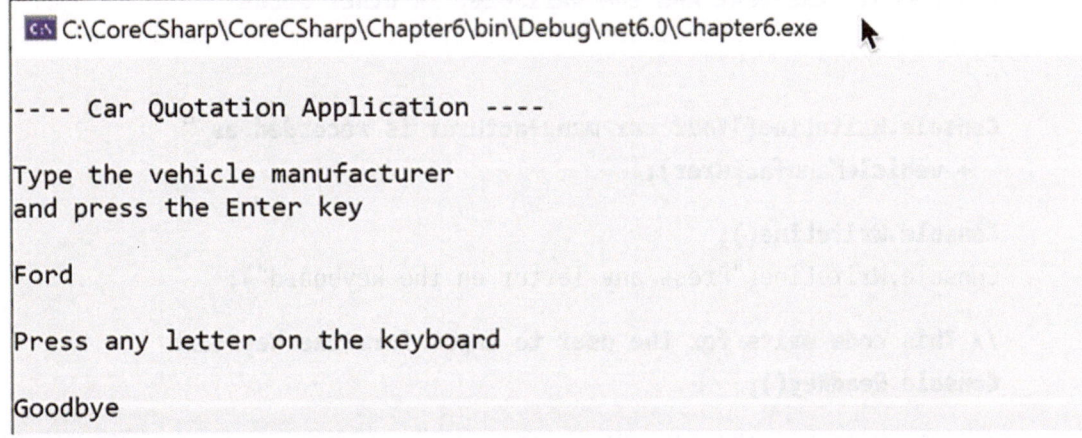

Figure 6-10. *Console output and user input*

37. Press the Enter key on the keyboard.

38. Press the Enter key again.

Display the vehicle manufacturer.

In the code we have read the string that the user input, Ford, using the **ReadLine()** method of the Console class and have assigned this string of data to the variable vehicleManufacturer, which we set up. This is great, but surely we want to use the value once we have it! We will now use the stored value containing the string Ford and print it to the console using the WriteLine() method.

39. Amend the code, as in Listing 6-7, to display the vehicleManufacturer value, which has been read from the console.

Listing 6-7. Displaying the vehicle manufacturer

```
vehicleManufacturer = Console.ReadLine();

Console.WriteLine();
/*
The next line of code tells the program to display the text
between the double quotes "" and to add on to this text
(indicated by the +) the value of the variable called
vehicleManufacturer which has been assigned the value
typed in by the user at the console (Ford). The + means to
concatenate the text and the variable, in other words
join them
*/
Console.WriteLine("Your car manufacturer is recorded as "
  + vehicleManufacturer);

Console.WriteLine();
Console.WriteLine("Press any letter on the keyboard");

// This code waits for the user to input form the keyboard
Console.ReadKey();

Console.WriteLine("Goodbye");
Console.ReadLine();
} // End of Main() method
```

40.   Click the File menu.

41.   Choose Save All.

42.   Click the Debug menu.

43.   Choose Start Debugging.

44.   Type Ford as the manufacturer name.

45.   Press the Enter key on the keyboard.

46.   Press the Enter key on the keyboard.

The message will appear showing us that the vehicle manufacturer is what we typed at the console, the Goodbye message appears, and the cursor will be flashing waiting for user input, as shown in Figure 6-11.

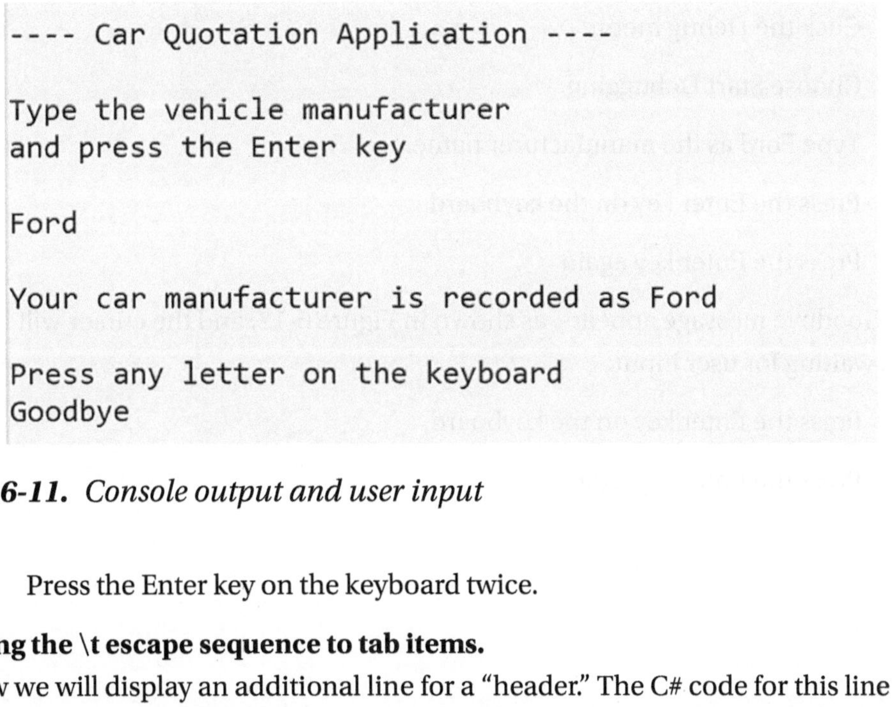

```
---- Car Quotation Application ----

Type the vehicle manufacturer
and press the Enter key

Ford

Your car manufacturer is recorded as Ford

Press any letter on the keyboard
Goodbye
```

Figure 6-11.   *Console output and user input*

47.   Press the Enter key on the keyboard twice.

Using the \t escape sequence to tab items.

Now we will display an additional line for a "header." The C# code for this line will use the **escape sequence \t** to **tab** the text on the line. The \t is an escape sequence that we might use to tab the output – in other words, leave a fixed amount of space, usually eight spaces at this position in the text.

48. Amend the code, as in Listing 6-8, to add the additional "header" line.

Listing 6-8. Using escape sequences when displaying to the console

```
String vehicleManufacturer;

Console.WriteLine();
Console.WriteLine("---- Car Quotation Application ----");
Console.WriteLine("\tCar\tInsurance\tApplication\n");
Console.WriteLine();
```

49. Click the File menu.

50. Choose Save All.

51. Click the Debug menu.

52. Choose Start Debugging.

53. Type Ford as the manufacturer name.

54. Press the Enter key on the keyboard.

55. Press the Enter key again.

The Goodbye message appears, as shown in Figure 6-12, and the cursor will be flashing, waiting for user input.

56. Press the Enter key on the keyboard.

57. Press the Enter key again.

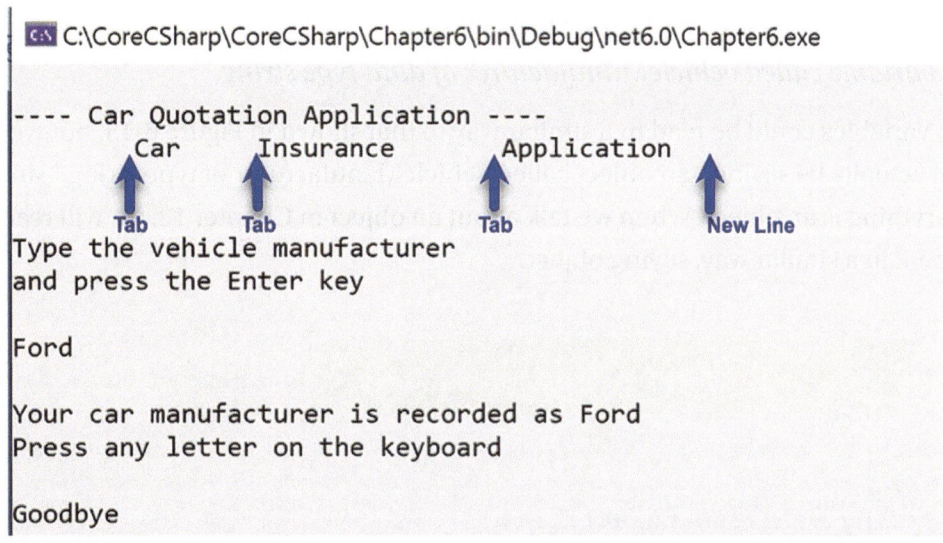

Figure 6-12. *Tab indentation and new line using escape sequences*

Figure 6-12 shows the tabbed space before the word Car and between the words Car and Insurance. Note how the space before the word Car is eight characters, and this is the space each tab takes up. We can then see that Car and five spaces take up the next eight tab spaces. As the word Insurance is nine characters, it uses the full eight spaces of a tab slot, and then it takes up one space in the next tab, so there are now seven spaces before the A of application.

Using the \n escape sequence to move to a new line.

In the `Console.WriteLine("\tCar\tInsurance\tApplication\n");` statement, which displays what is between the double quotes "", we have used another "strange" ending, **\n**. This is another **escape sequence,** and it means add a new line. So \n has a similar action to Console.WriteLine(), which also moves to a new line after writing its text.

Code Analysis

As we can see, the code includes extensive comments, which are aimed at explaining the code being used. For the code that we have just added, the following points are important:

- We have added a section within the Main() method where we declare the variables to be used in this Main() method of the program.

- In this section we have declared a variable called **vehicleManufacturer,** which will hold data of type **string.**

111

Read this line string vehicleManufacturer; as

a variable called vehicleManufacturer of data type string.

All variables could be read in a similar way to that shown in Figure 6-13, but we should actually be saying, "an object called vehicleManufacturer of type string," since in C# everything is an object. When we talk about an object in Chapter 13, we will read the statement in a similar way, saying object.

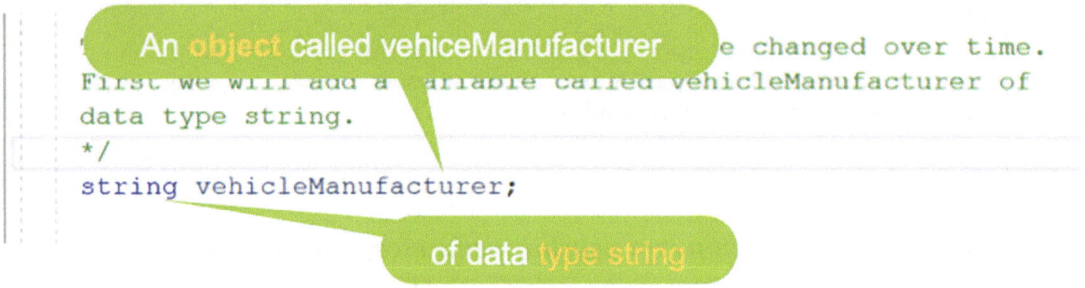

An object called vehiceManufacturer
... e changed over time.
First we will add a variable called vehicleManufacturer of data type string.
*/
string vehicleManufacturer;
of data type string

Figure 6-13. *Reading a type declaration*

- The vehicleManufacturer variable has been declared in the Main() method and will only be visible to code that is inside the open and close curly braces of the Main() method. This means that **the scope of the variable is the Main() method**, between the curly braces, as shown in Listing 6-9.

Listing 6-9. Variable scope

```
static void Main(string[] args)
{
   // The scope of the variable is the Main method,
   // between the curly braces
   String vehicleManufacturer;
}
```

- We have entered the statement Console.ReadLine() and it is included as part of the line `vehicleManufacturer = Console.ReadLine();`, which says that we want the variable vehicleManufacturer to be made equal to Console.ReadLine(). This is known as an **assignment**, where we assign a value to a variable. The variable is vehicleManufacturer and the value is whatever the user inputs at the console.

Read the line `vehicleManufacturer = Console.ReadLine();` like this:

The variable called vehicleManufacturer is assigned the value from Console.ReadLine().

- In the code we entered this statement:

```
Console.WriteLine("Your car manufacturer is recorded
as " + vehicleManufacturer);
```

This is an interesting line of code with three parts within the brackets ():

- The first part is what we have used before; it is simply text, **a string between double quotes ""**, and as we know this tells the program to display this exact text in the console.

- The second part is a **plus sign** (+) and we might be thinking this means add. Well, we are indeed correct, as the plus sign is being used here to say we want to add whatever comes after the plus sign to the text we have just written. This is called **concatenation** and we mentioned it earlier.

- The third part is the **name of the variable**, so the value that is entered at the console by the user, for example, Ford, is added to the end of the text "Your car manufacturer is recorded as "

This line means that the console will display Your car manufacturer is recorded as Ford, as shown in Figure 6-14.

```
Type the vehicle manufacturer
and press the Enter key

Ford

Your car manufacturer is recorded as Ford
Press any letter on the keyboard

Goodbye
```

Concatenated string with input value at the end

Figure 6-14. *Example of string concatenation*

The **plus sign (+) or plus symbol is used to add string parts together**. We can also use the more widely used term **concatenate** to refer to what the plus sign (+) does in this context. As we progress through the chapters, we will see that concatenation can be replaced with a more modern approach called **string interpolation**, and we will also see the plus sign (+) used as the mathematical plus where it will add two numerical values.

Amazing, we are now able to

- Write to the console.

- Read from the console.

- Set up a variable.

- Assign a value that has been read in from the console to a variable.

- Display text to the console, which is a concatenation of text and variables.

We will now amend the code to ask the user to input other details about the vehicle being insured. In this case it will be the model of the vehicle. This is the same process as we have already completed, and coding this will help reinforce our learning.

The steps are as follows:

- Set up a variable that will hold the data requested from the user. The variable will be of a particular data type, in this case string.

- Display a message to ask the user to input some data.

- Use the Console.ReadLine() method to get the data entered.

Note

In the preceding first bullet point, we have said that the data type will be **string**, but the data type for the vehicleManufacturer was **String** with a capital S, so what is the difference?

Well, **String** stands for **System.String,** and this type belongs to the .NET framework, which is the overarching framework for Microsoft languages such as C#, Visual Basic .NET, and F#. On the other hand, **string** is an alias in the C# language for System.String. This means that both String and string will work because they are compiled to **System. String**. As developers we can choose which of the two options to use and we can mix and match throughout our code. **BUT** this would not be a good example of clean code, so we should simply use the C# type, which is string rather than the .NET type, which is String.

58. Amend the code, as in Listing 6-10, by changing the vehicleManufacturer data type from String to string.

Listing 6-10. Using String or string

```
string vehicleManufacturer;

Console.WriteLine();
Console.WriteLine("---- Car Quotation Application ----");
Console.WriteLine("\tCar\tInsurance\tApplication\n");
```

Read and write the vehicle model.

59. Amend the code, as in Listing 6-11, by adding the string variable called vehicleModel.

Listing 6-11. Variable of data type string for the vehicle model

```
string vehicleManufacturer;

string vehicleModel;

Console.WriteLine();
Console.WriteLine("---- Car Quotation Application ----");
Console.WriteLine("\tCar\tInsurance\tApplication\n")
```

60. Amend the code, as in Listing 6-12, to ask for user input, read the user input, and assign it to the vehicleModel variable.

Listing 6-12. Read console input and assign it to a variable

```
Console.WriteLine("Your car manufacturer is recorded as "
  + vehicleManufacturer);

/*
In the next three lines we display a question for the user,
read whatever data the user inputs at the console, assign
this data to the variable called vehicleModel and write
out the concatenated text
*/
Console.WriteLine("What is the model of the vehicle?\n");

vehicleModel = Console.ReadLine();

Console.WriteLine("Press any letter on the keyboard ");

// This code waits for the user to input form the keyboard
Console.ReadLine();
```

61. Amend the code, as in Listing 6-13, to display the vehicleModel, which has been read from the console.

Listing 6-13. Displaying the vehicle model

```
vehicleModel = Console.ReadLine();

Console.WriteLine("You have told us that the vehicle " +
  "model is " + vehicleModel);

Console.WriteLine("Press any letter on the keyboard ");

// This code waits for the user to input form the keyboard
Console.ReadKey();

Console.WriteLine("Goodbye");
```

62. Click the File menu.

63. Choose Save All.

64. Click the Debug menu.

65. Choose Start Without Debugging.

66. Type Ford as the manufacturer name.

67. Press the Enter key on the keyboard.

68. Type Fiesta as the model name.

69. Press the Enter key on the keyboard.

70. Press the Enter key on the keyboard.

71. Press the Enter key on the keyboard.

We will see that the console window now displays the concatenated text for the model, as shown in Figure 6-15.

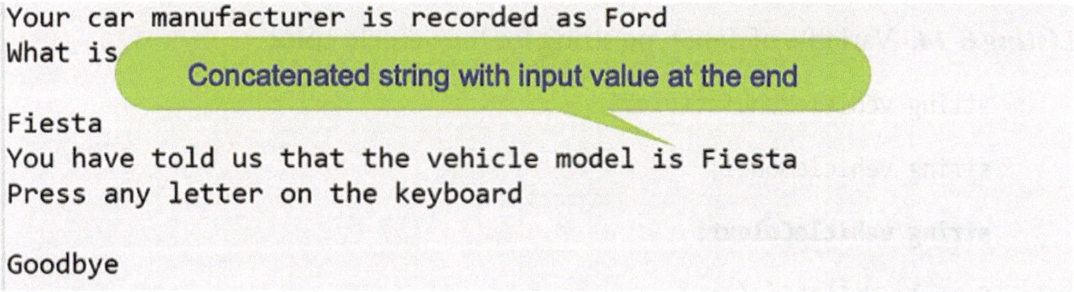

```
Your car manufacturer is recorded as Ford
What is                                              Concatenated string with input value at the end

Fiesta
You have told us that the vehicle model is Fiesta
Press any letter on the keyboard

Goodbye
```

Figure 6-15. *Example of string concatenation*

Note

When we are running the program, we should notice that after pressing the Enter key, when Goodbye appears, we are automatically being prompted to Press any key to close this window ..., as shown in Figure 6-16.

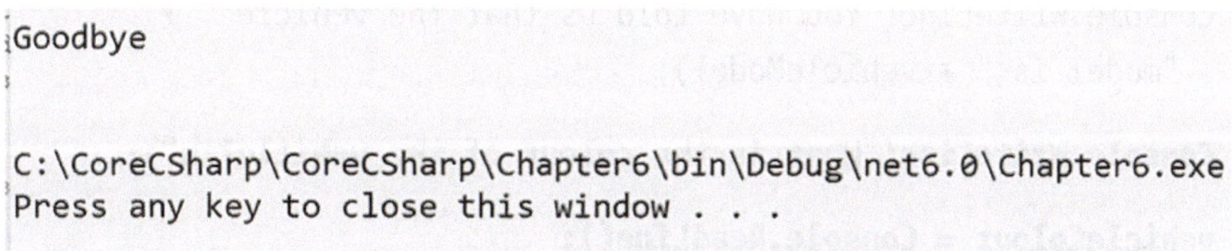

```
Goodbye


C:\CoreCSharp\CoreCSharp\Chapter6\bin\Debug\net6.0\Chapter6.exe
Press any key to close this window . . .
```

Figure 6-16. *Automatic waiting for a key press in debugging mode*

This is great, because in our code we now do not need to put the last line that is used to stop the console closing when we run the program. In the next programs, we will remove the additional line.

Read and write the vehicle color.

We will now amend the code to ask the user to input other details about the vehicle being insured. In this case it will be the color of the vehicle. Once again this is the same process as we have already completed, and coding this should help reinforce our learning.

The steps are as follows:

- Set up a variable that will hold the data requested from the user. The variable will be of a particular data type, in this case string.

- Display a message asking the user to input some data.

- Use the Console.ReadLine() method to get the data entered.

72. Amend the code, as in Listing 6-14, by adding the string variable called vehicleColour.

Listing 6-14. Variable of data type string for the vehicle color

```
string vehicleManufacturer;

string vehicleModel;

string vehicleColour;

Console.WriteLine();
Console.WriteLine("---- Car Quotation Application ----");
```

73. Amend the code, as in Listing 6-15, to ask for user input, read the user input, and assign it to the vehicleColour variable.

Listing 6-15. Read console input and assign it to a variable

```
Console.WriteLine("You have told us that the vehicle " +
  "model is " + vehicleModel);

Console.WriteLine("What is the colour of the vehicle?\n");

vehicleColour = Console.ReadLine();

Console.WriteLine("Press any letter on the keyboard ");
```

74. Amend the code, as in Listing 6-16, to display the vehicleColour value, which has been read from the console.

Listing 6-16. Displaying the vehicle color

```
Console.WriteLine("What is the colour of the vehicle?\n");
vehicleColour = Console.ReadLine();

Console.WriteLine("You have told us that the vehicle " +
    "colour is " + vehicleColour);

Console.WriteLine("Press any letter on the keyboard ");
```

Now we will remove the last lines of code that display the Goodbye message and the read line statement. This means that after the vehicle color message, there are no lines of code, just the end braces for the Main method, class, and namespace.

75. Amend the code, as in Listing 6-17, to remove the code lines.

Listing 6-17. Console.ReadLine() removed

```
Console.WriteLine("What is the colour of the vehicle?\n");
vehicleColour = Console.ReadLine();

Console.WriteLine("You have told us that the vehicle " +
    "colour is " + vehicleColour);

        } // End of Main() method
    } // End of Program class
} // End of Chapter6 namespace
```

76. Click the File menu.

77. Choose Save All.

78. Click the Debug menu.

79. Choose Start Without Debugging.

80. Type Ford as the manufacturer name.

81. Press the Enter key on the keyboard.

82. Type Fiesta as the model name.

83. Press the Enter key on the keyboard.

84. Type Blue as the vehicle color.

85. Press the Enter key on the keyboard.

Figure 6-17 shows the console window displaying the concatenated text for the color and the message to press any key to close this window.

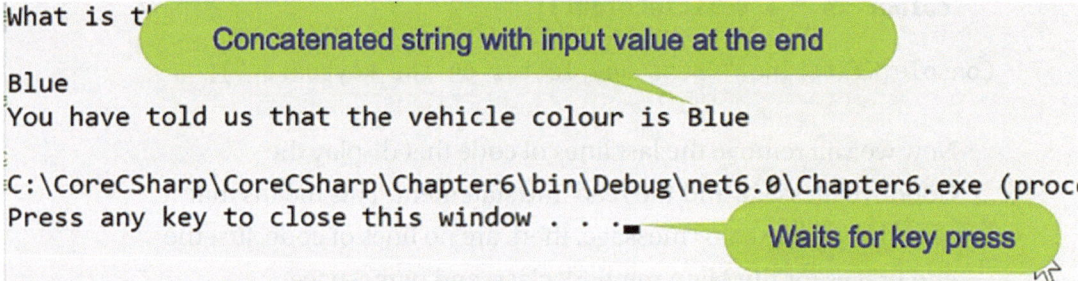

Figure 6-17. *Example of string concatenation and waiting for a key press*

86. Press the Enter key again to close the console window.

Something a Little Different with Our Variables

We will now amend the code to ask the user to input details about the age, in years, of the vehicle. We might use the age of the vehicle in a mathematical formula that will calculate the insurance premium to be charged. Once again this is the same process as we have already completed, **with one difference**: the variable is not of data type string – it will be of **data type int**.

So the steps are as follows:

- Set up a variable that will hold the data requested from the user. The variable will be of a particular data type – in this case it will be an int.

- Display a message asking the user to input some data.

- Use the Console.ReadLine() method to get the data entered.

This will be interesting as we will be accepting input from the console, and we have seen from the previous examples that console input is accepted as a string or String. So how can we now assign the string that the user enters for the age of the vehicle to the variable of data type int that we create to hold the data? We will see how to handle this shortly.

Read and write the vehicle age.

1. Amend the code, as in Listing 6-18, to add the variable we require.

Listing 6-18. Variable of data type int for the vehicle age

```
string vehicleManufacturer;
string vehicleModel;
string vehicleColour;

int vehicleAgeInYears;
```

2. Amend the code, as in Listing 6-19, to ask for user input, read the user input, and assign it to the vehicleAgeInYears variable.

Listing 6-19. Read console input and assign it to a variable

```
Console.WriteLine("You have told us that the vehicle " +
    "colour is " + vehicleColour);

Console.WriteLine("What is the age, in full years, of " +
    "the vehicle? \n");
vehicleAgeInYears = Console.ReadLine();

} // End of Main() method
} // End of Program class
} // End of Chapter6 namespace
```

3. Click the File menu.

4. Choose Save All.

All is not well in our code, as we can see from the red line under the Console. ReadLine. The red line indicates an error. The compiler is complaining.

5. Move the mouse over the red line and a pop-up message box appears, as shown in Figure 6-18.

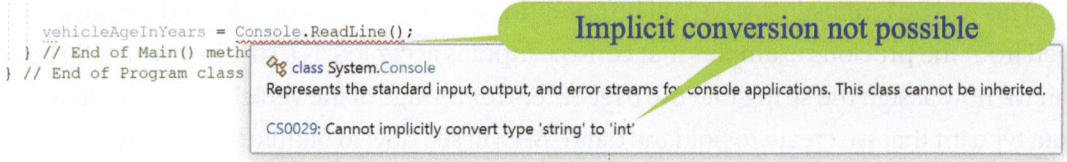

Figure 6-18. *Compiler error due to incorrect assignment*

The pop-up message box tries to tell us what the error is, so read the message carefully.

There is also an Error List window where we can see the error being displayed and this window can be viewed in different ways as shown in Figure 6-19. The Error List is a great way for us to see any errors in our code, and it offers us "tools" like the Filter icon or the drop-down list where we can choose if we want to display errors from the entire solution, the project, etc. It is really our choice as to how we wish to display the errors or the Error List, or we can hover over the underlined code.

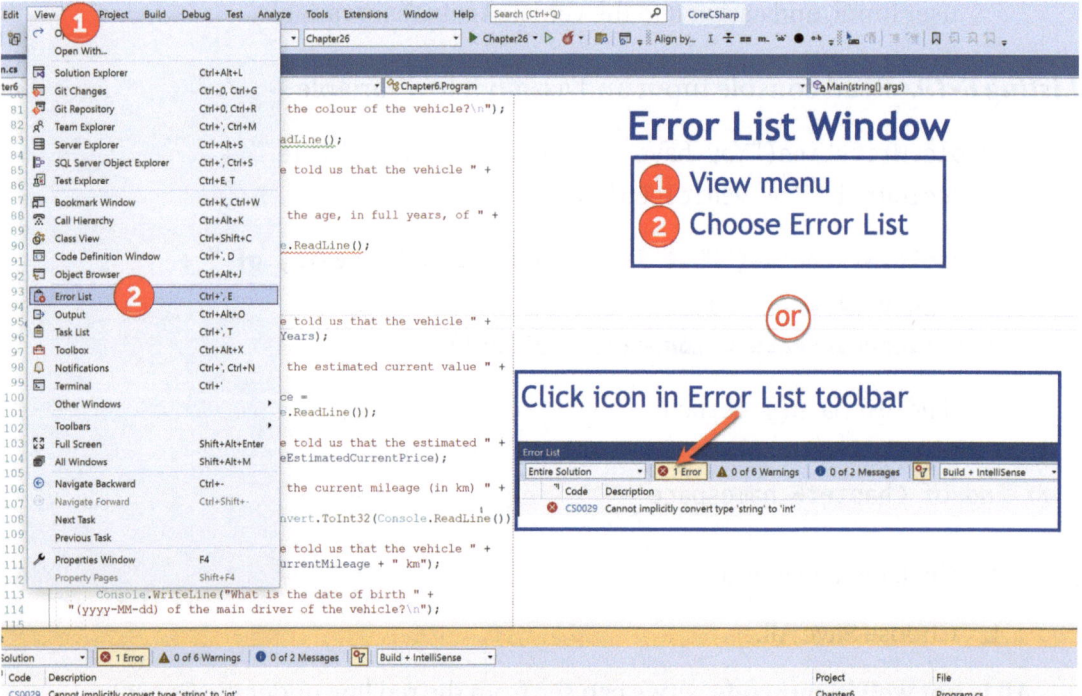

Figure 6-19. *Error List window*

As we program, we will make mistakes and the compiler will help us as much as it can to correct them. We will get used to the error messages and become familiar with their meaning and how to resolve the issues in our code. In this case the error message says

Cannot implicitly convert type 'string' to 'int'

Before we wrote the code for the vehicle age, we read the following:

So how can we now assign the string that the user enters for the age of the vehicle to the variable of data type int that we create to hold the data?

Now, that is exactly what the error message is saying to us. We now need to do something to the **string** we have read from the console and **convert it to data type int**. The compiler is telling us that it cannot do this conversion for us; it is not **implicit**. We must tell the compiler how to do it; we must be **explicit**.

Remember, we read earlier that when we want to convert from one data type to another data type, this can happen in one of two ways:

- **Implicit** conversion

  This means that we do not need to do anything as the conversion is automatically handled by our code. The compiler handles the conversion.

- **Explicit** conversion

  This means that we will need to code the data type conversion. It is not an automatic thing. The compiler will complain, through an error message, that it cannot handle the conversion.

Well, we have just seen an example in our code where an **implicit conversion** cannot happen; we will have to code the **explicit conversion**. This is a very straightforward process in C#, and we will use this type of conversion regularly. **This is not a conversion from one numeric data type to another numeric data type** as discussed earlier with narrowing and widening. **It is a conversion from a string to a numeric data type**. It is like a **parse**, where parse means to extract the data, so if the string was "10" then the parsed data would be 10.

6. Amend the code, as in Listing 6-20, to perform the variable conversion from data type string to data type int using the ToInt32() method.

Listing 6-20. Convert string input to an int using the Int32() method

```
    Console.WriteLine("What is the age, in full years, of " +
        "the vehicle? \n");
    vehicleAgeInYears = Convert.ToInt32(Console.ReadLine());
    } // End of Main() method
  } // End of Program class
} // End of Chapter6 namespace
```

Do we see any error message? No, we should not see an error.

Code Analysis

- We have just used another method, as we can see from the () in the code.

- The method is called ToInt32.

- As it is a method, it is written as ToInt32().

- The ToInt32() method has the keyword **Convert** in front of it followed by a full stop. As we have already learned, the full stop is dot notation in C# code and means that we want to use a variable or method of the **object** that appears to the left of the full stop, in our case the Convert object. We also know that Convert must be a class, which has variables and methods that we have access to.

- The Convert class methods will do conversions from one data type to another data type for us. We do not need to write our own code to do the conversions. This is a great example of ***reusable code***, where code is written once and can be reused as often as required. Some of the methods that are accessible to us from the Convert class are shown in Figure 6-20.

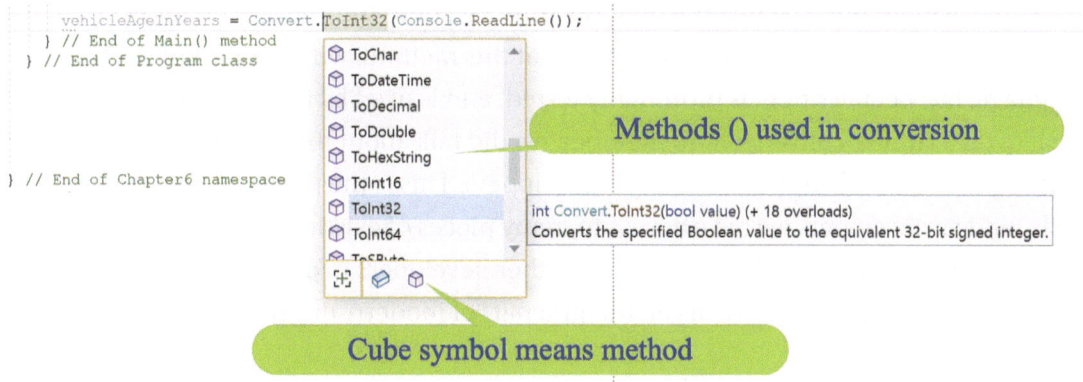

Figure 6-20. *Methods that are part of the Convert class*

- The ToInt32() method is used to convert from one data type to another data type, in our example from string to int, but we have to tell the method what is to be converted. We can clearly see this when, after typing the full stop, we click ToInt32 in the pop-up window, as shown in Figure 6-21.

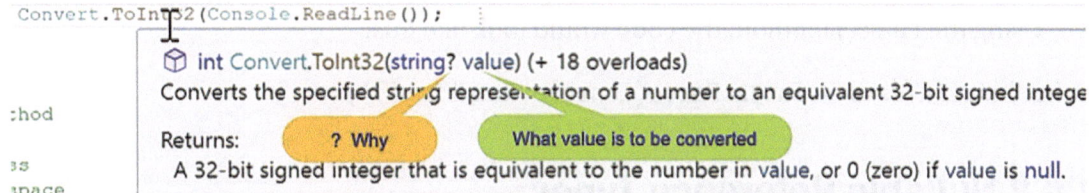

Figure 6-21. *ToInt32() method of the Convert class takes in a value*

- In Figure 6-21 we can see that between the brackets () it says `string? Value`. Later in this chapter we will see the meaning of the **?**.

- The method ToInt32() needs to be given a value. In other words the method accepts a value, an object, so it is a parameter method.

- The value given to the ToInt32() method is whatever line is read from the console. Hence, we have Console.ReadLine() between the brackets in the code `ToInt32(Console.ReadLine());`.

- Whatever is between the brackets of the ToInt32() method is converted to an integer, a 32-bit integer.

Great, we can now see that the method ToInt32() does the conversion for us. How? We do not need to know; we simply accept that this method, which is part of the C# language, has been written, is thoroughly tested, and is used by all developers when they wish to do a similar conversion. Remember, we did talk about this when we read about what the .NET is and what it offers us as developers. This is the power of using existing code, and as developers we have access to many pieces of existing code. Using existing code methods from .NET, the C# language, other developers in our organization, or other developers elsewhere forms an integral part of modern-day programming.

Note

As this Convert is a parse, we could also use another method to do the same thing as the Int32() method. The method is the `Int32.Parse()` method. The difference between the two methods is as follows:

- Using the .Parse() method for any data type will throw a null exception, error, if the string value to be parsed is null.

- Using the Convert. will not cause an exception for a null value.

- The ToInt32() method is slower than the Parse() method.

Using the Parse() method, the code would look like this:

```
vehicleAgeInYears = Int32.Parse(Console.ReadLine());
```

C# 8 Nullable Reference Types

- From the introduction of C# 8, every reference type is by default nullable in code that has opted into a **nullable aware context.** The nullable aware context has to be set up within the project.

- Within a nullable aware context, any reference type variable of type *Type* must be initialized with a non-null value. *Type* is just a generic name for any data type. Listing 6-21 and Figure 6-22 show the code and error.

Listing 6-21. Nullable reference type will cause a warning

```
/*
This will cause a warning as all reference types are
non-nullable by default. The warning will be similar to:
Converting null literal or possible null value to
non-nullable reference type.
*/
string policyId = null;
```

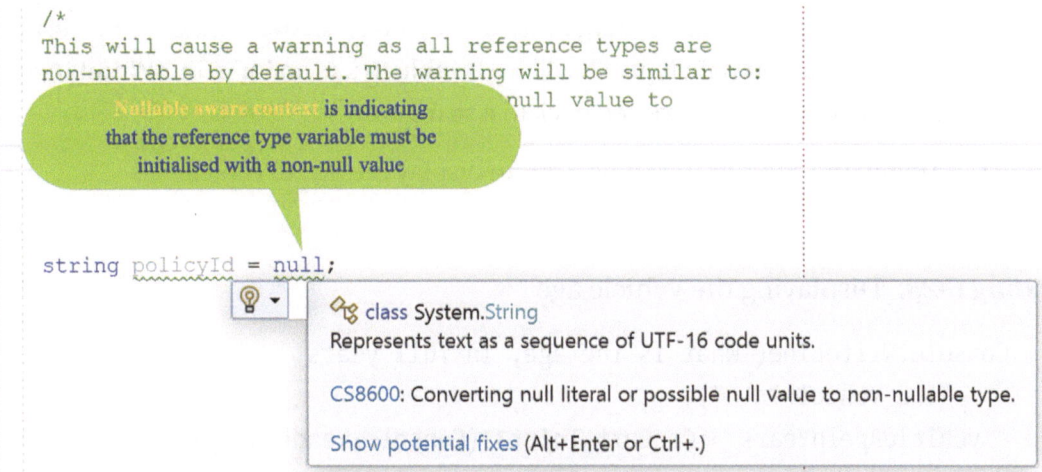

Figure 6-22. *Non-nullable type*

- Any reference type variable of type Type cannot be assigned a value that may be null.

- If we make the reference type of type **Type?,** then the variable can be initialized with a null value, or it can be assigned a null value.

  The example shown in Listing 6-22 will be fine because we have used the question mark, ?, which is the C# nullable allowed symbol.

Listing 6-22. Using the ?, C# nullable allowed, on a reference type

```
/*
This will cause a warning as all reference types are
non-nullable by default. The warning will be similar to:
```

```
Converting null literal or possible null value to
non-nullable reference type.
*/
string? policyId = null;
```

Earlier in Listing 6-4, we had the line of code vehicleManufacturer = Console.ReadLine(); and it was underlined indicating a warning in the non-aware context. We will see more of nullable reference types in Chapter 19.

Continuing from where we left off in Listing 6-20, we have corrected the code and the red underline has disappeared, so we just need to display a message to tell the user what has been read in. This will be interesting as we are reading a **string** from the console and then converting it to an **int** data type. So will we be able to use an int in our WriteLine() method, or will it need to be converted back to a string?

1. Amend the code, as in Listing 6-23, to display the age of vehicle message.

Listing 6-23. Displaying the vehicle age

```
Console.WriteLine("What is the age, in full years, of " +
    "the vehicle? \n");
  vehicleAgeInYears = Convert.ToInt32(Console.ReadLine());

  Console.WriteLine("You have told us that the vehicle " +
    "age is " + vehicleAgeInYears);

  } // End of Main() method
 } // End of Program class
} // End of Chapter6 namespace
```

Do we see any error message? No, we should not see an error.

2. Click the File menu.

3. Choose Save All.

4. Hover over the vehicleAgeInYears in the WriteLine() method and look at the message in the pop-up telling us it is an int, as shown in Figure 6-23.

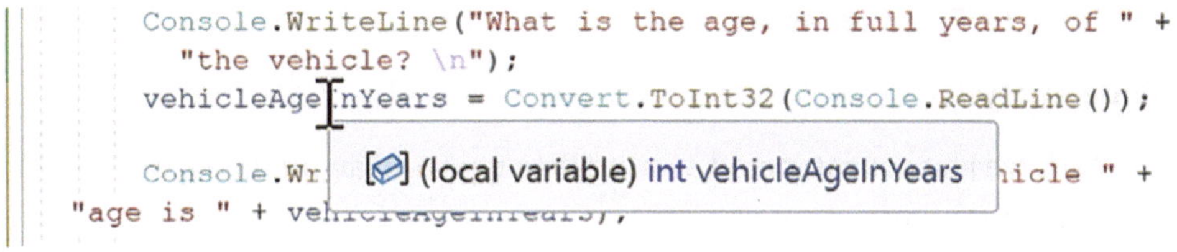

```
Console.WriteLine("What is the age, in full years, of " +
    "the vehicle? \n");
vehicleAgeInYears = Convert.ToInt32(Console.ReadLine());

Console.Wr    [symbol] (local variable) int vehicleAgeInYears    hicle " +
"age is " + vehicleAgeInYears);
```

Figure 6-23. *ToInt32()-converted input assigned to an int variable*

5.   Click the File menu.

6.   Choose Save All.

7.   Click the Debug menu.

8.   Choose Start Without Debugging.

9.   Type Ford as the manufacturer name.

10.   Press the Enter key on the keyboard.

11.   Type Fiesta as the model name.

12.   Press the Enter key on the keyboard.

13.   Type Blue as the vehicle color.

14.   Press the Enter key on the keyboard.

15.   Type 5 as the vehicle age.

16.   Press the Enter key on the keyboard.

Figure 6-24 shows the console with the concatenated text for the vehicle age.

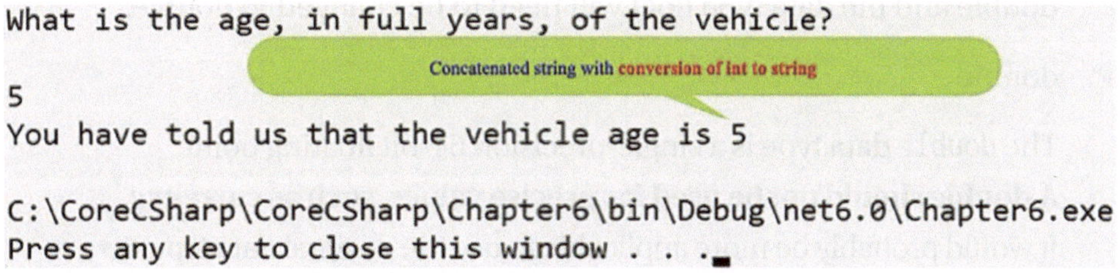

```
What is the age, in full years, of the vehicle?
                    Concatenated string with conversion of int to string
5
You have told us that the vehicle age is 5

C:\CoreCSharp\CoreCSharp\Chapter6\bin\Debug\net6.0\Chapter6.exe
Press any key to close this window . . .
```

Figure 6-24. *Implicit conversion in the Console.WriteLine()*

17. Press the Enter key again.

Code Analysis

- We have just concatenated a string data type and an int data type using the + concatenator.

- This works because the compiler does the conversion of the int data type to a string data type for us.

Amazing, we are now able to convert from one data type to another data type using the Convert class. We are able to use the ToInt32() method to convert a string to an int, and we should now be able to use the same concept for converting a string to another data type. We are also more familiar with the meaning of implicit and explicit conversions.

We will now amend the code to ask the user to input details about the value of the vehicle. This is the same process as we have already completed, so we will follow the same steps as before. Our main decision in this process will be what data type to use for the value of the vehicle that is input by the user. Three options could be considered:

- float

  The float data type is a single-precision 32-bit floating point. **A float should not be used for precise values, such as currency**. It would probably be more applicable to use the decimal data type. To initialize a float variable, we **must** use the suffix f or F, for example:

  ```
  float interest = 3.5F;
  ```

  If the suffix F or f is not declared, then the value will be treated as a double and the data type float will need to be changed to double.

- double

  The double data type is a single-precision 64-bit floating point. **A double should not be used for precise values, such as currency**. It would probably be more applicable to use the decimal data type. To initialize a double variable, we **can** use the suffix d or D, for example:

  ```
  double interest = 3.5d;
  ```

If the suffix D or d is not declared, then the value will be treated as a double. So double does not require the suffix "d" or "D" but they can be used.

- decimal

  The decimal type is a 128-bit data type. **The decimal data type is suitable for precise values such as currency**. To initialize a decimal variable, **we must use the suffix** m **or** M, for example:

  ```
  decimal interest = 3.5m;
  ```

  If the suffix m or M is not declared, then the value will be treated as a double and the data type decimal will need to be changed to double.

This can be summarized to say that, when choosing a data type for the value of the vehicle, it is our choice and depends on the accuracy we need for the value. Float is the least accurate, double is the next most accurate, and decimal is the most accurate. Here we can use any of the three, but for this example we will use decimal.

Read and write the vehicle estimated price.

18. Amend the code, as in Listing 6-24, by adding the variable called vehicleEstimatedCurrentPrice, which is of data type decimal.

Listing 6-24. Variable of data type decimal for the vehicle value

```
string vehicleColour;
int vehicleAgeInYears;
```

decimal vehicleEstimatedCurrentPrice;

19. Amend the code, as in Listing 6-25, to ask for user input, read the user input, and assign it to the vehicleEstimatedCurrentPrice variable.

Listing 6-25. Read console input and assign it to a variable

```
Console.WriteLine("You have told us that the vehicle " +
    "age is " + vehicleAgeInYears);

Console.WriteLine("What is the estimated current value " +
    "of the vehicle?\n");
vehicleEstimatedCurrentPrice =
    Convert.ToDecimal(Console.ReadLine());
} // End of Main() method
```

20. Amend the code, as in Listing 6-26, to display the vehicleEstimatedCurrentPrice value, which is read from the console.

Listing 6-26. Displaying the vehicle price

```
Console.WriteLine("What is the estimated current value " +
    "of the vehicle?\n");
vehicleEstimatedCurrentPrice =
    Convert.ToDecimal(Console.ReadLine());

Console.WriteLine("You have told us that the estimated " +
    "vehicle price is £ " + vehicleEstimatedCurrentPrice);
} // End of Main() method
} // End of Program class
} // End of Chapter6 namespace
```

21. Click the File menu.

22. Choose Save All.

23. Click the Debug menu.

24. Choose Start Without Debugging.

25. Type Ford as the manufacturer name.

26. Press the Enter key on the keyboard.

27. Type Fiesta as the model name.

28. Press the Enter key on the keyboard.

29. Type Blue as the vehicle color.

30. Press the Enter key on the keyboard.

31. Type 5 as the vehicle age.

32. Press the Enter key on the keyboard.

33. Type 6999.99 as the estimated vehicle value.

34. Press the Enter key on the keyboard.

Figure 6-25 shows the console with the output string, and the decimal value has been concatenated even though it is a decimal – this is an implicit conversion.

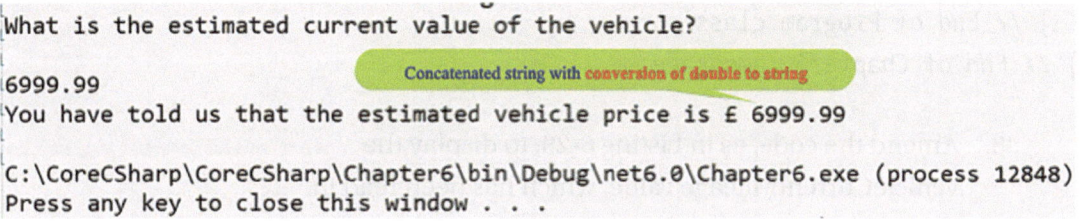

Figure 6-25. *Implicit conversion in the Console.WriteLine()*

35. Press the Enter key again.

Read and write the vehicle mileage.

We will now amend the code to ask the user to input details about the number of kilometers recorded on the odometer of the vehicle.

36. Amend the code, as in Listing 6-27, to add the variable to hold the mileage.

Listing 6-27. Variable of data type int for the vehicle mileage (km)

```
string vehicleColour;
int vehicleAgeInYears;
decimal vehicleEstimatedCurrentPrice;

int vehicleCurrentMileage;
```

37. Amend the code, as in Listing 6-28, to read the
     vehicleCurrentMileage value, which has been entered in the
     console.

Listing 6-28. Read console input and assign it to a variable

```
Console.WriteLine("You have told us that the estimated " +
    "vehicle price is £ " + vehicleEstimatedCurrentPrice);

Console.WriteLine("What is the current mileage (in km) " +
    "of the vehicle?\n");
vehicleCurrentMileage =Convert.ToInt32(Console.ReadLine());

} // End of Main() method
} // End of Program class
} // End of Chapter6 namespace
```

38. Amend the code, as in Listing 6-29, to display the
     vehicleCurrentMileage value, which has been read in.

Listing 6-29. Displaying the vehicle mileage

```
Console.WriteLine("What is the current mileage (in km) " +
    "of the vehicle?\n");
vehicleCurrentMileage =Convert.ToInt32(Console.ReadLine());

Console.WriteLine("You have told us that the vehicle " +
    "mileage is " + vehicleCurrentMileage + " km");

} // End of Main() method
} // End of Program class
} // End of Chapter6 namespace
```

Read and write the driver date of birth as a string.

We will now amend the code to ask the user to input the date of birth of the main
driver of the vehicle, but we should be aware that **dates are tricky to handle**. Initially
when we read the input it is a string, and we then convert it to a date. We use a data type
of **DateTime** for the variable.

39. Amend the existing code, as in Listing 6-30, by adding the DateTime variable called dateOfBirthOfMainDriver, which is of type DateTime.

Listing 6-30. Variable of data type DateTime for the driver date of birth

```
int vehicleAgeInYears;
decimal vehicleEstimatedCurrentPrice;
int vehicleCurrentMileage;

DateTime dateOfBirthOfMainDriver;
```

On hovering over the DateTime type, as shown in Figure 6-26, we can see what it represents, an instant in time, typically a date and time of the day.

```
DateTime dateOfBirthOfMainDriver;

Consol      readonly struct System.DateTime
Consol   Represents an instant in time, typically expressed as a date and time of day.
Consol
```

Figure 6-26. *DateTime type*

40. Amend the code, as in Listing 6-31, to ask the user to input the date, read the user input, and assign it to the dateOfBirthOfMainDriver variable.

Listing 6-31. Read console input and assign it to a variable

```
Console.WriteLine("You have told us that the vehicle " +
    "mileage is " + vehicleCurrentMileage + " km");

Console.WriteLine("What is the date of birth " +
"(yyyy-MM-dd) of the main driver of the vehicle?\n");

dateOfBirthOfMainDriver =
    DateTime.Parse(Console.ReadLine());
} // End of Main() method
} // End of Program class
} // End of Chapter6 namespace
```

Notice the use of the DateTime class and its associated Parse() method, which converts the string representation of a date and time to its DateTime equivalent.

41. Amend the code, as in Listing 6-32, to display the main driver date of birth, which has been read in.

Listing 6-32. Displaying the driver date of birth as type DateTime

```
dateOfBirthOfMainDriver =
    DateTime.Parse(Console.ReadLine());

    Console.WriteLine("You have told us that the main " +
        "driver was born on " + dateOfBirthOfMainDriver);
    } // End of Main() method
  } // End of Program class
} // End of Chapter6 namespace
```

42. Click the File menu.

43. Choose Save All.

44. Click the Debug menu.

45. Choose Start Debugging.

46. Type Ford as the manufacturer name.

47. Press the Enter key on the keyboard.

48. Type Fiesta as the model name.

49. Press the Enter key on the keyboard.

50. Type Blue as the vehicle color.

51. Press the Enter key on the keyboard.

52. Type 5 as the vehicle age.

53. Press the Enter key on the keyboard.

54. Type 6999.99 as the estimated vehicle value.

55. Press the Enter key on the keyboard.

56. Type 50000 as the number of kilometers on the odometer of the vehicle.

57. Press the Enter key on the keyboard.

58. Type 1998-01-01 as the date of birth for the main driver of the vehicle.

59. Press the Enter key on the keyboard.

Figure 6-27 shows the console with the output string, and the date value has been concatenated even though it is a date – this is an implicit conversion.

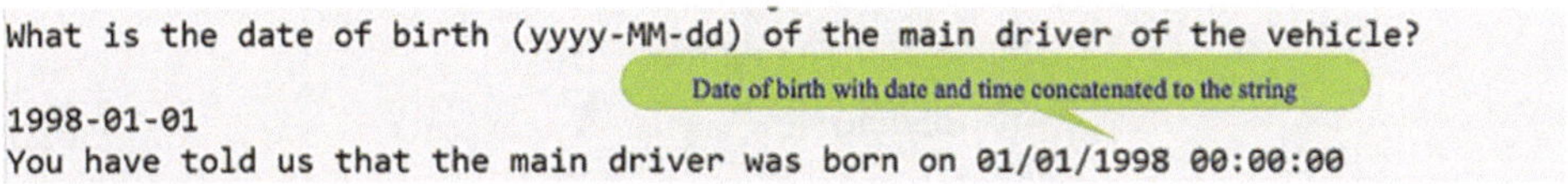

```
What is the date of birth (yyyy-MM-dd) of the main driver of the vehicle?

1998-01-01
You have told us that the main driver was born on 01/01/1998 00:00:00
```

Date of birth with date and time concatenated to the string

Figure 6-27. *DateTime type converted from type string*

60. Press the Enter key again.

Code Analysis

- We have used the data types int, decimal, and string, but now we have just used the data type of DateTime. This represents an instant in time, typically expressed as a date and time of day.

- When we read the console input, we have used the Convert class and selected the ToDateTime() method to perform the conversion.

- This works exactly the same way as our other explicit conversions.

- We have displayed the DateTime entered but it includes the time.

- If we do not want the time and simply want to display the date, then this will be possible since there is a method to do this.

- The method used to perform this "shortening" is **ToShortDateString().**

- This method belongs to the object called **DateTime.**

As we know, the variable dateOfBirthOfMainDriver is a DateTime variable; it is an object. If we add the full stop after the variable name in the WriteLine() method, we will see the variables and methods belonging to the DateTime object. Figure 6-28 shows this in action.

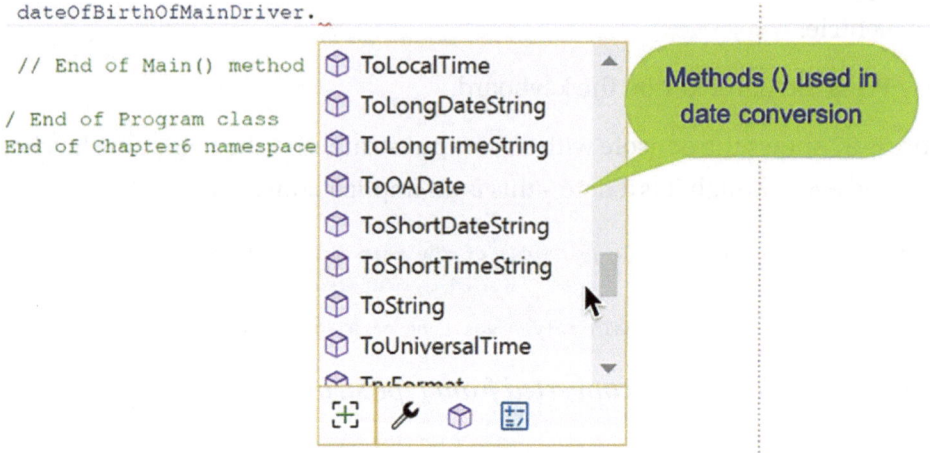

Figure 6-28. *Methods of the DateTime type struct*

- We can see that there are a number of methods available to us when we use the DateTime object. We can also see that there are a number of variables, the spanners, that are also available to us, for example, Minute, Month, and Ticks, as shown in Figure 6-29.

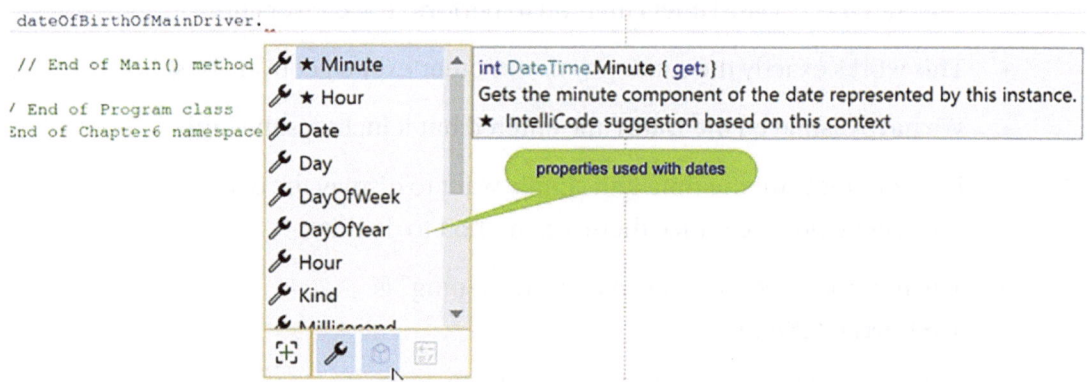

Figure 6-29. *Properties of the DateTime type struct*

We could be forgiven for thinking that DateTime is a class, as it has properties and methods. However, it is not a class; it is a **struct**, a structure. But let's forget about this for now and treat DateTime like a class with properties and methods, which we have access to. We will look at structs in a later chapter.

61. Amend the code, as in Listing 6-33, to display the short date of birth.

Listing 6-33. Displaying the driver date of birth as a short date

```
Console.WriteLine("You have told us that the main " +
    "driver was born on " + dateOfBirthOfMainDriver);

  Console.WriteLine("You have told us that the main " +
    "driver was born on "
    + dateOfBirthOfMainDriver.ToShortDateString());
  } // End of Main() method
 } // End of Program class
} // End of Chapter6 namespace
```

62. Click the File menu.

63. Choose Save All.

64. Click the Debug menu.

65. Choose Start Without Debugging.

66. Type Ford as the manufacturer name.

67. Press the Enter key on the keyboard.

68. Type Fiesta as the model name.

69. Press the Enter key on the keyboard.

70. Type Blue as the vehicle color.

71. Press the Enter key on the keyboard.

72. Type 5 as the vehicle age.

73. Press the Enter key on the keyboard.

74. Type 6999.99 as the estimated vehicle value.

75. Press the Enter key on the keyboard.

76. Type 50000 as the number of kilometers on the odometer of the vehicle.

77. Press the Enter key on the keyboard.

78. Type 1998-01-01 as the date of birth for the main driver of the vehicle.

79. Press the Enter key on the keyboard.

Figure 6-30 shows the console output with the short date format.

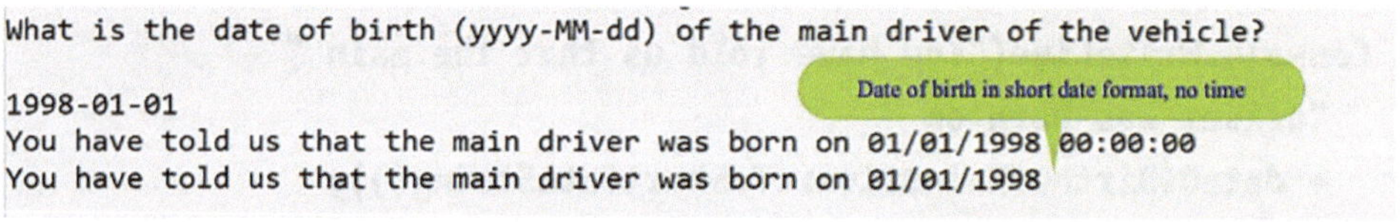

Figure 6-30. *DateTime type in short format converted from type string*

80. Press the Enter key again.

Chapter Summary

In this chapter we have learned about the very important programming concepts of **data types**, **variables,** and **conversions**. We have learned that

- There are value types in C# that include bool, byte, char, decimal, double, float, int, long, short, uint, and ushort.

- The value types in C# are referred to as **primitive types.** They are part of the language, they are built into the language, and we do not need to create them.

- C# is a programming language that is part of .NET, which also has other programming languages like F# and Visual Basic.

- There is a **Common Type System (CTS)** that exists in .NET and this means that we can use the programming language data types or those data types that belong to the Common Type System. We learned that string and String are the same as are double and Double and so on.

- Sometimes variables need to be converted from one data type to another data type and this is either done **explicitly** or **implicitly.**

- There are conversions called **widening conversions** where the converted data changes from a smaller data type to a larger data type.

- There are conversions called **narrowing conversions** where the converted data changes from a larger data type to a smaller data type and data can be lost.

- The Convert class has methods such as `ToInt32()` to help us convert between data types.

- Using a dot, a period, after a class name will display the accessible variables and methods that exist in the class.

- **Variables** in our code have a **scope.**

- Use of comments is important.

- Escape sequences such as \n and \t are useful for presentation of data in the console.

- Data can be read from and written to the console.

- There is a C# DateTime data type, object, that allows us to do things like using a method such as `ToShortDateString()` to convert a DateTime to a shortened version of the date, where only the date part is displayed and no time is shown.

We should also be aware that C# has other data types and we will use them as required by our code.

We have made great progress in such a short period of study, and in finishing this chapter and increasing our knowledge, we are advancing to our target.

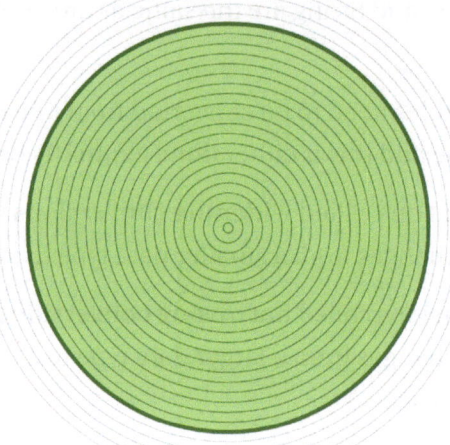

Our target is getting closer

CHAPTER 7

Casting and Parsing

Data Types, Casting, and Parsing

We learned in Chapter 6 that we can declare variables with a data type and then assign values to them in our code. We learned that we can accept user input and assign the input value to a variable, and we saw that there are times when we will need to convert a variable from one data type to another. In this context we learned about narrowing and widening conversions, and we used a conversion from an int to a byte, which involved casting, for example, (byte).

In C#, casting is a method used to convert one data type to another. Casting is used as an explicit conversion and tells the compiler what to do, but we need to be aware that there may be a loss of data. So we use casting to achieve a numeric conversion where the destination data type we are assigning the value to is of a lesser precision. **Casting is a conversion from one numeric data type to another numeric data type** as discussed earlier with narrowing and widening.

If we think back to what we have read about the numeric data types, we will see that we start with a less precise data type, sbyte, and we move up to the most precise **ulong** data type as shown in Table 7-1.

© Gerard Byrne 2022
G. Byrne, *Target C#*, https://doi.org/10.1007/978-1-4842-8619-7_7

Table 7-1. *Integral types*

Integral types			
byte	**Byte**	1	May contain integers from 0 to 255
sbyte	**SByte**	1	Signed byte from −128 to 127
short	**Int16**	2	Ranges from −32,768 to 32,767
ushort	**UInt16**	2	Unsigned, ranges from 0 to 65,535
int	**Int32**	4	Ranges from −2,147,483,648 to 2,147,483,647
uint	UInt32	4	Unsigned, ranges from 0 to 4,294,967,295
long	**Int64**	8	Ranges from −9,223,372,036,854,775,808 to 9,223,372,036,854,775,807
ulong	**UInt64**	8	Unsigned, ranges from 0 to 18,446,744,073,709,551,615

So taking a data type in Table 7-1 and trying to assign it to a variable with a data type above it in the table means we are moving to a less precise format and therefore we must use a cast, casting. Now we will code an example of int to short.

Add a new project to hold the code for this chapter.

1. Right-click the solution CoreCSharp.

2. Choose Add.

3. Choose New Project, as shown in Figure 7-1.

Figure 7-1. *Adding a new C# project*

4. Choose Console App from the listed templates as shown in Figure 7-2.

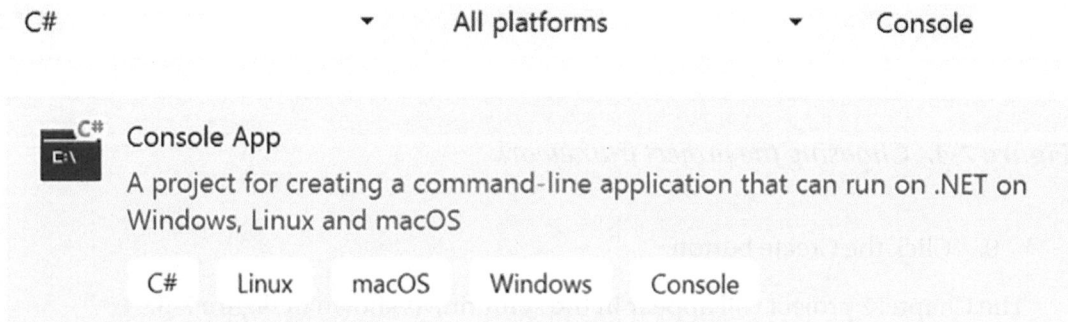

Figure 7-2. *Selecting a new C# console project*

5. Click the Next button.

6. Name the project Chapter7, leaving it in the same location, as shown in Figure 7-3.

Configure your new project

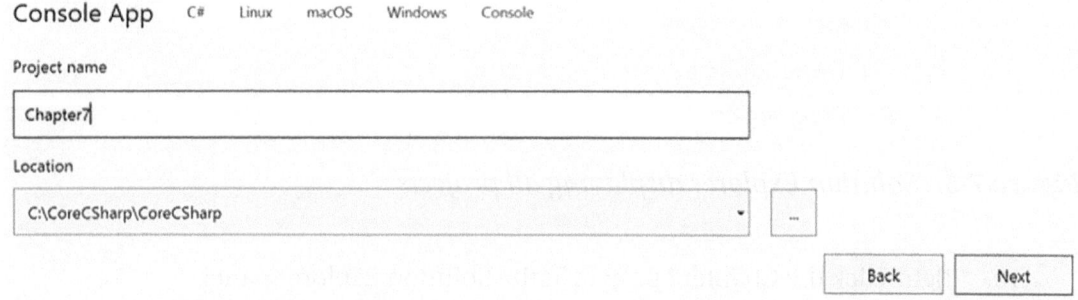

Figure 7-3. *Naming a new C# console project*

7. Click the Next button.

8. Choose the framework to be used, which in our projects will be .NET 6.0 or higher, as shown in Figure 7-4.

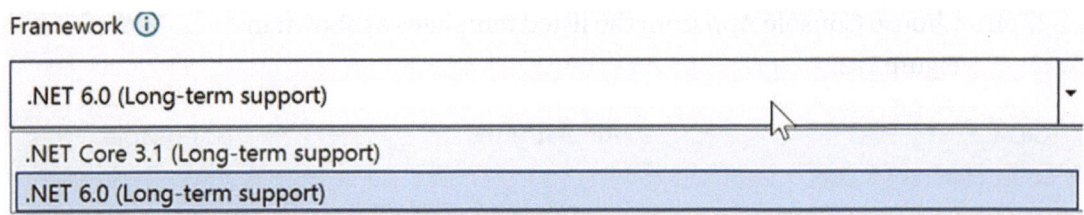

Figure 7-4. *Choosing the project framework*

9. Click the Create button.

The Chapter7 project will appear in the solution, as shown in Figure 7-5.

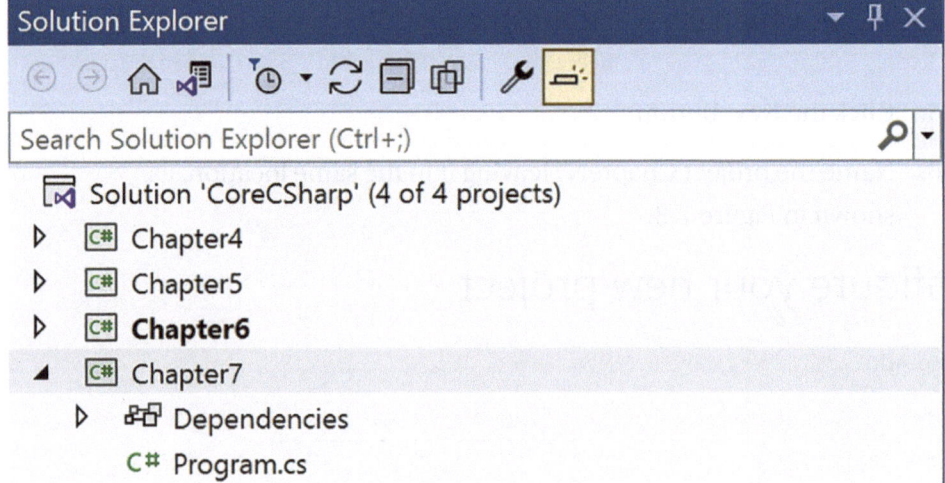

Figure 7-5. *Solution Explorer displaying all projects*

10. Right-click the Chapter7 project in the Solution Explorer panel.

11. Click the Set as Startup Project option.

Figure 7-6 shows that the Chapter7 project name has been made to have bold text, indicating that it is the new startup project and that it is the Program.cs file within it that will be executed when we run the debugging.

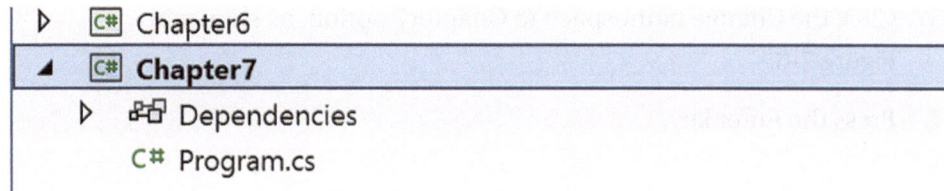

Figure 7-6. *Solution Explorer displaying the startup project*

**We will now copy the code from the Program.cs file in Chapter6 to the Program.
cs file in Chapter7.**

1. Double-click the Program.cs file in the Chapter6 project.

2. Highlight ALL the code within the program, yes, including the
    namespace and Main method.

3. Choose Copy.

4. Double-click the Program.cs file in the Chapter7 folder.

5. Highlight the existing code and delete it.

6. Right-click inside the blank editor window.

7. Choose Paste.

Now, the namespace is called Chapter6 so we will rename it as Chapter7. We have a
choice of ways to rename the namespace to Chapter7, but we will select the same one as
we did in the last chapter.

1. Right-click the word Chapter6, as shown in Figure 7-7.

2. Choose Quick Actions and Refactorings, as shown in Figure 7-7.

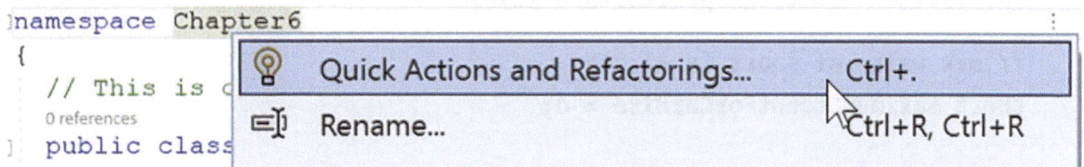

Figure 7-7. *Renaming the namespace using Quick Actions and Refactorings*

3. Click the Change namespace to Chapter7 option, as shown in Figure 7-8.

4. Press the Enter key.

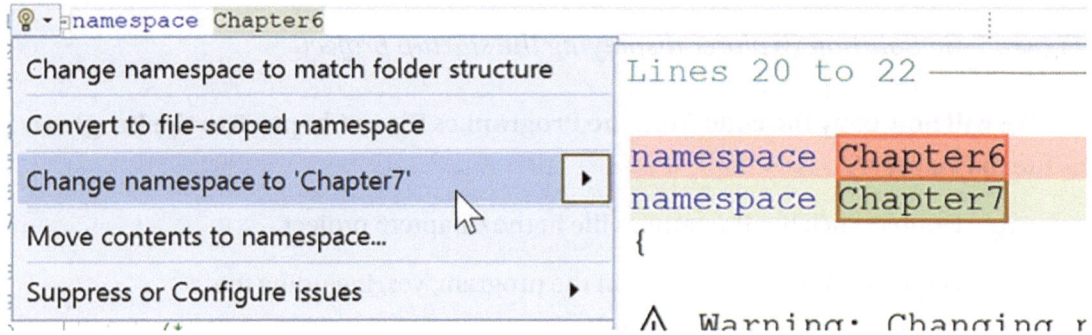

Figure 7-8. *Renaming the namespace to match the project name*

The namespace will now have been renamed to Chapter7.

We will amend the code by adding two new variables, one of data type int and called maximumAmountForRepairCosts and the other of data type short and called maximumAmountForCarHire.

1. Amend the code to add the two variables, as in Listing 7-1.

Listing 7-1. Two variables of types int and short with initial values

```
int vehicleCurrentMileage;
DateTime dateOfBirthOfMainDriver;

// max value of int is 2,147,483,647
int maximumAmountForRepairCosts = 32767;

// max value of short is 32,767
short maximumAmountForCarHire = 0;
```

2. Click the File menu.

3. Choose Save All.

We will now assign the value of the maximumAmountForRepairCosts variable to the variable called maximumAmountForCarHire.

4. Amend the code, as in Listing 7-2.

Listing 7-2. Assign one variable value to another variable

```
Console.WriteLine("You have told us that the main " +
  "driver was born on "
  + dateOfBirthOfMainDriver.ToShortDateString());

/*
Now we are trying to put the int variable
maximumAmountForRepairCosts into the short variable
maximumAmountForCarHire but this is not possible without
something being changed.
This is where the cast comes into play.
*/
maximumAmountForCarHire = maximumAmountForRepairCosts;

  } // End of Main() method
 } // End of Program class
} // End of Chapter7 namespace
```

5. Amend the code, as in Listing 7-3, to display the
    values of maximumAmountForRepairCosts and
    maximumAmountForCarHire.

Listing 7-3. Display messages including the variables

```
maximumAmountForCarHire = maximumAmountForRepairCosts;

Console.WriteLine("The int variable " +
  "maximumAmountForRepairCosts has a value of "
  + maximumAmountForRepairCosts);

Console.WriteLine();
Console.WriteLine("The short variable " +
  "maximumAmountForCarHire has a value of "
  + maximumAmountForCarHire);

  } // End of Main() method
```

```
} // End of Program class
} // End of Chapter7 namespace
```

As we see in Figure 7-9, the variable called maximumAmountForRepairCosts within the assignment statement is underlined with red. So we need to fix this issue, once we understand what is causing the error.

6. Hover over the red underline and read the pop-up message, as in Figure 7-9.

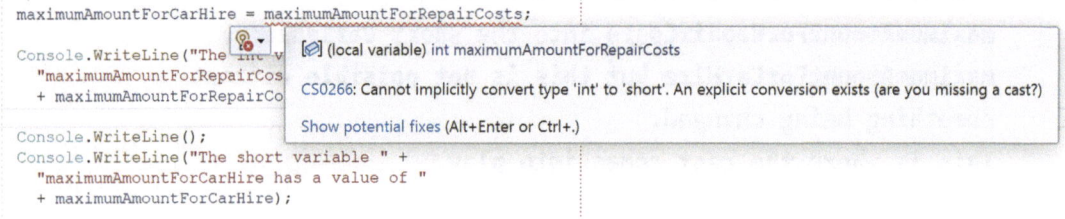

Figure 7-9. *Hovering over the error to see the help message*

In the error message, we are being told that maximumAmountForRepairCosts cannot be implicitly converted from an int data type to a short data type. Even though the error message does not specifically say it, the cause of the error is that we are trying to perform a narrowing conversion, and this cannot be done implicitly. We must perform the conversion with an explicit conversion, a **cast** in this case. If we look carefully, we will see that we are asked the question: "are you missing a cast?" This means that we can perform the conversion using a cast and we will be casting the maximumAmountForRepairCosts variable, which is of data type int, so it fits into a data type short.

7. Amend the code, as in Listing 7-4, to perform the casting.

Listing 7-4. Cast int type to short type

```
maximumAmountForCarHire = (short)maximumAmountForRepairCosts;

Console.WriteLine("The int variable " +
    "maximumAmountForRepairCosts has a value of "
    + maximumAmountForRepairCosts);
```

Now we should see that the red underline error has disappeared. We have fixed the conversion issue by using a **cast** to make the value of the variable of data type int into a short value.

Now, running this application with the int variable being set to have its maximum value of 32767 will be fine. This means the **casting will take place without loss of accuracy, on this occasion**.

8. Click the File menu.

9. Choose Save All.

10. Click the Debug menu.

11. Choose Start Without Debugging.

12. Type Ford as the manufacturer name.

13. Press the Enter key on the keyboard.

14. Type Fiesta as the model name.

15. Press the Enter key on the keyboard.

16. Type Blue as the vehicle color.

17. Press the Enter key on the keyboard.

18. Type 5 as the vehicle age.

19. Press the Enter key on the keyboard.

20. Type 6999.99 as the estimated vehicle value.

21. Press the Enter key on the keyboard.

22. Type 50000 as the number of kilometers on the odometer of the vehicle.

23. Press the Enter key on the keyboard.

24. Type 1998-01-01 as the date of birth for the main driver of the vehicle.

25. Press the Enter key on the keyboard.

Figure 7-10 shows the console window and we can see that the casting has worked.

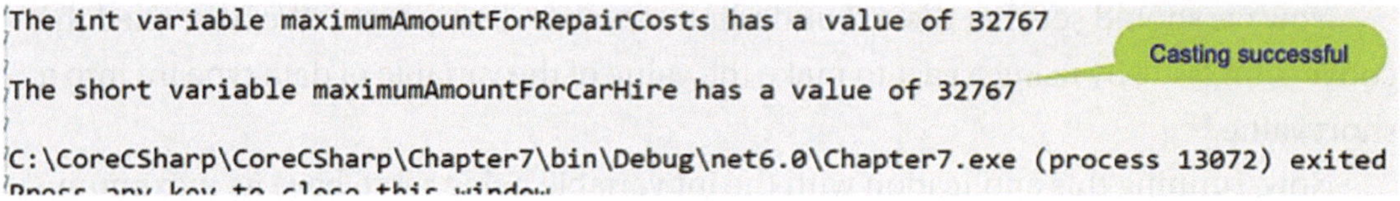

```
The int variable maximumAmountForRepairCosts has a value of 32767

The short variable maximumAmountForCarHire has a value of 32767

C:\CoreCSharp\CoreCSharp\Chapter7\bin\Debug\net6.0\Chapter7.exe (process 13072) exited
Press any key to close this window
```

Casting successful

Figure 7-10. *Casting int type to short type*

    26.   Press the Enter key to close the console window.

If we amend the code so that the int variable is set to have a value that is one more than the maximum value of the short data type, 32768, there will be an issue. This means the **casting will take place with loss of accuracy**.

We will now change the value of the int variable so that it is one more than the maximum value of a short data type. This will mean that when we cast the int variable, it will be too large for the variable maximumAmountForCarHire, data type short, to hold.

    27.   Amend the code as in Listing 7-5.

Listing 7-5. Assign a value of 32768 to a short – this is outside the type range

```
DateTime dateOfBirthOfMainDriver;

// max value of int is 2,147,483,647
int maximumAmountForRepairCosts = 32768;

// max value of short is 32,767
short maximumAmountForCarHire = 0;
```

    28.   Click the File menu.

    29.   Choose Save All.

    30.   Click the Debug menu.

    31.   Choose Start Without Debugging.

    32.   Click in the console window.

    33.   Type Ford as the manufacturer name.

    34.   Press the Enter key on the keyboard.

    35.   Type Fiesta as the model name.

36. Press the Enter key on the keyboard.

37. Type Blue as the vehicle color.

38. Press the Enter key on the keyboard.

39. Type 5 as the vehicle age.

40. Press the Enter key on the keyboard.

41. Type 6999.99 as the estimated vehicle value.

42. Press the Enter key on the keyboard.

43. Type 50000 as the number of kilometers on the odometer of the vehicle.

44. Press the Enter key on the keyboard.

45. Type 1998-01-01 as the date of birth for the main driver of the vehicle.

46. Press the Enter key on the keyboard.

We can now see that there is an output, as shown in Figure 7-11. There has not been a compile error, but **the result is not correct.**

```
The int variable maximumAmountForRepairCosts has a value of 32768    Casting successful???

The short variable maximumAmountForCarHire has a value of -32768

C:\CoreCSharp\CoreCSharp\Chapter7\bin\Debug\net6.0\Chapter7.exe (process 9716) exited
Press any key to close this window . . .
```

***Figure 7-11.** Casting appears to have worked successfully*

47. Change the value back to 32767 from 32768.

Amend the code to use a Boolean data type and use parsing for the conversion.

We will now amend the code to ask the user to input **True** or **False** at the console. Remember that the console input will be a string. We will then assign the console input to a variable of data type **bool.**

1. Amend the code, as in Listing 7-6, to add two new variables, one of data type string and the other of data type bool (Boolean).

Listing 7-6. Add variables of types string and bool

```
// max value of short is 32,767
short maximumAmountForCarHire = 0;

bool fullyComprehensiveRequirement = true;
```

2. Amend the code, as in Listing 7-7, to ask the user for input.

Listing 7-7. Ask for user input

```
Console.WriteLine("You have told us that the main " +
    "driver was born on " + dateOfBirthOfMainDriver);

Console.WriteLine("You have told us that the main " +
    "driver was born on "
    + dateOfBirthOfMainDriver.ToShortDateString());

Console.WriteLine("Do we require fully comprehensive" +
    " insurance (enter the word True or False)?\n");
```

3. Amend the code, as in Listing 7-8, to assign the value entered at the console to the variable fullyComprehensiveRequirement.

Listing 7-8. Read the string input and assign it to a variable

```
Console.WriteLine("You have told us that the main " +
    "driver was born on "
    + dateOfBirthOfMainDriver.ToShortDateString());

Console.WriteLine("Do we require fully comprehensive" +
    " insurance (enter the word True or False)?\n");

fullyComprehensiveRequirement = Console.ReadLine();
```

4. Amend the code, as in Listing 7-9, to display the value of the variable fullyComprehensiveRequirement, which is of data type bool.

Listing 7-9. Display the bool value

```
Console.WriteLine("Do we require fully comprehensive" +
  " insurance (enter the word True or False)?\n");

fullyComprehensiveRequirement = Console.ReadLine();


Console.WriteLine("It is " + fullyComprehensiveRequirement
  + " that we require fully comprehensive insurance");
```

As shown in Figure 7-12, there is a red underline under the statement Console. ReadLine(). So we need to fix the issue once we understand what is causing the error.

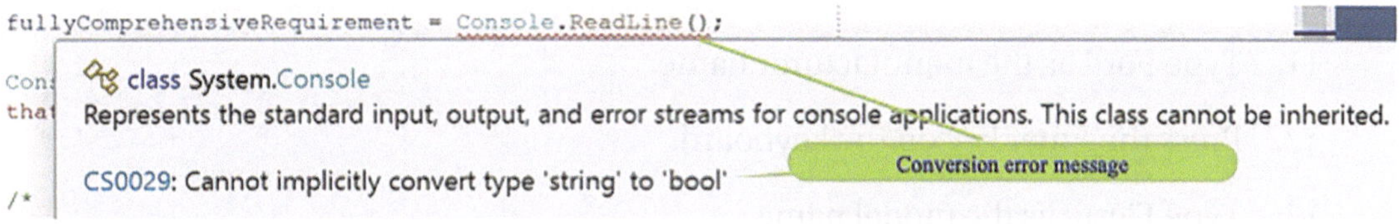

Figure 7-12. *Hovering over the error to see the help message*

Hovering over the word Console, we will be presented with an error message. We could also hover over the ReadLine() part of the statement and we will get a similar message. We are being told that fullyComprehensiveRequirement cannot be implicitly converted from a string data type to a bool data type. We need to fix the issue by performing a conversion as the message says. **There is no talking about a cast** as we saw in the previous example because this is not a conversion from one numeric data type to another numeric data type.

We can use the Parse() method, as discussed earlier. The **Parse() method** will be the `Boolean.Parse()` method, which accepts a string value and "converts," parses, it to a Boolean.

 5.   Amend the code, as in Listing 7-10, to perform the parsing.

Listing 7-10. Parse the string input to a bool

```
Console.WriteLine("Do we require fully comprehensive" +
  " insurance (enter the word True or False)?\n");

fullyComprehensiveRequirement =
  Boolean.Parse(Console.ReadLine());
```

```
Console.WriteLine("It is " + fullyComprehensiveRequirement
    + " that we require fully comprehensive insurance");
```

Now we should see that the red underline error has disappeared as we fixed the conversion issue.

6. Click the File menu.

7. Choose Save All.

8. Click the Debug menu.

9. Choose Start Without Debugging.

10. Click in the console window.

11. Type Ford as the manufacturer name.

12. Press the Enter key on the keyboard.

13. Type Fiesta as the model name.

14. Press the Enter key on the keyboard.

15. Type Blue as the vehicle color.

16. Press the Enter key on the keyboard.

17. Type 5 as the vehicle age.

18. Press the Enter key on the keyboard.

19. Type 6999.99 as the estimated vehicle value.

20. Press the Enter key on the keyboard.

21. Type 50000 as the number of kilometers on the odometer of the vehicle.

22. Press the Enter key on the keyboard.

23. Type 1998-01-01 as the date of birth for the main driver of the vehicle.

24. Press the Enter key on the keyboard.

25. Type **True** for the answer to the question. It is true that we require fully comprehensive insurance.

The output will be as shown in Figure 7-13.

```
Do we require fully comprehensive insurance (enter the word True or False)?
                     Boolean used
True
It is True that we require fully comprehensive insurance
```

Figure 7-13. *Boolean type as input*

We might also think of a **Convert.ToBoolean**() method to do the conversion, as in Listing 7-11. Yes, that would work.

Listing 7-11. Using the Convert class ToBoolean() method to parse

```
fullyComprehensiveRequirement =
  Boolean.Parse(Console.ReadLine());

fullyComprehensiveRequirement =
  Convert.ToBoolean(Console.ReadLine());

Console.WriteLine("It is " + fullyComprehensiveRequirement
  + " that you require fully comprehensive insurance");
```

We can therefore use

```
fullyComprehensiveRequirement =
  Boolean.Parse(Console.ReadLine());
```

or

```
fullyComprehensiveRequirement =
  Convert.ToBoolean(Console.ReadLine());
```

Chapter Summary

In this chapter we have learned about the particularly important programming concepts of parsing and casting and have seen the "subtle" difference between them. We have seen that in parsing we use the **wrapper** class that represents the data type, for example, Boolean, and we noted that this class, like all classes, starts with a capital letter. Each wrapper class has methods that will perform the parsing, for example, Parse(), and the method will be passed the name of the variable to be parsed, converted.

We are making really great progress, and we should keep it foremost in our programming thoughts that data types, casting, parsing, and conversions are a core programming concept and will be used throughout the chapters in this book, but more importantly, they are widely used in commercial applications.

We are making great progress in our programming of C# applications, and in finishing this chapter and increasing our knowledge, we are advancing to our target.

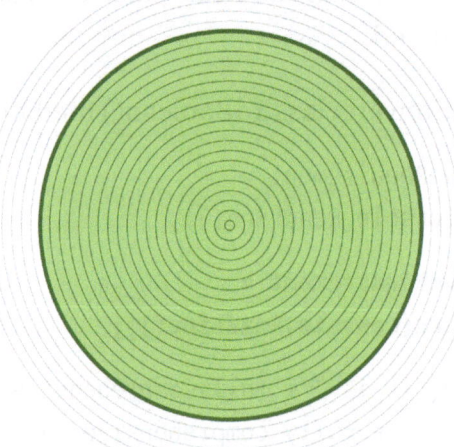

Our target is getting closer

CHAPTER 8

Arithmetic

Arithmetic Operations

We learned in Chapter 7 that variables can be "converted" from one numeric data type to another, which is referred to as **casting,** or from a string value to a numeric value, which is called **parsing**. Parsing uses methods from a wrapper class to convert the string data to a numeric data type value. These are important concepts and widely used in all programming languages by professional developers. As we develop our C# skills throughout the chapters, we will use these concepts, so it is worthwhile constantly reminding ourselves of the differences between casting and parsing and how they are used within C# code.

Arithmetic in Our Business Logic

The code, or business logic as it is often called, of many applications will have some degree of computation or calculation. In C# it is possible to perform operations on integers and other numerical data types, in the same way we can perform operations in normal mathematics.

We will probably be aware from our mathematics lessons at school that mathematical operations are performed in a specific order, and therefore we need to ensure that formulae are written in such a way that the mathematical operators work in the correct order. Based on this knowledge, we should recognize that calculations that involve combinations of mathematical operators such as add (+), subtract (–), multiply (*), and divide (/) can return a different value when the order is changed. The normal algebraic rules of **precedence** or **priority** apply in any programming language, including C#, and need to be thoroughly understood and applied. The precedence can be understood using the acronym BODMAS, which means

- **Brackets**
- p**O**wers

© Gerard Byrne 2022
G. Byrne, *Target C#*, https://doi.org/10.1007/978-1-4842-8619-7_8

- **D**ivision (division and multiplication have the same priority)

- **M**ultiplication

- **A**ddition (addition and subtraction have the same priority)

- **S**ubtraction

Another widely used acronym instead of BODMAS is PEMDAS, which means

- **P**arentheses

- **E**xponents

- **M**ultiplication

- **D**ivision (division and multiplication have the same priority)

- **A**ddition (addition and subtraction have the same priority)

- **S**ubtraction

To try and remember this acronym, people will use the mnemonic Please Excuse My Dear Aunt Sally, or another favorite is Please End My Day At School. Either acronym can be used and they mean the same thing.

As stated earlier it is vitally important that we get the correct answers when we execute calculations in our code. Therefore, we need to ensure that mathematical formulae are written correctly in our code. Big problems can be caused by, and for, developers when they code their formulae incorrectly. Often the coding errors in mathematical formulae are caused because developers misuse or do not use brackets ( ) to group expressions within their formulae.

Example 1

> **6 * 5 – 3**
>
> We could take this to mean (which is the correct interpretation based on the rules)
>
> **6 * 5** – This part is equal to 30.
>
> **30 – 3** – This part is equal to 27.
>
> If this was the intention, it should be written in a more clearly readable form as
>
> **(6 * 5) – 3**

Now the brackets make it clear that 6 is multiplied by 5 and the answer will have 3 subtracted from it to give an answer of 27.

Alternatively, we could take it to mean

5 – 3 – This part is equal to 2.

6 * 2 – This part is equal to 12.

If this was the intention, it should be written in a more clearly readable form as

6 * (5 – 3)

Now the brackets make it clear that 3 is subtracted from 5 and the answer is multiplied by 6 to give an answer of 12.

Example 2

$2 + 4 \times 3 - 1$ Multiply 4 by 3.

$2 + 12 - 1$ Add 2 and 12.

$14 - 1$ Subtract 1 from 14.

13

If we use brackets, it can make the visualization of the actual order much easier:

$2 + 4 \times 3 - 1$ can be written as $2 + (4 \times 3) - 1$.

Without brackets it can be harder to see what needs to be done in the formula. By using brackets ( ) to group expressions within the formula, we can make it much easier to understand. This idea of making code easier to read forms part of the concept of **clean code**. When we have clean code, we are more likely to have code that is easier to read and maintain.

Common Arithmetic Operators

Within C# we have access to a number of arithmetic operators, including those shown in the following, which we will use in this chapter and in many programs that we write:

Add +

Subtract -

Multiply *

Divide /

Modulus % the remainder

Integer Division

Integer division in any programming language, just as in mathematics, is an interesting operation in that we get an answer with a remainder, even if the remainder is 0. In programming, when two integer values are divided using the / operator, the result will be the **whole** part of the division and the **remainder** is not considered.

Example

19/5 will give an answer of 3.

As we can see this is the whole number part and there is no indication of the remainder. Where has the remainder of 4 gone? It has effectively been lost as we have not used the division operator in its full format. We need to use the division operator alongside the **modulus** operator (%). The modulus operator **%** gives the **remainder** after the division has been performed.

Example

19%5 will give an answer of 4.

Listing 8-1. Example code for division and modulus

```
Console.WriteLine("19 / 5 will give an answer of " + (19 / 5));

Console.WriteLine("19 % 5 will give an answer of " + (19 % 5));

Console.WriteLine("19 divided by 5 will give an answer of "
        + (19 / 5) + " remainder " + (19 % 5));
```

Therefore, to do a division properly, we need to combine the division and the modulus parts as shown in the last WriteLine() statement in Listing 8-1.

Now it is time for us to do some C# coding where the console application we code will use mathematical operators to perform arithmetic. We will read data input from the console using the `Console.ReadLine()` method and will write to the console using the `Console.WriteLine()` method. As we are dealing with mathematical operators, our data will need to be numerical, so our code will apply some conversion using the `Convert` class and the appropriate methods of this class, for example, `ToInt32()`. We will also apply some casting, particularly when undertaking division, which involves int data types.

In creating this C# application, we should use the same solution that we created for the earlier chapters, as we will still be able to see the code we have written for the previous chapters. The approach of keeping all our separate projects in one solution is a good idea while studying this book and coding the examples. Having already created some projects, we should be getting familiar with the process of project creation, and the whole idea of following a standard process to create the projects helps us reinforce our learning.

Add a new project to hold the code for this chapter.

1. Right-click the solution CoreCSharp.

2. Choose Add.

3. Choose New Project, as shown in Figure 8-1.

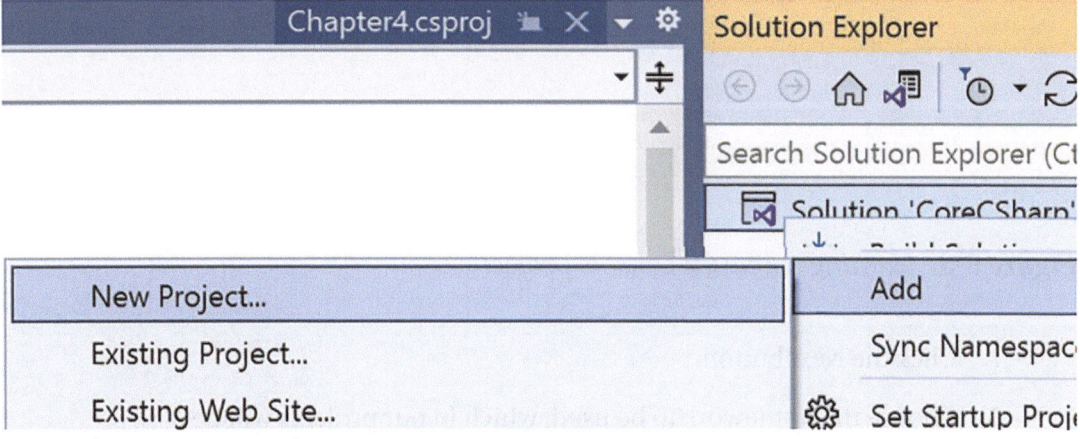

Figure 8-1. *Adding a new C# project*

4. Choose Console App from the listed templates that appear, as shown in Figure 8-2.

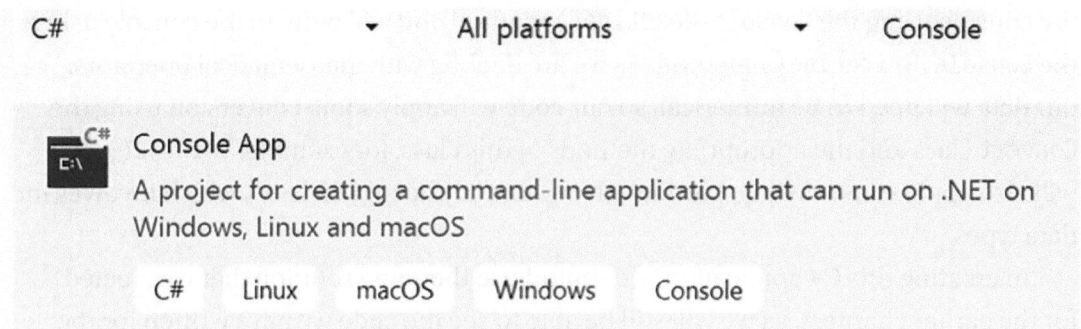

Figure 8-2. *Selecting a new C# console project*

5. Click the Next button.

6. Name the project Chapter8 and leave it in the same location, as shown in Figure 8-3.

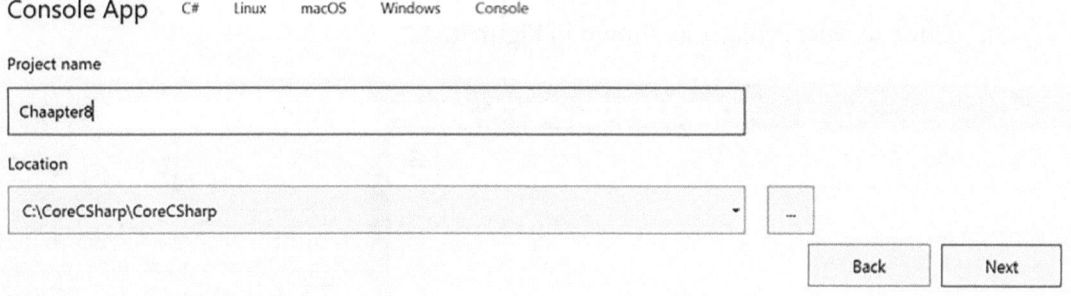

Figure 8-3. *Naming a new C# console project*

7. Click the Next button.

8. Choose the framework to be used, which in our projects will be .NET 6.0 or higher, as shown in Figure 8-4.

Framework ⓘ

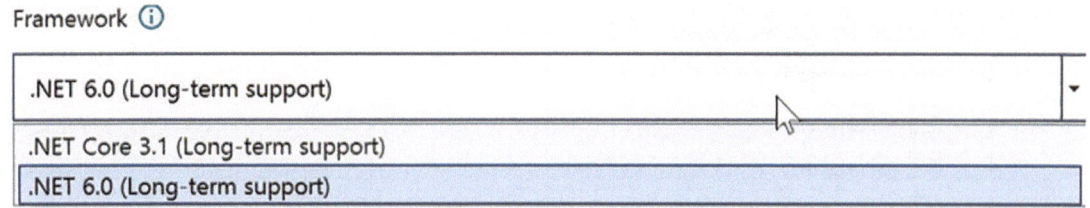

Figure 8-4. *Choosing the project framework*

9. Click the Create button.

Figure 8-5 shows the Chapter8 project within the solution called CoreCSharp.

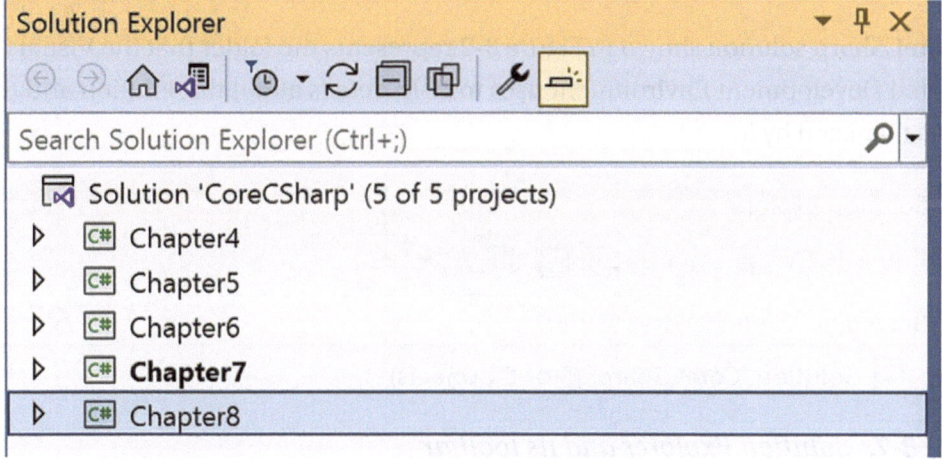

Figure 8-5. *Solution Explorer displaying all projects*

10. Right-click the Chapter8 project in the Solution Explorer panel.

11. Click the Set as Startup Project option.

Notice how the Chapter8 project name has been made to have bold text, as shown in Figure 8-6. This indicates that Chapter8 is the new startup project and it is the Program. cs file within it that will be executed when we debug.

Solution 'CoreCSharp' (5 of 5 projects)
▷   C# Chapter4
▷   C# Chapter5
▷   C# Chapter6
▷   C# Chapter7
▷   C# **Chapter8**

Figure 8-6. *Solution Explorer displaying the startup project*

Solution Explorer and Project Analysis

The CoreCSharp solution shown in Figure 8-7 represents the folder that the Visual Studio Integrated Development Environment uses to hold details about the solution and the projects managed by it.

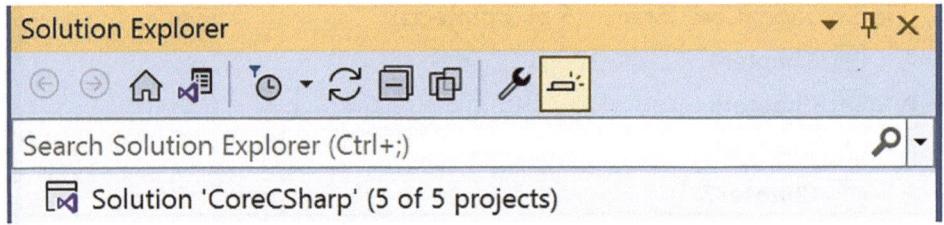

Figure 8-7. *Solution Explorer and its toolbar*

Inside the folder is a file called CoreCSharp, which is the solution file. If we look in the Windows File Explorer or the Finder on a Mac computer, where our projects are held, we will notice that the file type is **sln,** which represents a Visual Studio solution.

12.   Right-click the solution name.

13.   Choose Open Folder in File Explorer, or Finder on a Mac, as shown in Figure 8-8.

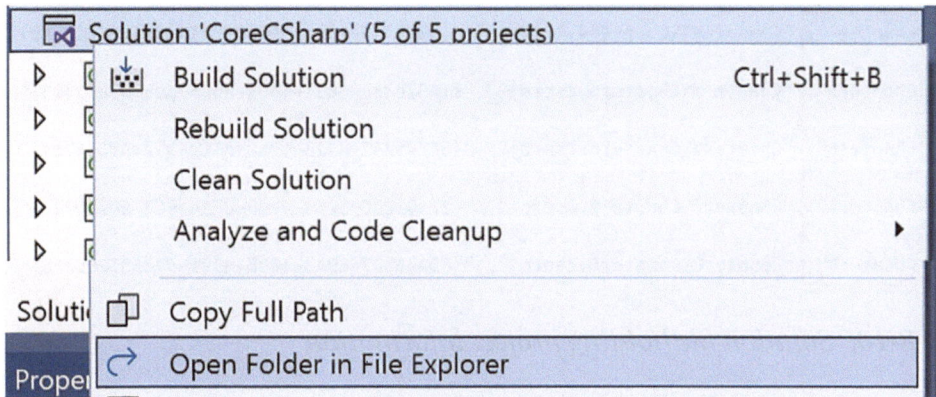

Figure 8-8. *Right-clicking the solution and opening the folder in the File Explorer window*

When the window opens, the CoreCSharp folder with the solution file will be displayed as shown in Figure 8-9.

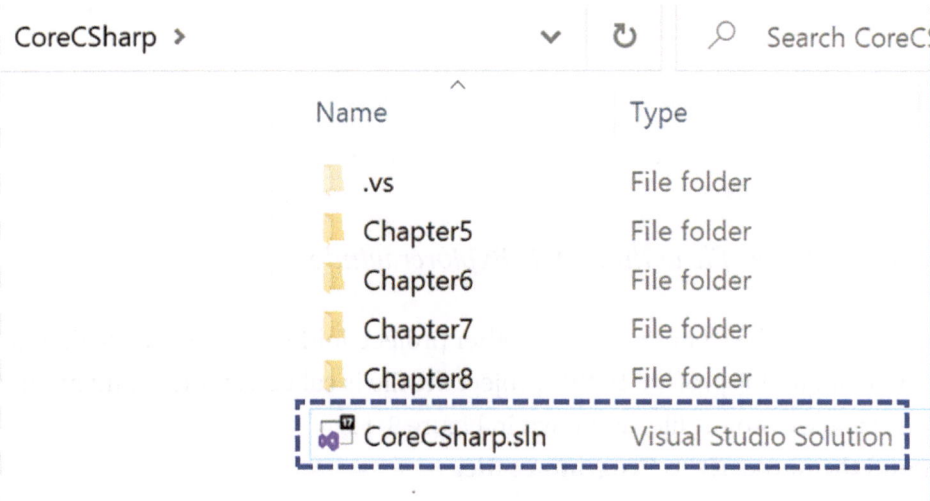

Figure 8-9. *Solution file within a File Explorer window*

The solution file holds information about the projects that are part of the overall solution. **There is no need for us to ever amend this file**. If we were to open the file in a text editor, we would see our solution has several projects, and this information is stored in the solution file as shown in Figure 8-10.

```
"Chapter4", "ConsoleV1\Chapter4.csproj", "{58BB44D7-8115-4F56-B720-2F52B8FD96A6}"

"Chapter5", "Chapter5\Chapter5.csproj", "{14B7833D-6637-4409-B68F-39EDD80711D3}"

"Chapter6", "Chapter6\Chapter6.csproj", "{68EB5222-A52B-4358-A1CD-D924A0C767E4}"

"Chapter7", "Chapter7\Chapter7.csproj", "{23392E5C-E2F3-4298-8F34-8C776D959787}"

"Chapter8", "Chapter8\Chapter8.csproj", "{B9A4BFD7-F9F3-409E-AD91-4706B72CD3F8}"
```

Figure 8-10. *Solution file holding project information*

14. Open the Chapter8 folder in File Explorer, or Finder on a Mac.

Name	Type	Size
bin	File folder	
obj	File folder	
Chapter8	CSPROJ File	1 KB
Program	CS File	1 KB

Figure 8-11. *Project file within a File Explorer window*

Looking inside the Chapter8, or any other project, folder reveals the file that holds information about this project. In this project the file is called Chapter8 and has a type of **csproj,** a visual C# project file, as shown in Figure 8-11.

Amend the name of the Program.cs file.

In each of the chapters so far, we have created a project within the solution, and we have accepted that Visual Studio creates a Program.cs file by default, which we have unassumingly used as a template, and added our own C# code to it. But might we want to have a different name from Program.cs? Well, we might, but if this is the file that contains the Main() method, the main entry point to our application, it would be unusual to rename it. Convention would be to have a Program.cs file with the Main() method contained within it. Future chapters will have multiple files within our project, and we will want to give them all **meaningful names** so we can quickly understand what their purpose is. So let us now rename the Program.cs file in our Chapter8 project, and then we will be able to use the same principle throughout the rest of the book chapters, so we have names that associate our code with the example application we are coding.

15. Double-click the Chapter8 Program.cs file in the Solution Explorer window to open it in the editor window.

16. Right-click the Chapter8 Program.cs file in the Solution Explorer window.

17. Choose Rename.

18. Change the name to Arithmetic.cs.

19. Press the Enter key.

Code Analysis

- If we have not switched off the top-level statements, as discussed in Chapters 4, 5, and 6, the new template in Visual Studio 2022, for a console application, is shown in the editor window.

- So the Visual Studio Integrated Development Environment is great at helping, but the unnecessary using statements it gives us do not fit well with the clean code concept. There is a programming concept known as **YAGNI,** which stands for **You Ain't Going To Need It**, and having the lines of code from the template code fits into this, so we will **remove** these two lines of code:

```
// See https://aka.ms/new-console-template for more information
Console.WriteLine("Hello, World!");
```

We should now be getting a better understanding of the structure for projects and solutions and, as we learn more, we will see how to add different classes to our projects, with only one class in each project containing the Main() method. Obviously, we will need to have different names for each class in a project, so **do we always want to have the Program.cs file, or would we like to rename it?** Well, it is possible for us to rename the file, so we will, for reinforcement purposes only, change the name of our Arithmetic. cs file in this project within the Solution Explorer.

20. Right-click the Arithmetic.cs file in the Solution Explorer window.

21. Choose Rename.

22.   Change the name to QuoteArithmetic.cs, as shown in Figure 8-12.

23.   Press the Enter key.

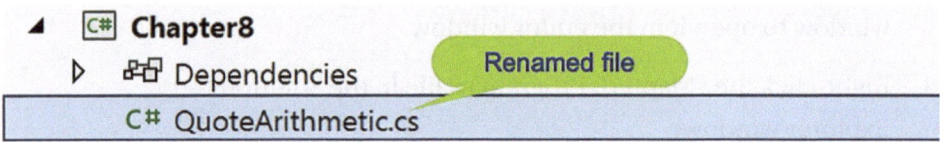

Figure 8-12. Program.cs file renamed

First, we will set up the code structure for the file, which will be the entry point for our application. This will be the same structure for most of our projects:

- First is a namespace.

- Inside the namespace will be a class – here it is QuoteArithmetic.

- Inside the class will be the Main() method.

The shortcut for creating the Main() method is to type **svm and press the Tab key twice.**

24.   In the QuoteArithmetic editor window, add the code in Listing 8-2.

Listing 8-2. QuoteArithmetic.cs structure with class and namespace

```
namespace Chapter8
{
  public class QuoteArithmetic
  {
    static void Main(string[] args)
    {
    } // End of Main() method
  } // End of QuoteArithmetic class
} // End of Chapter8 namespace
```

Now we will add the variables to be used in our code. In the code in Listings 8-2 and 8-3 and future listings, there are detailed comments to help us get a full understanding of the code. In this example all code is contained within the opening and closing curly braces, { }, of the Main() method.

25.   In the editor window, add the variables as shown in Listing 8-3.

Listing 8-3. Declaring the variables in the Main() method

```
namespace Chapter8
{
  public class QuoteArithmetic
  {
    static void Main(string[] args)
    {
      /*
      We will setup our variables that will be used in the
      mathematical calculation used to produce an insurance
      quotation for a vehicle.
      First we will setup the variables that will hold the user
      input and that will be used in calculating the quote
      */
      int vehicleAgeInYears;
      int vehicleCurrentMileage;

      /*
      For the quotation we will use 10000 kilometres as a base
      line for calculating a mileage factor. If the average
      kilometres travelled per year is above the base mileage of
      10000 the mileage factor will be above 1, if the average
      kilometres travelled per year is the lower than the base
      mileage of 10000 the mileage factor will be below 1
      */
      double quoteAverageExpectedKilometres = 10000;
      /*
      For the quotation we will use £100 as a base figure
      (this is just an example) and this figure will be
      multiplied by the mileage and age factors
      */
```

```
double quoteBaseRate = 100.00;

/*
For the quotation we will use 10 as a base figure for the
age of the vehicle (this is just an example).
If the vehicle is older than 10 years, the age factor
will be above 1.
If the vehicle is younger than 10 years the age factor
will be below 1
*/
int quoteBaseAge = 10;

/*
This variable will be used to hold the value of the
age factor
*/
double quoteAgeFactor;

/*
This variable holds the quote amount based on the age
factor and the base rate
*/
double quoteAgeFactorPremium;

/*
This variable holds the quote mileage factor based on the
number of kilometres travelled each year and how the
kilometres per year is a ratio of the average expected
10000 kilometres as decided by the insurance company
*/
double quoteMileageFactor;

/*
This variable holds the amount for the quote based only
on the mileage factor. The quote also has to take into
account the age of the vehicle
*/
double quoteMileageFactorPremium;
```

```
/*
This variable will hold the discount amount.
A discount will be applied to the quote based on the age
of the vehicle. The age of the vehicle is divided into 1
to get the discount. The decimal value is a representation
of the discount and will then be multiplied by the quote
value to get the actual discount in terms of £s
*/
double quoteDiscount;

/*
This variable holds the total of the age factor premium
and the mileage factor premium and will be used by the
discount calculation to get the discount amount
*/
double quoteAmountForPremium;

/*
This variable holds the final quotation value, the premium.
*/
double quoteFinalAmountForPremium;

    } // End of Main() method
  } // End of QuoteArithmetic class
} // End of Chapter8 namespace
```

Now we will write some information to the console and ask for user input.

26. Amend the code, as in Listing 8-4, adding print lines to the end of the code.

Listing 8-4. Displaying a message to the user

```
/*
This variable holds the final quotation value, the premium.
*/
double quoteFinalAmountForPremium;

Console.WriteLine();
```

```
    Console.WriteLine("---- Car Quotation Application ----");
    Console.WriteLine();
    Console.WriteLine("What is the age, in full years, of " +
        "the vehicle?\n");

    } // End of Main() method
  } // End of QuoteArithmetic class
} // End of Chapter8 namespace
```

Now we will

- Read the vehicle age input from the console and convert it to an int.

- Use the vehicle age to calculate an **age factor**, by dividing the base age that we set up as one of the variables by the vehicle age.

- Calculate the **premium**, based on the age factor and quote base rate of £100.

27. Amend the code, as in Listing 8-5, adding the lines to the end of the code.

Listing 8-5. Get user input for the vehicle age and perform calculations

```
Console.WriteLine("What is the age, in full years, of " +
    "the vehicle?\n");

/*
Perform the conversion, Parse, from string to int as we
will use the age of the vehicle in our calculation and
it needs to be numeric
*/
vehicleAgeInYears = Convert.ToInt32(Console.ReadLine());

/*
Perform the conversion from string to int as we will use
the age of the vehicle in our calculation and it needs
to be numeric
Example: For a 5 year old car the factor is 10/5 = 2
*/
quoteAgeFactor = (double)(quoteBaseAge) /
```

```
            (double)(vehicleAgeInYears);

/*
The quote amount based on the age is £100 multiplied by
the age factor
Example £100 * 2 = £200
*/
quoteAgeFactorPremium = quoteBaseRate * quoteAgeFactor;

  } // End of Main() method
 } // End of QuoteArithmetic class
} // End of Chapter8 namespace
```

Now we will

- Read the vehicle mileage input from the console and convert it to an int.

- Use the vehicle mileage and divide it by the age of the vehicle to get the average yearly mileage.

- Divide this value by 10000, which is the expected yearly mileage, to calculate a mileage factor.

- Calculate the premium based on the mileage factor and the quote base rate of £100.

28. Amend the code, as in Listing 8-6, to get the input and perform the two calculations.

Listing 8-6. Get user input for the mileage and perform calculations

```
quoteAgeFactorPremium = quoteBaseRate * quoteAgeFactor;

/*
Ask the user for the number of kilometres on the odometer
*/
Console.WriteLine("What is the current mileage (in km) " +
  "of the vehicle?\n");
vehicleCurrentMileage= Convert.ToInt32(Console.ReadLine());
```

```
    /*
    Calculate the mileage factor. This is based on the number
    of kilometres travelled each year and how the kilometres
    per year is a ratio of the average expected 10000
    kilometres as decided by the insurance company
    Example: For a 5 year old car with 60000km the factor is
                    (60000/5)/10000 = 12000/10000 = 1.2
    */
    quoteMileageFactor = (vehicleCurrentMileage /
      vehicleAgeInYears) / quoteAverageExpectedKilometres;

    /*
    The quote amount based on the mileage is £100
    multiplied by the mileage factor
    Example £100 * 1.2 = £120
    */
    quoteMileageFactorPremium = quoteBaseRate *
      quoteMileageFactor;

  } // End of Main() method
 } // End of QuoteArithmetic class
} // End of Chapter8 namespace
```

Now we will add the two values we have just calculated to give us the quote amount, the premium.

29.   Amend the code, as in Listing 8-7, to calculate the quote amount.

Listing 8-7. Calculate the quote amount for the premium

```
quoteMileageFactorPremium = quoteBaseRate *
  quoteMileageFactor;

/*
Calculate the quotation based on a base rate of £100.
This base rate is multiplied by the vehicle age factor
and by the vehicle mileage factor.
So, the older the vehicle the cheaper the quote or the
newer the vehicle the more expensive the quote.
```

The more kilometres travelled on average per year the more expensive the quote or the less kilometres travelled on average per year the cheaper the quote.
Example: For a 5 year old car, 60000km, age factor is 2 and mileage factor is 1.2
The quote is (£100*2) + (£100*1.2)= £200 + £120 = £320
*/

/*
The quote amount based on the age premium plus the mileage premium
Example £2000 + £120 = £320
*/
quoteAmountForPremium = quoteAgeFactorPremium + quoteMileageFactorPremium;

```
    } // End of Main() method
  } // End of QuoteArithmetic class
} // End of Chapter8 namespace
```

Now we will calculate the discount based on the calculated premium and the vehicle age.

30. Amend the code, adding a quote discount formula to the end of the code, as in Listing 8-8.

Listing 8-8. Calculate the quote discount and use casting

```
quoteAmountForPremium = quoteAgeFactorPremium +
  quoteMileageFactorPremium;
```

/*
The discount amount is based on the age of the vehicle
Example:
5 year old vehicle gives discount of 1/5 = 20 percent */
quoteDiscount = (1 / (double)vehicleAgeInYears) * quoteAmountForPremium;

```
    } // End of Main() method
```

```
    } // End of QuoteArithmetic class
} // End of Chapter8 namespace
```

Now we will calculate the quote amount after the discount is applied.

31. Amend the code, as in Listing 8-9, to perform the calculation for the final premium amount.

Listing 8-9. Calculate the quote final amount

```
quoteDiscount = (1 / (double)vehicleAgeInYears) *
  quoteAmountForPremium;

/*
The final quote with the discount applied
Example
5 year old vehicle gives discount of 100/5 = 20 percent
20% of £320 is £64.
So, the actual amount is £320 - £64 = £256
*/
quoteFinalAmountForPremium = quoteAmountForPremium -
  quoteDiscount;

    } // End of Main() method
  } // End of QuoteArithmetic class
} // End of Chapter8 namespace
```

32. Amend the code, as in Listing 8-10, to add some print lines displaying a quotation.

Listing 8-10. Display output information

```
quoteFinalAmountForPremium = quoteAmountForPremium -
  quoteDiscount;

Console.WriteLine("*******************************\n");
Console.WriteLine("Quotation is for 1 year from today\n");
Console.WriteLine("*******************************\n");
Console.WriteLine("The age of the vehicle is :\t\t" +
  vehicleAgeInYears);
```

```
Console.WriteLine("The age factor is for this vehicle " +
    "is : " + quoteAgeFactor);
Console.WriteLine();
Console.WriteLine("The average kilometres per year " +
    "is :\t" + (vehicleCurrentMileage / vehicleAgeInYears));
Console.WriteLine("The mileage factor is :\t\t\t" +
    quoteMileageFactor);
Console.WriteLine();
Console.WriteLine("The quotation is :\t\t\t£" +
    quoteAmountForPremium);
Console.WriteLine();
Console.WriteLine("The discount is :\t\t\t£" +
    quoteDiscount);
Console.WriteLine();
Console.WriteLine("The final discounted amount is :\t£" +
    quoteFinalAmountForPremium);
Console.WriteLine("*******************************\n");

    } // End of Main() method
  } // End of QuoteArithmetic class
} // End of Chapter8 namespace
```

33.   Click the File menu.

34.   Choose Save All.

35.   Click the Debug menu.

36.   Choose Start Without Debugging.

37.   Type 5 as the age of the vehicle.

38.   Press the Enter key on the keyboard.

39.   Type 60000 as the number of kilometers on the odometer.

40.   Press the Enter key on the keyboard.

Figure 8-13 shows the console window with the quotation details.

```
---- Car Quotation Application ----

What is the age, in full years, of the vehicle?

5
What is the current mileage (in km) of the vehicle?

60000
********************************

Quotation is for 1 year from today

********************************

The age of the vehicle is :              5
The age factor is for this vehicle is : 2

The average kilometres per year is :     12000
The mileage factor is :                  1.2

The quotation is :                       £320

The discount is :                        £64

The final discounted amount is :         £256
********************************
```

Figure 8-13. *Quotation output*

41. Press the Enter key to close the console window.

Now let us pose the question: Is the quotation amount correct?

- Well, we should have known what to expect, **before** we started the application.

- We need to know the formula before we code, but we should also have test data that would tell us what to expect for the final quote.

- If we followed a Test-Driven Development methodology, we would write tests first and then write the code that makes the tests pass.

It is imperative that we do not just accept that the console output is correct. An attitude of "It's in the console output, so it must be correct" is fundamentally wrong and a dangerous assumption. We need to verify the results. While we will not be using a Test-Driven Development approach, we still need to think like a software tester. Moving to a Test-Driven Development approach can only be achieved once we have built the core

C# programming skills, and after gaining these skills, Test-Driven Development is just a different methodology to writing the same C# code that we will be producing throughout the chapters in the book.

Let's check the mathematical calculations and see what the answer is:

quoteAgeFactor = 10/5 = 2.0

quoteAgeFactorPremium = £100 * 2.0 = £200

quoteMileageFactor = (60000/5)/ 10000 = 12000/10000 = 1.2

quoteMileageFactorPremium = £100 * 1.2 = £120

quoteAmountForPremium = £200 + £120 = £320

quoteDiscount = (1/5) * £320 = £64

quoteFinalAmountForPremium = £320 – £64 = £256

Formatting the Output

What we also see is that our output does not have two figures after the decimal point. The WriteLine() method merely prints out a line of code but does not format it. If we wish to have formatted text, we can use some "special" code.

The WriteLine() method can be used in a different way, not using the concatenation, +, version we have used up to now. We can keep all the output between double quotes "", and when we wish to have a variable included, we add a **placeholder** within the double quotes. The placeholder is used to represent the variable that will be included after the double quote, following a comma. Figures 8-14, 8-15, and 8-16 show the placeholder code and output for three different examples.

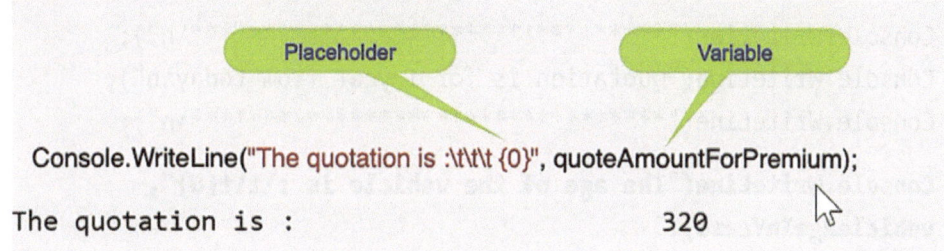

Figure 8-14. *WriteLine() with placeholder*

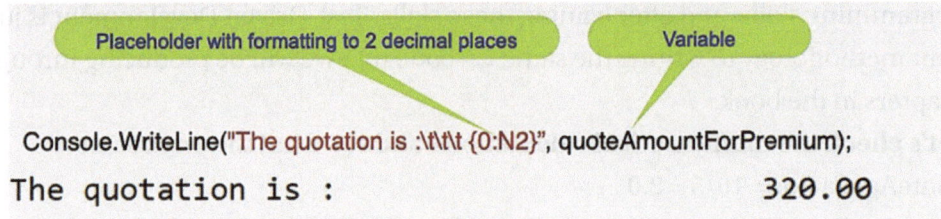

Figure 8-15. *WriteLine() with placeholder and formatting to two decimal places*

```
Console.WriteLine("The quotation is:" +"\t\t\t {0:C2}", quoteAmountForPremium);
The quotation is:                              £320.00
```

Figure 8-16. *WriteLine() with placeholder and currency formatting*

The placeholder(s) matches the variable(s) in the list after the ending double quote and comma. The placeholder can also control the number of decimal places.

1. Amend the code, as in Listing 8-11, replacing some WriteLine() methods with the new format containing placeholders.

Listing 8-11. Using placeholders

```
Console.WriteLine("*******************************\n");
Console.WriteLine("Quotation is for 1 year from today\n");
Console.WriteLine("*******************************\n");

Console.WriteLine("The age of the vehicle is :\t\t{0}",
vehicleAgeInYears);
Console.WriteLine("The age factor for this vehicle is :\t{0}",
quoteAgeFactor);
Console.WriteLine();

Console.WriteLine("The average kilometres per year is : \t{0:N2}",
(vehicleCurrentMileage / vehicleAgeInYears));
Console.WriteLine("The mileage factor is :\t\t\t{0:N2}",
quoteMileageFactor);
```

```
        Console.WriteLine();

        Console.WriteLine("The quotation is :\t\t\t{0:C2}",
        quoteAmountForPremium);

        Console.WriteLine();

        Console.WriteLine("The discount is :\t\t\t{0:C2}" , quoteDiscount);

        Console.WriteLine();

        Console.WriteLine("The final discounted amount is :\t{0:C2}",
        quoteFinalAmountForPremium);
        Console.WriteLine("********************************\n");
      } // End of Main() method
   } // End of QuoteArithmetic class
} // End of Chapter8 namespace
```

2.   Click the File menu.

3.   Choose Save All.

4.   Click the Debug menu.

5.   Choose Start Without Debugging.

6.   Type 5 as the age of the vehicle.

7.   Press the Enter key on the keyboard.

8.   Type 60000 as the number of kilometers on the odometer.

9.   Press the Enter key on the keyboard.

Figure 8-17 shows the console window with the quotation details formatted using decimal places and currency.

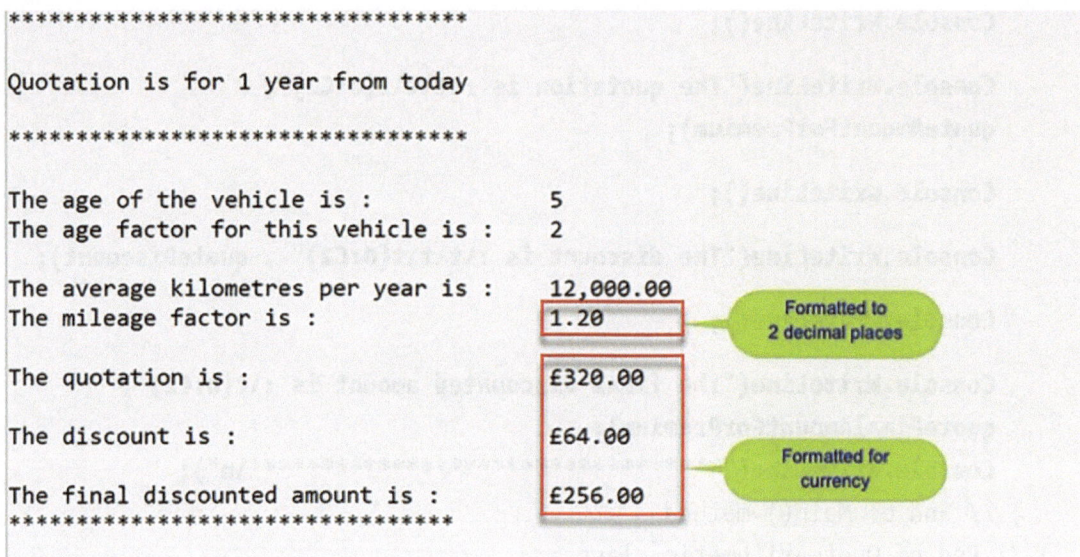

Figure 8-17. *Formatted output, two decimal places and currency*

10. Press the Enter key again to close the console window.

Other Operators

Table 8-1 shows two interesting arithmetic operators included with C#.

Table 8-1. *Add one and subtract one*

Two arithmetic operators that are included with C#
++ Means add one to the value
Example
double quoteMileageFactor = 1.2;
quoteMileageFactor ++;
quoteMileageFactor will now be 2.2.
We will see this operator when we come to code with iteration and loops.

(*continued*)

Table 8-1. *(continued)*

Two arithmetic operators that are included with C#

--   Means subtract one from the value

    Example

```
double quoteMileageFactor = 1.2;
quoteMileageFactor --;
```

    quoteMileageFactor will now be 0.2.

    We can use this operator when we code with iteration and loops.

Postfix increment operator

++   When the ++ appears after the variable name, the action occurs and then the variable value is incremented, so with post-increment, the operation is performed and then the increment happens.

```
double quoteMileageFactor = 1.2;

// 1.2 is displayed, the value then increases to 2.2
Console.WriteLine(quoteMileageFactor++);

// 2.2 will be displayed
Console.WriteLine(quoteMileageFactor);
```

Prefix increment operator

++   When the ++ appears before the variable name, the variable value is incremented before any action, so with pre-increment, the increment is performed and then the operation happens.

```
double quoteMileageFactor = 1.2;

// 2.2 is displayed, the value then increases to 2.2
Console.WriteLine(++quoteMileageFactor);

// 2.2 will be displayed
Console.WriteLine(quoteMileageFactor);
```

Apart from the mathematical operators +, –, *, /, and %, there are other operators included in C#. We will now look at what are called **assignment operators,** which store a value in the object on the left-hand side. Up to now in our code, we have used one operator, the = symbol, for example:

```
quoteAgeFactorPremium = quoteBaseRate * quoteAgeFactor;
```

The = operator is a **simple operator**. Now we will use the **compound assignment operators**. In the code examples in Table 8-2, we will see the use of the **compound assignment**, where an arithmetic operation is performed before the value is stored in the object on the left-hand side.

Table 8-2. *Compound assignment operators*

Compound assignment operators

+=   Means take the value on the right of the = and add it to the value of the object on the left of the =, storing the new value in the object on the left

Example
```
double quoteMileageFactor = 1.2;
quoteMileageFactor += 1;
```

quoteMileageFactor will now be 2.2.

-=   Means take the value on the right of the = and subtract it from the value of the object on the left of the =, storing the new value in the object on the left

Example
```
double quoteMileageFactor = 1.2;
quoteMileageFactor -= 1;
```

quoteMileageFactor will now be 0.2.

*=   Means take the value on the left of the = and multiply it by the value on the right of the =, storing the new value in the object on the left

Example
```
double quoteMileageFactor = 1.2;
quoteMileageFactor *= 2;
```

quoteMileageFactor will now be 2.4.

/=   Means take the value on the left of the = and divide it by the value on the right of the =, storing the new value in the object on the left

Example
```
double quoteMileageFactor = 1.2;
quoteMileageFactor /= 2;
```

quoteMileageFactor will now be 0.6.

We will now amend our existing code to use some of the operators we have just read about, starting with Listing 8-12.

Plus Equals (+=)

11. Add a new code statement that uses the += operator, as in Listing 8-12.

Listing 8-12. += operator

```
quoteMileageFactor = (vehicleCurrentMileage /
    vehicleAgeInYears) / quoteAverageExpectedKilometres;

quoteMileageFactor += 1;
```

12. Click the File menu.

13. Choose Save All.

14. Click the Debug menu.

15. Choose Start Without Debugging.

16. Type 5 as the age of the vehicle.

17. Press the Enter key on the keyboard.

18. Type 60000 as the number of kilometers on the odometer.

19. Press the Enter key on the keyboard.

Figure 8-18 shows the new calculations, after the increment of the variable quoteMileageFactor. We can see that the mileage factor has increased by 1 to become the value 2.2.

```
The average kilometres per year is :    12,000.00
The mileage factor is :                 2.20
```
Increased by 1
quoteMileageFactor +=1;

Figure 8-18. +=1

20. Press the Enter key to close the console window.

Minus Equals (-=)

21.   Amend the one code line, as Listing in 8-13, to use the -= operator.

Listing 8-13.   -= operator

```
quoteMileageFactor = (vehicleCurrentMileage /
    vehicleAgeInYears) / quoteAverageExpectedKilometres;

quoteMileageFactor -= 1;
```

22.   Click the File menu.

23.   Choose Save All.

24.   Click the Debug menu.

25.   Choose Start Without Debugging.

26.   Type 5 as the age of the vehicle.

27.   Press the Enter key on the keyboard.

28.   Type 60000 as the number of kilometers on the odometer.

29.   Press the Enter key on the keyboard.

Figure 8-19 shows the new calculations, after the decrement of the variable quoteMileageFactor. We can see that the mileage factor has decreased by 1 to become the value 0.2.

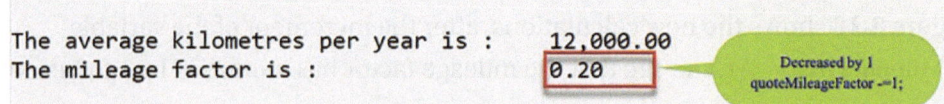

Figure 8-19.   -=1

30.   Press the Enter key to close the console window.

Multiply Equals (*=)

31.   Amend the one code line, as in Listing 8-14, to use the *= operator.

Listing 8-14. *= operator

```
quoteMileageFactor = (vehicleCurrentMileage /
  vehicleAgeInYears) / quoteAverageExpectedKilometres;

quoteMileageFactor *= 2;
```

32. Click the File menu.

33. Choose Save All.

34. Click the Debug menu.

35. Choose Start Without Debugging.

36. Type 5 as the age of the vehicle.

37. Press the Enter key on the keyboard.

38. Type 60000 as the number of kilometers on the odometer.

39. Press the Enter key on the keyboard.

Figure 8-20 shows the new calculations, after the increment of the variable quoteMileageFactor. We can see that the mileage factor has multiplied by 2, doubled, to become the value 2.4.

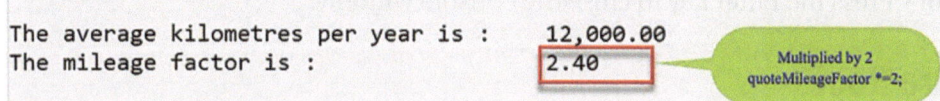
```
The average kilometres per year is :    12,000.00
The mileage factor is :                 2.40
```
Multiplied by 2
quoteMileageFactor *=2;

Figure 8-20. *= operator

40. Press the Enter key to close the console window.

Divide Equals (/=)

41. Amend the one code line, as in Listing 8-15, to use the /= operator.

Listing 8-15. /= operator

```
quoteMileageFactor = (vehicleCurrentMileage /
  vehicleAgeInYears) / quoteAverageExpectedKilometres;

quoteMileageFactor /= 2;
```

42.   Click the File menu.

43.   Choose Save All.

44.   Click the Debug menu.

45.   Choose Start Without Debugging.

46.   Type 5 as the age of the vehicle.

47.   Press the Enter key on the keyboard.

48.   Type 60000 as the number of kilometers on the odometer.

49.   Press the Enter key on the keyboard.

Figure 8-21 shows the new calculations, after the decrement of the variable quoteMileageFactor. We can see that the mileage factor has been divided by 2, halved, to become the value 0.6.

```
The average kilometres per year is :    12,000.00
The mileage factor is :                 0.60
```
Divided by 2
quoteMileageFactor /=2;

Figure 8-21. */= operator*

50.   Press the Enter key to close the console window.

Square Root

Here we will use the Math class and its Sqrt() method. The Sqrt() method accepts a numeric value, which is to be operated on.

51.   Amend the one code line, as in Listing 8-16, to use the Sqrt() method.

Listing 8-16. Square root

```
quoteMileageFactor = (vehicleCurrentMileage /
    vehicleAgeInYears) / quoteAverageExpectedKilometres;

quoteMileageFactor = Math.Sqrt(quoteMileageFactor);
```

52.   Click the File menu.

53.   Choose Save All.

54.   Click the Debug menu.

55.   Choose Start Without Debugging.

56.   Type 5 as the age of the vehicle.

57.   Press the Enter key on the keyboard.

58.   Type 60000 as the number of kilometers on the odometer.

59.   Press the Enter key on the keyboard.

Figure 8-22 shows the new calculations, after finding the square root of the variable quoteMileageFactor. We can see that the mileage factor has been calculated as the square root of 1.2, which is 1.1.

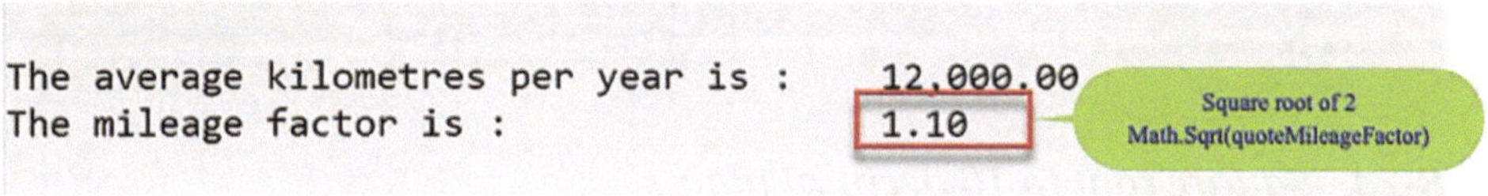

Figure 8-22. *Square Root*

60.   Press the Enter key to close the console window.

We will now change the format for the mileage factor, quoteMileageFactor, so we have 16 figures after the decimal point, just to illustrate that we do not necessarily always need or want to use two decimal places.

61.   Amend the code, changing the 2 to 16 in the line of code, as in Listing 8-17.

Listing 8-17. Square root to 16 decimal places

```
Console.WriteLine("The average kilometres per year is: " +
"\t{0:N2}", (vehicleCurrentMileage/vehicleAgeInYears));

Console.WriteLine("The mileage factor is :\t\t\t{0:N16}" ,
quoteMileageFactor);
```

62.   Click the File menu.

63.   Choose Save All.

64.   Click the Debug menu.

65.   Choose Start Without Debugging.

66.   Type 5 as the age of the vehicle.

67.   Press the Enter key on the keyboard.

68.   Type 60000 as the number of kilometers on the odometer.

69.   Press the Enter key on the keyboard.

Figure 8-23 shows the new calculations, after finding the square root of the variable quoteMileageFactor and displaying the output with 16 figures after the decimal point.

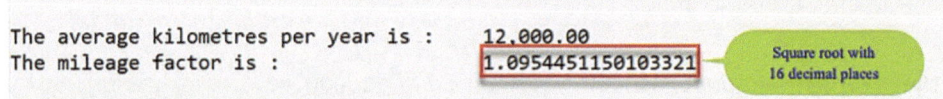

Figure 8-23. *Square root to 16 decimal places*

70.   Press the Enter key again to close the console window.

Note

The other calculations that depend on the quoteMileageFactor still have the same value. This should indicate to us that even though two decimal places were displayed, the underlying figure was more accurate than the two decimal places.

Chapter Summary

In this chapter we have learned about the very important concept of arithmetic operations, which will be widely used in real-world applications. We also saw that arithmetic performed on variables or values can result in inaccuracies because the display does not show the required number of decimal places. We then saw the use of the {0:D}, {0:2D}, and {0:C} type placeholders where we could specify the number of decimal places required in the output. Besides the popular arithmetic operators +, -, *, and /, we also saw some "strange" operators, +=, -=, *=, and /=.

We are making great progress in our programming of C# applications and we should be proud of our achievements. In finishing this chapter and increasing our knowledge, we are advancing to our target.

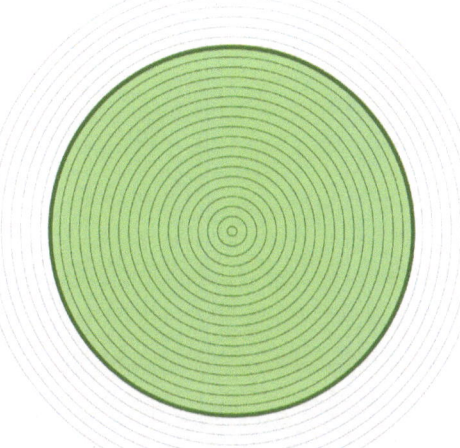

Our target is getting closer

CHAPTER 9

Selection

Arithmetic Operations

We learned in Chapter 8 that we could apply arithmetic operations on some variables and use the {0:D} and {0:C} type placeholders to specify the number of decimal places required in the output. We also investigated the use of less familiar arithmetic operators such as +=, -=, *=, and /=. In this chapter we will use comparison operators, some of which will look similar to arithmetic operators.

Selection

In this chapter we will learn about the very important concept of selection and its use within an application. However, the concept of selection should be familiar to us through our everyday life. Many of the things we do in everyday life require us to make decisions, and often we will be directed down one path or another. Figure 9-1 illustrates such a scenario.

© Gerard Byrne 2022
G. Byrne, *Target C#*, https://doi.org/10.1007/978-1-4842-8619-7_9

Figure 9-1. *Everyday decision using a yes-or-no scenario*

In a similar manner, the programs we, and every developer, write will normally require us to make decisions. Decisions in our code will change the execution flow depending on the decision made, as shown in Figure 9-1. Figure 9-1 indicates that

- A **yes** decision changes execution down the yes path.

- A **no** decision changes execution down the no path.

In Figure 9-1 the execution eventually returns to a common path, Go to the shops. In programming, making decisions can be achieved in a number of ways, and we will now look at the use of the **SELECTION** statements within C#.

Comparison Operators

To build our program code to make decisions, we need to make use of comparison operators to construct a condition. The operators we can use are familiar mathematical expressions, for example, less than, greater than, and equal to. Table 9-1 shows the symbols used in C# for the operators.

Table 9-1. *Comparison operators*

Symbol	Meaning
<	Less than
<=	Less than or equal to
>	Greater than
>=	Greater than or equal to
==	Equal to
!=	Not equal to
&&	Logical AND
||	Logical OR
!	Logical NOT

It is important we fully understand that when testing if one piece of data is equal to another, **we use the double equals (= =)**, because, as mentioned previously, a single equal symbol (=) is an assignment operation.

The primary selection constructs we will use in our C# code will be

- if

- if-else

- if else if construct

- switch

We will also look at the logical operators AND (&&), || (OR), and ! (NOT).

if Statement

The **if** construct is used whenever a choice has to be made between two alternative actions. The construct will enable a block of code to be executed depending upon whether or not a condition is true. If the condition is not true, it is false, and the code does not execute the block of code associated with the if statement. It just moves to the next code statement. The general format of the **if construct** is

```
if (condition)
{
   // perform these statements when condition is true
}
```

In simple terms all we are doing with the if construct is saying "Is something true?" – is it true or is it false? So the statement

if(condition) means if(true).

Remember true is a `bool` or `Boolean` data type.

In most programs selection will be a key element, but for an insurance program, selection statements may include

- Checking the maximum years of no claims a driver has and informing the user

    That the value is within the **years of no claims** limit and will be used – this is the true part

Or

    To just move to the next code statement

- Checking the maximum amount that can be charged to a credit card and informing the user

    That the insurance amount is under or equal to the credit card limit and can be processed – this is the true part

or

    To just move to the next code statement

if-else Statement

The general format of the **if-else construct** is

```
if (condition)
{
  // perform these statements when condition is true
}
else
{
  // perform these statements when condition is false
}
```

In simple terms all we are doing with the if-else construct is saying "Is something true or is it false?" – is it true or is it false? So the statement

if(condition) means if(true).

else means it is not true – it is false.

Remember false is also a `bool` or `Boolean` data type.

The else part of the if-else construct may be omitted depending on requirements, but if it is omitted, it becomes an if statement, which is what we looked at first.

Using the same insurance program criteria as we had in the preceding if statement, we can see how the if-else construct could be applied. The program selection statements may include

- Checking the maximum years of no claims a driver has and informing the user that

  The value is within the years of no claims limit and will be used – this is the true part.

or

  The value is over the years of no claims limit and will be reduced to 10 years – this is the else part, the false part.

- Checking the maximum amount that can be charged to a credit card and informing the user that

  The insurance amount is under or equal to the credit card limit and can be processed.

or

  The insurance amount is over the credit card limit and the user will need to call the company to give additional information.

The **if-else** statement is used to make a selection within a program, and the following points are important in understanding the format of the if-else statement:

- The if statement will test if a particular *condition* statement is true, for example:

```
if (yearsofnoclaims > 10)
```

- If the condition is true, then the program will execute a block of code within the curly braces following it, for example:

```
if (yearsofnoclaims > 10)
{
  // This block of code will be executed if the
  // yearsofnoclaims is greater than 10
}
```

- If the condition is false, then the program will execute a different block of code, the else part, that handles a false condition executed when the statement is not true, for example:

```
if (yearsofnoclaims > 10)
{
  // This block of code will be executed if the
  // yearsofnoclaims is greater than 10
}
else
{
  // This block of code will be executed if the
  // yearsofnoclaims is
  // less than or equal to 10
}
```

- It is essential that the two different blocks of code are clearly indicated, and to ensure this, we use the curly braces:

  { opening (left) curly brace

  } closing (right) curly brace

- The two different blocks of code are separated using the **else** keyword:

```
if (yearsofnoclaims > 10)
{
  BLOCK ONE
  // This block of code will be executed if the
  // yearsofnoclaims is greater than 10
}
```

```
else
{
  BLOCK TWO
 // This block of code will be executed if the
 // yearsofnoclaims is less than or equal to 10
}
```

switch Statement

A switch statement can have a number of advantages over the equivalent if-else statements including being easier to

- Read

- Debug

- Maintain

In using a switch construct, we will have multiple cases, and the matching case will be the one that will have its code executed. Switch also has some disadvantages depending on the version of C# we use. From C# 7.0 we can use pattern matching, but for now we will concentrate on the switch statement for C# 6 or earlier where the matching expression uses the data types char, string, and bool, an integral numeric type, or an enum type.

The general format of the **switch construct** is

```
switch (expression)
{
  case 1:
    {
      statements;
      break;
    }
  case 2:
    {
      statements;
      break;
    }
```

```
    default:
      {
        statements;
        break;
      }
      break;
  } // End of switch statement
```

We will now use the same insurance program criteria as used in the preceding if and if-else constructs and explore how the switch construct could be applied. The program selection statements may include

- Checking the maximum years of no claims a driver has and informing the user that

    - If the value is 0 years, the discount is 0%.

    - If the value is 5 years, the discount is 5%.

    - If the value is 10 years, the discount is 10%.

As a switch statement, this would be

```
    switch (years_of_no_claims)
    {
      case 0:
        {
          discount = 0.00;
          break;
        }
      case 5:
        {
          discount = 5.00;
          break;
        }
      case 10:
        {
          discount = 10.00;
          break;
        }
```

```
default:
  {
    discount = 0.00;
    break;
  }
} // End of switch statement
```

Let's code some C# and build our programming muscle.

The if Construct

We will now use the **if construct** that has one block of code, between the curly braces, that is executed if the condition inside the brackets evaluates as Boolean true. If the condition evaluates to Boolean false, then, with the if construct, there is no other block of code associated with it, so the next line in the program after the close curly brace is executed. The evaluation to Boolean true would be equivalent to the area highlighted by the green dotted rectangle in Figure 9-2, the pathway to the left.

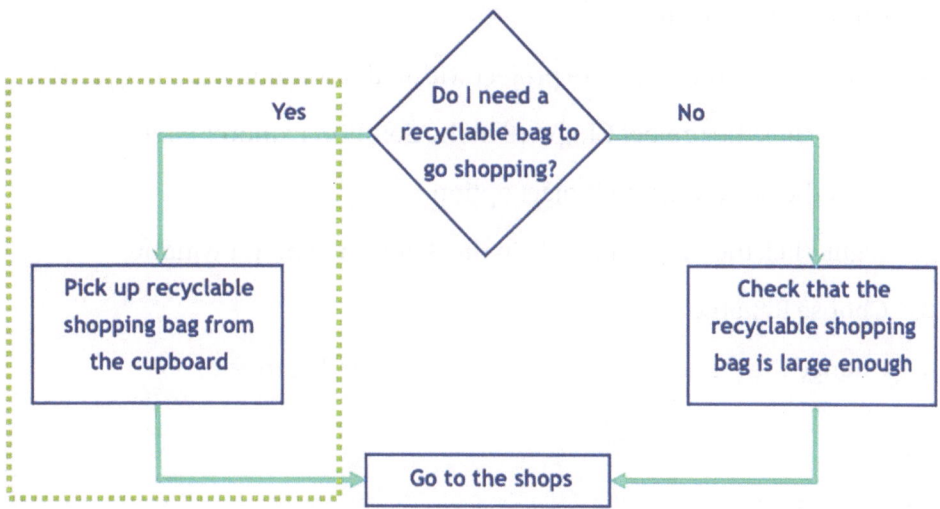

Figure 9-2. *The Boolean true section*

We should use the same solution that we created for the earlier chapters, as we will still be able to see the code we have written for the previous chapters. The approach of keeping all our separate projects in one solution is a good idea while studying this book and coding the examples.

This chapter, while concentrating on selection, will use an insurance quote example and build on our learning from the previous chapters. Now having created five projects, we should be confident with the process of creating projects inside a solution.

Add a new project to hold the code for this chapter.

1. Right-click the solution CoreCSharp.

2. Choose Add.

3. Choose New Project.

4. Choose Console App from the listed templates that appear.

5. Click the Next button.

6. Name the project Chapter9 and leave it in the same location.

7. Click the Next button.

8. Choose the framework to be used, which in our projects will be .NET 6.0 or higher.

9. Click the Create button.

Now we should see the Chapter9 project within the solution called CoreCSharp.

10. Right-click the project Chapter9 in the Solution Explorer panel.

11. Click the Set as Startup Project option.

12. Right-click the Program.cs file in the Solution Explorer window.

13. Choose Rename.

14. Change the name to Selection.cs, as shown in Figure 9-3.

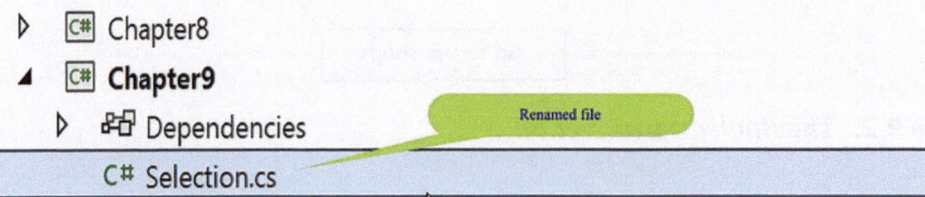

Figure 9-3. *Program.cs file renamed*

15.   Press the Enter key.

16.   Double-click the Selection.cs file to open it in the editor window.

Now we can set up the code structure with a namespace, and inside it will be the Selection class, and inside the class will be the Main() method. **The shortcut for creating the Main() method is to type svm and press the Tab key twice.** We will also create a variable inside the Main() method.

17.   Amend the code as shown in Listing 9-1.

Listing 9-1. Selection – setting up variables within the Main() method

```
// Program Description:    C# program to perform selection
// Author:                 Gerry Byrne
// Date of creation:       01/10/2021

namespace Chapter9
{
  internal class Selection
  {
    static void Main(string[] args)
    {
      // Set up variables to be used in the quote application
      int yearsOfNoClaims;
    } // End of Main() method
  } // End of Selection class
} // End of Chapter9 namespace
```

18.   Amend the code to request user input and then convert it to an int, as in Listing 9-2.

Listing 9-2. Request user input and convert from string to int

```
// Set up variables to be used in the quote application
int yearsOfNoClaims;

/* Read the user input and convert it to an int */
Console.WriteLine("How many full years of no claims does the driver have?\n");
```

```
    yearsOfNoClaims = Convert.ToInt32(Console.ReadLine());
  } // End of Main() method
 } // End of Selection class
} // End of Chapter9 namespace
```

We will now add code that will

- Check if the number of years of no claims is greater than 10:

  - If this is true, execute some code.

  - Otherwise, move to the next set of code lines.

19. Amend the code, as in Listing 9-3.

Listing 9-3. Use the if construct to check if value is greater than 10

```
yearsOfNoClaims = Convert.ToInt32(Console.ReadLine());

/*
Now we will check if the years of no claims is greater
than 10 if it is true then we execute some lines of code
which exist between the curly braces, else the program
just moves to the next code line which is to read a key
*/
if (yearsOfNoClaims > 10)
{
  /*
  This block of code will be executed if the
  yearsOfNoClaims is more than 10
  */
  Console.WriteLine();
  Console.WriteLine("Years of no claims is more than 10");
}
  } // End of Main() method
 } // End of Selection class
} // End of Chapter9 namespace
```

20. Click the File menu.

21. Choose Save All.

22. Click the Debug menu.

23. Choose Start Without Debugging.

24. Type 10 as the number of full years of no claims.

25. Press the Enter key.

Figure 9-4 shows the console window with no additional data after the 10, as the code has evaluated that 10 is not greater than (>) 10, so it skips the if block of code and moves to the next line of code after the closing curly brace, which is the end of the code.

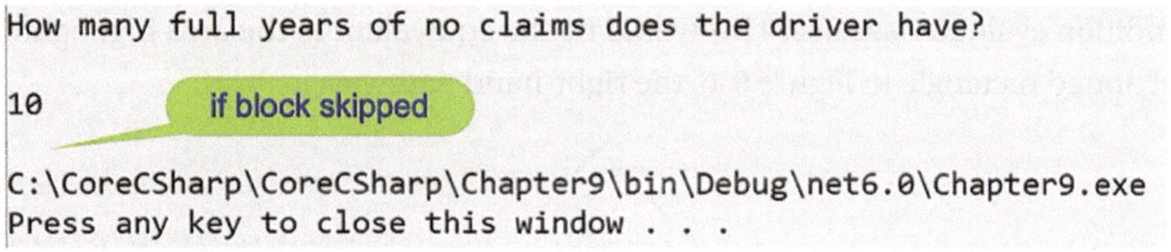

```
How many full years of no claims does the driver have?

10          if block skipped

C:\CoreCSharp\CoreCSharp\Chapter9\bin\Debug\net6.0\Chapter9.exe
Press any key to close this window . . .
```

***Figure 9-4.** If block skipped*

26. Press the Enter key to close the console window.

27. Click the Debug menu.

28. Choose Start Without Debugging.

The console window will appear and ask the question.

29. Type 20 and press the Enter key.

The console window will appear as shown in Figure 9-5.

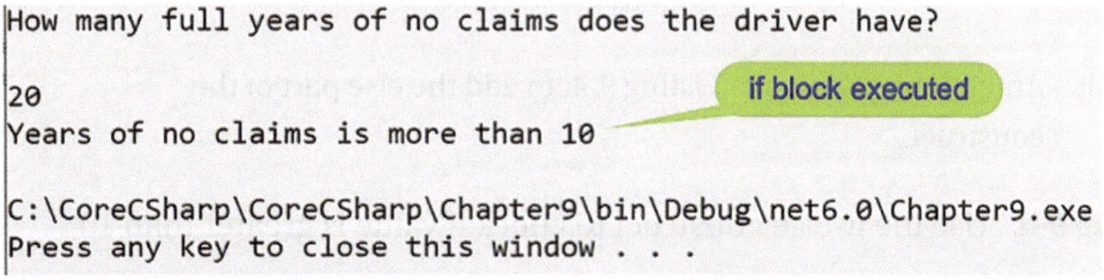

```
How many full years of no claims does the driver have?

20                          if block executed
Years of no claims is more than 10

C:\CoreCSharp\CoreCSharp\Chapter9\bin\Debug\net6.0\Chapter9.exe
Press any key to close this window . . .
```

***Figure 9-5.** If block executed*

The code has evaluated that 20 is greater than (>) 10 so it **executes the if block** of code and then it moves to the next line of code, which is the end of the code.

30.   Press the Enter key to close the console window.

The if-else Construct

We will now use the **if-else construct,** which is an extension of the if construct we have just used. In the if construct, we had one block of code, between the curly braces, that was executed when the condition inside the brackets evaluated to true. When the condition evaluated to false, the block of code was passed over, and the next line in the program was executed. Now, in the if-else construct, there will be a second block of code, with its own set of curly braces. This second block of code will be executed when the condition evaluates as false. This would be the equivalent to the area highlighted by the red dotted rectangle in Figure 9-6, the right-hand pathway.

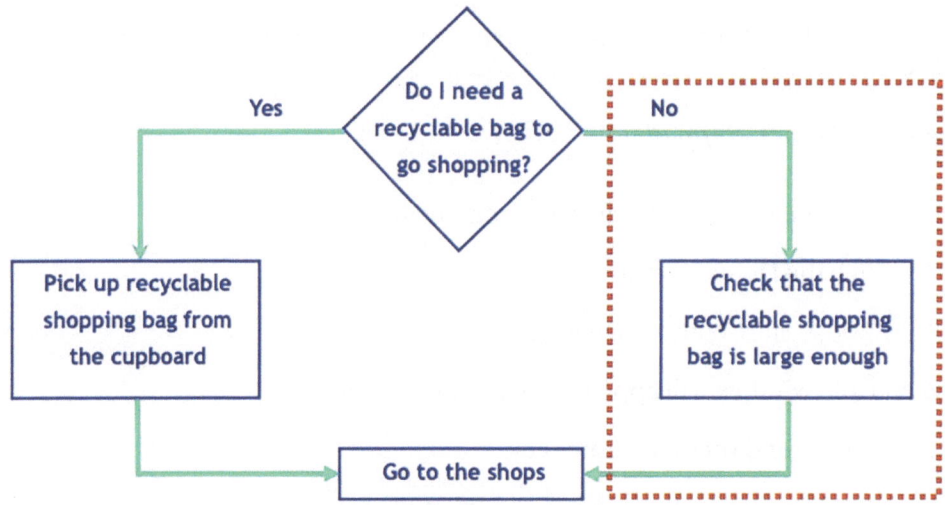

Figure 9-6. *The Boolean false section*

31.   Amend the code, as in Listing 9-4, to add the else part of the construct.

Listing 9-4. Use the if-else construct to check if value is greater than 10

```
if (yearsOfNoClaims > 10)
{
    /*
```

```
    This block of code will be executed if the
    yearsofnoclaims is more than 10
    */
    Console.WriteLine("Years of no claims is more than 10");
}// End of true block of code in the if construct
else
{
/*
This block of code will be executed if the yearsofnoclaims
is not more than 10. We need to be careful when we are
dealing with boundaries and in this example we should
realise that the >10 means 11, 12, 13 etc. The not greater
than 10 then means 10, 9, 8 etc. In other words, 10 is
included in the else part. We could also use >= 10 if we
wanted 10 to be included in the true section
    */

    Console.WriteLine("Years of no claims is less than " +
      "or equal to 10");
} // End of false block of code in the if construct

} // End of Main() method
```

32. Click the File menu.

33. Choose Save All.

34. Click the Debug menu.

35. Choose Start Without Debugging.

36. Type 20 as the number of full years of no claims.

Figure 9-7 shows the console window, and we can see that **the true block of code has been executed**.

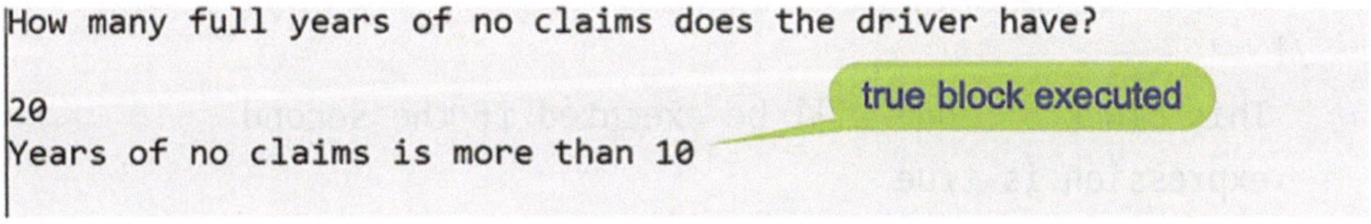

Figure 9-7. *If block executed – this is the true part*

37. Press the Enter key to close the console window.

38. Click the Debug menu.

39. Choose Start Without Debugging.

40. Type 10 as the number of full years of no claims.

Figure 9-8 shows the console window, and we can see that *the false, else, block of code has been executed*.

```
How many full years of no claims does the driver have?

10                                                    false block executed
Years of no claims is less than or equal to 10
```

Figure 9-8. *If block skipped – this is the false part*

41. Press the Enter key to close the console window.

The if else if Construct

The if-else construct we have used has two blocks of code, one for the Boolean true and the other for the Boolean false. However, what would happen if we had other choices when the first condition was not true? Well, the C# language provides us with a solution, which is an extension of the if-else construct. The if part of the construct can be followed by an **else if** statement. The general format will be

```
if (first expression is true)
{
    /*
       This block of code will be executed if the first
       expression is true
    */
}
else if (second expression is true)
{
    /*
       This block of code will be executed if the second
       expression is true
    */
}
```

```
else if (third expression is true)
{
    /*
      This block of code will be executed if the third
      expression is true
    */
}
else
{
    /*
      This block of code will be executed if the first
      expression, second expression and third expression
      are all false
    */
}
```

42. Amend the code, as in Listing 9-5, to add the else if parts of the construct, replacing the existing else code block.

Listing 9-5. Adding the else if parts of the if-else construct

```
if (yearsOfNoClaims > 10)
{
 /*
 This block of code will be executed if the
 yearsofnoclaims is more than 10
 */
  Console.WriteLine("Years of no claims is more than 10");
}// End of true block of code in the if construct
else if (yearsOfNoClaims > 8)
{
 /*
 This block of code will be executed if the
 yearsofnoclaims is more than 8 which means 9, 10, 11,
 12 etc. However, if yearsofnoclaims is 11, 12 etc it
 will have been detected in the yearsofnoclaims > 10
```

```
   block so really it will only be the 9 and 10 that will
   be detected in this block
   */
Console.WriteLine("Years of no claims is either 9 or 10");
} // End of first false block of code in the if construct
else if (yearsOfNoClaims > 6)
{
   /*
   This block of code will be executed if the yearsofnoclaims
   is more than 6 which means 7, 8, 9, 10 etc. However,
   if yearsofnoclaims is 9, 10 etc it will have been
   detected in the yearsofnoclaims > 8 block so really it
   will only be the 7 and 8 that will be detected in
   this block
   */
   Console.WriteLine("Years of no claims is either 7 or 8");
} // End of second false block of code in the if construct
else if (yearsOfNoClaims > 4)
{
   /*
   This block of code will be executed if the
   yearsofnoclaims is more than 4 which means 5, 6, 7,
   8 etc. However, if yearsofnoclaims is 7, 8 etc it will
   have been detected in the yearsofnoclaims > 6 block so
   really it will only be the 5 and 6 that will be detected
   in this block
   */
   Console.WriteLine("Years of no claims is either 5 or 6");
} // End of third false block of code in the if construct
else if (yearsOfNoClaims > 2)
{
   /*
   This block of code will be executed if the
   yearsofnoclaims is more than 2 which means 3, 4, 5,
   6 etc. However, if yearsofnoclaims is 5, 6 etc it will
```

```
    have been detected in the yearsofnoclaims > 4 block so
    really it will only be the 3 and 4 that will be detected
    in this block
    */
      Console.WriteLine("Years of no claims is either 3 or 4");
    } // End of fourth false block of code in the if construct
    else
    {
      /*
      This block of code will be executed if the
      yearsofnoclaims is not more than 2.
      For this block of code to be executed none of the
      conditions above must have been true (and none of the
      blocks of code were executed)
      */
      Console.WriteLine("Years of no claims is 2, 1, 0 " +
        "\n or indeed a negative number of years " +
        "\n because of a penalty being enforced on our
policy");           } // End of final false block of code in the if
construct
} // End of Main() method
  } // End of Selection class
} // End of Chapter9 namespace
```

43. Click the File menu.

44. Choose Save All.

45. Click the Debug menu.

46. Choose Start Without Debugging.

The console window will appear and ask the question. Now we can
try the values 10, 8, 6, 4, and 2, which will test the five else blocks. We will
start with 10.

47. Type 10 as the number of full years of no claims.

48. Press the Enter key.

Figure 9-9 shows the console window and we can see that **the first else if block of code has been executed**.

```
How many full years of no claims does the driver have?

10                                          else block 1 executed
Years of no claims is either 9 or 10

C:\CoreCSharp\CoreCSharp\Chapter9\bin\Debug\net6.0\Chapter9.exe
```

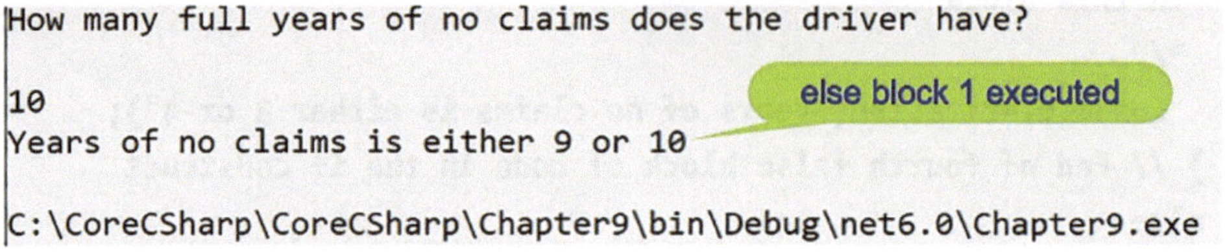

Figure 9-9. *First else if block executed*

49.   Press the Enter key to close the console window.

Start the program again.

50.   Click the Debug menu.

51.   Choose Start Without Debugging.

52.   Type 8 as the number of full years of no claims.

53.   Press the Enter key.

Figure 9-10 shows the console window and we can see that ***the second else if block of code has been executed***.

```
How many full years of no claims does the driver have?

8                                           else block 2 executed
Years of no claims is either 7 or 8

C:\CoreCSharp\CoreCSharp\Chapter9\bin\Debug\net6.0\Chapter9.exe
```

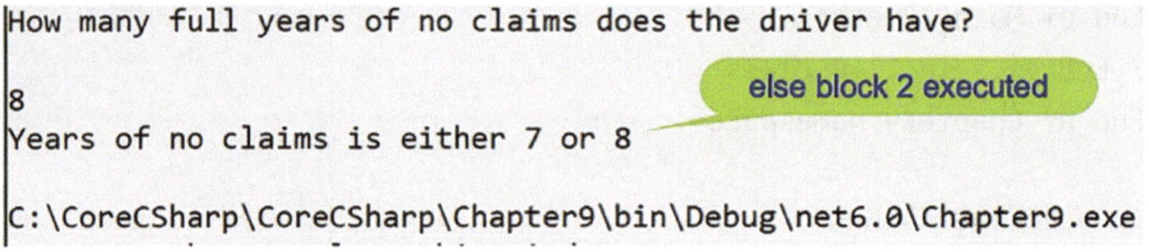

Figure 9-10. *Second else if block executed*

54.   Press the Enter key to close the console window.

Start the program again.

55.   Click the Debug menu.

56.   Choose Start Without Debugging.

57.   Type 6 as the number of full years of no claims.

58.   Press the Enter key.

Figure 9-11 shows the console window and we can see that **the third else if block of code has been executed**.

```
How many full years of no claims does the driver have?

6                                            else block 3 executed
Years of no claims is either 5 or 6

C:\CoreCSharp\CoreCSharp\Chapter9\bin\Debug\net6.0\Chapter9.exe
```

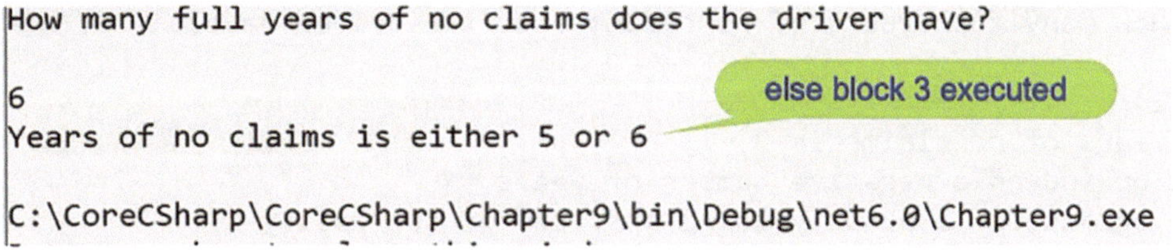

Figure 9-11. *Third else if block executed*

59.   Press the Enter key to close the console window.

Start the program again.

60.   Click the Debug menu.

61.   Choose Start Without Debugging.

62.   Type 4 as the number of full years of no claims.

63.   Press the Enter key.

Figure 9-12 shows the console window and we can see that **the fourth else if block of code has been executed**.

```
How many full years of no claims does the driver have?

4                                            else block 4 executed
Years of no claims is either 3 or 4

C:\CoreCSharp\CoreCSharp\Chapter9\bin\Debug\net6.0\Chapter9.exe
```

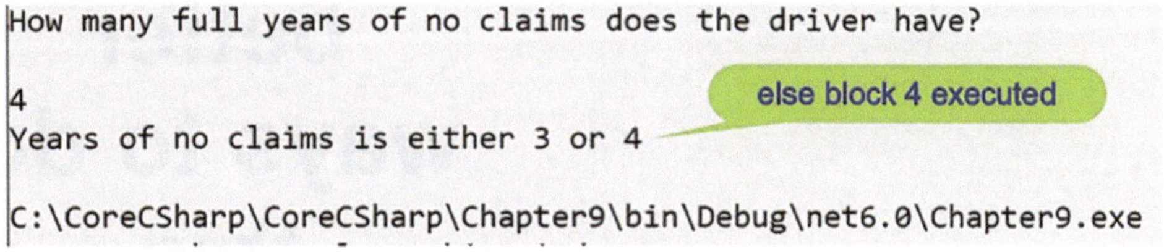

Figure 9-12. *Fourth else if block executed*

64.   Press the Enter key to close the console window.

Start the program again.

65.   Click the Debug menu.

66.   Choose Start Without Debugging.

67.   Type 2 as the number of full years of no claims.

68.   Press the Enter key.

Figure 9-13 shows the console window and we can see that ***the fifth else if block of code has been executed***.

```
How many full years of no claims does the driver have?

2
Years of no claims is 2, 1, 0                    else block5 executed
 or indeed a negative number of years
 because of a penalty being enforced on our policy

C:\CoreCSharp\CoreCSharp\Chapter9\bin\Debug\net6.0\Chapter9.exe
```

Figure 9-13. *Fifth else if block executed*

69. Press the Enter key to close the console window.

As we can see, the code works fine, and our test values have shown the correct blocks of code were executed. If we formatted the code differently, we could see why the if else if construct is often called the if else ladder. The code moves into the right for each section as shown in Figure 9-14.

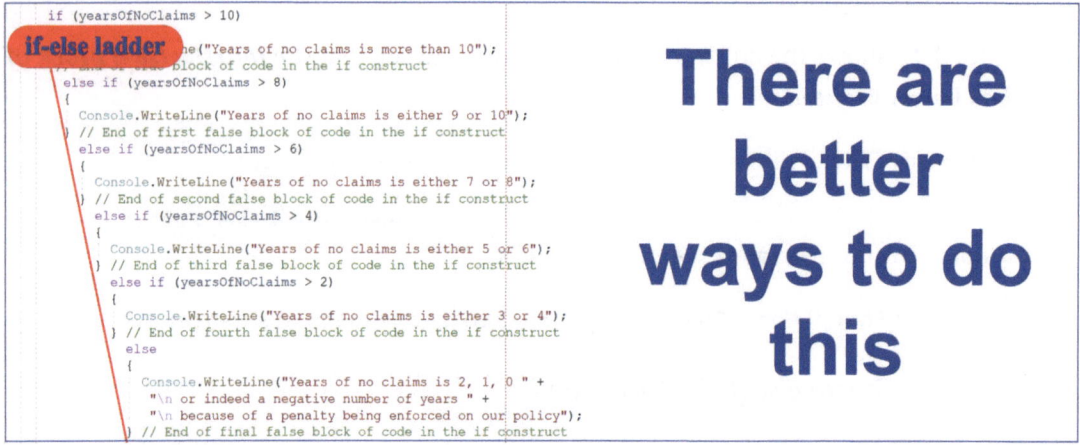

Figure 9-14. *If else ladder*

So do we think the code is OK because it executes properly?

We might say yes, but that would mean we are only concerned about the code execution. Let's think differently and consider code readability, maintainability, and efficiency. These aspects of code also play an important role in the code development process. It is not aways about our view; there may be others involved in the process. We must take a wider view of code development and not just think about our own small worldview. By thinking wider, we will think about others who are required to read our code, those who will have to maintain our code, and those who will use the code.

The previous code can indeed be made better in terms of readability and maintainability, by using another selection construct called the **switch construct**. It is important for us to understand that, in terms of efficiency, the switch construct is not always faster than the if else if construct.

The switch Construct

The **switch construct** is an alternative to the if-else construct we have just used in our code. As we read earlier, the general format of the **switch construct** is

```
switch (expression)
{
  case 1:
    {
      statements;
      break;
    }
  case 2:
    {
      statements;
      break;
    }
  default:
    {
      statements;
      break;
    }
    break;
} // End of switch statement
```

We will now apply this format to the if else if construct code we have just written. To do this we will create a new class in the project and make this new class the startup class.

1. Right-click the Chapter9, Selection, project.

2. Choose Add.

3. Choose Class.

4. Name the class Switch.cs.

5. Click the Add button.

The Switch class code will appear in the editor window and will be similar to Listing 9-6. Remember using System is intrinsic and may not be displayed.

Listing 9-6. Class template when adding a class

```
using System;

namespace Chapter9
{
  internal class Switch
  {
  } // End of Switch class
} // End of Chapter9 namespace
```

As the Main() method has not been created automatically, we will create a Main() method within the class by typing svm and pressing the Tab key twice. We will also delete the unwanted imports.

6. Amend the code as in Listing 9-7.

Listing 9-7. Main() method added and unused imports removed

```
using System;

namespace Chapter9
{
  internal class Switch
  {
    static void Main(string[] args)
    {
    } // End of Main() method
```

```
} // End of Switch class
} // End of Chapter9 namespace
```

Now we need to set this class as the startup class for the project.

7. Right-click the Chapter9 project in the Solution Explorer panel.

8. Choose Properties from the pop-up menu.

9. Choose the Chapter9.Switch class in the Startup object drop-down list, as shown in Figure 9-15.

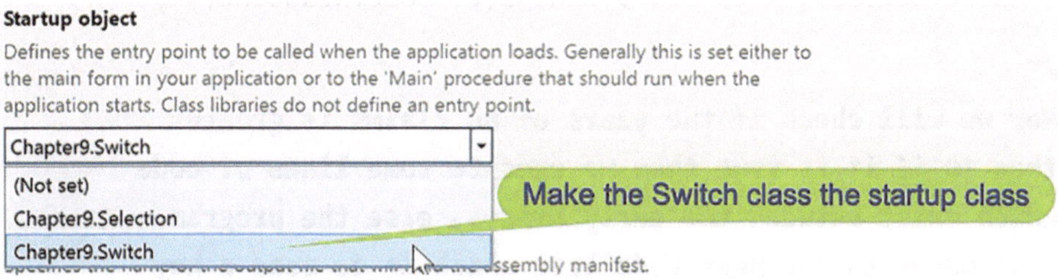

Figure 9-15. *Changing the startup class in the C# project*

10. Close the Properties window.

Now we will add the variables that will be used in our code. Firstly, we will set up a variable for the years of no claims and then add the code that will ask the user for input, read the console input, and convert it to data type int. In the code there are detailed comments to help us get a full understanding of the code.

11. Amend the code, as in Listing 9-8.

Listing 9-8. Ask for user input and convert the string input to int

```
static void Main(string[] args)
{
    /*
    We will setup our variables that will be used in
    the quote application
    */
    int yearsOfNoClaims;

    /* Read the user input and convert it to an int */
```

```
Console.WriteLine("How many full years of no claims " +
  "does the driver have?\n");

yearsOfNoClaims = Convert.ToInt32(Console.ReadLine());
} // End of Main() method
```

12. Amend the code, as in Listing 9-9, to add the switch construct.

Listing 9-9. The switch construct

```
yearsOfNoClaims = Convert.ToInt32(Console.ReadLine());

/*
Now we will check if the years of no claims is greater
than 10 if it is true then we execute some lines of code
which exist between the curly braces, else the program
just moves to the next code line which is to read a key
*/
switch (yearsOfNoClaims)
{
  case 11:
  case 12:
  case 13:
  case 14:
  case 15:
   /*
   This block of code will be executed if the
   yearsOfNoClaims is more than 10
   */
   Console.WriteLine("Years of no claims is more" +
     " than 10 but less than 16");
   break;
  case 9:
  case 10:
   /*
   This block of code will be executed if the
```

```
    yearsOfNoClaims is either 9 or 10
    */
    Console.WriteLine("Years of no claims is either" +
      " 9 or 10");
    break;
case 7:
case 8:
    /*
    This block of code will be executed if the
    yearsOfNoClaims is either 7 or 8
    */
    Console.WriteLine("Years of no claims is either 7 or 8");
    break;
case 5:
case 6:
    /*
    This block of code will be executed if the
    yearsOfNoClaims is either 5 or 6
    */
    Console.WriteLine("Years of no claims is either 5 or 6");
    break;
case 3:
case 4:
    /*
    This block of code will be executed if the
    yearsOfNoClaims is either 3 or 4
    */
    Console.WriteLine("Years of no claims is either 3 or 4");
    break;
default:
    /*
    This block of code will be executed if the
    yearsOfNoClaims is not one of the values in the case
    statements 4 to 15. That means if the value is more than
    15 or less than 4 this block will be executed.
```

```
    We need to think, is this what we really want. Certainly
    it does not give us the same result as the if else-if
    */
    Console.WriteLine("Years of no claims is either less " +
      "than 3 or greater than 15");
    break;
   } // End of switch construct
  } // End of Main() method
 } // End of Switch class
} // End of Chapter9 namespace
```

13. Click the File menu.

14. Choose Save All.

15. Click the Debug menu.

16. Choose Start Without Debugging.

The console window will appear and ask the question. Now we can try the values 15, 10, 8, 6, 4, and 2, which will test the six case blocks. We will start with 15.

17. Type 15 and press the Enter key.

Figure 9-16 shows the console window, and we can see that the first case block of code has been executed.

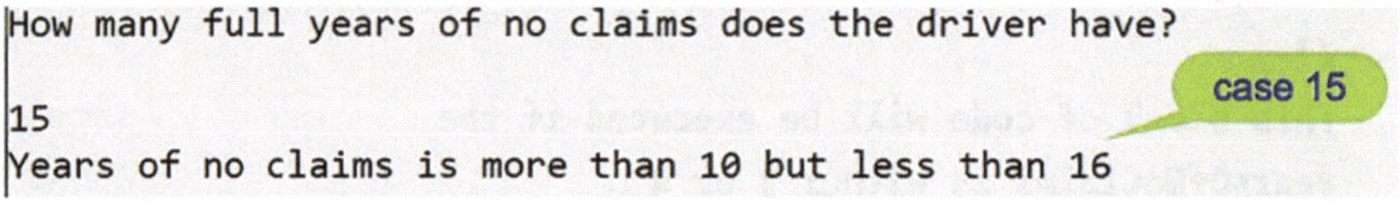

```
How many full years of no claims does the driver have?

                                                    case 15
15
Years of no claims is more than 10 but less than 16
```

Figure 9-16. Switch case 15

18. Press the Enter key to close the console window.

Start the program again.

19. Click the Debug menu.

20. Choose Start Without Debugging.

21. Type 10 and press the Enter key.

Figure 9-17 shows the console window, and we can see that the second case block of code has been executed.

```
How many full years of no claims does the driver have?

10                                              case 10
Years of no claims is either 9 or 10
```

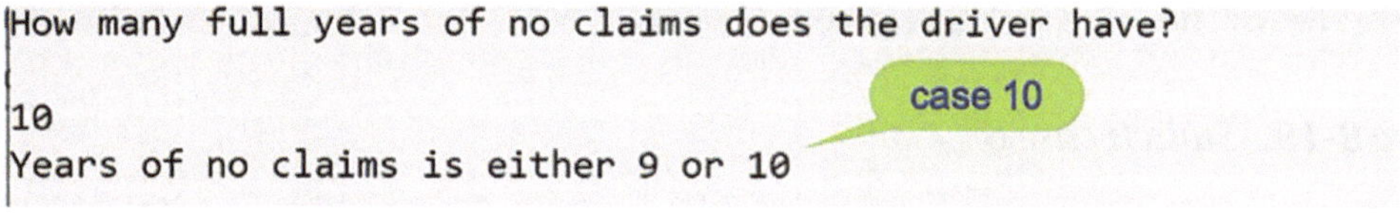

Figure 9-17. Switch case 10

22.   Press the Enter key to close the console window.

Start the program again.

23.   Click the Debug menu.

24.   Choose Start Without Debugging.

25.   Type 8 and press the Enter key.

Figure 9-18 shows the console window, and we can see that the third case block of code has been executed.

```
How many full years of no claims does the driver have?

8                                               case 8
Years of no claims is either 7 or 8
```

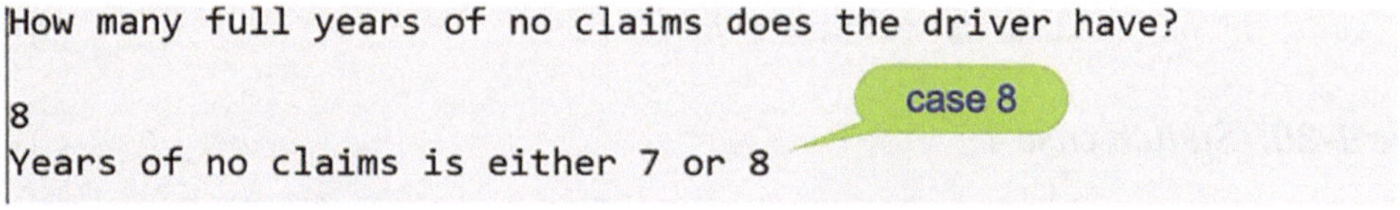

Figure 9-18. Switch case 8

26.   Press the Enter key to close the console window.

Start the program again.

27.   Click the Debug menu.

28.   Choose Start Without Debugging.

29.   Type 6 and press the Enter key.

Figure 9-19 shows the console window, and we can see that the fourth case block of code has been executed.

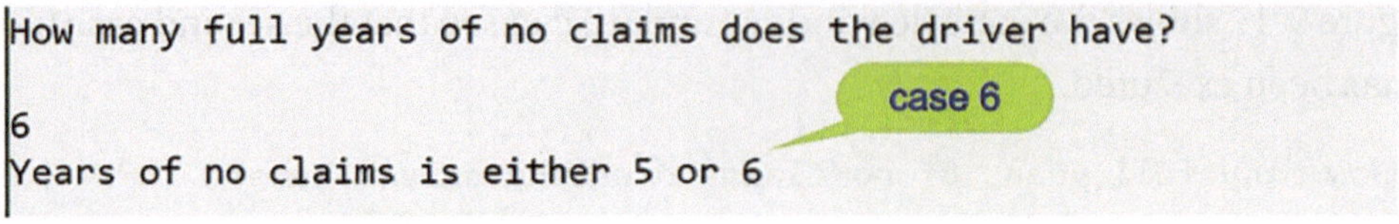

```
How many full years of no claims does the driver have?
                                                    case 6
6
Years of no claims is either 5 or 6
```

Figure 9-19. *Switch case 6*

30.   Press the Enter key to close the console window.

Start the program again.

31.   Click the Debug menu.

32.   Choose Start Without Debugging.

33.   Type 4 and press the Enter key.

Figure 9-20 shows the console window, and we can see that the fifth case block of code has been executed.

```
How many full years of no claims does the driver have?
                                                    case 4
4
Years of no claims is either 3 or 4
```

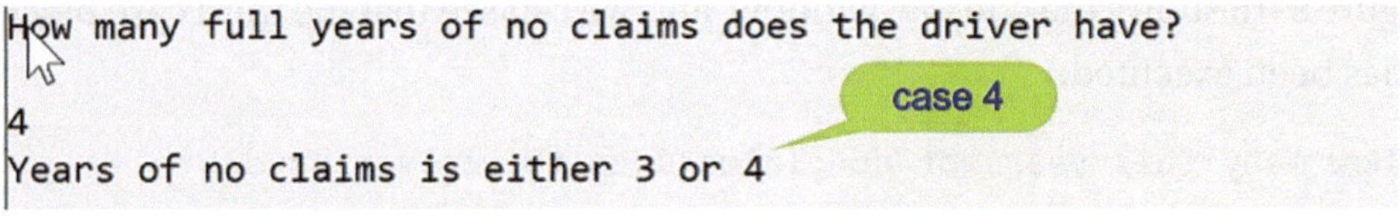

Figure 9-20. *Switch case 4*

34.   Press the Enter key to close the console window.

Start the program again.

35.   Click the Debug menu.

36.   Choose Start Without Debugging.

37.   Type 2 and press the Enter key.

Figure 9-21 shows the console window, and we can see that the sixth case block, the default block, of code has been executed.

```
How many full years of no claims does the driver have?
                                                default case
2
Years of no claims is either less than 3 or greater than 15
```

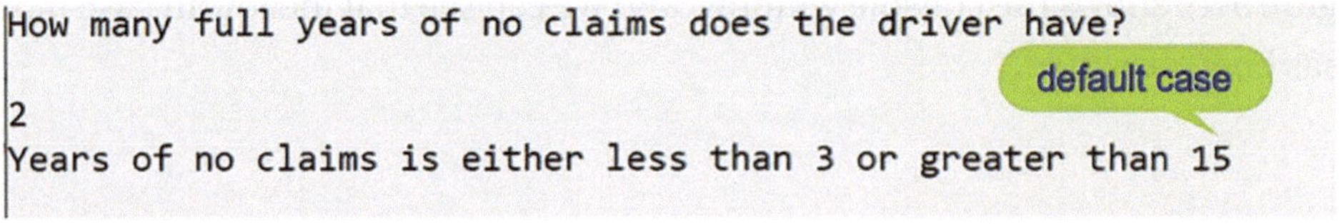

Figure 9-21. *Switch case default*

38. Press the Enter key to close the console window.

The switch construct is a replacement for the if else if construct.

As we might see, the only issue in our case construct code arises for the equivalent of yearsOfNoClaims >10:

- In the if else if, the yearsOfNoClaims >10 handled values 11, 12, 13, 14, 15, 16, 17, etc.

- In the switch statement, we had to individually state case 11, case 12, case 13, case 14, case 15, etc. But to do this for all values above 10 would be a long and wasteful process.

- So we may need to think of a better way to do this. We might use an if statement in the default block to check if the value is less than 3 or greater than 15 or just use the if else if construct.

- The case construct in C# 6 or lower does not always allow for the use of a range of numbers or even >10 as the case. The switch statement should not be used for condition checking.

C# 7

From C# 7 we can use a **when clause** to specify an additional condition that must be satisfied for the case statement to evaluate to true. The when clause can be any expression that returns a Boolean value, true or false.

The switch Construct Using when

We will now apply this format to the code we wrote for the case construct. To do this we will create a new class in the project and make this new class the startup class.

1. Right-click the Chapter9 project.

2. Choose Add.

3. Choose Class.

4. Name the class Switch7Onwards.cs.

5. Click the Add button.

6. Create a Main() method within the class, as this was not produced automatically, and delete the unwanted imports, as in Listing 9-10.

Listing 9-10. The class with the Main() method

```
namespace Chapter9
{
  internal class Switch7Onwards
  {
    static void Main(string[] args)
    {

    } // End of Main() method
  } // End of Switch7Onwards class
} // End of Chapter9 namespace
```

Now we need to set this class as the startup class for the project.

7. Right-click the Chapter9 project in the Solution Explorer panel.

8. Choose Properties from the pop-up menu.

9. Choose the Chapter9.Switch7Onwards class in the Startup object drop-down list, as shown in Figure 9-22.

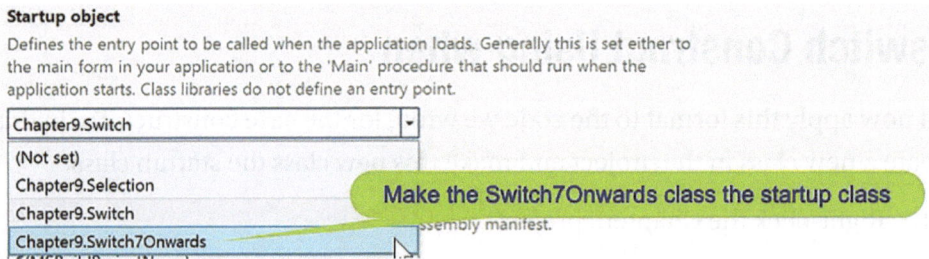

Figure 9-22. *Changing the startup class in the C# project*

10. Close the Properties window.

11. Amend the code, as in Listing 9-11, to add the code with the new **when** format for the first case block.

Listing 9-11. First case block with the when clause

```
using System;

namespace Chapter9
{
  internal class Switch7Onwards
  {
    static void Main(string[] args)
    {
      /*
      We will setup our variables that will be used in
      the quote application
      */
      int yearsOfNoClaims;

      /* Read the user input and convert it to an int */
      Console.WriteLine("How many full years of no claims does the driver
      have?\n");
      yearsOfNoClaims = Convert.ToInt32(Console.ReadLine());

      /*
      Now we will check if the years of no claims is greater
      than 10
      * if it is true then we execute some lines of code
        which exist between the curly braces, else the program
        just moves to the next code line which is to read a key
      */
      switch (yearsOfNoClaims)
      {
        case int numberOfYearsEntered when (yearsOfNoClaims > 10):
        /*
        This block of code will be executed if the
        yearsofnoclaims is more than 10
        */
        Console.WriteLine("Years of no claims is more than 10");
        break;
```

```
    } // End of switch construct
```

```
  } // End of Main() method
 } // End of Switch7Onwards class
} // End of Chapter9 namespace
```

Note

The line of code that has the when clause in it tells the compiler that we want this case block to execute when the yearsOfNoClaims value is greater than 10.

   12. Amend the code, as in Listing 9-12, to add the new when format for the second case block.

Listing 9-12. Second case block with the when clause

```
Console.WriteLine("Years of no claims is more than 10");
 break;

case int numberOfYearsEntered when (yearsOfNoClaims > 8):
 /*
 This block of code will be executed if the
 yearsofnoclaims is more than 8 which means 9, 10, 11,
 12 etc. However if yearsofnoclaims is 11, 12 etc it
 will have been detected in the case above where the
 condition  yearsofnoclaims > 10is used.
 */
 Console.WriteLine("Years of no claims is either 9 or 10");
 break;
 } //End of switch construct

  } // End of Main() method
 } // End of Switch7Onwards class
} // End of Chapter9 namespace
```

The when clause tells the compiler that we want this case block to execute when the yearsOfNoClaims value is greater than 8 and less than 11.

We will now repeat the use of the when statement for the other case elements.

   13. Amend the code, as in Listing 9-13, to add the new format for the remaining case blocks.

Listing 9-13. Completed code with all when clauses

```
Console.WriteLine("Years of no claims is either 9 or 10");
  break;

case int numberOfYearsEntered when (yearsOfNoClaims > 6):
  /*
  This block of code will be executed if the
  yearsofnoclaims is more than 6 which means 7, 8, 9,
  10 etc. However if yearsofnoclaims is 9, 10 etc it will
  have been detected in the case above where the condition
  yearsofnoclaims > 8 is used.
  */
  Console.WriteLine("Years of no claims is either 7 or 8");
  break;

case int numberOfYearsEntered when (yearsOfNoClaims > 4):
/*
This block of code will be executed if the
  yearsofnoclaims is more than 4 which means 5, 6, 7,
  8 etc. However if yearsofnoclaims is 7, 8 etc it will
  have been detected in the case above where the condition
  yearsofnoclaims > 4 is used.
  */
  Console.WriteLine("Years of no claims is either 5 or 6");
  break;

case int numberOfYearsEntered when (yearsOfNoClaims > 2):
  /*
  This block of code will be executed if the
  yearsofnoclaims is more than 2 which means 3, 4, 5,
  6 etc.. However if yearsofnoclaims is 5, 6 etc it will
  have been detected in the case above where the condition
  yearsofnoclaims > 2 is used.
  */
  Console.WriteLine("Years of no claims is either 3 or 4");
  break;
```

```
        default:
        /*
        This block of code will be executed if the
        yearsofnoclaims is not more than 2. For this block of
        code to be executed none of the conditions above must
        have been true (and none of the blocks of code were
        executed*/
        Console.WriteLine("Years of no claims is 2, 1, 0 " +
          "\n or indeed a negative number of years " +
          "\n because of a penalty being enforced on our policy");
        break;
      } // End of switch construct
    } // End of Main() method
  } // End of Switch7Onwards class
} // End of Chapter9 namespace
```

14. Click the File menu.

15. Choose Save All.

16. Click the Debug menu.

17. Choose Start Without Debugging.

The console window will appear and ask the question. Now we can try the values 15, 10, 8, 6, 4, and 2, which will test the six case blocks. We will start with 15.

18. Type 15 and press the Enter key.

Figure 9-23 shows the console window and we can see that the first case block of code has been executed.

```
How many full years of no claims does the driver have?

15                    case int numberOfYearsEntered when (yearsOfNoClaims > 10):
Years of no claims is more than 10
```

Figure 9-23. *Case when > 10 executed*

19.   Press the Enter key to close the console window.

20.   Start the program again by clicking the Debug menu.

21.   Choose Start Debugging.

22.   Type 10 and press the Enter key.

Figure 9-24 shows the console window and we can see that the second case block of code has been executed.

```
How many full years of no claims does the driver have?
                              case int numberOfYearsEntered when (yearsOfNoClaims > 8):
10
Years of no claims is either 9 or 10
```

Figure 9-24. *Case when > 8 executed*

23.   Press the Enter key to close the console window.

Repeat the input process for the values 8, 6, 4, and 2.

switch with Strings

The C# switch programs we have been writing have switches using an integer. We have therefore executed one block of code, or another, based on the integer value in the case statement. C# also allows us to use the case construct with a **string**. When we use a string, the construct is the same as we have already coded, but the string must be enclosed in double quotes "".

We will now use a string in the case construct. To do this we will amend the Switch.cs program, so the data read from the console is not converted to an int – we will just keep it as a string. To achieve this, we will also need to change the data type of the variable yearsOfNoClaims from int to string. Rather than changing the existing Switch class, we will create a copy of the class, rename it, and then change the code in the copied class. This is a great technique, as we can reuse existing code and save lots of time having to start a program from "scratch."

24.   Right-click the Switch class.

25.   Choose Copy.

26.   Right-click the Chapter9 project.

27. Choose Paste.

 The new file Switch – Copy.cs will be added to the project.

28. Right-click the Switch – Copy.cs file.

29. Choose Rename.

30. Type SwitchString.cs as the new name for this class.

31. Make sure this new class is open in the editor window, not the
      original class.

Looking at the code for the new class in the editor window, we will see an error line
under the class name in the code, as shown in Figure 9-25. This is because the class
name does not match the name of the file, class, in the Solution Explorer panel and the
class name Switch is therefore already in existence in the Chapter9 namespace.

Figure 9-25. *Class code has not been renamed as shown by the error*

Although it says a class called Switch exists, which is correct, we just need to rename
the class to match the name we gave it, SwitchString.

We can right-click the word Switch and choose rename, but do not check the
boxes that appear and ask about renaming other things as this may also rename the
original class. If we did this, we would have two classes with the same name in the same
namespace, and we read in Chapter 3 that this is not allowed.

32. Amend the word Switch in the editor window to say
      SwitchString.cs.

33. Amend the code as shown in Listing 9-14 to change the data type
      of the variable to string instead of int.

Listing 9-14. Change variable type from int to string

```
static void Main(string[] args)
{
  /*
  We will setup our variables that will be used in
  the quote application  */
  string yearsOfNoClaims;
```

34. Amend the code as shown in Listing 9-15 to remove the
    conversion of the data input by the user, as we want this to remain
    a string, which is the default for console input.

Listing 9-15. Remove the conversion from string to int

```
string yearsOfNoClaims;

/* Read the user input and convert it to an int */
Console.WriteLine("How many full years of no claims " +
  "does the driver have?\n");

yearsOfNoClaims = Console.ReadLine();
```

The code line was yearsOfNoClaims = Convert.ToInt32(Console.ReadLine());,
and we have removed the conversion from string to Int32.

35. Amend the code as shown in Listing 9-16 to add the new format
    for the first case block. This will mean enclosing the numbers in
    double quotes as they are being entered as strings.

Listing 9-16. Case statements accepting string values (double quotes)

```
switch (yearsOfNoClaims)
{
  case "11":
  case "12":
  case "13":
  case "14":
  case "15":
```

36.   Amend the code as shown in Listing 9-17 to add the new format
for the second and remaining case blocks.

Listing 9-17. All case statements accepting string values (double quotes)

```
switch (yearsOfNoClaims)
{
   case "11":
   case "12":
   case "13":
   case "14":
   case "15":
    /*
    This block of code will be executed if the
    yearsofnoclaims is more than 10
    */
    Console.WriteLine("Years of no claims is more" +
       " than 10 but less than 16");
    break;
   case "9":
   case "10":
    /*
    This block of code will be executed if the
    yearsofnoclaims is either 9 or 10
    */
    Console.WriteLine("Years of no claims is either" +
       " 9 or 10");
    break;
   case "7":
   case "8":
    /*
    This block of code will be executed if the
    yearsofnoclaims is either 7 or 8
    */
    Console.WriteLine("Years of no claims is either 7 or 8");
    break;
```

```
case "5":
case "6":
 /*
 This block of code will be executed if the
 yearsofnoclaims is either 5 or 6
 */
 Console.WriteLine("Years of no claims is either 5 or 6");
 break;
case "3":
case "4":
 /*
 This block of code will be executed if the
 yearsofnoclaims is either 3 or 4
 */
 Console.WriteLine("Years of no claims is either 3 or 4");
 break;
default:
 /*
 This block of code will be executed if the
 yearsofnoclaims is not one of the values in the case
 statements 4 to 15. That means if the value is more than
 15 or less than 4 this block will be executed.
 We need to think, is this what we really want. Certainly
 it does not give us the same result as the if else-if
 */
 Console.WriteLine("Years of no claims is either less " +
    "than 3 or greater than 15");
 break;
 } //End of switch construct    } // End of Main() method
} // End of SwitchString class
} // End of Chapter9 namespace
```

37. Right-click the Chapter9 project in the Solution Explorer panel.

38. Choose Properties from the pop-up menu.

39. Choose the SwitchString class in the Startup object drop-down list, as shown in Figure 9-26.

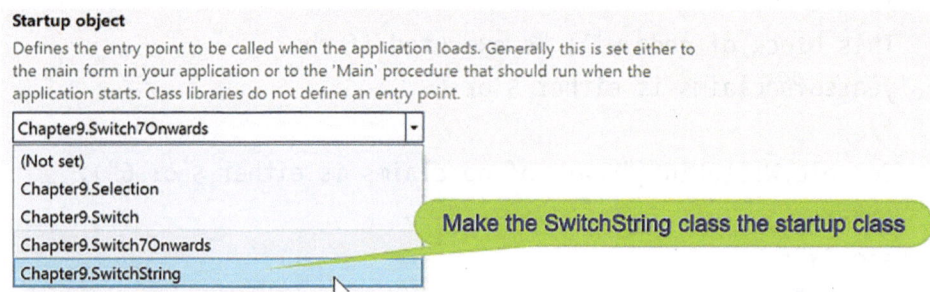

Figure 9-26. *Set the startup class*

40. Click the File menu.

41. Choose Save All.

42. Click the Debug menu.

43. Choose Start Without Debugging.

The console window will appear and ask the question. Now we can try the values 15, 10, 8, 6, 4, and 2, which will test the six case blocks. We will start with 15.

44. Type 15 and press the Enter key.

Figure 9-27 shows the console window and we can see that the first case block of code that uses the string has been executed.

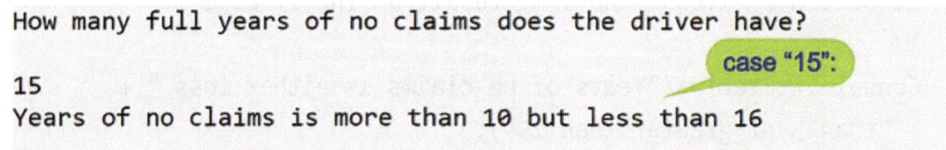

Figure 9-27. *Switch case 15*

45. Press the Enter key to close the console window.

Start the program again.

46. Click the Debug menu.

47. Choose Start Without Debugging.

48.   Type 10 and press the Enter key.

Figure 9-28 shows the console window and we can see that the second case block of code that uses the string has been executed.

```
How many full years of no claims does the driver have?

10                                          case "10":
Years of no claims is either 9 or 10
```

Figure 9-28. *Switch case 10*

49.   Press the Enter key to close the console window.

Start the program again.

50.   Click the Debug menu.

51.   Choose Start Without Debugging.

52.   Type 8 and press the Enter key.

Figure 9-29 shows the console window and we can see that the third case block of code that uses the string has been executed.

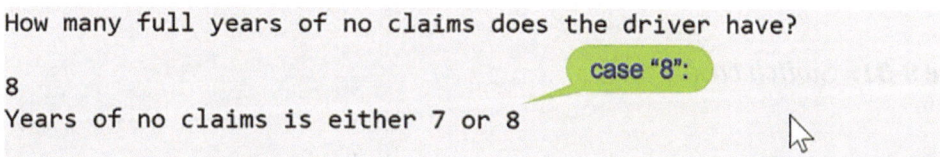

```
How many full years of no claims does the driver have?
                                          case "8":
8
Years of no claims is either 7 or 8
```

Figure 9-29. *Switch case 8*

53.   Press the Enter key to close the console window.

Start the program again.

54.   Click the Debug menu.

55.   Choose Start Without Debugging.

56.   Type 6 and press the Enter key.

Figure 9-30 shows the console window and we can see that the fourth case block of code that uses the string has been executed.

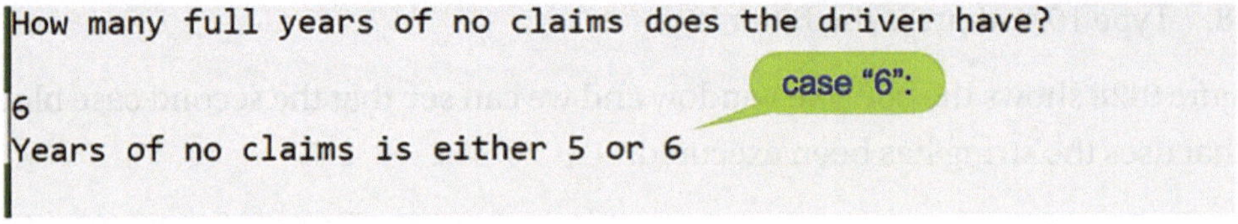

```
How many full years of no claims does the driver have?

6                                            case "6":
Years of no claims is either 5 or 6
```

Figure 9-30. *Switch case 6*

57. Press the Enter key to close the console window.

Start the program again.

58. Click the Debug menu.

59. Choose Start Without Debugging.

60. Type 4 and press the Enter key.

Figure 9-31 shows the console window and we can see that the fifth case block of code that uses the string has been executed.

```
How many full years of no claims does the driver have?

4                                            case "4":
Years of no claims is either 3 or 4
```

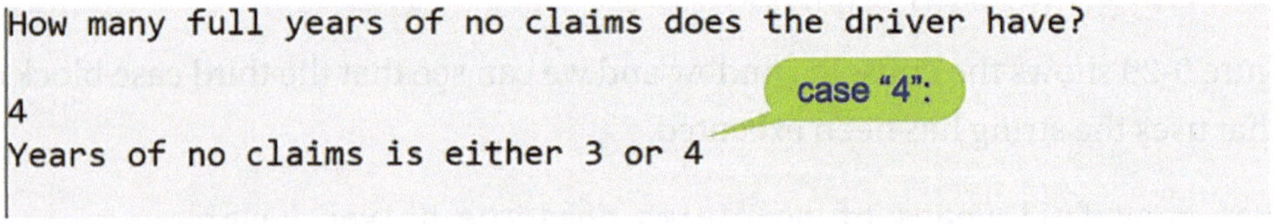

Figure 9-31. *Switch case 4*

61. Press the Enter key to close the console window.

Start the program again.

62. Click the Debug menu.

63. Choose Start Without Debugging.

64. Type 2 and press the Enter key.

Figure 9-32 shows the console window and we can see that the sixth case block, the default block, of code that uses the string has been executed.

```
How many full years of no claims does the driver have?
2                                                        default:
Years of no claims is either less than 3 or greater than 15
```

Figure 9-32. *Switch case default*

65. Press the Enter key to close the console window.

switch with Strings

Additional Example

We should remember the coding technique for displaying data using placeholders that we applied earlier:

- The placeholder has the format **placeholders {}.**

- Each placeholder has a number contained in the open and close braces.

- The number represents the position of the variable name, which is in the comma-separated list at the end of the statement.

- The variables are numbered starting with a 0, then a 1, etc. This means the numbers are zero indexed.

The placeholder format is very neat and means we do not have to keep opening and closing the double quotes to insert the concatenation + symbol. This new example will reinforce selection using the switch statement with string values.

1. Right-click the Chapter9 project.

2. Choose Add.

3. Choose Class.

4. Name the class SwitchStringVehicleModel.cs.

5. Click the Add button.

6. Amend the code as shown in Listing 9-18 to add the required variables and make use of the new WriteLine() format within the switch construct.

Listing 9-18. Switch using strings and using WriteLine() with placeholders

```
namespace Chapter9
{
  internal class SwitchStringVehicleModel
  {
    static void Main()
    {
      /*
      In this section we declare the two variables of data type
      string that we will use throughout the program code.
      */
      string vehicleModel;
      string vehicleManufacturer;

      Console.WriteLine();
      Console.WriteLine("What is the model of the vehicle?\n");

      /*
      In this section we read the user input from the console.
      The console input is by default a string data type which
      means we can directly assign the value to the string
      variable called vehicleModel. */
      vehicleModel = Console.ReadLine();

      /*
      In this section we use the string variable called
      vehicleModel in the case statement to decide which block
      of code will be executed. The blocks of code therefore
      will be based on the model of the vehicle and the code will
      set the value of the variable called vehicleManufacturer.
      */
      switch (vehicleModel)
      {
```

```
    case "Edge":
    case "Fiesta":
    case "Focus":
    case "Kuga":
    case "Mondeo":
    case "Mustang":
      vehicleManufacturer = "Ford";
      break;
    case "Astra":
    case "Corsa":
    case "Insignia":
    case "Viva":
      vehicleManufacturer = "Vauxhall";
      break;
    case "Altima":
    case "Juke":
    case "Sentra":
      vehicleManufacturer = "Nissan";
      break;
    case "C-Class":
    case "E-Class":
    case "S-Class":
    case "GLA":
    case "GLC":
    case "GLE":
      vehicleManufacturer = "Mercedes Benz";
      break;
    default:
      vehicleManufacturer = "unknown";
      break;
}
/*
Here we will write the same message to the console in two
different ways so we can use a new technique
*/
```

```
        /*
        In this statement we are writing data to the console in
        our normal way with a concatenated (joined) string and
        this works fine
        */
        Console.WriteLine("\nThe " + vehicleModel + " " +
           "manufacturer is " + vehicleManufacturer);

        /*
        In this statement we are writing data to the console in a
        different way using a string which has placeholders {}.
        Each place holder has a number and this number represents
        the position of the variable name which is in the comma
        separated list at the end of the statement. The variables
        are numbered starting with a 0 then a 1 etc (zero indexed)
        and are at the end of the statement.
        The example below effectively means
        Console.WriteLine("\nThe vehicleModel manufacturer is
        vehicleManufacturer ");
        This new format is very neat and means we do not have to
        keep opening and closing the double quotes and having the
        concatenation + symbol.
        */
        Console.WriteLine("\nThe {0} manufacturer is {1} ",
           vehicleModel, vehicleManufacturer);

    } // End of Main() method
  } // End of SwitchStringVehicleModel class
} // End of Chapter9 namespace
```

7. Right-click the Chapter9 project in the Solution Explorer panel.

8. Choose Properties from the pop-up menu.

9. Choose the SwitchStringVehicleModel.cs class in the Startup object drop-down list.

10. Click the File menu.

11. Choose Save All.

12. Click the Debug menu.

13. Choose Start Without Debugging.

The console window will appear and ask the question. Now we can try the string values **Mustang**, **Corsa**, **Juke**, **S-Class,** and **Pacifica,** which will test the five case blocks. We will start with Mustang.

14. Type Mustang and press the Enter key.

Figure 9-33 shows the console window and we can see that the first case block of code has been executed, and the different WriteLine() formats have output the same message, but one has used concatenation and the other has used the placeholders.

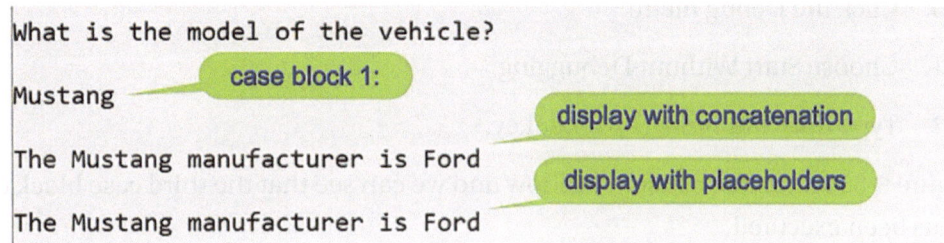

Figure 9-33. *Switch case block 1*

15. Press the Enter key to close the console window.

Start the program again.

16. Click the Debug menu.

17. Choose Start Without Debugging.

18. Type Corsa and press the Enter key.

Figure 9-34 shows the console window and we can see that the second case block of code has been executed.

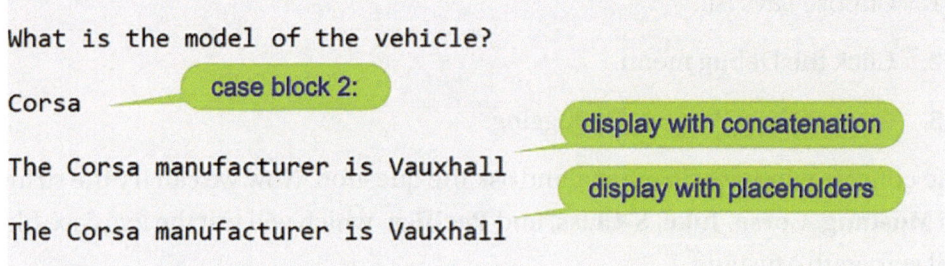

Figure 9-34. *Switch case block 2*

19.   Press the Enter key to close the console window.

Start the program again.

20.   Click the Debug menu.

21.   Choose Start Without Debugging.

22.   Type Juke and press the Enter key.

Figure 9-35 shows the console window and we can see that the third case block of code has been executed.

```
What is the model of the vehicle?
                case block 3:
Juke
                        display with concatenation
The Juke manufacturer is Nissan
                        display with placeholders
The Juke manufacturer is Nissan
```

Figure 9-35. *Switch case block 3*

23.   Press the Enter key to close the console window.

Start the program again.

24.   Click the Debug menu.

25.   Choose Start Without Debugging.

26.   Type S-Class and press the Enter key.

Figure 9-36 shows the console window and we can see that the fourth case block of code has been executed.

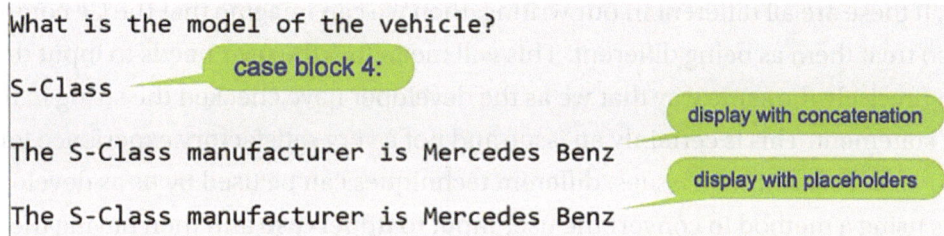

Figure 9-36. *Switch case block 4*

27.   Press the Enter key to close the console window.

Start the program again.

28.   Click the Debug menu.

29.   Choose Start Without Debugging.

30.   Type Pacifica and press the Enter key.

Figure 9-37 shows the console window and we can see that the fifth case block, the default case block, of code has been executed.

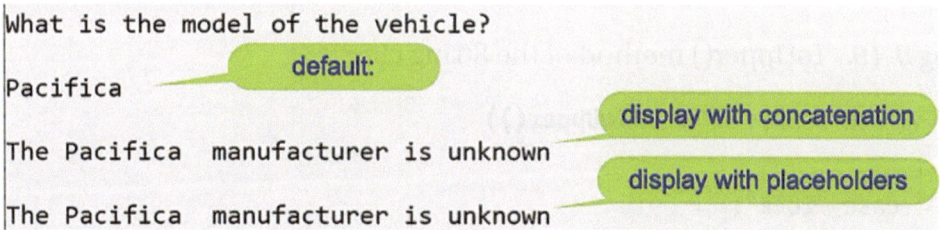

Figure 9-37. *Switch case block 5 – the default case block*

31.   Press the Enter key to close the console window.

An issue to be considered when using strings with the case statement is that checking is case sensitive. This should be no surprise to us really, as we will be familiar with writing and will know that these are all different strings:

- Mustang

- MUSTANG

- mustang

- mUSTANG

So, if these are all different in our writing, then we can imagine that the C# compiler will also treat them as being different. This will mean that the user needs to input the data in precisely the same way that we as the developer have checked the string in the switch statement. This is certainly an issue and not a very satisfactory experience for the end user. To avoid such issues, different techniques can be used by us as developers, such as using a method to convert the user input to **uppercase** and then having the case statements have uppercase text. The uppercase method belongs to the String class and is called ToUpper(), as shown in Figure 9-38.

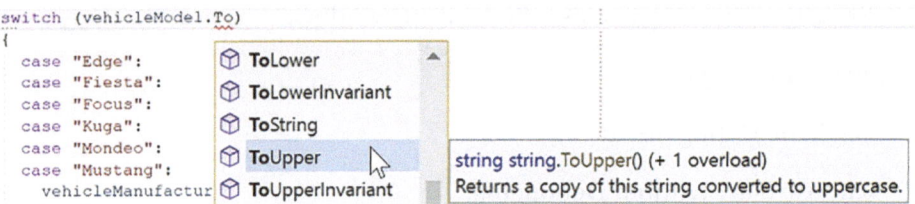

Figure 9-38. *The ToUpper() method from the String class*

We will see more of this in Chapter 15 on string handling, but as a "taster," this might be coded as shown in Listing 9-19.

Listing 9-19. ToUpper() method of the String class

```
switch (vehicleModel.ToUpper())
{
  case "EDGE":
  case "FIESTA":
  case "FOCUS":
  case "KUGA":
  case "MONDEO":
  case "MUSTANG":
    vehicleManufacturer = "Ford";
    break;
```

If the user inputs any string, it will be converted to uppercase when the switch statement is executed. So, if the user enters **mUsTaNg,** the code will convert it to uppercase **MUSTANG** and the case statement will find the correct manufacturer. We could also use the ToUpper() method on the output, as shown in Listing 9-20, and the output would show uppercase letters as shown in Figure 9-39.

Listing 9-20. ToUpper() method of the String class

```
Console.WriteLine("\nThe {0} manufacturer is {1} ",
    vehicleModel.ToUpper(), vehicleManufacturer);
```

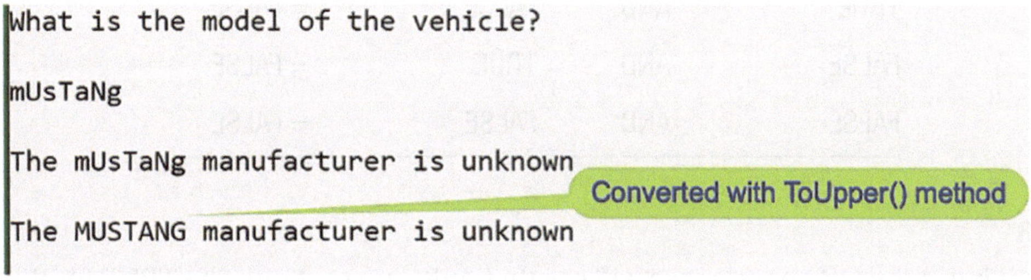

```
What is the model of the vehicle?

mUsTaNg

The mUsTaNg manufacturer is unknown                 Converted with ToUpper() method

The MUSTANG manufacturer is unknown
```

Figure 9-39. *The ToUpper() method from the String class*

For now, do not worry about this uppercase and lowercase.

Logical Operators

We said earlier

We will also look at the logical operators AND (&&), || (OR), and ! (NOT).

Well, now is the time to use them, by building on the if construct we have learned.

AND

Looking at the AND operator, we will see that both parts must be TRUE for the whole statement to be TRUE. Listing 9-21 shows the AND in an if construct, even though in C# coding we will not use the word AND.

Listing 9-21. Simplified version of an AND operator

```
if (yearsOfNoClaims > 10 AND policyHolderAge > 50)
{
    // Some business logic
}
```

Looking at Table 9-2, we can see all the possibilities for an AND operator when there are two parts.

Table 9-2. *The AND, &&, operator*

First part	Operator	Second part	Result
TRUE	AND	TRUE	= TRUE
TRUE	AND	FALSE	= FALSE
FALSE	AND	TRUE	= FALSE
FALSE	AND	FALSE	= FALSE

OR

Looking at the OR operator, we will see that only one part must be TRUE for the whole statement to be TRUE. Listing 9-22 shows the OR in an if construct, even though in C# coding we will not use the word OR.

Listing 9-22. Simplified version of an OR operator

```
if (yearsOfNoClaims > 10 OR policyHolderAge > 50)
{
  // Some business logic
}
```

Looking at Table 9-3, we can see all the possibilities for an OR operator.

Table 9-3. *The OR, !!, operator*

First part	Operator	Second part	Result
TRUE	OR	TRUE	= TRUE
TRUE	OR	FALSE	= TRUE
FALSE	OR	TRUE	= TRUE
FALSE	OR	FALSE	= FALSE

NOT

Looking at the NOT operator, we will see that the current value becomes the opposite of what it is: TRUE becomes FALSE and FALSE becomes TRUE. An example of using NOT in the if construct is shown in Listing 9-23.

Listing 9-23. Simplified version of a NOT, !, operator

```
if (!yearsOfNoClaims > 10)
{
  // Some business logic
}
```

Looking at Table 9-4, we can see all the possibilities for a NOT operator.

Table 9-4. *The NOT, !, operator*

Operator	First part	Result
NOT	TRUE	= FALSE
NOT	FALSE	= TRUE

In C# the logical operators will only evaluate the second part of the expression if it is necessary. "Why?" we might ask. Well, we will see from the following examples that it makes sense to use this **short-circuit** evaluation to save needless evaluation.

AND

In our truth table, Table 9-2, we saw that the only combination that evaluates to TRUE is when both parts of the expression are TRUE. So we can short-circuit any combinations that start with a FALSE:

if(6>7 AND 9<10) equates to if(FALSE AND TRUE), which equates to FALSE.

As the first part evaluates to FALSE there is no point in evaluating the second part.

OR

In our truth table, Table 9-3, we saw that a TRUE or a FALSE as the first part could lead to an overall evaluation of TRUE. So we cannot short-circuit when using the OR construct.

Let's code some C# and build our programming muscle.

Using the AND Operator

1. Right-click the Chapter9 project.

2. Choose Add.

3. Choose Class.

4. Name the class SelectionAnd.cs.

5. Click the Add button.

6. Amend the code to add the Main() method as in Listing 9-24.

Listing 9-24. Adding the Main() method

```
namespace Chapter9
{
  internal class SelectionAnd
  {
    static void Main(string[] args)
    {

    } // End of Main() method
  } // End of SelectionAnd class
} // End of Chapter9 namespace
```

Now we need to set this class as the startup class.

7. Right-click the Chapter9 project in the Solution Explorer panel.

8. Choose Properties from the pop-up menu.

9. Choose the SelectionAnd.cs class in the Startup object drop-down list.

10. Close the Properties window.

11. Amend the code to add the variables required, as in Listing 9-25.

Listing 9-25. Adding the variables

```
static void Main(string[] args)
{
  /*
  We will setup our variables that will be used in
  the quote application
  */
  int yearsOfNoClaims;
  int ageOfDriver;
} // End of Main() method
```

12. Amend the code, as in Listing 9-26, to request user input for the years of no claims and convert it to an int.

Listing 9-26. Accept user input and convert to an int

```
int yearsOfNoClaims;
int ageOfDriver;

/* Read the user input and convert it to an int */
Console.WriteLine("How many full years of no claims does the driver
have?\n");

yearsOfNoClaims = Convert.ToInt32(Console.ReadLine());
} // End of Main() method
```

13. Amend the code, as in Listing 9-27, to request user input for the driver age and convert it to an int.

Listing 9-27. Accept user input and convert to an int

```
yearsOfNoClaims = Convert.ToInt32(Console.ReadLine());

Console.WriteLine("What is the current age of the driver?\n");

ageOfDriver = Convert.ToInt32(Console.ReadLine());
} // End of Main() method
```

Now we will check if the number of years of no claims is greater than 10 and if the age of the driver is greater than 40:

- If these are both true, we execute code in the if block.

- Otherwise, move to the else block and execute the code in this block.

14. Amend the code, as in Listing 9-28.

Listing 9-28. Use selection through an if-else statement

```
ageOfDriver = Convert.ToInt32(Console.ReadLine());

/*
Now we will check if the years of no claims is greater
than 10 AND if the age of the driver is greater than 40.
```

251

```
If both are TRUE we have the Boolean expression
TRUE AND TRUE which equates to TRUE and we then we
execute some lines of code which exist between the
curly braces of the code block, otherwise the program
moves to the else code block and execute some lines of
code in this code block
*/
if (yearsOfNoClaims > 10 && ageOfDriver > 40)
{
/*
   This block of code will be executed if both
   parts of the condition are TRUE
*/
   Console.WriteLine("This quote is eligible for a 10% discount");
} // End of true part
else
{
/*
This block of code will be executed if the one
part of the condition is FALSE
*/
   Console.WriteLine("This quote is ineligible for a discount");
} // End of false part
} // End of Main() method
} // End of SelectionAnd class
} // End of Chapter9 namespace
```

Testing TRUE AND TRUE

15.   Click the File menu.

16.   Choose Save All.

17.   Click the Debug menu.

18.   Choose Start Without Debugging.

19.   Click in the console window.

20.   Type 20 as the number of years of no claims.

21.   Press the Enter key on the keyboard.

22.   Type 50 as the current age of the driver.

23.   Press the Enter key on the keyboard.

Figure 9-40 shows the console window with the message that a discount is applicable, as 20 is greater than 10 AND 50 is greater than 40.

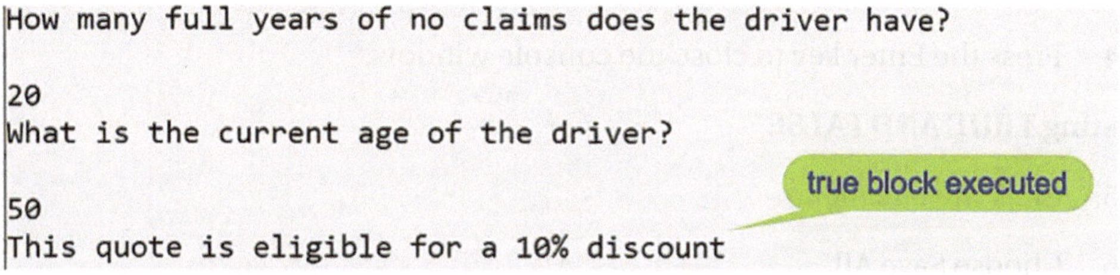

```
How many full years of no claims does the driver have?

20
What is the current age of the driver?
                                                true block executed
50
This quote is eligible for a 10% discount
```

Figure 9-40. *True section of if-else executed*

24.   Press the Enter key to close the console window.

Testing FALSE AND TRUE

25.   Click the File menu.

26.   Choose Save All.

27.   Click the Debug menu.

28.   Choose Start Without Debugging.

29.   Click in the console window.

30.   Type 10 as the number of years of no claims.

31.   Press the Enter key on the keyboard.

32.   Type 50 as the current age of the driver.

33.   Press the Enter key on the keyboard.

Figure 9-41 shows the console window with the message that no discount is applicable, as 50 is greater than 40 BUT 10 is not greater than 10.

```
How many full years of no claims does the driver have?

10
What is the current age of the driver?

50
This quote is ineligible for a discount
```
false block executed

Figure 9-41. *False section of if-else executed*

34.   Press the Enter key to close the console window.

Testing TRUE AND FALSE

35.   Click the File menu.

36.   Choose Save All.

37.   Click the Debug menu.

38.   Choose Start Without Debugging.

39.   Click in the console window.

40.   Type 20 as the number of years of no claims.

41.   Press the Enter key on the keyboard.

42.   Type 30 as the current age of the driver.

43.   Press the Enter key on the keyboard.

Figure 9-42 shows the console window with the message that no discount is applicable as 20 is greater than 10 BUT 30 is not greater than 40.

```
How many full years of no claims does the driver have?

20
What is the current age of the driver?

30
This quote is ineligible for a discount
```
false block executed

Figure 9-42. *False section of if-else executed*

44. Press the Enter key to close the console window.

Let's code some C# and build our programming muscle.

Using the OR Operator

1. Right-click the Chapter9 project.

2. Choose Add.

3. Choose Class.

4. Name the class SelectionOR.cs.

5. Click the Add button.

6. Create a Main() method within the class, as this was not produced automatically. Type svm and press Tab twice, and then delete the unwanted imports.

   Now we need to set this class as the startup class.

7. Right-click the Chapter9 project in the Solution Explorer panel.

8. Choose Properties from the pop-up menu.

9. Choose the SelectionOR class in the Startup object drop-down list.

10. Close the Properties window.

11. Open the SelectionAnd file and copy the code from within the Main() method.

12. Move back to the SelectionOR file in the editor and paste the copied code between the open and close curly braces, {}, of the Main() method.

   We will amend the code to use the logical operator OR rather than the logical operator AND. Within the copied code, we will change the && to || and change the comments to match. This means our code will

- Check if the number of years of no claims is greater than 10 OR if the age of the driver is greater than 40:

  If these are both true, we execute code in the if block.

  If one of these is true, we execute code in the if block.

  Otherwise, move to the else block and execute the code in this block.

13. Amend the code, as in Listing 9-29.

Listing 9-29. Use the OR (||) instead of the AND (&&)

```
ageOfDriver = Convert.ToInt32(Console.ReadLine());

/*
Now we will check if the years of no claims is greater
than 10 OR if the age of the driver is greater than 40.
If both are TRUE we have the Boolean expression
TRUE AND TRUE which equates to TRUE or if one of them
is TRUE we have the Boolean expression TRUE OR FALSE
or FALSE OR TRUE which equates to TRUE and we then we
execute some lines of code which exist between the curly
braces of the code block, otherwise the program moves
to the else code block and executes some lines of code
in this code block
*/

if (yearsOfNoClaims > 10 || ageOfDriver > 40)
{
  /*
    This block of code will be executed if one
    part of the condition are TRUE
  */
  Console.WriteLine("This quote is eligible for a 10% discount");
} // End of true part
else
{
  /*
```

```
    This block of code will be executed if the one
    part of the condition is FALSE
    */
    Console.WriteLine("This quote is ineligible for a discount");
  } // End of false part
```

Testing TRUE OR TRUE

14.   Click the File menu.

15.   Choose Save All.

16.   Click the Debug menu.

17.   Choose Start Without Debugging.

18.   Click in the console window.

19.   Type 20 as the number of years of no claims.

20.   Press the Enter key on the keyboard.

21.   Type 50 as the current age of the driver.

22.   Press the Enter key on the keyboard.

Figure 9-43 shows the console window with the message that a discount is applicable as 20 is greater than 10 OR 50 is greater than 40. In this case both are TRUE, which equates to TRUE.

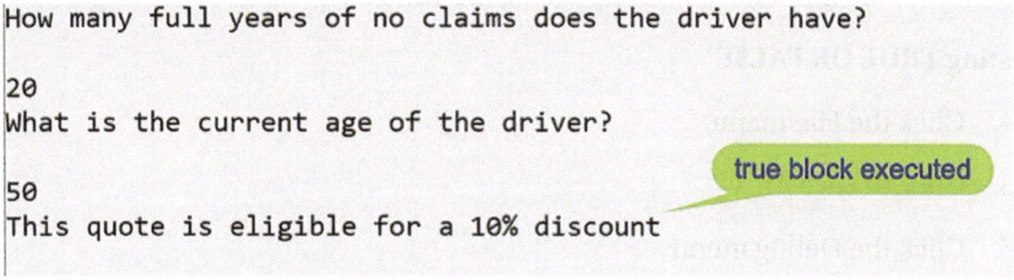

```
How many full years of no claims does the driver have?

20
What is the current age of the driver?

                                               true block executed
50
This quote is eligible for a 10% discount
```

Figure 9-43.   *True section of if-else executed*

23.   Press the Enter key to close the console window.

Testing FALSE OR TRUE

24.   Click the File menu.

25. Choose Save All.

26. Click the Debug menu.

27. Choose Start Without Debugging.

28. Click in the console window.

29. Type 10 as the number of years of no claims.

30. Press the Enter key on the keyboard.

31. Type 50 as the current age of the driver.

32. Press the Enter key on the keyboard.

Figure 9-44 shows the console window with the message that a discount is applicable as 10 is not greater than 10 (FALSE) OR 50 is greater than 40 (TRUE). In this case we have FALSE OR TRUE, which equates to TRUE.

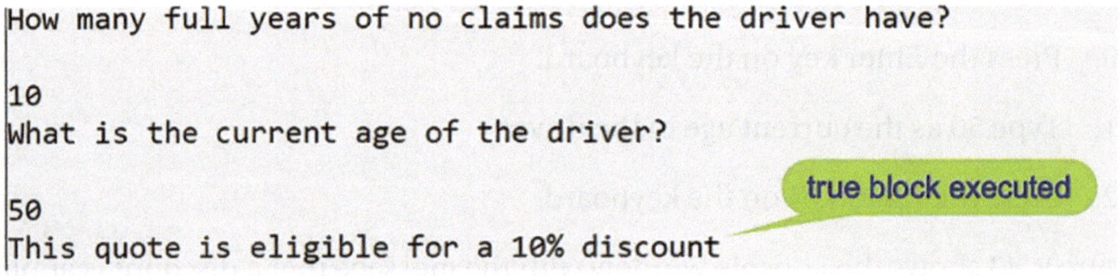

```
How many full years of no claims does the driver have?

10
What is the current age of the driver?
                                                    true block executed
50
This quote is eligible for a 10% discount
```

Figure 9-44. *True section of if-else executed*

33. Press the Enter key to close the console window.

Testing TRUE OR FALSE

34. Click the File menu.

35. Choose Save All.

36. Click the Debug menu.

37. Choose Start Without Debugging.

38. Click in the console window.

39. Type 20 as the number of years of no claims.

40. Press the Enter key on the keyboard.

41.   Type 30 as the current age of the driver.

42.   Press the Enter key on the keyboard.

Figure 9-45 shows the console window with the message that a discount is applicable as 20 is greater than 10 (TRUE) OR 30 is not greater than 40 (FALSE). In this case we have TRUE OR FALSE, which equates to TRUE.

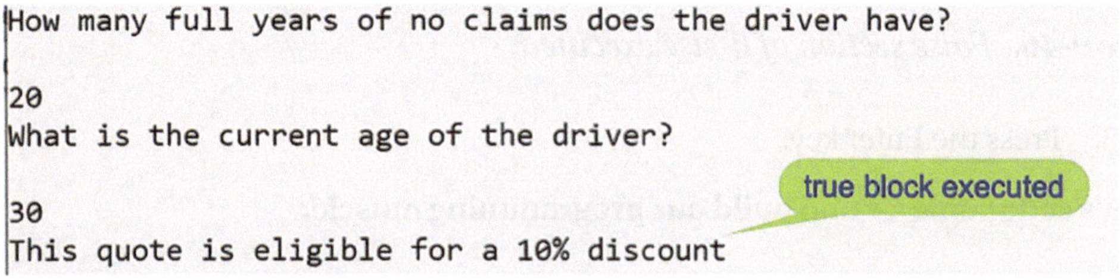

```
How many full years of no claims does the driver have?

20
What is the current age of the driver?
                                                    true block executed
30
This quote is eligible for a 10% discount
```

Figure 9-45. *True section of if-else executed*

43.   Press the Enter key to close the console window.

Testing FALSE OR FALSE

44.   Click the File menu.

45.   Choose Save All.

46.   Click the Debug menu.

47.   Choose Start Without Debugging.

48.   Click in the console window.

49.   Type 10 as the number of years of no claims.

50.   Press the Enter key on the keyboard.

51.   Type 30 as the current age of the driver.

52.   Press the Enter key on the keyboard.

Figure 9-46 shows the console window with the message that a discount is not applicable as 10 is not greater than 10 (FALSE) OR 30 is not greater than 40 (FALSE). In this case we have FALSE OR FALSE, which equates as FALSE.

```
How many full years of no claims does the driver have?

10
What is the current age of the driver?

30
This quote is ineligible for a discount
```

false block executed

Figure 9-46. *False section of if-else executed*

53. Press the Enter key.

Let's code some C# and build our programming muscle.

Using the NOT Operator

1. Right-click the Chapter9 project.

2. Choose Add.

3. Choose Class.

4. Name the class SelectionNOT.cs.

5. Click the Add button.

6. Create a Main() method within the class, as this was not produced automatically, and delete the unwanted imports.

Remember the shortcut to create the Main() method is to type svm and then press the Tab key twice. Now we need to set this class as the startup class.

7. Right-click the Chapter9 project in the Solution Explorer panel.

8. Choose Properties from the pop-up menu.

9. Choose the SelectionNOT class in the Startup object drop-down list.

10. Close the Properties window.

11. Open the SelectionOR file and copy the code within the Main() method.

12. In the Main() method of the SelectionNOT file, paste the copied code.

Now we will amend the code to use the logical operator NOT. We will

- Change the || to && (change the OR to an AND).

- Add brackets around the expression.

- Add the !, NOT, in front of the brackets.

- Leave the comments the same.

The if (!(yearsOfNoClaims > 10 && ageOfDriver > 40)) code line means we are checking if the number of years of no claims is greater than 10 AND if the age of the driver is greater than 40:

- If these are both true, the expression in the brackets equates to true but we negate it (!) to false, and we do not execute the code in the if block.

- If one of these is false, the expression in the brackets equates to false but we negate it (!) to true, and we execute the code in the if block.

- If these are both false, the expression in the brackets equates to false but we negate it (!) to true, and we execute the code in the if block.

We will now change to an **AND** expression, add an extra set of brackets () around it, and put a !, NOT, before the new brackets. We will leave the comments as they are.

13. Amend the code, as in Listing 9-30.

Listing 9-30. Use the NOT (!) operator

```
if (!(yearsOfNoClaims > 10 && ageOfDriver > 40))
{
  /*
    This block of code will be executed if one
    parts of the condition are TRUE
  */
  Console.WriteLine("This quote is eligible for a 10% discount");
} // End of true part
```

Testing TRUE AND TRUE

14.   Click the File menu.

15.   Choose Save All.

16.   Click the Debug menu.

17.   Choose Start Without Debugging.

18.   Click in the console window.

19.   Type 20 as the number of years of no claims.

20.   Press the Enter key on the keyboard.

21.   Type 50 as the current age of the driver.

22.   Press the Enter key on the keyboard.

Figure 9-47 shows the console window with the message that a discount is not applicable as we have an overall TRUE negated to a FALSE (20 is greater than 10 AND 50 is greater than 40, which means TRUE negated to FALSE, so no discount is applicable).

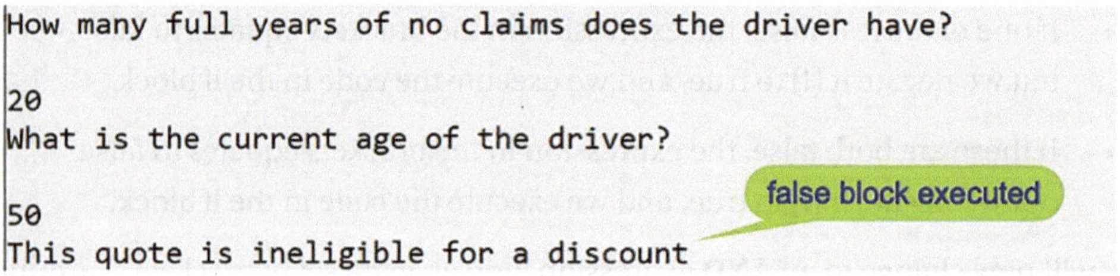

```
How many full years of no claims does the driver have?

20
What is the current age of the driver?
                                            false block executed
50
This quote is ineligible for a discount
```

Figure 9-47. *False section of if-else executed*

23.   Press the Enter key.

Testing FALSE AND TRUE
Start the program again.

24.   Click the Debug menu.

25.   Choose Start Without Debugging.

26.   Click in the console window.

27.   Type 10 as the number of years of no claims.

28.   Press the Enter key on the keyboard.

29.   Type 50 as the current age of the driver.

30.   Press the Enter key on the keyboard.

Figure 9-48 shows the console window with the message that a discount is applicable as we have an overall FALSE negated to a TRUE (10 is not greater than 10 AND 50 is greater than 40, which means FALSE negated to TRUE, so a discount is applicable).

```
How many full years of no claims does the driver have?

10
What is the current age of the driver?
                                                        true block executed
50
This quote is eligible for a 10% discount
```

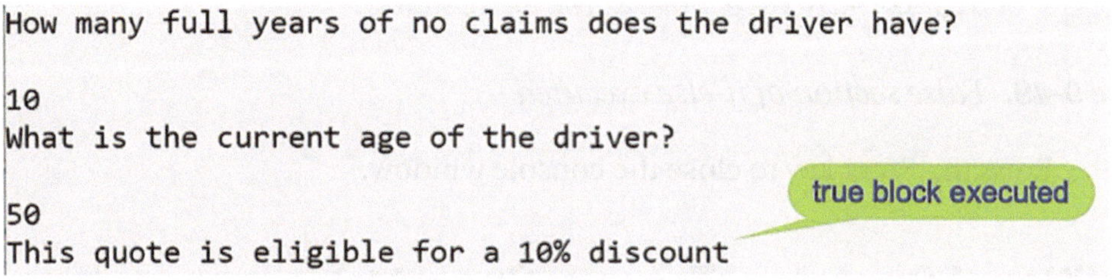

Figure 9-48. *False section of if-else executed*

31.   Press the Enter key to close the console window.

Testing TRUE AND FALSE

Start the program again.

32.   Click the Debug menu.

33.   Choose Start Without Debugging.

34.   Click in the console window.

35.   Type 20 as the number of years of no claims.

36.   Press the Enter key on the keyboard.

37.   Type 30 as the current age of the driver.

38.   Press the Enter key on the keyboard.

Figure 9-49 shows the console window with the message that a discount is applicable as we have an overall FALSE negated to a TRUE (20 is greater than 10 AND 30 is not greater than 40, which means FALSE negated to TRUE, so a discount is applicable).

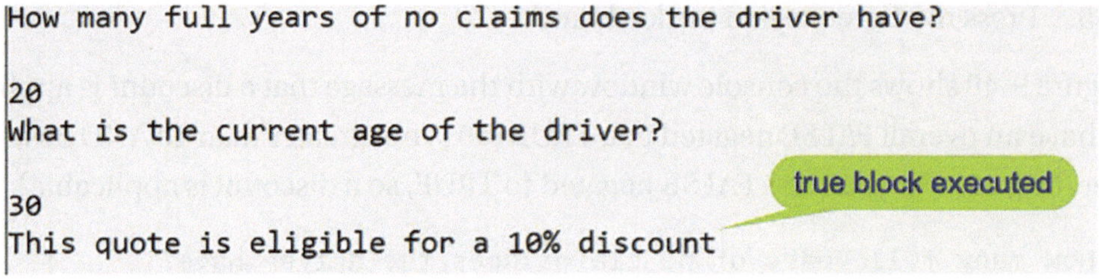

```
How many full years of no claims does the driver have?

20
What is the current age of the driver?

30
This quote is eligible for a 10% discount
```

true block executed

Figure 9-49. *False section of if-else executed*

39.   Press the Enter key to close the console window.

Conditional Operator (Ternary Operator)

Earlier, we used the if-else construct where there is one block of code executed if the condition is true and another block executed if the condition is false. The code we used is shown in Listing 9-31, with the comments removed.

Listing 9-31. if-else construct

```
if (yearsOfNoClaims > 10)
{
  Console.WriteLine("Years of no claims is more than 10");
}// End of true block of code in the if construct
else
{
  Console.WriteLine("Years of no claims is less than or " +
    "equal to 10");
} // End of false block of code in the if construct
```

However, there is another way to do the if-else construct, using the C# conditional operator, or **ternary** operator as it is also known. The ternary conditional operator will evaluate the Boolean expression and return either true or false. The syntax for the ternary conditional operator is

Condition ? First Expression : Second Expression

So analyzing this syntax, we will see that

- **Condition** is a "statement" that must evaluate to true or false.

- If the condition is **true,** the **First Expression** gets executed.

- If the condition is **false,** the **Second Expression** gets executed.

Looking at our if-else example, we could say

Condition is yearsOfNoClaims > 10

First Expression is Console.WriteLine("Years of no claims is more than 10");

Second Expression is Console.WriteLine("Years of no claims is less than or equal to 10");

If we follow this syntax, then our code could be written as

```
yearsOfNoClaims > 10 ? "Years of no claims is more than 10" :
                "Years of no claims is less than or equal to 10";
```

But let's see how we actually write it.

Let's code some C# and build our programming muscle.

1. Right-click the Chapter9 project.

2. Choose Add.

3. Choose Class.

4. Name the class Ternary.cs.

5. Click the Add button.

6. Create a Main() method within the class, as this was not produced automatically, and delete the unwanted imports.

Remember the shortcut to create the Main() method is to type svm and then press the Tab key twice. Now we need to set this class as the startup class.

7. Right-click the Chapter9 project in the Solution Explorer panel.

8. Choose Properties from the pop-up menu.

9. Choose the Ternary class in the Startup object drop-down list.

10. Close the Properties window.

Now we will amend the code to use the ternary conditional operator.

11. Amend the code as in Listing 9-32.

Listing 9-32. Ternary operator

```
namespace Chapter9
{
  internal class Ternary
  {
    static void Main(string[] args)
    {
    /*
    We will setup our variables that will be used in
    the quote application
    */
    int yearsOfNoClaims;

    /* Read the user input and convert it to an int */
    Console.WriteLine("How many full years of no claims" +
      " does the driver have?\n");
    yearsOfNoClaims = Convert.ToInt32(Console.ReadLine());

    // Assign the result of the ternary to a string variable
    string message = yearsOfNoClaims > 10 ?
              "Years of no claims is more than 10" :
              "Years of no claims is less than or equal to 10";

    // Display the result of the ternary condition
    Console.WriteLine(message);
    } // End of Main() method
  } // End of Ternary class
} // End of Chapter9 namespace
```

12. Click the File menu.

13. Choose Save All.

14.   Click the Debug menu.

15.   Choose Start Without Debugging.

16.   Click in the console window.

17.   Type 5 as the number of years of no claims.

18.   Press the Enter key on the keyboard.

Figure 9-50 shows the console window with the message for the FALSE block as 5 is not greater than 10.

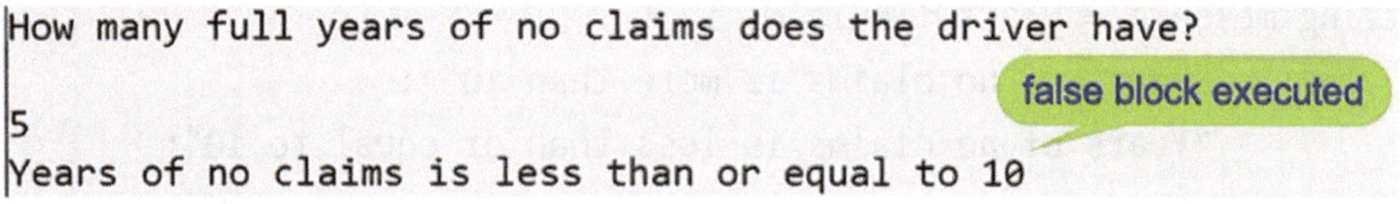

```
How many full years of no claims does the driver have?

5
Years of no claims is less than or equal to 10
```

false block executed

Figure 9-50. *False section of ternary executed*

19.   Press the Enter key to close the console window.
      Start the program again.

20.   Click the Debug menu.

21.   Choose Start Without Debugging.

22.   Click in the console window.

23.   Type 15 as the number of years of no claims.

24.   Press the Enter key on the keyboard.

Figure 9-51 shows the console window with the message for the TRUE block as 15 is greater than 10.

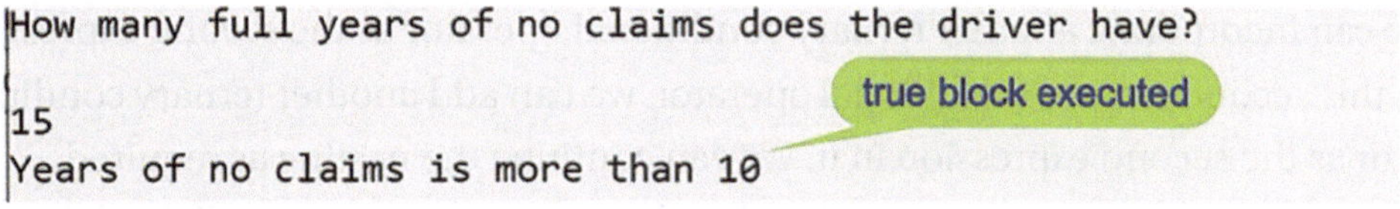

```
How many full years of no claims does the driver have?

15
Years of no claims is more than 10
```

true block executed

Figure 9-51. *True section of ternary executed*

25.   Press the Enter key to close the console window.

Code Analysis

We said earlier

If we follow this syntax, then our code could be written as

yearsOfNoClaims > 10 ? "Years of no claims is more than 10" : "Years of no claims is less than or equal to 10";

But we have written the code using an assignment as in Listing 9-33.

Listing 9-33. Ternary operator

```
// Assign the result of the ternary to a string variable
string message = yearsOfNoClaims > 10 ?
          "Years of no claims is more than 10" :
          "Years of no claims is less than or equal to 10";
```

Not putting the assignment causes the error message as shown in Figure 9-52.

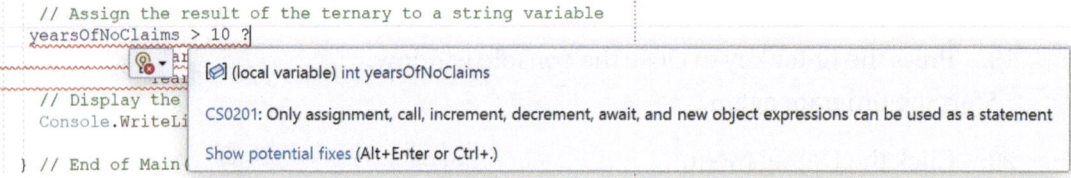

Figure 9-52. *Ternary error message when not assigned*

So our quote was slightly inaccurate as we need to assign the ternary to a value.

Nested Ternary Conditional Operator

We saw that the ternary conditional operator syntax was

Condition ? First Expression : Second Expression

We can incorporate another ternary conditional operator as the second expression, and in this second ternary conditional operator, we can add another ternary conditional operator as the second expression in it. We can continue the nesting as required. Warning: This can get complex to read and understand, as we are essentially doing an if-elseif-elseif and so on.

We will now amend the code, as in Listing 9-34, to do the same thing as our if else if example but using the ternary operator.

26.   Amend the code as in Listing 9-34.

Listing 9-34. Ternary operator

```
// Assign the result of the ternary to a string variable
string message = yearsOfNoClaims > 10 ?
        "Years of no claims is more than 10" :
        "Years of no claims is less than or equal to 10";

// Display the result of the ternary condition
Console.WriteLine(message);

// Assign the result of the ternary to a string variable
string newMessage = yearsOfNoClaims > 10 ?
        "Years of no claims is more than 10" :
        yearsOfNoClaims > 8 ?
        "Years of no claims is either 9 or 10" :
        yearsOfNoClaims > 6 ?
        "Years of no claims is either 7 or 8" :
        yearsOfNoClaims > 4 ?
        "Years of no claims is either 5 or 6" :
        yearsOfNoClaims > 2 ?
        "Years of no claims is either 3 or 4" :
        "Years of no claims is 2, 1, 0 \n " +
        "or indeed a negative number of years \n " +
        "because of a penalty being enforced on our policy";

    // Display the result of the new ternary condition
    Console.WriteLine(newMessage);
    } // End of Main() method
  } // End of Ternary class
} // End of Chapter9 namespace
```

Before we run the code, let us look at the nested ternary conditional operator in a more readable form:

yearsOfNoClaims > 10 ? **"Years of no claims is more than 10"** :

yearsOfNoClaims > 8 ? **"Years of no claims is either 9 or 10"** :

yearsOfNoClaims > 6 ? "**Years of no claims is either 7 or 8**" :

yearsOfNoClaims > 4 ? "**Years of no claims is either 5 or 6**" :

yearsOfNoClaims > 2 ? **"Years of no claims is either 3 or 4"**: **"Years of no claims is 2, 1, 0 \n or indeed a negative number of years \n because of a penalty being enforced on our policy"**;

- The second expression of the first ternary is ternary starting with yearsOfNoClaims > 8.

- The second expression of the second ternary is ternary starting with yearsOfNoClaims > 6.

- The second expression of the third ternary is ternary starting with yearsOfNoClaims > 4.

- The second expression of the fourth ternary is ternary starting with yearsOfNoClaims > 2.

27.   Click the File menu.

28.   Choose Save All.

29.   Click the Debug menu.

  The console window will appear and ask the question. Now we can try the values 10, 8, 6, 4, and 2, which will test the five ternary sections. We will start with 10.

30.   Type 10 as the number of years of no claims.

31.   Press the Enter key on the keyboard.

Figure 9-53 shows the console window, and we can see that the false part of the first ternary section has executed and there is another ternary and the true section of this ternary has been executed:

yearsOfNoClaims > 8 ? "Years of no claims is either 9 or 10"

```
How many full years of no claims does the driver have?
                                          1st nested ternary true executed
10
Years of no claims is less than or equal to 10
Years of no claims is either 9 or 10
```

Figure 9-53. *Nested ternary – first part executed*

32. Press the Enter key to close the console window.

Start the program again.

33. Click the Debug menu.

34. Choose Start Without Debugging.

35. Type 8 and press the Enter key.

The console window will appear, as shown in Figure 9-54, and we can see that the false part of the first ternary section has executed, there is another ternary and the false section of this ternary has been executed, and there is another ternary and the true section of this has been executed:

yearsOfNoClaims > 6 ? "Years of no claims is either 7 or 8"

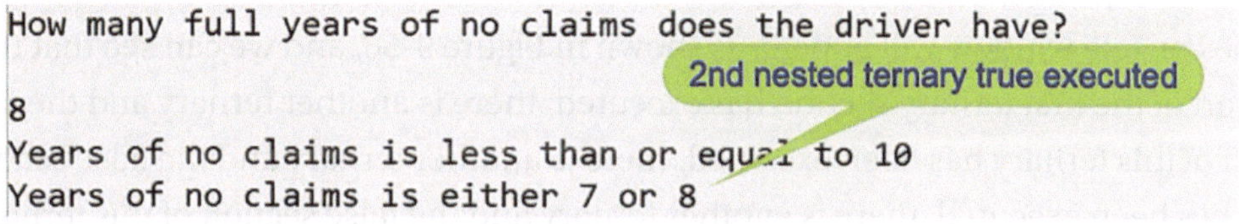

Figure 9-54. *Nested ternary – second part executed*

36. Press the Enter key to close the console window.

Start the program again.

37. Click the Debug menu.

38. Choose Start Without Debugging.

39. Type 6 and press the Enter key.

The console window will appear, as shown in Figure 9-55, and we can see that the false part of the first ternary section has executed, there is another ternary and the false section of this ternary has been executed, there is another ternary and the false section of this has been executed, and there is another ternary and the true section of this ternary has been executed:

yearsOfNoClaims > 4 ? "Years of no claims is either 5 or 6" :

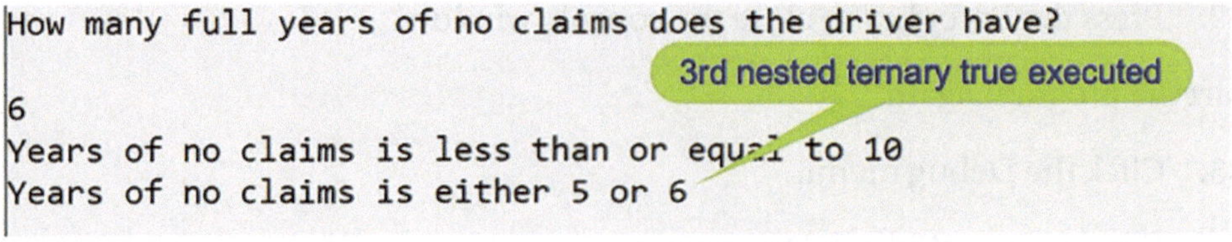

```
How many full years of no claims does the driver have?

6
Years of no claims is less than or equal to 10
Years of no claims is either 5 or 6
```
3rd nested ternary true executed

***Figure 9-55.** Nested ternary – third part executed*

40. Press the Enter key to close the console window.

Start the program again.

41. Click the Debug menu.

42. Choose Start Without Debugging.

43. Type 4 and press the Enter key.

The console window will appear, as shown in Figure 9-56, and we can see that the false part of the first ternary section has executed, there is another ternary and the false section of this ternary has been executed, there is another ternary and the false section of this has been executed, there is another ternary and the false section of this ternary has been executed, and there is another ternary and the true section of this ternary has been executed:

yearsOfNoClaims > 2 ? "Years of no claims is either 3 or 4":

```
How many full years of no claims does the driver have?

4
Years of no claims is less than or equal to 10
Years of no claims is either 3 or 4
```
4th nested ternary true executed

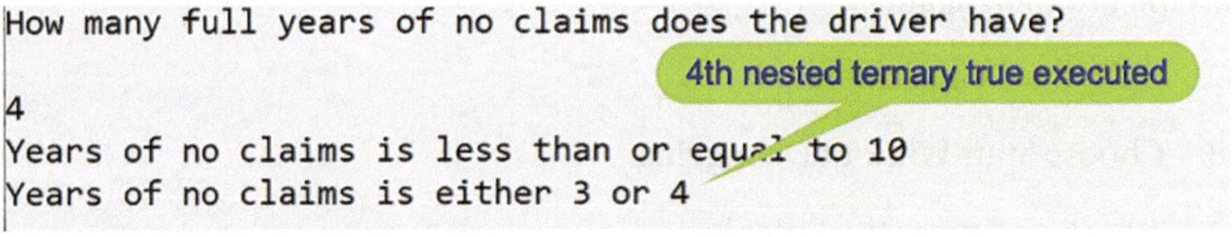

***Figure 9-56.** Nested ternary – fourth part executed*

44. Press the Enter key to close the console window.

Start the program again.

45. Click the Debug menu.

46. Choose Start Without Debugging.

47.   Type 2 and press the Enter key.

The console window will appear as shown in Figure 9-57 and we can see that the final ternary false section has been executed.

```
How many full years of no claims does the driver have?

2                          5th nested ternary true executed
Years of no claims is less than or equal to 10
Years of no claims is 2, 1, 0
 or indeed a negative number of years
 because of a penalty being enforced on our policy
```

Figure 9-57. *Nested ternary – fifth part executed*

48.   Press the Enter key to close the console window.

Whoa, whoa, let us catch our breath after that nested ternary code block. The code works and gives us the same results as the if else if code block. However, are we thinking that this ternary code looks confusing compared with the if else if code block? Remember we talked about clean code, so if we see this as confusing and not as readable as the if else if code block, we should not use it. **We have choice in how we write our code, but we have a responsibility to make the code readable and easy to maintain.**

Chapter Summary

In this chapter we have learned about a very important programming concept called selection and have seen that

- Selection in C# can have different formats, including

  The **if** construct

  The **if-else** construct

  The **if else if** construct

  The **switch** construct and the case label

  Ternary conditional operator

- The case construct can use numeric or string data types.

- The case label is case sensitive.

- the ternary conditional operator can replace the if else construct

- There is a different way to display data to the console with the use of "placeholders" {}.

- C# has a string handling class with useful methods, one of which is the ToUpper() method.

- We can have more than one class in a package.

We are making great progress in our programming of C# applications and we should be proud of our achievements. In finishing this chapter and increasing our knowledge, we are advancing to our target.

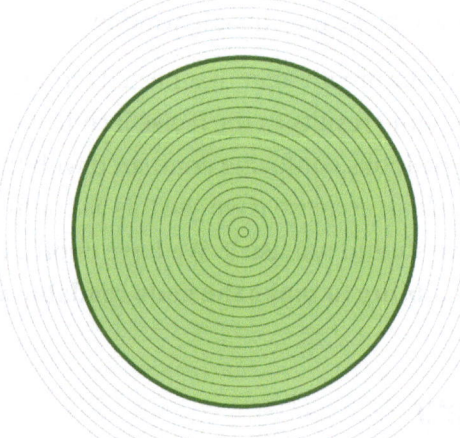

Our target is getting closer

CHAPTER 10

Iteration

Iteration and Loops

We learned in Chapter 9 that selection is a particularly important programming concept in all programming languages. To use selection in our C# code, we have several construct options, and the best construct option to choose will depend on the particular task the code has to perform. The different construct options for selection are the if construct, the if-else construct, the if else if construct, and the switch construct with its case label. The switch construct can use numeric or string data types, and when we use strings, it is based on a case-sensitive comparison. To help in using strings with the switch construct, we can make use of the ToUpper() or ToLower() method of the String class. We also learned that displaying data to the console could be achieved using "placeholders," {}, within the WriteLine() method.

In terms of the project structure, we learned that not only can we have multiple projects but within a project we can have multiple classes, each needing to have a unique name, but only one of the classes can be the startup class with the Main() method.

Introduction to Iteration

Many of the things we do in everyday life require iteration. Think about when we wish to make a number of slices of toast in our toaster. The instructions could be as follows:

- Take a slice of bread from the recyclable packaging.

- Put the slice of bread in the toaster.

- Pull the toaster lever down to start the heating process.

- When the toast pops up, remove the slice of toast from the toaster.

- Put the slice of toast on a plate.

© Gerard Byrne 2022
G. Byrne, *Target C#*, https://doi.org/10.1007/978-1-4842-8619-7_10

- **Repeat** the process the required number of times.

Think about when we are brushing our teeth – we move the toothbrush left and right, up and down, the required number of times. The movements show that we **repeat** specific actions. Even thinking about how often we should be cleaning our teeth, we should be **repeating** the process at least twice **every** day.

The concept of iteration is important in programming and the C# language offers different structures to perform iteration. In this chapter we will look at the C# iteration constructs, also called loops, including those listed in Table 10-1.

Table 10-1. *Iteration constructs and concepts*

C# iteration constructs (loops)	
The **for** loop	The **do** loop
The **while** loop	The **foreach** loop

The principle of iteration is to repeat a sequence of C# instructions, a number of times. The sequence is a block of code. The number of times the iteration repeats is determined by the type of loop structure, as we will see when we code each type of loop structure. We can also change how the iteration acts by using the break or continue statement, and we will look at these in our code examples.

For Loop

First, we will look at the **for loop** structure, which allows us to repeat a sequence of instructions a set number of times. The for statement repeats the block of code, a number of lines of code, until a Boolean expression evaluates to true.

The format of the for loop is shown in the following:

```
for(<Start value>; <Condition>; <increment value>)
{
    <statements>
}
```

There are three parts to the for construct:

- Start value – Which will be of data type int.

- Condition – Which will equate to true or false.

- Increment – Which will change the start value by a specified amount, which could be a positive value or a negative value. Using a positive value will mean an increment, while using a negative value will mean a decrement, a negative increment if we wish to say that

Example:

```
for (int counter = 0; counter < 2; counter++)
{
     block of code statements
}
```

In this example code

- A local variable called **counter** is set up inside the brackets ().

- The counter **variable** will be used as the loop counter and helps to decide how many times the block of code is executed.

- The variable is created as an integer and set to have an **initial value of 0**, but 0 does not have to be the starting point. **This is the first part of the for loop, the start value.**

- The loop counter is **compared** with the value 2, and if it is less than 2, the execution of the block of code continues. **This is the second part of the for loop, the condition.**

- The loop counter is **incremented**, increased, by 1. **This is the third part of the for loop, the increment – we could also decrement.**

- Each section is separated by a semicolon ;.

- All of this is enclosed in the brackets ().

- The block of code to be executed the required number of times is enclosed between open and close curly braces {}.

If required, the for construct can be exited early, by using the keyword **break,** and we can move to the next iteration in the loop by using the keyword **continue**.
Note:

If required, the for construct can be exited early, by using the keyword **return** *or indeed by using the less favored keyword* **goto**.

Add a new project to hold the code for this chapter

1. Right-click the solution CoreCSharp.

2. Choose Add.

3. Choose New Project.

4. Choose Console App from the listed templates that appear.

5. Click the Next button.

6. Name the project Chapter10 and leave it in the same location.

7. Click the Next button.

8. Choose the framework to be used, which in our projects will be .NET 6.0 or higher.

9. Click the Create button.

Now we should see the Chapter10 project within the solution called CoreCSharp.

10. Right-click the Chapter10 project in the Solution Explorer panel.

11. Click the Set as Startup Project option.

Notice how the Chapter10 project name has been made to have bold text, indicating that it is the new startup project and that it is the Program.cs file within it that will be executed when we run the debugging.

12. Right-click the Program.cs file in the Solution Explorer window.

13. Choose Rename.

14. Change the name to Iteration.cs.

15. Press the Enter key.

16. Double-click the Iteration.cs file to open it in the editor window.

Now we can set up the code structure with a namespace, and inside it will be the Iteration class, and inside the class will be the Main() method. The shortcut for creating the Main() method is to type svm and press the Tab key twice.

17. In the editor window, add the code in Listing 10-1.

Listing 10-1. Class template with the Main() method

```
namespace Chapter10
{
  internal class Iteration
  {
    static void Main(string[] args)
    {
    } // End of Main() method
  } // End of Iteration class
} // End of Chapter10 namespace
```

When a vehicle is involved in an accident and requires repair, it could go to a repair center that has been nominated by the insurance company. When the repairs are completed, the repair center will recoup their costs from the insurance company. We will now develop a program that will ask the user from the repair shop to enter the details required by the insurance company. The details will be

- The repair shop unique id (string)

- The vehicle insurance policy number (string)

- The claim amount (double)

- The date of the claim (string)

Now we will add the variables that will be used in our code. In the following code, there are detailed comments to help us get a full understanding of the code.

Let's code some C# and build our programming muscle.

18. Amend the code to add the variables we will require as in Listing 10-2.

Listing 10-2. Add the variables

```
using System;

namespace Chapter10
{
  internal class Iteration
  {
```

```
    static void Main(string[] args)
    {
      /*
      Set up the variables to be used in the quote application
      The details will be:
          - the repair shop unique id              (string)
          - the vehicle insurance policy number    (string)
          - the claim amount and                   (double)
          - the date of the claim                  (string)
      */
      string repairShopID;
      string vehiclePolicyNumber;
      string claimDate;
      double claimAmount;

    } // End of Main() method
  } // End of Iteration class
} // End of Chapter10 namespace
```

19. Amend the code, as in Listing 10-3, to include a for construct that will iterate twice.

Listing 10-3. Add the for loop

```
    string repairShopID;
    string vehiclePolicyNumber;
    string claimDate;
    double claimAmount;

    for(int claimsCounter = 0; claimsCounter < 2; claimsCounter++)
    {
    } // End of for loop

  } // End of Main() method
```

We will now ask the user to input the repair shop id, accept the input, keep it as a string, and assign the value to the variable called repairShopID.

20.   Amend the code, as in Listing 10-4.

Listing 10-4. Ask for the repair shop id and assign it to a variable

```
for(int claimsCounter = 0;claimsCounter < 2;claimsCounter++)
{
 /*
 Read the user input for the repair shop id and
 keep it as a string
 */
 Console.WriteLine("What is your repair shop id?\n");
 repairShopID = Console.ReadLine();

} // End of for loop

} // End of Main() method
```

We will now ask the user to input the vehicle policy number, accept the input, keep it as a string, and assign the value to the vehiclePolicyNumber variable.

21.   Amend the code, as in Listing 10-5.

Listing 10-5. Ask for the policy number and assign it to a variable

```
Console.WriteLine("What is your repair shop id?\n");
repairShopID = Console.ReadLine();

/*
Read the user input for the vehicle policy number
and keep it as a string
*/
Console.WriteLine("What is the vehicle policy number?\n");
vehiclePolicyNumber = Console.ReadLine();
} // End of for loop
```

We will now ask the user to input the repair amount, accept the input, convert it to a double, and assign the value to the variable called claimAmount.

22.   Amend the code, as in Listing 10-6.

Listing 10-6. Ask for the amount being claimed and assign it to a variable

```
vehiclePolicyNumber = Console.ReadLine();

/*
Read the user input for the repair amount and
convert it to a double
*/
Console.WriteLine("What is the amount being claimed" +
  " for the repair?\n");
claimAmount = Convert.ToDouble(Console.ReadLine());

} // End of for loop
```

We will now ask the user to input the repair date, accept the input, keep it as a string, and assign the value to the variable called claimDate, which is of type string.

23.   Amend the code, as in Listing 10-7.

Listing 10-7. Ask for the repair date and assign it to a variable

```
Console.WriteLine("What is the amount being claimed" +
  " for the repair?\n");
claimAmount = Convert.ToDouble(Console.ReadLine());

/*
Read the user input for the repair date
*/
Console.WriteLine("What was the date of the repair?\n");
claimDate = Console.ReadLine();

} // End of for loop
```

We will now display the details that have been entered by the user. The displaying of the details will occur at the end of each iteration, and therefore we will have two displays.

24.   Amend the code, as in Listing 10-8.

Listing 10-8. Display the details as entered by the user

```
Console.WriteLine("What was the date of the repair?\n");
claimDate = Console.ReadLine();

Console.WriteLine("The details entered for repair "
  + (claimsCounter + 1) + " are");
Console.WriteLine("Repair shop id:\t" + repairShopID);
Console.WriteLine("Policy number:\t" +vehiclePolicyNumber);
Console.WriteLine("Claim amount:\t" + claimAmount);
Console.WriteLine("Claim date:\t" + claimDate);

} // End of for loop
```

When the code is executed, the user will be asked to input two sets of details:

- The counter will start at 0 and the block of code is executed.

- Then the counter is incremented to 1 and the block of code is executed.

- When it is incremented to 2, it will be checked against the comparator (claimsCounter < 2); and as it is not less than 2, the loop will be exited.

25. Click the File menu.

26. Choose Save All.

27. Click the Debug menu.

28. Choose Start Without Debugging.

29. Click in the console window.

The console window will appear and ask the user to input the repair shop id.

30. Type RS000001 and press the Enter key.

The console will now ask the user to input the vehicle policy number.

31. Type VP000001 and press the Enter key.

The console will now ask the user to input the claim amount.

32. Type 1999.99 and press the Enter key.

The console will now ask the user to input the date of the repair

33.   Type 2021/10/01 and press the Enter key.

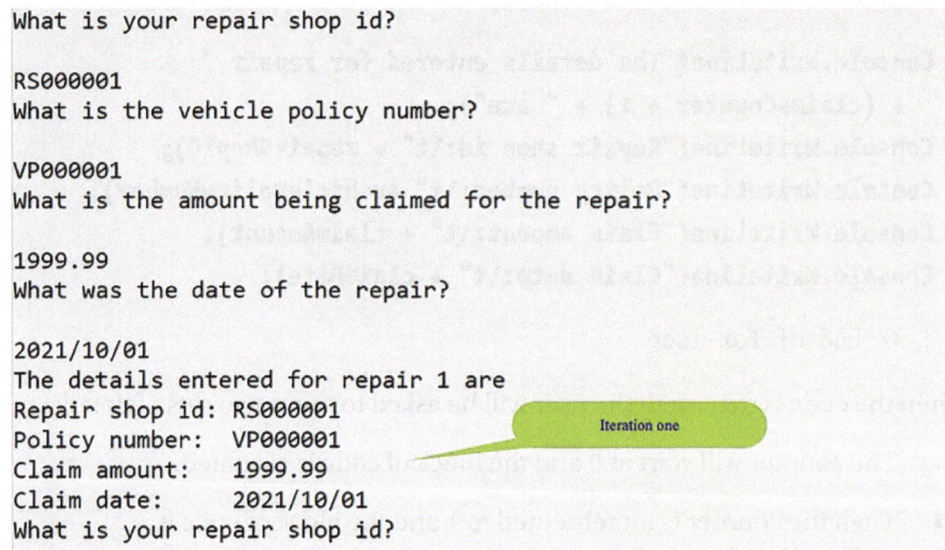

```
What is your repair shop id?

RS000001
What is the vehicle policy number?

VP000001
What is the amount being claimed for the repair?

1999.99
What was the date of the repair?

2021/10/01
The details entered for repair 1 are
Repair shop id: RS000001
Policy number:  VP000001          Iteration one
Claim amount:   1999.99
Claim date:     2021/10/01
What is your repair shop id?
```

Figure 10-1. *Iteration 1*

Iteration 1 is now completed; the block of code has been executed, as shown in Figure 10-1. The claims counter will now be incremented by 1 and become a 1. The comparison is made to see if the claims counter value is less than 2, and as it is, the iterations continue.

The console window will now ask the user to input the repair shop id.

34.   Type RS000001 and press the Enter key.

The console will now ask the user to input the vehicle policy number.

35.   Type VP001234 and press the Enter key.

The console will now ask the user to input the claim amount.

36.   Type 2500.99 and press the Enter key.

The console will now ask the user to input the date of the repair.

37.   Type 2021/10/01 and press the Enter key.

```
The details entered for repair 2 are
Repair shop id: RS000001
Policy number:  VP001234                    Iteration two
Claim amount:   2500.99
Claim date:     2021/10/01
```

Figure 10-2. *Iteration 2*

Iteration 2 is now completed; the block of code has been executed for the second time, as shown in Figure 10-2. The claims counter will now be incremented by 1 and become a 2. The comparison is made to see if the claims counter value is less than 2, and as it is not, the iterations will end. The code will now move to the next line, which waits for the user to press a key.

38.   Press any key to close the console window.

Thinking about the code applications we have completed, we should see that all the details we entered are lost. In the next chapter, we will look at storing the details in an array, so they will be available for the lifetime of the running application, but in this chapter, we are concentrating on iterations.

The iteration works fine, but we could improve the situation by adhering to the principle of writing clean and maintainable code:

- In the loop we have used a **hard-coded value** in the comparator, that is, the 2.

- In this case 2 is known as a "**magic number**," as it just appears.

- Ideally, we need to set up a constant that will store the value for the number of times that the loop is to be executed.

- We will now amend the code in two stages, just to show clearly the process of developing code that is more maintainable.

The first stage will be to

- Set up a constant called **NumberOfClaimsBeingMade** of data type int.

- Assign the value 2 to the variable.

- Remove the hard-coded 2 from the loop and replace it with the variable NumberOfClaimsBeingMade.

39. Amend the code, as in Listing 10-9, to implement variable declaration and value assignment.

Listing 10-9. Set up a variable and assign it a value

```
double claimAmount;

/*
Set up a constant called NumberOfClaimsBeingMade
of data type int and assign the variable the value 2
*/
const int NumberOfClaimsBeingMade = 2;

for(int claimsCounter = 0;claimsCounter < 2;claimsCounter++)
{
  /*
  Read the user input for the repair shop id and
  keep it as a string
  */
  Console.WriteLine("What is your repair shop id?\n");
  repairShopID = Console.ReadLine();
```

40. Click the File menu.

41. Choose Save All.

42. Amend the code, as in Listing 10-10, to remove the hard-coded number, the magic number, from the for loop and replace it with the variable name.

Listing 10-10. Remove the magic number

```
/*
Set up a constant called NumberOfClaimsBeingMade
of data type int and assign the constant the value 2
*/
const int NumberOfClaimsBeingMade = 2;
```

```
for(int claimsCounter = 0;claimsCounter <
                NumberOfClaimsBeingMade; claimsCounter++)
{
  /*
  Read the user input for the repair shop id and
  keep it as a string
  */
  Console.WriteLine("What is your repair shop id?\n");
  repairShopID = Console.ReadLine();
```

43. Click the File menu.

44. Choose Save All.

If we ran the program, we would see nothing has changed but our code is a little better, as we have used a constant in the loop. However, the code will still have to be amended if the user is required to enter a different number of claims than 2. Our code can be improved by removing the assigned value of 2 and replacing it with a value entered by the user. We will need to make the constant into a variable to do this. This will mean the code is written once and does not need to be changed, as the control lies with the value typed in by the user. Writing highly maintainable code is very important.

The second stage will therefore be to

- Ask the user to input the number of claims they wish to make.

- Read the value from the console.

- Assign the converted value to the **variable** numberOfClaimsBeingMade.

45. Amend the code, as in Listing 10-11, to implement these changes. Start with removing the initial value of 2 and deleting the const keyword and then change the PascalCase to camelCase for the variable. Remember to change the case of the variable inside the brackets of the for (int claimsCounter = 0; claimsCounter < numberOfClaimsBeingMade; claimsCounter++).

Listing 10-11. Remove the initial value

```
double claimAmount;

/*
Set up a variable called numberOfClaimsBeingMade
of data type int and assign the variable the value 2
*/
int numberOfClaimsBeingMade;
```

46. Amend the code, as in Listing 10-12, to ask the user to input the number of claims.

Listing 10-12. Input the number of claims

```
int numberOfClaimsBeingMade;

/*
Read the user input for the number of claims being
made and convert the string value to an integer data type
*/
Console.WriteLine("How many claims are being made?\n");
numberOfClaimsBeingMade=Convert.ToInt32(Console.ReadLine());

/*
As we are using a variable in the loop our code is
flexible and can be used for any number of claims.
An ideal situation and good code.
*/
```

47. Click the File menu.

48. Choose Save All.

49. Click the Debug menu.

50. Choose Start Without Debugging.

51. Click in the Console window.

The console window will appear and ask the user how many claims they wish to make.

52.   Type 2 and press the Enter key.

The console window will appear and ask the user to input the repair shop id.

53.   Type RS000001 and press the Enter key.

The console will now ask the user to input the vehicle policy number.

54.   Type VP000001 and press the Enter key.

The console will now ask the user to input the claim amount.

55.   Type 1999.99 and press the Enter key.

The console will now ask the user to input the date of the repair

56.   Type 2021/10/01 and press the Enter key.

```
How many claims are being made?

2
What is your repair shop id?

RS000001
What is the vehicle policy number?

VP000001
What is the amount being claimed for the repair?

1999.99
What was the date of the repair?

2021/10/01
The details entered for repair 1 are
Repair shop id: RS000001                          Iteration one
Policy number:  VP000001
Claim amount:   1999.99
Claim date:     2021/10/01
What is your repair shop id?
```

Figure 10-3. *Iteration 1 having used cleaner code*

Iteration 1 is now completed as shown in Figure 10-3. The claims counter will now be incremented by 1 and become a 1. The comparison is made to see if the claims counter value is less than 2, and as it is, the iterations continue.

The console window will now ask the user to input the repair shop id.

57.   Type RS000001 and press the Enter key.

The console will now ask the user to input the vehicle policy number.

58.   Type VP001234 and press the Enter key.

The console will now ask the user to input the claim amount.

59.   Type 2500.99 and press the Enter key.

The console will now ask the user to input the date of the repair

60.   Type 2021/10/01 and press the Enter key.

```
The details entered for repair 2 are
Repair shop id: RS000001
Policy number:  VP001234                    Iteration two
Claim amount:   2500.99
Claim date:     2021/10/01
```

Figure 10-4. *Iteration 2 having used cleaner code*

Iteration 2 is now completed; the block of code has been executed for the second time, as shown in Figure 10-4. The claims counter will now be incremented by 1 and become a 2. The comparison is made to see if the claims counter value is less than 2, and as it is not, the iterations will end. The code will now move to the next line, which waits for the user to press a key.

61.   Press any key to close the console window.

Wow! Very good! We have a nice little application handling multiple claims from any user, and we are not hard-coding values and using magic numbers.

Break Statement

Control of the for loop is determined by the three sections shown in Figure 10-5.

```
        section 1            section 2            section 3

for(<Start value>; <Condition>; <increment value>)

{

<statements>

 }
```

Figure 10-5. *The three sections of a for loop*

- The first section determines the start value of the counter.

- The second section determines when the loop has completed enough iterations.

- The third section increments the counter.

However, the control may be modified by using the **break** statement, which forces a loop to exit immediately.

We will create a variable called maximumNumberOfClaims and assign it the initial value of 1. This means that for this example the user will now be able to enter only one claim – it's just an example. Then we will check inside the loop if the counter has reached the value set for the maximumNumberOfClaims, that is, 1. If the value of the counter has reached 1, the loop will be exited.

1. Amend the code, as in Listing 10-13, by adding the new variable called maximumNumberOfClaims.

Listing 10-13. Create the variable maximumNumberOfClaims

```
/*
Set up a variable called numberOfClaimsBeingMade
of data type int and assign the variable the value 2
*/
int numberOfClaimsBeingMade;

int maximumNumberOfClaims = 1;
```

2. Amend the code, as in Listing 10-14, to implement this break
    statement within an if selection block.

Listing 10-14. Using an if construct with a break statement

```
for (int claimsCounter = 0;claimsCounter <
                numberOfClaimsBeingMade; claimsCounter++)
{
  /*
  We will use the if statement to perform a boolean test
  and if the test produces a true value we will break out
  of the loop. There is no else part to the if statement
  so if the boolean test produces a false value the loop
  simply continues executing the block of code
  */
    if (claimsCounter == maximumNumberOfClaims)
    {
    /*
    We have reached the maximum number of claims allowed
    in one session so we will break out of the loop early
    */
      Console.WriteLine("Breaking out of the loop?\n");
      break;
    } // End of if section
  /*
  Read the user input for the repair shop id and
  keep it as a string
  */
  Console.WriteLine("What is your repair shop id?\n");
  repairShopID = Console.ReadLine();
```

3. Amend the code, as in Listing 10-15, to display a message that the
    application has finished.

Listing 10-15. Display a message showing that the application has ended

```
    } // End of for loop

    Console.WriteLine("End of program\n");
  } // End of Main() method
 } // End of Iteration class
} // End of Chapter10 namespace
```

4. Click the File menu.

5. Choose Save All.

6. Click the Debug menu.

7. Choose Start Without Debugging.

The console window will appear, as shown in Figure 10-6, and ask the user how many claims they wish to make. Remember we have set a variable that will stop the iteration when the counter is 1, so the number entered here will be irrelevant!

8. Type 3 and press the Enter key.

The console window will now ask the user to input the repair shop id.

9. Type RS000001 and press the Enter key.

The console will now ask the user to input the vehicle policy number.

10. Type VP000001 and press the Enter key.

The console will now ask the user to input the claim amount.

11. Type 2500.99 and press the Enter key.

The console will now ask the user to input the date of the repair.

12. Type 2021/10/01 and press the Enter key.

13. Press the Enter key again to continue and close the console window.

The **break** statement has been executed and we are not asked for any further entries as the loop was exited, as in Figure 10-6.

```
How many claims are being made?

3
What is your repair shop id?

RS000001
What is the vehicle policy number?

VP000001
What is the amount being claimed for the repair?

2500.99
What was the date of the repair?

2021/10/01
The details entered for repair 1 are
Repair shop id: RS000001
Policy number:  VP000001
Claim amount:   2500.99
Claim date:     2021/10/01
Breaking out of the loop?

End of program
```

break executed

Figure 10-6. *The break statement executes*

Continue Statement

Control of the loop may also be modified by using the **continue** statement. The continue statement forces the code to move to the next iteration in the loop. So the loop continues, skipping the rest of the code in the current iteration, unlike the break statement where the loop is exited with no more iterations taking place.

Let's look at a sample scenario where the number of claims to be entered is 3:

- We will enter 3 for the number of claims to be made.

- When the counter starts, the value will be set to 0.

- When the check is made, it performs a division by 2.

- When the division is applied, the remainder is evaluated to see if it is a 0.

- If the remainder is 0, the counter number is an even number, so the code will stop this iteration and continue to the next iteration, if there is one.

- So, for the first iteration, the number is even, and no questions will be asked.

- The counter is incremented by 1 and will now have a value of 1.

- When the check is made, it performs a division by 2.

- The remainder is evaluated to see if it is 0; in this case it will not be 0 – it will be 1.

- So the questions will be asked.

- The counter is incremented by 1 and will now have a value of 2.

- When the check is made, it performs a division by 2.

- The remainder is evaluated to see if it is 0; in this case it will be 0.

- So the questions will not be asked.

- The counter is incremented by 1 and will now have a value of 3.

- The loop will be ended as the loop has been executed three times, but only once was the counter an odd number, so the questions were only asked once. We skipped out of the existing loop twice through the use of the continue statement.

14. Amend the code, as in Listing 10-16, by changing the value of the variable maximumNumberOfClaims to 5 so that we never actually come to the break statement.

Listing 10-16. Set the value of the variable

```
/*
Set up a variable called numberOfClaimsBeingMade
of data type int and assign the variable the value 2
*/
int numberOfClaimsBeingMade;

int maximumNumberOfClaims = 5;
```

15. Amend the code, as in Listing 10-17, to add a line at the start of the for loop that displays the counter's current value.

Listing 10-17. Display the counter value

```
for (int claimsCounter = 0;claimsCounter <
               numberOfClaimsBeingMade; claimsCounter++)
{
  Console.WriteLine("The current value of the counter is :" +
  claimsCounter + "\n");
```

16.   Amend the code, as in Listing 10-18, to implement this continue
statement.

Listing 10-18. Use the continue in an if statement

```
    Console.WriteLine("Breaking out of the loop?\n");
    break;
} // End of if section

/*
We will use the if statement to perform a boolean test
and if the test produces a true value we continue with
the loop but will skip out of this current iteration.
In this example we will check if the value of the
counter is even (when we divide by 2 the remainder is 0).
If it is an even number we will skip the rest of this
iteration by using the continue statement. There is
no else part to the if statement so if the boolean test
produces a false value the loop carries on executing
the block of code
*/
if (claimsCounter % 2 == 0)
{
/*
We have an even number so the continue is executed
*/
  continue;
}
```

```
    /*
    Read the user input for the repair shop id and
    keep it as a string
    */
    Console.WriteLine("What is your repair shop id?\n");
  repairShopID = Console.ReadLine();
```

17. Click the File menu.

18. Choose Save All.

19. Click the Debug menu.

20. Choose Start Without Debugging.

The console window will appear and ask the user to input the number of claims to be made.

21. Type 3 and press the Enter key.

The console window will show that the current value of the claims counter is 0 and will then immediately show that the current value of the claims counter is 1, as in Figure 10-7. This means no block of code was executed the first time, as the value 0 of the claims counter was an even number, and as such the continue statement was executed, putting the code to the next iteration, skipping the code in the current iteration.

```
How many claims are being made?

3
The current value of the counter is :0

The current value of the counter is :1    Code continues

What is your repair shop id?
```

Figure 10-7. *The counter value of 0 is even so the code continues*

As the value of the claims counter is now 1, and this is not an even number, the block of code in the current iteration is executed, so the questions are asked.

22. Type RS000001 for the repair shop id and press the Enter key.

The console will now ask the user to input the vehicle policy number.

   23.   Type VP000001 and press the Enter key.

The console will now ask the user to input the claim amount.

   24.   Type 1999.99 and press the Enter key.

The console will now ask the user to input the date of the repair.

   25.   Type 2021/10/01 and press the Enter key.

Iteration 1 is now completed; the block of code has been executed. The claims counter will now be incremented by 1 and become a 2.

The claims counter value of 2 is an even number, and as such the continue statement was executed, putting the code to the next iteration, skipping the code in the current iteration. The claims counter will now be incremented by 1 and become a 3, and as this is not less than the numberOfClaimsBeingMade, the loop has completed and will be exited.

   26.   Press the Enter key again to continue and close the console window.

While Loop

When we use a **while loop,** it will check a condition and then continue to execute a block of code if the condition evaluates to true. As the condition is evaluated at the start, before each execution, it is possible that the while loop will not execute the block of code at all. The while loop is said to "execute zero or more times." So, yes, it is possible that the loop does not execute the block of code.

Like the for construct, the while loop can be exited early, by using the keyword **break,** and we can move to the next iteration in the loop by using the keyword **continue**.

Note:

*If required, the while construct can be exited early, by using the keyword **return** or indeed by using the less favored keyword **goto**.*

```
while (<Condition>)
{
<statements>
 }
```

Example:

```
int counter = 0;
while (counter < 2)
{
  block of code to be executed
  counter++
} // End of while iteration
```

Code Analysis

In the example

- A variable called counter is set up outside the while loop. It cannot be created inside the brackets () as it can be in the for loop.

- The variable is initialized before entering the while loop.

- The loop counter is compared with the value 2, and if it is less than 2, the execution of the block of code continues.

- The loop counter is increased, incremented, by 1.

- The Boolean test is enclosed inside the brackets ().

- The block of code to be executed the required number of times is enclosed between opening and closing curly braces {}.

- When the condition is TRUE, the statements in the braces will execute.

- Once the statements have executed, control returns to the beginning of the while loop to check the condition again.

- When the condition is FALSE, the while statements in the braces are skipped, and execution begins after the closing brace of that block of code.

We will use the same example for this exercise as we did in the for loop exercise. To avoid having to enter the code again, we can copy and paste from the last program as we use a while loop.

1. Right-click the Chapter10 project.

2. Choose Add.

3. Choose Class.

4. Name the class WhileIteration.cs.

5. Click the Add button.

6. Create a Main() method within the class, as this was not
    produced automatically, and delete the unwanted imports as in
    Listing 10-19.

Remember the shortcut to create the Main() method is to type svm and then press
the Tab key twice.

Listing 10-19. Add the Main() method to the class template

```
using System;

namespace Chapter10
{
  internal class WhileIteration
  {
    static void Main(string[] args)
    {
    } // End of Main() method
  } // End of WhileIteration class
} // End of Chapter10 namespace
```

7. Right-click the Chapter10 project in the Solution Explorer panel.

8. Choose Properties from the pop-up menu.

9. Choose the WhileIteration class in the Startup object drop-
    down list.

10. Close the Properties window.

11. Amend the code, as in Listing 10-20, to set up and initialize the
    variables. Copy the code from the last program where possible.

Listing 10-20. Add the variables

```
static void Main(string[] args)
{
  /*
  Set up the variables to be used in the quote application
  The details will be:
      - the repair shop unique id           (string)
      - the vehicle insurance policy number (string)
      - the claim amount and                (double)
      - the date of the claim               (DateTime)
  */
  string repairShopID;
  string vehiclePolicyNumber;
  double claimAmount;
  DateTime claimDate;
  int numberOfClaimsBeingMade;
  int maximumNumberOfClaims = 0;
  int numberOfClaimsEntered = 0;

} // End of Main() method
```

12. Amend the code, as in Listing 10-21, to ask the user how many
     claims are being made and read the input value.

Listing 10-21. Ask for user input and read the input value

```
int numberOfClaimsEntered = 0;

/*
Read the user input for the number of claims being
made and convert the string value to an integer data type
*/
Console.WriteLine("How many claims are being made?\n");
numberOfClaimsBeingMade= Convert.ToInt32(Console.ReadLine());

  } // End of Main() method
 } // End of WhileIteration class
} // End of Chapter10 namespace
```

13. Amend the code, as in Listing 10-22, to include the start of a while loop.

Listing 10-22. While loop construct

```
Console.WriteLine("How many claims are being made?\n");
numberOfClaimsBeingMade= Convert.ToInt32(Console.ReadLine());

/*
Here we use the while iteration which uses a Boolean test
to see if the number of claims entered by the user so far
is less than the number of claims being made. If the
comparison equates to true then the while loop block of
code is executed. If the comparison equates
to false then the while loop block of code is not executed.
As we are using a variable in the loop our code is
flexible and can be used for any number of claims.
An ideal situation and good code.
*/
while (numberOfClaimsEntered < numberOfClaimsBeingMade)
{
} // End of while loop
} // End of Main() method
} // End of WhileIteration class
} // End of Chapter10 namespace
```

14. Amend the code, as in Listing 10-23, to read the user input from within the while loop. Copy the code from the last program.

Listing 10-23. Read user input for the four values required

```
while (numberOfClaimsEntered < numberOfClaimsBeingMade)
{
/*
Read the user input for the repair shop id and keep
it as a string
*/
```

```
        Console.WriteLine("What is your repair shop id?\n");
        repairShopID = Console.ReadLine();

        /*
        Read the user input for the vehicle policy number
        and keep it as a string
        */
        Console.WriteLine("What is the vehicle policy number?\n");
        vehiclePolicyNumber = Console.ReadLine();

        /*
        Read the user input for the repair amount and
        convert it to a double
        */
        Console.WriteLine("What is the amount being claimed " +
          " for the repair?\n");
        claimAmount = Convert.ToDouble(Console.ReadLine());

        /*
        Read the user input for the repair date and
        convert it to a Date
        */
        Console.WriteLine("What was the date of the repair?\n");
        claimDate = Convert.ToDateTime(Console.ReadLine());

      } // End of while loop
      } // End of Main() method
    } // End of WhileIteration class
  } // End of Chapter10 namespace
```

We will now display the details that have been entered and then close the while loop. Remember to try and copy the code from the last program and make the small amendment to the first line, which shows the "counter."

15. Amend the code, as in Listing 10-24.

Listing 10-24. Displaying the details entered

```
Console.WriteLine("What was the date of the repair?\n");
claimDate = Convert.ToDateTime(Console.ReadLine());

Console.WriteLine("The details entered for " +
    "repair " + (numberOfClaimsEntered + 1) + " are");

Console.WriteLine("Repair shop id:\t" + repairShopID);
Console.WriteLine("Policy number:\t" + vehiclePolicyNumber);
Console.WriteLine("Claim amount:\t" + claimAmount);
Console.WriteLine("Claim date:\t" + claimDate);

    /* Increment the loop counter by 1 */
    numberOfClaimsEntered++;

    } // End of while loop
  } // End of Main() method
 } // End of WhileIteration class
} // End of Chapter10 namespace
```

When the code is executed, the user will be asked to input the number of claims to be entered. We will enter 2. When the code is executed, the user will therefore be asked to input two sets of details:

- The counter in the while loop will be the variable called numberOfClaimsEntered, which will start at 0.

- At the start of the while loop, the numberOfClaimsEntered is compared to the variable numberOfClaimsBeingMade, which is 2.

- The comparison produces a true value and the block of code is executed.

- The numberOfClaimsEntered variable is incremented by 1 – it is now 1.

- The numberOfClaimsEntered is now 1 and is compared to the variable numberOfClaimsBeingMade, which is 2.

- The comparison produces a true value and the block of code is executed.

- The numberOfClaimsEntered variable is incremented by 1 – it is now 2.

- The numberOfClaimsEntered is now 2 and is compared to the variable numberOfClaimsBeingMade, which is 2.

- The comparison produces a false value and the block of code is not executed.

16.   Click the File menu.

17.   Choose Save All.

18.   Click the Debug menu.

19.   Choose Start Without Debugging.

20.   Click in the console window.

The console window appears and asks the user how many claims are to be made.

21.   Type 2 and press the Enter key.

The console window will appear and ask the user to input the repair shop id.

22.   Type RS000001 and press the Enter key.

The console will now ask the user to input the vehicle policy number.

23.   Type VP000001 and press the Enter key.

The console will now ask the user to input the claim amount.

24.   Type 1999.99 and press the Enter key.

The console will now ask the user to input the date of the repair.

25.   Type 2021/10/01 and press the Enter key.

```
How many claims are being made?

2
What is your repair shop id?

RS000001
What is the vehicle policy number?

VP000001
What is the amount being claimed  for the repair?

1999.99
What was the date of the repair?

2021/10/01
The details entered for repair 1 are
Repair shop id: RS000001
Policy number:  VP000001
Claim amount:   1999.99
Claim date:     01/10/2021 00:00:00
What is your repair shop id?
```
Iteration one

Figure 10-8. *Iteration 1*

Iteration 1 is now completed; the block of code has been executed, as shown in Figure 10-8. The claims counter will now be incremented by 1 and become a 1. The comparison is made to see if the claims counter value is less than 2, and as it is, the iterations continue.

The console window will now ask the user to input the repair shop id.

26.   Type RS000001 and press the Enter key.

The console will now ask the user to input the vehicle policy number.

27.   Type VP001234 and press the Enter key.

The console will now ask the user to input the claim amount.

28.   Type 2500.99 and press the Enter key.

The console will now ask the user to input the date of the repair.

29.   Type 2021/10/01 and press the Enter key.

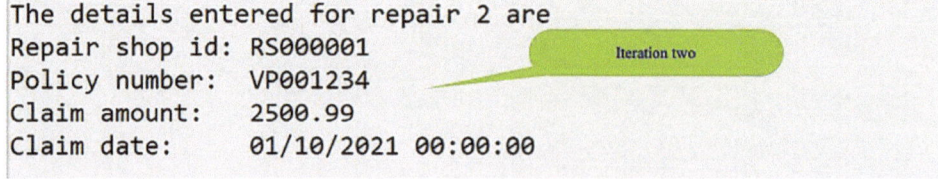

```
The details entered for repair 2 are
Repair shop id: RS000001
Policy number:  VP001234
Claim amount:   2500.99
Claim date:     01/10/2021 00:00:00
```
Iteration two

Figure 10-9. *Iteration 2*

The code will now move to the next line after the while loop, which waits for the user to press a key, as shown in Figure 10-9.

30.   Press any key to close the console window.

Break Statement

Control of the while loop is determined by the Boolean section, as shown in Figure 10-10.

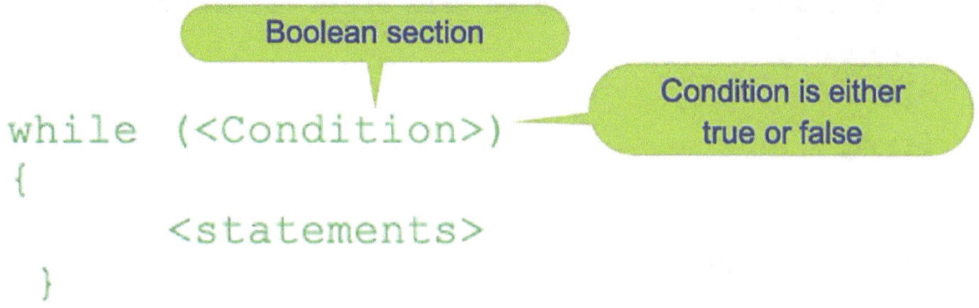

Figure 10-10. *The Boolean section*

The Boolean section determines if the counter has reached its limit; however, the control may be modified by using the **break** statement, which forces a loop to exit immediately.

We will now add a break statement as we did with the for loop. We have a variable called maximumNumberOfClaims, which is set to the value 0. This means for this example the user will not be able to enter any values – it's just an example. Now we will check inside the while condition if the number of claims entered has reached the maximumNumberOfClaims, that is, 0. If the value of the counter has reached 0, the loop will be exited, and the break is executed.

31.   Amend the code, as in Listing 10-25, to implement this break statement using an if construct inside the while loop.

Listing 10-25. Break statement inside an if construct

```
while (numberOfClaimsEntered < numberOfClaimsBeingMade)
{
    /*
    We will use the if statement to perform a boolean
    test and if the test produces a true value we will
    break out of the loop. If the boolean test produces a
```

```
false value the loop simply continues executing the
block of code
*/
if (numberOfClaimsEntered == maximumNumberOfClaims)
{
  /*
  We have reached the maximum number of claims
  allowed in one session so we will break out of the
  loop early
  */
  break;
}
```

32. Click the File menu.

33. Choose Save All.

34. Click the Debug menu.

35. Choose Start Without Debugging.

36. Type 3 for the number of claims being made, as shown in Figure 10-11.

Remember, we have set a variable that will stop the iteration when the number of claims entered is 0, the maximum number of claims allowed, so the number of claims we say we wish to enter will be irrelevant!

37. Press the Enter key to continue and close the console window.

The **break** statement has been executed and we are not asked any of the questions, as the loop was exited as shown in Figure 10-11.

```
How many claims are being made?

3
C:\CoreCSharp\CoreCSharp\Chapter1            break statement executed        0\Chapter10.exe
Press any key to close this window . . ._
```

Figure 10-11. *Break statement executed*

38. Press the Enter key again to continue and close the console window.

Continue Statement

Control of the while loop may also be modified by using the **continue** statement. The continue statement forces the code to move to the next iteration in the loop. So the loop continues, skipping the rest of the code in the current iteration, unlike the break statement where the loop is exited with no more iterations taking place. This is the same as we saw in the for loop. We will now add a continue statement, and we will use the same sample scenario as used in the for loop, where the number of claims to be entered is keyed in as 3.

39. Amend the code, as in Listing 10-26, by changing the value of the variable maximumNumberOfClaims to 5.

Listing 10-26. Change the value of the variable

```
DateTime claimDate;
int numberOfClaimsBeingMade;

// was int maximumNumberOfClaims = 0;
int maximumNumberOfClaims = 5;

int numberOfClaimsEntered = 0;
```

40. Amend the code, as in Listing 10-27, to add a line at the start of the while loop that informs us of the counter's current value.

Listing 10-27. Display the counter value

```
while (numberOfClaimsEntered < numberOfClaimsBeingMade)
{
Console.WriteLine("The current value of the counter is :" +
numberOfClaimsEntered + "\n");
```

In the next piece of code, we will increment the variable called numberOfClaimsEntered using the ++ operator. If we did not do this, we would be in an infinite loop because its initial value of 0 would never change and this value is checked in the brackets of the while statement to see if it is less than the variable numberOfClaimsBeingMade, which has been set to 5, so this will always be true and the code in the while block will always execute.

Continuing from this, we will highlight differences between the for and while iteration constructs:

- The for loop knows in advance how many times it will iterate, but the while loop does not know.

- The for loop has an initialization step, whereas the while loop does not.

- The for loop uses an increment or decrement step, which in our code was claimsCounter++, for (int claimsCounter = 0; claimsCounter < numberOfClaimsBeingMade; claimsCounter++), whereas the while loop does not and we have to add our own, numberOfClaimsEntered++.

41. Amend the code, as in Listing 10-28, to implement this continue statement, after the end of the if statement.

Listing 10-28. Implement the continue statement

```
if (numberOfClaimsEntered == maximumNumberOfClaims)
{
  /*
  We have reached the maximum number of claims
  allowed in one session so we will break out of the
  loop early
  */
  break;
}

/*
We will use the if statement to perform a boolean test
and if the test produces a true value we continue with
the loop but will skip out of this current iteration.
In this example we will check if the value of the
counter is even (when we divide by 2 the remainder is 0).
If it is an even number we will skip the rest of this
iteration by using the continue statement.
There is no else part to the if statement so if the
```

```
boolean test produces a false value the loop carries
on executing the block of code
*/
if (numberOfClaimsEntered % 2 == 0)
{
 /*
We have reached the maximum number of claims allowed
in one session so we will break out of the loop early.

Increment the loop counter by 1

This is an important statement as we are increasing the
value of the numberOfClaimsEntered and the while loop
only knows when to stop iterating when the
numberOfClaimsEntered is not less than the
numberOfClaimsBeingMade. So, if we do not increment the
value it will remain constant and we will be in an
infinite loop. NOT Good.
In the for iteration we had the 'counter' handled in
the at the top of the iteration using claimsCounter++

 for (int claimsCounter = 0; claimsCounter <
 numberOfClaimsBeingMade; claimsCounter++)
*/
 numberOfClaimsEntered++;
 continue;
} // End of second if construct

 /*
Read the user input for the repair shop id and keep
it as a string
*/
Console.WriteLine("What is your repair shop id?\n");
repairShopID = Console.ReadLine();
```

42.   Click the File menu.

43.   Choose Save All.

44. Click the Debug menu.

45. Choose Start Without Debugging.

The console window will appear and ask the user to input the number of claims to be made as shown in Figure 10-12.

46. Type 3 and press the Enter key.

Figure 10-12 shows the console window, which displays the current value of the claims counter as 0. The console window will immediately show that the current value of the claims counter is 1. This means no block of code was executed the first time, as the 0 value of the numberOfClaimsEntered counter was an even number. Consequently, the continue statement was executed, putting the code into the next iteration, skipping the code in the current iteration. As the value of the counter is now 1, and this is not an even number, the block of code in the current iteration is executed. So the questions are asked.

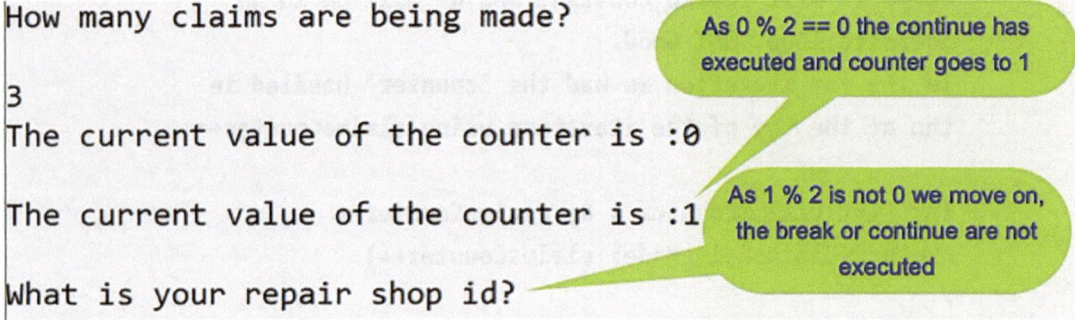

Figure 10-12. *Continue statement executed*

47. Type RS000001 and press the Enter key.

The console will now ask the user to input the vehicle policy number.

48. Type VP000001 and press the Enter key.

The console will now ask the user to input the claim amount.

49. Type 1999.99 and press the Enter key.

The console will now ask the user to input the date of the repair

50. Type 2021/10/01 and press the Enter key.

Now the counter value is 2, which is an even number, so the continue statement was executed, putting the code to the next iteration, skipping the code in the current iteration. The counter is incremented by 1 and becomes 3, and as this is not less than the variable numberOfClaimsBeingMade, the loop has completed and will be exited as shown in Figure 10-13.

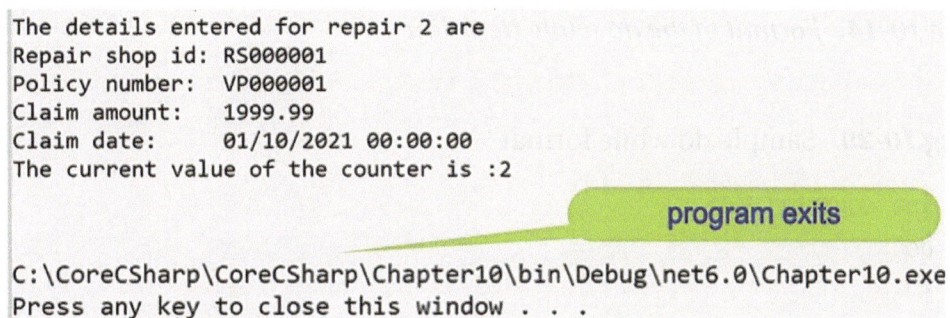

```
The details entered for repair 2 are
Repair shop id: RS000001
Policy number:  VP000001
Claim amount:   1999.99
Claim date:     01/10/2021 00:00:00
The current value of the counter is :2
```
program exits
```
C:\CoreCSharp\CoreCSharp\Chapter10\bin\Debug\net6.0\Chapter10.exe
Press any key to close this window . . .
```

***Figure 10-13.** Program exits*

51. Press the Enter key again to continue and close the console window.

Do (While) Loop

The **do loop** is like the while loop, except it has the Boolean check at the end rather than the start. This means that the do loop is guaranteed to execute at least once, unlike the while loop that may never be executed. Remember the "execute zero or more times" phrase associated with the while loop. The do while loop will check a condition at the end of the first iteration and then continue to execute the loop if the Boolean condition evaluates as true.

Like the for and while constructs, the do while loop can be exited early, by using the keyword **break,** and we can move to the next iteration in the loop by using the keyword **continue**.

Note:

*If required, the do while construct can be exited early, by using the keyword **return** or indeed by using the less favored keyword **goto**.*

The format of the do while loop is shown in Figure 10-14 and Listing 10-29.

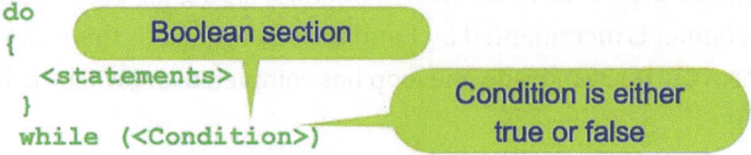

Figure 10-14. *Format of the do while iteration*

Listing 10-29. Sample do while format

```
int counter = 0;
do
{
  Block of code
  counter++
} while (counter < 2);
```

Code Analysis

In Listing 10-29

- A variable called counter is set up outside the do while loop. It cannot be created inside the brackets () as it can be in the for loop.

- The variable is initialized before entering the do while loop.

- The block of code between the {} braces is executed.

- Inside the block of code the counter is incremented.

- The loop counter is compared with the value 2, and if it is less than 2, the execution of the block of code will continue. In other words when the condition is true, the statements in the braces will execute.

- Once the condition is true, control returns to the beginning of the do while loop.

- When the condition is false, the statements in the braces are skipped, and execution begins after the closing brace of that block of code, the next code statement.

We will use the same example for this exercise as we did in the while loop exercise. To avoid having to enter the code again, we can copy and paste code as required.

1. Right-click the Chapter10 project in the Solution Explorer panel.

2. Choose Add.

3. Choose Class.

4. Name the class DoWhileIteration.cs.

5. Click the Add button.

6. Amend the code, as in Listing 10-30, to add the Main() method.

Listing 10-30. Main() method in the class template

```
namespace Chapter10
{
  internal class DoWhileIteration
  {
    static void Main(string[] args)
    {

    } // End of Main() method
  } // End of DoWhileIteration class
} // End of Chapter10 namespace
```

9. Amend the code, as Listing 10-31, to add the variables we will use.

Listing 10-31. Add the required variables

```
static void Main(string[] args)
{
  /*
  Set up the variables to be used in the quote application
```

315

```
        The details will be:
            - the repair shop unique id            (string)
            - the vehicle insurance policy number  (string)
            - the claim amount and                 (double)
            - the date of the claim                (DateTime)
        */
        string repairShopID;
        string vehiclePolicyNumber;
        DateTime claimDate;
        double claimAmount;

        int numberOfClaimsBeingMade;

        /*
        This variable will be used to maintain a count for the
        number of claims that have been entered by the user
        */
        int numberOfClaimsEntered = 0;

    } // End of Main() method
  } // End of DoWhileIteration class
} // End of Chapter10 namespace
```

10. Amend the code, as in Listing 10-32, to request user input and assign the input value to the variable numberOfClaimsBeingMade.

Listing 10-32. Request user input and convert it

```
/*
This variable will be used to maintain a count for the
number of claims that have been entered by the user
*/
int numberOfClaimsEntered = 0;

/*
Read the user input for the number of claims being made
and convert the string value to an integer data type
*/
```

```
Console.WriteLine("How many claims are you wishing to make?\n");
numberOfClaimsBeingMade = Convert.ToInt32(Console.ReadLine());

} // End of Main() method
```

11. Amend the code, as in Listing 10-33, to add the do while loop.

Listing 10-33. Add the do while loop

```
numberOfClaimsBeingMade = Convert.ToInt32(Console.ReadLine());

    /*
    Here we use the do iteration which means at least one
    iteration will be performed. The do iteration uses a
    Boolean test after iteration one to see if the number of
    claims entered by the user so far is less than the number
    of claims being made. If the comparison equates to true
    then the do loop block of code is executed again. If the
    comparison equates to false then the do loop block of
    code is not executed. As we are using a variable in the
    loop our code is flexible and can be used for any
    number of claims. An ideal situation and good code.
    */
    do
    {
      Console.WriteLine("The current value of the counter is :" +
      numberOfClaimsEntered + "\n");

      /*
      Read the user input for the repair shop id and
      keep it as a string
      */
      Console.WriteLine("What is your repair shop id?\n");
      repairShopID = Console.ReadLine();

      /*
      Read the user input for the vehicle policy number
      and keep it as a string
      */
```

```
Console.WriteLine("What is the vehicle policy number?\n");
vehiclePolicyNumber = Console.ReadLine();

/*
Read the user input for the repair amount and
convert it to a double
*/
Console.WriteLine("What is the amount being claimed for the
repair?\n");
claimAmount = Convert.ToDouble(Console.ReadLine());

/*
Read the user input for the repair date and
convert it to a Date
*/
Console.WriteLine("What was the date of the repair?\n");
claimDate = Convert.ToDateTime(Console.ReadLine());

Console.WriteLine("The details entered for repair " +
(numberOfClaimsEntered + 1) + " are");

Console.WriteLine("Repair shop id:\t" + repairShopID);
Console.WriteLine("Policy number:\t" + vehiclePolicyNumber);
Console.WriteLine("Claim amount:\t" + claimAmount);
Console.WriteLine("Claim date:\t" + claimDate);

/* Increment the loop counter by 1 */
numberOfClaimsEntered++;
} while (numberOfClaimsEntered < numberOfClaimsBeingMade);

} // End of Main() method
```

When the code is executed, the user will be asked to input the number of claims being made. We will enter 2 and the user will therefore be asked to input two sets of details. The sequence of events will be as follows:

- The block of code is executed immediately. Remember the statement associated with the do while loop: "execute at least once."

- The counter in the do while loop will be the variable called numberOfClaimsEntered, which will start at 0 as it enters the loop.

- At the end of the block of code, the variable called numberOfClaimsEntered is incremented and is now 1.

- At the end of the do while loop, the numberOfClaimsEntered is compared with the variable numberOfClaimsBeingMade, which is 2.

- The comparison is true and the block of code is executed again.

- The numberOfClaimsEntered variable is incremented by 1 – it is now 2.

- At the end of the do while loop, the numberOfClaimsEntered is compared with the variable numberOfClaimsBeingMade, which is 2.

- The comparison produces a false value and the block of code is not executed again.

12. Click the File menu.

13. Choose Save All.

14. Right-click the Chapter10 project in the Solution Explorer panel.

15. Choose Properties.

16. Select the DoWhileIteration from the drop-down menu of the Startup object.

17. Close the Properties window.

18. Click the Debug menu.

19. Choose Start Without Debugging.

The console window will appear and ask the user how many claims they wish to make.

20. Type 2 and press the Enter key.

The console window will appear and ask the user to input the repair shop id.

21. Type RS000001 and press the Enter key.

The console will now ask the user to input the vehicle policy number.

22.   Type VP000001 and press the Enter key.

The console will now ask the user to input the claim amount.

23.   Type 1999.99 and press the Enter key.

The console will now ask the user to input the date of the repair.

24.   Type 2021/10/01 and press the Enter key.

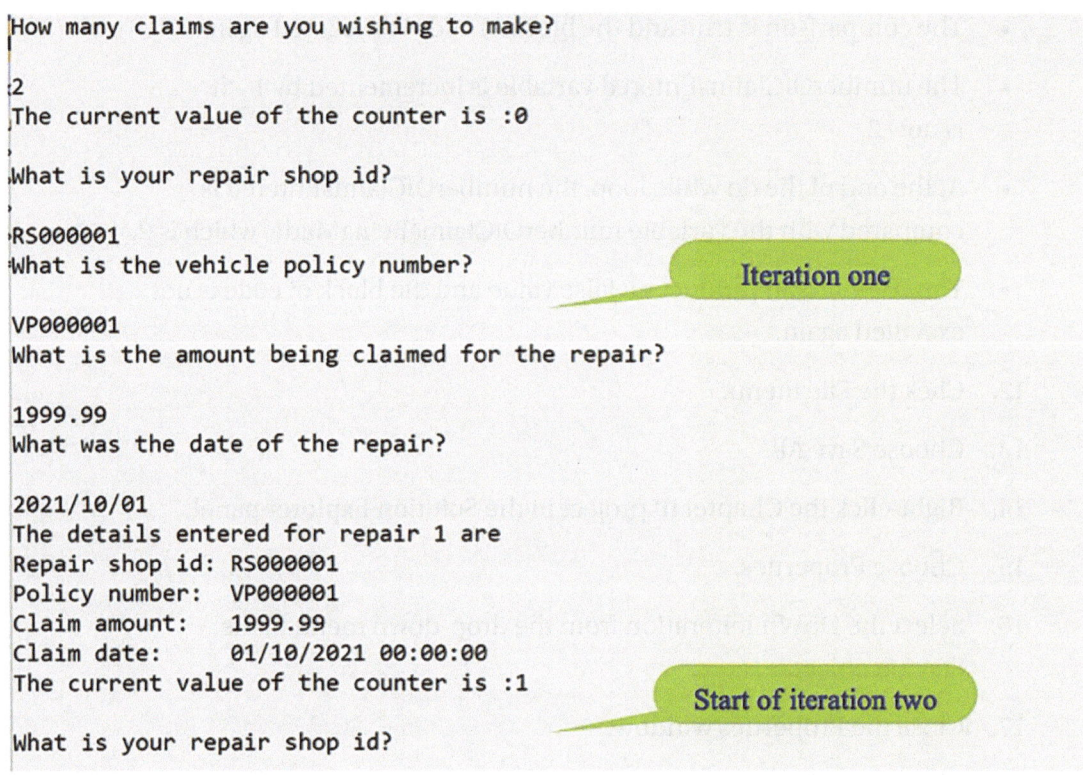

```
How many claims are you wishing to make?

2
The current value of the counter is :0

What is your repair shop id?

RS000001
What is the vehicle policy number?                    Iteration one

VP000001
What is the amount being claimed for the repair?

1999.99
What was the date of the repair?

2021/10/01
The details entered for repair 1 are
Repair shop id: RS000001
Policy number:  VP000001
Claim amount:   1999.99
Claim date:     01/10/2021 00:00:00
The current value of the counter is :1
                                                   Start of iteration two
What is your repair shop id?
```

Figure 10-15. *Iteration 1*

Figure 10-15 shows that iteration 1 is now completed; the block of code has been executed. The claims counter has been incremented by 1 and is now 1. The comparison is made to see if the claims counter value is less than 2, and as it is, the iterations continue.

The console window will now ask the user to input the repair shop id.

25.   Type RS000001 and press the Enter key.

The console will now ask the user to input the vehicle policy number.

26.   Type VP001234 and press the Enter key.

The console will now ask the user to input the claim amount.

27.   Type 2500.99 and press the Enter key.

The console will now ask the user to input the date of the repair.

28.   Type 2021/10/01 and press the Enter key.

```
The details entered for repair 2 are
Repair shop id: RS000001
Policy number:  VP001234
Claim amount:   2500.99
Claim date:     01/10/2021 00:00:00        Program exits

C:\CoreCSharp\CoreCSharp\Chapter10\bin\Debug\net6.0\Chapter10.exe)in\Debug\net6.0
Press any key to close this window . . .
```

Figure 10-16. *Iteration 2*

The code will now move to the next line after the while loop, which waits for the user to press a key, as shown in Figure 10-16.

29.   Press any key to close the console window.

Break Statement

Control of the do while loop is determined by the Boolean section as shown:

```
  do
{
   < statements >
} while (< Condition >)
          Boolean section
```

The Boolean section determines if the counter has reached its limit. However, the control may be modified by using the break statement, where the break statement forces a do while loop to exit immediately. We will now add a break statement in the same way as we did with the for and while loops. We will create a variable called maximumNumberOfClaims and set its value to 0. Now we will check inside the while condition if the counter has reached the value set for the maximumNumberOfClaims, that is, 0. If the value of the counter has reached 0, the loop will be exited.

30. Amend the code, as in Listing 10-34, to add a variable to hold the maximum number of claims.

Listing 10-34. Add a new variable

```
int numberOfClaimsBeingMade;

/*
This variable will be used to maintain a count for the
number of claims that have been entered by the user
*/
int numberOfClaimsEntered = 0;

int maximumNumberOfClaims = 0;
```

31. Amend the code, as in Listing 10-35, to implement the break statement.

Listing 10-35. Implement the break statement within an if construct

```
do
{
  Console.WriteLine("The current value of the counter is :" +
  numberOfClaimsEntered + "\n");

  /*
  We will use the if statement to perform a boolean
  test and if the test produces a true value we will
  break out of the loop. If the boolean test produces
  a false value the loop simply continues executing the
  block of code
  */
```

```
if (numberOfClaimsEntered == maximumNumberOfClaims)
{
 /*
 We have reached the maximum number of claims allowed
 in one session so we will break out of the loop early
 */
  break;
}
```

32. Click the File menu.

33. Choose Save All.

34. Click the Debug menu.

35. Choose Start Without Debugging.

36. When the console window appears, type 3 as the number of claims we wish to make.

Remember, we have set a variable that will stop the iteration when the counter is 0, so the number entered here will be irrelevant to the extent that the loop will definitely be entered, and the break statement will be executed.

37. Press the Enter key to continue and close the console window.

```
How many claims are you wishing to make?

3
The current value of the counter is :0
                                        break statement has been executed
C:\CoreCSharp\CoreCSharp\Chapter10\bin\Debug\net6.0\Chapter10.exe
Press any key to close this window . . .
```

Figure 10-17. *Program exits*

Figure 10-17 shows that the break statement has been executed and we are not asked any of the questions as the loop was exited.

Continue Statement

Control of the do while loop may also be modified by using the **continue** statement. The continue statement forces the code to move to the next iteration in the loop. So the loop continues, skipping the rest of the code in the current iteration, unlike the break statement where the loop is exited with no more iterations taking place. This is the same as we saw in the for and while loops. We will now add a continue statement in the same way as we did with the for loop. We will use the same sample scenario as used in the for loop, where the number of claims to be entered is keyed in as 3.

38. Amend the code, as Listing 10-36, to change the value of the maximumNumberOfClaims variable.

Listing 10-36. Change the variable value

```
double claimAmount;
int numberOfClaimsBeingMade;

/*
This variable will be used to maintain a count for the
number of claims that have been entered by the user
*/
int numberOfClaimsEntered = 0;
int maximumNumberOfClaims = 5;
```

39. Amend the code, as Listing 10-37, to implement this continue statement within an if construct.

Listing 10-37. Implement the continue statement inside an if construct

```
if (numberOfClaimsEntered == maximumNumberOfClaims)
{
 /*
 We have reached the maximum number of claims allowed
 in one session so we will break out of the loop early
 */
  break;
}
```

```
/*
We will use the if statement to perform a boolean test
and if the test produces a true value we will continue
with the loop but will skip out of this current
iteration. In this example we will check if the value
of the counter is even (when we divide by 2 the
remainder is 0). If it is an even number we will skip
the rest of this iteration by using the continue
statement. There is no else part to the if statement so
if the boolean test produces a false value the loop
carries on executing the block of code
*/
if (numberOfClaimsEntered % 2 == 0)
{
  /*
  We have reached the maximum number of claims allowed
  in one session so we will break out of the loop early.
  Increment the loop counter by 1
  */
  numberOfClaimsEntered++;
  continue;
}

/*
Read the user input for the repair shop id and
keep it as a string
*/
Console.WriteLine("What is your repair shop id?\n");
```

40. Click the File menu.

41. Choose Save All.

42. Click the Debug menu.

43. Choose Start Without Debugging.

The console window will appear and ask the user to input the number of claims to be made.

44.   Type 3 and press the Enter key.

The console window will show that the current value of the claims counter is 0, and it will immediately show that the current value of the claims counter is 1. This means no block of code was executed the first time, as the 0 value of the numberOfClaimsEntered counter was an even number and as such the continue statement was executed, putting the code into the next iteration, skipping the code in the current iteration.

As the value of the counter is 1 and not an even number, the code in the current iteration is executed and the questions are asked, as shown in Figure 10-18.

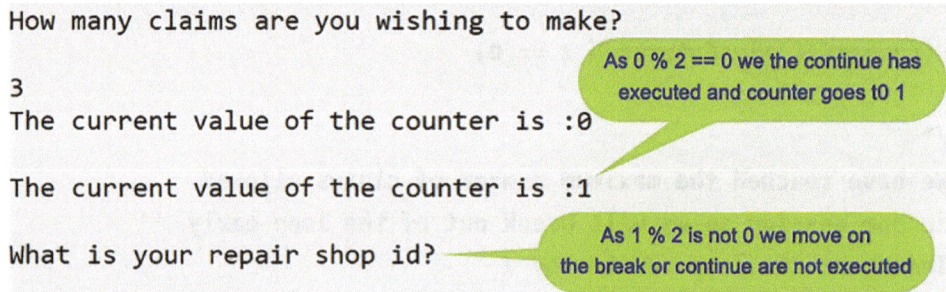

```
How many claims are you wishing to make?

3
The current value of the counter is :0

The current value of the counter is :1

What is your repair shop id?
```

As 0 % 2 == 0 we the continue has executed and counter goes t0 1

As 1 % 2 is not 0 we move on the break or continue are not executed

Figure 10-18.   *Current iteration is executed*

The console window will appear and ask the user to input the repair shop id.

45.   Type RS000001 and press the Enter key.

The console will now ask the user to input the vehicle policy number.

46.   Type VP000001 and press the Enter key.

The console will now ask the user to input the claim amount.

47.   Type 1999.99 and press the Enter key.

The console will now ask the user to input the date of the repair.

48.   Type 2021/10/01 and press the Enter key.

Iteration 1 is now complete; the block of code has been executed. The counter will now be incremented by 1 and become a 2. The counter value of 2 is an even number, and as such the continue statement was executed, putting the code to the next iteration, skipping the code in the current iteration. The counter will now be incremented by 1 and become a 3, and as this is not less than the numberOfClaimsBeingMade, the do while loop has completed and will be exited, as shown in Figure 10-19.

```
The details entered for repair 2 are
Repair shop id: RS000001
Policy number:  VP000001
Claim amount:   1999.99
Claim date:     01/10/2023 00:00:00
The current value of the counter is :2
                                                    program exits

C:\CoreCSharp\CoreCSharp\Chapter10\bin\Debug\net6.0\Chapter10.exe
Press any key to close this window . . .
```

Figure 10-19. *Iterations completed*

49. Press the Enter key again to continue and close the console window.

We will learn about another widely used iteration, the foreach iteration, when we study arrays in the next chapter.

Chapter Summary

In this chapter we have learned about a very important programming concept called iteration. We have learned that

- Iteration in C# can be completed in different ways, using different constructs including

  - The for loop

  - The while loop

  - The do loop

  - The foreach loop, which will be covered more in the next chapter

  - The break statement

  - The continue statement

- We can have more than one class in a project.

We are making great progress in our programming of C# applications and we should be proud of our achievements. In finishing this chapter and increasing our knowledge, we are advancing to our target.

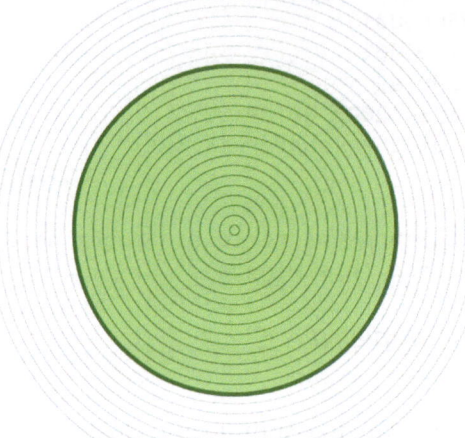

Our target is getting closer

CHAPTER 11

Arrays

Arrays: A Data Structure

We learned in Chapter 10 that iteration is a very important programming concept in all programming languages. To use iteration in our C# code, we have a number of construct options, and the best construct option to choose will depend on the particular task the code has to perform. The different constructs for iteration are the for construct, the while construct, the do while construct, and the foreach construct. Within the constructs, there are options to break out of the iterations completely or to break out of a particular iteration using the continue keyword. In terms of the project structure, we once again used the ability to have multiple classes within a package where each class must have a unique name.

We read earlier that when data was entered into our applications, it was stored temporarily. Now we will look at storing data in a structured and **more "permanent"** way using an array. An array is a list of data items, all of which must have the same type. We could also describe it as a **collection** of data items, each of the same type. We could have an array that contains a

- List of integers

- List of real numbers

- List of characters

- List of strings

If we think about a C# application that is applicable to a business that sells household products, it may contain arrays for

329

© Gerard Byrne 2022

G. Byrne, *Target C#*, https://doi.org/10.1007/978-1-4842-8619-7_11

- Surface cleaners   -   This could be a list of strings.
- Hand soaps   -   This could be a list of strings.
- Product codes   -   This could be a list of integers.

If we think about a C# application that is applicable to a business that sells insurance, it may contain arrays for

- Insurance types   -   This could be a list of strings.
- Account numbers   -   This could be a list of integers.
- Insurance premiums   -   This could be a list of doubles.
- Vehicle manufacturers   -   This could be a list of strings.
- Vehicle models   -   This could be a list of strings.

An array is therefore a list of related items that can be treated by C# as one **object**. For now, we could say that an array is a number of variables that can be treated as one object. So, when we think of an array, we should understand that we are dealing with individual variables or objects, but with the added advantage of them being organized for us in one object.

If we have the array object with the data items "lumped" together into one object, we are said to have what is called a **data structure**. In programming, data structures may be very complex or more simplistic and will be in the form of a sequence of data items such as a data **record** or **array**. In a program for a playing card game, like solitaire, we might want to keep a record that holds information about a card, that is, the suit and the value. This means we will have two fields in the record. With the C# programming language, we have access to data structures that we can use to accommodate this type of record. Such structures in C# include an **array** and a data structure called a **struct**.

When declaring an array in C#, we must abide by some basic rules:

- The array must be assigned a **data type.**

- After the data type will be an **open square bracket** followed by a **closing square bracket.**

- The square brackets can come immediately after the data type, **or** there can be a space after the data type, just before the opening square bracket.

- The array will have a single name, which is called its **identifier.**

- The array is of **fixed size** and cannot be made bigger or smaller, so it is not a dynamic structure.

When we initialize or populate the array, we must ensure that each item in the array is of the same data type, as identified by the data type assigned to the array. We therefore say that an array is **homogenous**, having similarity in structure.

When we wish to access an item in the array, we must refer to the item by a **subscript** or **index,** which gives its position within the array. In C#, arrays are **zero indexed,** which means that the first element of the array has an index of zero. Arrays are common across nearly all programming languages and in each language they are used in a similar manner. However, C# has a few things that are different and are worth noting at the outset:

- The square brackets come after the data type, for example, `string[]`, and not after the identifier.

- Putting the brackets after the identifier, for example, `string claimAmounts[]`,is not permitted.

- The size of the array is not part of its type, and this means we can declare an array using initial values, for example, `string[] claimAmounts = { "Home", "Auto", "Life" };`.

In C# there is support for the following array types:

- Single-dimensional arrays

- Multidimensional arrays

- Jagged arrays (also known as an array of arrays)

We will look at single-dimensional arrays in more detail and will see how to

- Declare the array.

- Initialize the array.

- Reference the members of the array.

We will see that there are different ways to declare and create arrays and different ways to initialize arrays, so it is important at the outset to understand that we will find our own preferred option from the various approaches. Each approach will have its advantages and disadvantages, but as a developer we will usually have a preferred option. On the other hand, as a developer we will spend much of our time maintaining code rather than writing new code, and often the code we maintain has not been written by us, so we need to understand all the approaches.

Single-Dimensional Arrays

A single-dimensional or one-dimensional array is a list of data items all of the same data type. It can be thought of as a type of linear array. At the start of this chapter, we read that a C# application for a business that sells insurance could contain arrays for

- Insurance types   - This could be a list of strings.
- Account numbers   - This could be a list of integers.
- Insurance premiums   - This could be a list of doubles.
- Vehicle manufacturers   - This could be a list of strings.
- Vehicle models   - This could be a list of strings.

Taking this theme a little further, we could see that the arrays could contain

- A list of insurance types of data type string, for example:

```
{ "Auto", "SUV 4x4", "Motorcycle", "Motorhome", "Snowmobile",
"Boat"};
```

Another way to think of the single-dimensional array is as a table with rows and columns. In the case of a single-dimensional array, there will only be a single row with the required number of columns as shown in Table 11-1.

Table 11-1. *Representation of the insuranceTypes single-dimensional array*

Array name	[0]	[1]	[2]	[3]	[4]	[5]
insuranceTypes	Auto	SUV 4x4	Motorcycle	Motorhome	Snowmobile	Boat

Now, based on what was stated earlier about the basic rules to be abided by when declaring an array, we could write the code to declare, create, and populate the array for this example as

```
String[] insuranceTypes = new String[6];
```
insuranceTypes[0]   =   "Auto";

insuranceTypes[1]   =   "SUV 4x4";

insuranceTypes[2]   =   "Motorcycle";

insuranceTypes[3]   =   "Motorhome";

insuranceTypes[4]   =   "Snowmobile";

insuranceTypes[5]   =   "Boat";

- A list of account numbers (integers):

  { 000001, 001122, 002233, 003344, 004455, 005566};

Thinking of this single-dimensional array as a row with columns, it could be represented as shown in Table 11-2.

Table 11-2. *Representation of the accountNumber single-dimensional array*

Array name	[0]	[1]	[2]	[3]	[4]	[5]
accountNumber	000001	001122	002233	003344	004455	005566

Now, based on what was stated earlier about the basic rules to be abided by when declaring an array, we could write the code to declare, create, and populate the array for this example as

```
int[] accountNumber = new int[6];
```
accountNumber [0]   =   000011;

accountNumber [1]   =   001122;

accountNumber [2]   =   002233;

accountNumber [3]   =   003344;

accountNumber [4]   =   004455;

accountNumber [5]   =   005566;

- A list of insurance costs (doubles):

    `{ 104.99, 105.99, 106.99, 107.99, 108.99, 109.99};`

Thinking of this single-dimensional array as a row with columns, it could be represented as shown in Table 11-3.

Table 11-3. *Representation of the insurancePremiums single-dimensional array*

Array name	[0]	[1]	[2]	[3]	[4]	[5]
insurancePremiums	104.99	105.99	106.99	107.99	108.99	109.99

Now, based on what was stated earlier about the basic rules to be abided by when declaring an array, we could write the code to declare, create, and populate the array for this example as

```
double[] insurancePremiums = new double[6];
insurancePremiums [0]      =        104.99;
insurancePremiums [1]      =        105.99;
insurancePremiums [2]      =        106.99;
insurancePremiums [3]      =        107.99;
insurancePremiums [4]      =        108.99;
insurancePremiums [5]      =        109.99;
```

Now that we have the concept of an array being a collection, a container, or a store for items of the same data type, we can look at how to code the implementation of an array. Like many things in life, we have choices. So C# gives us choices, different techniques, that allow us to set up and use arrays.

Choice 1: Declaring and Creating an Array in Two Stages

Stage 1: Declare

In C#, the single-dimensional arrays we have just considered can be declared as

```
string[] insuranceTypes;
int[] accountNumber;
double[] insurancePremiums;
```

When we say that we are **declaring** an array in C#, we are actually saying that **we want to use an array that will consist of items of the data type stated,** but it will not exist yet.

Stage 2: Create

Now, when an array has been declared, it needs to be **created**. To create the array, it must be **instantiated**, and this can be achieved by using the **new** keyword syntax.

The single-dimensional arrays we have just considered can be created as shown:

string[] insuranceTypes;			**declaration**
insuranceTypes	=	new string[6];	**creation**
int[] accountNumber;			**declaration**
accountNumber	=	new int[6];	**creation**
double[] insurancePremiums;			**declaration**
insurancePremiums	=	new double[6];	**creation**

In instantiating the array, we are setting aside the required memory resources for the array of the specified size and data type.

Choice 2: Declaring and Creating an Array in One Stage

In C#, the single-dimensional arrays we have just considered can be **declared** and **created** in one stage as

Declaration		Creation
string[] insuranceTypes	=	new string[6];
int[] accountNumber	=	new int[6];
double[] insurancePremiums	=	new double[6];

In each line of code, we are

- Declaring the data type of the array – string, int, or double

- Stating that the array is single dimensional – this is the [ ] part

- Giving the array its name – insuranceTypes, accountNumber, or insurancePremiums

- Instantiating the array with the new keyword

- Stating that it will contain six elements

The statement

```
string[] insuranceTypes = new string[6];
```

creates an array that can hold six strings and sets the array name as insuranceTypes. The newly created array is automatically filled with nulls. In C#, a newly created array is always filled with the default value as shown in Table 11-4.

Table 11-4. *Default values for the types used with arrays*

Value type	Default value
bool	false
byte	0
short	0
int	0
long	0L
float	0.0F
double	0.0D
char	'\0'
decimal	0.0M
sbyte	0
uint	0
ulong	0
ushort	0
String	null

The statement

```
int[] accountNumber = new int[6];
```

creates an array that can hold six integer values and sets the array name as accountNumber. The newly created array is automatically filled with zeros, as shown in Figure 11-1.

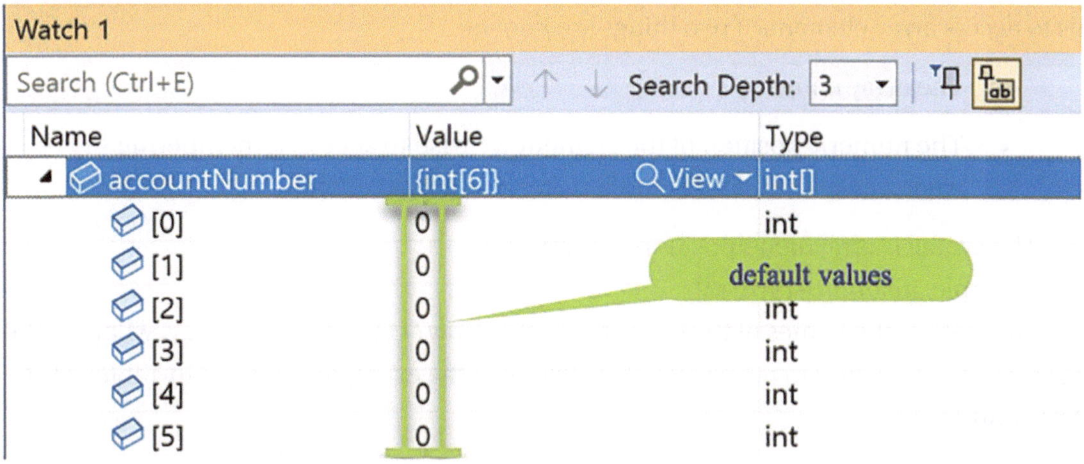

Figure 11-1. *Array filled with default values for the int type*

The statement

```
double[] accountNumber = new double[6];
```

creates an array that can hold six double values and sets the array name as accountNumber. The newly created array is automatically filled with 0 values as shown in Figure 11-2.

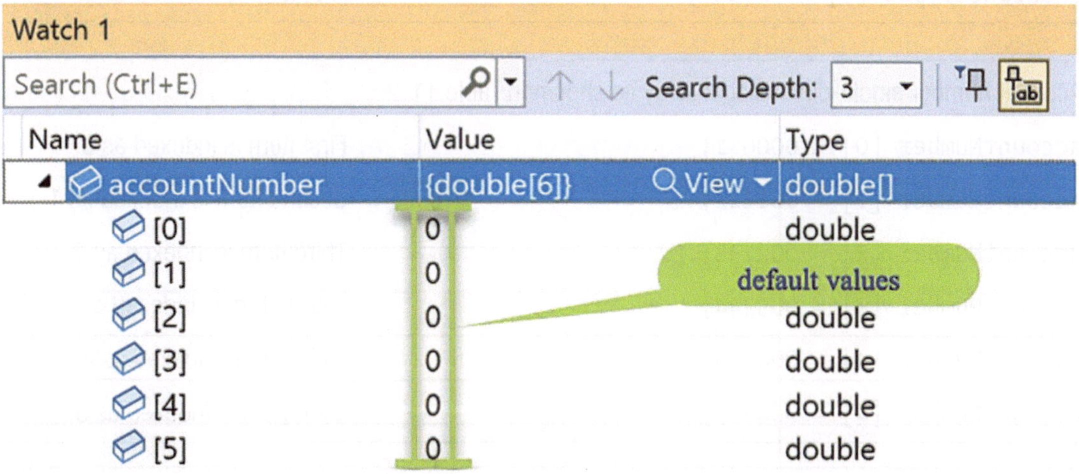

Figure 11-2. *Array filled with default values for the double type*

Referencing the Array Elements

Now that we have declared, created, and instantiated arrays, we need to have a way to access the elements of the arrays so we can use them in our code as required. C# allows us to access array elements if two things are known:

- The array name

- The numeric position of the element we wish to access, remembering what was said earlier about C# using zero-based referencing

The syntax is arrayname[position in array − 1]

Example: insuranceTypes[2]

So what are the names of the elements in the array? Or, put another way, what are the names of the variables in the array? We will look at the examples we used in Tables 11-1, 11-2, and 11-3.

Insurance type single-dimensional array as shown in Table 11-1:

insuranceTypes [0] = "Auto";	First item is indexed as 0.
insuranceTypes [1] = "SUV 4x4";	Second item is indexed as 1.
insuranceTypes [2] = "Motorcycle";	Third item is indexed as 2.
insuranceTypes [3] = "Motorhome";	Fourth item is indexed as 3.
insuranceTypes [4] = "Snowmobile";	Fifth item is indexed as 4.
insuranceTypes [5] = "Boat";	Sixth item is indexed as 5.

Account number single-dimensional array as shown in Table 11-2:

accountNumber [0] = 000011;	First item is indexed as 0.
accountNumber [1] = 001122;	Second item is indexed as 1.
accountNumber [2] = 002233;	Third item is indexed as 2.
accountNumber [3] = 003344;	Fourth item is indexed as 3.
accountNumber [4] = 004455;	Fifth item is indexed as 4.
accountNumber [4] = 004455;	Sixth item is indexed as 5.

Insurance cost single-dimensional array as shown in Table 11-3:

`insurancePremium [0] = 104.99;`	First item is indexed as 0.
`insurancePremium [1] = 105.99;`	Second item is indexed as 1.
`insurancePremium [2] = 106.99;`	Third item is indexed as 2.
`insurancePremium [3] = 107.99;`	Fourth item is indexed as 3.
`insurancePremium [4] = 108.99;`	Fifth item is indexed as 4.
`insurancePremium [4] = 109.99;`	Sixth item is indexed as 5.

Add a new project to hold the code for this chapter.

1. Right-click the solution CoreCSharp.

2. Choose Add.

3. Choose New Project.

4. Choose Console App from the listed templates that appear.

5. Click the Next button.

6. Name the project Chapter11 and leave it in the same location.

7. Click the Next button.

8. Choose the framework to be used, which in our projects will be .NET 6.0 or higher.

9. Click the Create button.

Now we should see the Chapter11 project within the solution called CoreCSharp.

10. Right-click the project Chapter11 in the Solution Explorer panel.

11. Click the Set as Startup Project option.

Notice how the Chapter11 project name has been made to have bold text, indicating that it is the new startup project and that it is the Program.cs file within it that will be executed when we run the debugging.

12. Right-click the Program.cs file in the Solution Explorer window.

13. Choose Rename.

14. Change the name to Arrays.cs.

15. Press the Enter key.

16. Double-click the Arrays.cs file to open it in the editor window.

Now we can set up the code structure with a namespace, and inside it will be the Arrays class, and inside the class will be the Main() method. The shortcut for creating the Main() method is to type svm and press the Tab key twice.

17. In the editor window, add the code in Listing 11-1.

Listing 11-1. Class template with the Main() method

```
namespace Chapter11
{
  internal class Arrays
  {
    static void Main(string[] args)
    {
    } // End of Main() method
  } // End of Arrays class
} // End of Chapter11 namespace
```

Note that the class name matches the filename, **Arrays.**

As we have seen earlier and have coded as an example, when a vehicle is involved in an accident and has to be repaired, the repair shop is required to supply specific details to the insurance company so they can be reimbursed for the costs. The details required are

- The repair shop unique id, data type string

- The vehicle insurance policy number, data type string

- The claim amount, data type double

- The date of the claim, data type Date

When we coded this program as part of the last chapter on iteration, we were aware that any data entered was not stored by the program code. We were made aware that this "flaw" would be rectified using an array. So now the time has come to amend the last program so that the data entered by the repair shop will be stored, for the duration that the program runs. It will not be available after the program is closed; that is why we marked the word permanent as **"permanent"** at the start of the chapter, indicating that permanent relates to the duration of the application run rather than forever. If we require the data after the application is exited, we could store the data in a text file or database, and later in Chapter 16, we will see how to store data permanently in a file.

To store the data in an array, we will

- **Declare an array,** having decided what data type the array will hold.

  Remember the information at the start of this chapter when we read that an array can only hold variables of the same data type – an array is homogenous. We have strings, a double, and a Date, so what data type will we use? Well, one answer is the string data type. This will mean that the Date will have to be converted to a string value. We could even have a separate array for each data type, but for simplicity we are just going to use data type string.

- Use a name for the array. Here we will use the name **repairShopClaims.**

- **Create the array** using the new keyword and stating the size of the array.

- Add the values to the array in the correct position.

Let's code some C# and build our programming muscle.

18. Amend the code, as in Listing 11-2, to declare and create the array that will hold the eight items of data input by the user.

Listing 11-2. Declare and create the array with eight values

```
static void Main(string[] args)
{
    /*
    The array is going to hold the data for 2 claims.
    Each claim has four pieces of information. The number
    of data items is therefore 2 multiplied by 4 = 8.
    So, we will make the array for this example of size 8.
    Not the best way to do things, but fine for now.
    */
    string[] repairShopClaims = new String[8];
} // End of Main() method
```

19.   Amend the code, as in Listing 11-3, to add the variables to be used.

Listing 11-3. Add the variables

```
string[] repairShopClaims = new String[8];

/*
We will setup our variables that will be used in the
quote application. The details will be:
•     the repair shop unique id (string)
•     the vehicle insurance policy number (string)
•     the claim amount (string)
•     the date of the claim (string)
*/
string repairShopID;
string vehiclePolicyNumber;
string claimAmount;
DateTime claimDate;
int numberOfClaimsBeingMade;
int numberOfClaimsEntered = 0;
int arrayPositionCounter = 0;
} // End of Main() method
```

Now we will ask the user to input the number of claims being made, read the user input, convert it to an int, and assign it to the numberOfClaimsBeingMade variable.

20.   Amend the code, as in Listing 11-4.

Listing 11-4. Ask user for number of claims and convert it to an integer

```
int numberOfClaimsEntered = 0;
int arrayPositionCounter = 0;

/*
Read the user input for the number of claims being made
and convert the string value to an integer data type
*/
```

```
Console.WriteLine("How many claims are being made?\n");
numberOfClaimsBeingMade = Convert.ToInt32(Console.ReadLine());
} // End of Main() method
```

Now we will include the start of a do while loop, which will iterate as many times as the user requested and display the current value of the counter for reference.

21.   Amend the code, as in Listing 11-5.

Listing 11-5. Adding the start of a do while loop

```
numberOfClaimsBeingMade = Convert.ToInt32(Console.ReadLine());

/*
As we are using a variable in the loop our code is
flexible and can be used for any number of claims.
An ideal situation and good code.
*/
do
{
  Console.WriteLine("The current value of the " +
    "counter is :" +numberOfClaimsEntered + "\n");
} // End of Main() method
```

Now we will ask the user to input the repair shop id, read the user input, and assign the input to the variable repairShopID.

22.   Amend the code, as in Listing 11-6.

Listing 11-6. Ask user for repair shop id and read the value

```
do
{
  Console.WriteLine("The current value of the " +
    "counter is :" +numberOfClaimsEntered + "\n");

  /*
  Read the user input for the repair shop id and keep
  it as a string
  */
```

```
Console.WriteLine("What is your repair shop id?\n");
repairShopID = Console.ReadLine();
} // End of Main() method
```

When the code is executed and the user has entered the details, we need to store these details in the array at position 0. We will now add the user input to the array in position 0 and then increment the arrayPositionCounter that is being used to track the positions at which the items go in the array.

23.   Amend the code, as in Listing 11-7.

Listing 11-7. Add input to the array and increment the counter

```
Console.WriteLine("What is your repair shop id?\n");
repairShopID = Console.ReadLine();

/*
Write the first input value to the array and then
increment the value of the arrayPositionCounter by 1.
*/
repairShopClaims[arrayPositionCounter] = repairShopID;
arrayPositionCounter++;
} // End of Main() method
```

Now we will ask the user to input the vehicle policy number, read the user input, and assign the input to the variable vehiclePolicyNumber.

24.   Amend the code, as in Listing 11-8.

Listing 11-8. Ask user for policy number and read the value

```
repairShopClaims[arrayPositionCounter] = repairShopID;
arrayPositionCounter++;

/*
Read the user input for the vehicle policy number
and keep it as a string
*/
Console.WriteLine("What is the vehicle policy number?\n");
vehiclePolicyNumber = Console.ReadLine();
} // End of Main() method
```

When the code is executed and the user has entered the details, we need to store these details in the array at position 1. We will now add the user input to the array in position 1 and then increment the arrayPositionCounter that is being used to track the positions at which the items go into the array.

25.   Amend the code, as in Listing 11-9.

Listing 11-9. Add input to the array and increment the counter

```
Console.WriteLine("What is the vehicle policy number?\n");
vehiclePolicyNumber = Console.ReadLine();

/*
Write the second input value to the array and then
increment the value of the arrayPositionCounter by 1
*/
repairShopClaims[arrayPositionCounter] = vehiclePolicyNumber;
    arrayPositionCounter++;
  } // End of Main() method
```

Now we will ask the user to input the claim amount, read the user input, and assign the input to the variable claimAmount.

26.   Amend the code, as in Listing 11-10.

Listing 11-10. Ask user for claim amount and read the value

```
repairShopClaims[arrayPositionCounter] = vehiclePolicyNumber;
arrayPositionCounter++;

/*
Read the user input for the repair amount and assign
it the variable claimAmount
*/
Console.WriteLine("What is the amount being claimed " +
  "for the repair?\n");
claimAmount = Console.ReadLine();
  } // End of Main() method
```

When the code is executed and the user has entered the details, we need to store these details in the array we have set up at position 2. We will now add the user input to the array in position 2 and then increment the arrayPositionCounter that is being used to track the positions at which the items go into the array.

27.   Amend the code, as in Listing 11-11.

Listing 11-11. Add input to the array and increment the counter

```
Console.WriteLine("What is the amount being claimed " +
  "for the repair?\n");
claimAmount = Console.ReadLine());

/*
Write the third input value to the array and then
increment the value of the arrayPositionCounter by 1
*/
repairShopClaims[arrayPositionCounter] = claimAmount;
arrayPositionCounter++;
} // End of Main() method
```

28.   Amend the code, as in Listing 11-12, to ask the user to input the date of the claim and then read the user input.

Listing 11-12. Ask user for claim date, read the value, and convert it to a Date

```
repairShopClaims[arrayPositionCounter] = claimAmount;
arrayPositionCounter++;

/*
Read the user input for the repair date and assign
it to the claimDate variable
*/
Console.WriteLine("What was the date of the repair?\n");
claimDate = Convert.ToDateTime(Console.ReadLine());
} // End of Main() method
```

When the code is executed and the user has entered the details, we need to store these details in the array we have set up at position 3. Now we will add the user input, converted to a string, to the array in position 3 and then increment the arrayPositionCounter that is being used to track the positions at which the items go into the array

29.   Amend the code, as in Listing 11-13.

Listing 11-13. Add input to the array and increment the counter

```
Console.WriteLine("What was the date of the repair?\n");
claimDate = Convert.ToDateTime(Console.ReadLine());

/*
Write the fourth input value to the array and then
increment the value of the arrayPositionCounter by 1
*/
repairShopClaims[arrayPositionCounter] = claimDate.ToString();
arrayPositionCounter++;
} // End of Main() method
```

Now we have accepted all the data required for the first claim. But before getting details for the second claim, we need to increment the numberOfClaimsEntered counter that is being used to hold the value of the number of claims that have been entered.

30.   Amend the code, as in Listing 11-14.

Listing 11-14. Increment the numberOfClaimsEntered counter

```
repairShopClaims[arrayPositionCounter] = claimDate.ToString();
arrayPositionCounter++;

/* Increment the loop counter by 1 */
numberOfClaimsEntered++;
} // End of Main() method
```

31.   Amend the code, as in Listing 11-15, to finish the do while loop by adding the Boolean condition to be tested.

Listing 11-15. Complete the do while iteration construct

```
        /* Increment the loop counter by 1 */
        numberOfClaimsEntered++;

    } while (numberOfClaimsEntered < numberOfClaimsBeingMade);
    } // End of Main() method
  } // End of Arrays class
} // End of Chapter11 namespace
```

Depending on the number of claims the user wishes to make, the do while loop will be executed again the required number of times. This is great, but our only problem will be verifying that the details have been stored in the array. This now offers us a great opportunity to use the last type of iteration, **foreach**, that was mentioned in the last chapter.

foreach Loop

We can use a **foreach loop** as an efficient way to iterate through an array or any collection. Unlike the other iteration constructs we looked at in the previous chapter – for, while, and do – there is no need for an index counter, as the foreach statement takes control and manages the required number of iterations. The foreach loop helps us as developers by reducing the amount of code we need to write. On the other hand, we do not actually have a counter variable to work with if we wish to use it in a display line or for some other reason. The format of the foreach loop is

```
foreach (var item in collection)
{
    <statements>
}
```

In this generic example code

- **var** represents the data type of the array or collection items but we can use any data type from the C# language.

- **item** is a **variable** representing the member of the array. The item in the array at the current position.

- The name **item** is a variable name, and we can call it whatever we like, for example, thememberofthearray.

- **in** is a keyword and must be used in this position.

- **collection** represents the name of the array or collection we wish to iterate.

Applying this to the preceding program we have coded, we would have the code for the iteration statement as shown in Listing 11-16.

Listing 11-16. foreach loop

```
foreach (var itemInTheClaimsArray in repairShopClaims)
{
  Console.WriteLine("The item in the array is:" +
    "\t" + itemInTheClaimsArray + "\n");
}
```

Looking at this specific example

- **var** represents the data type of the array or collection items.

- **item** has been replaced with the variable name **itemInTheClaimsArray.**

- **in** is the keyword.

- **repairShopClaims** represents the collection.

- In the write line statement, the variable **itemInTheClaimsArray** has been displayed.

We will now amend our code to iterate the array and display the items in the array as a way of confirming that the data entered by the user has been stored in the array.

32. Amend the code, as in Listing 11-17, to add the foreach iteration.

Listing 11-17. foreach iteration

```
} while (numberOfClaimsEntered < numberOfClaimsBeingMade);

foreach (var itemInTheClaimsArray in repairShopClaims)
{
```

```
    Console.WriteLine("The item in the array is:" +
        "\t" + itemInTheClaimsArray + "\n");
}
} // End of Main() method
```

33. Click the File menu.

34. Choose Save All.

35. Click the Debug menu.

36. Choose Start Without Debugging.

The console window will appear and ask the user to input the number of claims to be made.

37. Type 2 and press the Enter key.

38. Type RS000001 for the repair shop id and press the Enter key.

The console will now ask the user to input the vehicle policy number.

39. Type VP000001 and press the Enter key.

The console will now ask the user to input the claim amount.

40. Type 1999.99 and press the Enter key.

The console will now ask the user to input the date of the repair.

41. Type 2021/10/01 and press the Enter key.

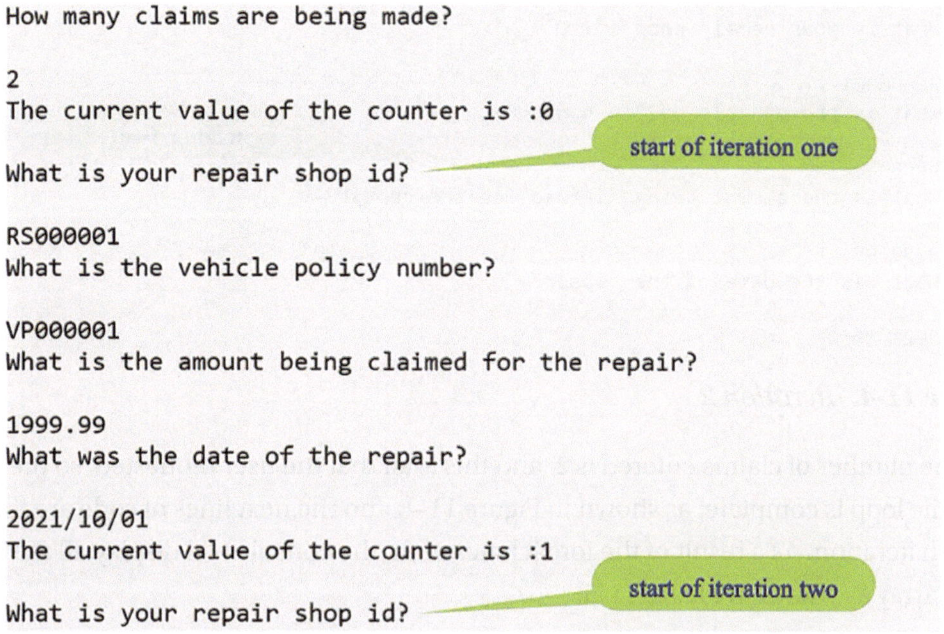

```
How many claims are being made?

2
The current value of the counter is :0

What is your repair shop id?

RS000001
What is the vehicle policy number?

VP000001
What is the amount being claimed for the repair?

1999.99
What was the date of the repair?

2021/10/01
The current value of the counter is :1

What is your repair shop id?
```

start of iteration one

start of iteration two

Figure 11-3. *Iteration 1*

Iteration 1 is now completed; the block of code has been executed. The counter will now be incremented by 1 and become a 1. The questions are asked again for the second claim, as shown in Figure 11-3.

42. Type RS000001 for the repair shop id and press the Enter key.

The console will now ask the user to input the vehicle policy number.

43. Type VP000002 and press the Enter key.

The console will now ask the user to input the claim amount.

44. Type 2999.99 and press the Enter key.

The console will now ask the user to input the date of the repair.

45. Type 2021/10/01 and press the Enter key.

```
What is your repair shop id?

RS000001
What is the vehicle policy number?

VP000002
What is the amount being claimed for the repair?

2999.99
What was the date of the repair?

2021/10/01
```

iteration two

Figure 11-4. *Iteration 2*

The number of claims entered is 2, and this is all that the user requested, so the do while loop is complete, as shown in Figure 11-4, and the next lines of code are the foreach iteration. As a result of the foreach iteration, the console will display all the items in the array as shown in Figure 11-5.

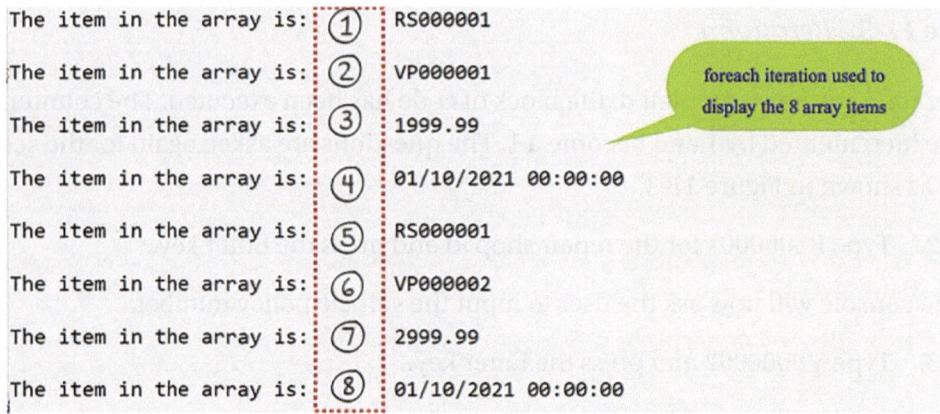

```
The item in the array is:  ①  RS000001

The item in the array is:  ②  VP000001                foreach iteration used to
                                                       display the 8 array items
The item in the array is:  ③  1999.99

The item in the array is:  ④  01/10/2021 00:00:00

The item in the array is:  ⑤  RS000001

The item in the array is:  ⑥  VP000002

The item in the array is:  ⑦  2999.99

The item in the array is:  ⑧  01/10/2021 00:00:00
```

Figure 11-5. *Foreach iteration shows the eight array items*

Figure 11-5 confirms that the array holds the data entered by the user since the foreach iteration has been used to display the array items. Our array is a single-dimensional array holding items of data type string.

46.   Press any key to close the console window.

Now that we have the basics of an array, we can now explore arrays further and see some of the possible errors associated with them.

Add a new class to hold the code for this example.

1. Right-click the Chapter11 project in the Solution Explorer panel.

2. Choose Add.

3. Choose Class.

4. Name the class ArrayErrors.cs.

5. Click the Add button.

6. Create a Main() method within the class, as this was not produced automatically, and delete the unwanted imports.

The shortcut to create the Main() method is to type svm and then press the Tab key twice. Now we need to set this class as the startup class.

7. Right-click the Chapter11 project in the Solution Explorer panel.

8. Choose Properties from the pop-up menu.

9. Choose the ArrayErrors.cs class in the Startup object drop-down list.

10. Close the Properties window.

We will now create a program that will declare and create an array whose size will be determined by the number of entries the user is making. Remember that the array size has to be known at compile time; otherwise, we will get an error. In this program we will keep the code straightforward and only ask the user for the vehicle policy number and the odometer reading.

11. Amend the code, as in Listing 11-18, to declare and create the array using a variable for the size of the array.

Listing 11-18. Create a variable and use it for the array size

```
static void Main(string[] args)
{
    /*
    We will setup our variables that will be used in the
    application. The number of entries being made will
    determine the size of the array
```

```
*/
int numberOfEntriesBeingMade;

/*
The array is going to hold the data for a number of
vehicles and their corresponding odometer readings.
Each entry will be a vehicle policy number and the
number of kilometres shown on the odometer. This means
that the size of the array will be twice the number of
entries being made by the repair shop.
*/
string[] odometerReadings = new string[numberOfEntriesBeingMade * 2];
} // End of Main() method
```

We should note that as we have not initialized the numberOfEntriesBeingMade variable, we get an error as shown in Figure 11-6.

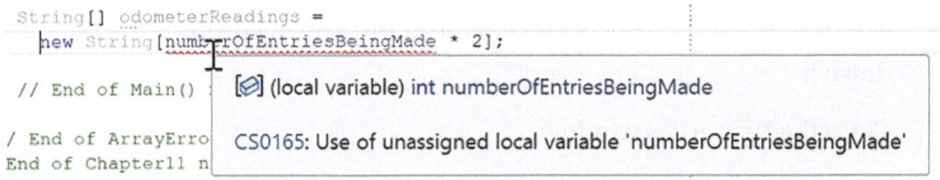

Figure 11-6. *Error when variable not initialized*

The error message shown in Figure 11-6 is saying that we cannot use an unassigned variable for the array size. So we will simply add a line of code that will ask the user to input the number of entries they are going to make and assign this value to the variable. Now the program will be happy as it will have a value for the variable – the variable is not unassigned. What we can see is that even though the actual value of the variable is not known, the program is happy as it will know the value before the array is created.

We will now ask the user to input the number of entries being made, read this value from the console, convert it to data type int, and assign the value to the variable called numberOfEntriesBeingMade. We will insert this code after the declaration of the array.

12. Amend the code, as in Listing 11-19.

Listing 11-19. Read the user input – after array declaration

```
string[] odometerReadings =
            new string[numberOfEntriesBeingMade * 2];
/*
Read the user input for the number of entries being
made and convert the string value to an integer data type
*/
Console.WriteLine("How many entries are you wishing to make?\n");
numberOfEntriesBeingMade = Convert.ToInt32(Console.ReadLine());
} // End of Main() method
```

We still see a red underline under the variable **numberOfEntriesBeingMade,** and this is understandable as the value read from the console is only known after the line of code that tries to declare and create the array. This is an error as the size needs to be known at compile time, **now,** not at runtime.

13. Amend the code, as in Listing 11-20, to move the block of code we have just entered to above the array declaration statement.

Listing 11-20. Read the user input – before array declaration

```
int numberOfEntriesBeingMade;

/*
Read the user input for the number of entries being
made and convert the string value to an integer data type
*/
Console.WriteLine("How many entries are you wishing to make?\n");
numberOfEntriesBeingMade = Convert.ToInt32(Console.ReadLine());

/*
The array is going to hold the data for a number of
vehicles and their corresponding odometer readings.
Each entry will be a vehicle policy number and the
number of kilometres shown on the odometer. This means
```

```
that the size of the array will be twice the number of
entries being made by the repair shop.
*/
string[] odometerReadings = new string[numberOfEntriesBeingMade * 2];
```

Great, the red underline has disappeared, and the compiler is happy. **So now we know that we must tell the compiler the size of the array to make it happy.** We can use a variable, but this must be known when the array is declared and created.

Now we will ask the user to input the value for the vehicle policy number followed by the odometer reading and this will be repeated the number of times requested by the user. For this we will use a do while loop. This code will be very similar to the code from the last code example.

14.   Amend the code, as in Listing 11-21, to add the other variables we will use.

Listing 11-21. Adding the extra variables we require

```
static void Main(string[] args)
{
  /*
        We will setup our variables that will be used in the
        application. The number of entries being made will
        determine the size of the array
        */
  int numberOfEntriesBeingMade;

  int numberOfEntriesEntered = 0;
  int arrayPositionCounter = 0;
  int odometerReadingForVehicle;

  string vehiclePolicyNumber;
```

15.   Amend the code, as in Listing 11-22, to add the loop and the questions.

Listing 11-22. Adding the do while loop and the user questions

```
string[] odometerReadings =
                new string[numberOfEntriesBeingMade * 2];

/*
As we are using a variable in the loop our code is
flexible and can be used for any number of claims.
An ideal situation and good code.
*/
do
{
  Console.WriteLine("The current value of the counter is :" +
  numberOfEntriesEntered + "\n");

  /*
  Read the user input for the vehicle policy number
  and keep it as a string
  */
  Console.WriteLine("What is the vehicle policy number?\n");
  vehiclePolicyNumber = Console.ReadLine();

  /*
  Write this first input value to the array and then
  increment the value of the arrayPositionCounter by 1
  */
  odometerReadings[arrayPositionCounter] = vehiclePolicyNumber;
  arrayPositionCounter++;

  /* Read the user input for the odometer reading */
  Console.WriteLine("What is the odometer reading?\n");
  odometerReadingForVehicle = Convert.ToInt32(Console.ReadLine());

  /*
  Write the second input value to the array and then
  increment the value of the arrayPositionCounter by 1
  */
```

```
odometerReadings[arrayPositionCounter] = odometerReadingForVehicle.
ToString();
arrayPositionCounter++;

/* Increment the loop counter by 1 */
numberOfEntriesEntered++;
} while (numberOfEntriesEntered < numberOfEntriesBeingMade);
} // End of Main() method
```

16. Amend the code, as in Listing 11-23, to add the iteration construct and display the array values.

Listing 11-23. Adding the foreach iteration to display the array values

```
/* Increment the loop counter by 1 */
 numberOfEntriesEntered++;
} while(numberOfEntriesEntered < numberOfEntriesBeingMade);

foreach(string itemInTheodometerReadingsArray in
                                    odometerReadings)
 {
   Console.WriteLine("The item in the array is: \t" +
   itemInTheodometerReadingsArray + "\n");
 } // End of foreach construct
} // End of Main() method
```

17. Click the File menu.

18. Choose Save All.

19. Click the Debug menu.

20. Choose Start Without Debugging.

21. Type 2 for the number of entries to be made.

22. Press the Enter key.

23. Type VP000001 for the vehicle policy number.

24. Press the Enter key.

The console will now ask the user to input the vehicle odometer reading.

25.   Type 10000.

26.   Press the Enter key.

27.   Type VP000002 for the vehicle policy number.

28.   Press the Enter key.

29.   Type 20000.

30.   Press the Enter key.

Figure 11-7 shows the two iterations, and Figure 11-8 shows the array items.

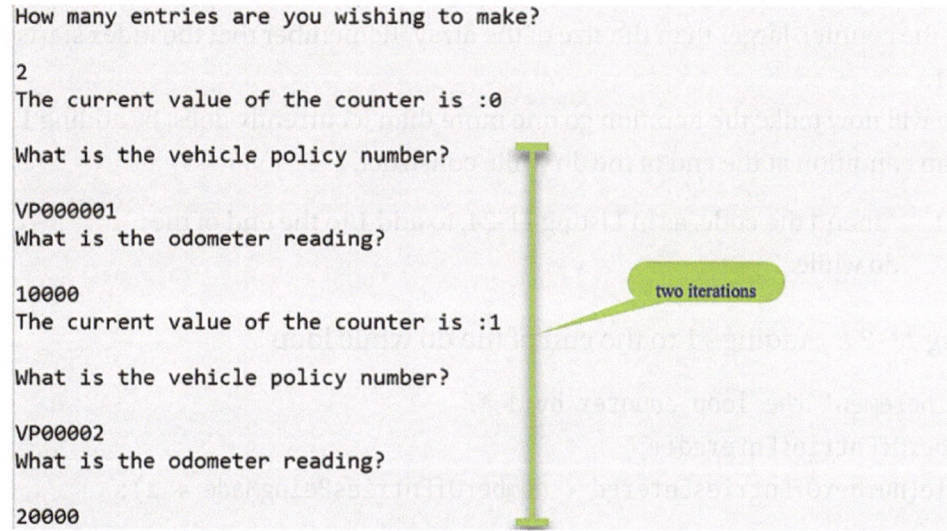

Figure 11-7. *Both iterations completed*

```
The item in the array is:          VP000001

The item in the array is:          10000

The item in the array is:          VP000002

The item in the array is:          20000


C:\CoreCSharp\CoreCSharp\Chapter11\bin\Debug\net6.0\Chapter11.exe
Press any key to close this window . . ._
```

Figure 11-8. *Foreach iteration displays the array items*

The array will therefore hold the string values as shown in Table 11-5.

Table 11-5. *Array depiction*

[0]	[1]	[2]	[3]
VP000001	10000	VP000002	20000

IndexOutOfBounds Exception

An array is of fixed size, and if we try to read or write a value that is outside the boundary of the array, we will be causing an exception. In C# the error is known as an **IndexOutOfBounds exception** because it happens when we have made the value of the index, the counter, larger than the size of the array. Remember that the index starts at 0, not 1.

We will now make the iteration go one more than it currently does, by adding 1 to the Boolean condition at the end of the do while construct.

31. Amend the code, as in Listing 11-24, to add 1 to the end of the do while.

Listing 11-24. Adding +1 to the end of the do while loop

```
/* Increment the loop counter by 1 */
numberOfEntriesEntered++;
} while(numberOfEntriesEntered < numberOfEntriesBeingMade + 1);
```

32. Click the File menu.

33. Choose Save All.

34. Click the Debug menu.

35. Choose Start Without Debugging.

36. Type 2 for the number of entries to be made.

37. Press the Enter key.

38. Type VP000001 for the vehicle policy number.

39. Press the Enter key.

The console will now ask the user to input the vehicle odometer reading.

40. Type 10000.

41. Press the Enter key.

42. Type VP000002 for the vehicle policy number.

43. Press the Enter key.

44. Type 20000.

45. Press the Enter key.

46. Type VP000003 for the vehicle policy number.

47. Press the Enter key.

Our array was made to have a size of

2 entries multiplied by the 2 values in each entry = 4

This means that the positions available in the array are

odometerReadings[0]

odometerReadings[1]

odometerReadings[2]

odometerReadings[3]

Our variable is 4, and we are therefore trying to write to position

odometerReadings[4]

This means our index of 4 is out of bounds, as 3 is the maximum boundary limit.

Figure 11-9 shows the resulting runtime error.

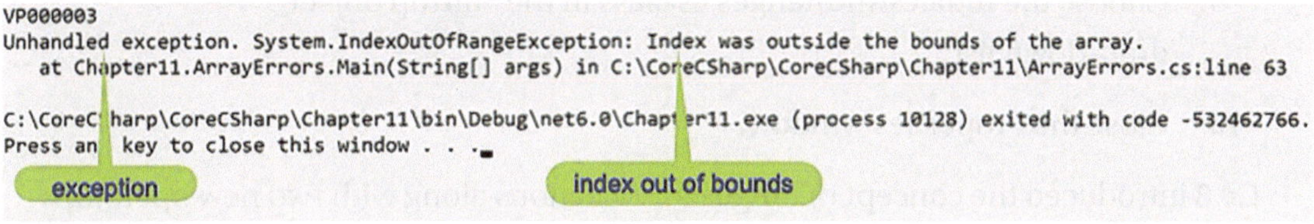

```
VP000003
Unhandled exception. System.IndexOutOfRangeException: Index was outside the bounds of the array.
   at Chapter11.ArrayErrors.Main(String[] args) in C:\CoreCSharp\CoreCSharp\Chapter11\ArrayErrors.cs:line 63

C:\CoreCSharp\CoreCSharp\Chapter11\bin\Debug\net6.0\Chapter11.exe (process 10128) exited with code -532462766.
Press any key to close this window . . ._
```
        exception   index out of bounds

Figure 11-9. *Array out-of-bounds exception*

We will now change the test back to its original value, no +, as in Listing 11-25.

Listing 11-25. Removing the +1 from the end of the do while loop

```
/* Increment the loop counter by 1 */
numberOfEntriesEntered++;
} while(numberOfEntriesEntered < numberOfEntriesBeingMade);
```

48. Click the File menu.

49. Choose Save All.

Ranges and Indices: C# 8 and Above

Add a new class to hold the code for this example.

1. Right-click the project Chapter11 in the Solution Explorer panel.

2. Choose Add.

3. Choose Class.

4. Name the class IndicesAndRanges.cs.

5. Click the Add button.

6. Create a Main() method within the class, as this was not produced automatically, and delete the unwanted imports.

Remember the shortcut to create the Main() method is to type svm and then press the Tab key twice.

Now we need to set this class as the startup class.

7. Right-click the Chapter11 project in the Solution Explorer panel.

8. Choose Properties from the pop-up menu.

9. Choose the IndicesAndRanges.cs class in the Startup object drop-down list.

10. Close the Properties window.

C# 8 introduced the concept of ranges to collections along with two new operators. When using ranges, we now have the **index** and the **range,** which can be used to index and slice the collection. Both index and range are part of the System namespace. When we think about what we have done so far with arrays, we have worked from the start of the zero-indexed array and never really thought about starting from the end of the array, and we use the index of the element or elements when we need access to them. Now, in C# 8 we have been given an **index expression** that allows us to access the collection from the end. The hat operator, ^, means **"index from end,"** so ^2 would give us the second element from the end. The syntax is the ^ followed by an integer value or a variable that can be converted to an integer, and we should still be aware that we can still get an IndexOutOfRange exception if we use an incorrect integer value.

Also, in C# there was no easy way to access a range or a slice of the collection, but we could use commands like Skip() and Take(), which belong to the Language-Integrated Query (LINQ) library. An example of these would be

```
string[] policyType = { "Home", "Auto", "Life", "Boat" };
```

```
var policies = policyType.Skip(2).Take(1);
```

```
Console.WriteLine("Skip 2 and take 4 gives the values");
foreach (var category in policies)
{
  Console.WriteLine(category);
}
```

Running this code would mean Home and Auto are skipped and then Life is taken and it is displayed within the foreach construct. But interestingly if we are to code either of these two lines

```
var policies = policyType.Skip(12).Take(1);
var policies = policyType.Skip(2).Take(10);
```

the fact that we have tried to skip 12 on line 1 when there are only 4 items and take 12 on line 2 when there are only 2 items remaining does not cause an out-of-range exception. However, if the source was null, we would get a System.ArgumentNullException: Value cannot be null error.

C# 8 however changes things, and we are now able to use the new range operator, **start..howmany**, and we can leave out the start or the end. The **..** syntax is called the **range operator**.

Let's code some C# and build our programming muscle.

11. Amend the code, as in Listing 11-26, to declare and initialize the array.

Listing 11-26. Declare and create the array

```
namespace Chapter11
{
  internal class IndicesAndRanges
```

```
  {
    static void Main(string[] args)
    {
      Console.WriteLine("**** C# 8 Indices and Ranges ****");
      Console.WriteLine("Ranges and indices provide a succinct ");
      Console.WriteLine("syntax for accessing single elements ");
      Console.WriteLine("or ranges in a sequence ");
      Console.WriteLine("*******************");
      /*
      Declare and initialise the array of employees
      and their salary
      */
        String[] employeeAndSalary = { "Gerry Byrne", "20000.55",
          "Peter Johnston", "30000.00", "Ryan Jones", "50000.00" };
    } // End of Main() method
  } // End of IndicesAndRanges class
} // End of Chapter11 namespace
```

We will amend the code to iterate the array and use the **index from end** within the console output. In this example we use ^**(employeeAndSalary.Length – (counter)),** which means

- Find the length of the array.

- Subtract the counter value from it, for example, 6 – 0 = 6.

- But with the ^ it becomes ^6, which means from the end take the sixth element, which we know is really the first item in the array or index zero.

12. Add the new code within the Main() method, as in Listing 11-27.

Listing 11-27. Iterate the array and use the hat operator, index from end

```
/*
Using the index from end operator ^ indicates we wish
to start at the end of the sequence
Counting from the beginning means we start at 0
Counting from the end means we start at 1
```

```
*/
for (int counter = 0; counter < employeeAndSalary.Length;
 counter++)
{
Console.WriteLine($"The element positioned {counter} from the end of the
array is {employeeAndSalary[^(counter+1)]}");
}
} // End of Main() method
```

13.   Click the File menu.

14.   Choose Save All.

15.   Click the Debug menu.

16.   Choose Start Without Debugging.

Figure 11-10 shows the array has been read using the ^ operator. We see the **index from end value and the value stored at that position.**

```
**** C# 8 Indices and Ranges ****
Ranges and indices provide a succinct
syntax for accessing single elements
or ranges in a sequence
********************
The element positioned 0 from the end of the array is 50000.00
The element positioned 1 from the end of the array is Ryan Jones
The element positioned 2 from the end of the array is 30000.00
The element positioned 3 from the end of the array is Peter Johnston
The element positioned 4 from the end of the array is 20000.55
The element positioned 5 from the end of the array is Gerry Byrne
```

Figure 11-10.   *Using the hat operator ^, "index from end"*

17.   Press the Enter key to close the console window.

18.   Amend the code, as in Listing 11-28, to use the index from end to display the second element from the end of the array.

Listing 11-28. Using the index from end, ^, to display the second element

```
    for (int counter = 0; counter < employeeAndSalary.Length;
        counter++)
    {
Console.WriteLine($"The element positioned {counter} from the end of the
array is {employeeAndSalary[^(counter+1)]}");
    }

    Console.WriteLine();
    Console.WriteLine("* ^ index from the end operator *");
    /*
    Using the index feature.
    ^ indicates we wish to start at the end
    In the first example we use the traditional position index
    In the second example we use the index from
    */
    Console.WriteLine($"Element index 2 is {employeeAndSalary[2]} and the
    second item from the end is {employeeAndSalary[4]}");

    Console.WriteLine($"Element index 2 is {employeeAndSalary[^4]} and
    the second item from the end is {employeeAndSalary[^2]}");
    Console.WriteLine();
  } // End of Main() method

 } // End of IndicesAndRanges class
} // End of Chapter11 namespace
```

19. Click the File menu.

20. Choose Save All.

21. Click the Debug menu.

22. Choose Start Without Debugging.

The console will show the array elements as shown in Figure 11-11. We see the output line repeated as we have used the traditional method and the equivalent ^, **index from end**.

```
* ^ index from the end operator *
Element index 2 is Peter Johnston and the second item from the end is Ryan Jones
Element index 2 is Peter Johnston and the second item from the end is Ryan Jones

C:\CoreCSharp\CoreCSharp\Chapter11\bin\Debug\net6.0\Chapter11.exe (process 5572) exited
Press any key to close this window . . .
```

Figure 11-11. *Traditional index and the hat operator*

23. Press the Enter key to close the console window.

24. Amend the code, as in Listing 11-29, to use the length and index from end to display the last element of the array.

Listing 11-29. Using the length and index from end, ^

```
Console.WriteLine($"Element index 2 is " +
  $"{employeeAndSalary[^4]} and the second item from" +
  $" the end is {employeeAndSalary[^2]}");
Console.WriteLine();

Console.WriteLine("* Length and ^ index from end operator*");
/*
Using the index feature. ^ indicates we wish to start
at the end. In the first example we use the length to
help find the last item. In the second example we use the
indices to find the last item
*/
Console.WriteLine($"The last item of the array is {employeeAndSalary[
employeeAndSalary.Length - 1]}");

Console.WriteLine($"The last item of the array is
{employeeAndSalary[^1]}");
Console.WriteLine();
} // End of Main() method
```

25. Click the File menu.

26. Choose Save All.

27.   Click the Debug menu.

28.   Choose Start Without Debugging.

Figure 11-12 shows the console with the last item of the array.

```
* Length and ^ index from end operator*
The last item of the array is 50000.00
The last item of the array is 50000.00
```

Figure 11-12.   *Length and the hat operator*

29.   Press the Enter key to close the console window.

Range

In this code we will look at the traditional method **GetRange()**, from the LINQ library, to get a sequence of values from the array. We will also use the **Skip()** and **Take()** methods, which are also from the LINQ library. We will then use the **new range operator ..** to locate elements.

We will amend the code to use the ToList() and GetRange() methods to display the items from the list within the given range. Read the comments to help with understanding the code.

30.   Amend the code as in Listing 11-30.

Listing 11-30.   Using the ToList() and GetRange() methods

```
Console.WriteLine($"The last item of the array " +
  $"is {employeeAndSalary[^1]}");
Console.WriteLine();

/*
Using the range feature. Range represents a sub range of
a sequence. A range specifies the start and end of a range.
Ranges are exclusive, meaning the end isn't included in
the range. The range [0..^0] represents the entire range.
Equally [0..sequence.Length] represents the entire range.
In the first example we use the traditional method to find
```

```
the length. In the second example we use the indices to
find the last item
*/
Console.WriteLine(" GetRange and ToList *");
Console.WriteLine("Range represents a sub range of a sequence");

var employees = employeeAndSalary.ToList().GetRange(2, 4);

foreach (var item in employees)
{
  Console.WriteLine($"After using GetRange() the array item is
  {item}");
}

Console.WriteLine();
} // End of Main() method
```

31. Click the File menu.

32. Choose Save All.

33. Click the Debug menu.

34. Choose Start Without Debugging.

Figure 11-13 shows the console displaying the array elements starting at element 2, the third item, and taking four items, which is up to element 5, the sixth item.

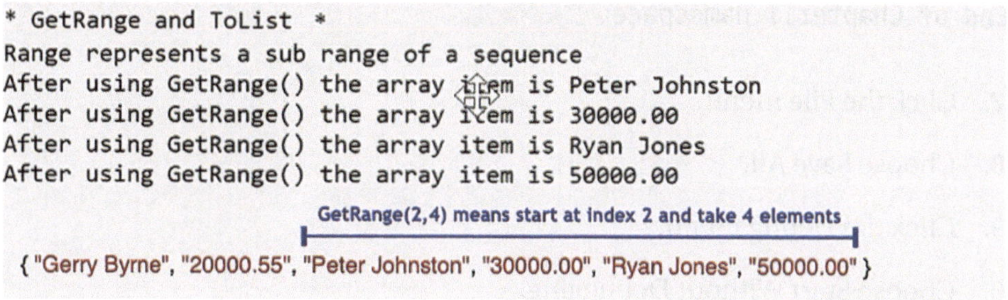

Figure 11-13. *GetRange() and ToList() methods start at the third item for four items*

35. Press the Enter key to close the console window.

36. Amend the code, as in Listing 11-31, to use the Skip() and Take() methods and display the items.

Listing 11-31. Using the Skip() and Take() methods

```
Console.WriteLine();

Console.WriteLine("* Skip and Take * ");
/*
Using the skip and take features.
In the first example we use the traditional method to
find the length. In the second example we use the indices
to find the last item
*/

var someemployees = employeeAndSalary.Skip(2).Take(4);

foreach (var item in someemployees)
{
  Console.WriteLine($"After using Skip() and Take() the array item is
  {item}");
}
Console.WriteLine();
} // End of Main() method

} // End of IndicesAndRanges class
} // End of Chapter11 namespace
```

37. Click the File menu.

38. Choose Save All.

39. Click the Debug menu.

40. Choose Start Without Debugging.

The console, as shown in Figure 11-14, will show the array elements.

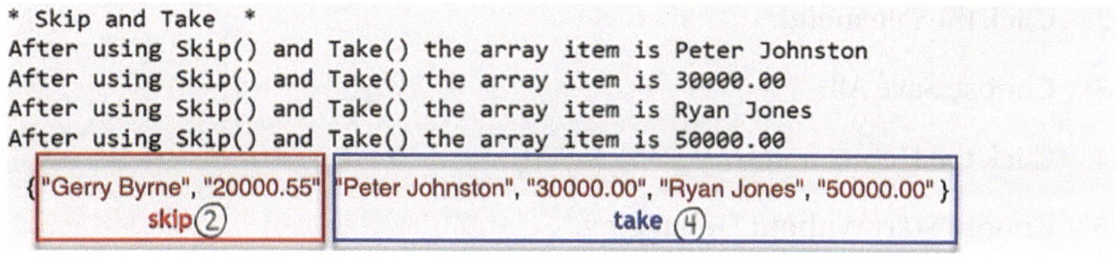

```
* Skip and Take  *
After using Skip() and Take() the array item is Peter Johnston
After using Skip() and Take() the array item is 30000.00
After using Skip() and Take() the array item is Ryan Jones
After using Skip() and Take() the array item is 50000.00
```

{ "Gerry Byrne", "20000.55" | "Peter Johnston", "30000.00", "Ryan Jones", "50000.00" }
skip ②   take ④

Figure 11-14. *Skip() and Take() methods*

41.   Amend the code to use the range operator and display the items.

Listing 11-32. Using the range operator [2..^2]

```
foreach (var item in someemployees)
{
  Console.WriteLine($"After using Skip() and " +
    $"Take() the array item is {item}");
}
Console.WriteLine();

Console.WriteLine("* Range operator *");
/*
Using the range operator .., specifies the start and end
of a range as its operands. A range specifies the start
and end of a range. Ranges are exclusive, meaning the
end isn't included in the range.
The range [0..^0] represents the entire range.
In this example we use start at index 2 and
stop at the element 2 from the end
*/

var someemployeeswithindices = employeeAndSalary[2..^2];

foreach (var item in someemployeeswithindices)
{
  Console.WriteLine($"Starting at index 2 and stopping at the element
    before 2 from the end the array item is { item }");
}
} // End of Main() method
```

42. Click the File menu.

43. Choose Save All.

44. Click the Debug menu.

45. Choose Start Without Debugging.

The console, as shown in Figure 11-15, shows the result from using the range operator.

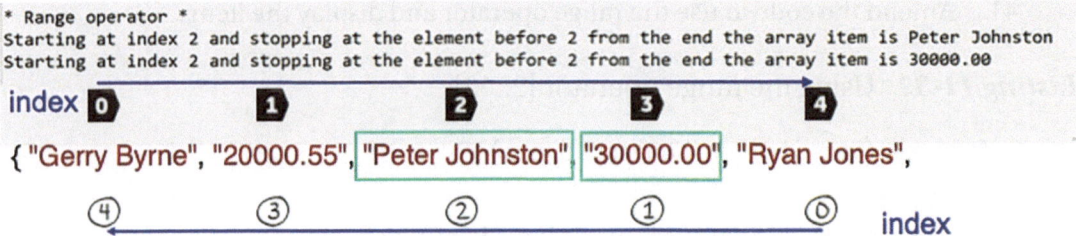

Figure 11-15. *Range operator [2.. ^2]*

Chapter Summary

In this chapter we have learned about the particularly important programming concept called arrays. We have learned that in C#

- Arrays are used to hold a collection of items all of the same data type.

- An array is homogeneous.

- Arrays are of fixed size. Once we declare the size of the array, it cannot be altered.

- Arrays hold the data for the duration that the program runs.

- There are single-dimensional arrays, which we have used in this chapter, but there are also multidimensional arrays.

- Items in an array are referenced by their index, also called the subscript.

- The indexes start at 0, not 1 – arrays are zero indexed.

- The foreach loop is an ideal iterator to use with arrays; however, it is not suitable if we need to reference a counter since no counter exists in the foreach construct.

- If we try to exceed the maximum index of the array, we will get an IndexOutOfBounds exception.

- There are different ways to access the elements of the array using the range features like the hat operator, ^, which means "index from end," and the range operator .., which effectively lets us "slice" the array.

- We can have more than one class in a project.

We are making great progress in our programming of C# applications and we should be proud of our achievements. In finishing this chapter and increasing our knowledge, we are advancing to our target.

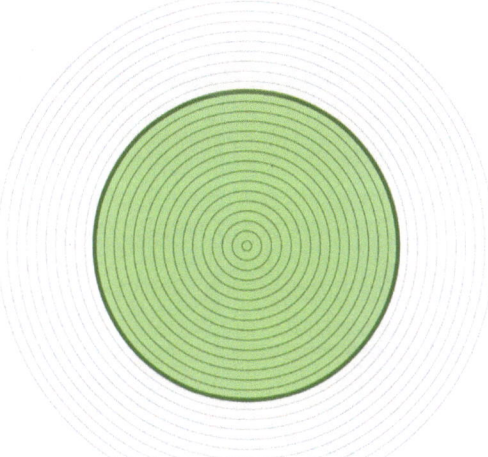

Our target is getting closer

CHAPTER 12

Methods

Methods: Modularization

We learned in Chapter 11 that arrays are a very important programming structure when we need to "store" a collection of data, variables or objects, of the same data type. We saw that arrays in C# are of a fixed size. Once we declare the size of the array, it cannot be altered. Each item in an array can be referenced using its index, which is also called its subscript, and we can use the foreach loop to iterate the array items. With the foreach iteration, we do not need to use a counter as the foreach construct handles the indexing for us. If we wish to reference an index in an iteration, we can use the more traditional for, while, or do while iteration. We also learned that we could cause an IndexOutOfBounds exception if we are not careful in our coding.

Methods: Concepts of Methods and Functions

Most commercial programs will involve large amounts of code, and from a maintenance and testing perspective, it is essential that the program has a good structure. Well-written and organized programs allow those who maintain or test them to

- Follow the code and the flow of events easier.

- Find things quicker.

Just look at Figure 12-1 and think which image fits with the description of finding things easier.

© Gerard Byrne 2022
G. Byrne, *Target C#*, https://doi.org/10.1007/978-1-4842-8619-7_12

Figure 12-1. *Organized or not?*

Would we say the right-hand image? We might say that in the right-hand image, there is a sense of organization, there is space to see things, and there is a sense of calm. The left-hand image, we might say, gives a sense of confusion, clutter, and not caring. We do not want our code to look or feel like the left-hand image.

One way to help structure the program code is to break it into small functional parts with each part performing only one task. When we have a functional part, which does one specific thing, it may be possible for that functional part to be used by other parts of the program. These small functional parts can be thought of as **subprograms** or **methods** or **functions,** or sometimes they are called **procedures**. The words *function* and *method* are often used interchangeably. If we think about functions in mathematics, for example, we can have mathematical functions such as square root, sin, cos, and tan, as shown in Figure 12-2.

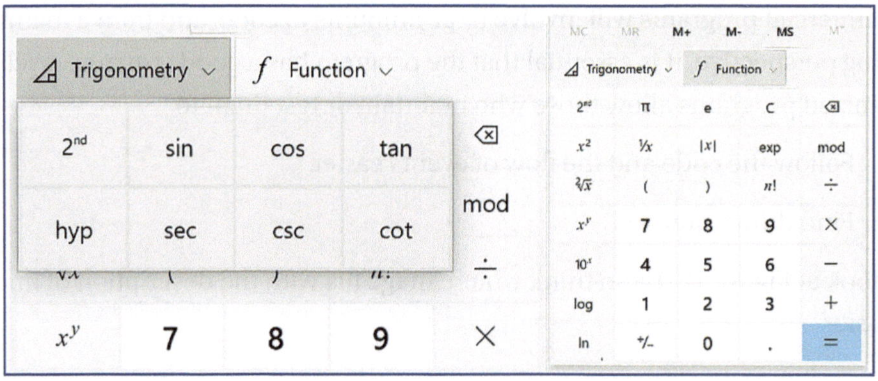

Figure 12-2. *Method or function?*

According to the Microsoft site

A method is a code block that contains a series of statements. A program causes the statements to be executed by calling the method and specifying any required method arguments.

In C#, every executed instruction is performed in the context of a method. The Main() method is the entry point for every C# application, and it is called by the Common Language Runtime (CLR) when the program is started.

Some Points Regarding Methods

- **A method begins with an access modifier**. The access modifier will determine the visibility of the method from another class. If we set the access modifier as

  - **public**, the method is accessible inside the class it is created in and is available from outside this class

  - **private**, the method is only accessible inside the class it is created in

  - **protected**, the method is only accessible inside the class it is in or in a class that is derived from the class

  - **internal**, the method is only accessible inside the same assembly but not from another assembly

- A method access modifier is followed by the method **return type**. The return type means the data type of the object that is being returned by the method. We can return any of the data types we have looked at, for example, int, float, double, char, string, or bool. Or we can return a type that we have defined. If the method will not return a value, then the return type is said to be void – the keyword void still needs to appear .

- The return type is followed by the **method name.** The method name should follow good coding principles and let the reader know what the method is doing, simply by reading the name.

- The method name is followed by open and close brackets ().

- Inside the brackets () there may be a **list of parameters**. The parameters are variables that will hold any values passed to the method. The parameters will have a data type, which will be stated in front of the parameter name. The list of parameters is enclosed in parentheses (). Not every method will accept parameters; they are optional. So the method can contain no parameters – they can be referred to as parameterless methods.

- The parentheses **()** are followed by opening and closing curly braces **{}.** Inside the curly braces is where the code, business logic, goes.

- Methods are coded inside the class but outside the Main method, if there is a Main method in the class.

Figure 12-3 shows the general format of a method with a specific method also shown.

General format for a method	Specific example of a method
access ret-type name (parameter-list) { // body of method }	```public void Hello()` `{` `Console.WriteLine("Hello World")` `}```

Figure 12-3. *General format for a method, with a specific example*

Examples

We will go into the structure more as we progress, but for now, we will look at three examples that fit the preceding rules:

1. public void CalculateCommission()

   - Here the access modifier is **public.**

   - The method will not return a value; it therefore returns **void.**

   - The method name is **CalculateCommission.**

   - The method has **no parameters**, so it takes in no values, no variables or objects.

2. private double CalculateCommission()

   - Here the access modifier is **private.**

   - The method will return a value, which is of data type double.

- The method name is **CalculateCommission.**

- The method has no parameters, so it takes in no variables or objects – it is parameterless.

3. private double CalculateCommission(double salesAmount, double commissionRate)

    - Here the access modifier is **private.**

    - The method will return a value, which is of data type double.

    - The method name is **CalculateCommission.**

    - The method accepts, takes in, **two parameters**. The first parameter is called **salesAmount,** which has a data type of double; and the second parameter is called **commissionRate,** which has a data type of double.

Some Other Important Points

- A method can contain one or more statements.

- A method name can use any valid identifier that we want.

- A method name should not be a C# keyword.

- The method name is used to call the method, and when we call the method, we are asking the method to execute its code and then return to the code that made the call.

- There is a very important method called **Main( )** and it **is reserved** for the method that begins execution of your program.

In Figure 12-4, MethodOne() is called from within the Main() method. The application code will look outside the Main() method for a method with the name MethodOne(). When it finds MethodOne(), it executes the lines of code within it and then returns to the code within the Main() method.

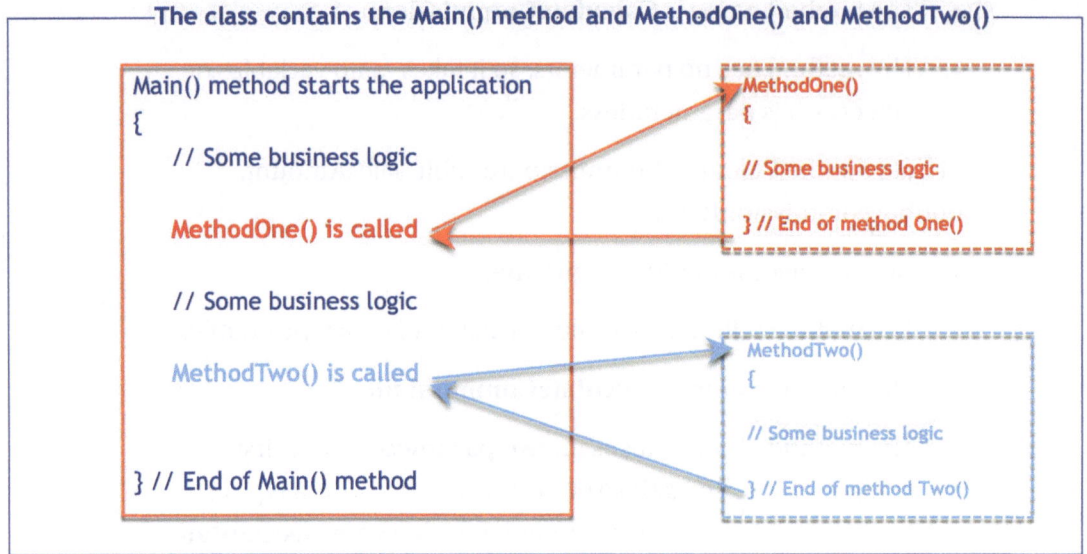

Figure 12-4. *Main() method that calls two methods*

After returning from MethodOne(), the next lines of code, indicated as some business logic in the code in Figure 12-4, are executed until the second method, MethodTwo(), is called. When MethodTwo() is called, the application code will again look outside the Main() method, but this time for a method with the name MethodTwo(). When it finds MethodTwo(), it executes the lines of code within it and then returns to the code within the Main() method.

Even looking at this simplified flow diagram, we get a sense that

- Methods can be kept separate from the main code and called as required.

- The methods are coded outside the Main() method.

- Methods are small blocks of code, as we can see from the dotted areas in Figure 12-4.

Modern programming style dictates that a method should do one thing and one thing only. Methods that do more than one thing should be split into further methods. As a caveat we need to be mindful that creating every method to do one thing can actually make the code less readable and possibly harder to maintain, so we have to strike a balance and be realistic, and that is part of being a developer. Essentially, we have three types of methods, and we will look at these now to see how they are used, their similarities, and their differences.

Three Types of Methods

- **Void method**

Listing 12-1. Void method

```
public void CalculateCommission();
```

> The code in Listing 12-1 is what we looked at earlier, and we saw that this type of method executed code and did not return any value – it is a void method.

- **Value method**

Listing 12-2. Value method

```
private double CalculateCommission();
```

> The code in Listing 12-2 is what we looked at earlier, and we saw that this type of method executed code and then returned a value. The value it returns is a variable, and the variable must have a data type that matches the return type stated after the access modifier and before the method signature. In this example we are returning a value of type double – it is a value method.

- **Parameter method**

Listing 12-3. Parameter method

```
private double CalculateCommission(double salesAmount, double
commissionRate);
```

> The code in Listing 12-3 is what we looked at earlier, and we saw that this type of method accepted one or more parameters. The parameters are just variables or objects, so they have a data type, and we give them a name of our choosing. The method executes code, which will probably use the variables passed in as parameters. Otherwise, why would we accept the parameters? The method can also return a value, in which case it is also a value method, or it may not return a value, in which case it is also a void method. This is a parameter method.

In Listing 12-2 the return type is a double, so the method is a value method, but it accepts, takes in, no value, so it is also a parameterless method.

In Listing 12-3 the return type is a double, so the method is a value method, and it accepts, takes in, two values of data type double, so it is also a parameter method.

In Listing 12-4 the return type is a void, so the method is a void method, and it accepts, takes in, one value of data type double, so it is also a parameter method.

Listing 12-4. Void/parameter method

```
private void CalculateCommission(double salesAmount);
```

Interestingly all the methods in Listings 12-1, 12-2, 12-3, and 12-4 have the same name, CalculateCommission, but they return different types or accept different parameters. We will talk about this later when we discuss method overloading.

Void Methods

When we call a method, the lines of code within the method are implemented. In Figure 12-4 we saw that when MethodOne() was called, the program looked for MethodOne(), the lines of code were executed, and control of the program was returned to the main program.

When a method does not return a value, it is said to be a void method. The declaration void indicates that the function returns no value to the caller. It is important to realize that every function declaration specifies a return type, even if it's void.

An example of a void method is shown in Listing 12-5.

Listing 12-5. Void method

```
public void OdometerReading()
{
    /// Ask the user to input the value on the odometer
    Console.WriteLine("What is the odometer reading");
```

```
    // Read the value entered by the user
    odometerReadingEntered = int.Parse(Console.ReadLine());
}
```

Code Analysis

- The method has an **access modifier** of **public** so the method will be available to all code inside the class or from outside the class.

- The **return type** is **void** so the method will not return any value, and we will therefore not see the last line of code in the method saying **return, but we should be aware that the return is still there and the compiler infers it. We can also have the return statement at any position in the method, but code following it will not be executed.**

- The name of the method is **OdometerReading.**

- The open and close parentheses follow the name and are empty, which means that the method has no parameters, accepts no values.

- The open and close curly braces follow the parentheses, and it is between these braces that the business logic, the code, goes.

- The business logic code is very simple as it displays a message to the user through the Console.WriteLine() method.

- It reads the user input from the console using the Parse() method.

- The Parse() method accepts a parameter, which in this case is Console.ReadLine() - in other words, whatever is entered at the console.

- The input is converted to an int, as we have used int.Parse() to convert.

The format for calling the method, using it, is by using the method name followed by the open and close parentheses as shown in Listing 12-6.

Listing 12-6. Calling the void method

```
OdometerReading();
```

Add a new project to hold the code for this chapter.

1. Right-click the solution CoreCSharp.

2. Choose Add.

3. Choose New Project.

4. Choose Console App from the listed templates that appear.

5. Click the Next button.

6. Name the project Chapter12 and leave it in the same location.

7. Click the Next button.

8. Choose the framework to be used, which in our projects will be .NET 6.0 or higher.

9. Click the Create button.

Now we should see the Chapter12 project within the solution called CoreCSharp.

10. Right-click the project Chapter12 in the Solution Explorer panel.

11. Click the Set as Startup Project option.

Notice how the Chapter12 project name has been made to have bold text, indicating that it is the new startup project and that it is the Program.cs file within it that will be executed when we run the debugging.

12. Right-click the Program.cs file in the Solution Explorer window.

13. Choose Rename.

14. Change the name to MethodsVoid.cs.

15. Press the Enter key.

16. Double-click the MethodsVoid.cs file to open it in the editor window.

Now we can set up the code structure with a namespace, and inside it will be the MethodsVoid class, and inside the class will be the Main() method. The shortcut for creating the Main() method is to type svm and press the Tab key twice.

17. In the editor window, add the code in Listing 12-7.

Listing 12-7. Class template when adding a class

```
namespace Chapter12
{
  internal class MethodsVoid
  {
    static void Main(string[] args)
    {

    } // End of Main() method

  } // End of MethodsVoid class
} // End of Chapter12 namespace
```

We are now going to use the same code that we created for the Arrays.cs program, but we will make the code more maintainable by creating methods. Our methods for this example will be void methods.

Listing 12-8 is the code from the Arrays.cs program but with the original comments removed and a new comment added for each block of code that will become a method in our new program. This is an example to illustrate that methods can be used to modularize our code, but remember the caveat we mentioned earlier about striking a balance between all methods doing one thing and having readable and maintainable code.

Do not type the following code; it is for reference only and is the same as we coded in the last chapter. It is here merely to show which blocks of code will become methods.

Listing 12-8. Program code

```
static void Main(string[] args)
{
  /****************** METHOD ONE ****************/
  Console.WriteLine("How many claims are being made?\n");
  numberOfClaimsBeingMade = Convert.ToInt32(Console.ReadLine());

  do
  {
    /******************METHOD TWO ****************/
    Console.WriteLine("The current value of the " +
      "counter is :" + numberOfClaimsEntered + "\n");
```

```
/********************METHOD THREE *****************/
Console.WriteLine("What is your repair shop id?\n");
repairShopID = Console.ReadLine();

/********************METHOD FOUR *****************/
repairShopClaims[arrayPositionCounter] = repairShopID;
arrayPositionCounter++;

/********************METHOD FIVE *****************/
Console.WriteLine("What is the vehicle policy number?\n");
vehiclePolicyNumber = Console.ReadLine();

/********************METHOD SIX *****************/
repairShopClaims[arrayPositionCounter] = vehiclePolicyNumber;
arrayPositionCounter++;

/********************METHOD SEVEN *****************/
Console.WriteLine("What is the amount being claimed " +
  "for the repair?\n");
claimAmount = Convert.ToDouble(Console.ReadLine());

/********************METHOD EIGHT *****************/
repairShopClaims[arrayPositionCounter] = claimAmount.ToString();
arrayPositionCounter++;

/********************METHOD NINE *****************/
Console.WriteLine("What was the date of the repair?\n");
claimDate = Convert.ToDateTime(Console.ReadLine());

/********************METHOD TEN *****************/
repairShopClaims[arrayPositionCounter] =
                        claimDate.ToString();
arrayPositionCounter++;

/* Increment the loop counter by 1 */
numberOfClaimsEntered++;

} while (numberOfClaimsEntered < numberOfClaimsBeingMade);
```

```
/*******************METHOD ELEVEN *****************/
foreach (var itemInTheClaimsArray in repairShopClaims)
{
  Console.WriteLine("The item in the array is:" +
    "\t" + itemInTheClaimsArray + "\n");
} // End of foreach iteration

} // End of Main() method
```

For this application

- We will start by creating the variables to be used in the code. The variables will be created at the class level, inside the class and outside any methods. Later we will make local variables rather than class variables.

- In creating the class-level variables, we will use the keyword **static** before each variable data type, because our Main() method is static, but when we study classes and objects in Chapter 13, we will have class-level variables that are not static, but that's for a later discussion.

- In terms of the word static, we will see more about it in Chapter 13, but for now just accept that **static means belonging to this class.**

- Creating variables at the class level means that all the methods of the class will have access to them.

- As we are on a chapter about creating and using methods, we will want to have easy access to the variables, but once we understand a bit more about methods, we will change the approach of using class-level variables and make use of local variables instead.

Note

We still have the code from the Arrays.cs class so we can copy and paste the code into this MethodsVoid.cs class, as we need it.

18. Amend the code, as in Listing 12-9, to declare and create the array at the class level, remembering to use the keyword static.

Listing 12-9. Declare and create the array

```
using System;

namespace Chapter12
{
  internal class MethodsVoid
  {
    /*
    The array is going to hold the data for 2 claims.
    Each claim has four pieces of information. The number of
    data items is therefore 2 multiplied by 4 = 8.
    So, we will make the array for this example of size 8.
    Not the best way to do things but fine for now.
    */
    static string[] repairShopClaims = new string[8];

    static void Main(string[] args)
    {
    } // End of Main() method
  } // End of MethodsVoid class
} // End of Chapter12 namespace
```

19. Amend the code, as in Listing 12-10, to create the variables at the
    class level. We must add the word static in front of the data type.

Listing 12-10. Create the variables using the static keyword

```
static string[] repairShopClaims = new string[8];

/*
We will setup our variables that will be used in the
quote application. The details will be:
•   the repair shop unique id (string)
•   the vehicle insurance policy number (string)
•   the claim amount (double)
•   the date of the claim (date)
*/
```

```
static string repairShopId;
static string vehiclePolicyNumber;
static double claimAmount;
static DateTime claimDate;
static int numberOfClaimsBeingMade;
static int numberOfClaimsEntered = 0;
static int arrayPositionCounter = 0;

static void Main(string[] args)
{
} // End of Main() method
```

Note

Methods are created outside the Main() method but inside the class. We can add the methods above the Main() method or below it. Here we will add the methods below the Main() method, so we need to be careful and make sure to add the methods below the Main() method but still inside the class, which is indicated by the second last curly brace }. The last curly brace } represents the end of the namespace.

We will now create the first method that will hold the code asking the user how many claims will be made and then collecting the user input from the console.

20. Amend the code, as in Listing 12-11, to create the first method, which will be called HowManyClaimsAreBeingMade().

Listing 12-11. Create method 1 outside the Main() method

```
} // End of Main() method

/*************************************************
All the methods will be located here.
They are outside the main but inside the class
*************************************************/
/***************** METHOD ONE *****************/
public static void HowManyClaimsAreBeingMade()
{
  /*
  Read the user input for the number of claims being made
  and convert the string value to an integer data type
  */
```

```
Console.WriteLine("How many claims are being made?\n");
numberOfClaimsBeingMade = Convert.ToInt32(Console.ReadLine());
} // End of HowManyClaimsAreBeingMade() method
```

```
} // End of MethodsVoid class
} // End of Chapter12 namespace
```

Remember to add the rest of the methods below the Main method and just above the class curly brace }.

21. Amend the code, as in Listing 12-12, to create the second method, which will be called CurrentValueOfCounter().

Listing 12-12. Create method 2 outside the Main() method

```
/***************** METHOD TWO *****************/
public static void CurrentValueOfCounter()
{
  Console.WriteLine("The current value of the counter " +
    "is :" +numberOfClaimsEntered + "\n");
  } // End of CurrentValueOfCounter() method
```

```
  } // End of MethodsVoid class
} // End of Chapter12 namespace
```

22. Amend the code, as in Listing 12-13, to create the third method, which will be called ReadTheRepairShopId().

Listing 12-13. Create method 3 outside the Main() method

```
/***************** METHOD THREE *****************/
public static void ReadTheRepairShopId()
{
  Console.WriteLine("What is your repair shop id?\n");
  repairShopId = Console.ReadLine();
  }// End of ReadTheRepairShopId() method
```

```
  } // End of MethodsVoid class
} // End of Chapter12 namespace
```

23. Amend the code, as in Listing 12-14, to create the fourth method, which will be called WriteRepairShopIdToTheArray().

Listing 12-14. Create method 4 outside the Main() method

```
/****************** METHOD FOUR ******************/
public static void WriteRepairShopIdToTheArray()
{
  repairShopClaims[arrayPositionCounter] = repairShopId;
  arrayPositionCounter++;
} // End of WriteRepairShopIdToTheArray() method

} // End of MethodsVoid class
} // End of Chapter12 namespace
```

24. Amend the code, as in Listing 12-15, to create the fifth method, which will be called ReadTheVehiclePolicyNumber().

Listing 12-15. Create method 5 outside the Main() method

```
/****************** METHOD FIVE ******************/
public static void ReadTheVehiclePolicyNumber()
{
  Console.WriteLine("What is the vehicle policy number?\n");
  vehiclePolicyNumber = Console.ReadLine();
} // End of ReadTheVehiclePolicyNumber() method

} // End of MethodsVoid class
} // End of Chapter12 namespace
```

25. Amend the code, as in Listing 12-16, to create the sixth method, which will be called WriteVehiclePolicyNumberToTheArray().

Listing 12-16. Create method 6 outside the Main() method

```
/****************** METHOD SIX ******************/
public static void WriteVehiclePolicyNumberToTheArray()
{
  repairShopClaims[arrayPositionCounter]=vehiclePolicyNumber;
  arrayPositionCounter++;
```

391

```
} // End of WriteVehiclePolicyNumberToTheArray() method
```

```
} // End of MethodsVoid class
} // End of Chapter12 namespace
```

26. Amend the code, as in Listing 12-17, to create the seventh method, which will be called ReadTheAmountBeingClaimed().

Listing 12-17. Create method 7 outside the Main() method

```
/****************** METHOD SEVEN ******************/
public static void ReadTheAmountBeingClaimed()
{
  Console.WriteLine("What is the amount being " +
    "claimed for the repair?\n");
  claimAmount = Convert.ToDouble(Console.ReadLine());
} // End of ReadTheAmountBeingClaimed() method
```

```
} // End of MethodsVoid class
} // End of Chapter12 namespace
```

27. Amend the code, as in Listing 12-18, to create the eighth method, which will be called WriteClaimAmountToTheArray().

Listing 12-18. Create method 8 outside the Main() method

```
/****************** METHOD EIGHT ******************/
public static void WriteClaimAmountToTheArray()
{
  repairShopClaims[arrayPositionCounter]
             = claimAmount.ToString();
  arrayPositionCounter++;
} // End of WriteClaimAmountToTheArray() method
```

```
} // End of MethodsVoid class
} // End of Chapter12 namespace
```

28. Amend the code, as in Listing 12-19, to create the ninth method, which will be called ReadTheRepairDate().

Listing 12-19. Create method 9 outside the Main() method

```
/****************** METHOD NINE ****************/
public static void ReadTheRepairDate()
{
  Console.WriteLine("What was the date of the repair?\n");
  claimDate = Convert.ToDateTime(Console.ReadLine());
} // End of method ReadTheRepairDate() method

 } // End of MethodsVoid class
} // End of Chapter12 namespace
```

29. Amend the code, as in Listing 12-20, to create the tenth method, which will be called WriteRepairDateToTheArray().

Listing 12-20. Create method 10 outside the Main() method

```
/****************** METHOD TEN *****************/
public static void WriteRepairDateToTheArray()
{
  repairShopClaims[arrayPositionCounter]
             = claimDate.ToString();
  arrayPositionCounter++;
} // End of method WriteRepairDateToTheArray() method

 } // End of MethodsVoid class
} // End of Chapter12 namespace
```

30. Amend the code, as in Listing 12-21, to create the eleventh method, which will be called DisplayAllItemsInTheArray().

Listing 12-21. Create method 11 outside the Main() method

```
/****************** METHOD ELEVEN *****************/
public static void DisplayAllItemsInTheArray()
{
  foreach (var itemInTheClaimsArray in repairShopClaims)
  {
    Console.WriteLine("The item in the array " +
```

```
            "is:\t" + itemInTheClaimsArray + "\n");
      }
   } // End of method DisplayAllItemsInTheArray() method

} // End of MethodsVoid class
} // End of Chapter12 namespace
```

Now we have created the methods, each executing a small amount of code. We can call any method, at any time, from within the Main() method in the program class or indeed from any method. In the next chapter, we will see how we could call the methods from within a different class.

We will now

- Call method 1 from within the Main() method.

- Add a do while iteration in the Main() method.

- Call methods 2–10 from within the do while iteration.

- Call method 11 from outside the do while iteration but within the Main() method.

31. Amend the code, as in Listing 12-22.

Listing 12-22. Create the method calls from within the Main() method

```
static void Main(string[] args)
{
   // Call the method that asks how many claims will be entered
   HowManyClaimsAreBeingMade();

   do
   {
      // Call the methods as required
      CurrentValueOfCounter();
      ReadTheRepairShopId();
      WriteRepairShopIdToTheArray();
      ReadTheVehiclePolicyNumber();
      WriteVehiclePolicyNumberToTheArray();
      ReadTheAmountBeingClaimed();
      WriteClaimAmountToTheArray();
```

```
ReadTheRepairDate();
WriteRepairDateToTheArray();

/* Increment the loop counter by 1 */
numberOfClaimsEntered++;
} while (numberOfClaimsEntered < numberOfClaimsBeingMade);

} // End of Main() method
```

32. Amend the code, as in Listing 12-23, by adding, within the Main() method and outside the do while iteration, a call to the display method.

Listing 12-23. Call method 11 to display the data

```
/* Increment the loop counter by 1 */
numberOfClaimsEntered++;
} while (numberOfClaimsEntered < numberOfClaimsBeingMade);

DisplayAllItemsInTheArray();
} // End of Main() method
```

33. Click the File menu.

34. Choose Save All.

35. Click the Debug menu.

36. Choose Start Without Debugging.

37. Click in the console window.

The console window will appear and ask the user how many claims are being made.

38. Type 2 and press the Enter key.

The console window will appear and ask the user to input the repair shop id.

39. Type RS000001 and press the Enter key.

The console will now ask the user to input the vehicle policy number.

40. Type VP000001 and press the Enter key.

The console will now ask the user to input the claim amount.

41. Type 1999.99 and press the Enter key.

The console will now ask the user to input the date of the repair.

42. Type 2021/10/01 and press the Enter key.

The console window will now ask the user to input the repair shop id.

43. Type RS000001 and press the Enter key.

The console will now ask the user to input the vehicle policy number.

44. Type VP001234 and press the Enter key.

The console will now ask the user to input the claim amount.

45. Type 2500.99 and press the Enter key.

The console will now ask the user to input the date of the repair.

46. Type 2021/10/01 and press the Enter key.

Iteration 2 is now completed; the block of code has been executed for the second time. The claims counter will now be incremented by 1 and become a 2. The comparison is made to see if the claims counter value is less than 2, and as it is not, the iterations will end. Figure 12-5 shows the output from the application.

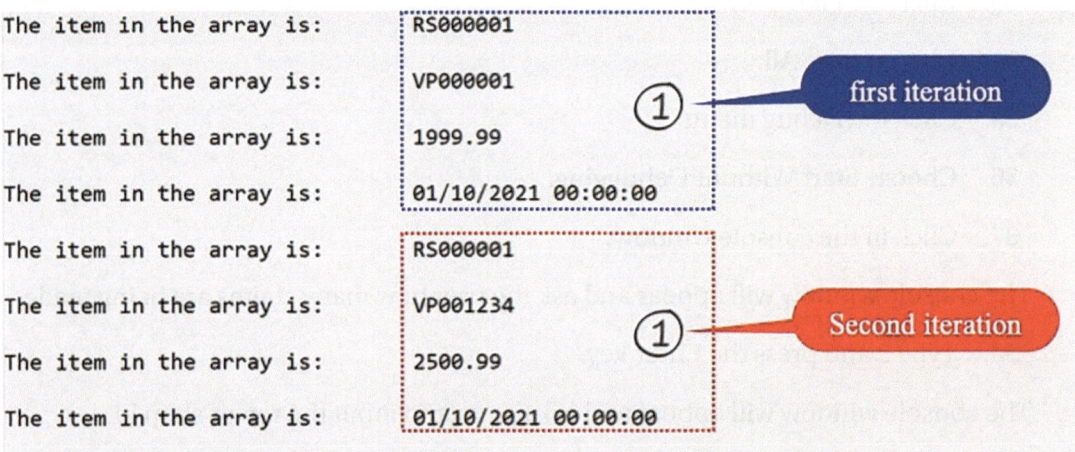

Figure 12-5. *Application output using void methods to modularize the code*

The output shown in Figure 12-5 verifies that the array actually does hold the data entered by the user as we have iterated the array and displayed the eight values. Our array is a single-dimensional array holding items of data type string.

47.   Press any key to close the console window.

So now we have refactored our original arrays code and created **methods** that have small amounts of code. The code is much neater as all we have in the Main() method are a series of calls to the methods. The methods sit outside the Main() method, but still inside the class. This is now a good example of modern programming where methods are an essential feature of maintainable code – it is **modularization**. With the code being decomposed into small methods, it is a relatively easy process to test these small code blocks. We could improve the code, but this is a great starting point for modularized code.

Value Methods

In the previous example when we called a method, the lines of code within the method were implemented and then control of the program was returned to the main program, to the calling statement. When a method is required to return a value to the calling statement, it is said to be a **value method**. When we return a value, we have learned from the start of our programming the applications in this book that all variables have a **data type** – for example, int, double, or string – and these data types are part of the C# programming language. In the last chapter we looked at arrays, and the arrays we created held objects that had a data type. So a value method could return a built-in data type such as int or double, or it could return our own data type such as an array that we have created. In looking at void methods, we used the return type void in front of the method signature as in Listing 12-24.

Listing 12-24. Void method

```
public void GetScoreDetails();
```

But when we have a value method that returns a variable or object of a specific data type, we must state the data type in front of the method signature as in Listing 12-25.

Listing 12-25. Value methods

```
public int GetScoreDetails();
public double GetScoreDetails();
public string GetScoreDetails();
```

Every method declaration specifies a return type, even if it's void.

Listing 12-26. Value method sample code

```
public int GetScoreDetails()
{
  // Ask the user to input the Score for Game One
  Console.WriteLine("What is the Score for Game One");

  // Read the Score for Game One
  scoreInGameOne = int.Parse(Console.ReadLine());

  return scoreInGameOne
}
```

Listing 12-26 Code Analysis

- The method has an **access modifier** of **public** so the method will be available to all code inside the class or from outside the class.

- The **return type** is **int** so the method will return a variable that must be of data type int, and the last line of code in the method, usually, says **return** followed by the variable or object name, but remember we read earlier that we can return from anywhere in the method.

- The name of the method is **GetScoreDetails.**

- The open and close parentheses () follow the name and are empty, indicating that the method accepts no parameters.

- The open and close curly braces follow the parentheses and it is between these braces that the business logic goes.

- The code uses the Console.WriteLine() method to display a message for the user.

- The user input is then read from the console using the int.**Parse()** method.

- The Parse() method accepts a parameter, which in this case is Console.ReadLine() – in other words, whatever is entered at the console.

- The input is converted to an int as we have used int.Parse() to convert.

- In the final line of code, the variable is returned, and it is of data type int.

The format for calling the method is by using the method name followed by the open and close parentheses, `GetScoreDetails();`.

Before we start coding an example of a value method, let us pause to think about the difference between a void method and value method as shown in Table 12-1.

Table 12-1. *Difference between void and value methods*

	Void method	Value method
Signature	Will contain the keyword void	Will contain the keyword belonging to the data type being returned
Code	Will not contain a return keyword in the code	Will contain a return keyword in the code

Create and Use Value Methods

1. Right-click the class called MethodsVoid.cs within the Chapter12 project in the Solution Explorer panel.

2. Choose Copy.

3. Right-click the Chapter12 project in the Solution Explorer panel.

4. Choose Paste.

5. Right-click the MethodsVoid – Copy.cs file, which is the copied file.

6. Choose Rename.

7. Name the class MethodsValue.cs.

8. Ensure that the MethodsValue.cs file is open in the editor window.

9. Rename the class in the open editor window from MethodsVoid to MethodsValue.

10. Right-click the Chapter12 project in the Solution Explorer panel.

11. Choose Properties from the pop-up menu.

12. Choose the MethodsValue.cs class in the Startup object drop-down list.

13. Close the Properties window.

We will now amend the code using some ordered steps:

- In the required methods, change the keyword void to the data type that is to be returned.

- In the required methods, add a return statement followed by the variable name being returned as the last line of the method.

We should be aware that if a method returns a value to a calling statement, then the returned value should be used for something. In other words, what use would the line of code in Listing 12-27 be if we called the method and it returned a value of 2?

Listing 12-27. Value method called and returned value not assigned to a variable

```
HowManyClaimsAreBeingMade();
```

The answer to our question is no use at all. We need to assign the returned value to a variable or use it in some other way, and we will do this from within the Main() method where the call is made.

Now we will change the void methods to value methods by adding the return type on the first line and then returning the value as the last line of the method.

14. Amend method 1, HowManyClaimsAreBeingMade(), as in Listing 12-28.

Listing 12-28. Method 1 return type changed and a return statement added

```
/****************** METHOD ONE ****************/
public static int HowManyClaimsAreBeingMade()
{
 /*
 Read the user input for the number of claims being made
 and convert the string value to an integer data type
 */
 Console.WriteLine("How many claims are being made?\n");
 numberOfClaimsBeingMade = Convert.ToInt32(Console.ReadLine());
 return numberOfClaimsBeingMade;
} // End of HowManyClaimsAreBeingMade() method
```

15. Amend the calling statement in the Main() method to assign the returned value to a variable as in Listing 12-29.

Listing 12-29. Call the method and assign the returned value to a variable

```
static void Main(string[] args)
{
    // Call the method that asks how many claims will be entered
    numberOfClaimsBeingMade = HowManyClaimsAreBeingMade();

    do
```

Looking at this line, we will see there is room for improvement in the code:

- The variable numberOfClaimsBeingMade is the class-level variable and we are assigning it the value returned from the method HowManyClaimsAreBeingMade().

- The HowManyClaimsAreBeingMade() method uses the same numberOfClaimsBeingMade class-level variable and has assigned it the value entered by the user.

- Therefore, we could make the method code better by simply returning the value read in from the console as entered by the user rather than assigning it to the variable. This simple change helps illustrate good coding. We should also understand that variables should be declared, scoped, only where they are required, that is, local scope rather than "global."

16. Amend the method 1 code to comment the assignment statement and return the converted input as in Listing 12-30.

Listing 12-30. Comment the assignment and amend the return statement

```
/****************** METHOD ONE *****************/
public static int HowManyClaimsAreBeingMade()
{
/*
Read the user input for the number of claims being made
and convert the string value to an integer data type
*/
Console.WriteLine("How many claims are being made?\n");
//numberOfClaimsBeingMade =Convert.ToInt32(Console.ReadLine());
return Convert.ToInt32(Console.ReadLine());
} // End of HowManyClaimsAreBeingMade() method
```

The original line of code has been commented out, but it could be completely removed as shown in Listing 12-31. Remember **YAGNI – You Ain't Going to Need It**. It's all part of the clean code ethos.

17. Remove the commented line so the method has the code as in Listing 12-31.

Listing 12-31. Commented assignment removed

```
/****************** METHOD ONE *****************/
public static int HowManyClaimsAreBeingMade()
{
/*
Read the user input for the number of claims being made
and convert the string value to an integer data type
*/
```

```
Console.WriteLine("How many claims are being made?\n");
return Convert.ToInt32(Console.ReadLine());
} // End of HowManyClaimsAreBeingMade() method
```

Amending the method to return the input is a good example of **refactoring** our code with the aim of making the code better. We will now follow the same process for some of the other methods, making them value methods and removing the line of code that is not required.

18.   Amend method 3, ReadTheRepairShopId(), as in Listing 12-32.

Listing 12-32. Method 3 return type changed and a return statement added

```
/***************** METHOD THREE *****************/
public static string ReadTheRepairShopId()
{
  Console.WriteLine("What is your repair shop id?\n");
  return Console.ReadLine();
}// End of ReadTheRepairShopId() method
```

19.   Amend the calling statement in the Main() method to assign the returned value to a variable as in Listing 12-33.

Listing 12-33. Call the method and assign the returned value to a variable

```
do
{
// Call the methods as required
CurrentValueOfCounter();

repairShopId = ReadTheRepairShopId();

WriteRepairShopIdToTheArray();
```

20.   Amend method 5, ReadTheVehiclePolicyNumber(), as in Listing 12-34.

Listing 12-34. Method 5 return type changed and a return statement added

```
/****************** METHOD FIVE *****************/
public static string ReadTheVehiclePolicyNumber()
{
  Console.WriteLine("What is the vehicle policy number?\n");
  return Console.ReadLine();
} // End of ReadTheVehiclePolicyNumber() method
```

21. Amend the calling statement in the Main() method to assign the returned value to a variable as in Listing 12-35.

Listing 12-35. Call the method and assign the returned value to a variable

```
do
{
// Call the methods as required
CurrentValueOfCounter();
repairShopID = ReadTheRepairShopId();
WriteRepairShopIdToTheArray();

vehiclePolicyNumber = ReadTheVehiclePolicyNumber();
WriteVehiclePolicyNumberToTheArray();
```

22. Amend method 7, ReadTheAmountBeingClaimed (), as in Listing 12-36.

Listing 12-36. Method 7 amended to return a value

```
/****************** METHOD SEVEN *****************/
public static double ReadTheAmountBeingClaimed()
{
  Console.WriteLine("What is the amount being " +
    "claimed for the repair?\n");
  return Convert.ToDouble(Console.ReadLine());
} // End of ReadTheAmountBeingClaimed() method
```

23. Amend the calling statement in the Main() method to assign the returned value to a variable as in Listing 12-37.

Listing 12-37. Call the method and assign the returned value to a variable

```
do
{
// Call the methods as required
CurrentValueOfCounter();
repairShopID = ReadTheRepairShopId();
WriteRepairShopIdToTheArray();

vehiclePolicyNumber = ReadTheVehiclePolicyNumber();
WriteVehiclePolicyNumberToTheArray();

claimAmount = ReadTheAmountBeingClaimed();
WriteClaimAmountToTheArray();
```

24. Amend method 9, ReadTheRepairDate(), to return the user input value as shown in Listing 12-38.

Listing 12-38. Method 9 return type changed and a return statement added

```
/***************** METHOD NINE *****************/
public static DateTime ReadTheRepairDate()
{
  Console.WriteLine("What was the date of the repair?\n");
  return Convert.ToDateTime(Console.ReadLine());
}// End of method ReadTheRepairDate()
```

25. Amend the calling statement in the Main() method to assign the returned value to a variable as in Listing 12-39.

Listing 12-39. Call the method and assign the returned value to a variable

```
claimAmount = ReadTheAmountBeingClaimed();
WriteClaimAmountToTheArray();

claimDate = ReadTheRepairDate();
WriteRepairDateToTheArray();

/* Increment the loop counter by 1 */
numberOfClaimsEntered++;
} while (numberOfClaimsEntered < numberOfClaimsBeingMade);
```

26. Click the File menu.

27. Choose Save All.

28. Click the Debug menu.

29. Choose Start Without Debugging.

30. Click in the console window.

The console window will appear and ask the user how many claims are being made.

31. Type 2 and press the Enter key.

The console window will appear and ask the user to input the repair shop id.

32. Type RS000001 and press the Enter key.

The console will now ask the user to input the vehicle policy number.

33. Type VP000001 and press the Enter key.

The console will now ask the user to input the claim amount.

34. Type 1999.99 and press the Enter key.

The console will now ask the user to input the date of the repair.

35. Type 2021/10/01 and press the Enter key.

The console window will now ask the user to input the repair shop id.

36. Type RS000001 and press the Enter key.

The console will now ask the user to input the vehicle policy number.

37. Type VP001234 and press the Enter key.

The console will now ask the user to input the claim amount.

38. Type 2500.99 and press the Enter key.

The console will now ask the user to input the date of the repair.

39. Type 2021/10/01 and press the Enter key.

The number of claims entered is 2, and this is all that the user requested, so the do while loop is complete, and the next lines of code are the foreach iteration. As a result of the foreach iteration, the console will display all the items in the array as shown in Figure 12-6.

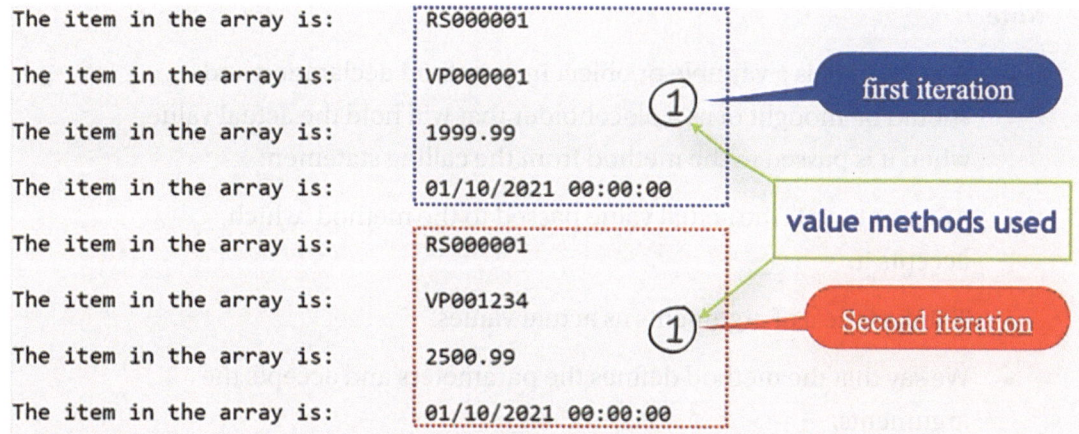

```
The item in the array is:          RS000001

The item in the array is:          VP000001

The item in the array is:          1999.99

The item in the array is:          01/10/2021 00:00:00

The item in the array is:          RS000001

The item in the array is:          VP001234

The item in the array is:          2500.99

The item in the array is:          01/10/2021 00:00:00
```

C:\CoreCSharp\CoreCSharp\Chapter12\bin\Debug\net6.0\Chapter12.exe (process
Press anv kev to close this window . . ._

Figure 12-6. *Application output using value methods to modularize the code*

40.   Press any key to close the console window.

So now we have changed some of the methods to make them **value methods.** A value method means a value, which has a data type, is returned from the method. When creating a value method and we talk about a method signature, **the method signature does not contain the data type being returned, but the data type being returned appears before the method name.**

This is great. We now have void and value methods within our code, and we will continue with the last main method type, the parameter method, which will also be a void or a value method.

Parameter Methods

It is possible to have our methods accept a value or multiple values and then use these values within the body of the method as part of the business logic processing. We could have a method that accepts two integer values and uses them in a multiplication or a method that accepts a string value and a quote amount and displays the two values. In using a parameter method, we pass it **actual values**, as **arguments,** when we call the method. When we are creating the parameter method, the parameters, and their data type, are enclosed as part of the method signature. When the arguments, actual values, are passed to the method, the method accepts these arguments, and their values are assigned to the parameters in the accepting method.

Note

- A parameter is a variable or object in a method declaration and should be thought of as a placeholder that will hold the actual value when it is passed to the method from the calling statement.

- An argument is the actual value passed to the method, which accepts it.

- Think of the a of **arguments** as actual values.

- We say that the method defines the parameters and accepts the arguments.

In using parameter methods, the calling method needs only to know what data type needs to be passed; it does not need to know what the method does with these values in its business logic. Figure 12-7 depicts the black box idea for a method that accepts values and outputs a result.

Parameter method that is also a value

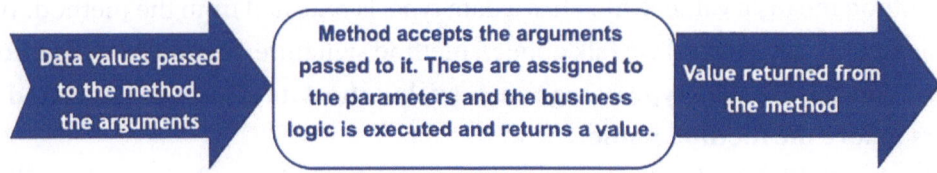

Figure 12-7. *Method is passed values and uses these in its business logic*

By providing the method with the required input data, the method produces the required answer, the value to be returned. To obtain the correct answer, we must ensure that the correct input arguments are provided:

- The right number of input arguments

- The correct type of arguments

- The correct order of the arguments

Example

By setting up the input data as the

- Number of items

- Cost per item

the result of a multiplication can be produced. The method will use the input data, perform its business logic and calculations, and produce a result.

The values passed into the method are known as **arguments**. The method is said to take them as its **parameters**, as shown in Figure 12-8.

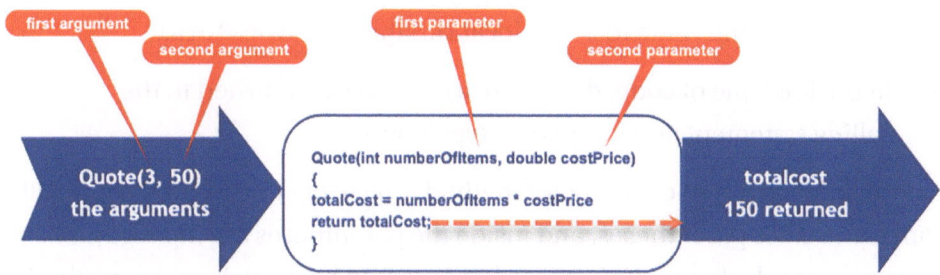

Parameter method that is also a value

Figure 12-8. *Method accepting arguments as its parameters*

An example of a value method is shown in Listing 12-40.

Listing 12-40. Parameter method that accepts one parameter

```
public double AccumulateClaimAmount(double totalOfAllClaims, double
claimAmount)
{
  double newTotal = totalOfAllClaims + claimAmount;

  return newTotal;
}
```

Listing 12-40 Code Analysis

- The method has an **access modifier** of **public** so the method will be available to all code inside the class or from outside the class.

- The **return type** is **double** so the method will return a variable that must be of data type double, and therefore the last line of code in the method will contain the keyword **return** followed by the variable name.

- The name of the method is AccumulateClaimAmount.

- The open and close parentheses () follow the name and hold two arguments passed to the method, and they are called `totalOfAllClaims` and `claimAmount`, which are of data type double.

- The open and close curly braces follow the parentheses, and it is between these braces that the business logic is coded.

- The business logic adds the variable values that have been passed in and assigns the value to a new local variable called `newTotal`.

- In the final line of code, the `newTotal` variable is returned to the calling statement and it is of data type double.

The format for calling the parameter method is by using the method name followed by the open and close parentheses, and inside the parentheses are the arguments, the values. In our example there is only one value accepted by the parameter method so we will be passing one argument, as in Listing 12-41.

Listing 12-41. Calling the parameter method and passing it a value

```
AccumulateClaimAmount(1000);
```

Now before we start coding an example of a parameter method, pause, and think about how a parameter method is associated with a void method and a value method. Table 12-2 shows the association.

Table 12-2. *Parameter method association with void and value methods*

	Parameter method	
Signature	May contain the keyword void	May contain the keyword belonging to the data type being returned
Code	May not contain a return keyword on the last line of code	May contain a return keyword on the last line of code
Arguments	Will contain one or more arguments	

Before we start adding new parameter methods to complete our code, let us think back to what we said earlier:

As we are on a chapter about creating and using methods, we will want to have easy access to the variables, but once we understand a bit more about methods, we will change the approach of using class-level variables and make use of local variables instead.

So now we have come to the stage where we can tidy our code and make more use of local variables and discard the class-level variables. The general steps we will use to create local variables when we can will be as follows:

- In the do while construct where we call the method, we are assigning the value returned from the value method to a class-level variable, so we will move the class-level variable to within the do while so it is local.

- Change the newly moved variable from having static in front of it, as the do while and therefore this variable are inside a static Main() method.

- Next, we will pass the variable to the value method used to write the value to the array; we pass the value as an argument when we call the method.

- We then need to make the value method used to write to the array into a parameter method so it can accept the argument being passed to it.

- We then will use the parameter of the parameter method in writing to the array rather than using the class-level variable.

We will start with fixing the call to the ReadTheRepairShopId() method, and the other fixes will follow the same process.

1. Highlight the line of code declaring the class-level variable repairShopId, as in Listing 12-42.

Listing 12-42. Highlight the static variable – repairShopId

```
static string repairShopId;
static string vehiclePolicyNumber;
static double claimAmount;
static DateTime claimDate;
```

2. Right-click and choose Cut.

3. Paste the copied code into the line within the do while construct
   so we are assigning this copied variable to the value returned from
   the method ReadTheRepairShopId(), as shown in Listing 12-43.

Listing 12-43. Static variable is assigned the returned value from the method

```
do
{
  // Call the methods as required
  CurrentValueOfCounter();
  static string repairShopId = ReadTheRepairShopId();

  WriteRepairShopIdToTheArray();
```

Notice that the keyword static is underlined as an error, and if we hover over the red
underline or look in the Error List window, we will see that it tells us that "The modifier
'static' is not valid for this." We need to remove the keyword static as we are inside the
static Main() method.

4. Remove the keyword static as in Listing 12-44.

Listing 12-44. Static has been removed from the variable

```
do
{
  // Call the methods as required
  CurrentValueOfCounter();
  string repairShopId = ReadTheRepairShopId();
  WriteRepairShopIdToTheArray();
```

5. Within the do while construct, call the
    WriteRepairShopIdToTheArray() method but pass the variable
    repairShopId as an argument, as in Listing 12-45.

Listing 12-45. Pass the value as an argument to the method

```
do
{
  // Call the methods as required
  CurrentValueOfCounter();
  string repairShopId = ReadTheRepairShopId();
  WriteRepairShopIdToTheArray(repairShopId);
```

Notice that the WriteRepairShopIdToTheArray() method name is underlined as an error, and if we hover over the red underline or look in the Error List window, we will see that it tells us that "No overload for method 'ReadTheRepairShopId' takes 1 arguments." So the WriteRepairShopIdToTheArray() method, method 4, currently does not accept any values. It is not a parameter method; it is just a void method. We need to make the method into a parameter method that accepts one string value.

6. Amend method 4 so that is accepts a string parameter, which we
    will call repairShopId. Method 4 is now as in Listing 12-46.

Listing 12-46. Make the method a parameter method

```
/****************** METHOD FOUR ******************/
public static void WriteRepairShopIdToTheArray(string repairShopId)
{
  repairShopClaims[arrayPositionCounter] = repairShopId;
  arrayPositionCounter++;
} // End of WriteRepairShopIdToTheArray() method
```

With these steps completed, we have now removed a class-level variable and used a local variable instead, and we have created a parameter method, which is called and passed the value of the local variable. We will now repeat this process for the policy number, claim amount, and claim date.

7. Highlight the line of code declaring the class-level variable
    vehiclePolicyNumber, as in Listing 12-47.

413

Listing 12-47. Highlight the static variable – vehiclePolicyNumber

```
static string vehiclePolicyNumber;
static double claimAmount;
static DateTime claimDate;
```

8. Right-click and choose Cut.

9. Paste the copied code into the line within the do while construct so we are assigning this copied variable to the value returned from the method ReadTheVehiclePolicyNumber() and remove the static, as shown in Listing 12-48.

Listing 12-48. Static variable is assigned the returned value from the method

```
do
{
  // Call the methods as required
  CurrentValueOfCounter();
  string repairShopId = ReadTheRepairShopId();
  WriteRepairShopIdToTheArray(repairShopId);

  string vehiclePolicyNumber = ReadTheVehiclePolicyNumber();
  WriteVehiclePolicyNumberToTheArray();
```

10. Within the do while construct, call the WriteVehiclePolicyNumberToTheArray() method but pass the variable vehiclePolicyNumber as an argument, as in Listing 12-49.

Listing 12-49. Pass the value as an argument to the method

```
do
{
  // Call the methods as required
  CurrentValueOfCounter();
  string repairShopId = ReadTheRepairShopId();
  WriteRepairShopIdToTheArray(repairShopId);

  string vehiclePolicyNumber = ReadTheVehiclePolicyNumber();
  WriteVehiclePolicyNumberToTheArray(vehiclePolicyNumber);
```

11.   Amend method 6 so that is accepts a string parameter, which we
will call vehiclePolicyNumber. Method 6 is now as in Listing 12-50.

Listing 12-50. Make the method a parameter method

```
/****************** METHOD SIX ******************/
public static void WriteVehiclePolicyNumberToTheArray(string
vehiclePolicyNumber)
{
  repairShopClaims[arrayPositionCounter] = vehiclePolicyNumber;
  arrayPositionCounter++;
} // End of WriteVehiclePolicyNumberToTheArray() method
```

We will now repeat this process for the claim amount.

12.   Highlight the line of code declaring the class-level variable
claimAmount, as in Listing 12-51.

Listing 12-51. Highlight the static variable – claimAmount

```
static double claimAmount;
static DateTime claimDate;
```

13.   Right-click and choose Cut.

14.   Paste the copied code into the line within the do while construct
so we are assigning this copied variable to the value returned from
the method ReadTheAmountBeingClaimed() and remove the
static, as shown in Listing 12-52.

Listing 12-52. Static variable is assigned the returned value from the method

```
do
{
  // Call the methods as required
  CurrentValueOfCounter();
  string repairShopId = ReadTheRepairShopId();
  WriteRepairShopIdToTheArray(repairShopId);
```

```
string vehiclePolicyNumber = ReadTheVehiclePolicyNumber();
WriteVehiclePolicyNumberToTheArray(vehiclePolicyNumber);

double claimAmount = ReadTheAmountBeingClaimed();
WriteClaimAmountToTheArray();
```

15. Within the do while construct, call the
    WriteClaimAmountToTheArray() method but pass the variable
    claimAmount as an argument, as in Listing 12-53.

Listing 12-53. Pass the value as an argument to the method

```
do
{
  // Call the methods as required
  CurrentValueOfCounter();
  string repairShopId = ReadTheRepairShopId();
  WriteRepairShopIdToTheArray(repairShopId);

  string vehiclePolicyNumber = ReadTheVehiclePolicyNumber();
  WriteVehiclePolicyNumberToTheArray(vehiclePolicyNumber);

  double claimAmount = ReadTheAmountBeingClaimed();
  WriteClaimAmountToTheArray(claimAmount);
```

16. Amend method 8 so that is accepts a parameter of type double,
    which we will call claimAmount. Method 8 is now as in
    Listing 12-54.

Listing 12-54. Make the method a parameter method

```
/****************** METHOD EIGHT ******************/
public static void WriteClaimAmountToTheArray(double claimAmount)
{
  repairShopClaims[arrayPositionCounter]
            = claimAmount.ToString();
  arrayPositionCounter++;
} // End of WriteClaimAmountToTheArray() method
```

We will now repeat this process for the claim date.

17. Highlight the line of code declaring the class-level variable claimDate as in Listing 12-55.

Listing 12-55. Highlight the static variable – claimDate

```
static DateTime claimDate;
```

18. Right-click and choose Cut.

19. Paste the copied code into the line within the do while construct so we are assigning this copied variable to the value returned from the method ReadTheRepairDate() and remove the static, as shown in Listing 12-56.

Listing 12-56. Static variable is assigned the returned value from the method

```
do
{
  // Call the methods as required
  CurrentValueOfCounter();
  string repairShopId = ReadTheRepairShopId();
  WriteRepairShopIdToTheArray(repairShopId);

  string vehiclePolicyNumber = ReadTheVehiclePolicyNumber();
  WriteVehiclePolicyNumberToTheArray(vehiclePolicyNumber);

  double claimAmount = ReadTheAmountBeingClaimed();
  WriteClaimAmountToTheArray(claimAmount);

  DateTime claimDate = ReadTheRepairDate();
  WriteRepairDateToTheArray();
```

20. Within the do while construct, call the WriteRepairDateToTheArray() method but pass the variable claimDate as an argument, as in Listing 12-57.

Listing 12-57. Pass the value as an argument to the method

```
do
{
  // Call the methods as required
  CurrentValueOfCounter();
  string repairShopId = ReadTheRepairShopId();
  WriteRepairShopIdToTheArray(repairShopId);

  string vehiclePolicyNumber = ReadTheVehiclePolicyNumber();
  WriteVehiclePolicyNumberToTheArray(vehiclePolicyNumber);

  double claimAmount = ReadTheAmountBeingClaimed();
  WriteClaimAmountToTheArray(claimAmount);

  DateTime claimDate = ReadTheRepairDate();
  WriteRepairDateToTheArray(claimDate);
```

21. Amend method 10 so that it accepts a parameter of type double,
     which we will call claimDate. Method 10 is now as in Listing 12-58.

Listing 12-58. Make the method a parameter method

```
/******************* METHOD TEN ******************/
public static void WriteRepairDateToTheArray(DateTime claimDate)
{
  repairShopClaims[arrayPositionCounter]
             = claimDate.ToString();
  arrayPositionCounter++;
} // End of method WriteRepairDateToTheArray() method
```

These changes have made a real difference to our code because we have reduced the
number of class-level variables, made good use of local variables, and used parameter
methods. Yes, we could go further and get rid of the other three class-level variables,
but for now this is excellent progress, and we can progress with some more parameter
methods.

We will now add some parameter methods to the existing code where

- The parameter method will accept two arguments, both of type double.

- The values passed in will be the values of the claim being made and the existing total of all claims.

- The method will use the values passed into it to find the new total of all the claims being made.

- We will create a method that accepts the accumulated total of the claims and works out how much of the accumulated total is value-added tax (VAT).

- The VAT amount will be included in the accumulated total, and the formula for the calculation is shown in Listing 12-59.

Listing 12-59. Formula for calculating value-added tax

```
vatamount = accumulated total passed in / 1.20;
```

We will add a parameter method called **AccumulateClaimAmount()**, which has two parameters, one called **claimAmountPassedIn** and the other called **totalOfAllClaims** of data type double.

22. Add method 12, a new parameter method, as in Listing 12-60.

Listing 12-60. Add a new parameter method

```
/****************** METHOD TWELVE ******************/
public static double AccumulateClaimAmount(double
claimAmountPassedIn, double totalOfAllClaims)
{
    totalOfAllClaims += claimAmountPassedIn;
    return totalOfAllClaims ;
}// End of method AccumulateClaimAmount()
} // End of MethodsValue class
} // End of Chapter12 namespace
```

The method accumulates the total of all repair claims being entered by the user, so we also need to create the variable to hold this total. Here we have named the variable totalOfAllClaims, and we will declare this as a method-level variable assigning it an initial value of 0.00, as shown in Listing 12-61.

Listing 12-61. Add the new method-level variable

```
static void Main(string[] args)
{
 // Call the method that asks how many claims will be entered
  numberOfClaimsBeingMade = HowManyClaimsAreBeingMade();
  double totalOfAllClaims = 0.00;

  do
  {
```

Now we need to call the AccumulateClaimAmount() method, which we have just created, and pass it the claim amount, which has been entered, and the current total of all claims. This method just adds the value to the existing total value of all claims.

23. Amend the code to call the method, passing the claim amount and the current claims total as the arguments, as in Listing 12-62.

Listing 12-62. Call the parameter method from within the do while construct

```
do
 {
// Call the methods as required
CurrentValueOfCounter();
string repairShopId = ReadTheRepairShopId();
 WriteRepairShopIdToTheArray(repairShopId);

 string vehiclePolicyNumber = ReadTheVehiclePolicyNumber();
   WriteVehiclePolicyNumberToTheArray(vehiclePolicyNumber);

   double claimAmount = ReadTheAmountBeingClaimed();
   WriteClaimAmountToTheArray(claimAmount);

   totalOfAllClaims = AccumulateClaimAmount(claimAmount, totalOfAllClaims);
```

```
DateTime claimDate = ReadTheRepairDate();
WriteRepairDateToTheArray(claimDate);

/* Increment the loop counter by 1 */
numberOfClaimsEntered++;
} while (numberOfClaimsEntered < numberOfClaimsBeingMade);
```

Now we need to create

- A value method that accepts the total of all claims as a parameter and then determines the VAT based on this value

- A method-level variable to hold the VAT value

- A void method that accepts the total of all claims and the VAT amount and displays a confirmation invoice showing the

  - Total of the claims without VAT

  - Total amount of VAT

  - Total of the claims including VAT

24. Amend the code, as in Listing 12-63, to include the method-level variable.

Listing 12-63. Add an additional local variable to hold the VAT amount

```
static void Main(string[] args)
{
 // Call the method that asks how many claims will be entered
  numberOfClaimsBeingMade = HowManyClaimsAreBeingMade();
  double totalOfAllClaims = 0.00;
  double vatAmount =0.00;

  do
  {
```

25. Amend the code to add the value and parameter method, method 13, as in Listing 12-64.

Listing 12-64. Add additional method to determine the VAT amount

```
/****************** METHOD THIRTEEN ******************/
public static double DetermineVATAmount(double
totalValueOfClaimsPassedIn, double vatAmount)
{
  vatAmount = totalValueOfClaimsPassedIn -
                     (totalValueOfClaimsPassedIn / 1.20);
  return vatAmount;
} // End of method DetermineVATAmount()
} // End of MethodsValue class
} // End of Chapter12 namespace
```

26. Amend the code in the Main() method to call the newly created VAT method, passing it the total value of the claims and the VAT amount, as in Listing 12-65.

Listing 12-65. Call the new method passing it the two arguments

```
} while (numberOfClaimsEntered < numberOfClaimsBeingMade);

vatAmount = DetermineVATAmount(totalOfAllClaims, vatAmount);

DisplayAllItemsInTheArray();

} // End of Main() method
```

27. Amend the code in the Main() method, as in Listing 12-66, to display the total of all claims.

Listing 12-66. Display the total of all claims

```
} while (numberOfClaimsEntered < numberOfClaimsBeingMade);

vatAmount = DetermineVATAmount(totalOfAllClaims, vatAmount);

DisplayAllItemsInTheArray();

Console.WriteLine("The total amount claimed is:\t" + totalOfAllClaims);

} // End of Main() method
```

Now we can create the void method that accepts the total of all claims and the VAT amount and displays the invoice receipt.

28. Amend the code to add the new void method, method 14, which accepts the two arguments – it's a parameter method, as in Listing 12-67.

Listing 12-67. Create the new method to display the invoice details

```
/******************** METHOD FOURTEEN ******************/
public static void DisplayInvoiceReceipt(double
        totalValueOfClaimsPassedIn, double vatPassedIn)
{
  Console.WriteLine("\nInvoice for vehicle repairs\n");
  Console.WriteLine("Nett claim\t" + (totalValueOfClaimsPassedIn -
  vatPassedIn) + "\n");
  Console.WriteLine("VAT amount\t" + vatPassedIn + "\n");
  Console.WriteLine("Total amount\t" + totalValueOfClaimsPassedIn
  + "\n");
} // End of method DisplayInvoiceReceipt()
} // End of MethodsValue class
} // End of Chapter12 namespace
```

29. Amend the Main() method code to call the method as in Listing 12-68.

Listing 12-68. Call the method to display the total of all claims

```
} while (numberOfClaimsEntered < numberOfClaimsBeingMade);

vatAmount = CalculateVATAmount(totalOfAllClaims);

DisplayAllItemsInTheArray();

Console.WriteLine("The total amount claimed is:\t" +
totalOfAllClaims);

DisplayInvoiceReceipt(totalOfAllClaims, vatAmount);
} // End of Main() method
```

Now we will run the code and use claim values that will make it easy to test if the code works properly. If we make two claim values, as shown in Table 12-3, we can check that our output matches.

Table 12-3. *Test data*

	Net amount	VAT amount	Total amount
	1000	200	1200
	2000	400	2400
Totals	3000	600	3600

30. Click the File menu.

31. Choose Save All.

32. Click the Debug menu.

33. Choose Start Without Debugging.

34. Click in the console window.

The console window will appear and ask for the number of entries being made.

35. Type 2 and press the Enter key.

The console window will appear and ask the user to input the repair shop id.

36. Type RS000001 and press the Enter key.

The console will now ask the user to input the vehicle policy number.

37. Type VP000001 and press the Enter key.

The console will now ask the user to input the claim amount.

38. Type 1200.00 and press the Enter key.

The console will now ask the user to input the date of the repair.

39. Type 2021/10/01 and press the Enter key.

The console window will now ask the user to input the repair shop id.

40. Type RS000001 and press the Enter key.

The console will now ask the user to input the vehicle policy number.

41.   Type VP001234 and press the Enter key.

The console will now ask the user to input the claim amount.

42.   Type 2400.00 and press the Enter key.

The console will now ask the user to input the date of the repair.

43.   Type 2021/10/01 and press the Enter key.

The invoice receipt will be displayed as shown in Figure 12-9.

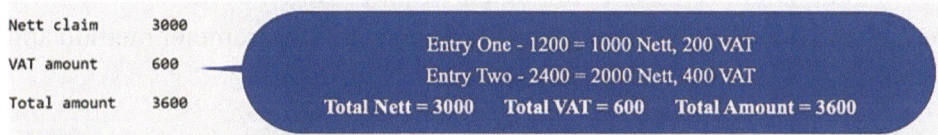

Figure 12-9. Application output

44.   Press any key to close the console window.

So now we have added parameter methods. Some of the parameter methods – methods 4, 6, 8, 10, 12, and 13 – are also value methods because they return a value, but method 14 is a void method and a parameter method.

We now have the trio of methods – void, value, and parameter – within our code. Now we are really beginning to see how code modularization works and how it can help by making the methods do one thing, which can be tested. We are also learning to think about using local variables rather than class-level variables.

Method Overloading

In C# we can have **more than one method with the same name** if we follow a few essential rules:

- The number of arguments must be different.

    For example, vatAmount(double claimAmount, double vatRate)

    vatAmount(double claimAmount, double vatRate, string vatCode)

- The types of arguments are different.

  For example, vatAmount(double claimAmount, double vatRate)

  vatAmount(double claimAmount, float vatRate)

- The order of arguments is different.

  For example, vatAmount(double claimAmount, double vatRate)

  vatAmount(double vatRate, double claimAmount)

Method overloading is a form of **polymorphism**, different forms of the same object. We will now code a new overloaded method to display a different invoice receipt. The new method, method 15, will accept three arguments. It is a parameter method and it is almost the same code as the last display method.

45. Amend the code to add method 15, as in Listing 12-69.

Listing 12-69. Method with three parameters to display a receipt

```
/****************** METHOD FIFTEEN *****************/
public static void DisplayInvoiceReceipt(double
totalValueOfClaimsPassedIn, double vatPassedIn, string
messagePassedIn)
{
Console.WriteLine("******************************");
Console.WriteLine("\nInvoice for vehicle repairs\n");
Console.WriteLine("Nett claim\t" + (totalValueOfClaimsPassedIn -
vatPassedIn) + "\n");
Console.WriteLine("VAT amount\t" + vatPassedIn + "\n");
Console.WriteLine("Total amount\t" + totalValueOfClaimsPassedIn + "\n");
Console.WriteLine(messagePassedIn);

Console.WriteLine("******************************");
} // End of method DisplayInvoiceReceipt

} // End of MethodsValue class
} // End of Chapter12 namespace
```

46.   Amend the Main() method code to call the method as in
      Listing 12-70.

Listing 12-70. Call the method to display the new invoice format

```
DisplayInvoiceReceipt(totalOfAllClaims, vatAmount);

DisplayInvoiceReceipt(totalOfAllClaims, vatAmount, "\t" +
  "Thank you for your claims\n\tthey will be processed today");

} // End of Main() method
```

47.   Click the File menu.

48.   Choose Save All.

49.   Click the Debug menu.

50.   Choose Start Without Debugging.

51.   Click in the console window.

The console window will appear and ask for the number of entries being made.

52.   Type 2 and press the Enter key.

The console window will appear and ask the user to input the repair shop id.

53.   Type RS000001 and press the Enter key.

The console will now ask the user to input the vehicle policy number.

54.   Type VP000001 and press the Enter key.

The console will now ask the user to input the claim amount.

55.   Type 1200.00 and press the Enter key.

The console will now ask the user to input the date of the repair.

56.   Type 2021/10/01 and press the Enter key.

The console window will now ask the user to input the repair shop id.

57.   Type RS000001 and press the Enter key.

The console will now ask the user to input the vehicle policy number.

58.   Type VP001234 and press the Enter key.

The console will now ask the user to input the claim amount.

59.   Type 2400.00 and press the Enter key.

The console will now ask the user to input the date of the repair.

60.   Type 2021/10/01 and press the Enter key.

The invoice receipt will be displayed as shown in Figure 12-10.

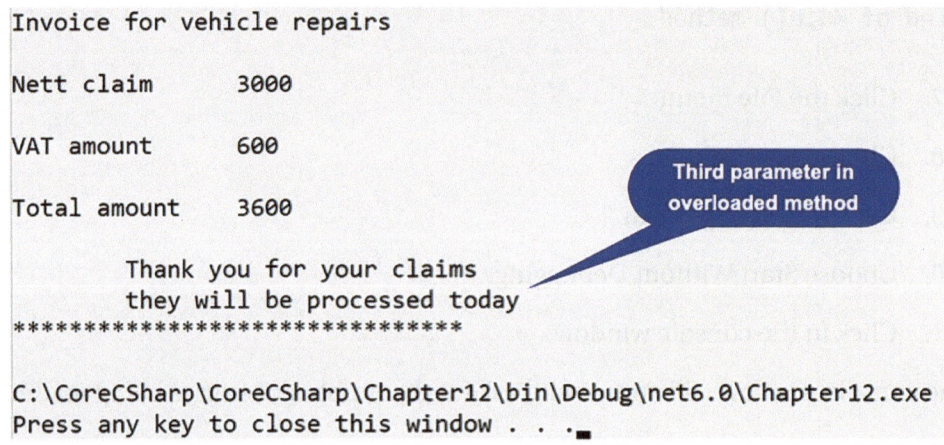

Figure 12-10. *Application output*

61.   Press any key to close the console window.

So now we have added an overloaded method, method 15. It is overloaded because

- It has the same name as the DisplayInvoiceReceipt method, method 14.

- It has three arguments, whereas the other DisplayInvoiceReceipt method, method 14, has two arguments.

Now for something a little different, and I mean different!

C# 7 Local Function

The local function is a feature introduced in C# 7. What we have covered in terms of methods, and methods being created outside the Main() method, applies not just to C# but other languages like Java. We have also seen that it is good practice to modularize our code and use methods that are small and do one thing. This is all part of the concept of **clean code** and the concept of **separation of concern** (SOC). There is also a concept in programming called the **SOLID** principles, where the S stands for single responsibility, for a class. But maybe we should also think about single responsibility for a method. When we use a **Test-Driven Development** approach to programming, we are expected to test methods, and we expect those methods to do one thing.

Now, when it comes to methods in C# 7 and above, we can have what is called a local function, which is a function within a method. Sorry. What happened to the "a method should do one thing and we should have separation of concern and clean code that is easy to maintain"? Well, as the developer, we can decide if it is appropriate to use the local function, and we may choose to use it, but we might choose not to use it.

One thing we should remember is that the methods we have used all exist inside a class. We have learned that methods and fields or properties belong to classes and alongside this we can have local variables, which are only accessible within a method and do not need to be accessed in the class or from other classes. "Traditionally," the method itself is accessible within the class and from outside the class, but C# 7 introduced us to **local functions,** and C# 8 introduced us to the **static local function,** both of which we will look at and explore.

A local function is a function declared within an existing method. The local function, as we might deduct from the name "local," is only accessible within the method, ensuring tight control. Or, if we want to use some "fancy" terminology, the method encapsulates the functionality of the function. We can think of it like this: the local function is a private function to the method it is encapsulated in. When we see the local function, we should immediately associate it with the context of the method. The local function will not have an access modifier, like public, as this would be irrelevant since the local function is only available within the method. An uncomplicated example of a local function is shown in Listing 12-71.

Listing 12-71. Local function

```
void simpleLocalFunction()
{
  Console.WriteLine($"A local function inside a method");
}
```

1. Right-click the Chapter12 project.

2. Choose Add.

3. Choose Class.

4. Name the class LocalFunctions.cs.

5. Click the Add button.

6. Create a Main() method within the class, as this was not produced automatically, and delete the unwanted imports, as in Listing 12-72.

Remember the shortcut to create the Main() method is to type svm and then press the Tab key twice.

Listing 12-72. Add the Main() method to the class template

```
namespace Chapter12
{
  internal class LocalFunctions
  {
    static void Main(string[] args)
    {
    }// End of Main() method

  } // End of LocalFunctions class
} // End of Chapter12 namespace
```

7. Right-click the Chapter12 project in the Solution Explorer panel.

8. Choose Properties from the pop-up menu.

9. Choose the LocalFunctions class in the Startup object drop-down list.

10. Close the Properties window.

We will now create a static method called CalculateRepairCostIncludingVAT() that will

- Accept a repair cost.

- Return a value based on

  - The repair cost

  - The value that will be returned from the **local function** CalculateVATAmount(), which we will create and which will be passed the variable holding the repair amount.

11. Amend the code to add a CalculateRepairCostIncludingVAT() static method, as in Listing 12-73.

Listing 12-73. Add the static method CalculateRepairCostIncludingVAT()

```
}// End of Main() method

/*
Method that takes in the pre-VAT amount and calculates
the post VAT amount
*/
public static double CalculateRepairCostIncludingVAT(double
repairAmountPassedIn)
{
    return repairAmountPassedIn + CalculateVATAmount(repairAmount
    PassedIn);

} // End of calculateRepairCostIncludingVAT method
} // End of LocalFunctions class
} // End of Chapter12 namespace
```

We will now create the **local function** called **CalculateVATAmount,** which accepts a value representing the repair cost of type double. Remember this is a local function and is therefore created in an existing method, which in our example is the CalculateRepairCostIncludingVAT() method.

12. Amend the CalculateRepairCostIncludingVAT() method to include our local function, as in Listing 12-74.

Listing 12-74. Create the local function called CalculateVATAmount

```
public double CalculateRepairCostIncludingVAT(double
        repairAmountPassedIn)
{
  return repairAmountPassedIn +
        CalculateVATAmount(repairAmountPassedIn);

  /*
  FUNCTION that takes in the pre-VAT amount and
  calculates the VAT amount. This is a local function, a
  function within a method.
  */
  double CalculateVATAmount(double repairAmount)
  {
    double vatamount = repairAmount * 20 / 100;
    return vatamount;
  } // End of local function CalculateVATAmount
} // End of calculateRepairCostIncludingVAT method
```

We will now amend the Main() method to

- Add the method-level variables we need.

- Call the CalculateRepairCostIncludingVAT() method, passing it the cost of repair value.

- Display a message to show the total cost.

13. Now add code within the Main() method to add the variables we need, as in Listing 12-75.

Listing 12-75. Add the method-level variables within the Main() method

```
static void Main(string[] args)
{
  double costOfRepair = 350.00;
  double vatRate = 20;
}// End of Main() method
```

14. Now call the CalculateRepairCostIncludingVAT method, as in Listing 12-76, passing it the variable for the repair cost and assigning the returned value to a new local variable called costOfRepairWithVAT.

Listing 12-76. Call the CalculateRepairCostIncludingVAT method and assign it

```
double costOfRepair = 350.00;
double vatRate = 20;

double costOfRepairWithVAT =  CalculateRepairCostIncludingVAT(costOf
Repair);
  }// End of Main() method
```

15. Now display the value returned from the method call, as in Listing 12-77.

Listing 12-77. Display a message to include the total cost

```
static void Main(string[] args)
{
  double costOfRepair = 350.00;
  double vatRate = 20;

  double costOfRepairWithVAT = CalculateRepairCostIncludingVAT(cost
OfRepair);

  Console.WriteLine($"For a repair costing ${costOfRepair:0.00}
  the cost including VAT at {vatRate}% will be
  ${costOfRepairWithVAT:0.00}");

  }// End of Main() method
```

16. Click the File menu.

17. Choose Save All.

18. Click the Debug menu.

19. Choose Start Without Debugging.

Figure 12-11 shows the console window displaying the total cost with the VAT included.

```
For a repair costing $350.00 the cost including VAT at 20% will be $420.00

C:\CoreCSharp\CoreCSharp\Chapter12\bin\Debug\net6.0\Chapter12.exe (process 1404)
Press any key to close this window . . ._
```

Figure 12-11. *Application output having used the local function*

C# 8 Static Local Function

While C# 7 introduced the local function, it was further developed in C# 8 with the introduction of the static local function. The concept of a static local function is to ensure that it cannot reference variables from the enclosing method, and if it does, the compiler will complain, throw an error. To make the method static, we add the keyword static to the method "signature." We will now amend our last code example to

- Demonstrate a static local function.

- Show that a class-level static variable can be accessed from within a static local function.

- Show that outer method variables are not accessible within a static local function.

The steps to show this will be as follows:

- Move the vatRate variable to the class level and make it private static.

- Make the Main() method private.

- Make the CalculateRepairCostIncludingVAT() method private.

- Make the local function CalculateVATAmount static.

The code shown in the Listing 12-78 has additional and amended comments to help us understand the changes.

20.   Amend the code as in Listing 12-78, which applies the steps set
       out previously.

Listing 12-78. Static local function accessing static class variable

```
namespace Chapter12
{
  internal class LocalFunctions
  {
    /*
    Make a static class level variable
    We are able to use a static class level variable within
    our local functions and within our static local functions
    */
    private static double vatRate = 20;

    // Make the Main() method private
    private static void Main(string[] args)
    {
      double costOfRepair = 350.00;

      double costOfRepairWithVAT = CalculateRepairCostIncludingVAT(cost
      OfRepair);

      Console.WriteLine($"For a repair costing ${costOfRepair:0.00}
      the cost including VAT at {vatRate}% will be
      ${costOfRepairWithVAT:0.00}");

    }// End of Main() method

    /*
    Now we have a private method that takes in private variable
    holding the pre-private VAT amount and the calculates
    the post-private VAT amount
    */
```

```
private static double CalculateRepairCostIncludingVAT(double
repairAmountPassedIn)
{
  return repairAmountPassedIn + CalculateVATAmount(repairAmount
  PassedIn);

  /*
  FUNCTION that takes in the pre-VAT amount and
  calculates the VAT amount. This is a local function, a
  function within a method.
  This local function is static and we have access to the
  static class level variable vatAmount
  We do not have access to the outer method, in this case
  the Main() method, variables as we would see if we tried
  to use the variable costOfRepair in our formula
  */
  static double CalculateVATAmount(double repairAmount)
  {
    double vatamount = repairAmount * 20 / 100;
    return vatamount;
  } // End of local function CalculateVATAmount

} // End of calculateRepairCostIncludingVAT method
} // End of LocalFunctions class

} // End of Chapter12 namespace
```

Running the code again gives us the same output, as in Figure 12-11, but we have applied the use of static local functions and shown how they can access static class-level variables. The other thing to demonstrate is that static local functions cannot access outer method variables.

21. Amend the code, as in Listing 12-79, to make the formula use the variable costOfRepair, which exists in the Main() method, the outer method.

Listing 12-79. Amend the formula to use the outer method variable

```
static double CalculateVATAmount(double repairAmount)
 {
   double vatamount = repairAmount * costOfRepair * 20 / 100;
    return vatamount;
 } // End of local function CalculateVATAmount
```

22. Hover over the red underline on the costOfRepair and note that we are being told that this variable does not exist in the current context, as in Figure 12-12.

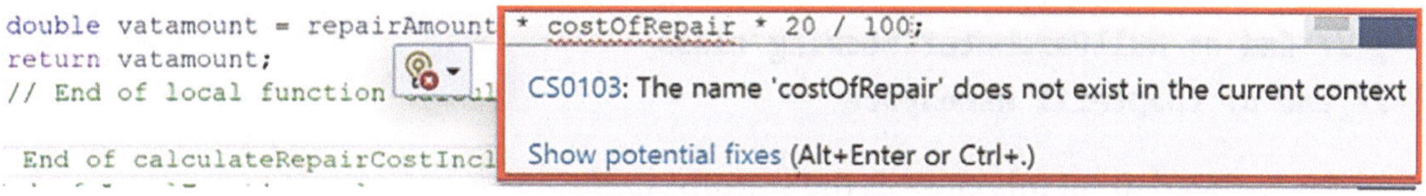

Figure 12-12. *Static local function cannot access outer method variable*

23. Change the formula back to its original format.

C# 10 Null Parameter Checking

We have seen how a method can accept parameters, but what would happen if a parameter was null? Well, C# 10 helps us handle this with the introduction of the null parameter checking.

Add a new class to hold the code for this example.

1. Right-click the project Chapter12 in the Solution Explorer panel.

2. Choose Add.

3. Choose Class.

4. Name the class NullParameterChecking.cs.

5. Click the Add button.

6. Create a Main() method within the class, as this was not produced automatically, and delete the unwanted imports, as in Listing 12-80.

The shortcut to create the Main() method is to type svm and then press the Tab key twice.

Listing 12-80. Create the Main() method

```
namespace Chapter12
{
  internal class NullParameterChecking
  {
    static void Main(string[] args)
    {
    } // End of Main() method
  } // End of NullParameterChecking class
} // End of Chapter12 namespace
```

Now we need to set this class as the startup class.

7. Right-click the Chapter12 project in the Solution Explorer panel.

8. Choose Properties from the pop-up menu.

9. Choose the NullParameterChecking.cs class in the Startup object drop-down list.

10. Close the Properties window.

11. Amend the code to add a variable to hold a string value representing a vehicle registration and assign it a value, as in Listing 12-81.

Listing 12-81. Add a variable to hold the vehicle registration

```
static void Main(string[] args)
{
  string vehicleRegistration = "ABC 1234";
} // End of Main() method
```

We will now amend the code to

- Create a method called DisplayInvoice(), which will accept three values and check if the first value is null:

    - If the value is null, display an error message.

    - If it is not null, display a "receipt."

- Call the DisplayInvoice() method and pass it the three values.

12. Amend the code, as in Listing 12-82, to call the DisplayInvoice() method, which we will create next, and pass it three values, the first of which is the variable we set up for the vehicle registration.

Listing 12-82. Call the DisplayInvoice() method passing in three values

```
static void Main(string[] args)
{
  string vehicleRegistration = "ABC 1234";

  DisplayInvoice(vehicleRegistration, 10000, 2000);
} // End of Main() method
```

13. Amend the code to create the DisplayInvoice() method outside the Main() method, as in Listing 12-83.

Listing 12-83. Create the DisplayInvoice() method accepting three values

```
} // End of Main() method

public static void DisplayInvoice(string vehicleRegistration,
  double repairTotal, double vatAmount)
{
  if (vehicleRegistration == null)
  {
    Console.WriteLine("\nNull value error message\n");
  } // End of if block
  else
```

```
    {
        Console.WriteLine("\nInvoice for vehicle repairs\n");
        Console.WriteLine("Vehicle registration\t" +
                            vehicleRegistration + "\n");
        Console.WriteLine("Repair amount\t\t$" +
                                repairTotal + "\n");
        Console.WriteLine("VAT amount\t\t$" +
                                vatAmount + "\n");
    } // End of else block
    } // End of DisplayInvoice() method
} // End of NullParameterChecking class
} // End of Chapter12 namespace
```

14. Click the File menu.

15. Choose Save All.

16. Click the Debug menu.

17. Choose Start Without Debugging.

Figure 12-13 shows the console window, which displays the receipt.

```
Invoice for vehicle repairs

Vehicle registration    ABC 1234

Repair amount           $10000

VAT amount              $2000

C:\CoreCSharp\CoreCSharp\Chapter12\bin\Debug\net6.0\Chapter12.exe
Press any key to close this window . . .
```

Figure 12-13. *Application output receipt*

18. Press the Enter key to close the console window.

But now let us see what happens when a null value is used.

19. Amend the code to assign null to the variable holding the vehicle registration, as in Listing 12-84.

Listing 12-84. Make the variable have a null value

```
static void Main(string[] args)
{
  string vehicleRegistration = null;
  //string vehicleRegistration = "ABC 1234";

  DisplayInvoice(vehicleRegistration, 10000, 2000);
```

20. Click the File menu.

21. Choose Save All.

22. Click the Debug menu.

23. Choose Start Without Debugging.

Figure 12-14 shows the console window displaying the null error message.

```
Null value error message


C:\CoreCSharp\CoreCSharp\Chapter12\bin\Debug\net6.0\Chapter12.exe
Press any key to close this window . . .
```

Figure 12-14. *Application showing that the value is null*

24. Press the Enter key to close the console window.

C# 10 Null Parameter Checking Approach

In C# 10.0 we can use the ArgumentNullException.ThrowIfNull() method instead of using the if selection construct.

25. Amend the code to use the ArgumentNullException.ThrowIfNull() method on the vehicle registration variable, as in Listing 12-85.

Listing 12-85. Use the ArgumentNullException.ThrowIfNull() method

```
namespace Chapter12
{
  internal class NullParameterChecking
  {
    static void Main(string[] args)
    {
      // string vehicleRegistration = "ABC 1234";
      string vehicleRegistration = null;
      DisplayInvoice(vehicleRegistration, 10000, 2000);

    } // End of Main() method

    public static void DisplayInvoice(string vehicleRegistration, double
    repairTotal, double vatAmount)
    {
      ArgumentNullException.ThrowIfNull(vehicleRegistration);

      Console.WriteLine("\nInvoice for vehicle repairs\n");
      Console.WriteLine("Vehicle registration\t" + vehicleRegistration
      + "\n");
      Console.WriteLine("Repair amount\t\t$" + repairTotal + "\n");
      Console.WriteLine("VAT amount\t\t$" + vatAmount + "\n");

    } // End of DisplayInvoice() method
  } // End of NullParameterChecking class
} // End of Chapter12 namespace
```

26. Click the File menu.

27. Choose Save All.

28. Click the Debug menu.

29. Choose Start Without Debugging.

The console window will appear, as shown in Figure 12-15, and display the exception message specifying the parameter causing the problem.

```
Unhandled exception. System.ArgumentNullException: Value cannot be null. (Paramet ^
er 'vehicleRegistration')
   at System.ArgumentNullException.Throw(String paramName)
   at System.ArgumentNullException.ThrowIfNull(Object argument, String paramName)

   at Chapter12.NullParameterChecking.DisplayInvoice(String vehicleRegistration,
Double repairTotal, Double vatAmount) in C:\CoreCSharp\CoreCSharp\Chapter12\NullP
arameterChecking.cs:line 21
   at Chapter12.NullParameterChecking.Main(String[] args) in C:\CoreCSharp\CoreCS
harp\Chapter12\NullParameterChecking.cs:line 11

C:\CoreCSharp\CoreCSharp\Chapter12\bin\Debug\net6.0\Chapter12.exe (process 2252)
exited with code -532462766.
Press any key to close this window . . ._
```

Figure 12-15. *Exception message received when attempting to display the receipt*

Chapter Summary

So, finishing this chapter on methods, we now have coded our own

- Void methods

- Value methods

- Parameter methods

- Overloaded methods

However, we have also used methods in this code that we did not write. In fact, we have been using methods that we did not write from the first program we wrote in this course. The first real line of code we entered was WriteLine();.

WriteLine() is a method. In this line of code, there is no text in the () brackets so no text is written to the console, but a new line is taken. So the WriteLine() method will move to a new line once it prints its content. How does it work? Well, we do not have to worry because we did not write the code and will not have to maintain the method code – it is part of the C# framework. When we go to answer the question, "How does it work?" simply answer it like this: **don't know, don't care.** What this really means is as developers we should not get involved with methods that are developed to help us and have been tested and proved reliable. They work. We just use them to build our application code.

Other examples of methods we did not write but have used in our code include

`Write()` – Does not move to a new line once it prints its content

`ReadLine()` – Accepts no arguments

`Parse()` – Accepts no arguments

`nextDouble()` – Accepts no arguments

`WriteLine("Message")` – A parameter method that accepts one argument

Now, thinking about the methods we have created and the methods we have not created but have used, they all have one thing in common, and this commonality will lead us into the next chapter. **The common thing about them is that they all live inside a class; they are part of a class.** When we code an example like this

```
 public class MethodsV2
{
}
```

it says that the code contained between the opening curly brace { and the closing curly brace } is within the class. All our code is inside the class, apart from the import statements. So a takeaway from this chapter is that **a class contains**

- **Methods**

- **Variables**

We also saw that we can have a local function, a function within a method, and we can even make the function a static function. Finally, we looked at the concept of handling a null parameter being passed to a method by using the ThrowIfNull() method, which accepts the parameter being checked.

We are making great progress in our programming of C# applications and we should be proud of our achievements. In finishing this very important chapter, we are ready to look at classes, and while we have increased our knowledge further, we are advancing to our target.

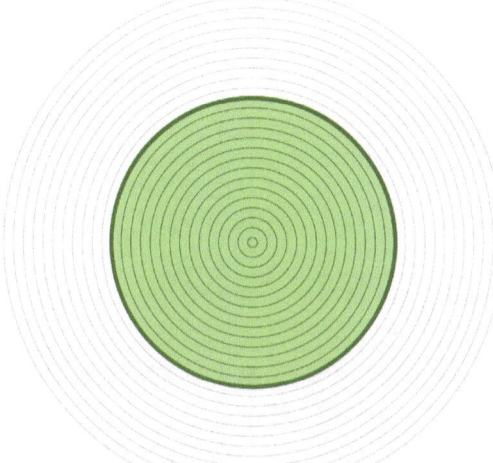

Our target is getting closer

CHAPTER 13

Classes

Classes and Objects in OOP

We learned in Chapter 12 that methods belong inside classes and classes consist of variables and methods. We saw that there are a number of different method types that can be used in our code. The method types we can create or use are

- Void methods that return no value and simply execute code

- Value methods that return a value of a specific data type after executing

- Parameter methods that take actual values as their parameters and that may or may not return a value of a specific data type after executing

- Overloaded methods, which are methods with the same name but different parameters

There are many methods used in our code, which are not written by us, for example, WriteLine(), Write(), ReadLine(), ToDouble(), ToInt32(), and ToDateTime(). The methods we have created and the methods we have not created but have used all have one thing in common:

They all live inside a class; they are part of a class.

It is the commonality of classes that this chapter will be concentrating on. The crucial takeaway from the last chapter and a vital thing to remember in this chapter is that a class contains

- Methods
- Variables

447

© Gerard Byrne 2022
G. Byrne, *Target C#*, https://doi.org/10.1007/978-1-4842-8619-7_13

When we create our own classes, they act in the same way as the classes in .NET or any other classes in that they can be reused, usually by creating instances of them, to create one or more objects.

A Class Is a Data Structure

In the software development world, there are many programming languages and many different types of program. Some languages and programs are what can be called legacy languages and legacy programs. COBOL is one such legacy programming language, but it is still a very powerful language that widely exists in many commercial applications. On the other hand, other languages are popular and use the latest methods or features in object-oriented programming (OOP). With traditional languages like COBOL, developers often coded the programs as a set of instructions that followed a sequence, and hence it was called sequential programming. With object-oriented programming (OOP), there is now a focus on structuring the code more and using objects. This is achieved by organizing or capturing the code in logically related methods and data objects called classes. This process of organizing or capturing the data and methods is called **encapsulation**.[1]

Our classes will contain fields, and sometimes these fields, as we have read before, can be referred to as members or variables or properties or instance variables. For simplicity we should just think of them as variables. In this chapter we are now going to elaborate on what can be held within a class, and we can categorize these as either:

- Data members that store data associated with the class or data associated with an instance of the class, the object. We can simply think of them as a **variable** if they are private or protected and as a **field** if they are public.

- Function members that are used to execute code. They are the **methods** we use to hold our code.

In a class we can have different types, and when trying to learn about classes and objects, it is very important that we understand what the types are and what their role is, so we will look at these in more detail now.

---

[1] **Encapsulation** is the concept of making packages that hold all the things we need. In object-oriented programming, we can create classes that store all the variables and methods. The methods will be used to manipulate the data we have stored.

Type 1: Fields

A field is a variable of any data type that is declared directly in our class. A field will usually store data that needs to be accessible to more than one method in the class and must be stored for longer than the lifetime of any single method. In relation to some of the examples we have used so far, we have had:

- A class called QuoteArithmetic that held details about an insurance quote and had fields that represented the

  - Age of the vehicle in terms of years. It was called `vehicleAgeInYears`.

  - Current mileage of the vehicle. It was called `vehicleCurrentMileage`.

- A class called MethodsV1 that held details about an insurance claim and had fields that represented the

  - id of the repair shop making the claim. It was called `repairShopID`.

  - Claim amount. It was called `claimAmount`.

When we declare these fields at the class level, they can be used by more than one method of our class. The variables are said to have a **class scope** within the class. On the other hand, when the field will be used by only one method within the class, we should ensure that the variable is declared inside the method, and therefore it is said to have a method scope. A field is declared within the class block by identifying

- The **access level** of the field, for example, public or private

- The **type** of the field, for example, double, string, etc.

- The **name** of the field, for example, premium

Examples of the fields are shown in Tables 13-1 and 13-2.

Table 13-1. *A class with a public field*

Example	Explanation
| ```
public class QuoteArithmetic
{
 public int vehicleAgeInYears;
}
``` | • Access modifier is public.<br>• Type is int.<br>• Name is vehicleAgeInYears. |

Table 13-2. *A class with a private field*

Example	Explanation
| ```
public class MethodsV1
{
 private String repairShopID;
}
``` | • Access modifier is private.<br>• Type is String.<br>• Name is repairShopID. |

Type 2: Constants

The value of a variable can change throughout the lifetime of the application. In C# when a variable is declared using the **const** keyword, the value cannot be modified. In essence, it is a **constant** value, and a constant value will therefore not change during the lifetime of the application and is always known to the compiler at runtime. A constant is declared within the class block by

- Identifying the **access level** of the field, for example, public or private.

- Adding the **const** modifier.

- Identifying the **type** of the field, for example, double, String, etc.

- Identifying the name of the field. In C# the naming convention may be to use PascalCase for class names, method names, and constants or readonly variables, whereas in Java the naming convention could be to use capital letters for the name of a constant, for example, BASEINSURANCEAMOUNT. Ultimately it is a convention, rather than a must-do.

- Setting its fixed value.

Examples of constant values are shown in Tables 13-3 and 13-4.

Table 13-3. *A class with a constant field with public access*

Example	Explanation
| ```
public class QuoteArithmetic
{
 public const int
 maximumDriverAge=100;
}
``` | • Access modifier is public.<br>• Modifier const makes it a constant value.<br>• Type is int.<br>• Name is maximumDriverAge.<br>• Value is fixed to 100. |

Table 13-4. *A class with a constant field with private access*

Example	Explanation
| ```
public class MethodsV1
{
 private const double
 minimumQuote=100.00;
}
``` | • Access modifier is private.<br>• Modifier const makes it a constant value.<br>• Type is double.<br>• Name is minimumQuote.<br>• Value is fixed at 100.00. |

Type 3: Methods

Methods form a large part of the C# language. Our C# application will start its execution from within the **Main**() method, so in our code the Main() method will exist in one of our classes and forms the entry point for the application being developed. As developers we use methods to modularize our code and make it easier to read and maintain. More importantly, methods form the basis for the vitally important concept of Test-Driven Development (TDD), where the idea is to test a unit of code, which is usually a method. In Test-Driven Development we write tests first before we write our classes and methods – yes, that is strange. With Test-Driven Development the tests themselves are methods, which are inside a class, called the test class. So once again we see the importance of classes with methods and variables.

When we create methods, we are really developing blocks of code that perform an action, and we can say that methods hold our business logic. A method is declared within the class block by identifying

- The access level of the method

- Optional modifiers such as abstract, sealed, static, override, and virtual

- The return type of the method

- The name of the method

- Any parameters that are passed into the method

Listing 13-1. Example method code snippet

```
// Method 1
public static void HowManyClaimsAreBeingMade()
{
  /*
  Read the user input for the number of claims being made
  and convert the string value to an integer data type*/
  Console.WriteLine("How many claims are being made?\n");
  numberOfClaimsBeingMade = Convert.ToInt32(Console.ReadLine());
} // End of HowManyClaimsAreBeingMade() method
```

Analysis of the Method Code in Listing 13-1

- **Access level** of the method is **public.**

- The **static** modifier has been applied to the method, and we will learn more about static in this chapter.

- The **return type** of the method is **void** – it does not return anything.

- The **name** of the method is **HowManyClaimsAreBeingMade.**

- No parameters are passed into the method – it is parameterless.

Type 4: Properties

As we saw in Tables 13-1, 13-2, 13-3, and 13-4, it is possible to set the field access modifier as public or private. Private fields are referred to as variables and public fields are referred to as fields. The reason for setting the field as private is to ensure that it cannot be accessed directly from outside the class, by another class. We may therefore wonder how we can read the value of a variable or write a value to a variable from outside its class if it is set as private. Well, the answer is by using a **property,** which is a mechanism that allows for reading and writing, getting or setting, of the variable.

Properties are declared in the class block by specifying the access level of the variable, followed by the type of the property, followed by the name of the property, and followed by a code block that can declare a **get accessor** and/or a **set accessor**.

- Get accessor, getter

  A get accessor method used to read the value of a private field is called a **getter.** The method is used to return a value to outside classes; it is a read method and the method will be used as shown in Listing 13-2.

Listing 13-2. Example code snippet for a getter

```
public class Methods
{
  double totalOfAllClaims;

  public double TotalOfAllClaims
  {
    get
    {
      return totalOfAllClaims;
    }
  }
} //End of class
```

So, in essence, the getter method gets the value of a field, variable, and returns the value to the calling statement. In Listing 13-2 we can see that the getter is used to get the value of the field totalOfAllClaims. The get accessor returns this value to the statement that calls it.

- Set accessor, setter

A set accessor method used to write a value to a private field is called a **setter**. The method is used to accept a value from outside the class and the method will be used as shown in Listing 13-3.

Listing 13-3. Example code snippet for a setter

```
public class Methods
{
  double totalOfAllClaims;
  public double TotalOfAllClaims
  {
    get
    {
      return totalOfAllClaims;
    }
    set
    {
        totalOfAllClaims = value;
    }
  }
} //End of class
```

So, in essence, the setter method sets the value of a field. In Listing 13-3 we can see that the setter is used to set the value of the field totalOfAllClaims. The set accessor assigns the new value to the field.

Type 5: Constructor

We now know that fields with an access modifier of private can have their value amended using a setter. There is also a very special method that can exist in a class and can be used for the purpose of initializing the values of the fields or writing some code. This special method is called a **constructor** and will be created by the developer.

Default Constructor

If we do not want to initialize the fields, they will have the default value for the data type of the particular field, for example, the int data type has a default of 0 and the double data type has a default of 0.00. When we choose not to develop a constructor and therefore leave the default values for the fields, there is still a constructor in the class; it is called a **default constructor** and it will not be visible.

Analysis of the Constructor Code in Figure 13-1

- Here we have created an instance of the class MethodsV1 – we are instantiating the class.

- This instantiation passes in no values, arguments, to the class called MethodsV1, as there are no values between the open and close brackets ().

- This means that the default constructor has been used and the fields of the class will have the default value for their data type.

```
public class Test
{
  public static void Main(String[] args)
  {
    // Instantiate the class using the default constructor
    MethodsV1 myInstanceOfMethodsV1 = new MethodsV1();
  } // End of Main() method
} // End of class
```

Instantiate using the default constructor

Figure 13-1. *Instantiate the class using the default constructor, no values*

Custom Constructor

If we want to initialize the fields so they do not have their default values, we need to create our own constructor. Once we create our own constructor method, the default constructor no longer exists, but we could still manually add a default constructor. Figure 13-2 shows the custom constructor.

```
public class MethodsV1
{
    string repairShopId;
    double claimAmount;

    public MethodsV1(string repairShopId, double claimAmount)
    {
        repairShopId = repairShopId;
        claimAmount = claimAmount;
```

custom constructor with 2 parameters

no return type

parameter one of type string

parameter two of type double

```
    } // End of constructor

} // End of MethodsV1 class
```

Figure 13-2. *Creating the custom constructor*

The **constructor** "method" is used to initialize the value of the fields in the class. It may be used to initialize all the fields or just some of them. A constructor has the following features (we will refer to Figure 13-2):

- It must have the **same name as the class** – in this example it is MethodsV1.

- It must have an access modifier of public.

- It has **no return type**, not even void.

- It has parameters, and they are of the same type as the fields that are to be initialized. Here we have a string followed by a double.

The **constructor**, method, is "activated" when the class is created. We will see more about this as we code the examples in this chapter. The way a class is "activated" is by creating an **instance of the class.** The reason we use an instance of the class is because the class itself is a **template** and should not be used directly.

In the code shown in Figure 13-2, we could have used the keyword **this** to refer to the fields of the class, and we would do this to differentiate between the field of the class and the parameter of the method. But wait a minute! Could we not have named the parameters of the method different from the field names of the class and then avoided using the this keyword? Yes, of course we could, but in terms of clean code and convention, using the same name for the variables can be seen as preferential, and therefore we use the this keyword. We can think of this as referring to the current object, the field of the class we are in.

Analysis of the Constructor Code in Figure 13-3

- This instantiation passes in two values, arguments, to the constructor of the MethodsV1 class.

- As we can see from the two values between the open and close brackets (), we are passing in one string, "RS1234", followed by one double, 2999.50, to the constructor of the class called MethodsV1.

- The values, arguments, are passed to the constructor, which has been created, and the constructor accepts these arguments as its parameters.

- The values are of types string and double in this specific order.

- Remember, the default constructor accepts no values.

- Since we are using a custom constructor, we know that the default constructor does not exist.

```
public class Test
{
  public static void Main(String[] args)   custom constructor is called and passed 2 arguments
  {
    // Instantiate the class using a custom constructor
MethodsV1 myInstanceOfMethodsV1=new MethodsV1("RS1234", 2999.50);
      } // End of Main() method
} // End of Test class              instance of the class
      the actual class
```

Figure 13-3. *Instantiate the class using a custom constructor, values passed.*

The class code to go with this instantiation could be as shown in Figure 13-2 and reproduced here as Listing 13-4.

Listing 13-4. Class with custom constructor

```
public class MethodsV1
{
  String repairShopId;
  double claimAmount;

  public MethodsV1(string repairShopId, double claimAmount)
```

```
  {
    this.repairShopId = repairShopId;
    this.claimAmount = claimAmount;
  } // End of constructor
} // End of class
```

Analysis of the Constructor Code in Listing 13-4 and Figure 13-3

- Figure 13-3 shows that when the class is instantiated, the first argument is the value "RS1234".

- This argument is accepted by the repairShopId parameter, as in Listing 13-4, and the default value of the repairShopId field is overwritten. The value becomes "RS1234".

- Figure 13-3 shows that when the class is instantiated, the second argument is the value 2999.50.

- This argument is accepted by the claimAmount parameter, as in Listing 13-4, and the default value of the claimAmount field is overwritten. The value becomes 2999.50.

- The constructor, as in Listing 13-4, therefore uses the arguments passed to it to initialize the fields.

- this.repairShopId, in Listing 13-4, refers to the field repairShopID of the class.

- The field repairShopID, in Listing 13-4, is therefore assigned the value "RS1234".

- this.claimAmount, in Listing 13-4, refers to the field claimAmount of the class.

- The field claimAmount, in Listing 13-4, is therefore assigned the value 2999.50.

Since there is a constructor method in this example, it means that the default constructor no longer exists – it has been overwritten.

Constructor Overloading

In C# it is possible to use overloading of constructors, and the concept of overloading constructors is the same as the method overloading that exists in the C# language, which we looked at in the previous chapter. Overloading means that it is possible for us to have constructors with the same name, the name of the class, but which take a different set of input parameters. This is comparable to the overloading of methods that we looked at in the last chapter. Listing 13-5 shows code where we have three constructors. The first constructor has two parameters of type string followed by a double. The second constructor has only one parameter of type string. The third constructor has only one parameter of type double. Remember a constructor has the same name as the class, so all three constructors are called MethodsV1. Constructors also have no return type.

Listing 13-5. Constructor overloading – more than one custom constructor

```
public class MethodsV1
{
 String repairShopId;
 double claimAmount;

 public MethodsV1(string repairShopId, double claimAmount)
 {
   this.repairShopId = repairShopId;
   this.claimAmount = claimAmount;
 }// End of constructor with parameters of type String and double

 public MethodsV1(string repairShopId)
 {
   this.repairShopId = repairShopId;
 }// End of constructor with a parameter of type String

public MethodsV1(double claimAmount)
 {
   this.claimAmount = claimAmount;
 }// End of constructor with a parameter of type double

} // End of class MethodsV1
```

As we read earlier, many commercial programs will involve large amounts of code, and from a maintenance and testing perspective, it is essential that the program has a good structure. Well-written and organized programs allow those who maintain or test them to

- Follow the code and the flow of events easier.

- Find things quicker.

Let's recap what we have seen in Chapter 12:

To structure the program code better, we could break the code into small functional parts, each part performing one task. When we have a functional part, which does one particular thing, it may be possible for that functional part to be used by other parts of the program.

In the last chapter on methods, we created methods that performed one task, and then the methods were called as required. Well, this section will develop this concept even further.

Suppose we have developed a program with the following methods:

- AgentCommission()

- AgentBonus()

- CustomerPersonalDetails()

- CustomerVehicleDetails()

Suppose all the methods are inside a class and outside the Main() method. Now, this would be fine, and the code could work, and it's similar to what we did when coding in Chapter 12. But, looking closely at the method names, we might suggest that they **relate to two distinct categories or groups, an Agent and a Customer**.

If this is the case, we should think, *Would it not be better if each method was placed inside a class that related to its category?* This would mean that our code could now look something like the three classes shown in Listings 13-6, 13-7, and 13-8.

Class 1

The class in Listing 13-6 is the main entry point into the application and is used to start the program as it has the Main() method.

Listing 13-6. Class with the Main() entry point

```
public class Insurance
{
  public static void Main(String[] args)
  {
    //Some code to call the methods in the other class(es)
  } // End of Main() method
} // End of Insurance class
```

Class 2

The class in Listing 13-7 has the methods and fields associated with an Agent; it does not have a Main() method as only one class in our application can have the entry point.

Listing 13-7. Class for the Agent

```
public class Agent
{
  public static void AgentCommission()
  {
    //Some business logic code to calculate the commission
  } // End of AgentCommission method

  public static void AgentBonus()
  {
    //Some business logic code to calculate the bonus
  }// End of AgentBonus method

}// End of Agent class
```

Class 3

This class in Listing 13-8 has the methods and fields associated with a Customer; it does not have a Main() method as only one class in our application can have the entry point.

Listing 13-8. Class for the Customer

```
public class Customer
{
  public static void CustomerPersonalDetails()
  {
      //Some code to read in the customer personal details
  }// End of CustomerPersonalDetails method

  public static void CustomerVehicleDetails()
  {
      //Some code to read in the customers vehicle details
  }// End of CustomerVehicleDetails method
}// End of Customer class
```

Our code is now organized into classes and into methods within the classes. More importantly, the distinct classes hold methods and fields that have a similar purpose. This is a good starting point, and we might, even at this stage, think we could have completed the separation process in a different way. We could, and that is part of the "joy" of programming, as developers think in different ways, and no one way is the right way.

While coding the examples in each of the previous chapters, we have seen at least one property of a class, and we have used methods that belonged to different classes. Listing 13-9 shows the Length property of the Arrays class, and we should notice that the Length property does not contain the opening and closing parentheses () – it is not a method.

Listing 13-9. Length property of the Arrays class

```
for (int counter = 0; counter < employeeAndSalary.Length; counter++)
{
  Console.WriteLine($"The element positioned at {counter} is
  {^(employeeAndSalary.Length - (counter))} from the end of the array");
}
```

Listing 13-10 shows the Parse() method of the Int32 class, and we should notice that the method does contain the opening and closing parentheses () – it is a method.

Listing 13-10. Parse method of the Int32 class – also the ReadLine() method

```
return Int32.Parse(Console.ReadLine());
```

When using the method called Parse(), some things to note are as follows:

- When the line of code in Listing 13-10 is entered into the Integrated Development Environment (IDE) and the full stop is typed after the word Int32, a pop-up window appears.

- The pop-up window displays the methods and fields that are part of the Int32 class.

- The methods have the cube icon.

- The fields have the spanner icon, but there are no fields for Parse.

- The constants have the rectangle with lines icon.

- However, some Integrated Development Environments use the symbols M for a method and F for a field.

- The Int32 class has only methods that are associated with 32-bit integers.

In Figure 13-4 we can see the methods, in particular the Parse() method. We can also see that the Int32 class has methods and constants – it has no fields.

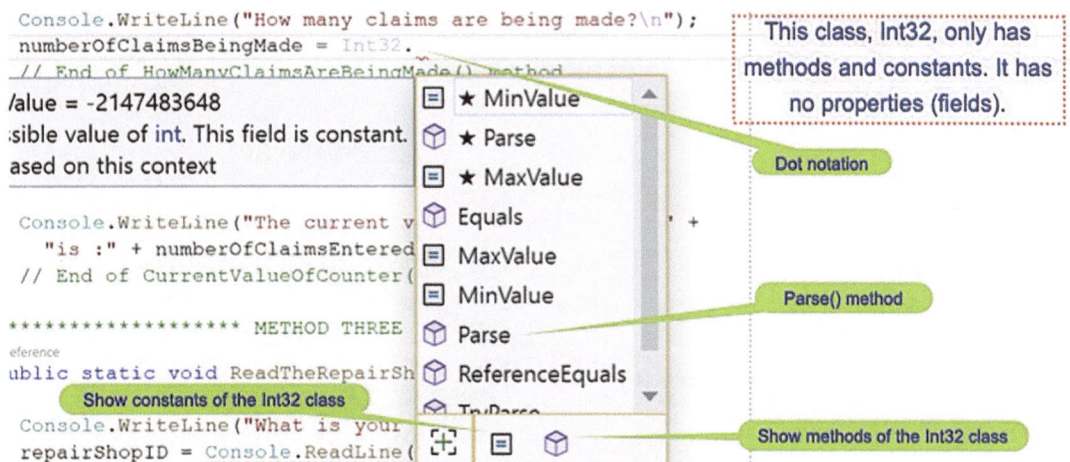

Figure 13-4. *Int32 class with its methods and constants*

Listing 13-11. Sqrt() method from the Math class

```
double answer = Math.Sqrt(9.00);
```

In Listing 13-11 we have used the method called Sqrt(), which belongs to the class called Math:

- When the code in Listing 13-11 is entered into the Integrated Development Environment (IDE) and the full stop is typed after the word Math, a pop-up window appears.

- The pop-up window displays any methods and fields that are part of the Math class.

- The methods have the cube icon.

- The fields would have the spanner icon, but Math has no fields.

- The constants have the rectangle with the lines, for example, PI and Tau.

- The Math class has only methods that are associated with mathematics.

In Figure 13-5 we can see the methods, cube icon, in particular the Sqrt() method that accepts a double as an argument.

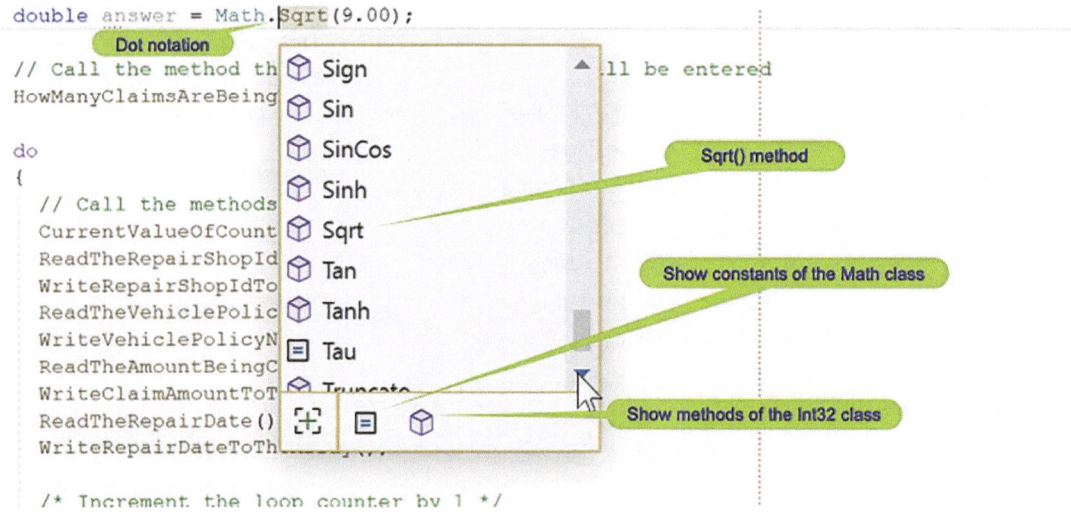

Figure 13-5. *Math class with its methods*

Great, now we can think of methods that come with C# and from the imports, not just being coded in one class but in numerous classes. With these classes there is a high degree of code separation. We call it **separation of concern** (SoC), where associated methods are kept together, and this is what we can do – we have done this in Chapter 12. Think about separation of concern using these real-world examples.

In a school there are different roles:

- The head teacher

- The senior teachers

- The teachers

- The administration staff

- The facilities staff

- The canteen staff

All roles have separate concerns, but all concerns serve one purpose, to keep the school working.

In a hospital there are different roles:

- The consultants

- The doctors

- The nurses

- The care assistants

- The administration staff

- The facilities staff

- The catering staff

All roles have separate concerns, but all concerns serve one purpose, to keep the hospital functioning.

Let's code some C# and build our programming muscle.

Now it is time for us to code some classes with methods and show the separation of concern working in our application. We will be programming the same application that we have just completed in Chapter 12, so we can choose to copy and paste code as required, but the following instructions assume that we are starting again with no code.

Add a new project to hold the code for this chapter.

1. Right-click the solution CoreCSharp.

2. Choose Add.

3. Choose New Project.

4. Choose Console App from the listed templates that appear.

5. Click the Next button.

6. Name the project Chapter13 and leave it in the same location.

7. Click the Next button.

8. Choose the framework to be used, which in our projects will be .NET 6.0 or higher.

9. Click the Create button.

Now we should see the Chapter13 project within the solution called CoreCSharp.

10. Right-click the project Chapter13 in the Solution Explorer panel.

11. Click the Set as Startup Project option.

Notice how the Chapter13 project name has been made to have bold text, indicating that it is the new startup project and that it is the Program.cs file within it that will be executed when we run the debugging.

12. Right-click the Program.cs file in the Solution Explorer window.

13. Choose Rename.

14. Change the name to ClaimApplication.cs.

15. Press the Enter key.

16. Double-click the ClaimApplication.cs file to open it in the editor window.

Now we can set up the code structure with a namespace, and inside it will be the ClaimApplication class, and inside the class will be the Main() method. The shortcut for creating the Main() method is to type svm and press the Tab key twice.

17. In the editor window, add the code in Listing 13-12.

Listing 13-12. Class with the Main() method

```
namespace Chapter13
{
  internal class ClaimApplication
  {
    static void Main(string[] args)
    {
    } // End of Main() method

  } // End of ClaimApplication class
} // End of Chapter13 namespace
```

Now we have a class with a Main() method. We can follow points 18–21 in the following to set it as the Startup object, but as this is the only class with a Main() method in this startup project, it will automatically be used as the Startup object.

18. Right-click the Chapter13 project in the Solution Explorer panel.

19. Choose Properties from the pop-up menu.

20. Choose the Chapter13.ClaimApplication class in the Startup object drop-down list.

21. Close the Properties window.

Add the ClaimDetails class, which has no Main() method.

22. Right-click the Chapter13 project in the Solution Explorer window.

23. Choose Add.

24. Choose New Item.

25. Choose Class.

26. Change the name to ClaimDetails.cs.

27. Click the Add button.

The **ClaimDetails** class code will appear in the editor window and will be similar to Listing 13-13.

Listing 13-13. ClaimDetails class with no Main() method

```
namespace Chapter13
{
  internal class ClaimDetails
  {
  } // End of ClaimDetails class
} // End of Chapter13 namespace
```

We are now going to use the same code, with some small changes, that we created for the MethodsValue program, but the methods will be contained within the ClaimDetails class and will be called from within the ClaimApplication class, which contains the Main() method. This will now ensure that we have some degree of separation. Remember that the methods were numbered, so the following instructions will reference the methods by their number. We will then code further classes to reinforce the concept of classes and objects.

28.   Amend the code, as in Listing 13-14, to create the required class-level variable.

Listing 13-14. Add the class-level variable

```
namespace Chapter13
{
  internal class ClaimDetails
  {
    int numberOfClaimsEntered;

  } // End of ClaimDetails class
} // End of Chapter13 namespace
```

REMEMBER

We have the code for the methods in the MethodsValue.cs class, so copy and paste and remove the static keyword.

29.   Amend the ClaimDetails code, as in Listing 13-15, to add method 1. Notice that static has been removed.

Listing 13-15. Add method 1

```
internal class ClaimDetails
{
   int numberOfClaimsBeingMade;

   /****************** METHOD ONE ******************/
   public int HowManyClaimsAreBeingMade()
   {
     /*
     Read the user input for the number of claims being made
     and convert the string value to an integer data type
     */
     Console.WriteLine("How many claims are being made?\n");
     return Convert.ToInt32(Console.ReadLine());
   } // End of HowManyClaimsAreBeingMade() method

} // End of ClaimDetails class
```

30. Click the File menu.

31. Choose Save All.

Now that we have the method, we should be able to refer to it from the other class called ClaimApplication. We should take note that the full name of the method will have to contain the class name, but as we said earlier, to use the ClaimDetails class, we make an instance of it. We do not use the original class as it is the template. We will therefore create an instance of the class from within the Main() method of the ClaimApplication class.

32. Amend the ClaimApplication class, as in Listing 13-16, to create an instance of the ClaimDetails class.

Listing 13-16. Create an instance of the ClaimDetails class

```
internal class ClaimApplication
{
   static void Main(string[] args)
```

```
    {
       ClaimDetails myClaimDetailsInstance = new ClaimDetails();
    } // End of Main() method

  } // End of ClaimApplication class
```

33. Amend the Main() method to call the
    HowManyClaimsAreBeingMade() method, method 1, and assign
    it to the numberOfClaimsBeingMade variable, as in Listing 13-17.

Listing 13-17. Call the HowManyClaimsAreBeingMade() method

```
static void Main(string[] args)
{
    ClaimDetails myClaimDetailsInstance = new ClaimDetails();

    int numberOfClaimsBeingMade = myClaimDetailsInstance.
    HowManyClaimsAreBeingMade();

} // End of Main() method
```

This clearly shows the concept of classes:

- A class without a Main() method has been created to hold methods
  and fields.

- From another class, which has a Main() method, an instance of the
  class containing the methods is created.

- Using the instance of the class, we have access to the methods
  and fields of the class that have the public access modifier and are
  not static, that is, they belong to the instance of the class, not the
  class itself.

- Adding the full stop after the instance name means those methods
  and fields that are accessible will be displayed. This is called the dot
  notation.

This means that we could create as many methods as we like in the class and
create as many classes as we like. This idea of separating our code into methods and
our methods into classes is exactly what a C# application should look like when it is
being coded.

Let us just emphasize a few points that are crucial if we are to fully understand and use classes and objects:

- The word static in front of a method or field of a class means that the method or field belongs to the class it is declared in.

- When we make an instance of the class, we will not be able to access the static fields or the static methods using the instance name.

- Static fields and methods are available directly inside the class they are declared in.

- To access a static field or a static method, we use the class name, not the name of the instance of the class.

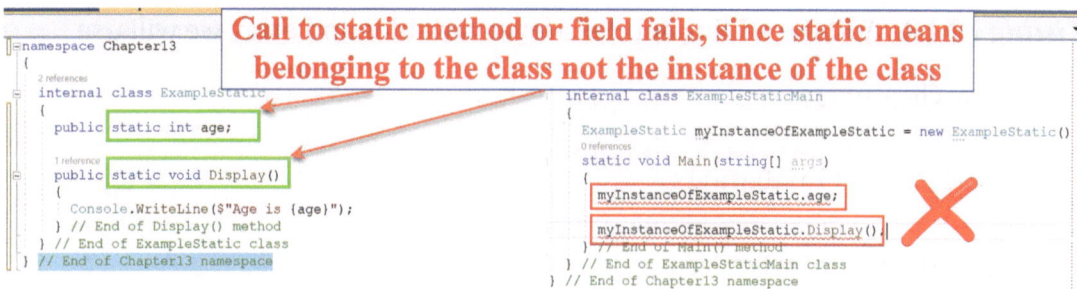

Figure 13-6. *Static fields and methods not accessible from a class instance*

Now check that the method is being read correctly.

34. Click the File menu.

35. Choose Save All.

36. Click the Debug menu.

37. Choose Start Without Debugging.

The console window will appear, as shown in Figure 13-7, and ask the user to input the number of claims to be made. The method from the class without the Main() method has been called from the class with the Main() method.

38. Type 2 and press the Enter key.

39. Press the Enter key.

```
How many claims are being made?

2

C:\CoreCSharp\CoreCSharp\Chapter13\bin\Debug\net6.0\Chapter13.exe
Press any key to close this window . . .
```

Figure 13-7. *Method called from another class*

This is excellent! Our method has been called from another class. We will now add more fields and methods to the ClaimDetails class.

40.   Amend the ClaimDetails class, as in Listing 13-18, to add the additional fields we require and initialize the existing variable to 0.

Listing 13-18. Add the additional class-level variables and array we will use

```
namespace Chapter13
{
  internal class ClaimDetails
  {
    int numberOfClaimsEntered = 0;
    static int arrayPositionCounter = 0;

    /*
    The array is going to hold the data for 2 claims.
    Each claim has four pieces of information. The number of
    data items is therefore 2 multiplied by 4 = 8.
    So, we will make the array for this example of size 8.
    Not the best way to do things but fine for now.
    */
    static string[] repairShopClaims = new string[8];

    /***************** METHOD ONE *****************/
    public int HowManyClaimsAreBeingMade()
    {
```

41.   Amend the ClaimDetails code, as in Listing 13-19, to add method 2 after method 1. Notice that static has been removed.

Listing 13-19. Add method 2

```
/***************** METHOD TWO *****************/
public void CurrentValueOfCounter()
{
  Console.WriteLine("The current value of the counter is :" +
  numberOfClaimsEntered + "\n");
} // End of CurrentValueOfCounter() method
} // End of ClaimDetails class
} // End of Chapter13 namespace
```

42.   Amend the ClaimDetails code, as in Listing 13-20, to add method
      3 after method 2. Notice that static has been removed.

Listing 13-20. Add method 3

```
/***************** METHOD THREE *****************/
public string ReadTheRepairShopId()
{
  Console.WriteLine("What is your repair shop id?\n");
  return Console.ReadLine();
}// End of ReadTheRepairShopId() method

} // End of ClaimDetails class
} // End of Chapter13 namespace
```

43.   Amend the ClaimDetails code, as in Listing 13-21, to add method
      4 after method 3. Notice that static has been removed.

Listing 13-21. Add method 4

```
/***************** METHOD FOUR *****************/
public void WriteRepairShopIdToTheArray(string repairShopId)
{
  repairShopClaims[arrayPositionCounter] = repairShopId;
  arrayPositionCounter++;
} // End of WriteRepairShopIdToTheArray() method

} // End of ClaimDetails class
} // End of Chapter13 namespace
```

44. Amend the ClaimDetails code, as in Listing 13-22, to add method 5 after method 4. Notice that static has been removed.

Listing 13-22. Add method 5

```
/****************** METHOD FIVE ****************/
public string ReadTheVehiclePolicyNumber()
{
  Console.WriteLine("What is the vehicle policy number?\n");
  return Console.ReadLine();
} // End of ReadTheVehiclePolicyNumber() method

} // End of ClaimDetails class
} // End of Chapter13 namespace
```

45. Amend the ClaimDetails code, as in Listing 13-23, to add method 6 after method 5. Notice that static has been removed.

Listing 13-23. Add method 6

```
/****************** METHOD SIX ****************/
public void WriteVehiclePolicyNumberToTheArray(string
vehiclePolicyNumber)
{
  repairShopClaims[arrayPositionCounter] = vehiclePolicyNumber;
  arrayPositionCounter++;
} // End of WriteVehiclePolicyNumberToTheArray() method

} // End of ClaimDetails class
} // End of Chapter13 namespace
```

46. Amend the ClaimDetails code, as in Listing 13-24, to add method 7 after method 6. Notice that static has been removed.

Listing 13-24. Add method 7

```
/****************** METHOD SEVEN ******************/
public double ReadTheAmountBeingClaimed()
{
  Console.WriteLine("What is the amount being claimed for the
  repair?\n");
  return Convert.ToDouble(Console.ReadLine());
} // End of ReadTheAmountBeingClaimed() method

  } // End of ClaimDetails class
} // End of Chapter13 namespace
```

47. Amend the ClaimDetails code, as in Listing 13-25, to add
     method 8 after method 7. Notice that static has been removed.

Listing 13-25. Add method 8

```
/****************** METHOD EIGHT ******************/
public void WriteClaimAmountToTheArray(double claimAmount)
{
  repairShopClaims[arrayPositionCounter] = claimAmount.ToString();
  arrayPositionCounter++;
} // End of WriteClaimAmountToTheArray() method

  } // End of ClaimDetails class
} // End of Chapter13 namespace
```

48. Amend the ClaimDetails code, as in Listing 13-26, to add method
     9 after method 8. Notice that static has been removed.

Listing 13-26. Add method 9

```
/****************** METHOD NINE ******************/
public DateTime ReadTheRepairDate()
{
  Console.WriteLine("What was the date of the repair?\n");
  return Convert.ToDateTime(Console.ReadLine());
}// End of method ReadTheRepairDate() method
```

```
}  // End of ClaimDetails class
}  // End of Chapter13 namespace
```

49. Amend the ClaimDetails code, as in Listing 13-27, to add method 10 after method 9. Notice that static has been removed.

Listing 13-27. Add method 10

```
/****************** METHOD TEN ******************/
public void WriteRepairDateToTheArray(DateTime claimDate)
{
  repairShopClaims[arrayPositionCounter] = claimDate.ToString();
  arrayPositionCounter++;
} // End of method WriteRepairDateToTheArray() method

}  // End of ClaimDetails class
}  // End of Chapter13 namespace
```

50. Amend the ClaimDetails code, as in Listing 13-28, to add method 11 after method 10. Notice that static has been removed.

Listing 13-28. Add method 11

```
/****************** METHOD ELEVEN ******************/
public void DisplayAllItemsInTheArray()
{
  foreach (var itemInTheClaimsArray in repairShopClaims)
  {
    Console.WriteLine("The item in the array is:\t" +
    itemInTheClaimsArray + "\n");
  }
} // End of method DisplayAllItemsInTheArray()
}  // End of ClaimDetails class
}  // End of Chapter13 namespace
```

51. Amend the ClaimDetails code, as in Listing 13-29, to add method 12 after method 11. Notice that static has been removed.

Listing 13-29. Add method twelve

```
/***************** METHOD TWELVE ****************/
public double AccumulateClaimAmount(double
claimAmountPassedIn, double totalOfAllClaims)
{
  totalOfAllClaims += claimAmountPassedIn;
  return totalOfAllClaims;
}// End of method AccumulateClaimAmount()
} // End of ClaimDetails class
} // End of Chapter13 namespace
```

52. Amend the ClaimDetails code, as in Listing 13-30, to add method
    13 after method 12. Notice that static has been removed.

Listing 13-30. Add method 13

```
/***************** METHOD THIRTEEN ****************/
public double DetermineVATAmount(double totalValueOfClaimsPassedIn,
double vatAmount)
{
  vatAmount = totalValueOfClaimsPassedIn - (totalValueOfClaimsPassedIn
  / 1.20);
  return vatAmount;
} // End of method DetermineVATAmount()
} // End of ClaimDetails class
} // End of Chapter13 namespace
```

53. Amend the ClaimDetails code, as in Listing 13-31, to add method
    14 after method 13. Notice that static has been removed.

Listing 13-31. Add method 14

```
/***************** METHOD FOURTEEN ****************/
public void DisplayInvoiceReceipt(double
       totalValueOfClaimsPassedIn, double vatPassedIn)
{
  Console.WriteLine("\nInvoice for vehicle repairs\n");
```

```
    Console.WriteLine("Nett claim\t" + (totalValueOfClaimsPassedIn -
    vatPassedIn) + "\n");
    Console.WriteLine("VAT amount\t" + vatPassedIn + "\n");
    Console.WriteLine("Total amount\t" + totalValueOfClaimsPassedIn
    + "\n");
  } // End of method DisplayInvoiceReceipt()
 }  // End of ClaimDetails class
}  // End of Chapter13 namespace
```

54. Amend the ClaimDetails code, as in Listing 13-32, to add method
    15 after method 14. Notice that static has been removed.

Listing 13-32. Add method 15

```
/******************* METHOD FIFTEEN *****************/
public void DisplayInvoiceReceipt(double
totalValueOfClaimsPassedIn, double vatPassedIn, string
messagePassedIn)
{

  Console.WriteLine("*****************************");
  Console.WriteLine("\nInvoice for vehicle repairs\n");
  Console.WriteLine("Nett claim\t" + (totalValueOfClaimsPassedIn -
  vatPassedIn) + "\n");
  Console.WriteLine("VAT amount\t" + vatPassedIn + "\n");
  Console.WriteLine("Total amount\t" + totalValueOfClaimsPassedIn
  + "\n");
  Console.WriteLine(messagePassedIn);

  Console.WriteLine("*****************************");
 } // End of method DisplayInvoiceReceipt
}  // End of ClaimDetails class
}  // End of Chapter13 namespace
```

Code Analysis

Now, let's stop and think what we have just done:

- We have created a new class without a Main() method – it is called ClaimDetails.

- We have added the fields that we will use in the methods of the class.

- We have added the original methods we had in the MethodsValue class in the last chapter.

- We have created a class called ClaimApplication with a Main() method.

- In the Main() method we have

  - Created an instance of the ClaimDetails class

  - Accessed the method called HowManyClaimsAreBeingMade() by using the name of the class instance we created, followed by a full stop (dot notation), and then selecting the method

We will now continue with the code in the ClaimApplication class.

55. Amend the code, as in Listing 13-33, in the ClaimApplication class, to add the rest of the fields we will need in this class.

Listing 13-33. Add the two additional fields we need in the Main() method class

```
static void Main(string[] args)
{
    double vatAmount = 0.00, totalOfAllClaims = 0.00;

    ClaimDetails myClaimDetailsInstance = new ClaimDetails();

    int numberOfClaimsBeingMade
        = myClaimDetailsInstance.HowManyClaimsAreBeingMade();
} // End of Main() method
```

56. Now add the do while loop within the Main() method, as in Listing 13-34.

Listing 13-34. Add the do while construct

```
int numberOfClaimsBeingMade
  = myClaimDetailsInstance.HowManyClaimsAreBeingMade();

/*
As we are using a variable in the loop our code is
flexible and can be used for any number of claims.
An ideal situation and good code.
*/
do
{

} while (numberOfClaimsEntered < numberOfClaimsBeingMade);


} // End of Main() method
```

Now we will call the method that will read the repair shop id, remembering that the method does not exist in the class we are in. We will need to call it using the instance of the class that we created, myClaimDetailsInstance. Remember, after we enter the instance name and type the dot, the list of fields and methods of the class will appear if they are accessible, so we should select the method rather than typing it.

If the list of fields and methods of the class do not appear, then there is something wrong with the code. Go back and check it.

57.   Add the code in Listing 13-35, to call the repair shop id method.

Listing 13-35. Call the ReadTheRepairShopId() method from the other class

```
do
{
  /*
   Call the methods as required assigning returned
   values to method level variables
  */
  string repairShopId = myClaimDetailsInstance.ReadTheRepairShopId();

} while (numberOfClaimsEntered < numberOfClaimsBeingMade);
```

This once again clearly shows the concept of classes. Using the instance of the class, we have access to the methods and fields of the class that have the public access modifier and are not static. The dot notation, a full stop after the instance name of the class, shows us those methods and fields that are accessible, as shown in Figure 13-8.

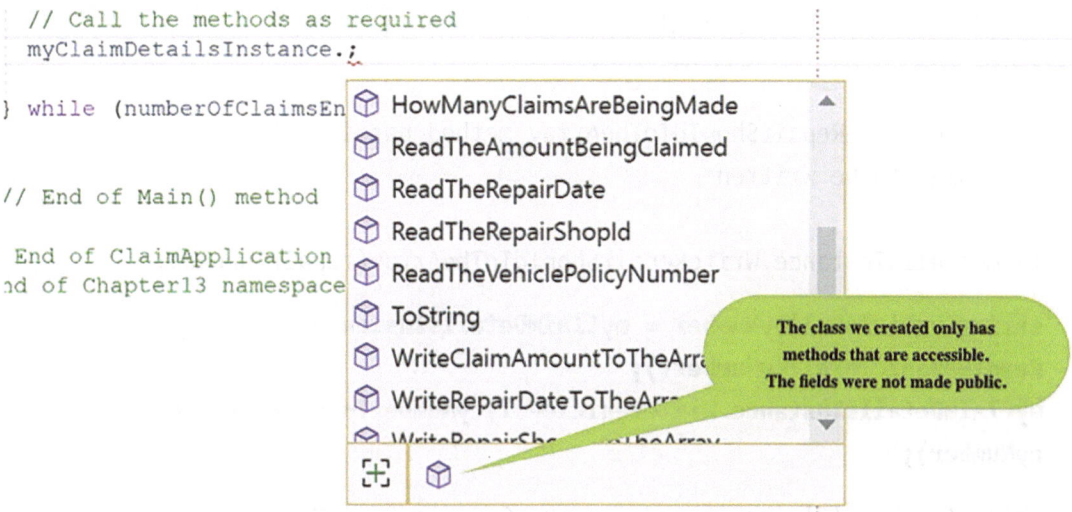

Figure 13-8. *Methods in the ClaimDetails class that are accessible*

58. Add the code in Listing 13-36, to call the method to write the repair shop id to the array.

Listing 13-36. Call the WriteRepairShopIdToTheArray() method

```
do
{
  /*
  Call the methods as required assigning returned
  values to method level variables
  */
  string repairShopId = myClaimDetailsInstance.ReadTheRepairShopId();

  /*
  Call the WriteRepairShopIdToTheArray method passing it
  the value to be written
  */ myClaimDetailsInstance.WriteRepairShopIdToTheArray(repairShopId);
```

481

```
    } while (numberOfClaimsEntered < numberOfClaimsBeingMade);
```

59. Add the code in Listing 13-37, to call the two methods we require
     to read the policy number and then write it to the array.

Listing 13-37. Call the read and write policy number methods

```
/*
Call the WriteRepairShopIdToTheArray method passing it
the value to be written
*/
myClaimDetailsInstance.WriteRepairShopIdToTheArray(repairShopId);

string vehiclePolicyNumber = myClaimDetailsInstance.
ReadTheVehiclePolicyNumber();
myClaimDetailsInstance.WriteVehiclePolicyNumberToTheArray(vehiclePoli
cyNumber);

} while (numberOfClaimsEntered < numberOfClaimsBeingMade);
```

60. Add the code in Listing 13-38, to call the two methods we require
     to read the amount being claimed and then write it to the array
     and then call the method that accumulates the total for all claims.

Listing 13-38. Call the read and write claim amount methods

```
string vehiclePolicyNumber = myClaimDetailsInstance.
ReadTheVehiclePolicyNumber();
myClaimDetailsInstance.WriteVehiclePolicyNumberToTheArray(vehiclePoli
cyNumber);

double claimAmount = myClaimDetailsInstance.ReadTheAmountBeingClaimed();
myClaimDetailsInstance.WriteClaimAmountToTheArray(claimAmount);

totalOfAllClaims = myClaimDetailsInstance.AccumulateClaimAmount(claimAmo
unt, totalOfAllClaims);

} while (numberOfClaimsEntered < numberOfClaimsBeingMade);
```

61.   Add the code in Listing 13-39, to call the two methods we require to read the repair date and then write it to the array.

Listing 13-39. Call the read and write claim date methods

```
totalOfAllClaims = myClaimDetailsInstance.AccumulateClaimAmount(claimAm
ount, totalOfAllClaims);

DateTime claimDate = myClaimDetailsInstance.ReadTheRepairDate();
myClaimDetailsInstance.WriteRepairDateToTheArray(claimDate);

} while (numberOfClaimsEntered < numberOfClaimsBeingMade);
```

Now we have the bulk of the work done because we have our methods in one class and we have called the methods from the other class with the Main() method to get the user input and store the details in an array.

The numberOfClaimsEntered variable in the ClaimDetails class is private and cannot be accessed from the ClaimApplication class so we will need to make it available through its property accessor.

62.   The start of the Main() method should be as shown in Listing 13-40.

Listing 13-40. Remove the method-level variable

```
static void Main(string[] args)
{
    double vatAmount = 0.00, totalOfAllClaims = 0.00

    ClaimDetails myClaimDetailsInstance = new ClaimDetails();
```

63.   Add the code in Listing 13-41, to increment the number of claims that have been entered by one using the static field in the other class.

Listing 13-41. Increment the number of claims entered counter

```
DateTime claimDate = myClaimDetailsInstance.ReadTheRepairDate();
myClaimDetailsInstance.WriteRepairDateToTheArray(claimDate);

/* Increment the loop counter by 1 */
myClaimDetailsInstance.numberOfClaimsEntered++;

} while (numberOfClaimsEntered < numberOfClaimsBeingMade);
```

We will see an error message under the numberOfClaimsEntered, and if we hover over it, we see that the protection level is making it inaccessible, as in Figure 13-9.

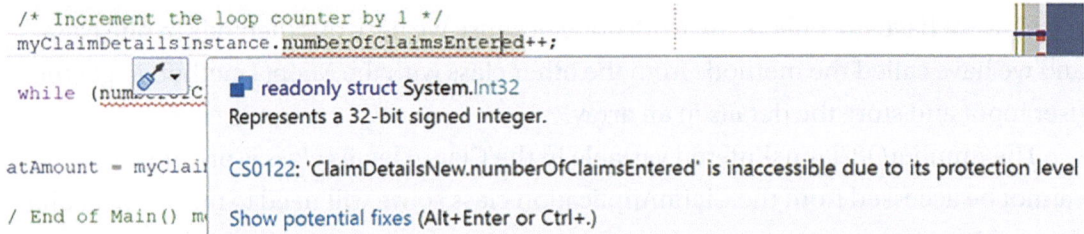

Figure 13-9. *Field not accessible*

We will now code a property with the getter and setter, which we looked at earlier.

64. Open the ClaimDetails class.

65. Right-click the numberOfClaimsEntered field.

66. Choose Quick Actions and Refactorings as shown in Figure 13-10.

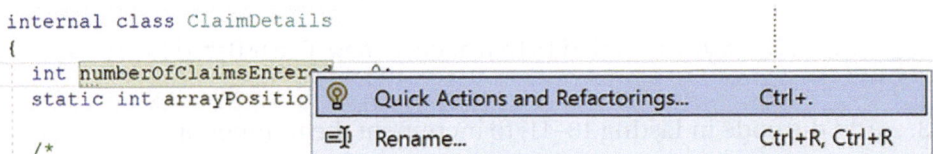

Figure 13-10. *Right-click the field and choose Quick Actions and Refactorings*

67. Choose Encapsulate field: numberOfClaimsEntered (but still use field) as shown in Figure 13-11.

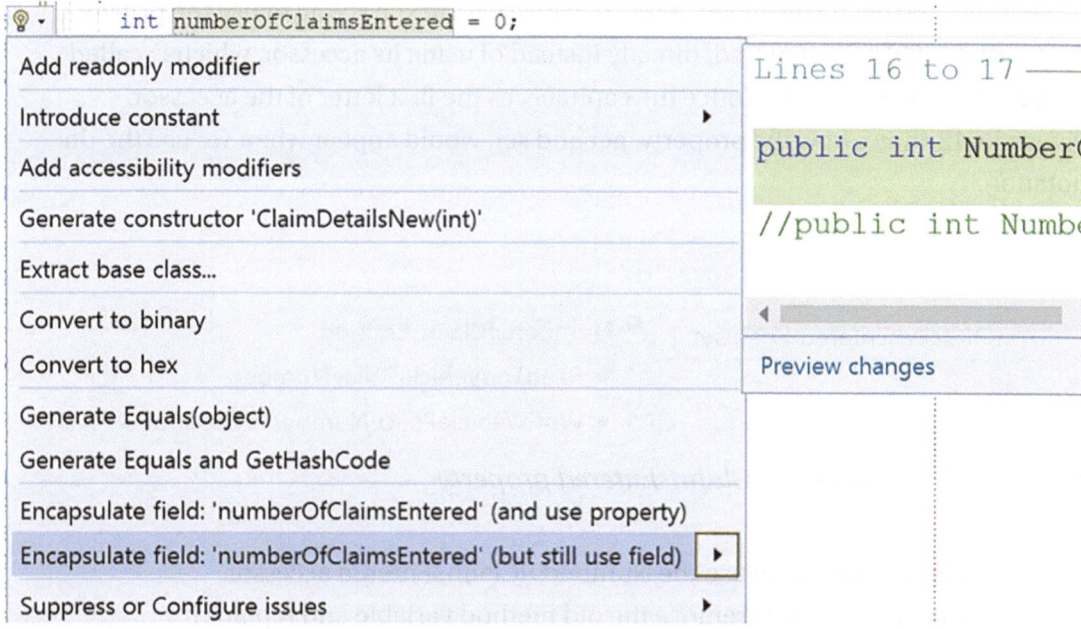

Figure 13-11. *Encapsulate the field*

The accessor is created for us in our code, and we can move it from the position it has been placed in if we wish to do so or reformat it so it is not all coded on one line, as in Listing 13-42.

Listing 13-42. The accessor for numberOfClaimsEntered is added to the class

```
static string[] repairShopClaims = new string[8];

public int NumberOfClaimsEntered
{
  get => numberOfClaimsEntered;
  set => numberOfClaimsEntered = value;
}

/****************** METHOD ONE ******************/
public int HowManyClaimsAreBeingMade()
{
```

68. Open the ClaimApplication class.

We will see that the error still exists because we are still trying to use the private field, numberOfClaimsEntered, directly instead of using its accessor, which is called NumberOfClaimsEntered. Notice the capital N as the first letter of the accessor. Figure 13-12 shows how the property, get and set, would appear when we use the dot notation.

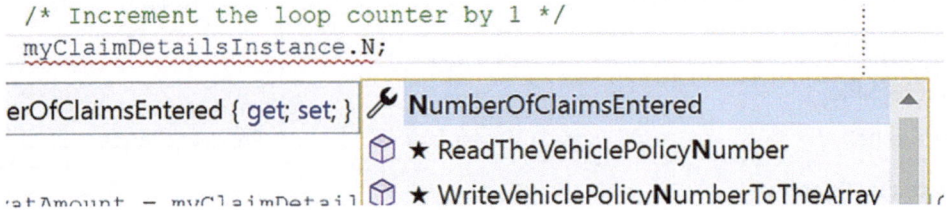

Figure 13-12. *NumberOfClaimsEntered property*

69.   Amend the call to use the NumberOfClaimsEntered accessor. Inside the while() remove the old method variable and replace it with the instance variable NumberOfClaimsEntered accessor, as in Listing 13-43.

Listing 13-43. The accessor NumberOfClaimsEntered is used (capital N)

```
DateTime claimDate = myClaimDetailsInstance.ReadTheRepairDate();
myClaimDetailsInstance.WriteRepairDateToTheArray(claimDate);

/* Increment the loop counter by 1 */
myClaimDetailsInstance.NumberOfClaimsEntered++;

} while (myClaimDetailsInstance.NumberOfClaimsEntered <
numberOfClaimsBeingMade);

    } // End of Main() method

  } // End of ClaimApplication class
} // End of Chapter13 namespace
```

Now we will

- Call the DetermineVATAmount() method, passing it the totalOfAllClaims and the vatAmount.

- Call the DisplayAllItemsInTheArray() method.

- Write the total of all claims to the console.

- Call one of the DisplayInvoiceReceipt() methods, passing it the totalOfAllClaims and the vatAmount.

- Call one of the DisplayInvoiceReceipt() methods, passing it the totalOfAllClaims, the vatAmount, and a message.

The two DisplayInvoiceReceipt methods have the same name but have different parameters, and this is referred to as method overloading.

70. Add the ClaimApplication code in Listing 13-44, to call the method that will display the invoice receipt based on the total of the claims, the VAT amount, and the message string.

Listing 13-44. Call the method that will display the invoice

```
} while (myClaimDetailsInstance.NumberOfClaimsEntered <
numberOfClaimsBeingMade);

vatAmount = myClaimDetailsInstance.DetermineVATAmount(totalOfAllClaims,
vatAmount);

myClaimDetailsInstance.DisplayAllItemsInTheArray();

Console.WriteLine("The total amount claimed is:\t" + totalOfAllClaims);

myClaimDetailsInstance.DisplayInvoiceReceipt(totalOfAllClaims,
vatAmount);

myClaimDetailsInstance.DisplayInvoiceReceipt(totalOfAllClaims,
vatAmount, "\t" + "Thank you for your claims\n\tthey will be processed
today");

  } // End of Main() method
 } // End of ClaimApplication class
} // End of Chapter13 namespace
```

Great. All the methods have been placed in one class, and then they are called from another class that has the Main() method. We could have made other classes and moved some of the methods to these classes, but we are just trying to appreciate that we can have separate classes with one class having its methods called from the main class. This is plenty to understand for now. We now need to test the structure.

71.   Click the File menu.

72.   Choose Save All.

73.   Click the Debug menu.

74.   Choose Start Without Debugging.

The console window will appear and ask the user to input the number of claims to be made.

75.   Type 2 and press the Enter key.

The console window will appear and ask the user to input the repair shop id.

76.   Type RS000001 for the repair shop id and press the Enter key.

The console will now ask the user to input the vehicle policy number.

77.   Type VP000001 and press the Enter key.

The console will now ask the user to input the claim amount.

78.   Type 1200 and press the Enter key.

The console will now ask the user to input the date of the repair.

79.   Type 2021/10/01 and press the Enter key.

The questions are asked again for the second claim.

80.   Type RS000001 for the repair shop id and press the Enter key.

The console will now ask the user to input the vehicle policy number.

81.   Type VP000002 and press the Enter key.

The console will now ask the user to input the claim amount.

82.   Type 3600 and press the Enter key.

The console will now ask the user to input the date of the repair.

83.   Type 2021/10/01 and press the Enter key.

The invoice receipt will be displayed as shown in Figure 13-13.

```
*********************************

Invoice for vehicle repairs

Nett claim      4000

VAT amount      800

Total amount    4800

        Thank you for your claims
        they will be processed today
*********************************

C:\CoreCSharp\CoreCSharp\Chapter13\bin\Debug\net6.0\Chapter13.exe (p
Press any key to close this window . . ._
```

Figure 13-13.   *Receipt, having used classes*

84.   Press the Enter key to close the console window.

This is the same application as MethodsValue() and the same invoice receipt, with different amounts. The big difference is the separation of the methods from the class that contains the Main() method.

This is just an example to show how classes work. It certainly is not a "polished" application, and it can be improved upon, but the important things to take away from what we have done so far are as follows:

- A class can contain **fields**.

- A class can contain **methods**.

- To use a class from within another class, we create an instance of the class – this is called **instantiation**.

- The instantiated class gives us access to the fields and methods of the class.

Constructor

In the ClaimApplication class, we made an instance of the ClaimDetails class so we could access the fields and methods of the class as shown in Listing 13-45.

Listing 13-45. Creating an instance of the class

```
ClaimDetails myClaimDetailsInstance = new ClaimDetails();
```

The new ClaimDetails() section of the code means we are not passing in any arguments to the class; this is why there are no values between the brackets (). This means we are calling the **default constructor,** and we read earlier that the **constructor** "method" can be used to initialize the value of the fields in the class. It may be used to initialize all the fields or some of them, or in the case of a default constructor, none of the fields are initialized – they just have their default values.

Refreshing what we read earlier, a constructor has the following features:

- It must have the same name as the class. We will therefore use the name ClaimDetails.

- It must have an access modifier of public.

- It does not have a return type, not even void.

- It takes in arguments of the same type as the fields being initialized.

Next

- We will create a constructor that has a DateTime parameter.

- The new constructor will therefore overwrite the default constructor.

- We will use a DateTime field with a readonly keyword, which means the field can only be assigned a value as part of the declaration or in a constructor in the same class. The readonly field can be assigned and reassigned multiple times within the field declaration and constructor.

- By setting the date field to the date read from the computer, we will not need to have the method that asks the user to input the date of the claim, method 9, so this method will not be called from the Main method.

- When we then write the date to the array, we will use the new DateTime field we are setting up in the class and initializing with the computer date.

- For now, we will leave the method in the ClaimDetails class.

1. In the ClaimDetails amend the code to add the readonly DateTime field and a constructor that will set the date field to the current computer date, as in Listing 13-46.

Listing 13-46. Add a new constructor that has a DateTime parameter

```
internal class ClaimDetails
{
  int numberOfClaimsEntered;
  readonly DateTime claimDate;
  static int arrayPositionCounter = 0;

  /*
The array is going to hold the data for 2 claims.
Each claim has four pieces of information. The number of
data items is therefore 2 multiplied by 4 = 8.
So, we will make the array for this example of size 8.
Not the best way to do things but fine for now.
*/
  static string[] repairShopClaims = new string[8];

  /*
The constructor has the same name as the class, it has an
access modifier of public, it takes an argument of data
type DateTime as this is the same data type as the field,
claimDate, that is being initialised, and it does not
return a value so there is no return type
*/
  public ClaimDetails(DateTime claimDate)
  {
    this.claimDate = Convert.ToDateTime(claimDate);
  } // End of constructor that takes in a date
```

Now that we have created the constructor, we can use it when creating the instance of the class from within the Main() method. If we look in the ClaimApplication class, we will now see that there is an error in the line that instantiates the ClaimDetails class. This is because there is no default constructor, and the new constructor expects a DateTime value to be passed to it. This can be seen in the message box that appears when we hover over the red underscore. We will do the fix "manually" so do not click Create constructor fix.

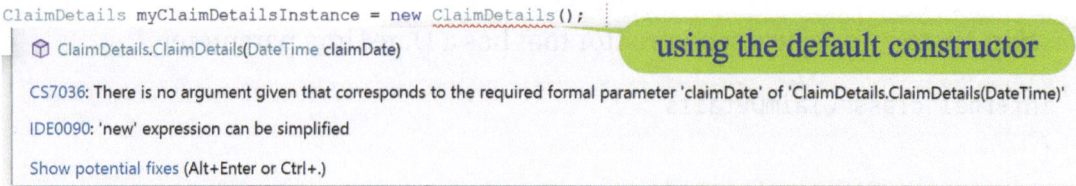

Figure 13-14. *Error because we now have no default constructor*

2.   Amend the ClaimApplication code, as in Listing 13-47, to read the date from the computer.

Listing 13-47. Read the date from the computer

```
static void Main(string[] args)
{
    double vatAmount = 0.00, totalOfAllClaims = 0.00;

    // Read the date from the computer clock
    DateTime localDate = DateTime.Now;

    ClaimDetails myClaimDetailsInstance = new ClaimDetails();
```

3.   Amend the code, as in Listing 13-48, to pass the DateTime to the constructor.

Listing 13-48. Use the custom constructor, passing in the DateTime

```
// Read the date from the computer clock
DateTime localDate = DateTime.Now;

ClaimDetails myClaimDetailsInstance = new ClaimDetails(localDate);
```

4.   As we now have the date, we do not need to ask the user to input the date. The method call can be removed or commented out, as it is not used, as in Listing 13-49.

Listing 13-49. Comment the line where the repair date reading method is called

```
totalOfAllClaims = myClaimDetailsInstance.AccumulateClaimAmount(claimAm
ount, totalOfAllClaims);

//DateTime claimDate = myClaimDetailsInstance.ReadTheRepairDate();
myClaimDetailsInstance.WriteRepairDateToTheArray(claimDate);

/* Increment the loop counter by 1 */
myClaimDetailsInstance.NumberOfClaimsEntered++;

} while (myClaimDetailsInstance.NumberOfClaimsEntered <
numberOfClaimsBeingMade);
```

Now we need to call the claimDate field from the ClaimDetails class but it is private, so we need to create the property with the get and set. This is the same process as we followed for the numberOfClaimsEntered field.

5.   Right-click the claimDate field in the ClaimDetails class.

6.   Choose Quick Actions and Refactorings.

7.   Choose Encapsulate field: claimDate (but still use field).

The accessor is created for us in our code, and we can move it from the position it has been placed in if we wish to do so. **As the field is readonly, the accessor only allows us to get the date, not set the date**.

8.   Now we need to call the DateTime field so we can write the date to the array. In the ClaimApplication, class amend the code to call the accessor, as in Listing 13-50.

Listing 13-50. Call the DateTime field through its property

```
totalOfAllClaims = myClaimDetailsInstance.AccumulateClaimAmount(
claimAmount, totalOfAllClaims);

//DateTime claimDate = myClaimDetailsInstance.ReadTheRepairDate();
myClaimDetailsInstance.WriteRepairDateToTheArray(myClaimDetails
Instance.ClaimDate);

/* Increment the loop counter by 1 */
```

In order to see the date being displayed, we need to iterate the array and display the items within it. Now we can test the code to ensure the constructor works. If it does, the array will be populated with the current date.

9. Click the File menu.

10. Choose Save All.

11. Click the Debug menu.

12. Choose Start Without Debugging.

The console window will appear and ask the user to input the number of claims to be made.

13. Type 2 and press the Enter key.

The console window will appear and ask the user to input the repair shop id.

14. Type RS000001 for the repair shop id and press the Enter key.

The console will now ask the user to input the vehicle policy number.

15. Type VP000001 and press the Enter key.

The console will now ask the user to input the claim amount.

16. Type 1200 and press the Enter key.

We have removed the call to the method that asks the user to input the date of the repair so we will not be asked for the date of the repair.

The questions are asked again for the second claim.

17. Type RS000001 for the repair shop id and press the Enter key.

The console will now ask the user to input the vehicle policy number.

18.   Type VP000002 and press the Enter key.

The console will now ask the user to input the claim amount.

19.   Type 3600 and press the Enter key.

The invoice receipt will be displayed as shown in Figure 13-15.

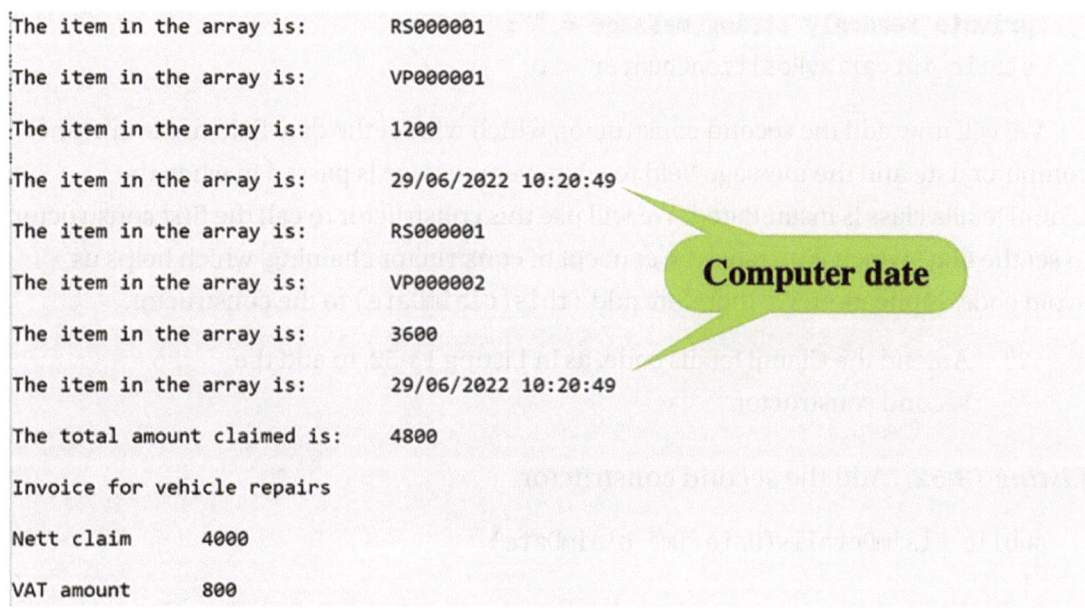

Figure 13-15. *The computer date is displayed*

20.   Press the Enter key to close the console window.

Another Constructor

We will now create a second constructor, which will set the date field and a message field of data type String. This new constructor will therefore be different from the first constructor, as it has two arguments as opposed to one, This is constructor overloading.

We will need to create an additional field called message of data type string and we will explicitly set it as private.

21.   Amend the ClaimDetails code, as in Listing 13-51, to add the field called message.

Listing 13-51. Add a String field and assign it a value

```
internal class ClaimDetails
  {
    int numberOfClaimsEntered = 0;
    readonly DateTime claimDate;
    private readonly string message = "";
    static int arrayPositionCounter = 0;
```

We will now add the second constructor, which will set the date field to the current computer date and the message field to whatever message is passed in when the ClaimDetails class is instantiated. We will use this constructor to call the first constructor to set the date, which illustrates the concept of constructor chaining, which helps us avoid code duplication. We therefore add :this(claimDate) to the constructor.

22. Amend the ClaimDetails code, as in Listing 13-52, to add the second constructor.

Listing 13-52. Add the second constructor

```
public ClaimDetails(DateTime claimDate)
  {
    this.claimDate = Convert.ToDateTime(claimDate);
  } // End of constructor that takes in a date

  /*
  This is a second constructor that accepts two
  arguments and the values that are passed to the constructor
  are used to set the value of the field called claimDate
  and the field called message. The constructor calls the
  first constructor to assign the value to the DateTime field
  As the constructor has two arguments it is different
  from the first constructor
  */
  public ClaimDetails(DateTime claimDate, string message):this(claimDate)
  {
    this.message = message;
  } // End of constructor that takes in a date and a message
```

Now we will look back at the call to the DisplayInvoiceReceipt() method in the ClaimApplication class that we added, shown in Listing 13-53.

Listing 13-53. Calling the method to display the invoice receipt

```
myClaimDetailsInstance.DisplayInvoiceReceipt(totalOfAllClaims, vatAmount,
"\t" + "Thank you for your claims\n\tthey will be processed today");
```

- Here we are calling the method DisplayInvoiceReceipt() and we have passed it a message, which the method uses to display the message.

- However, we have just created a constructor that accepts a message string and assigns this string value to the field called message.

- As we have the new constructor, we could pass our message at the time we instantiate the class, and the message will then exist in the class.

- We can then remove method 15 where we accepted the message.

- We can call method 14, which accepts only two parameters, not the message:

  ```
  DisplayInvoiceReceipt(double totalValueOfClaimsPassedIn,
  double vatPassedIn)
  ```

- We can then add an extra line to method 14 to display the message field because we have direct access to the field in the other class.

As the message is initialized as "", if there is no message created by our constructor, a blank line space will be written for the message. What this means is if we leave the original instantiation, which uses the first constructor, no message is passed in, so the message will use the value assigned to it, "".

23. Amend the ClaimDetails class code, as in Listing 13-54, to remove method 15 or simply comment the method code.

Listing 13-54. Comment all of method 15 (don't worry about YAGNI!)

```
///****************** METHOD FIFTEEN *****************/
//public void DisplayInvoiceReceipt(double
//totalValueOfClaimsPassedIn, double vatPassedIn, string
```

```
//messagePassedIn)
//{

//   Console.WriteLine("******************************");
//   Console.WriteLine("\nInvoice for vehicle repairs\n");
//   Console.WriteLine("Nett claim\t" + (totalValueOfClaimsPassedIn -
vatPassedIn) + "\n");
//   Console.WriteLine("VAT amount\t" + vatPassedIn + "\n");
//   Console.WriteLine("Total amount\t" + totalValueOfClaimsPassedIn
+ "\n");
//   Console.WriteLine(messagePassedIn);

//   Console.WriteLine("******************************");
//} // End of method DisplayInvoiceReceipt
  }  // End of ClaimDetails class
} // End of Chapter13 namespace
```

We will now see that the ClaimApplication class has an error as it is trying to use the DisplayInvoiceReceipt() method that has three arguments, as shown in Figure 13-16.

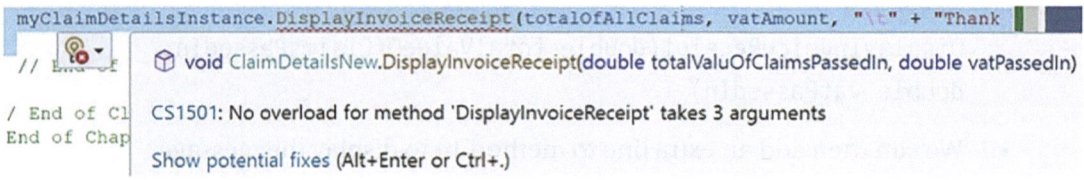

Figure 13-16. *Error as the method accepting three arguments does not exist*

Amend the code by removing the line that has the error. We are already calling the DisplayInvoiceReceipt() method in the line above this one.

24.   Amend the code to delete the line of code with the error. With this
      line removed, the code should be as shown in Listing 13-55.

Listing 13-55. Remove the second call to the DisplayInvoiceReceipt() method

```
vatAmount = myClaimDetailsInstance.DetermineVATAmount(totalOfAll
Claims, vatAmount);

myClaimDetailsInstance.DisplayAllItemsInTheArray();
```

```
Console.WriteLine("The total amount claimed is:\t" +
totalOfAllClaims);

myClaimDetailsInstance.DisplayInvoiceReceipt(totalOfAllClaims,
vatAmount);
} // End of Main() method
```

Now we need to change the instantiation code line, since it is currently using the constructor that accepts one parameter of type DateTime. In Listing 13-56 the new code line is shown above the old code line, which has been commented, and this is simply to help us understand what to do. If we are to stick with the YAGNI principle, we can just remove the commented line.

25. Now amend the instantiation code line, in the ClaimApplication class, to pass the two values to the new constructor, as in Listing 13-56.

Listing 13-56. Add the two arguments to the method call

```
static void Main(string[] args)
{
  double vatAmount = 0.00, totalOfAllClaims = 0.00;

  // Read the date from the computer clock
  DateTime localDate = DateTime.Now;

  ClaimDetails myClaimDetailsInstance = new ClaimDetails(localDate, "\
  tThank you for your claims \n\tthey will be processed today");

  // ClaimDetails myClaimDetailsInstance = new ClaimDetails(localDate);
  int numberOfClaimsBeingMade = myClaimDetailsInstance.
  HowManyClaimsAreBeingMade();
```

26. Amend the DisplayInvoiceReceipt() method in the ClaimDetails class to add the new line, which will print the message line, as in Listing 13-57.

Listing 13-57. Display the message

```
/******************* METHOD FOURTEEN *****************/
public void DisplayInvoiceReceipt(double totalValueOfClaimsPassedIn,
double vatPassedIn)
{
  Console.WriteLine("\nInvoice for vehicle repairs\n");
  Console.WriteLine("Nett claim\t" + (totalValueOfClaimsPassedIn -
  vatPassedIn) + "\n");
  Console.WriteLine("VAT amount\t" + vatPassedIn + "\n");
  Console.WriteLine("Total amount\t" + totalValueOfClaimsPassedIn + "\n");
  Console.WriteLine(message);
} // End of method DisplayInvoiceReceipt()
```

27. Open the ClaimApplication class.

28. Click the File menu.

29. Choose Save All.

30. Click the Debug menu.

31. Choose Start Without Debugging.

The console window will appear and ask the user to input the number of claims to be made.

32. Type 2 and press the Enter key.

The console window will appear and ask the user to input the repair shop id.

33. Type RS000001 for the repair shop id and press the Enter key.

The console will now ask the user to input the vehicle policy number.

34. Type VP000001 and press the Enter key.

The console will now ask the user to input the claim amount.

35. Type 1200 and press the Enter key.

We have removed the call to the method that asks the user to input the date of the repair so we will not be asked for the date of the repair.

The questions are asked again for the second claim.

36.   Type RS000001 for the repair shop id and press the Enter key.

The console will now ask the user to input the vehicle policy number.

37.   Type VP000002 and press the Enter key.

The console will now ask the user to input the claim amount.

38.   Type 3600 and press the Enter key.

The invoice receipt will be displayed as shown in Figure 13-17.

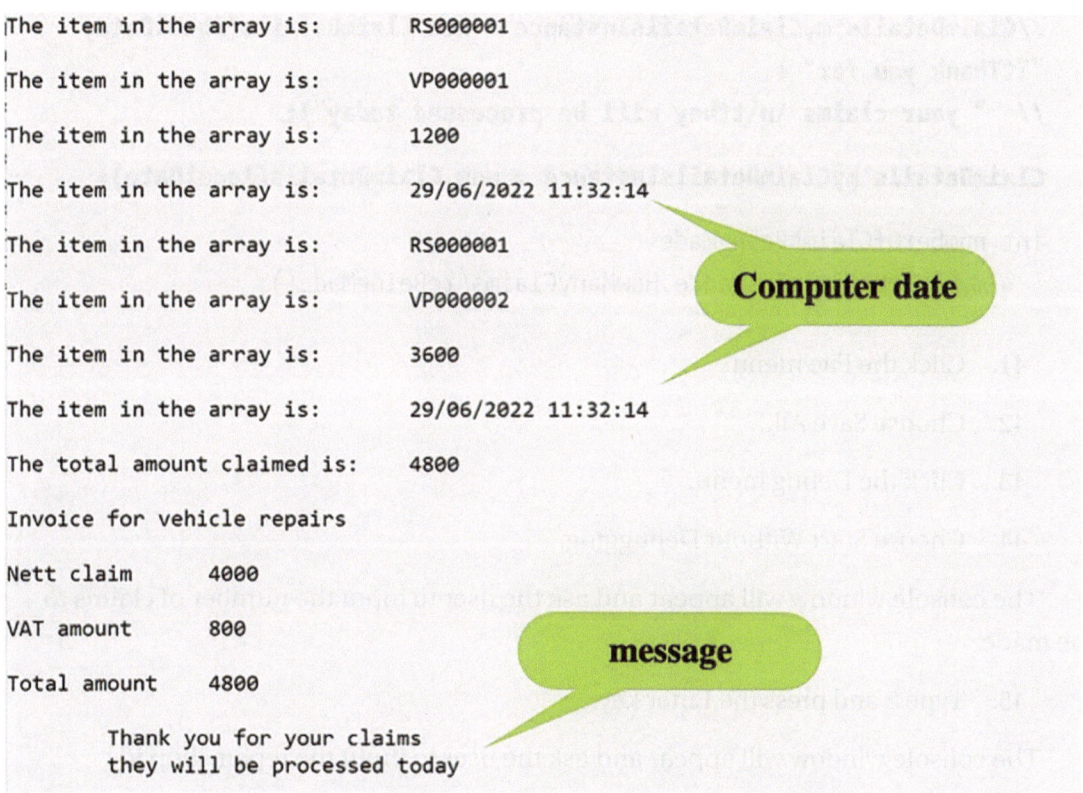

```
The item in the array is:       RS000001

The item in the array is:       VP000001

The item in the array is:       1200

The item in the array is:       29/06/2022 11:32:14

The item in the array is:       RS000001

The item in the array is:       VP000002              Computer date

The item in the array is:       3600

The item in the array is:       29/06/2022 11:32:14

The total amount claimed is:    4800

Invoice for vehicle repairs

Nett claim        4000

VAT amount        800                      message

Total amount      4800

       Thank you for your claims
       they will be processed today
```

Figure 13-17.   *The message and the computer date are displayed*

39.   Press the Enter key to close the console window.

Now we will amend the instantiation code line to pass only one value, the date, to the constructor. This means the first constructor will be used, and hence the message field will not be changed – it will have the value we entered, "".

40. Amend the instantiation code line to comment out the first call and add the new call to the constructor, as in Listing 13-58.

Listing 13-58. Use the constructor with one parameter

```
static void Main(string[] args)
 {
   double vatAmount = 0.00, totalOfAllClaims = 0.00;
   // Read the date from the computer clock
   DateTime localDate = DateTime.Now;

   //ClaimDetails myClaimDetailsInstance = new ClaimDetails(localDate,
   "\tThank you for" +
   //  " your claims \n\tthey will be processed today");

   ClaimDetails myClaimDetailsInstance = new ClaimDetails(localDate);

   int numberOfClaimsBeingMade
     = myClaimDetailsInstance.HowManyClaimsAreBeingMade();
```

41. Click the File menu.

42. Choose Save All.

43. Click the Debug menu.

44. Choose Start Without Debugging.

The console window will appear and ask the user to input the number of claims to be made.

45. Type 2 and press the Enter key.

The console window will appear and ask the user to input the repair shop id.

46. Type RS000001 for the repair shop id and press the Enter key.

The console will now ask the user to input the vehicle policy number.

47. Type VP000001 and press the Enter key.

The console will now ask the user to input the claim amount.

48. Type 1200 and press the Enter key.

We have removed the call to the method that asks the user to input the date of the repair so we will not be asked for the date of the repair.

The questions are asked again for the second claim.

49.   Type RS000001 for the repair shop id and press the Enter key.

The console will now ask the user to input the vehicle policy number.

50.   Type VP000002 and press the Enter key.

The console will now ask the user to input the claim amount.

51.   Type 3600 and press the Enter key.

The invoice receipt will be displayed as shown in Figure 13-18.

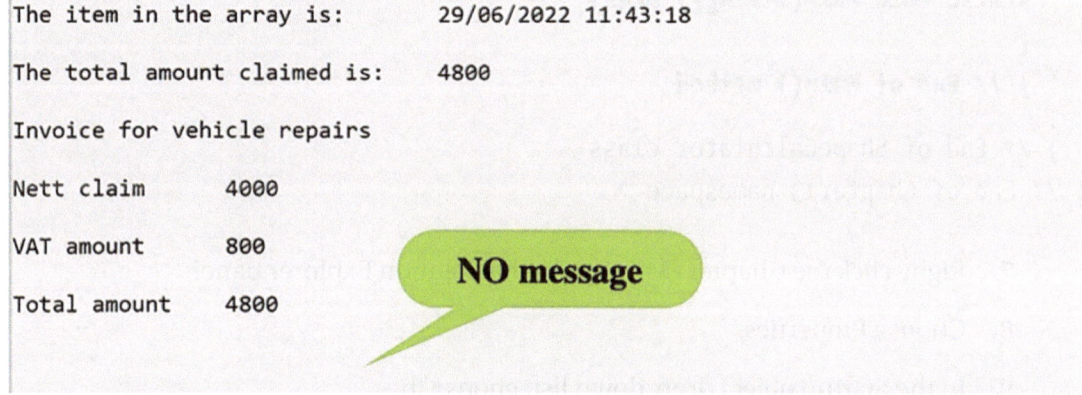

Figure 13-18. *No message displayed using the constructor with one parameter*

52.   Press the Enter key to close the console window.

Additional Example for Classes and Objects

Now we will consolidate what we have learned in the previous section regarding classes. Here we will take another example and create a class with methods and fields and call them from another class with a Main() method. The example we will use will involve some mathematical formulae and be related to shapes.

1.   Right-click the Chapter13 project.

2.   Choose Add.

3. Choose Class.

4. Name the class ShapeCalculator.cs.

5. Click the Add button.

6. Amend the code, as in Listing 13-59, by adding a Main() method.

Listing 13-59. Class with a Main() method as the entry point for the program

```
namespace Chapter13
{
  internal class ShapeCalculator
  {
    static void Main(string[] args)
    {
    } // End of Main() method

  } // End of ShapeCalculator class
} // End of Chapter13 namespace
```

7. Right-click the Chapter13 project in the Solution Explorer panel.

8. Choose Properties.

9. In the Startup object drop-down list, choose the ShapeCalculator file.

10. Close the Properties window.

CircleFormulae Class

1. Right-click the Chapter13 project.

2. Choose Add.

3. Choose Class.

4. Name the class CircleFormulae.cs.

5. Click the Add button.

6. Amend the code, as in Listing 13-60, by adding the start of a method that will calculate the area of a circle.

Listing 13-60. Class with NO Main() method

```
namespace Chapter13
{
  internal class CircleFormulae
  {
   /*
   This is a method that will ask the user to input the length
   of the radius of the circle, calculate the area of the circle
   and display the area of the circle in the console window
   */
   public void AreaOfCircle()
   {
   } //End of AreaOfCircle method

  } // End of CircleFormulae class
} // End of Chapter13 namespace
```

7. Amend the code, as in Listing 13-61, to create variables that will hold the radius and the area of the circle, setting their initial value to be 0.

Listing 13-61. Create and initialize the variables

```
  public void AreaOfCircle()
  {
    /*
    Create two variables of data type double to hold the
    value of the radius input by the user and the calculated
    area of the circle, initialise the two variables to zero
    */
    double radiusLength = 0;
    double areaOfCircle = 0;
   } //End of AreaOfCircle method
```

8. Amend the code, as in Listing 13-62, to ask the user to input the radius of the circle and assign the value to the radiusLength variable.

Listing 13-62. Read the radius input and convert it to type double

```
double areaOfCircle = 0;

// Read the user input for the size of the radius
Console.WriteLine("What size is the radius?\n");

radiusLength = Convert.ToDouble(Console.ReadLine());

} //End of AreaOfCircle method
```

Remember we talked about PI before as being a constant in the Math class.

9. Now add the code in Listing 13-63, to calculate the area of the circle.

Listing 13-63. Add the formula for the area of a circle

```
radiusLength = Convert.ToDouble(Console.ReadLine());

// Calculate the area of the circle with the formula
areaOfCircle = Math.PI * radiusLength * radiusLength;

} //End of AreaOfCircle method
```

We will now use the Format() method of the String class to display the output using two decimal places. There are other ways to display formatted data, and we will look at these in detail in Chapter 15. For now it is fine to use String.Format() to display our output.

10. Now add the code in Listing 13-64, to display the area and radius, using the Format() method.

Listing 13-64. Display the radius and area of the circle

```
// Calculate the area of the circle with the formula
areaOfCircle = Math.PI * radiusLength * radiusLength;
```

```
Console.WriteLine(String.Format("\nA circle with radius {0:0.#} has
an area of {1:0.##}",
  radiusLength, areaOfCircle));
```

```
} //End of AreaOfCircle method
```

Now that we have created a class with a method in it, we will be able to call the method from the Main() method in the ShapeCalculator class. But remember, we will need to instantiate the class rather than using the class template.

11. Open the ShapeCalculator class and create an instance of the CircleFormulae class, calling it myCircleFormulae, as in Listing 13-65.

Listing 13-65. Instantiate the CircleFormulae class using a default constructor

```
static void Main(string[] args)
{
  // Instantiate the CircleFormulae class
  CircleFormulae myCircleFormulae = new CircleFormulae();
} // End of Main() method
```

Now we need to call the AreaOfCircle() method from the other class. As we type **myCircleFormulae** and add the ., as shown in Figure 13-19, we should automatically see any accessible fields and methods that belong in the CircleFormulae class, or more correctly to the myCircleFormulae instance of the class. Remember a class is made up of fields and methods.

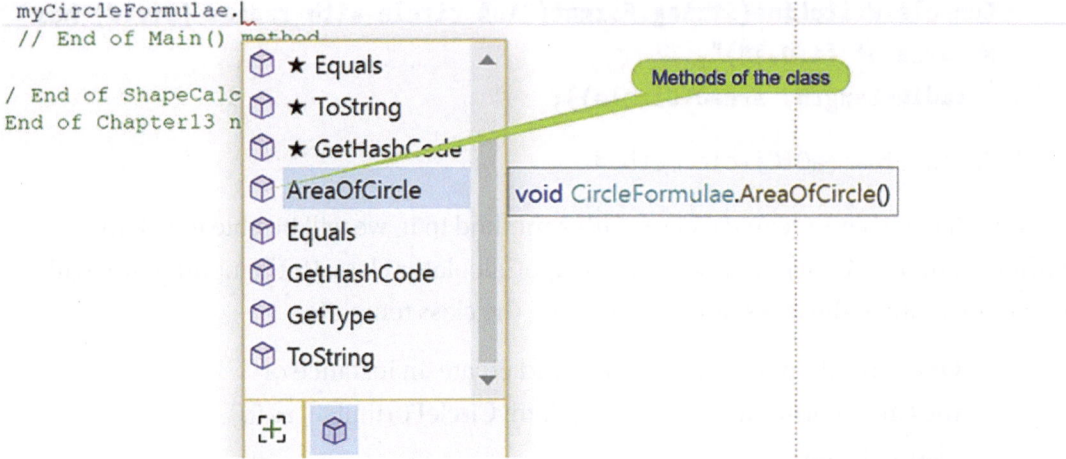

Figure 13-19. *Methods accessible in the CircleFormulae class – no fields exist*

12. Now add the code in Listing 13-66, to call the AreaOfCircle() method.

Listing 13-66. Call the AreaOfCircle() method that is in the other class

```
static void Main(string[] args)
{
    // Instantiate the CircleFormulae class
    CircleFormulae myCircleFormulae = new CircleFormulae();

    myCircleFormulae.AreaOfCircle();
} // End of Main() method
```

13. Click the File menu.

14. Choose Save All.

15. Click the Debug menu.

16. Choose Start Without Debugging.

The console window will appear and ask the user to input the radius of the circle.

17. Type 10 and press the Enter key.

The console window will show the area of the circle, as shown in Figure 13-20.

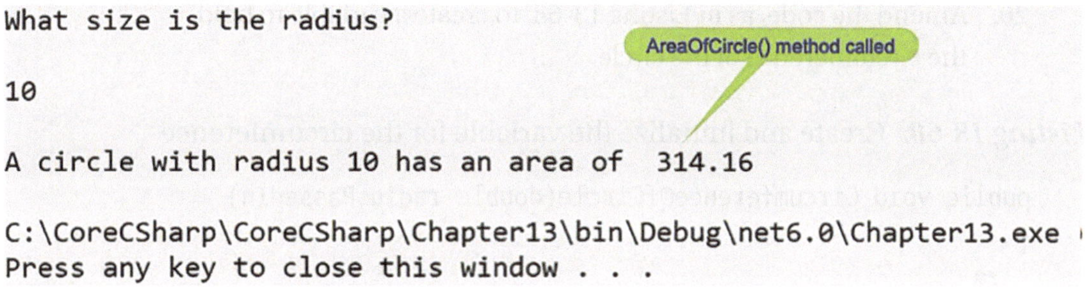

What size is the radius?

AreaOfCircle() method called

10

A circle with radius 10 has an area of 314.16

C:\CoreCSharp\CoreCSharp\Chapter13\bin\Debug\net6.0\Chapter13.exe
Press any key to close this window . . .

Figure 13-20. *AreaOfCircle() method called and working*

18.   Press the Enter key to close the console window.

This is excellent! Our method has been called from another class. We will now add another method, just after the AreaOfCircle method and inside the class, to calculate the circumference of the circle.

19.   Amend the code, as in Listing 13-67, in the CircleFormulae class to add the start of a method that will calculate the circumference of the circle.

Listing 13-67. Add a method to calculate the circumference of the circle

```
} //End of AreaOfCircle method

/*
This is a method that will accept the value of the radius
passed to it. The radius has been obtained in the
AreaOfCircle method and then the AreaOfCircle() method
will call this new CircumferenceOfCircle() method passing
it the value of the radius. This method will then calculate
the circumference and display the value in the console window
*/
public void CircumferenceOfCircle(double radiusPassedIn)
{
} // End of CircumferenceOfCircle method

} // End of CircleFormulae class
} // End of Chapter13 namespace
```

20. Amend the code, as in Listing 13-68, to create a variable to hold the circumference of the circle.

Listing 13-68. Create and initialize the variable for the circumference

```
public void CircumferenceOfCircle(double radiusPassedIn)
{
  /*
  Create a variable of data type double to hold the value
  calculated for the circumference of the circle.
  Initialise the variable to zero.
  We have the radius as it is passed into this method.
  */
  double circumferenceOfCircle = 0;
} // End of CircumferenceOfCircle method
```

21. Now add the code in Listing 13-69, to calculate the circumference.

Listing 13-69. Add the formula for the circumference of a circle

```
public void CircumferenceOfCircle(double radiusPassedIn)
{
  /*
  Create a variable of data type double to hold the value
  calculated for the circumference of the circle.
  Initialise the variable to zero.
  We have the radius as it is passed into this method.
  */
  double circumferenceOfCircle = 0;

  //Calculate the circumference with the formula
  circumferenceOfCircle = 2 * Math.PI * radiusPassedIn;
} // End of CircumferenceOfCircle method
```

22. Now add the code in Listing 13-70, to display the circumference and radius, using the Format() method.

Listing 13-70. Display the radius and circumference of the circle

```
double circumferenceOfCircle = 0;

//Calculate the circumference with the formula
circumferenceOfCircle = 2 * Math.PI * radiusPassedIn;

Console.WriteLine(String.Format("\nA circle with radius {0:0.#} has a
circumference of {1:0.##}", radiusPassedIn, circumferenceOfCircle));
} // End of CircumferenceOfCircle method
```

Now that we have created the second method, we will call it from the first method, AreaOfCircle(), passing it the radius that has been input by the user.

23.   In the AreaOfCircle() method, call the CircumferenceOfCircle()
method, as in Listing 13-71.

Listing 13-71. Call the CircumferenceOfCircle() method

```
Console.WriteLine(String.Format("\nA circle with radius {0:0.#} has
an area of  {1:0.##}", radiusLength, areaOfCircle));

/*
Now call the method which calculates the circumference
of the circle using the radius the user has input.
We call the method and pass the radius as a parameter.
*/
CircumferenceOfCircle(radiusLength);
} //End of areaOfCircle method
```

24.   Click the File menu.

25.   Choose Save All.

26.   Open the ShapeCalculator class.

27.   Click the Debug menu.

28.   Choose Start Without Debugging.

The console window will appear and ask the user to input the radius of the circle, as shown in Figure 13-21.

29.   Type 10 and press the Enter key.

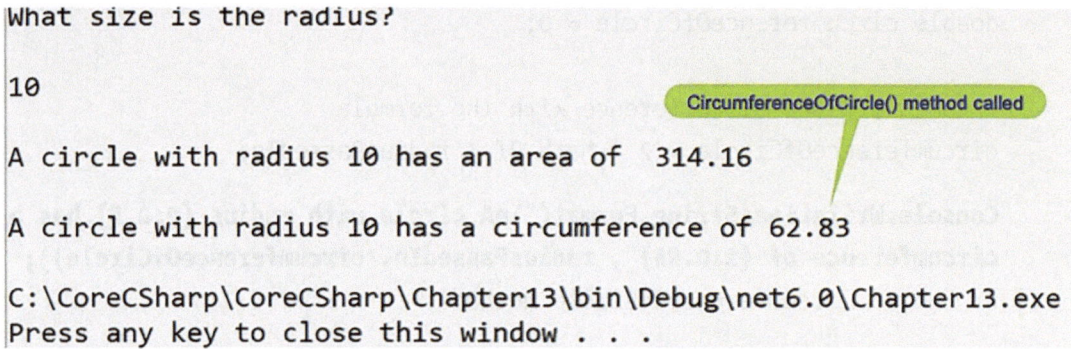

```
What size is the radius?

10

A circle with radius 10 has an area of  314.16

A circle with radius 10 has a circumference of 62.83

C:\CoreCSharp\CoreCSharp\Chapter13\bin\Debug\net6.0\Chapter13.exe
Press any key to close this window . . .
```

Figure 13-21. *CircumferenceOfCircle() method called and working*

30.   Press the Enter key to close the console window.

We see two decimal places in the circumference as we used 0.## in the Format() method. This is excellent! Our two methods that contain the business logic, the formulae, were created in a class and have been called from another class.

We can see that we have used the principle of "separation of concern," where we have kept our circle formulae separate from the class with the Main() method. We will now reinforce the principle of "separation of concern" by creating another class that will be related to a rectangle and will hold any formula related to a rectangle.

RectangleFormulae Class

1.   Right-click the Chapter13 project.

2.   Choose Add.

3.   Choose Class.

4.   Name the class RectangleFormulae.cs.

5.   Click the Add button.

We will create a method for the area of a rectangle. The formula for the area of a rectangle is the length multiplied by the breadth. This formula will therefore be our business logic. To calculate the area of the rectangle, we will ask the user to input the length and breadth of the rectangle they require.

6. Amend the code, as in Listing 13-72, by adding the start of a method that will calculate the area of a rectangle.

Listing 13-72. Creating the method for the area of a rectangle

```
namespace Chapter13
{
  internal class RectangleFormulae
  {
    /*
    This is a method that will ask the user to input the
    length of the rectangle, then ask them for the breadth of
    the rectangle, calculate the area of the rectangle and
    display the area of the rectangle in the console window
    */
    public void AreaOfRectangle()
    {
    } // End of AreaOfRectangle method

  } // End of RectangleFormulae class
} // End of Chapter13 namespace
```

7. Amend the code, as in Listing 13-73, to create variables to hold the length, breadth, and area of the rectangle and initialize them to 0.

Listing 13-73. Create and initialize the variables for the rectangle formulae

```
    public void areaOfRectangle()
    {
      /*
      Create three variables of data type double to hold the
      value of the length and breadth as input by the user and
      the calculated area of the rectangle.
      Initialise the three variables to zero.
      */
      double lengthOfRectangle = 0;
      double breadthOfRectangle = 0;
```

```
    double areaOfRectangle = 0;
} // End of AreaOfRectangle method
```

8. Amend the code, as in Listing 13-74, to ask the user to input the length and breadth of the rectangle and then convert the inputs to type double.

Listing 13-74. Ask for user input for length and breadth

```
double breadthOfRectangle = 0;
double areaOfRectangle = 0;

Console.WriteLine("\nWhat is the rectangle length?\n");
lengthOfRectangle = Convert.ToDouble(Console.ReadLine());

Console.WriteLine("\nWhat is the rectangle breadth?\n");
breadthOfRectangle = Convert.ToDouble(Console.ReadLine());

} // End of AreaOfRectangle method
```

9. Now add the code in Listing 13-75, to calculate the area of the rectangle.

Listing 13-75. Add the formula for the area of a rectangle

```
Console.WriteLine("\nWhat is the rectangle breadth?\n");
breadthOfRectangle = Convert.ToDouble(Console.ReadLine());

// Calculate the area of the rectangle with the formula
areaOfRectangle = lengthOfRectangle * breadthOfRectangle;
} // End of AreaOfRectangle method
```

10. Now add the code in Listing 13-76, to display the length, breadth, and area, using the Format() method.

Listing 13-76. Display the length, breadth, and area of the rectangle

```
// Calculate the area of the rectangle with the formula
areaOfRectangle = lengthOfRectangle * breadthOfRectangle;

// Display the rectangle details
Console.WriteLine(String.Format("\nA rectangle with length of {0:0.#}
and breadth of {1:0.#} has an area of {2:0.#}", lengthOfRectangle,
breadthOfRectangle, areaOfRectangle));

} // End of AreaOfRectangle method
```

Now that we have created another class with a method in it, we will be able to call the method from the Main() method in the ShapeCalculator class. Remember, we do not use the RectangleFormulae class directly; we make an instance of it.

11.   Open the ShapeCalculator class and create an instance of the RectangleFormulae class, as in Listing 13-77.

Listing 13-77. Instantiate the RectangleFormulae class

```
static void Main(string[] args)
{
  // Instantiate the CircleFormulae class
  CircleFormulae myCircleFormulae = new CircleFormulae();

  myCircleFormulae.areaOfCircle();

  RectangleFormulae myRectangleFormulae = new RectangleFormulae();
} // End of Main() method
```

Now we need to call the AreaOfRectangle() method from the other class. As we type **myRectangleFormulae** and add the ., as shown in Figure 13-22, we should automatically see any accessible fields and methods that belong in the RectangleFormulae class, or more correctly to the myRectangleFormulae instance of the class. Remember a class is made up of fields and methods.

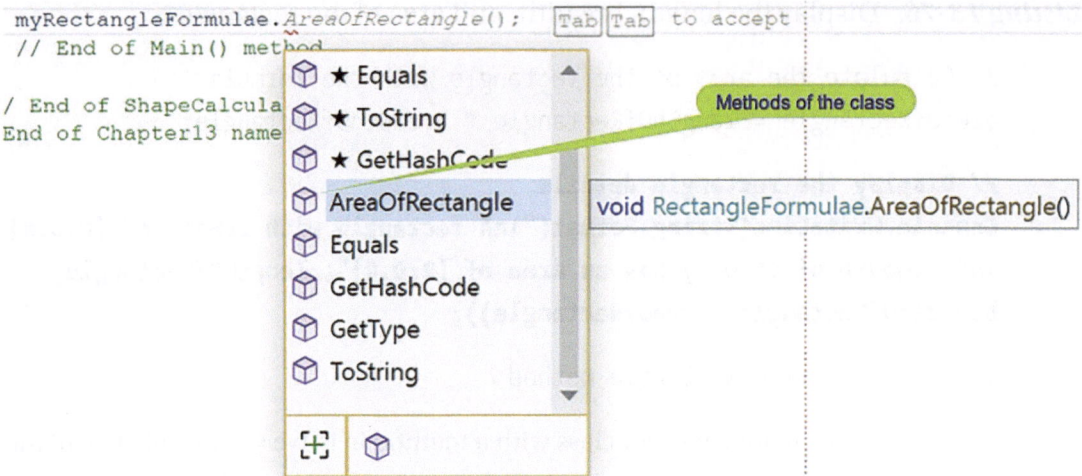

Figure 13-22. *Methods accessible in the RectangleFormulae class*

12. Now add the code in Listing 13-78, to call the AreaOfRectangle()
     method of our new instance class.

Listing 13-78. Call the AreaOfRectangle method

```
myCircleFormulae.AreaOfCircle();
RectangleFormulae myRectangleFormulae
= new RectangleFormulae();

myRectangleFormulae.AreaOfRectangle();
} // End of Main() method
```

13. Click the File menu.

14. Choose Save All.

15. Click the Debug menu.

16. Choose Start Without Debugging.

The console window will appear and ask the user to input the radius of the circle.

17. Type 10 and press the Enter key.

The console window will ask the user to input the length of the rectangle.

18. Type 10.5 and press the Enter key.

The console window will ask the user to input the breadth of the rectangle.

19. Type 20.5 and press the Enter key.

Figure 13-23 shows the console window with the areas of the circle and rectangle.

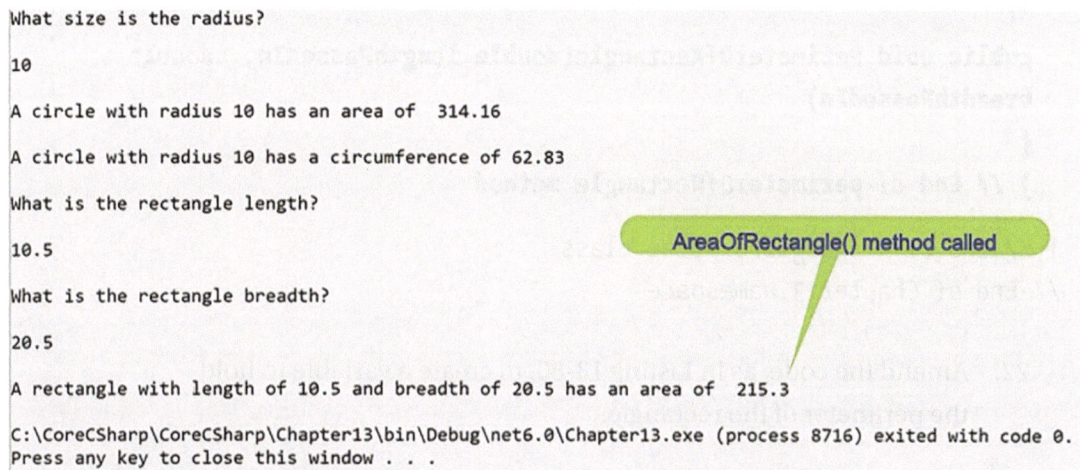

Figure 13-23. *AreaOfRectangle() method called and working*

20. Press the Enter key to close the console window.

We see one digit after the decimal point in the area of the rectangle as we used 0.# in the Format() method. This is excellent! Our method for the rectangle area has been called from another class. Now we will extend our RectangleFormulae class by adding another method, just after the method AreaOfRectangle() and inside the class, to calculate the perimeter of the rectangle.

21. Amend the code, as in Listing 13-79, in the RectangleFormulae class to add the method that will calculate the perimeter of the rectangle/

Listing 13-79. Add the PerimeterOfRectangle() method

```
    } // End of AreaOfRectangle method

/*
This is a method that will accept the values of the length
and breadth passed to it. Both values have been obtained in
the AreaOfRectangle method and then the AreaOfRectangle()
```

method will call this new PerimeterOfRectangle() method
passing it the values of the length and breadth.
This method will then calculate the perimeter and display
the value in the console window
*/
public void PerimeterOfRectangle(double lengthPassedIn,   double
breadthPassedIn)
{
} // End of perimeterOfRectangle method

```
  } // End of RectangleFormulae class
} // End of Chapter13 namespace
```

22. Amend the code, as in Listing 13-80, to create a variable to hold
the perimeter of the rectangle.

Listing 13-80. Add a variable that will hold the perimeter

```
public void PerimeterOfRectangle(double lengthPassedIn, double
breadthPassedIn)
    {
```
/*
Create a variable of data type double to hold the value
calculated for the perimeter of the rectangle. Initialise
the variable to zero. We have the length and breadth as
they are passed into this method
*/
double perimeterOfRectangle = 0;
```
    } // End of PerimeterOfRectangle method
```

23. Now add the code in Listing 13-81, to calculate the rectangle
perimeter.

Listing 13-81. Add the formula for the perimeter of the rectangle

```
double perimeterOfRectangle = 0;

//Calculate the perimeter of the rectangle with the formula
perimeterOfRectangle = 2 * (lengthPassedIn + breadthPassedIn);

} // End of PerimeterOfRectangle method
```

24. Now add the code in Listing 13-82, to display the perimeter of the rectangle.

Listing 13-82. Display the length, breadth, and perimeter of the rectangle

```
//Calculate the perimeter of the rectangle with the formula
perimeterOfRectangle = 2 * (lengthPassedIn + breadthPassedIn);

Console.WriteLine(String.Format("\nA rectangle with length of {0:0.##}
and breadth of {1:0.##} has a perimeter of {2:0.##}", lengthPassedIn,
breadthPassedIn, perimeterOfRectangle));

  } // End of PerimeterOfRectangle method
```

Now that we have created the second method for the rectangle, we will call it from the first method, AreaOfRectangle(), passing it the length and breadth.

25. In the AreaOfRectangle() method, add the code in Listing 13-83, to call the PerimeterOfRectangle() method.

Listing 13-83. Call the PerimeterOfRectangle() method

```
// Display the answer
Console.WriteLine(String.Format("\nA rectangle with length of {0:0.#}
and breadth of {1:0.#} has an area of  {2:0.#}", lengthOfRectangle,
breadthOfRectangle, areaOfRectangle));

/*
Now call the method which calculates the perimeter of the
rectangle using the length and breadth the user has input.
We call the method and pass the radius as a parameter
*/
```

`PerimeterOfRectangle(lengthOfRectangle, breadthOfRectangle);`

`} // End of AreaOfRectangle method`

26. Click the File menu.

27. Choose Save All.

28. Click the Debug menu.

29. Choose Start Without Debugging.

The console window will appear and ask the user to input the radius of the circle.

30. Type 10 and press the Enter key.

The console window will ask the user to input the length of the rectangle.

31. Type 10.5 and press the Enter key.

The console window will ask the user to input the breadth of the rectangle.

32. Type 20.5 and press the Enter key.

The console window, as shown in Figure 13-24, displays the perimeter of the rectangle.

```
What size is the radius?

10

A circle with radius 10 has an area of  314.16

A circle with radius 10 has a circumference of 62.83

What is the rectangle length?

10.5

What is the rectangle breadth?                    PerimeterOfRectangle() method called

20.5

A rectangle with length of 10.5 and breadth of 20.5 has an area of  215.3

A rectangle with length of 10.5 and breadth of 20.5 has a perimeter of  62

C:\CoreCSharp\CoreCSharp\Chapter13\bin\Debug\net6.0\Chapter13.exe (process 8280) exited with code 0.
Press any key to close this window . . .
```

Figure 13-24. PerimeterOfRectangle() method called and working

33. Press the Enter key to close the console window.

Chapter Summary

So, finishing this chapter on classes, we should remember what was covered in Chapter 12 on methods, because the two concepts are highly connected. Classes contain methods and fields, and we have created classes to hold methods and fields and have created separate classes when necessary, so that each class represents related items. We can access classes from the Main() method of another class, and in doing this we create a copy of the class. We use this instance, the copy of the class, to give us access to the methods and properties of the class.

We have come a long way from Chapter 1, and getting to this stage, where we can create and use our own classes, is an absolutely fantastic achievement for us in our learning. We are making fantastic progress in our programming of C# applications and we should be very proud of our achievements. In finishing this very important chapter, we have increased our knowledge further, and we are advancing to our target.

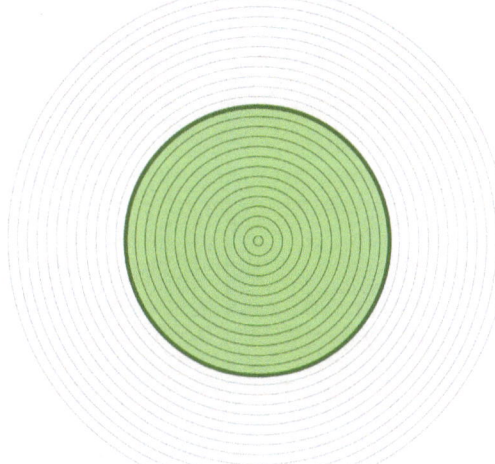

Our target is getting closer

CHAPTER 14

Interfaces

Interfaces and Abstract Classes

We learned in Chapter 13 that classes contain methods and fields. We also read in Chapter 12 on methods that

> *The methods we have not created but have used, they all have one thing in common.*

> *They all live inside a class; they are part of a class.*

We also said that

> *The crucial takeaway from the last chapter and a vital thing to remember in this chapter is that a class contains methods and variables.*

So, in the last chapter, we saw that methods form a large part of the classes we created or that exist in the C# language. This is great as it helped us modularize our code. But let us think more on a larger scale than one or two classes. Let us use two examples, so we can think about different developers creating separate classes and methods around the same "topic" or "idea."

Example 1

A number of developers are writing an ecommerce application that will work for different countries, and one of the methods required is to calculate the value-added tax for a product. Looking at the role of the developers, we see that

- Developer 1 is writing for country 1, so they develop their class called Billing and they create a method called **VatCalculation(),** where the business logic is to multiply the item price by 20% (0.2) and return the amount.

© Gerard Byrne 2022
G. Byrne, *Target C#*, https://doi.org/10.1007/978-1-4842-8619-7_14

- Developer 2 is writing for country 2, so they develop their class called Billing and they create a method called **TaxCalculation(),** where the business logic is to multiply the item price by 15% (0.15) and return the amount.

- Developer 3 is writing for country 3, so they develop their class called Billing and they create a method called **CalculateTax(),** where the business logic is to multiply the item price by 10% (0.10) and return the amount.

Now we should ask, "Why do we have three Billing classes all doing the same thing, which have a common method that calculates the VAT amount, but the method names are not the same?" Well, the answer is because we can! But is this a good example of standardization or clean code? Maybe not.

Now think about the same problem but where the three developers collaborate and discuss what they are about to do. They might suggest the methods they will use and the naming conventions. Sound like a plan? Well, this is where an **abstract class** or an **interface** could help. By using an abstract class or an interface, we can declare the **method signatures and return types** to be used, but not the code to be used, as the code will be decided by the individual developers and be appropriate to their situation.

In C#, a method signature is used by the C# compiler to ensure we have unique methods, that is, no two methods can have the same method signature. And we saw this when we looked at method overloading. We can now apply the concept of method signatures to an abstract class or interface because, within it we only declare the method signatures we require, not the actual body for the method. The actual body for the method will be supplied by the developer when the method is coded in a class that makes use of the abstract class or interface. Table 14-1 shows some method signatures.

Table 14-1. *Method signature examples*

Method signature	Description
CalculateTax(double itemPrice)	Method name is CalculateTax. Parameter is of type double.
CalculateTax(double itemPrice, int quantity)	Method name is CalculateTax. First parameter is of type double. Second parameter is of type int.

When we talk about a method signature, we are not including the return type of the method. We cannot have the same method signature with different return types.

When we discussed overloaded methods, we said they were methods with the same name but different parameters. There was no mention of the return type. Our two CalculateTax() methods, in Table 14-1, show an example of method overloading.

Example 2

A number of developers are writing an application for an online insurance company who insures computer hardware in a country with different regions. Each developer is assigned to a different region, and they must have methods that calculate the regional rate and the hardware rate, before calculating the quote. Looking at the role of the developers, we see that

- Developer 1 is writing for region A, so they develop their class called Quote and they create a method called **RegionalRateCalculation(),** where the business logic is to look up a struct and return the rate as a double for this region, for example, 0.05.

- Developer 2 is writing for region B, so they develop their class called Quote and they create a method called **RegionBRate(),** where the business logic is to look up the same struct and return the rate as a double for this region, for example, 0.10.

- Developer 3 is writing for region C, so they develop their class called Quote and they create a method called **CRate(),** where the business logic is to look up the same struct and return the rate as a double for this region, for example, 0.20.

There are therefore three classes called Quote all doing the same thing and having a common method that looks up the regional rate amount, but the method names are not the same. Surely, we can do better than this!

Well, this is where an **abstract class** or an **interface** could help.

The Interface or Abstract Class as a Manager

Example 3

Think about the abstract class or interface as being like a manager. In this scenario a manager gives three of their employees – Gerry, May, and June – the same request: order ten pizzas for the C# book launch at the "Build Your Core Programming Muscle" event tomorrow. So what might happen?

- Gerry orders ten margherita pizzas of size 10 inches.

- May orders five margherita and five pepperoni pizzas of size 16 inches.

- June orders four pepperoni, two BBQ chicken, and four vegetable pizzas of size 16 inches.

Brilliant! All three employees have fulfilled the manager request, so they all have one thing in common: they have ten pizzas. However, the implementation of the request for ten pizzas was very different as can be seen from the different selection of pizzas each employee has chosen. This is perfectly acceptable as the manager request has been fulfilled.

When we write code or when we look back at the developers in Examples 1 and 2, we can see that a "manager" could be useful to set some upfront guidelines. We should think of the abstract class or interface as the manager giving some guidelines. Now, we might ask ourselves, "How can we apply the manager concept to the preceding Examples 1 and 2?" Well, Figure 14-1 shows how we could apply the abstract class and the classes to the ecommerce application example. We will use the idea of the abstract class for now, but the same principles apply to using an interface, with some differences.

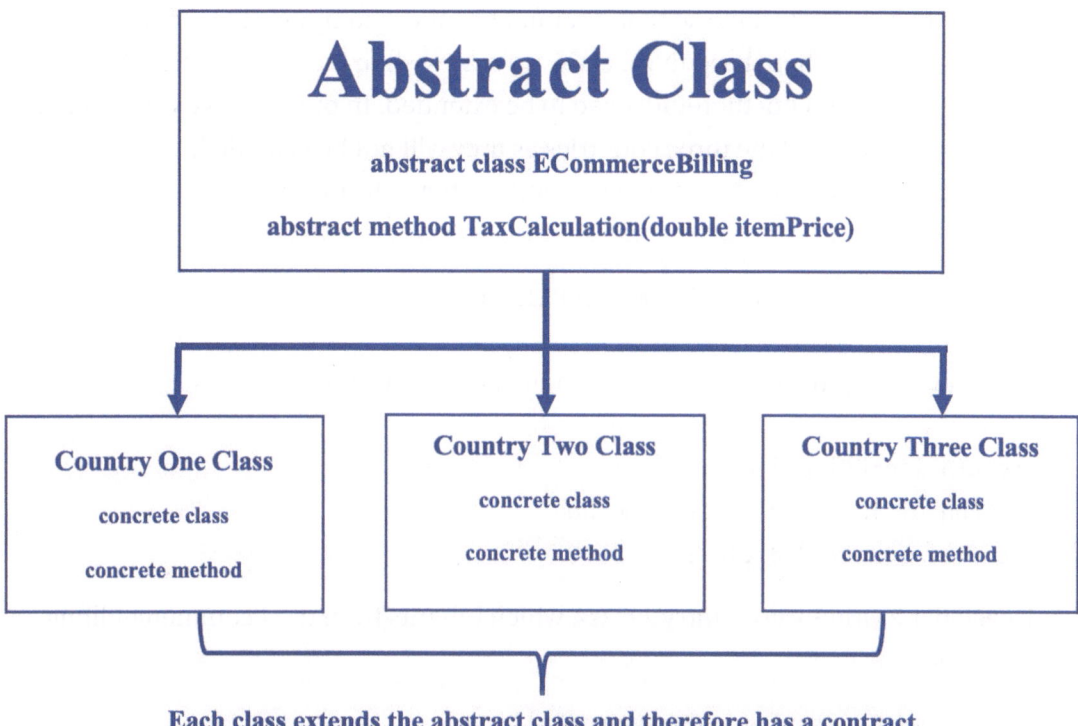

Each class extends the abstract class and therefore has a contract
to make the abstract methods concrete, by adding a body

Figure 14-1. *Hierarchy for the abstract and concrete classes*

Now let us look at the example code that could be used to satisfy the structure
shown in Figure 14-1. In looking at the application code, we will relate it to the manager
scenario. The manager gives three of their staff the same instructions in following a task:
"Use this **abstract class** when you write your class."

The abstract class is supplied as

```
public abstract class EcommerceBilling
{
  // abstract method
  public abstract double TaxCalculation(double itemPrice);
} // End of the abstract class
```

Now that the three developers have been given the abstract class, what might they do
with it when they write their code?

Sealed Class

We can make a class sealed so that it cannot be inherited by another class but it can still be instantiated. When designing a class, we may wish to indicate that the class is specialized and should not therefore need to be extended. In our example we will create sealed classes for each of the three countries as they will not be extended.

Developer 1 writes the country 1 class, which inherits from the EcommerceBilling abstract class:

```
public sealed CountryOne : EcommerceBilling
{
  public override double TaxCalculation(double itemPrice)
  {
    return itemPrice * 0.2;
  } // End of TaxCalculation() method
} // End of CountryOne class
```

Developer 2 writes the country 2 class, which inherits from the EcommerceBilling abstract class:

```
public sealed CountryTwo : EcommerceBilling
{
  public override double TaxCalculation(double itemPrice)
  {
    return itemPrice * 0.15;
  } // End of TaxCalculation() method
} // End of CountryTwo class
```

Developer 3 writes the country 3 class, which inherits from the EcommerceBilling abstract class:

```
public sealed CountryThree : EcommerceBilling
{
  public override double TaxCalculation(double itemPrice)
  {
    return itemPrice * 0.10;
  } // End of TaxCalculation() method
} // End of CountryThree class
```

All three classes have been developed by inheriting the EcommerceBilling abstract class, and therefore they are **contracted** to use the method called TaxCalculation(), which has a parameter of type double. Here, all three developers have written their classes and implemented the method as contracted to do so, but they have different business logic appropriate for their country, that is, 20%, 15%, or 10%. This is like the "manager" giving the instructions and the employees implementing them but with different business logic.

Brilliant! We have now seen, in theory, that an abstract class can be developed to have method signatures with a return type stated. What we should also see from the example code is that we are using an **abstract class, not a full class.** It is not a full class because **it is not complete**; it has **abstract methods, and these have no code**. An abstract class can also have concrete methods, methods with code. We refer to the incomplete class as an **abstract class,** whereas a full class is referred to as a **concrete class.** The preceding classes, CountryOne, CountryTwo, and CountryThree, are all concrete classes as they are complete.

As we have seen, the information in the base class, the abstract class, has only general methods, methods with a return type and a signature. It is incumbent on each implementing class, the derived class, to add its own details. The abstract class therefore decides the nature of the methods that any derived classes must implement, but it will not provide an implementation of any of the defined methods.

Abstract classes can therefore be defined as incomplete classes. Abstract classes have the following characteristics:

- The class is marked with the **abstract keyword.**

- They contain one or more incomplete methods called **abstract methods.**

- They provide the signature or declaration of the abstract methods; they leave the implementation of these methods to **derived** or **subclasses.**

- They **cannot be instantiated** as they are incomplete.

- They **cannot be static.**

- They can contain a **constructor.**

- Their methods are marked with the abstract keyword, as they are **abstract methods.**

- They can have **concrete methods**, that is, methods with a body of code.

- A class inheriting an abstract class must implement all the abstract methods in the abstract class, or it too must be declared as an abstract class.

- A class inheriting an abstract class and implementing all its abstract methods is called the **concrete class** of the abstract class.

- Methods in the inheriting class, the derived class, must include the keyword override before the method name when they are using the abstract methods.

- They cannot be used for multiple inheritance. In other words, if we have an EcommerceBilling abstract class and an EcommercePayment abstract class, then a derived class such as CountryOne could not implement both of these abstract classes:

```
public class CountryOne : EcommerceBilling, EcommercePayment
```

This line or any format does not work. There is no multiple inheritance.

Let's code some C# and build our programming muscle.

Add a new project to hold the code for this chapter.

1. Right-click the solution CoreCSharp.

2. Choose Add.

3. Choose New Project.

4. Choose Console App from the listed templates that appear.

5. Click the Next button.

6. Name the project Chapter14 and leave it in the same location.

7. Click the Next button.

8. Choose the framework to be used, which in our projects will be .NET 6.0 or higher.

9. Click the Create button.

Now we should see the Chapter14 project within the solution called CoreCSharp.

10.   Right-click the Chapter14 project in the Solution Explorer panel.

11.   Click the Set as Startup Project option.

Notice how the Chapter14 project name has been made to have bold text, indicating that it is the new startup project and that it is the Program.cs file within it that will be executed when we run the debugging.

Amend the name of the Program.cs file.

Remember the coding principle of "self-documenting" code? Of course we do. So let us now rename the Program.cs file.

12.   Right-click the Program.cs file in the Solution Explorer window.

13.   Choose Rename.

14.   Change the name to VATCalculator.cs.

15.   Press the Enter key.

16.   Amend the VATCalculator class, as in Listing 14-1, to have a namespace, class, and Main() method.

Listing 14-1. Class template with a Main() method

```
namespace Chapter14
{
  internal class VATCalculator
  {
    static void Main(string[] args)
    {
    } // End of Main() method

  } // End of VATCalculator class
} // End of Chapter14 namespace
```

17.   Right-click the Chapter14 project in the Solution Explorer panel.

18.   Choose Add.

19.   Choose Class.

20.   Name the class as AbstractVATCalculations.cs.

21. The AbstractVATCalculations.cs class code will appear in the editor window and will be similar to Listing 14-2.

Listing 14-2. Class – no methods, not yet an abstract class

```
namespace Chapter14
{
  internal class AbstractVATCalculations
  {
  } // End of AbstractVATCalculations class
} // End of Chapter14 namespace
```

22. Amend the code, as in Listing 14-3, to make it an abstract class using the keyword abstract.

Listing 14-3. Abstract class – no methods

```
namespace Chapter14
{
  internal abstract class AbstractVATCalculations
  {
  } // End of AbstractVATCalculations class
} // End of Chapter14 namespace
```

23. Amend the code, as in Listing 14-4, to add two abstract methods to the abstract class.

Listing 14-4. Abstract methods in the abstract class

```
  internal abstract class AbstractVATCalculations
  {
    /*
    Declare two incomplete methods which will be detailed in
    the inherited class. Each is an abstract method - a method
    signature and an access modifier
    */
    public abstract double CalculateVAT();
```

```
    public abstract double CalculateTotalPrice();

  } // End of AbstractVATCalculations class
} // End of Chapter14 namespace
```

Code Analysis

The AbstractVATCalculations class contains an abstract method CalculateVAT(), which could be used later to calculate the amount of VAT to be added to an item. The "body" of the method will be decided by the actual class that inherits the abstract class.

The CalculateVAT() method has therefore been declared as **abstract** so that any subclasses will need to provide their own criteria for calculating the VAT. We also have a CalculateTotalPrice() abstract method declared, and this will also need to be made into a concrete method that returns a value of type double.

Instantiate the Abstract Class?

Let's look and see what happens if we try to instantiate this abstract class from within the Main() method. Will it be OK, or will we get an error? Well, we did read earlier that we cannot instantiate an abstract class, so let us code an example and prove that this is true.

24.   Open the VATCalculator class and amend the code, as in Listing 14-5, to try and instantiate the AbstractVATCalculations abstract class.

Listing 14-5. Instantiate an abstract class

```
internal class VATCalculator
{
 static void Main(string[] args)
 {
 Console.WriteLine("We cannot instantiate an abstract class");

 AbstractVATCalculations taxCalc = new AbstractVATCalculations();

 } // End of Main() method

} // End of VATCalculator class
```

25. Hover over the red underline under the AbstractVATCalculations(), as shown in Figure 14-2, to reveal the error message that tells us we cannot create an instance of the abstract type or interface.

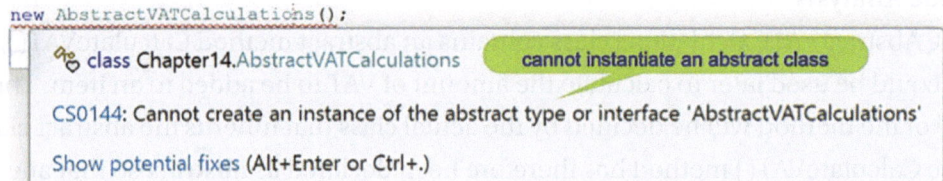

Figure 14-2. *Error message – cannot create an instance of an abstract class*

26. Remove the two lines of code we added in Listing 14-5, so that there is no code within the Main() method.

Create a class that inherits from the abstract class.

27. Right-click the Chapter14 project in the Solution Explorer panel.

28. Choose Add.

29. Choose Class.

30. Name the class as VATCalculations.cs.

31. The VATCalculations class code will appear and be similar to the code shown in Listing 14-6.

Listing 14-6. Concrete class template

```
namespace Chapter14
{
  internal class VATCalculations
  {
  } // End of VATCalculations class
} // End of Chapter14 namespace
```

32. Amend the VATCalculations class code, as in Listing 14-7, to add a member.

Listing 14-7. Add a member, field

```
internal class VATCalculations
{
  private double itemPrice;

} // End of VATCalculations class
} // End of Chapter14 namespace
```

33. Amend the VATCalculations class code, as in Listing 14-8, to add a constructor that will set the value of the member.

Listing 14-8. Add a constructor that overrides the default constructor

```
internal class VATCalculations
{
  private double itemPrice;

  public VATCalculations(double itemPrice)
  {
    this.itemPrice = itemPrice;
  } // End of VATCalculations constructor

} // End of VATCalculations class
} // End of Chapter14 namespace
```

34. Amend the VATCalculations code to inherit the AbstractVATCalculations class, as in Listing 14-9.

Listing 14-9. Make the class inherit the abstract class

```
namespace Chapter14
{
  internal class VATCalculations : AbstractVATCalculations
  {
    private double itemPrice;
```

There will be an error line under the VATCalculations class name because this class does not implement the method that was declared in the abstract class. We now need to implement the required method and complete the contract.

35. Amend the VATCalculations class code to implement the CalculateVAT() abstract method, as in Listing 14-10.

Listing 14-10. Add the code to implement the method CalculateVAT()

```
public VATCalculations(double itemPrice)
{
  this.itemPrice = itemPrice;
} // End of VATCalculations constructor

public override double CalculateVAT()
{
  return this.itemPrice * 0.20;
} // End of CalculateVAT() method

  } // End of VATCalculations class
} // End of Chapter14 namespace
```

36. Amend the VATCalculations class code to implement the CalculateTotalPrice() abstract method, as in Listing 14-11.

Listing 14-11. Add the code to implement the method CalculateTotalPrice()

```
public override double CalculateVAT()
{
  return this.itemPrice * 0.20;
} // End of CalculateVAT() method

public override double CalculateTotalPrice()
{
  return itemPrice + CalculateVAT();
} // End of CalculateTotalPrice() method
  } // End of VATCalculations class
} // End of Chapter14 namespace
```

Now we will instantiate the VATCalculations class, which has inherited from the AbstractVATCalculations abstract class, passing it the item price. We will then call the CalculateVAT() method and assign the returned VAT value to a variable, before displaying the VAT and the total price.

37.   Open the VATCalculator class and amend the code, as in
      Listing 14-12.

Listing 14-12. Instantiate the VATCalculations class

```
static void Main(string[] args)
    {
        VATCalculations myCalculations = new VATCalculations(100);

        double vatAmount = myCalculations.CalculateVAT();

        Console.WriteLine($"{"VAT due on the item is",-30} £{vatAmount}");

        Console.WriteLine($"{"The total item cost is",-30} £{myCalculations.
        CalculateTotalPrice()}\n");

    } // End of Main() method
```

38.   Click the File menu.

39.   Choose Save All.

40.   Click the Debug menu.

41.   Choose Start Without Debugging.

The console window will appear, as shown in Figure 14-3, displaying the total cost as 100 plus the 20% of 100, which is 20, giving the total of 120.

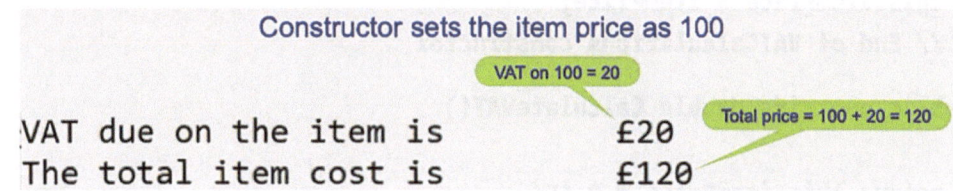

Figure 14-3. *Two methods have been implemented*

42.   Press the Enter key to close the console window.

Once we have an abstract class, we can develop as many concrete classes as we wish, with each class inheriting from the base abstract class. The only stipulation is that each concrete class must provide a definition for each abstract method. Let's code an example to demonstrate that when we create a new class that inherits the abstract class, we change the code in the class but the code in the Main() will be the same, except we instantiate the new class.

43. Right-click the Chapter14 project in the Solution Explorer panel.

44. Choose Add.

45. Choose Class.

46. Name the class as VATCalculationsFifteenPercent.cs.

47. Amend the code as in Listing 14-13.

Listing 14-13. Add the code and use 15%, which is 0.15

```
namespace Chapter14
{
  internal class VATCalculationsFifteenPercent : AbstractVATCalculations
  {
    private double itemPrice;

    public VATCalculationsFifteenPercent(double itemPrice)
    {
      this.itemPrice = itemPrice;
    } // End of VATCalculations constructor

    public override double CalculateVAT()
    {
      return this.itemPrice * 0.15;
    } // End of CalculateVAT() method

    public override double CalculateTotalPrice()
    {
      return itemPrice + CalculateVAT();
    } // End of CalculateTotalPrice() method

  } // End of VATCalculationsFifteenPercent class
} // End of Chapter14 namespace
```

48. Open the VATCalculator class that has the Main()
method and add the code to instantiate the newly created
VATCalculationsFifteenPercent and comment the first
instantiation, as in Listing 14-14.

Listing 14-14. Change the class being instantiated

```
static void Main(string[] args)
{
    //VATCalculations myCalculations = new VATCalculations(100);

    VATCalculationsFifteenPercent myCalculations = new
    VATCalculationsFifteenPercent(100);
```

49. Click the File menu.

50. Choose Save All.

51. Click the Debug menu.

52. Choose Start Without Debugging.

The console window will appear, as shown in Figure 14-4, displaying the total cost as
100 plus the 15% of 100, which is 15, giving the total of 115.

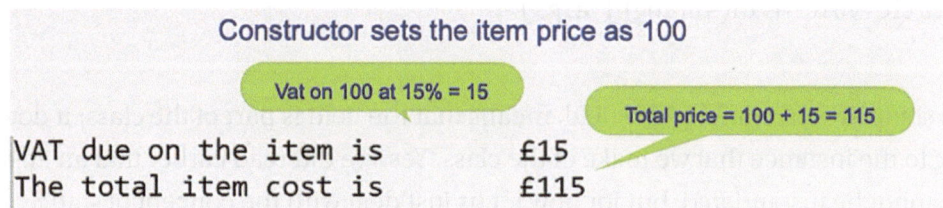

Figure 14-4. *Two methods have been implemented*

53. Press the Enter key to close the console window.

Static Members of the Abstract Class

When we have a static member in the abstract class, we can call it directly without having
to use the instance of the class. Let's really think hard about this one sentence, because it
is very important that we understand the meaning of static. In all the examples we have
coded up to now, we have used static. Two examples are shown in Listings 14-15 and 14-16.

Listing 14-15. The static keyword in the Main() method

```
public static void Main(string[] args)
{

} // End of Main() method
```

Listing 14-16. The static keyword with variables in program MethodsValue

```
internal class MethodsValue
{
    static String[] repairShopClaims = new String[8];
    static string repairShopID;
    static string vehiclePolicyNumber;
    static double claimAmount;
    static DateTime claimDate;
    static int numberOfClaimsBeingMade;
    static int numberOfClaimsEntered = 0;
    static int arrayPositionCounter = 0;
    static double totalOfAllClaims;
    static double vatAmount;

    static void Main(string[] args)
  {
```

So static, when related to the field, means that the field is part of the class; it does not belong to the instance that we make of the class. Yes, we did read earlier that an abstract class cannot be instantiated, but for now let us just deal with the concept of static.

In trying to understand static, let us think again of a manager scenario. The manager is a very busy person, so they decide to make two instances of themselves and give the instances their characteristics, except their mobile phone number. Looking at this we could represent it as shown in Table 14-2.

Table 14-2. *The manager characteristic and the instance characteristics*

Manager	myManagerInstance1	myManagerInstance2
Approve leave	Approve leave	Approve leave
Attend meeting	Attend meeting	Attend meeting
Answer calls		

The manager has reserved the answer calls characteristic. Only they can answer calls; the two instances can approve leaves and attend meetings. In terms of classes, we would say that

- Approve leave is an instance variable; it belongs to, or is only associated with, the instance of the class, not the actual class.

- Attend meeting is an instance variable; it belongs to, or is only associated with, the instance of the class, not the actual class.

- Answer calls is a static variable; it belongs to the class and not to any of the two instances of the class.

This is very useful for the manager, the manager class, as it can now keep a record of the number of calls directly. Now, as an employee who wants to have leave approved, we might go to manager instance 1 or manager instance 2. And in terms of writing C# code, we would say something like this:

```
myManagerInstance1.approveLeave
```

or

```
myManagerInstance1.approveLeave
```

But if we wanted to phone the manager, we would have to do this directly, and in terms of writing C# code, we would say something like this:

```
Manager.answerCall
```

Now, going back to abstract classes and our static variable, we are saying that it belongs to the abstract class. Remember, we cannot make an instance of an abstract class. Also, when we move on to look at interfaces shortly, we will see that we cannot instantiate an interface. Static equals fixed, does not move; it is stuck to the class or interface.

54.   Amend the AbstractVATCalculations class code, as in
Listing 14-17, to add a discount rate.

Listing 14-17. Add the variable discountRate

```
internal abstract class AbstractVATCalculations
 {
   public double discountRate = 0.10;

   /*
   Declare two incomplete methods which will be detailed in
   the inherited class. Each is an abstract method - a method
   signature and an access modifier
   */
   public abstract double CalculateVAT();
```

Now we will add a method in the AbstractVATCalculations class that contains the
formula to calculate the discount amount, based on the field discountRate. We could add
this method to the VATCalculations class, but if we think about this method, we will see
that it is logic that can be shared, so we will put it into the AbstractVATCalculations class.
This means we will be calling the abstract class method directly; there is no instance of
an abstract class.

55.   In the AbstractVATCalculations class, add the method, as in
Listing 14-18.

Listing 14-18. Add the code for the method CalculateDiscountedAmount()

```
   public abstract double CalculateVAT();

   public abstract double CalculateTotalPrice();

   public double CalculateDiscountedAmount()
   {
     return CalculateTotalPrice() * discountRate;
   } // End of CalculateDiscountedAmount() method
 } // End of AbstractVATCalculations class
} // End of Chapter14 namespace
```

56. In the VATCalculator class, amend the code, as in Listing 14-19, to call the method from within a WriteLine() method and set the instantiated class back to the original VATCalculations rather than VATCalculationsFifteenPercent.

Listing 14-19. Add the code to call the method in the abstract class

```
namespace Chapter14
{
  internal class VATCalculator
  {
    static void Main(string[] args)
    {
      VATCalculations myCalculations = new VATCalculations(100);

      //VATCalculationsFifteenPercent myCalculations = new
      VATCalculationsFifteenPercent(100);

      double vatAmount = myCalculations.CalculateVAT();

      Console.WriteLine($"{"VAT due on the item is",-30} £{vatAmount}");

      Console.WriteLine($"{"The total item cost is",-30} £{myCalculations.
      CalculateTotalPrice()}\n");

      Console.WriteLine($"{"The discounted amount is",-30}
      £{myCalculations.CalculateDiscountedAmount()}\n");

    } // End of Main() method
  } // End of VATCalculator class
} // End of Chapter14 namespace
```

57. Click the File menu.

58. Choose Save All.

59. Click the Debug menu.

60. Choose Start Without Debugging.

The console window will appear, as shown in Figure 14-5, displaying

- The total cost as 100 plus the 20% of 100, which is 20, giving the total item cost of 120.

- A discount of 10%, as per the static variable, of the 120, which is 12.

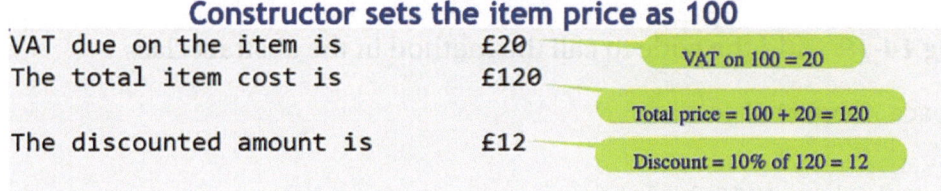

Figure 14-5. *The static variable has been accessed and worked correctly.*

61. Press the Enter key to close the console window.

Let's code another abstract class using the countries example.

We read in the earlier example the following:

A number of developers are writing an application for an online insurance company who insure computer hardware in a country with different regions. Each developer is assigned to a different region, and they must have methods that calculate the regional rate and the hardware rate, before calculating the quote.

Add a new folder to the Chapter 14 project to hold the code for this example.

1. Right-click the Chapter14 project name.

2. Choose Add.

3. Choose New Folder.

4. Name the folder Example2.

5. Right-click the Example2 folder.

6. Choose Add.

7. Choose Class.

8. Click the Add button.

9. Name the class EcommerceBilling.cs.

10. Click the Create button.

The EcommerceBilling.cs class code will appear in the editor window and will be similar to Listing 14-20.

Listing 14-20. New class template code

```
namespace Chapter14.Example2
{
  // abstract class
  internal class EcommerceBilling
  {

  } // End of EcommerceBilling class
} // End of Chapter14 namespace
```

11.   Amend the code, as in Listing 14-21, to make the class abstract and add an abstract method.

Listing 14-21. Make class abstract and add an abstract method

```
namespace Chapter14.Example2
{
  // abstract class
  internal abstract class EcommerceBilling
  {
   // abstract method
    public abstract double TaxCalculation(double itemPrice);

  } // End of EcommerceBilling class
} // End of Chapter14 namespace
```

This will mean that any class that uses this abstract class as its base class will have to implement the TaxCalculation() method by adding code to it, making it a concrete method in a concrete class.

Make the concrete classes, which have to inherit from the abstract class.

12.   Right-click the Example2 folder in the Solution Explorer panel.

13.   Choose Add.

14.   Choose Class.

15. Name the class as CountryOne.cs.

16. Amend the CountryOne class code to have it inherit the
    EcommerceBilling class, and then implement the method with
    some code specific to this country's tax rate for the item, as in
    Listing 14-22.

Listing 14-22. Country 1 class inherits the abstract class and implements
the method

```
namespace Chapter14.Example2
{
  internal class CountryOne : EcommerceBilling
  {
    public override double TaxCalculation(double itemPrice)
    {
      return itemPrice * 0.2;
    } // End of TaxCalculation() method

  } // End of CountryOne class
} // End of Chapter14.Example2 namespace
```

17. Right-click the Example2 folder in the Solution Explorer panel.

18. Choose Add.

19. Choose Class.

20. Name the class as CountryTwo.cs.

21. Amend the CountryTwo class code to have it inherit the
    EcommerceBilling class, and then implement the method with
    some code specific to this country's tax rate for the item, as in
    Listing 14-23.

Listing 14-23. Country 2 class inherits the abstract class and implements
the method

```
namespace Chapter14.Example2
{
```

```
internal class CountryTwo : EcommerceBilling
{
  public override double TaxCalculation(double itemPrice)
  {
    return itemPrice * 0.15;
  } // End of TaxCalculation() method

} // End of CountryTwo class
} // End of Chapter14.Example2 namespace
```

22. Right-click the project Example2 folder in the Solution Explorer panel.

23. Choose Add.

24. Choose Class.

25. Name the class as CountryThree.cs.

26. Amend the CountryThree class code to have it inherit the EcommerceBilling class, and then implement the method with some code specific to this country's tax rate for the item, as in Listing 14-24.

Listing 14-24. Country 3 class inherits the abstract class and implements the method

```
namespace Chapter14.Example2
{
  internal class CountryThree : EcommerceBilling
  {
    public override double TaxCalculation(double itemPrice)
    {
      return itemPrice * 0.10;
    } // End of TaxCalculation() method

  } // End of CountryThree class
} // End of Chapter14.Example2 namespace
```

Make the concrete class that will contain the Main method and use the three country classes, which have inherited from the abstract class.

27. Right-click the project Example2 folder in the Solution Explorer panel.

28. Choose Add.

29. Choose Class.

30. Name the class as EcommerceApplication.cs.

31. Amend the EcommerceApplication class code to have it contain a Main() method and one member of type double that will hold a price for an item, as in Listing 14-25.

Listing 14-25. Class with a Main() method and one member

```
namespace Chapter14.Example2
{
  internal class EcommerceApplication
  {
    static void Main(string[] args)
    {
      double itemPrice = 100.00;

    } // End of Main() method

  } // End of EcommerceApplication class
} // End of Chapter14.Example2 namespace
```

32. Right-click the Chapter14 project in the Solution Explorer panel.

33. Choose Properties from the pop-up menu.

34. Choose the Chapter14.Example2.EcommerceApplication class in the Startup object drop-down list, as shown in Figure 14-6.

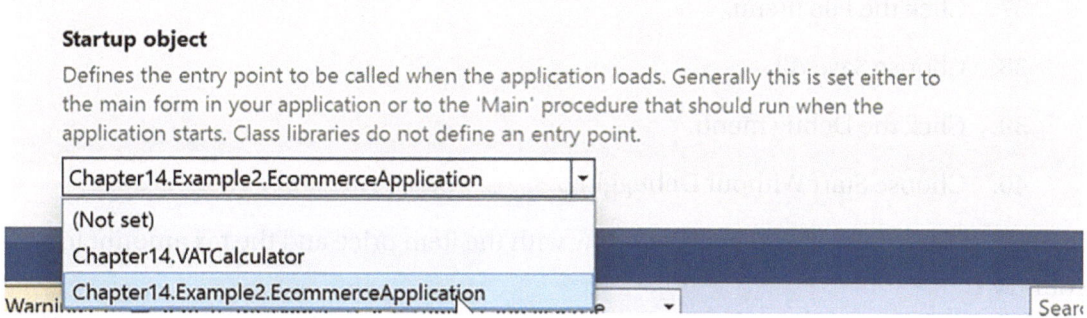

Startup object

Defines the entry point to be called when the application loads. Generally this is set either to the main form in your application or to the 'Main' procedure that should run when the application starts. Class libraries do not define an entry point.

```
Chapter14.Example2.EcommerceApplication        ▼
```
(Not set)
Chapter14.VATCalculator
Chapter14.Example2.EcommerceApplication

Warni...   Sear

Figure 14-6. *Changing the startup class in the C# project*

35. Amend the EcommerceApplication class code to have it instantiate the CountryOne class, as in Listing 14-26.

Listing 14-26. Instantiate the CountryOne class using the default constructor

```
static void Main(string[] args)
{
    double itemPrice = 100.00;

    CountryOne myCountryOne = new CountryOne();

} // End of Main() method
```

36. Amend the EcommerceApplication class code to have it display a message that includes a call to the method in the CountryOne class, as in Listing 14-27.

Listing 14-27. Display details of the item for CountryOne class

```
static void Main(string[] args)
{
    double itemPrice = 100.00;

    CountryOne myCountryOne = new CountryOne();

    Console.WriteLine($"The tax on an item of price £{itemPrice} is
    £{myCountryOne.TaxCalculation(itemPrice)}");
} // End of Main() method
```

37.   Click the File menu.

38.   Choose Save All.

39.   Click the Debug menu.

40.   Choose Start Without Debugging.

Figure 14-7 shows the console window with the item price and the tax amount for country 1.

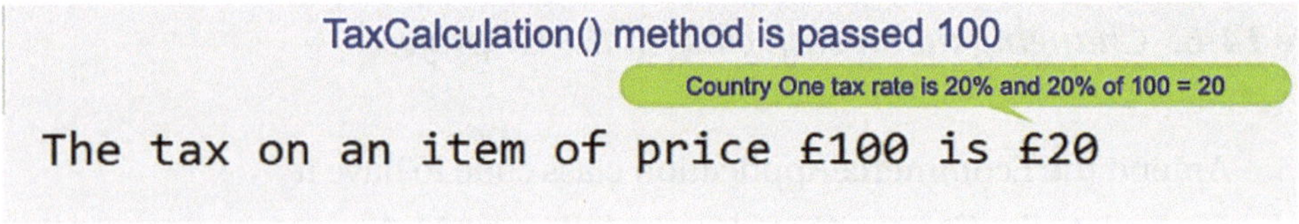

> TaxCalculation() method is passed 100
>
> Country One tax rate is 20% and 20% of 100 = 20
>
> The tax on an item of price £100 is £20

Figure 14-7. CountryOne output from the method

41.   Press the Enter key to close the console window.

42.   Amend the EcommerceApplication class code to have it instantiate the CountryTwo and CountryThree classes, as in Listing 14-28.

Listing 14-28. Instantiate the CountryTwo and CountryThree classes

```
static void Main(string[] args)
{
   double itemPrice = 100.00;

   CountryOne myCountryOne = new CountryOne();
   CountryTwo myCountryTwo = new CountryTwo();
   CountryThree myCountryThree = new CountryThree();
```

43.   Amend the EcommerceApplication class code to have it display messages that include calls to the methods in the CountryTwo and CountryThree classes, as in Listing 14-29.

Listing 14-29. Display details of the item for CountryTwo and CountryThree

```
CountryOne myCountryOne = new CountryOne();
CountryTwo myCountryTwo = new CountryTwo();
CountryThree myCountryThree = new CountryThree();

Console.WriteLine($"The tax on an item of price " +
$"£{itemPrice} is £{ myCountryOne.TaxCalculation(itemPrice)}");
```

```
Console.WriteLine($"The tax on an item of price £{itemPrice} is
£{myCountryOne.TaxCalculation(itemPrice)}");
```

Console.WriteLine($"The tax on an item of price £{itemPrice} is
£{myCountryTwo.TaxCalculation(itemPrice)}");

Console.WriteLine($"The tax on an item of price £{itemPrice} is
£{myCountryThree.TaxCalculation(itemPrice)}");
```
    } // End of Main() method
```

44.   Click the File menu.

45.   Choose Save All.

46.   Click the Debug menu.

47.   Choose Start Without Debugging.

The console window will appear, as Figure 14-8, and show the item price and the tax amount for each of the three countries.

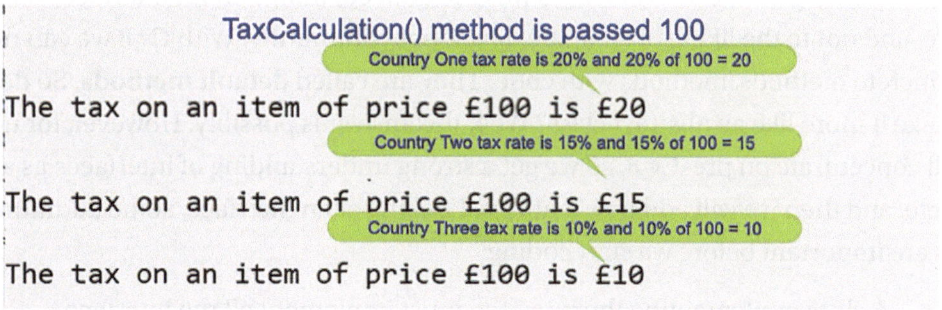

Figure 14-8. *All three methods, one from each class, have run.*

48.   Press the Enter key to close the console window.

Concept of an Interface

We have just used abstract classes, and we will now see that an interface is similar to an abstract class and is also used with abstraction and inheritance. There are some differences, however, and interfaces have the following characteristics:

- They are marked with the **interface** keyword.

- They contain one or more incomplete methods called interface methods, **but we do not use the keyword abstract as the compiler would complain.**

- They provide the signature or declaration of the abstract methods; they leave the implementation of these methods to the **class that implements the interface.**

- They **cannot be instantiated** as they are incomplete and they are interfaces.

- From C# 8 an interface **can have static members**, for example, vatRate = 0.25. This means that the vatRate member can be called directly from the interface without having an instantiation.

Now the interesting one. If we have used or read about C# interfaces compared with abstract classes up to C# 7, then we may have read the following statement:

They cannot have concrete methods, that is, methods with a body.

Yes, that message could probably be embedded in our inner mind, but, like all things, they change. Indeed, when C# 8 was introduced, things about interfaces did change, and not to the liking of all in the developer community. With C# 8 we can now add concrete methods, methods with code. They are called **default methods**. So does this make it more like an abstract class? Well, the answer is possibly. However, for now, we will concentrate on pre–C# 8, so we get a strong understanding of interfaces as a concrete, and then we will add new features. Looking at an interface, some additional points are important before we start coding:

- A class implementing the interface must implement all the interface methods in the interface class.

- They can be used for multiple inheritance. In other words, if we have an EcommerceBilling interface class and an EcommercePayment interface class, then a derived class such as CountryOne could implement both of these interfaces:

```
public class CountryOne : IEcommerceBilling, IEcommercePayment
```

This line works as we can implement more than one interface. Looking back at the example we had earlier in the abstract class, we can now show how we could do the same thing using an interface.

Example

The manager gives three of their staff the same instructions in following a task: "Use this **interface** when you write your class."

The interface is supplied as in Listing 14-30.

Listing 14-30. Sample interface from manager

```
// Interface
interface IEcommerceBilling
{
  // Abstract method in interface but no keyword abstract
  double TaxCalculation(double itemPrice);
}
```

Now that the three developers have been given the interface, what might they do with it when they write their code?

Developer 1 writes the CountryOne class, which inherits from the IEcommerceBilling interface as in Listing 14-31.

Listing 14-31. Developer 1's implementation of the interface

```
class CountryOne : IEcommerceBilling
{
  public double TaxCalculation(double itemPrice)
  {
    return itemPrice * 0.2;
  } // End of TaxCalculation() method
} // End of CountryOne class
```

Developer 2 writes the CountryTwo class, which inherits from the IEcommerceBilling interface as in Listing 14-32.

Listing 14-32. Developer 2's implementation of the interface

```
class CountryTwo : IEcommerceBilling
{
  public double TaxCalculation(double itemPrice)
  {
    return itemPrice * 0.15;
  } // End of TaxCalculation() method
} // End of CountryTwo class
```

Developer 3 writes the CountryThree class, which inherits from the IEcommerceBilling interface as in Listing 14-33.

Listing 14-33. Developer 3's implementation of the interface

```
class CountryThree : IEcommerceBilling
{
  public double TaxCalculation(double itemPrice)
  {
    return itemPrice * 0.10;
  } // End of taxCalculation() method
} // End of CountryThree class
```

All three classes have been developed by implementing the IEcommerceBilling interface, and therefore they are **contracted** to use the method called TaxCalculation(), which has a parameter of type double. Here, all three developers have written their classes and implemented the method as contracted to do so, but they have different business logic appropriate for their country, that is, 20%, 15%, or 10% is used depending on the developer and their country. This is like the "manager" giving the instructions and the employees implementing them, but with different business logic.

Brilliant! We have now seen that an interface or an abstract class can be developed to have method signatures with a return type stated. What we should also see from the example code is that we are using an **interface.** The preceding classes, CountryOne, CountryTwo, and CountryThree, are all concrete classes.

Add a **new folder** to the Chapter 14 project to hold the code for this example.

1. Right-click the Chapter14 project name.

2. Choose Add.

3. Choose New Folder.

4. Name the folder Example3Interfaces.

5. Right-click the Example3Interfaces folder.

6. Choose Add.

7. Choose New Item.

8. Choose Interface.

9. Name the class IEcommerceBilling.cs.

10. Click the Add button.

We are using the letter I to make it easy to see that this "class" is an interface. The use of an I as the initial letter is not essential, but the initial letter I will be used by many developers. Indeed, in the C# documentation, there are plenty of examples where the Microsoft developers have used the I to name an interface:

- In the TextWriter class documentation, we are told that it represents a writer that can write a sequential series of characters, that it is abstract, and that it implements **IDisposable** and **IAsyncDisposable.**

- In the String class documentation, we are told that the String represents text as a sequence of UTF-16 code units and that it implements **IEnumerable<Char>, IEnumerable, IComparable, IComparable<String>, IConvertible, IEquatable<String>,** and **ICloneable.**

Now continuing the example, we will see the **IEcommerceBilling.cs** class code will appear in the editor window and will be similar to Listing 14-34. Note the word **interface.**

Listing 14-34. New interface template code

```
namespace Chapter14.Example3Interfaces
{
  internal interface IEcommerceBilling
```

```
{

} // End of IEcommerceBilling interface
} // End of Chapter14.Example3Interfaces namespace
```

11. Amend the code, as in Listing 14-35, to add an "abstract method,"
     which means a return type and a signature.

Listing 14-35. New interface with an interface method

```
internal interface IEcommerceBilling
{
    // interface method
    double TaxCalculation(double itemPrice);

} // End of IEcommerceBilling interface
```

This will mean that any class using this interface will have to implement the
TaxCalculation() method by adding code to it.

Make the concrete classes, which have to inherit from the interface.

12. Right-click the project Example3Interfaces folder in the Solution
     Explorer panel.

13. Choose Add.

14. Choose Class.

15. Name the class as CountryOne.cs.

16. Click the Add button.

17. Amend the CountryOne class code, as in Listing 14-36, to have
     it inherit the IEcommerceBilling class and then implement the
     method with some code specific to this country's tax rate for
     the item.

Listing 14-36. Country 1 class inherits the interface and implements the method

```
namespace Chapter14.Example3Interfaces
{
    internal class CountryOne : IEcommerceBilling
```

```
  {
    public double TaxCalculation(double itemPrice)
    {
      return itemPrice * 0.2;
    } // End of taxCalculation() method

  } // End of CountryOne class
} // End of Chapter14.Example3Interfaces namespace
```

18. Right-click the project Example3Interfaces folder in the Solution Explorer panel.

19. Choose Add.

20. Choose Class.

21. Name the class as CountryTwo.cs.

22. Amend the CountryTwo class code, as in Listing 14-37, to have it inherit the IEcommerceBilling class and then implement the method with some code specific to this country's tax rate for the item.

Listing 14-37. Country 2 class inherits the interface and implements the method

```
namespace Chapter14.Example3Interfaces
{
  internal class CountryTwo :IEcommerceBilling
  {
    public double TaxCalculation(double itemPrice)
    {
      return itemPrice * 0.15;
    } // End of TaxCalculation() method

  } // End of CountryTwo class
} // End of Chapter14.Example3Interfaces namespace
```

23. Right-click the Example3Interfaces folder in the Solution Explorer panel.

24. Choose Add.

25. Choose Class.

26. Name the class as CountryThree.cs.

27. Amend the CountryThree class code, as in Listing 14-38, to have it inherit the IEcommerceBilling class and then implement the method with some code specific to this country's tax rate for the item.

Listing 14-38. Country 3 class inherits the interface and implements the method

```
namespace Chapter14.Example3Interfaces
{
  internal class CountryThree :IEcommerceBilling
  {
    public double TaxCalculation(double itemPrice)
    {
      return itemPrice * 0.10;
    } // End of TaxCalculation() method

  } // End of CountryThree class
} // End of Chapter14.Example3Interfaces namespace
```

Now we will make the class that will contain the Main method and use the three country classes, which have inherited from the interface.

28. Right-click the Example3Interfaces folder in the Solution Explorer panel.

29. Choose Add.

30. Choose Class.

31. Name the class as EcommerceApplication.cs.

32. Amend the EcommerceApplication class code to have it contain a Main() method and one member of type double, which will hold a price for an item, as in Listing 14-39.

Listing 14-39. Class with a Main() method and one member

```
namespace Chapter14.Example3Interfaces
{
  internal class EcommerceApplication
  {
    static void Main(string[] args)
    {
      double itemPrice = 100.00;

    } // End of Main() method


  } // End of EcommerceApplication class
} // End of Chapter14.Example3Interfaces namespace
```

33. Right-click the Chapter14 project in the Solution Explorer panel.

34. Choose Properties from the pop-up menu.

35. Choose the Chapter14.Example3Interfaces.
     EcommerceApplication class in the Startup object drop-down list,
     as shown in Figure 14-9.

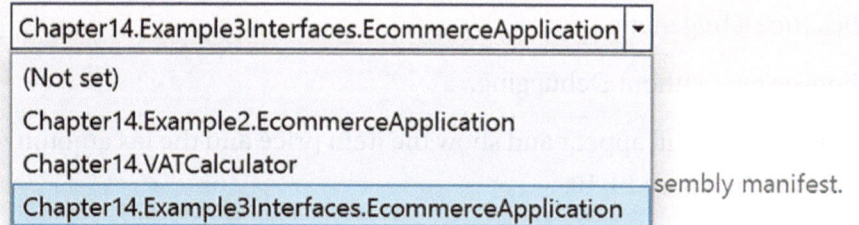

Startup object

Defines the entry point to be called when the application loads. Generally
this is set either to the main form in your application or to the 'Main'
procedure that should run when the application starts. Class libraries do not
define an entry point.

Chapter14.Example3Interfaces.EcommerceApplication ▾

(Not set)

Chapter14.Example2.EcommerceApplication

Chapter14.VATCalculator   sembly manifest.

Chapter14.Example3Interfaces.EcommerceApplication

Figure 14-9. *Changing the startup class in the C# project*

36. Amend the EcommerceApplication class code to have it
     instantiate the CountryOne class, as in Listing 14-40.

Listing 14-40. Instantiate the CountryOne class

```
static void Main(string[] args)
{
  double itemPrice = 100.00;

  CountryOne myCountryOne = new CountryOne();

} // End of Main() method
```

37.   Amend the EcommerceApplication class code to have it display
      a message that includes a call to the method in the CountryOne
      class, as in Listing 14-41.

Listing 14-41. Display details of the item for CountryOne class

```
static void Main(string[] args)
{
  double itemPrice = 100.00;

  CountryOne myCountryOne = new CountryOne();

  Console.WriteLine($"The tax on an item of price £{itemPrice} is
  £{myCountryOne.TaxCalculation(itemPrice)}");

} // End of Main() method
```

38.   Click the File menu.

39.   Choose Save All.

40.   Click the Debug menu.

41.   Choose Start Without Debugging.

The console window will appear and show the item price and the tax amount for
country 1, as shown in Figure 14-10.

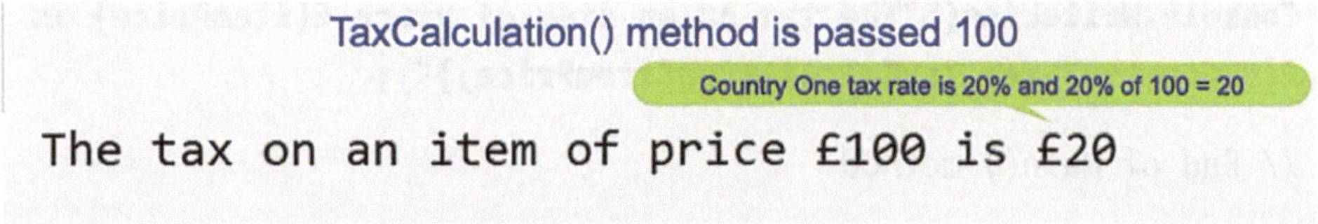

TaxCalculation() method is passed 100

Country One tax rate is 20% and 20% of 100 = 20

The tax on an item of price £100 is £20

Figure 14-10. *CountryOne output from the method*

42. Press the Enter key to close the console window.

43. Amend the EcommerceApplication class code to have it instantiate the CountryTwo and CountryThree classes, as in Listing 14-42.

Listing 14-42. Instantiate the CountryTwo and CountryThree classes

```
static void Main(string[] args)
{
  double itemPrice = 100.00;

  CountryOne myCountryOne = new CountryOne();
  CountryTwo myCountryTwo = new CountryTwo();
  CountryThree myCountryThree = new CountryThree();
```

44. Amend the EcommerceApplication class code to have it display messages that include calls to the methods in the CountryTwo and CountryThree classes, as in Listing 14-43.

Listing 14-43. Display details of the item for CountryTwo and CountryThree

```
CountryOne myCountryOne = new CountryOne();
CountryTwo myCountryTwo = new CountryTwo();
CountryThree myCountryThree = new CountryThree();

Console.WriteLine($"The tax on an item of price £{itemPrice} is
£{myCountryOne.TaxCalculation(itemPrice)}");

    Console.WriteLine($"The tax on an item of price £{itemPrice} is
    £{myCountryTwo.TaxCalculation(itemPrice)}");
```

```
Console.WriteLine($"The tax on an item of price £{itemPrice} is
£{myCountryThree.TaxCalculation(itemPrice)}");
} // End of Main() method
```

45.   Click the File menu.

46.   Choose Save All.

47.   Click the Debug menu.

48.   Choose Start Without Debugging.

The console window will appear, as Figure 14-11, and show the item price and the tax amount for each of the three countries.

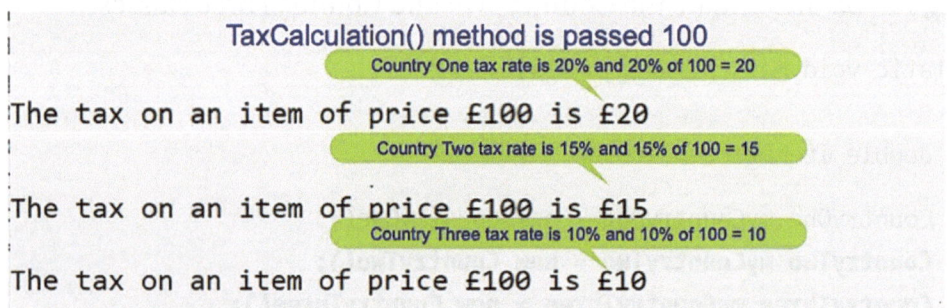

Figure 14-11.   *All three methods, one from each class, have run*

49.   Press the Enter key to close the console window.

Implementing Multiple Interfaces

When using interfaces, it is possible to implement multiple of them. In other words, if we have an IEcommerceBilling interface and an IEcommercePayment interface, then a class such as CountryOne could implement both of these interfaces. The syntax for this multiple inheritance would be

```
public class CountryOne : IEcommerceBilling, IEcommercePayment
```

So we will now code this and ensure that we can see the implementation of multiple interfaces by classes. The new IEcommercePayment interface will have three interface methods that will be used in the CountryOne class to calculate the extra charge on a transaction based on the card type and the transaction amount. There are only two card types for this example, credit card or debit card:

- The first method will accept the card type and the transaction amount and pass the transaction amount to either the credit card payment method or the debit card payment method and return the additional fee value to the calling method.

- The second method will be for the debit card payment fee, which will calculate 1%, 0.01, of the transaction amount and return the value to the calling method.

- The third method will be for the credit card payment fee, which will calculate 2%, 0.02, of the transaction amount and return the value to the calling method.

Create a second interface.

1. Right-click the **Example3Interfaces** folder.

2. Choose Add.

3. Choose New Item.

4. Choose Interface.

5. Name the interface IEcommercePayment.cs.

6. Click the Add button.

The IEcommercePayment.cs class code will appear in the editor window and will be similar to Listing 14-44. Note the word interface.

Listing 14-44. Interface template code

```
namespace Chapter14.Example3Interfaces
{
  internal interface IEcommercePayment
  {
  } // End of IEcommercePayment interface
} // End of Chapter14.Example3Interfaces namespace
```

7. Amend the code, as in Listing 14-45, to add the "abstract methods," which means a return type and a signature.

Listing 14-45. New interface with interface methods

```
namespace Chapter14.Example3Interfaces
{
  internal interface IEcommercePayment
  {
    // interface methods
    double PaymentMethod(String paymentType,
    double transactionAmount);
    double DebitCardPaymentFee(double debitAmount);
    double CreditCardPaymentFee(double creditAmount);

  } // End of IEcommercePayment interface
} // End of Chapter14.Example3Interfaces namespace
```

This will mean that any class implementing this interface will have to implement all three of the interface methods by adding code to them.

Make the concrete class CountryOne inherit from this interface.

8. Open the CountryOne class, which is in the **Example3Interfaces** folder.

9. Amend the CountryOne class code to have it inherit this new interface IEcommercePayment, as well as the original IEcommerceBilling interface, and then implement the methods with some code specific to this country, as in Listing 14-46.

Listing 14-46. Multiple inheritance and implementing all abstract methods

```
namespace Chapter14.Example3Interfaces
{
 internal class CountryOne : IEcommerceBilling, IEcommercePayment
  {
    public double TaxCalculation(double itemPrice)
    {
      return itemPrice * 0.2;
```

```
    } // End of taxCalculation() method

  public double PaymentMethod(String paymentType, double
     transactionAmount)
  {
    double cardFee;

    if (paymentType.Equals("Debit"))
    {
      cardFee = DebitCardPaymentFee(transactionAmount);
    } // End of if block
    else
    {
      cardFee = CreditCardPaymentFee(transactionAmount);
    }// End of else block

    return cardFee;
  } // End of paymentMethod() method

  public double DebitCardPaymentFee(double debitAmount)
  {
    return debitAmount * 0.01; // 1%
  } // End of debitCardPaymentFee() method

  public double CreditCardPaymentFee(double creditAmount)
  {
    return creditAmount * 0.02; // 2%
  } // End of creditCardPaymentFee() method

  } // End of CountryOne class
} // End of Chapter14.Example3Interfaces namespace
```

10.   Open the EcommerceApplication class, which is in the
      Example3Interfaces folder.

In the EcommerceApplication class, we will now

- Add a variable of type double called feeForUsingACard, which
  will hold the value passed back from the payment method in the
  CountryOne class.

- Call the PaymentMethod() method in the CountryOne concrete class, passing to it a credit card and an amount of 200.

- Display the returned fee amount from the method call. In this example for a credit card in this country, there is a 2% fee, so we should expect to get back 2% of 100, which is 2.

11. Amend the code, as in Listing 14-47.

Listing 14-47. Add a variable, calling the payment method from the class

```
static void Main(string[] args)
{
  double itemPrice = 100.00;
  double feeForUsingACard;

  CountryOne myCountryOne = new CountryOne();
  CountryTwo myCountryTwo = new CountryTwo();
  CountryThree myCountryThree = new CountryThree();

  Console.WriteLine($"The tax on an item of price " +
  $"£{itemPrice} is £{ myCountryOne.TaxCalculation(itemPrice)}");

  Console.WriteLine($"The tax on an item of price " +
  $"£{itemPrice} is £{ myCountryTwo.TaxCalculation(itemPrice)}");

  Console.WriteLine($"The tax on an item of price " +
  $"£{itemPrice} is £{ myCountryThree.TaxCalculation(itemPrice)}");

  feeForUsingACard = myCountryOne.PaymentMethod("Credit", itemPrice);

  Console.WriteLine($"The fee for using this card with this transaction
  amount is £{feeForUsingACard: 0.00}");

  } // End of Main() method
```

12. Click the File menu.

13. Choose Save All.

14. Click the Debug menu.

15. Choose Start Without Debugging.

The console window will appear as shown in Figure 14-12 and the card fee of 2.00 will be displayed.

```
The tax on an item of price £100 is £20
The tax on an item of price £100 is £15
The tax on an item of price £100 is £10
The fee for using this card with this transaction amount is £ 2.00
```

Credit card transaction fee = 2% of 100 = 2.00

Figure 14-12. *Card fee for CountryOne calculated*

16.   Press the Enter key to close the console window.

This is great. We have coded a nice example that has allowed us to use implementation of more than one interface.

As an extension to this example, we will code for the CountryTwo and CountryThree classes, so they inherit the IEcommercePayment interface, as in Listings 14-46 and 14-47. This is really the same process we used when CountryOne inherited the interface. The main difference would be using different percentage rates in each class if that was required:

- **For CountryTwo, the rates might be as follows:**

  - Debit card payment fee of 1.5%, 0.015, of the transaction amount

  - Credit card payment fee of 2.5%, 0.025, of the transaction amount

- **For CountryThree, the rates might be as follows:**

  - Debit card payment fee of 2.0%, 0.02, of the transaction amount

  - Credit card payment fee of 3.0%, 0.03, of the transaction amount

17.   Amend the code for the CountryTwo class, which is in the **Example3Interfaces** folder, as shown in Listing 14-48.

Listing 14-48. CountryTwo inheriting the interfaces and implementing methods

```
namespace Chapter14.Example3Interfaces
{
  internal class CountryTwo : IEcommerceBilling,IEcommercePayment
  {
    public double TaxCalculation(double itemPrice)
    {
```

```
      return itemPrice * 0.15;
    } // End of TaxCalculation() method

  public double PaymentMethod(String paymentType, double
  transactionAmount)
  {
    double cardFee;

    if (paymentType.Equals("Debit"))
    {
      cardFee = DebitCardPaymentFee(transactionAmount);
    } // End of if block
    else
    {
      cardFee = CreditCardPaymentFee(transactionAmount);
    }// End of else block

    return cardFee;
  } // End of PaymentMethod() method

  public double DebitCardPaymentFee(double debitAmount)
  {
    return debitAmount * 0.015; // 1.5%
  } // End of DebitCardPaymentFee() method

  public double CreditCardPaymentFee(double creditAmount)
  {
    return creditAmount * 0.025; // 2.5%
  } // End of CreditCardPaymentFee() method

  } // End of CountryTwo class
} // End of Chapter14.Example3Interfaces namespace
```

18. Amend the code for the CountryThree class, which is in the
    Example3Interfaces folder, as shown in Listing 14-49.

Listing 14-49. CountryThree inheriting the interfaces and implementing methods

```
namespace Chapter14.Example3Interfaces
{
  internal class CountryThree :IEcommerceBilling, IEcommercePayment
  {
    public double TaxCalculation(double itemPrice)
    {
      return itemPrice * 0.10;
    } // End of TaxCalculation() method

    public double PaymentMethod(String paymentType, double
    transactionAmount)
    {
      double cardFee;

      if (paymentType.Equals("Debit"))
      {
        cardFee = DebitCardPaymentFee(transactionAmount);
      } // End of if block
      else
      {
        cardFee = CreditCardPaymentFee(transactionAmount);
      }// End of else block

      return cardFee;
    } // End of PaymentMethod() method

    public double DebitCardPaymentFee(double debitAmount)
    {
      return debitAmount * 0.02; // 2%
    } // End of DebitCardPaymentFee() method

    public double CreditCardPaymentFee(double creditAmount)
    {
      return creditAmount * 0.03; // 3%
    } // End of CreditCardPaymentFee() method
```

```
} // End of CountryThree class
} // End of Chapter14.Example3Interfaces namespace
```

19. Open the EcommerceApplication class, which is in the
    Example3Interfaces folder.

20. Amend the code, as in Listing 14-50, to call the PaymentMethod()
    methods from the CountryTwo and CountryThree concrete
    classes, passing to them a credit card and an amount of 200, and
    have it display the returned fee amounts from each call.

For a credit card for CountryTwo, there is a 2.5% fee, so we should expect to get back
2.5% of 100, which is 2.5.

For a credit card for CountryThree, there is a 3.0% fee, so we should expect to get
back 3.0% of 100, which is 3.

Listing 14-50. EcommerceApplication card fee calls

```
feeForUsingACard = myCountryOne.PaymentMethod("Credit", itemPrice);

        Console.WriteLine($"The fee for using this card with this transaction
        amount is £{feeForUsingACard: 0.00}");

        feeForUsingACard = myCountryTwo.PaymentMethod("Credit", itemPrice);

        Console.WriteLine($"The fee for using this card with this transaction
        amount is £{feeForUsingACard: 0.00}");

        feeForUsingACard = myCountryThree.PaymentMethod("Credit", itemPrice);

        Console.WriteLine($"The fee for using this card with this transaction
        amount is £{feeForUsingACard: 0.00}");

    } // End of Main() method
  } // End of EcommerceApplication class
} // End of Chapter14.Example3Interfaces namespace
```

21. Click the File menu.

22. Choose Save All.

23.   Click the Debug menu.

24.   Choose Start Without Debugging.

The console window will appear as shown in Figure 14-13, and the card fee for each of the three countries based on the business logic implemented in each of the three country classes is displayed.

```
The tax on an item of price £100 is £20
The tax on an item of price £100 is £15                              Credit card transaction fee = 2% of 100 = 2.00
The tax on an item of price £100 is £10
The fee for using this card with this transaction amount is £ 2.00   Credit card transaction fee = 2.5% of 100 = 2.50
The fee for using this card with this transaction amount is £ 2.50
The fee for using this card with this transaction amount is £ 3.00   Credit card transaction fee = 3% of 100 = 3.00
```

Figure 14-13. *Card fee for all countries calculated*

25.   Press the Enter key to close the console window.

This is fantastic! We have coded a nice example with two interfaces containing interface methods, and we have three different classes that implemented the interfaces and their interface methods.

As we conclude this chapter on abstract classes and interfaces, let us think about the manager concept again. The manager, the abstract class or interface, dictates what they require through their abstract methods; and the employees, the concrete classes, implement all the abstract methods by making them concrete. Brilliant!

Yes, the idea of an abstract class or interface is great, and we have seen that they work well in code. BUT what happens if CountryTwo does not have credit cards, only debit cards? Well, one solution would be that the CountryTwo class will not have an if construct and simply call the DebitCardPaymentFee() method, as in Listing 14-51. The CreditCardPaymentFee() method could be left as it is or changed to, for example, return 0.00 – after all, it is never called. The problem with this "fix" is that whether it is a credit or debit transaction, the debit fee is charged, so all in all a poor development solution. But it is here to illustrate that a problem has been found because this country code needs to be different.

Listing 14-51. CountryTwo class with no if construct

```
public double PaymentMethod(String paymentType, double transactionAmount)
    {
        double cardFee;
```

```
    cardFee = DebitCardPaymentFee(transactionAmount);
    return cardFee;
} // End of PaymentMethod() method
```

So the real issue is that because the "manager," the interface, has three methods and developer 2 is told to inherit the IEcommercePayment interface, they must implement all three methods, even though they will not be using one or more of the methods. It's a contract that cannot be broken.

But did we not read in Chapter 8 the following?

*There is a programming concept known as **YAGNI,** which stands for **You Ain't Going To Need It.***

Yes, we did read this. So how does the interface and class design we have just suggested for CountryTwo fit with this concept? **It doesn't is the simple answer.** Now, how can we get around the YAGNI for developer 2 and their country 2 class? It is a strange but simplistic solution in which we develop interfaces with only one interface method and the implementing classes can then choose which interfaces they wish to implement. For developer 2 and their CountryTwo 2, they might follow a process similar to the following example.

Add a new folder to the Chapter14 project to hold the code for this example.

1. Right-click the solution Chapter14 project name.

2. Choose Add.

3. Choose New Folder.

4. Name the folder Example4Interfaces**.**

IEcommerceBilling Interface

We will now add a new interface, which will have only one interface method. As we do this example, we can copy and paste the relevant code from the existing interface from the Example3Interfaces project and simply change references from Example3 to Example4.

5. Right-click the Example4Interfaces folder.

6. Choose Add.

7. Choose New Item.

8.   Choose Interface.

9.   Name the interface IEcommerceBilling.cs.

10.   Click the Add button.

The IEcommerceBilling.cs class code will appear in the editor window.

11.   Amend the code to have the one interface method, as in Listing 14-52.

Listing 14-52.   Interface with only one interface method

```
namespace Chapter14.Example4Interfaces
{
  internal interface IEcommerceBilling
  {
    // interface method
    double TaxCalculation(double itemPrice);
  } // End of IEcommerceBilling interface
} // End of Chapter14.Example4Interfaces namespace
```

IPaymentMethod Interface

Add a new interface for the payment method, which has only one interface method.

1.   Right-click the Example4Interfaces folder.

2.   Choose Add.

3.   Choose New Item.

4.   Choose Interface.

5.   Name the interface IPaymentMethod.cs.

6.   Click the Add button.

The IPaymentMethod.cs class code will appear in the editor window.

7.   Amend the code to have the one interface method, as in Listing 14-53.

Listing 14-53. Interface with only one interface method

```
namespace Chapter14.Example4Interfaces
{
  internal interface IPaymentMethod
  {
    // Interface methods
    double PaymentMethod(String paymentType, double transactionAmount);
  } // End of IPaymentMethod interface
} // End of Chapter14.Example4Interfaces namespace
```

IDebitCardPayment Interface

Add a new interface for the debit card payment method, which has only one interface method.

8. Right-click the Example4Interfaces folder.

9. Choose Add.

10. Choose New Item.

11. Choose Interface.

12. Name the interface IDebitCardPayment.cs.

13. Click the Add button.

The IDebitCardPayment.cs class code will appear in the editor window.

14. Amend the code to have the one interface method, as in Listing 14-54.

Listing 14-54. Interface with only one interface method

```
namespace Chapter14.Example4Interfaces
{
  internal interface IDebitCardPayment
  {
    // Interface methods
    double DebitCardPaymentFee(double debitAmount);

  } // End of IDebitCardPayment interface
} // End of Chapter14.Example4Interfaces namespace
```

ICreditCardPayment Interface

Add a new interface for the credit card payment method, which has only one interface method.

15. Right-click the Example4Interfaces folder.

16. Choose Add.

17. Choose New Item.

18. Choose Interface.

19. Name the interface ICreditCardPayment.cs.

20. Click the Add button.

The ICreditCardPayment.cs class code will appear in the editor window.

21. Amend the code to have the one interface method, as in Listing 14-55.

Listing 14-55. Interface with only one interface method

```
namespace Chapter14.Example4Interfaces
{
  internal interface ICreditCardPayment
  {
    // interface method
    double CreditCardPaymentFee(double creditAmount);

  } // End of ICreditCardPayment interface
} // End of Chapter14.Example4Interfaces namespace
```

Now we have four interfaces, each with only one abstract method, and our concrete classes can now select which of the interfaces they wish to use. This will mean there is no need for a concrete class to have methods that it will not use. No more YAGNI.

Code the class CountryTwo.

22. Right-click the Example4Interfaces folder.

23. Choose Add.

24. Choose Class.

25.   Name the class CountryTwo.cs.

26.   Click the Add button.

This country does not have credit card payments, so it does not need to inherit the interface ICreditCardPayment. This concrete class will implement the abstract methods by adding code to the methods, making them concrete methods.

27.   Amend the code to implement the interface methods for the three interfaces that this class inherits from, as in Listing 14-56.

Listing 14-56. Implement the methods

```
namespace Chapter14.Example4Interfaces
{
  internal class CountryTwo : IEcommerceBilling,
                              IPaymentMethod, IDebitCardPayment
  {
    public double TaxCalculation(double itemPrice)
    {
      return itemPrice * 0.15;
    } // End of TaxCalculation() method

    public double PaymentMethod(String paymentType,
                                    double transactionAmount)
    {
      double cardFee;
      cardFee = DebitCardPaymentFee(transactionAmount);

      return cardFee;
    } // End of PaymentMethod() method

    public double DebitCardPaymentFee(double debitAmount)
    {
      return debitAmount * 0.02; // 2%
    } // End of DebitCardPaymentFee() method

  } // End of CountryTwo class

} // End of Chapter14.Example4Interfaces namespace
```

28.   Right-click the Example4Interfaces folder.

29.   Choose Add.

30.   Choose Class.

31.   Name the class as EcommerceApplication.cs.

We will now add the class containing the Main() method and call the PaymentMethod() method in the CountryTwo concrete class, passing it a debit card and an amount of 100, and have it display the returned fee amount. Before we run the application code, we should know what we expect as an answer. When using a debit card in this country, there is a 2% fee, so we should expect to get back 2% of 100, which is 2.

32.   Amend the EcommerceApplication class code, as in Listing 14-57.

Listing 14-57. Display the card fee

```
namespace Chapter14.Example4Interfaces
{
  internal class EcommerceApplication
  {
    static void Main(string[] args)
    {
      double itemPrice = 100.00;
      double feeForUsingACard;

      CountryTwo myCountryTwo = new CountryTwo();

      Console.WriteLine($"The tax on an item of price £{itemPrice} is
      £{myCountryTwo.TaxCalculation(itemPrice)}");

      feeForUsingACard = myCountryTwo.PaymentMethod("Debit", itemPrice);

      Console.WriteLine($"The fee for using this card with this transaction
      amount is £{feeForUsingACard: 0.00}");
    } // End of Main() method
  } // End of EcommerceApplication class
} // End of Chapter14.Example4Interfaces namespace
```

33. Right-click the Chapter14 project in the Solution Explorer panel.

34. Choose Properties from the pop-up menu.

35. Choose the Chapter14.Example4Interfaces.
EcommerceApplication class in the Startup object drop-down list,
as shown in Figure 14-14.

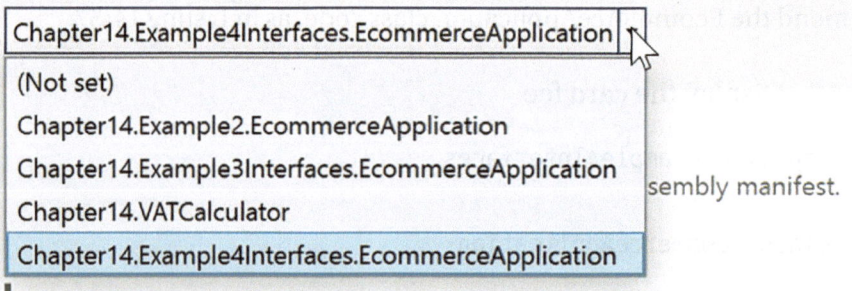

Startup object

Defines the entry point to be called when the application loads. Generally
this is set either to the main form in your application or to the 'Main'
procedure that should run when the application starts. Class libraries do not
define an entry point.

Chapter14.Example4Interfaces.EcommerceApplication

(Not set)

Chapter14.Example2.EcommerceApplication

Chapter14.Example3Interfaces.EcommerceApplication

Chapter14.VATCalculator

Chapter14.Example4Interfaces.EcommerceApplication

Figure 14-14. *Changing the startup class in the C# project*

36. Click the File menu.

37. Choose Save All.

38. Click the Debug menu.

39. Choose Start Without Debugging.

The console window will appear as Figure 14-15, and show the card fee of 2.00,
which we know is correct, because we did the calculation before we ran the code and
knew what the expected outcome should be. This 2.00 result is the same result as we got
from the previous code when we had not separated the abstract methods, as shown in
Figure 14-13, but now we have segregated our abstract methods in different interfaces.

```
The tax on an item of price £100 is £20
The tax on an item of price £100 is £15        Credit card transaction fee = 2% of 100 = 2.00
The tax on an item of price £100 is £10
The fee for using this card with this transaction amount is £ 2.00
```

Figure 14-15. *Card fee for country 2 calculated*

40.   Press the Enter key to close the console window.

Now we have a "solution", but in reality if we were to pass Credit to the CountryTwo
PaymentMethod() method, we would get the same result, which would not be what
we wanted. The correct solution would be to only have the IDebitCardPayment and
ICreditCardPayment interfaces and forget the IPaymentMethod interface. Then
CountryTwo only implements the IDebitCardPayment and cannot get access to the
ICreditCardPayment.

41.   Right-click the CountryTwo.cs file in the Example4Interfaces
      folder and choose Copy.

42.   Right-click the Example4Interfaces folder and choose paste.

43.   Rename the CountryTwo – Copy.cs file to CountryTwoDebit.cs.

44.   Amend the CountryTwoDebit.cs to remove the implementation of
      the IPaymentMethod as in Listing 14-58.

Listing 14-58. New CountryTwo class not implementing IPaymentMethod

```
namespace Chapter14.Example4Interfaces
{
  internal class CountryTwoDebit : IEcommerceBilling, IDebitCardPayment
  {
    public double TaxCalculation(double itemPrice)
    {
      return itemPrice * 0.15;
    } // End of TaxCalculation() method

    public double DebitCardPaymentFee(double debitAmount)
    {
      return debitAmount * 0.02; // 2%
    } // End of DebitCardPaymentFee() method

  } // End of CountryTwoDebit class

} // End of Chapter14.Example4Interfaces namespace
```

45. Amend the EcommerceApplication.cs code to add an additional variable called feeForUsingADebitCard, instantiate the new class, and call the method that calculates the fee, assigning the returned value to the variable we have created, as in Listing 14-59.

Listing 14-59. Instantiate the CountryTwoDebit class and find card fee

```
namespace Chapter14.Example4Interfaces
{
  internal class EcommerceApplication
  {
    static void Main(string[] args)
    {
      double itemPrice = 100.00;
      double feeForUsingACard, feeForUsingADebitCard;

      CountryTwo myCountryTwo = new CountryTwo();

      Console.WriteLine($"The tax on an item of price £{itemPrice} is
      £{myCountryTwo.TaxCalculation(itemPrice)}");

      feeForUsingACard = myCountryTwo.PaymentMethod("Debit", itemPrice);

      Console.WriteLine($"The fee for using this card with this transaction
      amount is £{feeForUsingACard: 0.00}");

      CountryTwoDebit myCountryTwoDebit = new CountryTwoDebit();

      feeForUsingADebitCard = myCountryTwoDebit.DebitCardPaymentFee
      (itemPrice);
      Console.WriteLine($"The fee for using a debit card with this
      transaction amount is £{feeForUsingADebitCard: 0.00}");
    } // End of Main() method

  } // End of EcommerceApplication class
} // End of Chapter14.Example4Interfaces namespace
```

46. Click the File menu.

47. Choose Save All.

48.   Click the Debug menu.

49.   Choose Start Without Debugging.

The console window will display the result as in Figure 14-16.

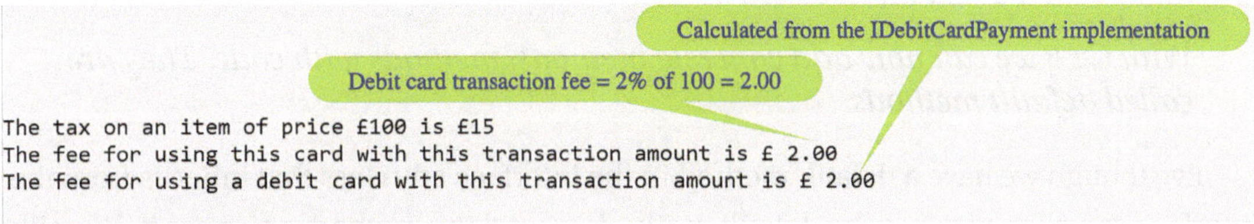

```
The tax on an item of price £100 is £15
The fee for using this card with this transaction amount is £ 2.00
The fee for using a debit card with this transaction amount is £ 2.00
```

Callout: Calculated from the IDebitCardPayment implementation

Callout: Debit card transaction fee = 2% of 100 = 2.00

Figure 14-16. *Card fee for CountryTwo calculated*

50.   Press the Enter key to close the console window.

We can now see that using segregation in our interfaces follows the same principle we read about when we dealt with methods and classes. In following this principle of segregation, we are writing clean code, avoiding issues around YAGNI, using the SOLID principles of interface segregation and single responsibility, and using another industry principle of programming to an interface.

Should we use an abstract class or an interface?

Whether we use an abstract class or an interface will depend on the needs we have or the application we are coding. As we have seen, abstract classes and interfaces are similar, but as we have seen there are differences, and it will be these differences that help us decide which is the best option. We need to consider a few things:

- An "abstract class" can have abstract methods and concrete methods.

    - We have seen that an abstract class contains abstract methods, but it can also contain concrete methods, therefore allowing classes that inherit from the abstract class to override or implement the methods.

    - On the other hand, we saw that an interface cannot contain concrete methods.

Do we want our class to implement from more than one "abstract class"?

- We have seen that a class can inherit only one abstract class.

- On the other hand, a class can inherit more than one interface – multiple inheritance.

But whoa! What did we read earlier?

With C# 8 we can now add concrete methods, methods with code. They are called default methods.

Eve though we have a default method in the interface any class that inherits from the interface can choose to use the default method, amend the method, or ignore it. We will now verify that it is possible to add a default method and see how this is implemented, or not, in a class.

Concept of Default Method in an Interface

We will now add a new folder to the project to hold the code for this example where we will code the interfaces with the default method.

1. Right-click the solution Chapter14 project name.

2. Choose Add.

3. Choose New Folder.

4. Name the folder Example5Interfaces.

IPolicy Interface

Now we will add a new interface containing interface methods.

5. Right-click the Example5Interfaces folder.

6. Choose Add.

7. Choose New Item.

8. Choose Interface.

9. Name the interface IPolicy.cs.

10. Click the Add button.

11. Amend the code to add the abstract methods and a default method, as in Listing 14-60.

Listing 14-60. Interface with abstract methods and a default method

```
namespace Chapter14.Example5Interfaces
{
  internal interface IPolicy
  {
    // abstract methods, method signature and return type
    void CreateAPolicy();
    void CloseAPolicy();

    // C# 8 allows us to have default implementations
    public void Print(string policyName)
    {
      Console.WriteLine($"The policy type created by the " +
        $"default interface implementation is {policyName}");
        }
  } // End of IPolicy interface

} // End of Chapter14.Example5Interfaces namespace
```

PolicyManager Class Inheriting from the IPolicy Interface

12. Right-click the Example5Interfaces folder.

13. Choose Add.

14. Choose Class.

15. Name the class PolicyManager.cs.

16. Click the Add button.

We will now have this PolicyManager class implement the IPolicy interface and make the abstract methods of the interface concrete, thereby ensuring the "contract" with the interface is applied.

17. Amend the code, as in Listing 14-61.

Listing 14-61. Concrete class implementing the abstract methods

```
namespace Chapter14.Example5Interfaces
{
internal class PolicyManager: IPolicy
{
// Implement the abstract method, make it a concrete method
public void CreateAPolicy()
{
        Console.WriteLine("Policy created");
} // End of CreateAPolicy() concrete method

// Implement the abstract method, make it a concrete method
public void CloseAPolicy()
{
        Console.WriteLine("Policy closed");
} // End of CloseAPolicy() concrete method

}//End of PolicyManager class that implements IPolicy interface

} // End of Chapter14.Example5Interfaces
```

Program Class with the Main() Method

18. Right-click the Example5Interfaces folder.

19. Choose Add.

20. Choose Class.

21. Name the class PolicyApplication.cs.

22. Click the Add button.

23. Amend the code to instantiate the PolicyManager class and call the concrete methods that we created in it as in Listing 14-62.

Listing 14-62. Main class, which uses the default method of the interface

```
namespace Chapter14.Example5Interfaces
{
  internal class PolicyApplication
  {
  public static void Main()
  {
    Console.WriteLine("C# 8 default methods in an Interface");

 // Instantiate the PolicyManager class
    IPolicy myPolicyManager = new PolicyManager();

 // Call the CreateAPolicy method from the PolicyManager instance
    myPolicyManager.CreateAPolicy();

 // Call the CloseAPolicy method from the PolicyManager instance
    myPolicyManager.CloseAPolicy();

 // Call the default method from the PolicyManager instance
    myPolicyManager.Print("Auto");

  } // End of Main() method

  } // End of PolicyApplication class
} // End of Chapter14.Example5Interfaces class
```

24. Right-click the Chapter14 project in the Solution Explorer panel.

25. Choose Properties from the pop-up menu.

26. Choose the Chapter14.Example5Interfaces.PolicyApplication class in the Startup object drop-down list, as shown in Figure 14-17.

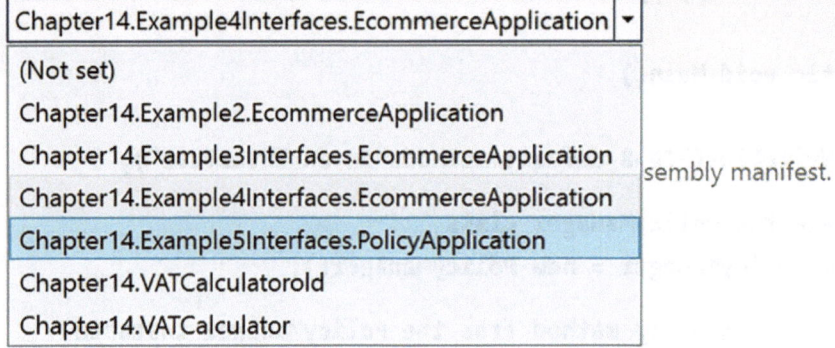

Startup object

Defines the entry point to be called when the application loads. Generally this is set
the main form in your application or to the 'Main' procedure that should run when
application starts. Class libraries do not define an entry point.

| Chapter14.Example4Interfaces.EcommerceApplication | ▾ |

| (Not set) |
| Chapter14.Example2.EcommerceApplication |
| Chapter14.Example3Interfaces.EcommerceApplication |
| Chapter14.Example4Interfaces.EcommerceApplication |
| Chapter14.Example5Interfaces.PolicyApplication |
| Chapter14.VATCalculatorold |
| Chapter14.VATCalculator |

sembly manifest.

Figure 14-17. *Set the startup project*

27. Click the File menu.

28. Choose Save All.

29. Click the Debug menu.

30. Choose Start Without Debugging.

The console window will appear, as shown in Figure 14-18, and display the message
from the default method of the interface.

> **myPolicyManager.Print("Auto");**
> **is using the Interface default method Print()**

```
C# 8 default methods in an Interface          The value passed to the default method of the Interface
Policy created
Policy closed
The policy type created by the overridden default interface method is Auto
```

Figure 14-18. *Default method of the interface has been executed*

31. Press the Enter key to close the console window.

The code has worked, and in the code line
```
IPolicy myPolicyManager = new PolicyManager();
```

we have used the interface IPolicy when instantiating, but what would happen if we were to use the PolicyManager class, which inherits from the IPolicy interface, and our code line would be

```
PolicyManager myPolicyManager = new PolicyManager
```

Well, let us see how this works out.

32. Amend the code to use PolicyManager rather than IPolicy, as shown in in Listing 14-63.

Listing 14-63. Instantiate using the class rather than the interface

```
public static void Main()
{
  Console.WriteLine("C# 8 default methods in an Interface");

  // Instantiate the PolicyManager class
  PolicyManager myPolicyManager = new PolicyManager();
```

We will see that we have a compile error in the amended code.

33. Hover over the red underline of the Print("Auto") in the line of code myPolicyManager.Print() as shown in Figure 14-19.

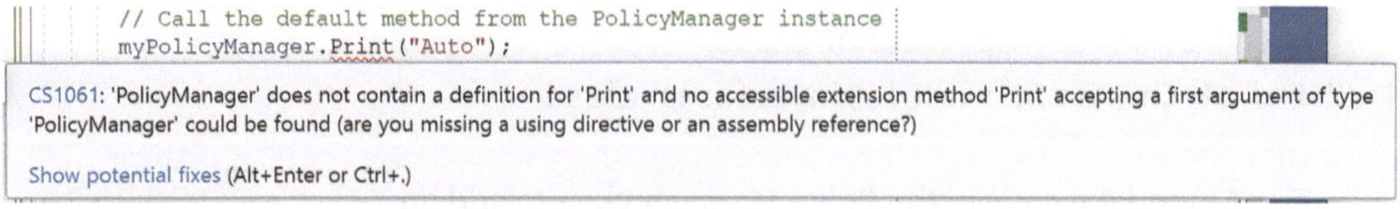

```
      // Call the default method from the PolicyManager instance
      myPolicyManager.Print("Auto");
```
CS1061: 'PolicyManager' does not contain a definition for 'Print' and no accessible extension method 'Print' accepting a first argument of type 'PolicyManager' could be found (are you missing a using directive or an assembly reference?)

Show potential fixes (Alt+Enter or Ctrl+.)

Figure 14-19. *Error, method not available*

The compile error tells us that the myPolicyManager object does not contain a Print() method. This is telling us that the default method is not accessible; in other words, the inherited class knows nothing about the default method of the interface. To make it accessible, we must use the interface, and we can achieve this in two different ways:

• We can go back to using the IPolicy in the instantiation:

```
// Instantiate the PolicyManager class
IPolicy myPolicyManager = new PolicyManager();
```

- We can **upcast** the myPolicyManager to an interface:

```
// Call the default method from the PolicyManager instance
 ((IPolicy)myPolicyManager).Print("Auto");
```

We will use the upcasting technique since we have not used this before with an interface. Upcasting follows the same principle as we used when casting with our data types. When we looked at casting in Chapter 7, we said

> *In C#, casting is a method used to convert one data type to another. Casting is used as an explicit conversion and tells the compiler what to do.*

34. Amend the code within the Main() method to use the upcasting, as shown in Listing 14-64.

Listing 14-64. Upcast the class to an interface

```
// Call the CloseAPolicy method from the PolicyManager instance
        myPolicyManager.CloseAPolicy();

// Call the default method from the PolicyManager instance
        ((IPolicy)myPolicyManager).Print("Auto");

    } // End of Main() method
  } // End of PolicyApplication class
} // End of Chapter14.Example5Interfaces class
```

35. Amend the code in the PolicyManager class to add an "overridden" version of the interface default method, as in Listing 14-65.

Listing 14-65. Override the default method of the interface

```
public void CloseAPolicy()
{
  Console.WriteLine("Policy closed");
} // End of CloseAPolicy() concrete method

/*
C# 8 allows us to have default implementations
*/
```

```
public void Print(string policyName)
{
 Console.WriteLine($"The policy type created by the overridden default
 interface method is {policyName }");
}

}//End of PolicyManager class that implements IPolicy interface
} // End of Chapter14.Example5Interfaces
```

36. Click the File menu.

37. Choose Save All.

38. Click the Debug menu.

39. Choose Start Without Debugging.

The console window will appear and show the message from the default method of the interface, as in Figure 14-20.

((IPolicy)myPolicyManager).Print("Auto")
is using the overridden version of the default method Print()

```
C# 8 default methods in an Interface
Policy created
Policy closed                    The overridden version is in the PolicyManager
The policy type created by the overridden default interface method is Auto
```

Figure 14-20. Default method has been overridden

40. Press the Enter key to close the console window.

We have seen that we can have a default implementation in our interface, but the class that implements the interface does not have to implement the default method – it is optional. When we talk about **"program to an interface"** as a design approach, we use the interface as our starting point. In using such a design approach, we will then have many classes that are dependent on the interface, and if we then decide to go back and amend the interface, we will impact all the dependent classes. So we would say that once the interface is designed, it is not open for amendments. However, as we have seen, C# 8 allows us to add default implementations to the interface, and this does not break any of the existing classes that implement the interface, since the default methods are optional. We therefore say that with C# 8 and above, the interface is expandable in terms of adding default methods.

Concept of Static Methods and Fields in an Interface

With C# 8 interfaces, we were introduced to another new feature in which we can have static members, methods, and fields. We read earlier the following:

Remember that static means belonging to the class or Interface.

So not only can a class have static members but an interface, from C# 8, can also have static members. We will now add a static member, field, to the IPolicy interface.

41. Amend the code, as in Listing 14-66, to declare a static field to the IPolicy interface that will be used to record the number of current policies.

Listing 14-66. Static field in an interface

```
using System;

namespace Chapter14.Example5Interfaces
{
  internal interface IPolicy
  {
    /*
    C# 8 allows us to have static members. Here we use a
    static field.
    Remember that static means belonging to the class or
    Interface.
    We can therefore call the methods and members of the
    interface directly.
    */
    static int policyCounter;
```

From within the Main() method, we will now call the policyCounter field directly from its location in the interface. We will call the policyCounter field twice, once when the policy is created and again when the policy is closed. The static nature of the field means there is only one version of the field; there is no copy made when the class is instantiated.

42.   Amend the PolicyApplication.cs class code, as in Listing 14-67.

Listing 14-67. Call the static field in an interface

```
using System;

namespace Chapter14.Example5Interfaces
{
  internal class PolicyApplication
  {
    public static void Main()
    {
      Console.WriteLine("C# 8 default methods in an Interface");

      // Instantiate the PolicyManager class
      PolicyManager myPolicyManager = new PolicyManager();

  // Call the CreateAPolicy method from the PolicyManager instance
      myPolicyManager.CreateAPolicy();

      // Increment the static policyCounter by 1
      IPolicy.policyCounter = IPolicy.policyCounter + 1;
      Console.WriteLine($"Policy created - there are now {IPolicy.
      policyCounter} policies");

  // Call the CloseAPolicy method from the PolicyManager instance
      myPolicyManager.CloseAPolicy();

      // Decrement the static policyCounter by 1
      IPolicy.policyCounter = IPolicy.policyCounter - 1;
      Console.WriteLine($"Policy closed - there are now {IPolicy.
      policyCounter} policies");

// Call the default method from the PolicyManager instance
      ((IPolicy)myPolicyManager).Print("Auto");

    } // End of Main() method

  } // End of Program class
} // End of Chapter14.Example5Interfaces class
```

43. Click the File menu.

44. Choose Save All.

45. Click the Debug menu.

46. Choose Start Without Debugging.

The console window will appear as shown in Figure 14-21. The console message shows that after the CreateAPolicy() method is called, we have one policy. Then the message shows that there are zero policies after the CloseAPolicy() method is called.

Figure 14-21. *Static field of the interface has been called.*

Chapter Summary

In this chapter we have tackled two large concepts, abstract classes and interfaces, and we have looked at the differences and similarities between them. We have also seen that since C# 8 the concept of an interface changed from being a template that could only have abstract methods to being capable of having default implementations with business logic. When creating a class that inherits from the interface with the default implementation, we do not have to use the default implementation, but if we do use it, we call it directly from the interface. In the previous chapter, we looked at classes and objects, and now we should appreciate that abstract classes and interfaces sit alongside classes. A class can decide to form a contract with an abstract class or interface, and then it will have to implement the abstract methods that are part of the contract. This has been a "big chapter" in terms of learning, but we are now really moving to coding at a higher level and seeing how applications are coded in the commercial world.

We are making fantastic progress in our programming of C# applications and we should be very proud of our achievements. In finishing this very important chapter, we have increased our knowledge further and we are advancing to our target.

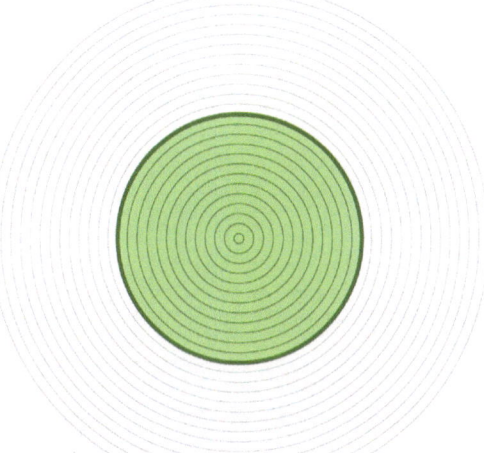

Our target is getting closer

CHAPTER 15

String Handling

String Handling and Manipulation

In the previous chapter, we gained knowledge of interfaces and abstract classes and their relationship with classes and objects. We saw that interfaces and abstract classes can be used to make classes have a consistency when they inherit from the interface or abstract class. We also read that many developers will program to an interface, showing that interfaces form an integral part of developing C# applications in a commercial environment.

In this chapter we will study in more detail the use of Strings and see how we can use and manipulate them within our C# code. Throughout our chapters we used Strings, and in many of our coding examples, we have seen how we can concatenate a string to another string or to a non-string data type, which has been converted to a string. When we look back to Chapter 6, we can see that string is not one of the primitive data types, whereas char is. So we know that String as a data type is special. Just look at the fact that we have used a capital S when writing it here. Having studied classes and objects in Chapter 13, we might also think that the capital S might suggest that it is a class, as classes by convention start with a capital letter. Indeed, we are correct in this assumption, and we would say that String is a class within .NET in the System namespace. The fully qualified name of the String class is `System.String,` and string in C# is a shortcut for System.String.

From the code we have already developed, we should be aware that strings are very important in C# applications, and we have taken strings and converted them to other data types so that they could be used in calculations. Such examples make us realize that not all data entered into our application will be as we require. Let us look at some examples to help us better understand this:

© Gerard Byrne 2022
G. Byrne, *Target C#*, https://doi.org/10.1007/978-1-4842-8619-7_15

- A customer may need to enter their personal details into an online form and submit the form so the data can be stored in a company database. However, the customer, like myself, might not be the best "typist" and may enter uppercase or lowercase or a mixture of cases when entering their details. Does the company really want to store this poorly formed string of data in its database? Probably not. In developing the code, we could convert the data to upper, to lower, or to proper case through our C# code, thereby standardizing the stored format.

- A customer may need to complete an online form and include their account number. As they enter their account number, they add an extra space at the start or end. In developing the code, we need to read this account number and check if it exists, before we let the customer see their account details. As the extra space is included, our code will not be able to match the account number. Our code must check for extra spaces at the start or end of a string and take appropriate action to correct the string.

- A customer may need to enter their credit card number, and it is known that this should be 16 digits with no spaces and in the correct format. As developers we need to check that there are 16 digits, not less or more, and in our code we will need to check that there is not a mixture of numbers and characters or even all characters.

- Data read from a text file might need to be dissected and parsed for various reasons such as getting the customer postcode or date of birth.

- Data being written to a database from our application needs to be validated, manipulated, and then written, to reduce the possibility of errors happening during the writing process.

In dealing with all the preceding situations, and many more, we can make use of string manipulation, yet another "tool" offered to us by .NET and one we will make good use of in many of our applications. The String class comes with its own methods and fields and we will now explore some of these. However, it is important to remember that all of the String methods and C# **operators that appear to modify a string actually return the results in a new string object**. We say that a string is *immutable.* Immutable means we cannot change the contents of a string, so what happens is that a new string object is created and the variable that pointed to the old string is now pointed to the new string object. Interestingly, if we think of strings in terms of memory usage and allocation, they are – to say the least – "poor."

Listing 15-1. Example string replacement

```
string accountNumber = "AB123456";
accountNumber = accountNumber.Replace("AB", "GB");
```

In Listing 15-1 we are trying to replace the characters AB with the characters GB in the string and assign the returned value to the string, but as the string accountNumber cannot be changed – it is immutable – a new string object is created and accountNumber is simply pointed to this new object in its new memory location, as shown in Figure 15-1.

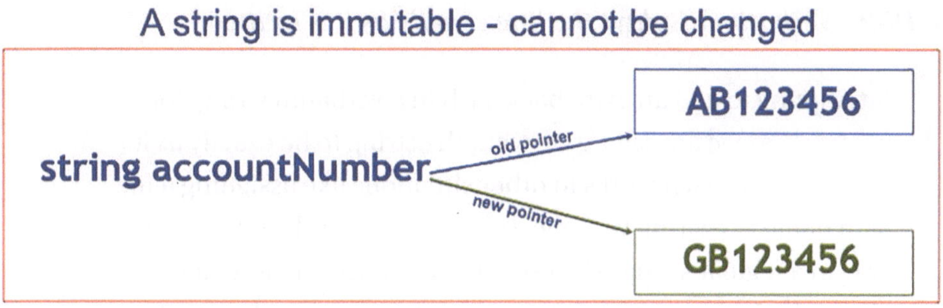

Figure 15-1. *Immutable string – new object is created*

String Literals

C# has two types of string literals, verbatim and regular strings:

- Verbatim string

  The first type of string literal is the verbatim string. When we create a verbatim string, there will be an @ symbol at the start of the string, informing the string constructor to ignore any escape characters and line breaks. Verbatim means exact, so when we use the @ symbol, we are saying, "Use the string exactly as it is written." We will see as we code examples in this chapter that escape characters are special characters, for example, \n represents a new line and \t represents a tab.

Listing 15-2. Example verbatim string

```
String  message = @"\n C# programming \t console applications";
Console.WriteLine(message);
```

> In Listing 15-2 the code includes the escape sequences \n and
> \t as part of the string, but they are not taken to mean new line
> and tab, because we have used the @ symbol. When the code is
> compiled and run, the output will be as shown in Figure 15-2.

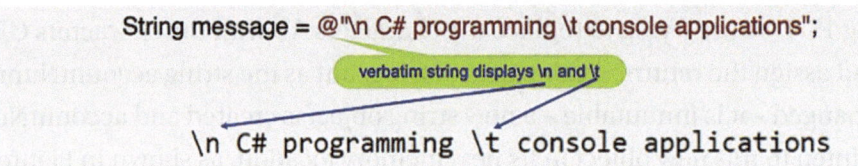

Figure 15-2. *Verbatim displays the line exactly as it is written*

> Attempting to add an extra backslash in a verbatim string does
> not work, as we are saying we want the string to be exactly as it
> is. The \\ approach works in other situations like assigning a file
> path name to a string variable, but it will not work with verbatim,
> only in a regular string. The escape sequences \\n and \\t in
> Listing 15-3 are part of the string, and the output will be as shown
> in Figure 15-3.

Listing 15-3. Example verbatim string using double backslash

```
String  message = @"\\n C# programming \\t console applications";
Console.WriteLine(message);
```

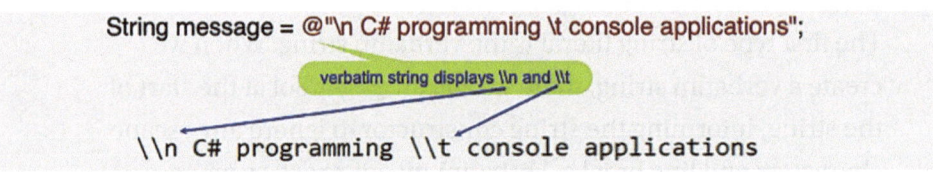

Figure 15-3. *Trying a double slash \\ does not work with verbatim*

- Regular string

    The second type of string literal is the regular string. When we create a regular string literal, it means the string will be read and special characters will need to be "escaped" with a \.

Listing 15-4. Example regular string

```
string message = "\n C# programming \t console applications";
Console.WriteLine(message);
```

The escape sequences \n and \t in Listing 15-4 are not taken as part of the string; they are to be taken to mean new line and tab. We have not used the verbatim symbol, @, so the output will be as shown in Figure 15-4.

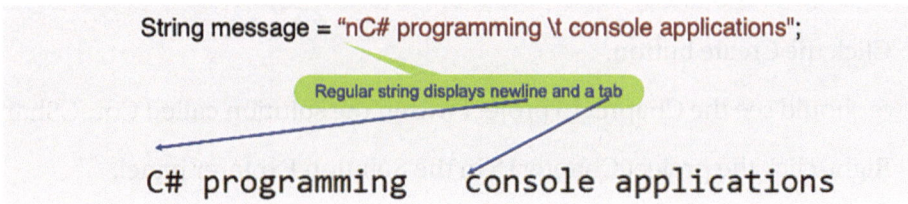

Figure 15-4. *Regular string*

If we want the \n and \t to be displayed when using a regular string, we use the \\, double backslash, as shown in Listing 15-5, and the output will be as shown in Figure 15-5.

Listing 15-5. Example regular string with double backslash

```
string message = "\\n C# programming \\t console applications";
Console.WriteLine(message);
```

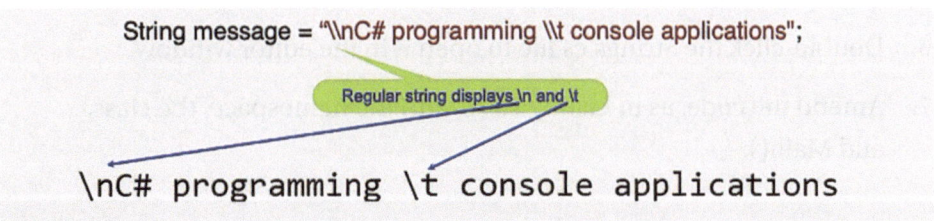

Figure 15-5. *Regular string with \\, a double backslash*

Let's code some C# and build our programming muscle.

Add a new project to hold the code for this chapter.

1. Right-click the solution CoreCSharp.

2. Choose Add.

3. Choose New Project.

4. Choose Console App from the listed templates that appear.

5. Click the Next button.

6. Name the project Chapter15 and leave it in the same location.

7. Click the Next button.

8. Choose the framework to be used, which in our projects will be .NET 6.0 or higher.

9. Click the Create button.

Now we should see the Chapter15 project within the solution called CoreCSharp.

10. Right-click the project Chapter15 in the Solution Explorer panel.

11. Click the Set as Startup Project option.

Notice how the Chapter15 project name has been made to have bold text, indicating that it is the new startup project and that it is the Program.cs file within it that will be executed when we run the debugging.

12. Right-click the Program.cs file in the Solution Explorer window.

13. Choose Rename.

14. Change the name to Strings.cs.

15. Press the Enter key.

16. Double-click the Strings.cs file to open it in the editor window.

17. Amend the code, as in Listing 15-6, with the namespace, the class, and Main().

Listing 15-6. Class with the Main() method

```
namespace Chapter15
{
  internal class Strings
  {
    static void Main(string[] args)
    {

    } // End of Main() method

  } // End of Strings class
} // End of Chapter15 namespace
```

We will now create code that uses String class methods and properties and demonstrates their use in practical examples. We will start with the Substring method.

Substring

The Substring() method has two forms that can be used:

- Substring(Int32 startposition)

  In this format the Substring method will retrieve a substring of the full string starting at the specified character position and continuing to the end of the string.

- Substring(Int32 startposition, Int32 length)

  In this format the Substring method will retrieve a substring starting at the specified character position and continuing for the specified number of characters as indicated by the length.

We will now create a string variable to hold a vehicle registration number. We will use the String data type, with a capital S, to emphasize the idea that we are dealing with a class. Remember we could use string or String.

1. Amend the code, as in Listing 15-7.

Listing 15-7. Set up a string and assign it a value

```
static void Main(string[] args)
{
  String myVehicleRegistration = "ZER 7890";
} // End of Main() method
```

We will now write the code to find the characters of the string from position 4 to the end of the string object.

2. Amend the code as in Listing 15-8.

Listing 15-8. Characters of the string starting at position 4

```
static void Main(string[] args)
{
  String myVehicleRegistration = "ZER 7890";

  /*
  Use the Substring() method to find the first string
  characters of the myVehicleRegistration string, starting
  at position 4 and reading to the end of the string.
  */
  Console.WriteLine("The characters from position 4 are: "
    + myVehicleRegistration.Substring(4));
```

3. Click the File menu.

4. Choose Save All.

5. Click the Debug menu.

6. Choose Start Without Debugging.

Figure 15-6 shows the console window displaying the characters of the zero-indexed string from position 4, the fifth element.

```
The characters from position 4 are: 7890

C:\CoreCSharp\CoreCSharp\Chapter15\bin\Debug\net6.0\Chapter15.exe
Press any key to close this window . . .
```

Figure 15-6. *Position 4 to the end of the string*

7.   Press the Enter key to close the console window.

Continuing with this code, we will add new code to demonstrate different string handling methods and features. We will add the code after the existing code, just above the end curly brace of the Main() method. We will continue now by coding the statements to find the characters from position 0 to position 2, the first three characters, of the myVehicleRegistration String object.

8.   Amend the code, as in Listing 15-9.

Listing 15-9. First three characters using Substring

```csharp
Console.WriteLine("The characters from position 4 are: "
  + myVehicleRegistration.Substring(4));

/*
Use the Substring() method to find the first 3 characters
of the myVehicleRegistration string.
Remember substring is inclusive of the char at the first
position but exclusive of the char at the end position we
say it is inclusive/exclusive
*/
Console.WriteLine("The first 3 characters are: "
  + myVehicleRegistration.Substring(0, 3));

  } // End of Main() method


  } // End of Strings class
} // End of Chapter15 namespace
```

9.   Click the File menu.

10. Choose Save All.

11. Click the Debug menu.

12. Choose Start Without Debugging.

Figure 15-7 shows the console window displaying the first three characters.

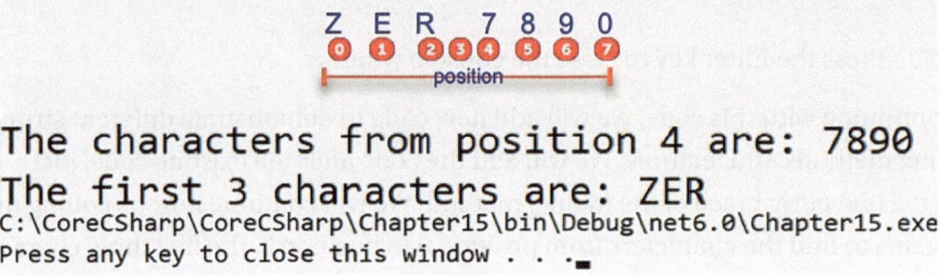

The characters from position 4 are: 7890
The first 3 characters are: ZER
C:\CoreCSharp\CoreCSharp\Chapter15\bin\Debug\net6.0\Chapter15.exe
Press any key to close this window . . .

Figure 15-7. *First three characters of the string*

13. Press the Enter key to close the console window.

Length

The Length property will return an integer that represents the number of char values in the string. The code behind the Length property will count spaces in the string as they are also characters.

1.   Amend the code to find the number of characters in the string called myVehicleRegistration, as in Listing 15-10.

Listing 15-10. Find the length of a string

```
Console.WriteLine("The first 3 characters are: "
  + myVehicleRegistration.Substring(0, 3));

/*
Use the Length property from the String class to find the
number of characters in the myVehicleRegistration object.
*/
```

```
Console.WriteLine("The number of characters is: "
    + myVehicleRegistration.Length);
```

```
} // End of Main() method
```

2. Click the File menu.

3. Choose Save All.

4. Click the Debug menu.

5. Choose Start Without Debugging.

Figure 15-8 shows the console window displaying the number of characters in the string as 8.

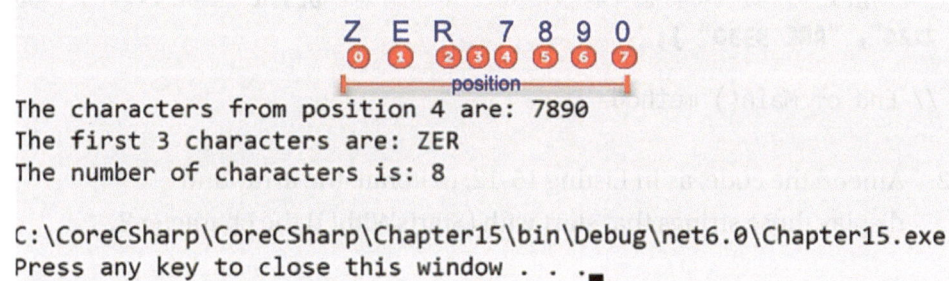

```
The characters from position 4 are: 7890
The first 3 characters are: ZER
The number of characters is: 8

C:\CoreCSharp\CoreCSharp\Chapter15\bin\Debug\net6.0\Chapter15.exe
Press any key to close this window . . .
```

***Figure 15-8.** The length of a string*

6. Press the Enter key to close the console window.

StartsWith()

In coding our insurance application, we might need to find a specific character or characters in a vehicle registration number since an accident involved a vehicle with the specific character(s). For this situation we could use the StartsWith() method. There are two forms of this method, method overloading, that we will use.

The StartsWith() method has two forms:

- StartsWith(Char)

  In this format the StartsWith() method will return a Boolean value of true or false, depending on whether the String object begins with the specific char or chars. The method starts at character 0.

605

- StartsWith(String)

    In this format the StartsWith() method will return a Boolean value
    of true or false, depending on whether the String object begins
    with the specific string. The method starts at character 0.

1. Amend the code, as in Listing 15-11, to add an array of strings.

Listing 15-11. Declare and create an array of strings

```
Console.WriteLine("The number of characters is: "
  + myVehicleRegistration.Length);

// Create an array of String objects
String[] myVehicleRegistrations = new String[] { "ZER 7890", "ZAC
7124", "ARC 3330" };

} // End of Main() method
```

2. Amend the code, as in Listing 15-12, to iterate the array and
   display those strings that start with (StartsWith()) the character Z.

Listing 15-12. Find strings that start with the character Z and display them

```
String[] myVehicleRegistrations = new String[] { "ZER 7890", "ZAC
7124", "ARC 3330" };

foreach (String registration in myVehicleRegistrations)
{
  if (registration.StartsWith('Z'))
  {
    Console.WriteLine(String.Format("\nThe registration {0} starts
    with the letter Z", registration));
  } // End of if block
  else
  {
    Console.WriteLine(String.Format("\nThe registration {0} does not
    start with the letter Z", registration));
```

```
    } // End of else block
   } // End of for each iteration

 } // End of Main() method
```

3. Click the File menu.

4. Choose Save All.

5. Click the Debug menu.

6. Choose Start Without Debugging.

Figure 15-9 shows the console window displaying each array member and stating if it begins with the character Z.

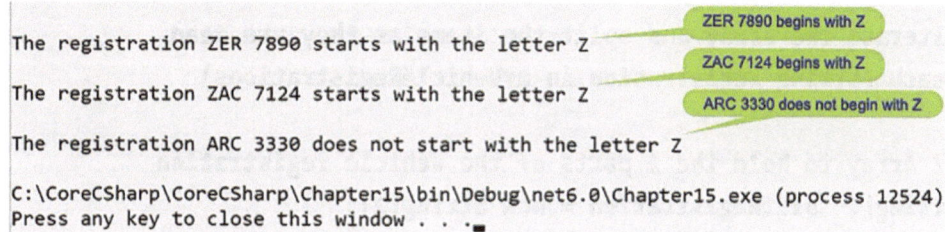

Figure 15-9. *Strings starting with Z*

7. Press the Enter key to close the console window.

Split()

In coding our insurance application, we might need to read a file or database, which contains data. The format of the file might be that each part is separated by a comma or a tab or a - or a space. We will need to find the data from within the file, and for this situation we could use the Split() method, which will split the data at the specified value. The Split() method will return an array of strings after it has split the string object at the specified expression. We will split each value in our registration array at the space, and we will put each of the parts of the split into a new array, which we will call splitRegistration. The Split() method has different options in the form of method overloads.

1. Amend the code, as in Listing 15-13.

Listing 15-13. Split the strings at the spaces

```
Console.WriteLine(String.Format("\nThe registration {0} starts with
the letter Z", registration));
} // End of if block
else
{
Console.WriteLine(String.Format("\nThe registration {0} does not
start with the letter Z", registration));
} // End of else block
} // End of for each iteration

// Iterate the array and split the items as they are read
foreach (String registration in myVehicleRegistrations)
{
    // Array to hold the 2 parts of the vehicle registration
    String[] splitRegistration = new String[2];

    // Split the array at the space
    splitRegistration = registration.Split(' ');

    Console.WriteLine(String.Format("\nPart 0 is {0}",
    splitRegistration[0]));
    Console.WriteLine(String.Format("\nPart 1 is {0}",
    splitRegistration[1]));
 } // End of iteration for splitting at the space character

} // End of Main() method
```

2. Click the File menu.

3. Choose Save All.

4. Click the Debug menu.

5. Choose Start Without Debugging.

Figure 15-10 shows the console window displaying each of the array members in their two parts, split at the space character.

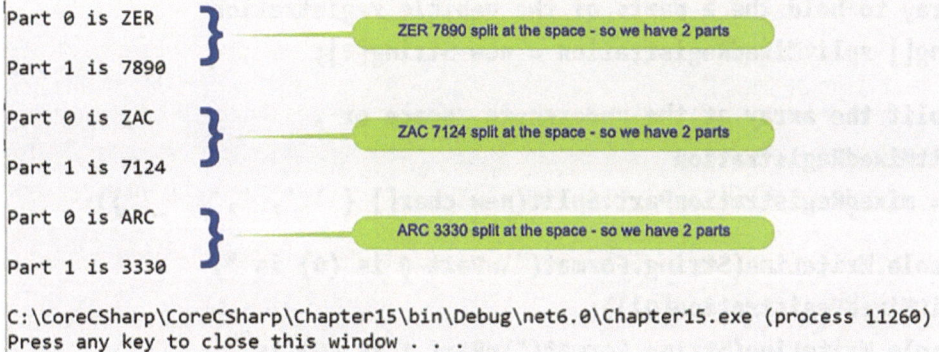

Part 0 is ZER
Part 1 is 7890
}   ZER 7890 split at the space - so we have 2 parts

Part 0 is ZAC
Part 1 is 7124
}   ZAC 7124 split at the space - so we have 2 parts

Part 0 is ARC
Part 1 is 3330
}   ARC 3330 split at the space - so we have 2 parts

C:\CoreCSharp\CoreCSharp\Chapter15\bin\Debug\net6.0\Chapter15.exe (process 11260)
Press any key to close this window . . .

Figure 15-10. *New strings created from original strings split at spaces*

6.   Press the Enter key to close the console window.

We can also split on multiple characters, delimiters, or regular expressions.

7.   Amend the code, as in Listing 15-14, to add a new array, called myMixedVehicleRegistrations.

Listing 15-14. Add a new array called myMixedVehicleRegistrations

```
// Create a new array of String objects
String[] myMixedVehicleRegistrations = new String[]{ "ZER 7890",
"ZAC_7124", "ARC,3330" };

} // End of Main() method
```

We will now iterate the new array, myMixedVehicleRegistrations, and split each String object member of the array at the underscore, space, or comma and put the result into the splitMixedRegistration array which we will create, as shown in Listing 15-15.

8.   Amend the code, as in Listing 15-15.

Listing 15-15. Split the strings at the required delimiters

```
String[] myMixedVehicleRegistrations = new String[]
{ "ZER 7890", "ZAC_7124", "ARC,3330" };

// Iterate the array and split the items as they are read
foreach (String mixedRegistrationPart in myMixedVehicleRegistrations)
{
```

```
// Array to hold the 2 parts of the vehicle registration
 String[] splitMixedRegistration = new String[2];

 // Split the array at the underscore, space or ,
  splitMixedRegistration
     = mixedRegistrationPart.Split(new char[] { ' ', ',', '_' });

 Console.WriteLine(String.Format("\nPart 0 is {0} is ",
 splitMixedRegistration[0]));
 Console.WriteLine(String.Format("\nPart 1 is {0} is ",
 splitMixedRegistration[1]));
 } // End of for each iteration

} // End of Main() method
```

9. Click the File menu.

10. Choose Save All.

11. Click the Debug menu.

12. Choose Start Without Debugging.

Figure 15-11 shows the console window displaying new strings.

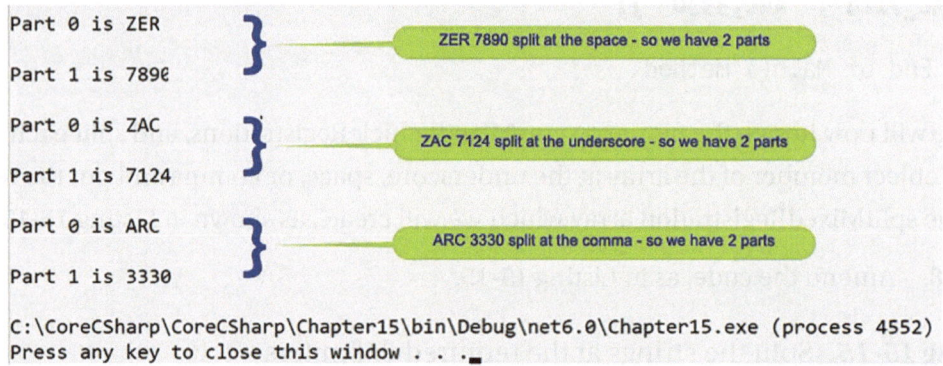

Figure 15-11. *New strings created from original strings split at the delimiters*

13. Press the Enter key to close the console window.

CompareTo()

In coding our insurance application, we might need to compare two strings. We could be asking a customer to enter their account reference and then comparing it with account references read from a file so we can display data related to this specific customer. To undertake the comparison, we could use the CompareTo() method of the String class. Interestingly, the CompareTo() method is an implementation of the interface method CompareTo() that exists in the interface IComparable. We have just completed a chapter on interfaces where we talked about interfaces and interface methods, and this is a great example of an implementation of an interface method.

In string handling the CompareTo() method will compare two string objects or strings and return an integer that indicates a position for the comparing string, as per the following rules:

- If the string being compared precedes the other string, it returns an integer less than zero.

- If the string being compared is in the same position as the other string, it returns a 0, zero.

- If the string being compared follows the other string, it returns an integer greater than zero.

When dealing with strings, the comparison is based on the lexical relationship between the two objects, which essentially means alphabetical order. We can think of it as the dictionary order of the word where digits come before letters and lowercase letters come before uppercase ones.

1. Amend the code, as in Listing 15-16, to add a new array called myDuplicateVehicleRegistrations with additional String objects.

Listing 15-16. New array

```
Console.WriteLine(String.Format("\nPart 1 is {0}" +
  " is ", splitMixedRegistration[1]));
} // End of for each iteration
```

```
// Create a new array of String objects
String[] myDuplicateVehicleRegistrations = new String[] { "ZER 7890",
"ZAC_7124", "ARC,3330", "ZER 7890", "ARC,3330", "zer 7890",
" zac_7124" };

} // End of Main() method
```

Finding Matching Strings

We will add code to iterate the new array and compare each String object with each of the other String objects and output a message to say if the Strings are the same. This will require an inner iteration.

2. Amend the code, as in Listing 15-17.

Listing 15-17. Iterate the array and find strings that are the same

```
// Create a new array of String objects
String[] myDuplicateVehicleRegistrations = new String[]
{ "ZER 7890", "ZAC_7124", "ARC,3330", "ZER 7890",
  "ARC,3330", "zer 7890", " zac_7124" };

// Iterate the array and split the items as they are read
for (int counter = 0; counter <
        myDuplicateVehicleRegistrations.Length; counter++)
{
  for (int innercounter = counter + 1; innercounter <
     myDuplicateVehicleRegistrations.Length; innercounter++)
  {
    if (myDuplicateVehicleRegistrations[counter].CompareTo(myDuplicate
    VehicleRegistrations[innercounter]) == 0)
    {
      Console.WriteLine(String.Format("\n{0} at index {1} is the same
      String as array index {2} {3}", myDuplicateVehicleRegistrations
      [counter],counter,innercounter,myDuplicateVehicleRegistrations
      [innercounter]));
    } // End of the if selection block
  } // End of for inner loop iteration
} // End of for each outer loop iteration

} // End of Main() method
```

3. Click the File menu.

4. Choose Save All.

5. Click the Debug menu.

6. Choose Start Without Debugging.

Figure 15-12 shows the console window displaying strings that have been compared as the same. This means a value less than zero was returned when the two strings were compared.

CompareTo()

```
ZER 7890 at index 0 is the same String as array index 3 ZER 7890

ARC,3330 at index 2 is the same String as array index 4 ARC,3330

C:\CoreCSharp\CoreCSharp\Chapter15\bin\Debug\net6.0\Chapter15.exe (process 6596)
Press any key to close this window . . ._
```

Figure 15-12. *Equal strings*

7. Press the Enter key to close the console window.

Finding Which Strings Precede Other Strings

We will add code at the end of the Main() method to iterate the new array and compare each String object with each of the other String objects, displaying a message when a string comes before, precedes, another string.

8. Amend the code, as in Listing 15-18.

Listing 15-18. Iterate the array and find strings that precede other strings

```
// Iterate the array and split the items as they are read
for (int counter = 0; counter < myDuplicateVehicleRegistrations.Length;
counter++)
{
  for (int innercounter = counter + 1; innercounter <
  myDuplicateVehicleRegistrations.Length; innercounter++)
  {
    if (myDuplicateVehicleRegistrations[counter].CompareTo(myDuplicate
    VehicleRegistrations[innercounter]) == 1)
    {
```

```
    Console.WriteLine(String.Format("\nString {0} comes after String
    {1}", myDuplicateVehicleRegistrations[counter],myDuplicateVehicle
    Registrations[innercounter]));
   } // End of if block
  } // End of for inner loop iteration
 } // End of for each outer loop iteration

} // End of Main() method
```

9.   Click the File menu.

10.   Choose Save All.

11.   Click the Debug menu.

12.   Choose Start Without Debugging.

Figure 15-13 shows the console window displaying the strings that come before other strings in the array.

```
String ZER 7890 comes after String ZAC_7124

String ZER 7890 comes after String ARC,3330

String ZER 7890 comes after String ARC,3330

String ZER 7890 comes after String zer 7890

String ZER 7890 comes after String  zac_7124

String ZAC_7124 comes after String ARC,3330

String ZAC_7124 comes after String ARC,3330

String ZAC_7124 comes after String  zac_7124

String ARC,3330 comes after String  zac_7124

String ZER 7890 comes after String ARC,3330

String ZER 7890 comes after String zer 7890

String ZER 7890 comes after String  zac_7124

String ARC,3330 comes after String  zac_7124

String zer 7890 comes after String  zac_7124
```

Figure 15-13. *Strings in the array that precede other strings*

13.   Press the Enter key to close the console window.

ToUpper() and ToLower()

In coding our insurance application, we might need to compare two strings, but we need to be sure the strings are in the correct case. There is no point in having the customer enter their account reference in mixed-case lettering and then trying to compare it for equality with our data, which is in uppercase. To solve this issue, we could use the ToUpper() method of the String class to convert the user input to match our uppercase data. We could equally apply the same principle to a scenario where we need to use lowercase.

In string handling the ToUpper() method will convert the characters of the string into uppercase characters, when there is an equivalent uppercase character.

In string handling the ToLower() method will convert the characters of the string into lowercase characters, when there is an equivalent lowercase character.

We will add code to convert the String objects to uppercase when we are comparing them. This code is the same iteration as we have just used, but we use the ToUpper() method on both strings being compared.

1. Add the code in Listing 15-19.

Listing 15-19. Convert both strings to uppercase using the ToUpper() method

```
/*
Iterate the array and compare the items, changing to
upper case, as they are read
*/
for (int counter = 0; counter <
        myDuplicateVehicleRegistrations.Length; counter++)
{
  for (int innercounter = counter + 1; innercounter <
          myDuplicateVehicleRegistrations.Length; innercounter++)
  {
    if(myDuplicateVehicleRegistrations[counter].ToUpper().
    CompareTo(myDuplicateVehicleRegistrations[innercounter].ToUpper()) == 0)
    {
      Console.WriteLine("With upper case {0} at index {1} is " +
      "the same String as {3} at index {2}\n",
      myDuplicateVehicleRegistrations[counter], counter,
```

```
     innercounter, myDuplicateVehicleRegistrations[innercounter]);
   }
 } // End of inner for iteration
} // End of outer for each iteration
} // End of Main() method
```

2. Click the File menu.

3. Choose Save All.

4. Click the Debug menu.

5. Choose Start Without Debugging.

Figure 15-14 shows the console window displaying the matching strings when conversion to uppercase has occurred.

```
With upper case ZER 7890 at index 0 is the same String as ZER 7890 at index 3

With upper case ZER 7890 at index 0 is the same String as zer 7890 at index 5

With upper case ARC,3330 at index 2 is the same String as ARC,3330 at index 4      ToUpper()

With upper case ZER 7890 at index 3 is the same String as zer 7890 at index 5
```

Figure 15-14. *Using ToUpper() before comparing strings*

6. Press the Enter key to close the console window.

We could amend the program code if we wished to test the ToLower() method.

Concat()

In many of the applications we have coded, we have concatenated a string and a non-string value using the + symbol. Another way to concatenate when we have only string values is to use the String.Concat() static method of the String class.

Concat() will concatenate multiple strings by appending the specified Strings. The String.Concat() method returns the newly combined String of characters.

We will now amend the code to create three string literals and concatenate the strings into a message of two sentences. The concatenation includes "hard-coded" string constants and an escape character, \n. Ensure there is a space before the G of Gerry in the insuredPerson string, as we will use it later in an example.

1. Add the code in Listing 15-20.

Listing 15-20. Using the Concat() method to join strings

```
String insuredPerson = " Gerry Byrne,";
String welcome = "thank you for taking out insurance with us.";
String insuranceType = "Home Insurance";
String myOfferDetails = String.Concat(insuredPerson, " ", welcome, "\n",
"You now have full ", insuranceType, ". ");

Console.WriteLine(String.Format("\n{0}", myOfferDetails));
} // End of Main() method
```

2. Click the File menu.

3. Choose Save All.

4. Click the Debug menu.

5. Choose Start Without Debugging.

Figure 15-15 shows the console window displaying the concatenated strings.

```
 Gerry Byrne, thank you for taking out insurance with us.
You now have full Home Insurance.
                                   4 strings concatenated into 1 string
C:\CoreCSharp\CoreCSharp\Chapter15\bin\Debug\net6.0\Chapter15.exe
Press any key to close this window . . ._
```

Figure 15-15. *Concatenating strings*

6. Press the Enter key to close the console window.

Trim()

We read at the start of the chapter about an example where a customer might enter
their account number and accidentally add an extra space at the start or end. We said
that our code would need to check for spaces at the start and end of the string input,
and this is what the Trim() method can do for us. The Trim() method will remove any
leading spaces, at the start, and any trailing spaces, at the end, from the string object.
The method will leave spaces that exist inside the string. There is also a TrimStart()

method, which is used to remove the occurrences of a set of characters from the start of the String object, while the TrimEnd() method is used to remove the occurrences of a set of characters from the end of a String object.

We will now amend the code to trim the space from the front of the insuredPerson string, remembering that we were told to insert a space before the Gerry Byrne part. We will then display the new string.

1.   Add the code in Listing 15-21, to apply the Trim() method to the myOfferDetails variable.

Listing 15-21. Remove the leading and trailing spaces using the Trim() method

```
String trimmedMyOfferDetails = myOfferDetails.Trim();
Console.WriteLine(String.Format("\n{0}", trimmedMyOfferDetails));

} // End of Main() method
```

2.   Click the File menu.

3.   Choose Save All.

4.   Click the Debug menu.

5.   Choose Start Without Debugging.

Figure 15-16 shows the console window displaying the concatenated strings, but the leading space has been removed.

```
 Gerry Byrne, thank you for taking out insurance with us.
You now have full Home Insurance.
          Leading space removed
Gerry Byrne, thank you for taking out insurance with us.
You now have full Home Insurance.

C:\CoreCSharp\CoreCSharp\Chapter15\bin\Debug\net6.0\Chapter15.exe
Press any key to close this window . . .
```

Figure 15-16. *Extra space at the front of the string trimmed*

6.   Press the Enter key to close the console window.

Replace()

In an application we may need to replace a character or characters with different characters, and this can be achieved using the Replace() method. We may need to replace 2023 with 2024 in a date string or replace Au with AU in all auto policies.

The Replace() method has two forms:

- Replace(old char, new char)

  In this format the method will replace all occurrences of the old character with the new character.

- Replace(old string, new string)

  In this format the method will replace all occurrences of the old string of characters with the new string of characters.

We will amend the code to use the Replace() method to replace a character in a string and then display the new string.

1. Amend the code, as in Listing 15-22.

Listing 15-22. Replace characters in a string; new string object is formed

```
String name = "Gerry Byrne";
String newName = name.Replace('e', 'E');
Console.WriteLine(String.Format("\n{0}", newName));

} // End of Main() method
```

2. Click the File menu.

3. Choose Save All.

4. Click the Debug menu.

5. Choose Start Without Debugging.

Figure 15-17 shows the console window displaying the string with the two lowercase e characters replaced with uppercase E characters.

```
GErry ByrnE        lower case e replaced with upper case E in the string Gerry Byrne

C:\CoreCSharp\CoreCSharp\Chapter15\bin\Debug\net6.0\Chapter15.exe
Press any key to close this window . . .
```

Figure 15-17. *Lowercase e replaced with uppercase E*

6. Press the Enter key to close the console window.

We will amend the code to use the Replace() method to replace a string of characters in a string and then display the new String.

7. Amend the code as in Listing 15-23.

Listing 15-23. Replace Gerry with GERARD

```
String name = "Gerry Byrne";
String newName = name.Replace('e', 'E');
Console.WriteLine(String.Format("\n{0}", newName));

String newCapitalName = name.Replace("Gerry", "GERARD");
Console.WriteLine(String.Format("\n{0}", newCapitalName));

    } // End of Main() method
```

8. Click the File menu.

9. Choose Save All.

10. Click the Debug menu.

11. Choose Start Without Debugging.

Figure 15-18 shows the console window displaying the string Gerry replaced by the string GERARD.

```
GERARD Byrne       The string Gerry replaced with the string GERARD in the string Gerry Byrne

C:\CoreCSharp\CoreCSharp\Chapter15\bin\Debug\net6.0\Chapter15.exe
Press any key to close this window . . .
```

Figure 15-18. *Gerry replaced with GERARD*

12. Press the Enter key to close the console window.

Contains()

In an application we may need to check if a string contains a char or a number of chars, and this can be achieved using the Contains() method. We may need to check if a policy id contains AU and then amend the monthly premium because auto insurance policies are due to be increased by 10%.

The Contains() method has two forms:

- Contains(char)

  In this format the method will return a value indicating if a specified character occurs within a string.

- Contains(string)

  In this format the method will return a value indicating if a specified string occurs within a string.

1. Amend the code, as in Listing 15-24, to use the Contains() method to see if the user has input the string Home in an answer to a question.

Listing 15-24. Checking if a string input contains the string Home

```
Console.WriteLine("What type of insurance do you require?\n");
  String clientInsuranceType = Console.ReadLine();

  if (clientInsuranceType.Contains("Home"))
  {
    Console.WriteLine("Home Insurance types are");
    Console.WriteLine("1. Building Only");
    Console.WriteLine("2. Content Only");
    Console.WriteLine("3. Building and Content Only");
  }
  else
  {
    Console.WriteLine("You have not chosen Home Insurance");
  }

} // End of Main() method
```

2. Click the File menu.

3. Choose Save All.

4. Click the Debug menu.

5. Choose Start Without Debugging.

Figure 15-19 shows the console window displaying the question.

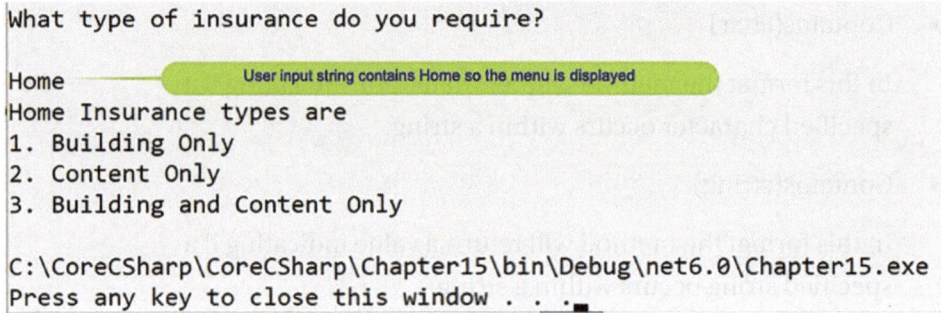

```
What type of insurance do you require?

Home ——————[ User input string contains Home so the menu is displayed ]
Home Insurance types are
1. Building Only
2. Content Only
3. Building and Content Only

C:\CoreCSharp\CoreCSharp\Chapter15\bin\Debug\net6.0\Chapter15.exe
Press any key to close this window . . .▪
```

Figure 15-19. *Home insurance types displayed*

6. Type Home in the console window and press the Enter key.

7. Press the Enter key to close the console window.

Figure 15-19 shows the types of home insurance because our input contained the string Home.

IndexOf( )

In our application we may wish to see if a string contains a specific character and at what position the character is located, and for this we use the IndexOf() method to check if a character is inside a string. An example might be when we are verifying a customer email address. We might want to check that it contains an @ symbol. If it does, we might be happy that the entry is a valid email address; otherwise, it is not. But we might also wish to verify that the @ is located at a specific position or index.

The IndexOf() method has two forms:

- IndexOf(char)

  In this format the method will return the zero-based index of the first occurrence of the specified char in the string object.

- IndexOf(string)

  In this format the method will return the zero-based index of the first occurrence of the specified string in the string object.

The IndexOf () method returns –1 if the character or string is not found.

1. Amend the code, as in Listing 15-25, to use the IndexOf() method to find the position of the @ char.

Listing 15-25. Check if IndexOf() returns –1

```
Console.WriteLine("Please enter your email address?\n");
string emailAddress = Console.ReadLine();
int intPosition = emailAddress.IndexOf("@");
if (intPosition == -1)
{
  Console.WriteLine("Not a valid email address - retype your email
  address");
}
else
{
  Console.WriteLine("Valid email address with the @ at position "
    + intPosition);
}
} // End of Main() method
```

2. Click the File menu.

3. Choose Save All.

4. Click the Debug menu.

5. Choose Start Without Debugging.

Figure 15-20 shows the console window asking for the email address.

```
Please enter your email address?
                        User input string contains @
gerry@anywhere.com
Valid email address with the @ at position 5

C:\CoreCSharp\CoreCSharp\Chapter15\bin\Debug\net6.0\Chapter15.exe
Press any key to close this window . . .
```

Figure 15-20. *Index of the character @*

6. Type an email address containing an @, **for example,** gerry@
    anywhere.com, and press the Enter key.

7. Press the Enter key to close the console window.

The text is checked only for an @ symbol, so this is not a very efficient email checker, but we receive a message that the email address is valid, as in Figure 15-20, because the @ symbol was located.

Insert()

In our application we may wish to see if a string contains a specific character or string of characters, and if it does not, then we might wish to insert the character or string of characters. .NET offers us the Insert() method to place characters inside a string. As an example, we might need to verify a customer account number by checking that it contains two letters at the start. If it does, the entry can be seen as a valid account number. If it does not, then we may wish to put the two letters in front of the number based on other information the user has also entered.

The format for the Insert() method means we must specify the zero-indexed position where the insertion will take place and we must also give the character or characters to be inserted. In this example we will check if the first two characters of a string are G and B, and if they are not, we insert the value GB at position 0.

1. Amend the code, as in Listing 15-26.

Listing 15-26. Use the Insert method to insert the characters GB at index 0

```
Console.WriteLine("What is your account number?\n");
string accountNumber = Console.ReadLine();

int intPositionG = accountNumber.IndexOf("G");
```

```
int intPositionB = accountNumber.IndexOf("B");

if (intPositionG == 0 && intPositionB == 1)
{
  Console.WriteLine("Valid account number\n" + "Character G was found at
  location " + intPositionG + "\nCharacter B was found at location " +
  intPositionB);
} // End of if section
else
{
  Console.WriteLine("Not a valid account number");
  accountNumber = accountNumber.Insert(0, "GB");
  Console.WriteLine("The account number is " + accountNumber);
} // End of else section

} // End of Main() method
```

- The code finds the position of the letter G in the string and assigns it to the variable intPositionG.

- The code finds the position of the letter B in the string and assigns it to the variable intPositionB.

- The next part uses the if statement to see if the letters G and B have been located at the start of the string in the positions 0 and 1.

- If they have been found, then a message is displayed saying that the account number is valid and telling us the position of the two letters.

- If the two letters are not found, then a message is displayed saying that the account number is invalid.

- The letters GB are then inserted into the string starting at position 0. Remember that we are using the Insert() method, not the Replace() method.

- The console will show the string with the GB added at the start.

2. Click the File menu.

3. Choose Save All.

4. Click the Debug menu.

5. Choose Start Without Debugging.

The console window will appear and ask the user to input their account number. We know it should begin with the string GB or, put another way, G should be the first character and B should be the second character. If this is not what is entered, the code will insert GB at the start of the entered string. Obviously, we could have used the Replace() method, but we are trying to understand the Insert() method.

6. Type AB123456, an invalid input, and press the Enter key.

Figure 15-21 shows the console window with GB prefixed to the string.

```
What is your account number?
                        User input string does not have G as the first character and B as the second character
AB123456                The Insert() method has inserted the letters GB starting at position 0
Not a valid account number
The account number is GBAB123456

C:\CoreCSharp\CoreCSharp\Chapter15\bin\Debug\net6.0\Chapter15.exe
Press any key to close this window . . .
```

Figure 15-21. *Insert GB as the first two characters if they are not already GB*

7. Press the Enter key to close the console window.

8. Click the File menu.

9. Choose Save All.

10. Click the Debug menu.

11. Choose Start Without Debugging.

12. Type GB123456, a valid input, and press the Enter key.

Figure 15-22 shows the console window with the indexes of G and B shown, after we have entered the input required.

```
What is your account number?
                            User input string does have G as the first character and B as the second character
GB123456
Valid account number
Character G was found at location 0
Character B was found at location 1

C:\CoreCSharp\CoreCSharp\Chapter15\bin\Debug\net6.0\Chapter15.exe
Press any key to close this window . . .
```

Figure 15-22. *No replacement needed*

13.   Press the Enter key to close the console window.

String.Format()

We will continue the use of the String class, but we will now look at how we have already used the Format() method of the String class to contain a string and placeholders for variables or objects.

In many of our code applications, we have displayed to the console using two different formats:

- The first format has been to use the Console.WriteLine() method where we have concatenated a string literal with a variable. In this case the variable becomes a string and is joined onto the string literal, and then the whole string is displayed. Listing 15-27 shows an example that we have already coded.

Listing 15-27. Using Console.WriteLine()

```
Console.WriteLine("The number of characters is: " + myVehicleRegistration.
Length);
```

- The second format has been to use the Console.WriteLine() method where we have included the String.Format() method to format the string. We use String.Format() when we wish to insert a variable, object, or expression within our string. Listing 15-28 shows an example that we have already coded.

627

Listing 15-28. Using String.Format()

```
Console.WriteLine(String.Format("\nThe registration {0} does not start with
the letter Z", registration));
```

The {0} is a placeholder within the format string. The 0 refers to the index of the object whose string value will be inserted at that position, and in Listing 15-28 this is the variable called registration. If the placeholder refers to an object that is not a string, then the ToString() method of the object will be called, and the object will be converted to a string, which is placed at the position of the placeholder.

We can have as many placeholders as we require so long as there is a matching object after the comma (,) following the end double quote. We say that there is an object list after the comma following the end double quote.

Formatting the Items in the String

When we use the placeholder like {0} in Listing 15-28, it refers to an object in the object list, and if the object is a string, this is an easy insertion. If we have a different data type to be inserted, like a double, we may wish to format it to two decimal places or some other type of formatting. With placeholders we can add some control to them, and in the widely used case of the double or float data type, we could do {0:d}. We can also use a similar approach for a time object, where we could do {1:t}, remembering that we can have more than one object in the string, and that is why we have the number 1 in the curly braces. There are a number of types in C# that are supportive of format strings, including all numeric types, dates, and times. Listing 15-29 shows some code examples, with comments, and their output.

1. Amend the code, as in Listing 15-29, to use some String.Format() methods.

Listing 15-29. Using String.Format() with formatting

```
// Format the number to 2 decimal places giving 99.97
Console.WriteLine(String.Format("Decimal: {0:0.00}", 99.9687));

// Format to scientific format 9.99E+002
// (E+002 is 10 to the power of 2 or 100)
Console.WriteLine(String.Format("Scientific: {0:E}", 999));

// Format to local currency format e.g. 2 decimal places
// and a £ symbol £99.97
Console.WriteLine(String.Format("Currency:{0:C}", 99.9687654));

// Format to percent 99 multiplied by 100 is 9900%.
Console.WriteLine(String.Format("Percent: {0:P}", 99));

DateTime localDate = DateTime.Now;

// Format the string as a short time
Console.WriteLine(String.Format("Short date:{0:t}", localDate));

// Format the string as a long time
Console.WriteLine(String.Format("Long date: {0:F}", localDate));

} // End of Main() method
```

2. Click the File menu.

3. Choose Save All.

4. Click the Debug menu.

5. Choose Start Without Debugging.

Figure 15-23 shows the console window after we have entered the inputs required.

Figure 15-23. *Output when using String.Format()*

6. Press the Enter key to close the console window.

String Interpolation

We will continue the use of the String class, but we will now look at how we can use string interpolation to format a string to be used in the WriteLine() method.

We have been coding using what is called **composite formatting**, which is fine, and we have used it successfully to display our output. However, from C# 6 the recommended way to do the same thing is by using **string interpolation** because it is more flexible and the code is easier to read. String interpolation introduces us to the use of the special character **$**, which identifies the string literal as an interpolated string. An interpolated string is a string literal that might contain interpolation expressions. Whoa, hold on. What does this word *interpolation* even mean? Well, it means

The insertion of something of a different

nature into something else

For us it is a fancy word for joining our strings with other non-string variables or values, and to build a string interpolation, we will have the following:

- The start as a $

- Next, open and close "" double quotes

- Then, inside the double quotes, our string

- Next to the string, open and close curly braces {} to hold an object

- Then, inside the open and close curly braces {}, the object and any formatting

- All this will be within the () of the WriteLine().

Listing 15-30 shows some code examples, with comments, and their output.

1. Amend the code, as in Listing 15-30.

Listing 15-30. Using string interpolation

```
// Format  the number to 2 decimal places giving 99.97
Console.WriteLine($"Decimal: {99.9687:0.00}");

// Format to scientific format giving 9.99E+002
// E+002 is 10 to the power of 2 or 100)
Console.WriteLine($"Scientific: {999:E}");

// Format to local currency format e.g. 2 decimal places
// and a £ symbol £99.97
Console.WriteLine($"Currency: {99.9687654:C}");

// Format to percent 99 multiplied by 100 is 9900%
Console.WriteLine($"Percent: {99:P}");

DateTime localDate2 = DateTime.Now;

// Format the string as a short time
Console.WriteLine($"Short time: {localDate2:t}");

// Format the string as a long time
Console.WriteLine($"Long date: {localDate2:F}");

} // End of Main() method
```

2. Click the File menu.

3. Choose Save All.

4. Click the Debug menu.

5. Choose Start Without Debugging.

Figure 15-24 shows the console and confirms that we get the same output as Figure 15-23, which uses the code shown in Listing 15-29, but we should be thinking that our code is easier to read and therefore will be easier to maintain.

```
Decimal: 99.97                                    Console.WriteLine($"Decimal: {99.9687:0.00}");
Scientific: 9.990000E+002                         Console.WriteLine($"Scientific: {999:E}");
Currency: £99.97                                  Console.WriteLine($"Currency: {99.968754:C}");
Percent: 9,900.00%                                Console.WriteLine($"Percent: {99:P}");
Short date: 11:25                                 Console.WriteLine($"Short date: {localDate2:t}");
Long date: 24 April 2022 11:25:14                 Console.WriteLine($"Long date: {localDate2:F}");
```

C:\CoreCSharp\CoreCSharp\Chapter15\bin\Debug\net6.0\Chapter15.exe
Press any key to close this window . . .

Figure 15-24. *Interpolation with a single object in the display line*

    6.   Press the Enter key to close the console window.

In the code of Listing 15-30, we have used one object in the interpolation, so let us code an example that uses more than one object.

    7.   Amend the code, as in Listing 15-31, to use multiple objects in the interpolation.

Listing 15-31. *Using string interpolation with more than one object*

```
Console.WriteLine($"Decimal: {99.9687654:0.00} Scientific: {999:E}
Currency: {99.9687654:C}");

Console.WriteLine($"The Short date is {localDate:t} while the long date is
{localDate:F}");

} // End of Main() method
```

    8.   Click the File menu.

    9.   Choose Save All.

  10.   Click the Debug menu.

  11.   Choose Start Without Debugging.

Figure 15-25 shows the console window displaying the formatted objects in each of the two display lines.

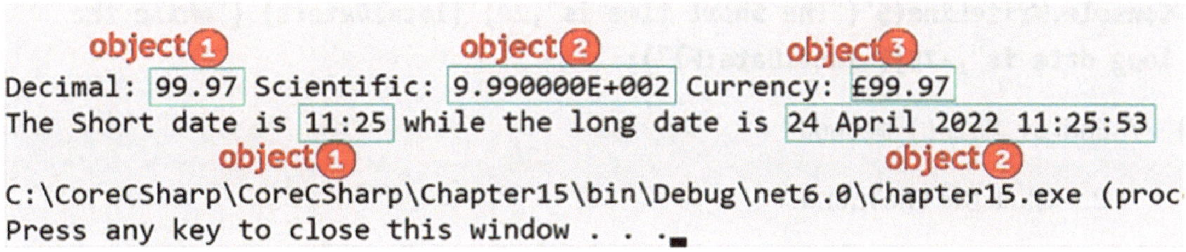

Figure 15-25. Interpolation with multiple objects in the display line

12.   Press the Enter key to close the console window.

String Interpolation: Spacing

We also have the option of controlling spacing within the interpolation by using the alignment component. This component uses a signed integer where

- A negative means align left.

- A positive means align right.

If there is a situation where the string is larger than the amount of spacing set aside, then the alignment is ignored and the length of the string will be used for the field width, therefore overriding the user-assigned numeric value. The padding required to make the string the correct alignment will consist of white spaces. Listing 15-32 shows some code examples, with comments, and their output.

1.   Amend the code, as in Listing 15-32, to use spacing in string interpolation.

Listing 15-32. Using string interpolation with control of spacing

```
/*
Spacing is achieved using - for left and + for right alignment
In this example we have the first string right aligned in its
20 spaces, the second string left aligned in its 25 spaces,
*/
 Console.WriteLine($"The Short time is {localDate:t} while the long date is
 {localDate:F}");
```

```
Console.WriteLine($"{"The Short time is",20} {localDate:t} {"while the
long date is",-25}{ localDate:F}");
```

`} // End of Main() method`

2. Click the File menu.

3. Choose Save All.

4. Click the Debug menu.

5. Choose Start Without Debugging.

Figure 15-26 shows the console window displaying, in the second line, the right- and left-aligned formatted objects.

```
The Short time is 19:52 while the long date is 30 June 2022 19:52:47
   The Short time is 19:52 while the long date is    30 June 2022 19:52:47
```
    20 right aligned   **25 left aligned**

Figure 15-26. *Second line is controlled using left and right alignment*

6. Press the Enter key to close the console window.

@ Verbatim

Sometimes in our strings, we will want to use characters such as a backslash, \ , and double quotes, " , but the compiler thinks they are code sequences and tries to "interpret" them. There will be other times when we want to use escape sequences such as \n for a new line and \t for a tab, and in order to achieve this we can use another backslash, \ , in front of the escape sequence. Often, we will see the \ in code that uses a path name for a file, **for example**:

`"C:\Desktop\Gerry\Code\test.cs"`

We will see this in the next chapter on file handling. In the path name we have backslashes and double quotes ", which can cause errors in our code. Listing 15-33 shows some code examples, with comments, and their output.

1. Amend the code, as in Listing 15-33, to use the double backslash in string interpolation.

Listing 15-33. Using \\ to make the compiler read the sequence literally

```
/*
Escape sequences
In this example we use the backslash in front of the \n which
is the escape sequence for a new line
*/
Console.WriteLine("Two character pair for a new line is \\n");

/*
Escape sequences
In this example we use the backslash in front of the starting
double quote " to indicate that we wish the " to be displayed
We then use the backslash in front of the \n which is the
escape sequence for a new line and we are saying we want this
\n to be displayed and finally we use the backslash in front
of the ending double quote " to indicate that we wish
the " to be displayed
*/
Console.WriteLine("Two character pair for a new line is \"\\n\" ");
} // End of Main() method
```

2. Click the File menu.

3. Choose Save All.

4. Click the Debug menu.

5. Choose Start Without Debugging.

Figure 15-27 shows the console window displaying the \n in the first display line and the double quotes and \n in the second line.

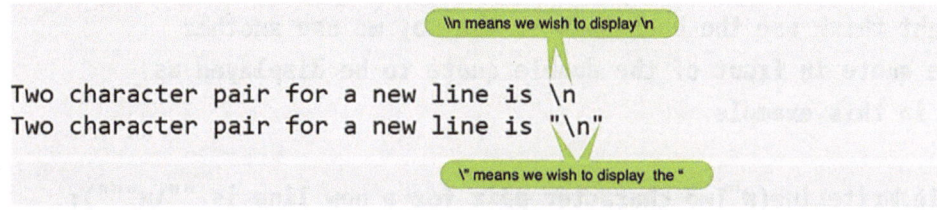

Figure 15-27. *Output from \\, double backslash sequence*

6.   Press the Enter key to close the console window.

Unfortunately we may have a number of these backslashes in our strings, and it can be tedious to type the string and it also makes the code hard to read, **for example:**

```
\"C:\\Desktop\\Gerry\\Code\\test.cs\"
```

So another way to do the same thing is to use verbatim, the @ symbol. Using the verbatim @ symbol means backslashes are not interpreted as escape characters. However, the downside is that we cannot have special characters in our string when using verbatim. Another idiosyncrasy is when we want to display a double quote. We need to precede the double quote with another double quote. Listing 15-34 shows the same code examples as Listing 15-33, with comments, and their output.

Listing 15-34. Using verbatim, @

```
/*
@ Verbatim
There is an alternative way to the \\ when we wish to display
or use a \
The alternative is to use a verbatim string which means we use
a regular string but we put a @ symbol before the opening
double quotes. The verbatim now treats all characters in a
literal way, just as they appear
*/
Console.WriteLine(@"Two character pair for a new line is \n");

/*
There is an exception when using the verbatim and that is when
we are wanting to display the double quote character ".
As the " indicates the start and the end of the verbatim string
how can we add them if we want to actually display them?
We might think use the backslash \. But no, we use another
double quote in front of the double quote to be displayed as
shown in this example.
*/
Console.WriteLine(@"Two character pair for a new line is ""\n""");
```

7.   Click the File menu.

8.   Choose Save All.

9.   Click the Debug menu.

10.   Choose Start Without Debugging.

Figure 15-28 shows the console window displaying the \n in the first display line and the double quotes and \n in the second line, but this time we have used the verbatim style.

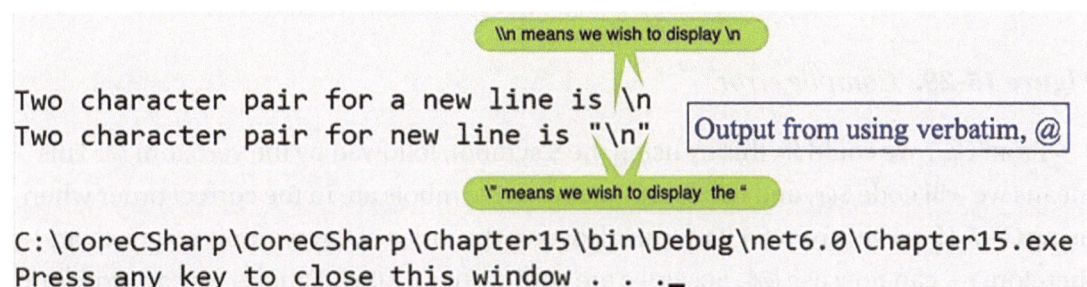

Figure 15-28.   *Output from using verbatim, @*

11.   Press the Enter key to close the console window.

Now we will look at using the verbatim, @, symbol alongside the string interpolation, $, symbol. We will see how C# 8, C# 10, and above handle the use and mixing of these symbols.

What About $@ or @$?

While coding an application, we may also have a need within the string interpolation to have double quotes around something, **for example**, we might want to display "\" as we saw in the last example using the verbatim. So, in the string interpolation, we might try to use the line of code as shown in Listing 15-35.

Listing 15-35.   Compile error when using "" within a verbatim string

```
Console.WriteLine($"Two character pair for a new line is ""\n""");
```

However, if we were to code this line, we would get a compile error, as shown in Figure 15-29. The reason for the error is we will have reached the match for the opening double quote when we are at the first double quote after the word *is*.

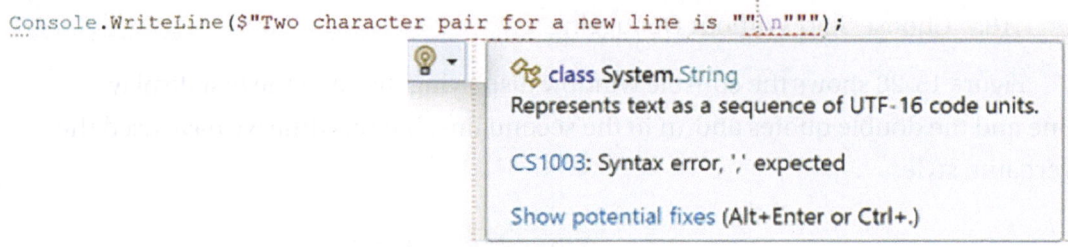

```
Console.WriteLine($"Two character pair for a new line is ""\n""");
```

class System.String
Represents text as a sequence of UTF-16 code units.

CS1003: Syntax error, ',' expected

Show potential fixes (Alt+Enter or Ctrl+.)

Figure 15-29. *Compile error*

From C# 7 we could fix this by using the $ symbol, followed by the verbatim @. This means we will code $@, and it is essential that the symbols are in the correct order when using C# 7. However, from C# 8 we can also have the order of the symbols reversed, and therefore we can now use @$. So, as we are coding for C# 10 and above, we can write our code as in Listing 15-36 or as in Listing 15-37, and the results will be the same, as shown in Figure 15-30.

Listing 15-36. In C# 7 we use $@

```
Console.WriteLine($@"Two character pair for a new line is ""\n""");
```

Listing 15-37. In C# 8 onward we can also use @$

```
Console.WriteLine(@$"Two character pair for a new line is ""\n""");
```

```
Two character pair for a new line is "\n"     Coding the statement with $@
Two character pair for a new line is "\n"     Coding the statement with @$

C:\CoreCSharp\CoreCSharp\Chapter15\bin\Debug\net6.0\Chapter15.exe
Press any key to close this window . . ._
```

Figure 15-30. *$@ or @$ gives the same output*

From all the different ways we have looked at to display to the console, we can choose which "format" to use. What we need to consider is which format suits our coding style while at the same time making the code easy to read and therefore easier to maintain. Having personal choice also comes with responsibility.

Const String Interpolation

Prior to C# 10 we could have constant strings, where a **const string** is a string that cannot be modified. Prior to C# 10 we had to concatenate const strings using the +, and we could not use const strings in string interpolation, with the $. However, from C# 10 this has changed, and we can now make use of const strings within a string interpolation.

Add a new class.

1. Right-click the Chapter15 project.

2. Choose Add.

3. Choose Class.

4. Name the class ConstantStrings.cs.

5. Amend the code, as in Listing 15-38, to create a Main() method within the class, as this was not produced automatically, and delete the unwanted imports.

Listing 15-38. Using const strings

```
namespace Chapter15
{
  internal class ConstantStrings
  {
    static void Main(string[] args)
    {
    } // End of Main() method
  } // End of ConstantStrings class
} // End of Chapter15 namespace
```

Now we will create four const strings, which we will use in a concatenation.

6. Create a series of four const strings, as in Listing 15-39.

Listing 15-39. Adding the four const strings

```
static void Main(string[] args)
{
  /*
  Prior to C# 10 we could have const strings and we
  had to concatenate them using the +
  */
  const string thankYou = "Thank you for purchasing insurance
  with us.\n";

  const string offerMessageHome = "As a thank you we are offering you 10%
  of your next Home insurance \n";

  const string offerMessageBuilding = "As a thank you we are offering you
  5% of your next Building insurance \n";

  const string redeemMessage = "Simply call us and we have this offer
  associated with your account\n ";
} // End of Main() method
```

Now we will create a new const string for a home message, which will be formed by concatenating three of the four const strings. We will then display the new home message const string.

7. Amend the code as in Listing 15-40.

Listing 15-40. Concatenating strings for a home message using the +

```
const string redeemMessage = "Simply call us and we have this offer
associated with your account\n ";

// Concatenation using +
const string homeMessage = thankYou + offerMessageHome + redeemMessage;

Console.WriteLine(homeMessage);
  } // End of Main() method
```

Now we will create a new const string for a building message, which will be formed by concatenating three of the four const strings. We will then display the new building message const string.

8.   Amend the code as in Listing 15-41.

Listing 15-41. Concatenating strings for a building message using the +

```
// Concatenation using +
const string homeMessage = thankYou + offerMessageHome + redeemMessage;

Console.WriteLine(homeMessage);

const string buildingMessage = thankYou + offerMessageBuilding +
redeemMessage;

Console.WriteLine(buildingMessage);
 } // End of Main() method
```

9.   Right-click the Chapter15 project in the Solution Explorer panel.

10.   Choose Properties from the pop-up menu.

11.   Choose the Chapter15.ConstantStrings class in the Startup object drop-down list, as shown in Figure 15-31.

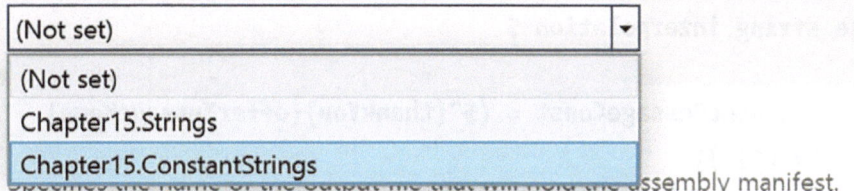

Startup object

Defines the entry point to be called when the application loads. Generally this is set either to the main form in your application or to the 'Main' procedure that should run when the application starts. Class libraries do not define an entry point.

(Not set)	▼

(Not set)

Chapter15.Strings

Chapter15.ConstantStrings

~~Specifies the name of the output file that will hold the~~ assembly manifest.

Figure 15-31. *Changing the startup class in the C# project*

12.   Close the Properties window.

13.   Click the File menu.

14.   Choose Save All.

15.   Click the Debug menu.

16.   Choose Start Without Debugging.

Figure 15-32 shows the console output displaying the concatenated const strings.

```
Thank you for purchasing insurance with us.
As a thank you we are offering you 10% of your next Home insurance
Simply call us and we have this offer associated with your account

Thank you for purchasing insurance with us.
As a thank you we are offering you 5% of your next Building insurance
Simply call us and we have this offer associated with your account


C:\CoreCSharp\CoreCSharp\Chapter15\bin\Debug\net6.0\Chapter15.exe (proc
Press any key to close this window . . .■
```

Figure 15-32. *Concatenating strings using the traditional +*

17.   Press the Enter key to close the console window.

Now we will use the const strings, but in an interpolated string. We will create a new home message const string and assign it the $ string interpolation, which uses the const strings. We will then display the new string to the console.

18.   Amend the code, as in Listing 15-42.

Listing 15-42. Interpolated string using const strings – home message

```
/*
From C# 10 we are allowed to concatenate const strings
with the string interpolation $
*/
const string homeMessageConst = ($"{thankYou}{offerMessageHome}
{redeemMessage}");

Console.WriteLine(homeMessageConst);
} // End of Main() method
```

Now we will create a new building message const string and assign it the $ string interpolation, which uses the const strings. We will then display the new string to the console.

19.   Amend the code, as in Listing 15-43.

Listing 15-43. Interpolated string using const strings – building message

```
const string homeMessageConst = ($"{thankYou}{offerMessageHome}
{redeemMessage}");

Console.WriteLine(homeMessageConst);

const string buildingMessageConst = $"{thankYou}{offerMessageBuilding}
{redeemMessage}";

Console.WriteLine(buildingMessageConst);
} // End of Main() method
```

If we look at our code and hover over the opening bracket (in the code

```
($"{thankYou}{offerMessageHome}{redeemMessage}");
```

there may be a warning, as shown in Figure 15-33, stating that we do not require the opening and closing brackets, but it is also fine to keep the brackets.

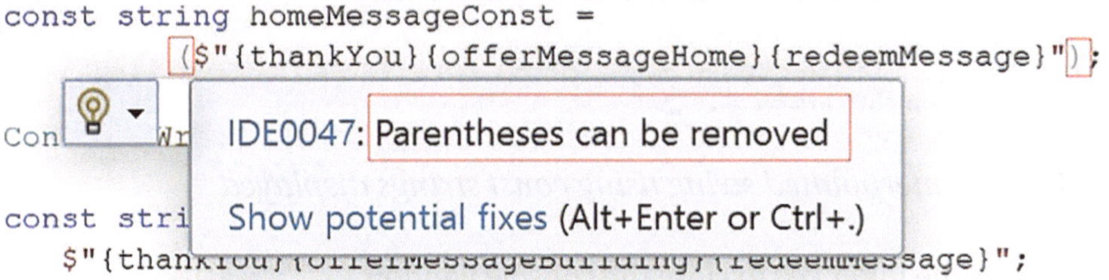

Figure 15-33. *Warning that parentheses are not required*

Also, if we are not using C# 10, we will see a message, as shown in Figure 15-34, that const strings in an interpolated string are not available.

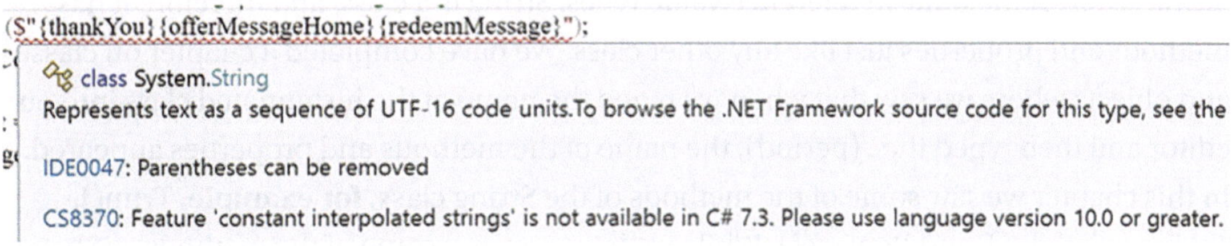

Figure 15-34. *Error – const strings not available in this language version*

20. Click the File menu.

21. Choose Save All.

22. Click the Debug menu.

23. Choose Start Without Debugging.

Figure 15-35 shows the console output displaying the interpolated string, which uses the const strings.

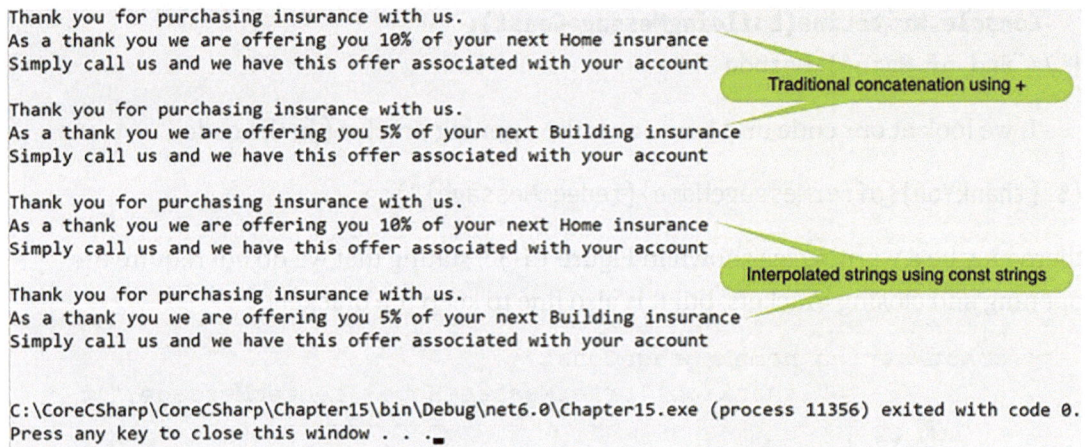

Figure 15-35. *Interpolated string using const strings displayed*

24. Press the Enter key to close the console window.

Chapter Summary

So, finishing this long chapter on string handling, we should remember that a string or String is one of the built-in reference value types. String is a class, and therefore it has methods and properties just like any other class. We have completed a chapter on classes and objects where we saw that when we typed the name of the instantiated class into our editor and then typed the . (period), the name of the methods and properties appeared. In this chapter we saw some of the methods of the String class, **for example,** Trim(), ToUpper(), Split(), and Replace(). While we have covered some of the methods, we have not covered them all, and we could investigate many more of the methods and their use. We have also covered different ways to write code in the WriteLine() method, and we have also looked at the newer features of C#, including constant interpolated strings and then constant strings within interpolated strings available from C# 10.

We are making fantastic progress in our programming of C# applications and we should be very proud of our achievements. In finishing this chapter, we have increased our knowledge further and we are advancing to our target.

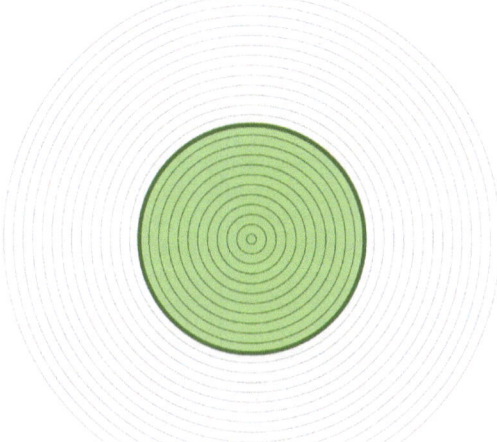

Our target is getting closer

645

CHAPTER 16

File Handling

File Handling

In the previous chapter, we gained knowledge of string handling and used many of the methods that belong to the String class. We saw some of the new features introduced in C# 10 that related to string handling, and now we will look at another important topic, file handling. File handling is an important skill since there are many uses for it in the commercial environment.

We learned throughout all the previous chapters about the core constructs of a C# program, and we have seen how to write data to an array. We also read that an array is used to temporarily store data in a data structure, but now we will look at how to store the data in the more permanent form of a text file. Once we have seen how to write to a text file, we should easily be capable of writing the data to a database, but for this book we will not get into the setting up of a database.

It is common for developers to interact with files within their applications. If we think about a game application, we will often see that the highest scores are stored, and the store could be a file located on the device where the game is being played. If the top ten scores are **written** to the file, then we can envisage that the file will have to be amended as new high scores are achieved. With a persistent store, such as a text file, the scores will be **read** after the device is restarted.

In the same manner when we use a web browser to visit a website, the site might store a cookie on our computer. The cookie could be a session cookie, which is stored temporarily and only exists for the duration of our browser session on this site, or it could be a persistent cookie where a small text file is saved on our computer. Text files are also widely used as log files, and a log file could consist of historical data related to things that occur. An example where we might encounter a log file could be historical data related to when we logged on to our insurance account or a bank account. The insurance company

© Gerard Byrne 2022
G. Byrne, *Target C#*, https://doi.org/10.1007/978-1-4842-8619-7_16

may record data related to the date and time of our log-in, the date and time when we logged out, and what parts of the account we used, for example, the payments window or the statements window. Or it might have been the documents window where we can see a PDF of our policy.

Within .NET we are provided with many "tools" to help us interact with the file system. Files provide a means by which our programs can store and access data. Within .NET the System.IO namespace offers us a collection of classes, methods, enumerations, and types to read and write data streams and files, using either a synchronous or asynchronous approach. In .NET all file handling operations require us to use the System.IO namespace.

An Overview of File Handling

We can think of a file as a series of bytes that exist as a collection of bytes in a named file on a persistent storage. Think of a file in terms of

- The file path, which contains

  - The drive the file is stored on, which could be a local drive or server

  - The directory the file is located in, within the drive – this may be a nested folder

In C#, when our application code is used to read in from a file or write out to a file, we will use a stream object, which can pass and receive data in the form of bytes. We can think of a stream as a series of bytes, and we will commonly use streams when we are reading or writing a large file where it is more efficient to read the file, chunk by chunk, or where we write to the file, chunk by chunk. Streams offer better performance in our application because in a write operation, the data is written to a stream first and held there until the device being written to is ready to accept the data. Equally, in a read operation, the chunks are sent to a stream as they are read from a file on the device, before they are used by the application requesting the data.

In using streams, it is not always about file streams being used to read from or write to a physical file, for example, a text file (.txt), an image file (.jpg, .jpeg, .bmp, .png), etc. Instead, we could use a different type of stream, and some of the possible stream types are shown in the following:

- Network – A network stream will be used to read from or write to a network socket, where a socket is one of the endpoints in a two-way network communication.

- Memory – A memory stream will be used to read or write bytes stored in memory.

- Pipe – A pipe stream will be used to read or write bytes from or to various processes.

- Buffer – A buffered stream is used to read or write bytes from or to other streams in order to enhance the performance of the operation.

The stream object offers us subclasses that can help when we have to work with any of the streams we have mentioned. Even though there are different classes for dealing with the different types of streams, there is some commonality. The common and regularly used methods will be the following:

- Read() method, which allows us to read data from a stream.

- Write() method, which allows us to write data to a stream.

- Close() method, which frees the file for other processes to use. Not closing the stream means other programs will not have access to the stream and its data.

- Seek() method, which allows us to change position within a stream. We can therefore use this method to read from or write to a position of our choice within the stream.

File Class

Now we will look at the File class, having read a little about streams. The C# File class provides static methods for file operations such as creating a file, copying a file, moving a file, and deleting a file. It also works with the FileStream class to read and write streams. So the File class and the FileStream class are different but work together. Table 16-1 shows some of the methods we might use.

Table 16-1. *File class methods*

Method	Description
AppendAllLines(filename, lines)	This method will be used to append lines to a file and then close the file. Should the file not exist, then the method will create the file for us, write the required lines to the new file, and then close the newly created file.
AppendAllText(filename, strig)	This method will be used to open a file and append the specified string to the file, closing the file when it has completed the task. Should the file not exist, then the method will create the file for us, write the required string to the new file, and then close the newly created file.
Exists(filename)	This method checks if the specified file exists.
ReadAllBytes(filename)	This method will be used to open a binary file and then read the contents of the file into a byte array before closing the file.
ReadAllLines(filename)	This method will be used to open a file and then read the contents of the file line by line before closing the file.
ReadAllText(filename)	This method will be used to open a file and then read the contents of the file as one block before closing the file.
WriteAllBytes(filename, byte[])	This method will be used to create a new file and then write the contents of the specified byte array to the file before closing the file. Should the file exist, then the method will overwrite it.
WriteAllLines(filename, String[])	This method will be used to create a new file and then write the contents of the specified String array to the file before closing the file. Should the file exist, then the method will overwrite it.
WriteAllText(filename, string)	This method will be used to create a new file and then write the contents of the specified string to the file before closing the file. Should the file exist, then the method will overwrite it.

In Chapter 12, we read the following point:

*In terms of the word **static**, we will see more about it in Chapter 13, but for now just accept that **static means belonging to this class**.*

In Chapter 13, we read the following points:

*Using the instance of the class, we have access to the methods and fields of the class that have the public access modifier and are not **static**.*

Adding the full stop after the instance name means those methods and fields that are accessible will be displayed. This is called the dot notation

Well, in .NET **the File class contains static methods,** and this means they belong to the File class, not any instance of the File class. So, when we wish to use the static methods, we will **not** need to make an instance of the File class to access and use these **methods. Yes, indeed, this is different from what we did in Chapter** 13, but it is a perfectly acceptable practice, and there are many classes that follow this paradigm.

In the following exercises, where we will use the File class from the System.IO namespace, we will be using the File class directly to access any methods. The format for calling the methods will be as follows: the word File followed by a period, followed by the method name, for example, File.ReadAllLines(), or File. followed by any of the static methods of the File class. A few of the static methods that will appear when the period is added in Visual Studio 2022 are shown in Figure 16-1.

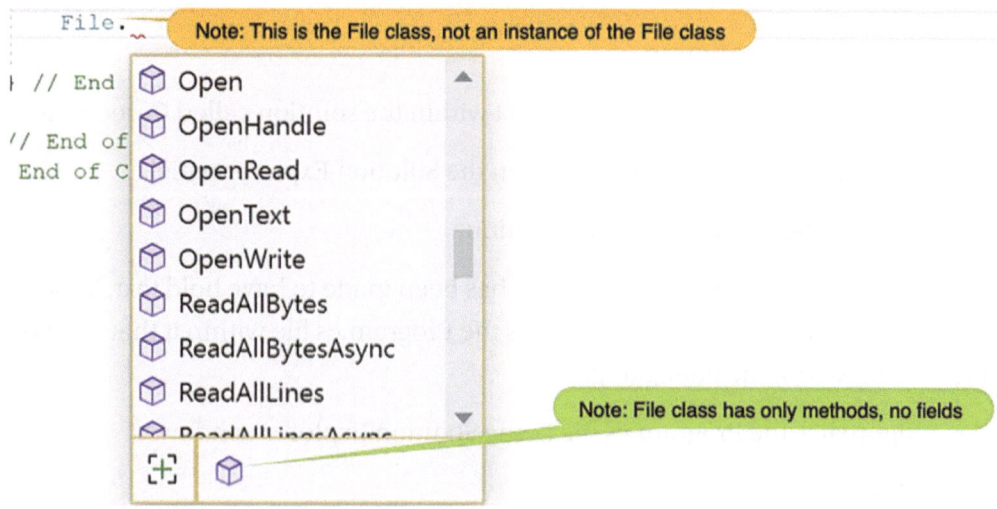

Figure 16-1. *File class methods*

Having gained some knowledge about classes and knowing that when we use the File class, we are using the class directly, we will know that we do not need to make an instance of the class. We can say this another way: we do not make an instance of the class.

Let's code some C# and build our programming muscle.

Add a new project to hold the code for this chapter.

1. Right-click the solution CoreCSharp.

2. Choose Add.

3. Choose New Project.

4. Choose Console App from the listed templates that appear.

5. Click the Next button.

6. Name the project Chapter16 and leave it in the same location.

7. Click the Next button.

8. Choose the framework to be used, which in our projects will be .NET 6.0 or higher.

9. Click the Create button.

Now we should see the Chapter16 project within the solution called CoreCSharp.

10. Right-click the Chapter16 project in the Solution Explorer panel.

11. Click the Set as Startup Project option.

Notice how the Chapter16 project name has been made to have bold text, indicating that it is the new startup project and that it is the Program.cs file within it that will be executed when we run the debugging.

12. Right-click the Program.cs file in the Solution Explorer window.

13. Choose Rename.

14. Change the name to FileHandling.cs.

15. Press the Enter key.

16. Double-click the FileHandling.cs file to open it in the editor window.

17. Amend the code as, in Listing 16-1, to have a namespace, a class, and a Main() method and import the System and System.IO namespaces.

Listing 16-1. Class template with the Main() method

```
namespace Chapter16
{
  internal class FileHandling
  {
    static void Main(string[] args)
    {
    } // End of Main() method

  } // End of FileHandling class
} // End of Chapter16 namespace
```

We will initially create a string variable to hold the name of the file being used. We will then write the code in a method that checks to see if a file exists, and when we run the application, we will see that a message appears telling us that the file does not exist. After this we will create the file and once again check that the file does exist.

18. Amend the code, as in Listing 16-2, to create string variables at the class level and assign the filenames to them.

Listing 16-2. String variable assigned the filename

```
namespace Chapter16
{
  internal class FileHandling
  {
    /*
    Create a variable to hold the file name. Here the file is
    in the current directory, which in this case means it will
    be in the Chapter 16 folder and then inside the bin folder
    of either the Debug or Release folder depending on how we
    have run the application, Start without debugging or Start
    with debugging which means it goes into the debug folder,
    build application means it will go into the Release folder
    */
```

```
const string policyDetailsFile = "policydetails.txt";
const string policyDetailsFileNew = "policydetailsnew.txt";
const string policyDetailsFileCopy = "policydetailscopy.txt";

static void Main(string[] args)
{
```

We will now create a method to check if a file exists using the Exists() method, and then we will call the method from the Main() method.

19.   Amend the code, as in Listing 16-3.

Listing 16-3. Create a method outside Main() and call it from inside Main()

```
static void Main(string[] args)
{
  CheckIfTheFileExists();
} // End of Main() method

public static void CheckIfTheFileExists()
{
  // Check if the file exists and display a message
  if (File.Exists(policyDetailsFile))
  {
    Console.WriteLine("Policy details file exists.");
  }
  else
  {
    Console.WriteLine("Policy details file does not exist.");
  }
}// End of CheckIfTheFileExists() method

} // End of FileHandling class
} // End of Chapter16 namespace
```

20.   Click the File menu.

21.   Choose Save All.

22.   Click the Debug menu.

23.   Choose Start Without Debugging.

Figure 16-2 shows the console window, which displays the message telling us the file does not exist.

```
Policy details file does not exist.

C:\CoreCSharp\CoreCSharp\Chapter16\bin\Debug\net6.0\Chapter16.exe
Press any key to close this window . . ._
```

Figure 16-2. *File does not exist message*

24.   Press the Enter key to close the console window.

We will now create a method that uses the Create() method to create a new file with a specified name and then call the method from the Main() method. The Create() method will create or overwrite a file with the filename given, and in doing so we are given a FileStream, which gives us read and write access to the file. Once the stream is opened, we need to be sure to close it using the Close() method or dispose of the stream in some other way.

25.   Amend the code, as in Listing 16-4, to create the method for creating the file.

Listing 16-4. Create a new file using the Create() method

```
}// End of CheckIfTheFileExists() method

public static void CreateTheFile()
{
  /*
  Create a file called policydetails.txt and close
  the stream that is opened for us
  */
  File.Create(policyDetailsFile).Close();
}// End of CreateTheFile() method
} // End of FileHandling class
} // End of Chapter16 namespace
```

26. Amend the code, as in Listing 16-5, to call the method from the Main() method.

Listing 16-5. Call our new method that creates the file

```
static void Main(string[] args)
{
  CheckIfTheFileExists();
  CreateTheFile();
} // End of Main() method
```

27. Click the File menu.

28. Choose Save All.

29. Click the Debug menu.

30. Choose Start Without Debugging.

The console window will now display the same "file does not exist" message. Just ignore this for now.

31. Press any key to close the console window that appears.

32. In the Solution Explorer click the Chapter16 project.

33. Click the Show All Files icon, as shown in Figure 16-3.

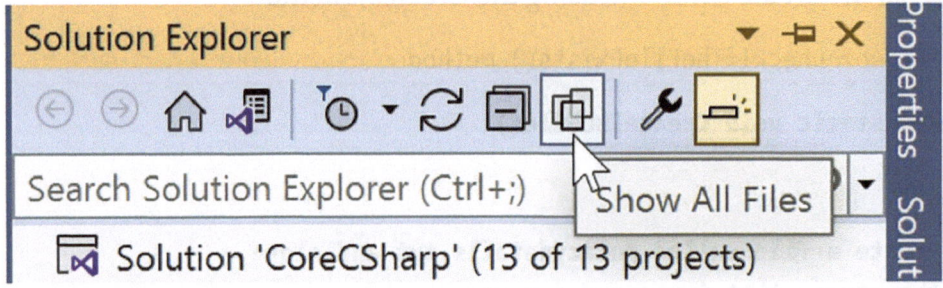

Figure 16-3. *Show All Files*

34. Click the Sync with Active Document button, if the icon is displayed, as shown in Figure 16-4.

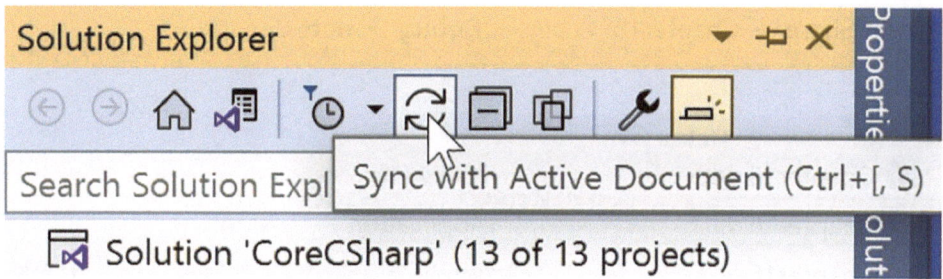

Figure 16-4. Refresh the project files view

35.   Expand the bin, Debug, and net6.0 folders.

The text file, which we wrote the code to create, should be displayed in the, initially hidden, net6.0 folder, which is inside the Debug folder, which is inside the bin folder, as shown in Figure 16-5.

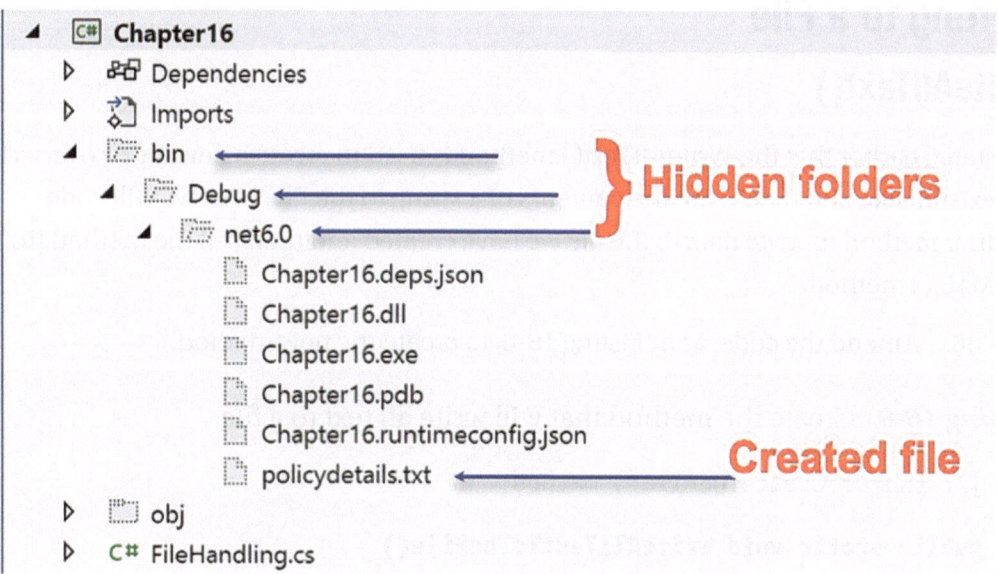

Figure 16-5. Text file has been written to its location

The file is not where we might initially have thought it would be. We must not always think about the code we are writing, and its location, but more about the compiled code and where it will be located. This is why our text file is located in the bin file, the binary file folder. Figure 16-6 shows the containing folder where we can see the text file, but also the Chapter16 application file, our program essentially.

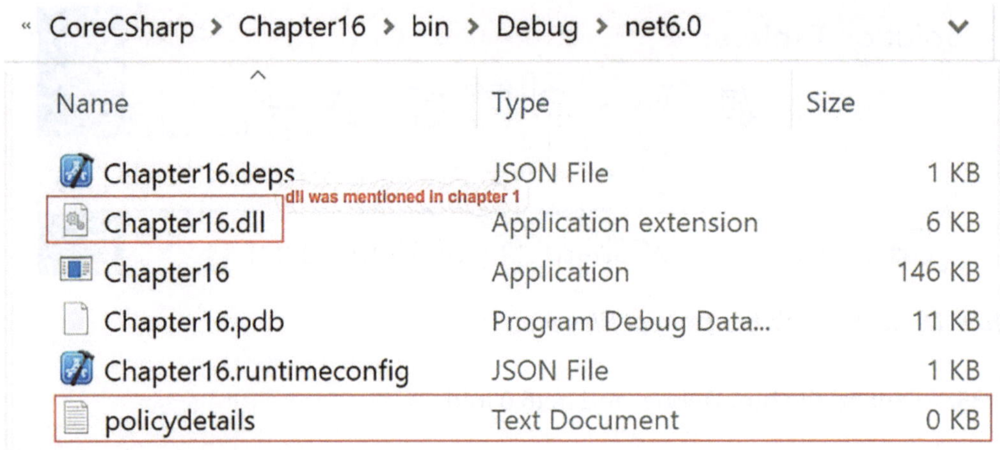

Figure 16-6. *Location of the compiled code*

Writing to a File

WriteAllText()

We stated earlier that the WriteAllText() method is used to create a new file or overwrite the existing file and then write the contents of a string to the file. Now we will code another method to write data to the file we have created and then call the method from the Main() method.

36. Amend the code, as in Listing 16-6, to create the new method.

Listing 16-6. Create the method that will write all text to a file

```
}// End of CreateTheFile() method

public static void WriteAllTextToTheFile()
{
  string policyDetailsMessage = "This file will hold details of the
  customer policies\r\n";
  File.WriteAllText(policyDetailsFile, policyDetailsMessage);
}// End of WriteAllTextToTheFile() method

} // End of FileHandling class
} // End of Chapter16 namespace
```

37.   Amend the code, as in Listing 16-7, to call the method from the
       Main() method.

Listing 16-7. Call our new method that writes text to the file

```
static void Main(string[] args)
{
  CheckIfTheFileExists();
  CreateTheFile();
  WriteAllTextToTheFile();
} // End of Main() method
```

38.   Click the File menu.

39.   Choose Save All.

40.   Click the Debug menu.

41.   Choose Start Without Debugging.

Figure 16-7 shows the console window, which displays the message telling us the file
exists, and now we will be able to check that the data has been written to it.

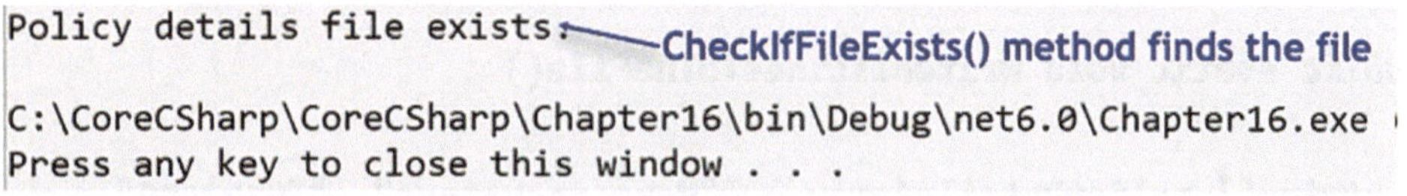

Figure 16-7. *File is found and can be written to*

42.   Press any key to close the console window that appears.

43.   In the Solution Explorer expand the Chapter16 project.

As we have just shown in Figure 16-7, the application code does create the file and
we get the message to confirm this. Looking in the file directory structure where our
Chapter16 project is located and then looking inside the net6.0 folder, within the Debug
folder, within the bin folder, we will see the text file has been created and the text has
been written to it.

44. Double-click the policydetails.txt file to open it in the editor window, as shown in Figure 16-8.

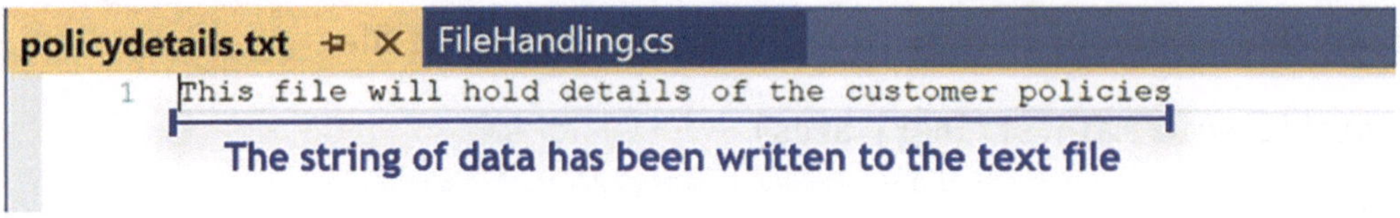

Figure 16-8. *Data written to the text file*

WriteAllLines()

We stated earlier that the WriteAllLines() method is used to create a new file or overwrite the existing file with the contents of a string array. Now we will code another method to write all the data from a string array to the file we have created and then call the method from the Main() method.

45. Amend the code, as in Listing 16-8, to create a method.

Listing 16-8. Create the method that will write the array contents to the text file

```
}// End of WriteAllTextToTheFile() method

public static void WriteAllLinesToTheFile()
{
  string[] policyDetailsArray = {"Home insurance", "ID123456",
  "199.99"};
  File.WriteAllLines(policyDetailsFile, policyDetailsArray);
}// End of WriteAllLinesToTheFile() method

  } // End of FileHandling class
} // End of Chapter16 namespace
```

46. Amend the code, as in Listing 16-9, to call the method from the Main() method.

Listing 16-9. Call our new method that writes all lines to the file

```
static void Main(string[] args)
{
  CheckIfTheFileExists();
  CreateTheFile();
  WriteAllTextToTheFile();
  WriteAllLinesToTheFile();
} // End of Main() method
```

47. Click the File menu.

48. Choose Save All.

49. Click the Debug menu.

50. Choose Start Without Debugging.

51. Press any key to close the console window that appears.

52. In the Solution Explorer click the Chapter16 project.

53. Double-click the policydetails.txt file to open it in the editor window, as shown in Figure 16-9.

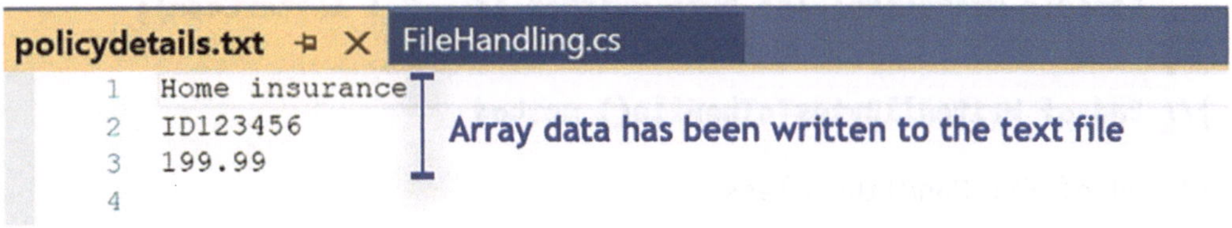

Figure 16-9. *Data from array written to the text file, overriding existing text*

WriteAllBytes()

We stated earlier that the WriteAllBytes method is used to create a new file or overwrite the existing file with the contents of a byte array. Now we will code another method where we will

- Create a string variable and assign it a string of text.

- Convert the string to bytes using the GetBytes() method from System. Text.Encoding.ASCII and place the bytes in a byte array.

- Use the WriteAllBytes() method to write the bytes to a new text file.

- Display the bytes by iterating the byte array and displaying each element, which will be a byte value from 0 to 255.

54. Amend the code, as in Listing 16-10, to create the method to perform the steps listed previously.

Listing 16-10. Create the method to write a byte array's contents to the text file

```
}// End of WriteAllLinesToTheFile() method

public static void WriteAllBytesToTheFile()
{
  string policyMessage = "All policies";
  byte[] policyMessageAsData =
  System.Text.Encoding.ASCII.GetBytes(policyMessage);

  File.WriteAllBytes(policyDetailsFile, policyMessageAsData);

  Console.WriteLine("The bytes written to the file are");
  foreach (byte letterCode in policyMessageAsData)
  {
    Console.WriteLine("The byte written is - " + letterCode);
  }
}// End of WriteAllBytesToTheFile() method

} // End of FileHandling class
```

55. Amend the code, as in Listing 16-11, to call the WriteAllBytesToTheFile() method from the Main() method.

Listing 16-11. Call our new method that writes a byte array's contents to the text file

```
static void Main(string[] args)
{
  CheckIfTheFileExists();
  CreateTheFile();
  WriteAllTextToTheFile();
```

```
    WriteAllLinesToTheFile();
    WriteAllBytesToTheFile();
} // End of Main() method
```

56. Click the File menu.

57. Choose Save All.

58. Click the Debug menu.

59. Choose Start Without Debugging.

The console window will appear, as shown in Figure 16-10, and display the ASCII byte values that are stored in the byte array.

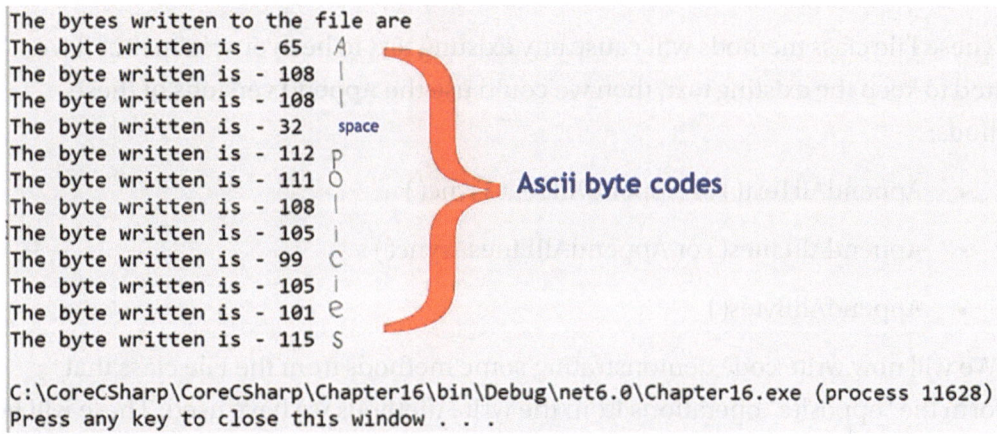

Figure 16-10. *The bytes from the byte array are displayed*

60. Press any key to close the console window that appears.

61. In the Solution Explorer click the Chapter16 project.

62. Double-click the policydetails.txt file to open it in the editor window, as shown in Figure 16-11, and see that the data is written to the file.

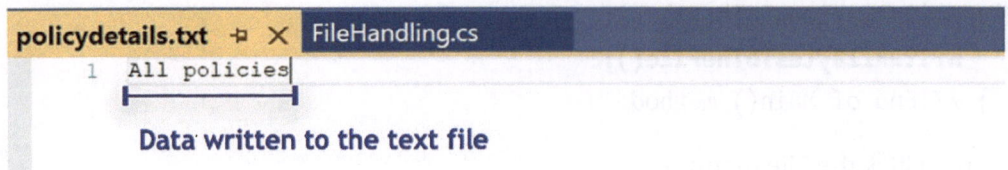

Data written to the text file

Figure 16-11. *Data from array written to the text file*

We have completed code demonstrating the following methods from the File class:

- WriteAllText()

- WriteAllLines()

- WriteAllBytes()

These File class methods will cause any existing text to be overwritten, but if we wanted to keep the existing text, then we could use the Append versions of these methods:

- AppendAllText() or AppendAllTextAsync()

- AppendAllLines() or AppendAllLinesAsync()

- AppendAllBytes()

We will now write code demonstrating some methods from the File class that perform the "opposite" operations from the write methods we have used. These will be read methods and we will be looking to use

- ReadAllText()

- ReadAllLines()

- ReadAllBytes()

There are also async versions of these three methods: ReadAllTextAsync(), ReadAllLinesAsync() and ReadAllBytesAsync().

Reading from a File

ReadAllText( )

We stated earlier that the ReadAllText() method is used to open a file and then read the contents of the file as one block, before closing the file. Now we will code another method to read all the text from a new file, which we will create, and then call the method from the Main() method.

Create the new text file.

1. Right-click the policydetails.txt file in the net6.0 folder, which is inside the Debug folder, inside the bin folder, in the Solution Explorer window.

2. Choose Copy.

3. Right-click the net6.0 folder.

4. Choose Paste.

5. Right-click the newly pasted policydetails – Copy.txt file.

6. Choose Rename.

7. Rename the file policydetailsnew.txt.

8. Double-click the policydetailsnew.txt file to open it in the editor window.

9. Amend the text file by adding some additional lines of text. Listing 16-12 shows some additional lines added to the one line that previously existed.

Listing 16-12. Additional lines added to the policydetailsnew.txt file

```
All policies
Policy AU123456
Policy HO987654
Policy BO234580
Policy LI675423
```

We will now add the new method to the FileHandling.cs file and then call it from the Main() method.

    10.   Amend the **FileHandling.cs** code, as in Listing 16-13, to create the method.

Listing 16-13. Create the method to read all contents of the text file

```
}// End of WriteAllBytesToTheFile() method

public static void ReadAllTextFromTheFile()
{
 // Open the file to be read from
 string textReadFromFile =
 File.ReadAllText(policyDetailsFileNew);
 Console.WriteLine("The data read is:\n" + textReadFromFile);
}// End of ReadAllTextFromTheFile() method

} // End of FileHandling class
} // End of Chapter16 namespace
```

    11.   Amend the code, as in Listing 16-14, to call the method from the Main() method.

Listing 16-14. Call our new method that reads all contents of the text file

```
static void Main(string[] args)
{
  CheckIfTheFileExists();
  CreateTheFile();
  WriteAllTextToTheFile();
  WriteAllLinesToTheFile();
  WriteAllBytesToTheFile();
  ReadAllTextFromTheFile();
} // End of Main() method
```

    12.   Click the File menu.

    13.   Choose Save All.

14. Click the Debug menu.

15. Choose Start Without Debugging.

The console window will appear, as shown in Figure 16-12, and show the contents of the file that has been read.

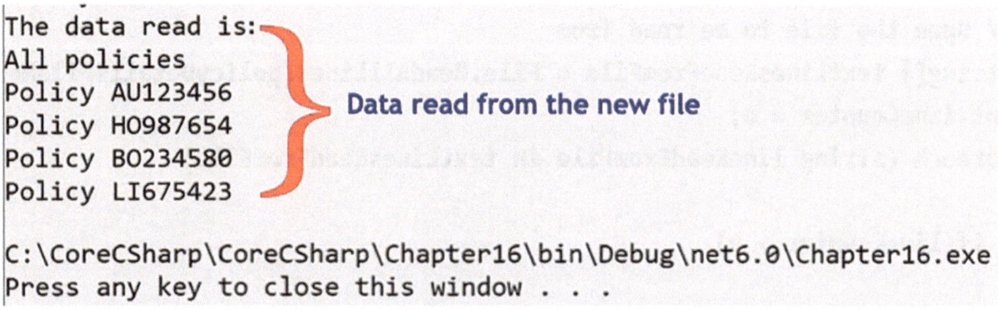

```
The data read is:
All policies
Policy AU123456        }  Data read from the new file
Policy HO987654
Policy BO234580
Policy LI675423

C:\CoreCSharp\CoreCSharp\Chapter16\bin\Debug\net6.0\Chapter16.exe
Press any key to close this window . . .
```

Figure 16-12. *Data read from the file is displayed*

16. Press any key to close the console window that appears.

ReadAllLines( )

We stated earlier that the ReadAllLines( ) method is used to open a file and then read the contents of the file line by line before closing the file. Now we will code another method to

- Read all the lines from the file we have created

- If it is the first line, display the text as it is.

- If it is not the first line, use the Substring( ) method to read the policy number part of the line, which starts at character 7.

- Display a message showing the policy number.

We will then call the method from the Main() method.

17. Amend the code, as in Listing 16-15, to create the method.

Listing 16-15. Create the method to read all lines of the text file

```
}// End of ReadAllTextFromTheFile() method

public static void ReadAllTextLinesFromTheFile()
{
  // Open the file to be read from
  string[] textLinesReadFromFile = File.ReadAllLines(policyDetailsFileNew);
  int lineCounter = 0;
  foreach (string lineReadFromFile in textLinesReadFromFile)
  {
    if(lineCounter > 0)
    {
      string policyNumber = lineReadFromFile.Substring(7);
      Console.WriteLine("The policy number is " + policyNumber);
    }
    else
    {
      Console.WriteLine(lineReadFromFile);
    }
    lineCounter++;
  }// End of foreach
}// End of ReadAllTextLinesFromTheFile() method

  } // End of FileHandling class
} // End of Chapter16 namespace
```

18. Amend the code, as in Listing 16-16, to call the method from the Main() method.

Listing 16-16. Call our new method that reads all lines of the text file

```
static void Main(string[] args)
{
  CheckIfTheFileExists();
  CreateTheFile();
  WriteAllTextToTheFile();
```

```
    WriteAllLinesToTheFile();
    WriteAllBytesToTheFile();
    ReadAllTextFromTheFile();
    ReadAllTextLinesFromTheFile();
} // End of Main() method
```

19. Click the File menu.

20. Choose Save All.

21. Click the Debug menu.

22. Choose Start Without Debugging.

23. Press any key to close the console window, as shown in Figure 16-13.

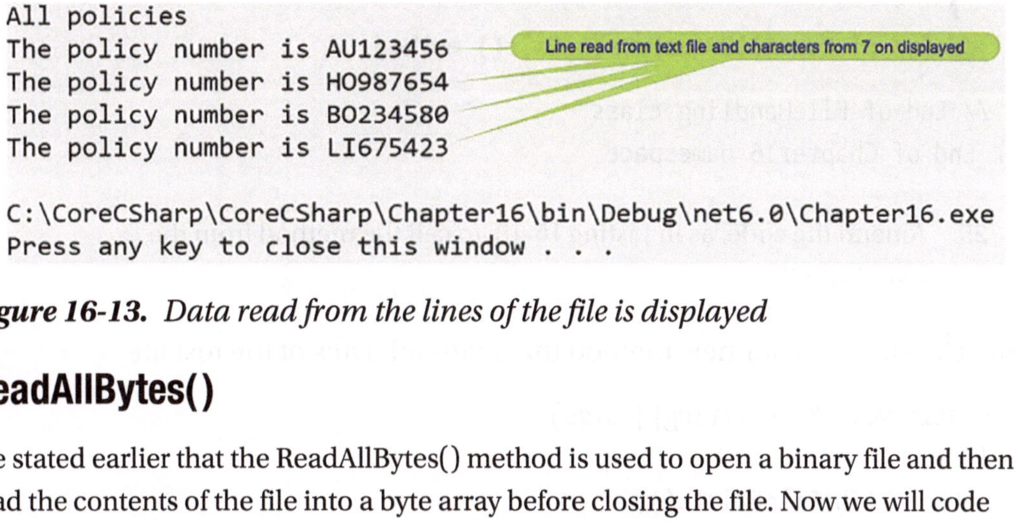

```
All policies
The policy number is AU123456 ──────   Line read from text file and characters from 7 on displayed
The policy number is HO987654
The policy number is BO234580
The policy number is LI675423

C:\CoreCSharp\CoreCSharp\Chapter16\bin\Debug\net6.0\Chapter16.exe
Press any key to close this window . . .
```

Figure 16-13. *Data read from the lines of the file is displayed*

ReadAllBytes()

We stated earlier that the ReadAllBytes() method is used to open a binary file and then read the contents of the file into a byte array before closing the file. Now we will code another method to read all the bytes from the file we created and add them to a byte array. We will then call the method from the Main() method.

24. Amend the code, as in Listing 16-17, to create the method.

Listing 16-17. Create the method to read all bytes of the text file

```
}// End of ReadAllTextLinesFromTheFile() method

public static void ReadAllBytesFromTheFile()
{
  /*
  Open the file to read from and read all the bytes placing
  them in a byte string
  */
  byte[] bytesReadFromTheFile = File.ReadAllBytes(policyDetails
  FileNew);
  foreach (byte byteReadFromFile in bytesReadFromTheFile)
  {
    Console.WriteLine("The byte is " + byteReadFromFile);
  }
}// End of ReadAllBytesFromTheFile() method

  } // End of FileHandling class
} // End of Chapter16 namespace
```

25. Amend the code, as in Listing 16-18, to call the method from the Main() method.

Listing 16-18. Call our new method that reads all bytes of the text file

```
static void Main(string[] args)
{
  CheckIfTheFileExists();
  CreateTheFile();
  WriteAllTextToTheFile();
  WriteAllLinesToTheFile();
  WriteAllBytesToTheFile();
  ReadAllTextFromTheFile();
  ReadAllTextLinesFromTheFile();
  ReadAllBytesFromTheFile();
} // End of Main() method
```

26. Click the File menu.

27. Choose Save All.

28. Click the Debug menu.

29. Choose Start Without Debugging.

30. Press any key to close the console window, as shown in Figure 16-14.

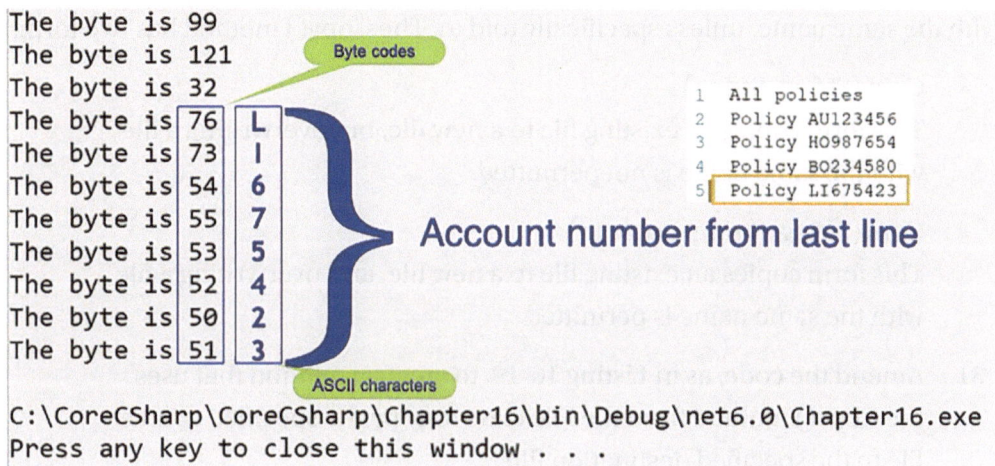

Figure 16-14. *Some of the data read from the file to a byte array*

Copy a File

Up to now we have been reading from and writing to files without any errors, exceptions, occurring. However, when we attempt to read and write files, things can go wrong, for example:

- The file might not exist.

- The file might be readonly when we attempt to write to it.

- The file may be damaged.

- We may have the filename spelled incorrectly.

C# gives us a try catch block that can help us avoid getting an exception error when we perform file handling processes. The C# try catch block uses the try and catch keywords, and the try catch block is placed around the code that we think could throw an exception. When an exception is thrown, the try catch block will handle the exception and therefore ensure that our application does not cause an unhandled exception. Since we are dealing with files and we are using the System.IO namespace, we can use the catch section to catch any IO exceptions.

Copy()

The Copy() method is used to copy an existing file to a new file, but it cannot overwrite a file with the same name, unless specifically told to. The Copy() method has two forms:

- Copy(String, String)
  This form copies an existing file to a new file, but overwriting a file with the same name is not permitted.

- Copy(String, String, Boolean)
  This form copies an existing file to a new file, and overwriting a file with the same name is permitted.

31. Amend the code, as in Listing 16-19, to create a method that uses the Copy() method from the File class to copy the specified source file to the specified destination file.

Listing 16-19. Create the method to copy the file

```
}// End of ReadAllBytesFromTheFile() method

public static void CopyAFile()
{
  // Use a try catch construct to catch any exceptions
  try
  {
    /*
    Copy the contents of the source file policydetailsnew.txt
    to the destination file policydetailscopy.txt
    */

    File.Copy(policyDetailsFileNew,policyDetailsFileCopy,true);
    Console.WriteLine("The copying process was successful.");
  } // End of try block
```

```
    catch (IOException exceptionFound)
    {
      Console.WriteLine("Copying failed with exception:");
      Console.WriteLine(exceptionFound.Message);
    } // End of catch block
  }// End of CopyAFile() method
} // End of FileHandling class
} // End of Chapter16 namespace
```

32. Amend the code, as in Listing 16-20, to call the method from the Main() method.

Listing 16-20. Call our new method that copies the file

```
static void Main(string[] args)
{
  CheckIfTheFileExists();
  CreateTheFile();
  WriteAllTextToAFile();
  WriteAllLinesToAFile();
  WriteAllBytesToAFile();
  ReadAllTextFromAFile();
  ReadAllTextLinesFromAFile();
  ReadAllBytesFromAFile();
  CopyAFile();
} // End of Main() method
```

33. Click the File menu.

34. Choose Save All.

35. Click the Debug menu.

36. Choose Start Without Debugging.

Figure 16-15 shows the output that indicates a successful copying process.

```
The byte is 50
The byte is 51                          Copy file success
The copying process was successful.

C:\CoreCSharp\CoreCSharp\Chapter16\bin\Debug\net6.0\Chapter16.exe
Press any key to close this window . . .
```

Figure 16-15. *File success message*

37.   Press any key to close the console window that appears.

Looking in the net6.0 folder, inside the Debug folder, inside the bin folder, we should see the file policydetailscopy as shown in Figure 16-16.

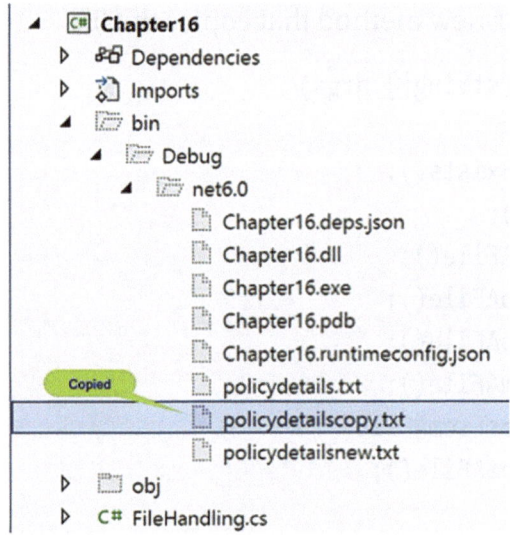

Figure 16-16. *File copied*

Delete a File

In a similar manner to reading a file or writing a file where we could get an exception, when we wish to delete a file, we could get an exception, so we will use the try catch block around the process used to delete a file.

Delete()

The Delete() method is used to delete an existing file.

38. Amend the code, as in Listing 16-21, to create a method that uses the Delete() method from the File class to delete the specified source file.

Listing 16-21. Create the method to delete the file

```
}// End of CopyAFile() method

public static void DeleteAFile()
{
  // Use a try catch construct to catch any exceptions
  try
  {
    // Delete the file policydetailscopy.txt
    File.Delete("policydetailscopy.txt");
    Console.WriteLine("The file deletion was successful.");
  } // End of try block
  catch (IOException exceptionFound)
  {
   Console.WriteLine("File deletion failed with exception:");
   Console.WriteLine(exceptionFound.Message);
  } // End of catch block
 }// End of DeleteAFile() method

} // End of FileHandling class
```

39. Amend the code, as in Listing 16-22, to call the method from the Main() method.

Listing 16-22. Call our new method that deletes a file

```
static void Main(string[] args)
{
  CheckIfTheFileExists();
  CreateTheFile();
```

```
            WriteAllTextToAFile();
            WriteAllLinesToAFile();
            WriteAllBytesToAFile();
            ReadAllTextFromAFile();
            ReadAllTextLinesFromAFile();
            ReadAllBytesFromAFile();
            CopyAFile();
            DeleteAFile();
        } // End of Main() method
```

40. Click the File menu.

41. Choose Save All.

42. Click the Debug menu.

43. Choose Start Without Debugging.

The output, as shown in Figure 16-17, shows the deletion was successful.

```
The copying process was successful.
The file deletion was successful.
```

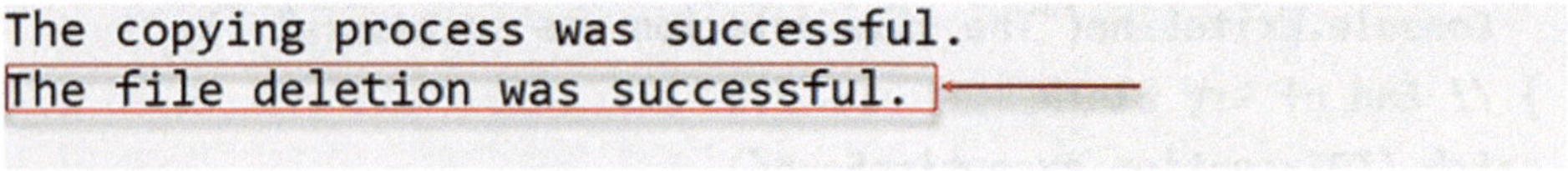

Figure 16-17. *Deletion successful*

44. Press any key to close the console window that appears.

Looking in the net6.0 folder, inside the Debug folder, inside the bin folder, we should see the copied file has been deleted as shown in Figure 16-18.

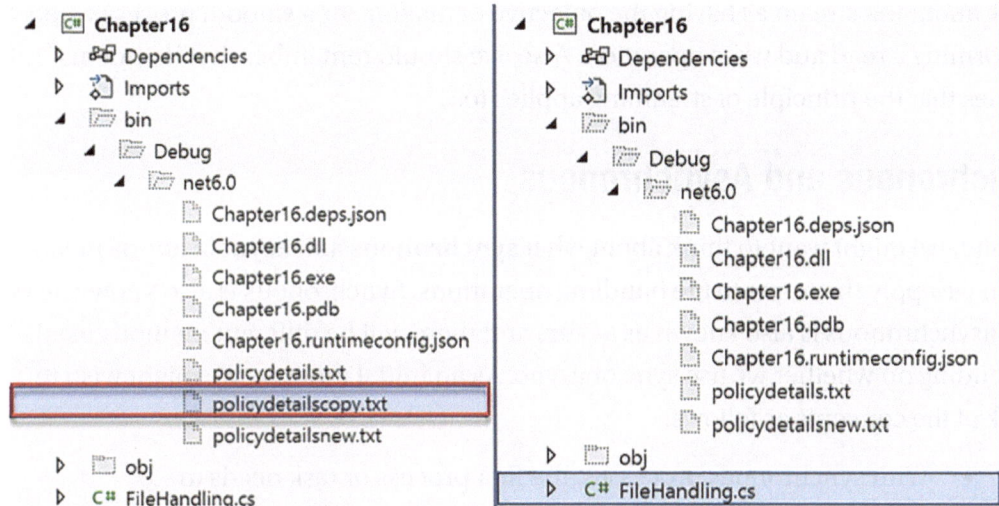

Figure 16-18. *File deleted*

StreamReader Class

The C# StreamReader class provides methods that allow us to read the characters of a file into a stream. There is also a StreamWriter class that allows us to write to a stream, and we will discuss this in the next section. StreamReader and StreamReader hide us from some of the complexities of streams, and we will look at this in the "FileStream" section.

Stream

First, we might want to think about what a stream is and why we would use one. Well, let's think about downloading a film from our favorite online store. Do we expect the whole video to be downloaded before we watch it? Well, the answer is probably not, and this is where the idea of a stream comes in. The stream will act as an intermediary, between the sender and the receiver, where the sender starts delivering the movie, chunk by chunk, and the stream accepts the chunk and starts to pass the data to the receiver. The speed at which the sender can send the movie data and the speed at which the receiving device can accept the data could well be different, so the stream holds the data and "feeds" the receiver at a speed that suits it. In the meantime, as this streaming process is taking place, we are able to start watching the movie as the first chunks have arrived, and the other chunks will be available when we need them. We should therefore think about the stream as having the objective of making for a smooth process when performing a read and write operation. Also, we should remember that it's not just movies that the principle of streaming applies to.

Synchronous and Asynchronous

Second, we might want to think about what **synchronous** and **asynchronous** mean when we apply the terms to file handling operations. Synchronous is also known as **sync,** and asynchronous is also known as **async**, and there will be different methods used depending on whether we use sync or async. As an initial thought, we might wish to think of the concepts as follows:

- With synchronous processes, the first process or task needs to complete before the next process starts. We therefore have the first process **"blocking"** other processes while it completes its task fully.

- With asynchronous processes, the first process or task does not need to complete before the next process starts. The processes can run in parallel. One process does not block the other processes, and we therefore will hear the term **"non-blocking"** in the context of asynchronous processing.

Now, if we think about synchronous and asynchronous approaches within our C# code, we might see that the synchronous approach could cause delays in the execution of a process or program. Many programmers will therefore use an asynchronous approach to overcome the delays. In programming we will hear mention of threading, the use of multiple threads where each thread will return after making a request, so that the program can get on with performing the other processes it has to perform.

Looking at another programming language called JavaScript, we will see that it is by default **synchronous** and single-threaded, meaning our JavaScript code could not create new threads and run in parallel. On the other hand, when Node.js was created, it introduced a non-blocking input and output (I/O) environment, and there is the concept of a **callback**, which is used to inform one process when its work has been completed. Think of it like the "chef" who takes the order for eggs and toast from child 1. They process the order by making the eggs and toast, and then they call the first child when their order is complete, a callback. We have probably experienced a callback or asynchronous process in our everyday life.

StreamReader Class Methods

StreamReader uses the TextReader class as its base class and has methods and one property that can help us perform operations on our stream of data. Table 16-2 shows some of the StreamReader methods we might use, but we should be aware that there are many overloads of these methods that can be used.

Table 16-2. *StreamReader class methods and property*

Method	Description
Read()	This method will be used to read the next set of characters from an input stream and then move to the next.
ReadAsync()	This method will be used to asynchronously read a sequence of bytes from a stream and then move to the next position in the stream to read the next sequence of bytes.
ReadLine()	This method will be used to read a line of characters from a stream returning the data read as a string.
ReadLineAsync()	This method will be used to read a line of characters from a stream in an asynchronous manner returning the data read as a string.
ReadToEnd()	Reads all characters from the current position to the end of the stream.
Property	
EndOfStream	This property of the class returns a value that indicates if we are at the end of the stream. It is a Boolean value, so it is either true or false.

StreamWriter Class

The C# StreamWriter class provides methods that allow us to write characters to a stream with specific encoding and by default uses UTF-8 encoding. UTF-8 is used as an encoding mechanism for Unicode, and Unicode is a standard that assigns a unique number to every character. UTF is an acronym for Unicode Transformation Format.

The StreamWriter class inherits from the TextWriter class so it makes use of the methods in this TextWriter class. Table 16-3 shows some of the StreamWriter methods we might use, but we should be aware that there are many overloads of these methods that can be used.

Table 16-3. *StreamWriter class methods and property*

Method	Description
Write()	This method will be used to write a sequence of bytes to a stream and then advance to the position after this sequence of bytes.
WriteAsync()	This method will be used to asynchronously write a sequence of bytes to a stream and then advance to the position in the stream after this sequence of bytes.
WriteLine()	This method will be used to write a formatted string and a new line to a stream.
WriteLineAsync()	This method will be used to asynchronously write a sequence of bytes to a stream followed by a line terminator.
Property	
EndOfStream	Gets a value that indicates if the current stream position is at the end of the stream. The return value is true if the current stream position is at the end of the stream; otherwise, it will be false.

Reading from a Stream

We will now use the StreamReader Read() method and the EndOfStream property in some code. Initially, we will create a method that uses the Read() method to read the specified text and then display the byte data. When we open a stream, we should always close it, so we will use the Close() method to do this.

1. Amend the code, as in Listing 16-23.

Listing 16-23. Read() and Peek() to read file characters, close StreamReader

```
}// End of DeleteAFile() method

public static void UseStreamReaderRead()
{
  try
  {
    if (File.Exists(policyDetailsFile))
```

```
    {
      // Create an instance of the StreamReader class
      StreamReader myStreamReader = new StreamReader(policyDetailsFile);

      /*
      Iterate the instance of the StreamReader while there
      is data, which means the Peek() method returns an
      integer greater than 0
      */
      while (myStreamReader.Peek() > 0)
      {
        Console.Write(myStreamReader.Read() + "\t");
      }
      myStreamReader.Close();
    }
    else
    {
    }
  }
  catch (Exception exceptionFound)
  {
    Console.WriteLine("Process failed with the exception:");
    Console.WriteLine(exceptionFound.Message);
  }
  Console.WriteLine();
}// End of UseStreamReaderRead() method

} // End of FileHandling class
} // End of Chapter16 namespace
```

2. Call the method from the Main() method, as in Listing 16-24.

Listing 16-24. Call our new method that reads the specified text

```
    CopyAFile();
    DeleteAFile();
    UseStreamReaderRead();
  } // End of Main() method
```

3. Click the File menu.

4. Choose Save All.

5. Click the Debug menu.

6. Choose Start Without Debugging.

The output, as shown in Figure 16-19, shows the bytes of the file that has been read. The file contains the words *All policies*, which is 12 characters, so we see 12 byte codes. Each of the bytes represents an ASCII character, for example, 65 is A and 32 is a space.

65	108	108	32	112	111	108	105	99	105	101	115
A	l	l	space	P	O	l	l	c	l	e	s

```
C:\CoreCSharp\CoreCSharp\Chapter16\bin\Debug\net6.0\Chapter16.exe (process 9856) exited with code 0.
Press any key to close this window . . .
```

Figure 16-19. *Bytes read from file – these bytes represent the string All policies*

7. Press any key to close the console window that appears.

Writing to a Stream

Rather than using the try catch block, we will use a different approach to illustrate that a **using** block can be used if we wish to have garbage collection (GC) handled for us. Using is very helpful and can be used with the StreamReader and StreamWriter classes. With the using block, we wrap the StreamWriter process inside it. Using handles disposal of any objects that are not required; it is not a try catch being used to catch exceptions, but rather a way to ensure disposal of objects we are not using.

We will discuss the using statement at the end of this chapter, but for now we will use the pre–C# 8 version of the using statement, and later we will see how there is an alternative way to use the using without the curly braces.

We will now use the StreamWriter WriteLine() method in some code along with the using block:

- We will create the using block.

- Using will be given an instance of the StreamWriter class.

- In creating the instance of the StreamWriter class, we will use the constructor, which will accept a true attribute, and this indicates that the content should be appended to the file, rather than overwriting the contents.

- We will use the WriteLine() method to write some lines to the file.

- We will also add an extra WriteLine() so our new data starts on a new line.

8. Amend the code, as in Listing 16-25.

Listing 16-25. Making use of the using block

```
}// End of UseStreamReaderRead() method

public static void UseStreamWriterWriteInUsingBlock()
{
  using (StreamWriter myStreamWriter =
                 new StreamWriter(policyDetailsFile, true))
  {
    try
    {
    if (File.Exists(policyDetailsFile))
    {
      myStreamWriter.WriteLine("");
      myStreamWriter.WriteLine("Auto insurance");
      myStreamWriter.WriteLine("ID987654");
      myStreamWriter.WriteLine("299.99");
      Console.WriteLine("The data has been written to file");
       }
       else
       {
       }
    }
     catch (Exception exceptionFound)
```

```
      {
        Console.WriteLine("Process failed with the exception:");
          Console.WriteLine(exceptionFound.Message);
        }
      } // End of using block
    }// End of UseStreamWriterWriteInUsingBlock() method
  } // End of FileHandling class
} // End of Chapter16 namespace
```

9. Call the method from the Main() method, as in Listing 16-26.

Listing 16-26. Call our new method

```
    DeleteAFile();
    UseStreamReaderRead();
    UseStreamWriterWriteInUsingBlock();
  } // End of Main() method
```

10. Click the File menu.

11. Choose Save All.

12. Click the Debug menu.

13. Choose Start Without Debugging.

14. Press any key to close the console window that appears.

15. Double-click the policydetails.txt file to open it in the editor window.

Figure 16-20 shows the lines of text have been added, but because of the other code we have, the policydetails.txt starts blank and our new method adds its data. We therefore do not see the effect of the true, which allows appending data to the file. If we wanted to see this append effect, we would need to comment out the other method calls in the Main() method. But for now, we will accept that appending has occurred.

Figure 16-20. *WriteLine() method inside a using block*

Great, the StreamWriter class has been used with its WriteLine() method to write data to the file.

Async Methods and Asynchronous Programming

When we use input and output operations such reading from and writing to a database or text file, we should consider using asynchronous programming. To assist in using asynchronous programming, the C# language offers us Task-based Asynchronous Pattern (TAP). This effectively means we do not have to worry about the callbacks we discussed earlier, as they will be handled for us. When we use this asynchronous pattern, two keywords are important, async and await. The important concepts to understand are as follows:

- We must use the **async** keyword to convert our method into an **async method**, which then allows us to use the await keyword within the body of the method. We should not use async on void methods, and we should use **Task** as the return type for non-void methods.

- The **await** keyword acts to put the caller on hold while the async method is performing what it needs to perform, but in the meantime our program can do other things until we get control back.

Listing 16-27 shows an example of using Task and await, while Listing 16-28 shows how we call the async method that returns a Task.

So how can using asynchronous programming help us when reading and writing files? Well, writing to a file in an asynchronous manner allows our program to continue doing other things while the file is being written to. If we are writing small files, the asynchronous approach will hardly be noticeable, but when the files become much larger, which will be the case in many business applications, it will make a big difference. The same principle applies when reading a large file in an asynchronous manner. Our program can get on with doing other things while it awaits the end of the reading process.

WriteLineAsync

We will now use the StreamWriter WriteLineAsync() method to write data. This is almost the same code as in Listing 16-25, but we are using a **WriteLineAsync()** method instead of the ordinary WriteLine() method, and we will still have our code in a using block. We read earlier that the WriteLineAsync() method is used to asynchronously write a sequence of bytes to a stream followed by a line terminator.

16.   Amend the code as in Listing 16-27.

Listing 16-27. Writing data asynchronously with WriteLineAsync()

```
}// End of UseStreamWriterWriteInUsingBlock() method

public static async Task<int> WriteCharactersAsynchronously()
{
  int count = 0;
  using (StreamWriter myStreamWriter = File.
  CreateText("asynctextfile.txt"))
  {
    await myStreamWriter.WriteLineAsync("Life insurance");
    await myStreamWriter.WriteLineAsync("LF123456");
    await myStreamWriter.WriteLineAsync("99.99");
    count += 3;
  }
  return count;
}// End of WriteCharactersAsynchronously() method

} // End of FileHandling class
} // End of Chapter16 namespace
```

17.   Call the method from the Main() method, as in Listing 16-28.

Listing 16-28. Call our new method that writes data asynchronously

```
UseStreamWriterRead();
UseStreamWriterWriteInUsingBlock();
Task<int> task = WriteCharactersAsynchronously();
} // End of Main() method
```

18. Click the File menu.

19. Choose Save All.

20. Click the Debug menu.

21. Choose Start Without Debugging.

22. Press any key to close the console window that appears.

23. Double-click the asynctextfile.txt file, in the net6.0 folder, to open it in the editor window.

Figure 16-21 shows the lines of text have been added, just like in the last example, but this time using an asynchronous method. Remember that we will not see any real difference when the code runs because we will be writing small amounts of data.

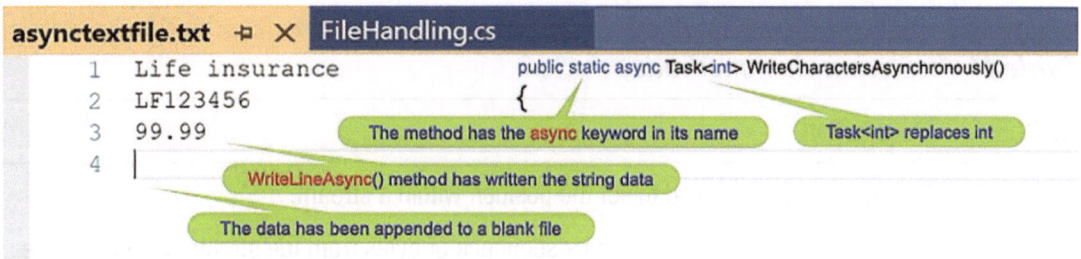

***Figure 16-21.** Data written to new file in an asynchronous manner*

FileStream

When looking at this section, we need to be aware that we have used the StreamReader and StreamWriter classes and they have shielded us from certain "complexities." Now we are going to see how we can do things that the StreamReader and StreamWriter shield us from.

FileModes

A file stream needs to understand the file mode to be used, and the FileMode enumeration holds the modes. For now, we will not concern ourselves with what an enumeration is, as we will have a full chapter on enumerations later in the book. The FileMode fields assist us in manipulating files. Table 16-4 shows some of the constants included in the FileMode enum, along with a short description, while Table 16-5 shows some of the stream methods we might see,

Table 16-4. *The FileMode fields, which dictate the file mode*

Field	Description
Open	This will open the file.
OpenOrCreate	This will open the file if it exists and creates a new file if it does not exist.
Append	This will open the file and seeks the end of the file. If the file does not exist, it will be created.
Create	This will create a new file, and if the file already exists, it will be overwritten.
CreateNew	This will create a new file, and if the file already exists, an exception is thrown – more about this shortly.
Truncate	This will open a file and truncate it so the size is zero bytes.

Table 16-5. *Stream class methods*

Method	Description
Seek()	This method will be used to set the position within a stream.
Read()	This method will be used to read a sequence of bytes from the stream and then move by the number of bytes read to the new position within the stream.
ReadAsync()	This method will be used to asynchronously read a sequence of bytes from the stream and then move by the number of bytes read to the new position within the stream.
Write()	This method will be used to write a sequence of bytes to the stream and then move by the number of bytes written to the new position within the stream.
WriteAsync()	This method will be used to asynchronously write a sequence of bytes to the stream and then move by the number of bytes written to the new position within the stream.

We will now create a method that will

- Create a byte array from a string of characters.

- Display the elements of the byte array.

- Create a file to hold the byte data and use an appropriate method to add the bytes to it.

- Use the Seek() method to move to a position in the FileStream, the stream.

- Read each byte from this new position to the end of the stream.

- Display the data that has been read.

Having displayed the byte elements, we will be able to confirm that the data is displayed from the new position found using the Seek() method.

24.   Amend the code, as in Listing 16-29, to create the method.

Listing 16-29. Using the Seek() method

```
} // End of WriteCharactersAsynchronously() method

public static void FileStreamSeekReadAndWrite()
{
  const string claimsFileName = "claims.dat";
  int startPosition = 6;

  // Create a string and then convert it to a byte array
  string claimantsName = "Gerry Byrne";

  byte[] claimantsByteArray =
   System.Text.Encoding.ASCII.GetBytes(claimantsName);

  Console.WriteLine("The bytes written to the file are");

  // Iterate the byte array and display each byte
  foreach (byte byteInTheArray in claimantsByteArray)
  {
    Console.WriteLine(byteInTheArray);
  } // End of foreach block

  Console.WriteLine("The bytes read from the file are");
  using (FileStream fileStream = new FileStream(claimsFileName,
  FileMode.Create))
  {
    for (int counter = 0; counter< claimantsByteArray.Length;
    counter++)
```

```
    {
      fileStream.WriteByte(claimantsByteArray[counter]);
    } // End of for block

    // Move to new position in the file stream
    fileStream.Seek(startPosition, SeekOrigin.Begin);

    for (int counter = 0; counter< fileStream.Length - startPosition;
    counter++)
    {
      Console.WriteLine(fileStream.ReadByte());
    } // End of for block
   } // End of using block
  } // End of FileStreamSeekReadAndWrite() method

 } // End of FileHandling class
} // End of Chapter16 namespace
```

25.   Call the method from the Main() method, as in Listing 16-30.

Listing 16-30. Call our new FileStreamSeekReadAndWrite() method

```
    UseStreamWriterWriteInUsingBlock();
    Task<int> task = WriteCharactersAsynchronously();
    FileStreamSeekReadAndWrite();
  } // End of Main() method
```

26.   Click the File menu.

27.   Choose Save All.

28.   Click the Debug menu.

29.   Choose Start Without Debugging.

Figure 16-22 shows the console output.

```
The bytes written to the file are
71
101
114
114
121
32
66   ◄———— start at position
121
114
110
101
The bytes read from the file are
66
121
114  ◄————characters at position 6, 7, 8, 9 and 10
110
101
C:\CoreCSharp\CoreCSharp\Chapter16\bin\Debug\net6.0\Chapter16.exe (process 5748) exited with code 0.
Press any key to close this window . . ._
```

Figure 16-22. *Data read from file starting at index 6*

30. Press any key to close the console window that appears.

Chapter Summary

So, finishing this chapter on file handling, we should be aware that C# file handling is taken care of by the namespace System.IO. We have used some of the methods of the File class including Exists(), Create(), ReadAllText(), WriteAllText(), Copy(), and Delete(). We also looked at the StreamReader class with methods such as Read(), ReadAsync(), and the synchronous and asynchronous concepts in programming. Likewise, we looked at the StreamWriter class and the methods WriteLine() and WriteLineAsync(). The FileStream class was then introduced when we looked at the Seek(), ReadByte(), and WriteByte() methods, but we should be aware that all stream types work in roughly the same way. We also looked at exception handling with the try catch code block and the using statement.

It is great to be able to read from and write to a text file, and we could in the future apply a similar concept to reading from and writing to a database.

We are making fantastic progress in programming our C# applications. We should be proud of our achievements. In finishing this very important chapter, we have increased our knowledge further and we are advancing to our target.

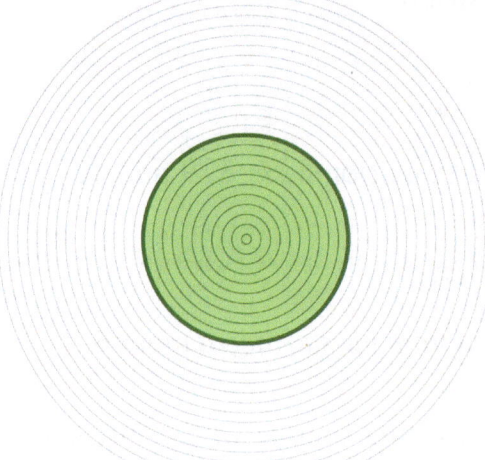

Our target is getting closer

CHAPTER 17

Exception Handling

Exceptions

In the previous chapter on file handling, we gained knowledge of different classes and methods that could be used to read from and write to a file. More importantly, when we used the methods CopyAFile(), DeleteAFile(), and UseStreamWriterRead(), we introduced the concept of the try catch block. In this chapter we will enhance our knowledge and skills in exception handling.

What Is an Exception?

We should think of an exception as an "exceptional event" that occurs when an application program is being executed. If we think about a time when we have seen an unhandled exception in our personal life, we will understand the consequences of such exception. What about when we have been dependent on information from a screen at an airport or railway station and the screen displayed a technical message of the unhandled exception? This may be an inconvenience to us, but thankfully it is unlikely to cause us any serious damage. However, what if we required the use of an emergency device in our home and the device screen displayed an exception! This situation may be more inconvenient or indeed life-threatening. Unfortunately, when we develop code, there are many different things within our code that can cause an exception. There can also be exceptions outside our code that will cause our code to stop working and are outside our control. Some examples of exceptions that we might encounter are the following:

- When the code is required to read a text file, as in Listing 17-1, but the text file is corrupted or not at the location, we get a FileNotFoundException. Figure 17-1 shows the exception when

© Gerard Byrne 2022
G. Byrne, *Target C#*, https://doi.org/10.1007/978-1-4842-8619-7_17

the file is not found because the filename has been entered as policydetail.txt instead of policydetails.txt.

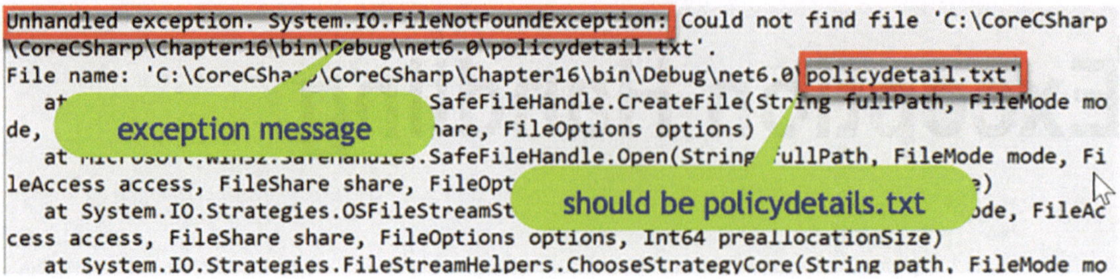

Figure 17-1. *FileNotFoundException – filename is incorrect*

Listing 17-1. Code will cause a FileNotFoundException

```csharp
internal class Exceptions
{
  static void Main(string[] args)
  {
    StreamReader myStreamReader = new
              StreamReader("policydetail.txt");

    while (myStreamReader.EndOfStream)
    {
      Console.Write(myStreamReader.Read() + "\t");
    }
    myStreamReader.Close();
  } // End of Main() class
} // End of Exceptions class
```

- When the code is required to read a database and the SQL server returns a SQL exception.

- When iterating an array and trying to go past the last item, we get an IndexOutOfRangeException, or out-of-bounds exception. Listing 17-2 shows code that gives an IndexOutOfRangeException as shown in Figure 17-2.

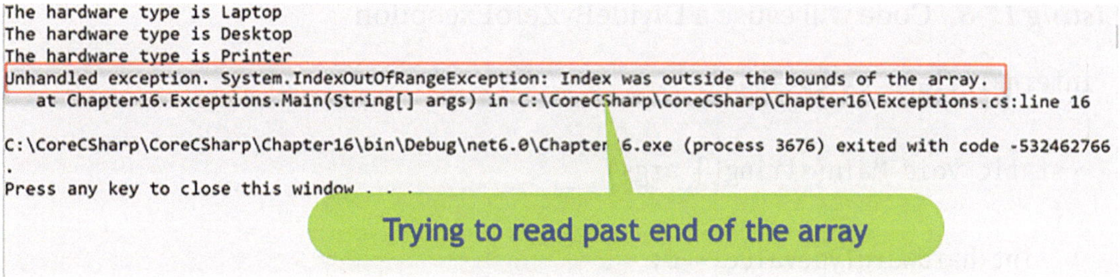

```
The hardware type is Laptop
The hardware type is Desktop
The hardware type is Printer
Unhandled exception. System.IndexOutOfRangeException: Index was outside the bounds of the array.
   at Chapter16.Exceptions.Main(String[] args) in C:\CoreCSharp\CoreCSharp\Chapter16\Exceptions.cs:line 16

C:\CoreCSharp\CoreCSharp\Chapter16\bin\Debug\net6.0\Chapter16.exe (process 3676) exited with code -532462766
.
Press any key to close this window . . .
```

Trying to read past end of the array

Figure 17-2. *Exception – index out of bounds*

Listing 17-2. Code will cause an IndexOutOfRangeException

```csharp
static void Main(string[] args)
{
  string[] hardwareTypes = new String[3];
  hardwareTypes[0] = "Laptop";
  hardwareTypes[1] = "Desktop";
  hardwareTypes[2] = "Printer";

  for (int counter = 0; counter < 4; counter++)
  {
  Console.WriteLine($"The hardware type is
  {hardwareTypes[counter]}");
  }
} // End of Main() class
} // End of Exceptions class
```

- Performing a calculation involving division that is dependent on the user input for the divisor. When a 0 is input by the user, the calculation will cause a DivideByZeroException. Listing 17-3 shows code that gives a divide-by-zero exception as shown in Figure 17-3.

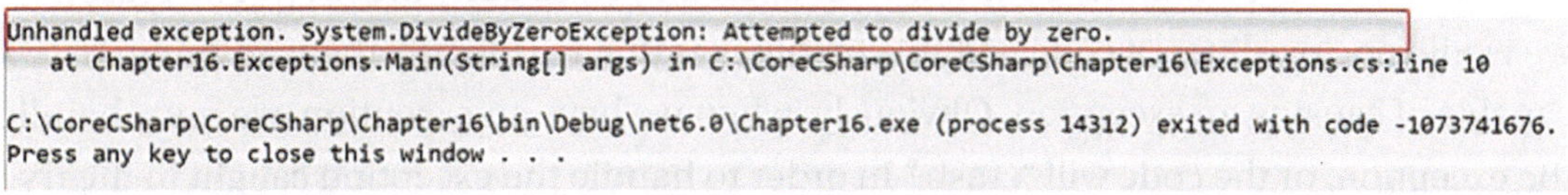

```
Unhandled exception. System.DivideByZeroException: Attempted to divide by zero.
   at Chapter16.Exceptions.Main(String[] args) in C:\CoreCSharp\CoreCSharp\Chapter16\Exceptions.cs:line 10

C:\CoreCSharp\CoreCSharp\Chapter16\bin\Debug\net6.0\Chapter16.exe (process 14312) exited with code -1073741676.
Press any key to close this window . . .
```

Figure 17-3. *Exception – divide-by-zero exception*

Listing 17-3. Code will cause a DivideByZeroException

```
internal class Exceptions
{
  static void Main(string[] args)
  {
    int hardwareTypeValue = 0;
    double premium = 100 / hardwareTypeValue;
    Console.WriteLine(premium);
  } // End of Main() class
} // End of Exceptions class
```

When we get a .NET exception, it is an object that holds information about the specific error. We can then access the object within our code and display whatever information we require.

When we code, we need to use exception handling when there is the possibility of an error happening, and we can use a number of different "tools," which include

- The **try** block, which is used to segment code that can cause an exception.

- The **catch** block(s), which is associated with the try block and handles the caught exception. This is an optional block if we have the try and finally blocks.

- A **finally** block, where we write code that will execute whether there is a caught exception or not. This is an optional block if we have the try and catch blocks.

We will now look in more detail at the try, catch, and finally blocks of code.

try

The try block will contain C# code between open and close curly braces {}. The reason we would enclose lines of code within a try block is that we identify them as being capable of causing an exception. Obviously, when we have an exception, we must handle the exception, or the code will "crash." In order to handle the exception caught in the try block, we must associate the try with a catch block. The syntax for the try block will be similar to

```
try
{
  // code statements that may cause an exception
}
```

catch

The catch block will contain C# code between open and close curly braces {}. The code will be used to handle the caught exception and could include displaying the details from the error object, for example, the stack trace or specific error message. We can have one catch block or more, but if we have only one catch block, then it can be used to handle all exceptions. If we have more than one catch block, when the try block has an error, it will be handled by the appropriate catch block. Looking back at our common exceptions, we might have a first catch block for a DivideByZeroException and a second one for a FileNotFoundException and so on. When the try block tries to divide by zero, then the first catch block will be executed:

```
Int numberOne = 5, numberTwo = 0;
try
{
  double answer = numberOne / numberTwo;
}
catch (DivideByZeroException)
{
  // code statements that handle DivideByZeroException
  Console.WriteLine("DivideByZeroException");
}
catch (FileNotFoundException)
{
  // code statements that handle FileNotFoundException
  //  Console.WriteLine("FileNotFoundException");
}
```

The important thing to remember about catch is that it can be used without accepting arguments, catch, and this means it will catch any type of exception. But the recommended usage is catch(), and the argument contains the exception details, and this is how we can use the exception details to display a message. Every exception inherits from SystemException, and therefore we can have a catch block that appears as catch(Exception). This Exception will therefore catch any exceptions not previously found. In this format the exception is not held in a variable and therefore cannot be used. When we use multiple catch blocks, we should always have a "fallback" for an exception we have not previously tried to catch. Amending the code for the previous example by assigning different values for numberOne and numberTwo and adding an array, when the code would try to read the array value outside the range, we will invoke the generic exception, catch(Exception):

```
int numberOne = 50, numberTwo = 10;
int[] claims = { 100, 200, 300 };
try
{
  double answer = numberOne / numberTwo;
  Console.WriteLine(claims[3]);
}
catch (DivideByZeroException)
{
  // code statements that handle DivideByZeroException
  Console.WriteLine("DivideByZeroException");
}
catch (FileNotFoundException)
{
  // code statements that handle FileNotFoundException
  Console.WriteLine("FileNotFoundException");
}
catch (Exception)
{
  Console.WriteLine("An exception was found");
}
```

finally

The finally block will contain C# code between open and close curly braces {}. The code will be used to execute whatever we wish to happen regardless of whether there was an exception or not. In other words, the finally block will always be executed, whereas the catch block is only executed if there is an exception it can handle. The syntax for the finally block will be similar to

```
finally
{
    // code statements that will be executed if there is an
        exception or if there is no exception
}
```

throw

When exceptions occur and are handled by the try, catch, and finally blocks, we are handling exceptions that have been **thrown** by the system at runtime. However, what would happen if we wanted to throw an exception manually in our code? Well, this is where the **throw** keyword comes to our assistance, and we will look at this concept later.

Now we will implement our theory of exceptions that we have just read, by creating some code.

Let's code some C# and build our programming muscle.

Add a new project to hold the code for this chapter.

1. Right-click the solution CoreCSharp.

2. Choose Add.

3. Choose New Project.

4. Choose Console App from the listed templates that appear.

5. Click the Next button.

6. Name the project Chapter17 and leave it in the same location.

7. Click the Next button.

8. Choose the framework to be used, which in our projects will be .NET 6.0 or higher.

9. Click the Create button.

Now we should see the Chapter17 project within the solution called CoreCSharp.

10. Right-click the project Chapter17 in the Solution Explorer panel.

11. Click the Set as Startup Project option.

Notice how the Chapter17 project name has been made to have bold text, indicating that it is the new startup project and that it is the Program.cs file within it that will be executed when we run the debugging.

12. Right-click the Program.cs file in the Solution Explorer window.

13. Choose Rename.

14. Change the name to ExceptionHandling.cs.

15. Press the Enter key.

16. Double-click the ExceptionHandling.cs file to open it in the editor window.

17. Amend the code, as in Listing 17-4, with the namespace, class, and Main() method and a try block with some code.

Listing 17-4. Class with the Main() method and try block

```
namespace Chapter17
{
  internal class ExceptionHandling
  {
    static void Main(string[] args)
    {
      try
      {
        int hardwareTypeValue = 0;
        double premium = 100 / hardwareTypeValue;
        Console.WriteLine(premium);
      } // End of try block
```

```
} //End of Main() method
```

```
} // End of ExceptionHandling class
} // End of Chapter17 namespace
```

The closing curly brace may be showing a red underline, as Figure 17-4, indicating an error, and hovering over the error would display a message that tells us we must use either a matching catch block or a finally block.

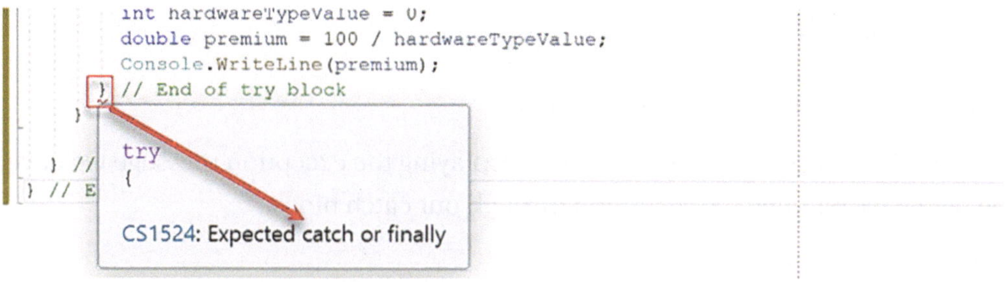

Figure 17-4. *Try block needs a catch or finally block*

If we think about this, it makes sense, because why would we try to find an exception and then do nothing about the exception? Not handling exceptions is a **root cause** for unreliable software applications, which cause business revenue losses and make the user experience unsatisfactory.

We will now create the catch block and add some code to handle any exception. Here we will simply display a message.

18. Amend the code, as in Listing 17-5.

Listing 17-5. Adding the catch block

```
static void Main(string[] args)
{
  try
  {
    int hardwareTypeValue = 0;
    double premium = 100 / hardwareTypeValue;
    Console.WriteLine(premium);
  } // End of try block
```

```
    catch
    {
      Console.WriteLine("Error - you cannot divide by zero");
    } // End of catch block
} //End of Main() method
```

19. Click the File menu.

20. Choose Save All.

21. Click the Debug menu.

22. Choose Start Without Debugging.

Figure 17-5 shows the console window displaying the exception message we have coded, when we handled the exception through our catch block.

```
Error - you cannot divide by zero
                                        Cannot divide by zero
C:\CoreCSharp\CoreCSharp\Chapter17\bin\Debug\net6.0\Chapter17.exe
Press any key to close this window . . .
```

Figure 17-5. *Catch block executes.*

23. Press the Enter key to close the console window.

Great, as the developer, we have caught the exception and "gracefully" handled it using the catch block, and our application can move to the next statements. But what was the actual exception? Well, we used the catch that accepted no arguments, and we displayed a message of our choice. We could have used the preferred catch option, which lets the catch accept an argument passed to it. In other words, the actual exception is passed and accepted as the parameter of the catch, and this will be more beneficial to us as we will be getting more details about the exception. In accepting the exception as its parameter, the catch will have been coded to assign the exception a name, and this could be ex or anything we would like to call it. In this example we will use ex, not a great name when we think about clean code, but we will discuss this issue later in the chapter.

We will now replace the existing catch block so that we have a new catch block that accepts the passed-in argument as its parameter and add some code to display the message that belongs to the exception.

24. Amend the code, as in Listing 17-6.

Listing 17-6. Catch method that accepts the exception as a parameter

```
try
{
  int hardwareTypeValue = 0;
  double premium = 100 / hardwareTypeValue;
  Console.WriteLine(premium);
} // End of try block
catch (Exception ex)
{
  Console.WriteLine($"Exception message is - {ex.Message}");
} // End of catch block
  } //End of Main() method
```

25. Click the File menu.

26. Choose Save All.

27. Click the Debug menu.

28. Choose Start Without Debugging.

Figure 17-6 shows the console window, which displays the exception message, which was passed from the actual system exception, which we called ex. We should notice that the message passed from the exception handler, Attempted to divide by zero, is similar to what we manually entered in our catch code. The important thing is that we can use the existing exception messages rather than having to create our own messages.

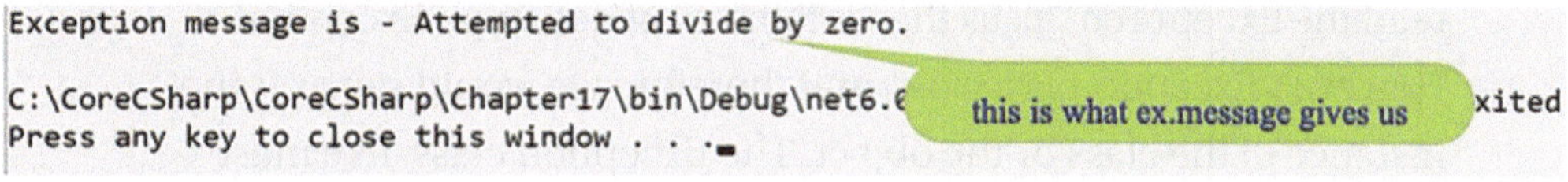

```
Exception message is - Attempted to divide by zero.

C:\CoreCSharp\CoreCSharp\Chapter17\bin\Debug\net6.6            xited
Press any key to close this window . . .
```
this is what ex.message gives us

Figure 17-6. *Exception message displayed*

29. Press the Enter key to close the console window.

Great, we have caught the exception and displayed the actual exception message, which came from the "generic" exception. But we could also catch more specific exceptions like the divide-by-zero exception, and we can use the general and specific together.

Multiple Exceptions

We can have more than one exception handler if we wish to and be more specific about the exception. In Listing 17-6 we saw that the catch accepted the exception as its parameter called ex. We then used the Message field from the ex instance in the console message using the code line

```
Console.WriteLine($"Exception message is - {ex.Message}");
```

While this was fine and the code worked, there are a couple of points to consider:

- Is it acceptable to call the parameter ex? What about clean code?

  Let's be honest. ex is not a very good name for a variable or parameter. What does ex tell us about its meaning or purpose? We have already read about clean code and self-documenting code, so maybe we should consider being more explicit about the name. Certainly, if we search for code snippets or solutions to problems on the World Wide Web, we will see the naming convention ex, but remember we must try and make our code more readable and more maintainable, not just for ourselves but for others who will have to work with our code. We can therefore be more explicit in our naming of the parameter, for example, exceptionFound, divideByZeroException, or fileNotFoundException.

- What does the ex really mean?

  As we have just said, ex is the parameter name and it is of type Exception. So, for simplicity and going back to Chapter 6, we could read the `Exception ex` as the variable ex of data type Exception. However, Exception is a class, and therefore we would say ex is the instance of the class or the object. The Exception class, like most classes, will be made up of methods and properties, and one of the properties is Message, which gets a message that describes the current exception. This concept of fields and methods within a class should be familiar to us because we have coded our own examples of classes and objects in Chapter 13 and we used fields and methods within them. Looking at the Exception class from the example code shown in Figure 17-7, we can see some methods and fields that exist within it.

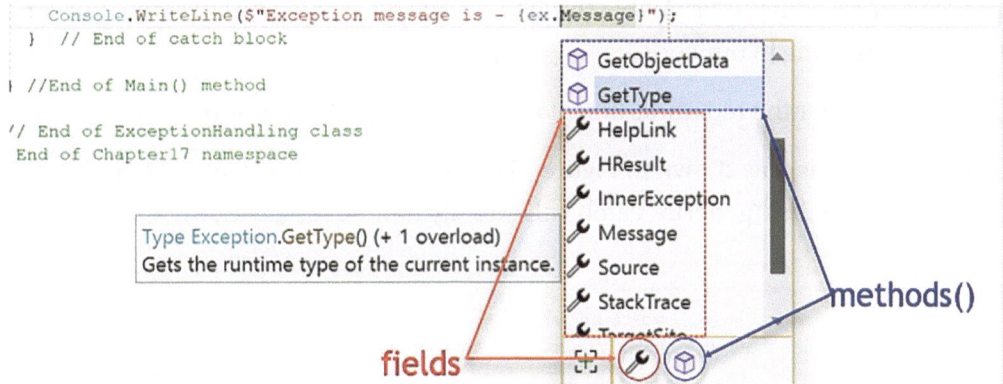

Figure 17-7. *Methods and fields of the Exception class*

We will now look at multiple exceptions, where we can prioritize the possible exceptions, starting with the more specific and moving to the more general, which is really what the ex was in Listing 17-6. Here we will just use the name DivideByZeroException with no instance of it being made.

    30.   Amend the code, as in Listing 17-7, to create another catch block that checks for the specific exception DivideByZeroException.

Listing 17-7. Multiple catch clauses

```
try
{
  int hardwareTypeValue = 0;
  double premium = 100 / hardwareTypeValue;
  Console.WriteLine(premium);
} // End of try block
catch (Exception ex)
{
 Console.WriteLine($"Exception message is - {ex.Message}");
 } // End of catch block
 catch (DivideByZeroException)
 {
   Console.WriteLine($"Divide By Zero Exception message");
 } // End of DivideByZeroException catch block
} //End of Main() method
```

In theory this seems a reasonable thing to do. We have two types of catch, but we have an error showing in our code.

31.   Hover over the red underline of the DivideByZeroException.

The error message, as shown in Figure 17-8, tells us that the second catch is unnecessary as the first "generic" catch will already handle the divide-by-zero exception.

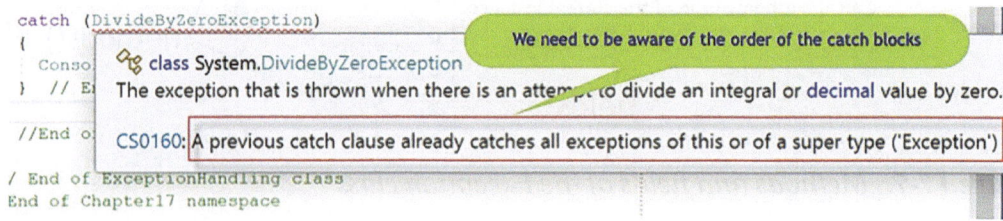

Figure 17-8. *Exception message displayed*

However, let us reverse the order of the catch blocks, as in Listing 17-8, putting the specific error first and then having the "generic" catch, and see what happens.

32.   Amend the code, as in Listing 17-8, to reverse the order of the catch() clauses.

Listing 17-8. Multiple catch clauses – reversed

```
} // End of try block

catch (DivideByZeroException)
{
  Console.WriteLine($"Divide By Zero Exception message");
} // End of DivideByZeroException catch block
catch (Exception ex)
{
Console.WriteLine($"Exception message is - {ex.Message}");
} // End of catch block
} //End of Main() method
```

The red underline will have disappeared because we have "**stacked**" the catch blocks in a hierarchical manner from the specific to the general.

33.   Click the File menu.

34.   Choose Save All.

35.   Click the Debug menu.

36.   Choose Start Without Debugging.

Figure 17-9 shows the console window displaying the specific exception message, which we have created. This shows that there is precedence in the catch blocks.

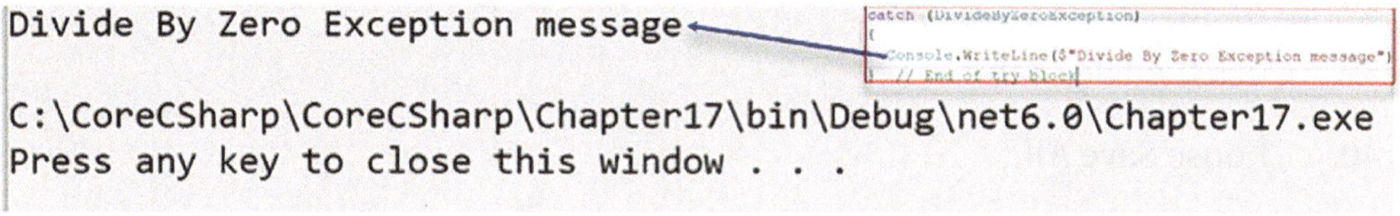

Figure 17-9. *First exception clause executed rather than the general exception*

37.   Press the Enter key to close the console window.

FileNotFoundException

We will now make a few changes so we can see the effect of the catch blocks being checked in sequential order. We will change the value of the variable hardwareTypeValue, as in Listing 17-9, from a 0 to a 10, and we will use code very similar to code we used in Chapter 16 to read the data from a file. However, we will use a filename that does not exist, and this will mean there will be a file-not-found exception.

38.   Amend the code inside the try block, as in Listing 17-9, to have code that attempts to read a file.

Listing 17-9. hardwareTypeValue=10 and read a text file that does not exist

```
try
{
    int hardwareTypeValue = 10;
    double premium = 100 / hardwareTypeValue;
    Console.WriteLine(premium);

    StreamReader myStreamReader = new
    StreamReader("policydetailsXXX.txt");
```

```
    while (myStreamReader.EndOfStream)
    {
        Console.Write(myStreamReader.Read() + "\t");
    }
    myStreamReader.Close();

} // End of try block
```

39.   Click the File menu.

40.   Choose Save All.

41.   Click the Debug menu.

42.   Choose Start Without Debugging.

We will see that the console window, as shown in Figure 17-10, now displays the general exception message. The first part of the message is the hard-coded text string, while the second part is the property from the ex instance of the Exception class.

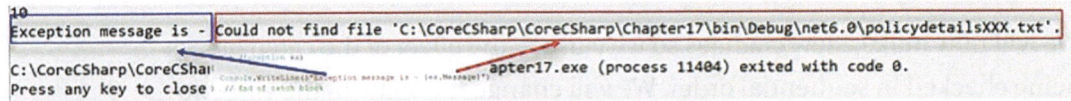

Figure 17-10. *General exception for file not found*

43.   Press the Enter key to close the console window.

Great, again we have caught the exception and displayed the "generic" exception message. But we could also catch the more specific exception like the file-not-found exception. We will now add a new catch block for the FileNotFoundException, coding it just before the "generic" catch block. Here we will use the name FileNotFoundException but we will use an instance of it, calling it exNoFile.

44.   Amend the code, as in Listing 17-10, to add the new catch block.

Listing 17-10. Add catch block for FileNotFoundException

```
} // End of try block
catch (DivideByZeroException)
{
    Console.WriteLine($"Divide By Zero Exception message");
```

```
} // End of DivideByZeroException catch block
catch (FileNotFoundException exNoFile)
{
  // Write the 'whole' exception
  Console.WriteLine(exNoFile);
} // End of FileNotFoundException catch block
catch (Exception ex)
{
Console.WriteLine($"Exception message is - {ex.Message}");
  } // End of catch block
} //End of Main() method
```

45. Click the File menu.

46. Choose Save All.

47. Click the Debug menu.

48. Choose Start Without Debugging.

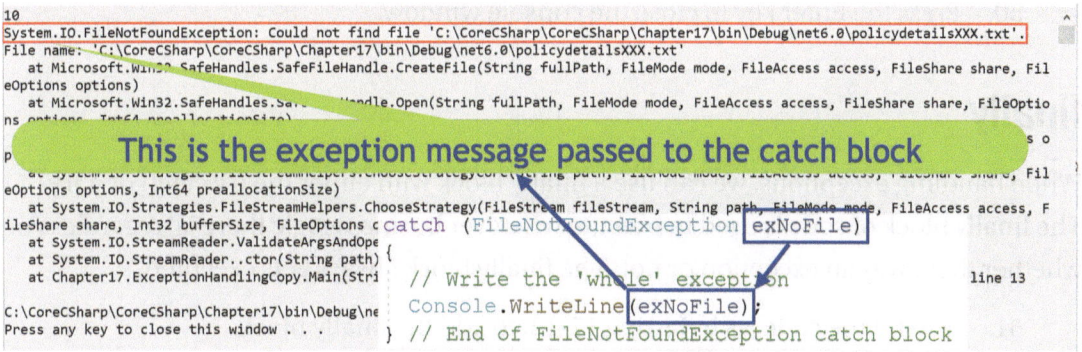

Figure 17-11. *Specific FileNotFoundException message displayed*

49. Press the Enter key to close the console window.

Figure 17-11 shows the console window displaying the specific exception, which we have created for the file not found. In this example we have displayed the whole exception in the WriteLine() method as we have simply used exNoFile, the instance of the Exception class, and this shows both the Message and StackTrace of the exception. In the example as shown in Figure 17-11, we used the ex.Message where Message was the property of the Exception class that gave us access to details about the cause of the exception. Figure 17-12 shows what we would see if we had used the code exNoFile.Message as in Listing 17-11.

Listing 17-11. Using the Message property of the exception

```
catch (FileNotFoundException exNoFile)
{
  // Write the exception Message property value
  Console.WriteLine(exNoFile.Message);
}// End of FileNotFoundException catch block
```

Figure 17-12. *FileNotFoundException.Message property message*

    50.   Press the Enter key to close the console window.

finally

When handling exceptions, we can use a finally block with either the try catch or a try. The finally block of code is used to execute whatever business logic there is, regardless of whether there was an exception or not. The finally block always gets executed.

    51.   Amend the code, as in Listing 17-12, to add the finally block.

Listing 17-12. Using the finally block

```
catch (Exception ex)
{
  Console.WriteLine($"Exception message is - {ex.Message}");
} // End of catch block
```

```
finally
{
  Console.WriteLine("Try catch blocks ended, tidying up");
}

  } //End of Main() method

} // End of ExceptionHandling class
} // End of Chapter17 namespace
```

52. Click the File menu.

53. Choose Save All.

54. Click the Debug menu.

55. Choose Start Without Debugging.

Figure 17-13 shows the console window, displaying at the end of the text the message from the finally block.

```
10
Could not find file 'C:\CoreCSharp\CoreCSharp\Chapter17\bin\Debug\net6.0\policydetailsXXX.txt'.
Try catch blocks ended, tidying up

C:\CoreCSharp\CoreCSharp\Chapter17\bin\Debug\net...\Chapter17.exe (process 11060) exited with code 0.
Press any key to close this window . . .
```

This is the text from the finally code block

Figure 17-13. *Finally block executed and message appearing at the end*

56. Press the Enter key to close the console window.

In one of our try blocks, we had code that was using the StreamReader to read a text file and, as is good practice, we closed the instance of the StreamReader, myStreamReader, when we had finished using it. The finally block would also be a location to code the Close() method, but the instance of the StreamReader would need to be moved to outside the try block. Otherwise, it would not be accessible. The example code for this finally block is shown in Listing 17-13, where we can see the instance of the StreamReader is moved to the class level and made static. We do not need to code this; it's merely for information and for demonstrating another way to use the finally block.

Listing 17-13. Using the finally block to use the Close() method

```
using System;

namespace Chapter17
{
  internal class ExceptionHandling
  {static StreamReader myStreamReader = new StreamReader
   ("policydetailsXXX.txt");
   static void Main(string[] args)
    {

      try
      {
        int hardwareTypeValue = 10;
        double premium = 100 / hardwareTypeValue;
        Console.WriteLine(premium);

        while (myStreamReader.EndOfStream)
        {
          Console.Write(myStreamReader.Read() + "\t");
        }
        myStreamReader.Close();

      } // End of try block
      catch (DivideByZeroException)
      {
        Console.WriteLine($"Divide By Zero Exception message");
      }  // End of DivideByZeroException catch block
      catch (FileNotFoundException exNoFile)
      {
        // Write the 'whole' exception
        Console.WriteLine(exNoFile);
      }// End of FileNotFoundException catch block
      catch (Exception ex)
```

```
    {
     Console.WriteLine($"Exception message is - {ex.Message}");
    }   // End of catch block
    finally
    {
       Console.WriteLine("Try catch blocks ended, tidying up");

       myStreamReader.Close();
    }
  } //End of Main() method
 } // End of ExceptionHandling class
} // End of Chapter17 namespace
```

StackTrace

Just like we used the Message property of the Exception class, we could also have used the StackTrace property, and we would get a different output to help us identify the exception cause. Using the code in Listing 17-14, we will get the exception message as shown in Figure 17-14. This is a more detailed message.

57.   Amend the code, as in Listing 17-14, to display the stack trace message.

Listing 17-14. Using the StackTrace property

```
catch (FileNotFoundException exNoFile)
{
   // Write the StackTrace exception
   Console.WriteLine(exNoFile.StackTrace);
}// End of FileNotFoundException catch block
```

58.   Click the File menu.

59.   Choose Save All.

60.   Click the Debug menu.

61.   Choose Start Without Debugging.

62.   Press the Enter key to close the console window.

```
10
    at Microsoft.Win32.SafeHandles.SafeFileHandle.CreateFile(String fullPath, FileMode mode, FileAccess
access, FileShare share, FileOptions options)
    at Microsoft.Win32.SafeHandles.SafeFileHandle.Open(String fullPath, FileMode mode, FileAccess access
, FileShare share, FileOptions options, Int64 preallocationSize)
    at System.IO.Strategies.OSFileStreamStrategy..ctor(String path, FileMode mode, FileAccess access, Fi
leShare share, FileOptions options, Int64 preallocationSize)
    at System.IO.Strategies.FileStreamHelpers.ChooseStrategyCore(String path, FileMode mode, FileAccess
access, FileShare share, FileOptions options, Int64 preallocationSize)
    at System.IO.Strategies.FileStreamHelpers.ChooseStrategy(FileStream fileStream, String path, FileMod
e mode, FileAccess access, FileShare share, Int32 bufferSize, FileOptions options, Int64 preallocationS
ize)
    at System.IO.StreamReader.ValidateArgsAndOpenPath(String path, Encoding encoding, Int32 bufferSize)
    at System.IO.StreamReader..ctor(String path)
    at Chapter17.ExceptionHandling.Main(String[] args) in C:\CoreCSharp\CoreCSharp\Chapter17\ExceptionHa
ndling.cs:line 15Try catch blocks ended, tidying up

C:\CoreCSharp\CoreCSharp\Chapter17\bin\Debug\net6.0\Chapter17.exe (process 12020) exited with code 0.
Press any key to close this window . . .
```

Figure 17-14. *Stack trace message*

throw

Rather than using the try, catch, and finally blocks to handle exceptions thrown at runtime, we can throw an exception manually in our code. Any exception that is derived from the Exception class can be thrown by us within our code, and we can choose where in the code to throw the exception.

When we throw our new exception, the class it belongs to must be based on the Exception class. In this example we will create a class for a hardware value being too high, and inside it, we will create our new exception. The code is added inside the namespace but outside the ExceptionHandling class.

63.   Amend the code, as in Listing 17-15, to add a class for our new exception, which has to inherit from the Exception base class.

Listing 17-15. New class HardwareValueException inside namespace

```
    } //End of Main() method
  } // End of ExceptionHandling class

  // Our custom exception for a value which is too high
  public class HardwareValueException : Exception
  {
    public HardwareValueException(string errormessage) :base(errormessage)
    {
    } // End of HardwareValueException constructor
```

} // End of HardwareValueException class

} // End of Chapter17 namespace

We will now use the newly created exception method, which accepts the user input for the hardware value and throws an exception if the value is too high.

64.   Amend the code, as in Listing 17-16.

Listing 17-16. New method inside the ExceptionHandling class outside Main()

```
} //End of Main() method
public static void CheckIfQuoteCanBeMade()
{
  Console.WriteLine("What is the value of the hardware to be insured?");
double hardwareValue = Convert.ToDouble(Console.ReadLine());
 try
 {
   if (hardwareValue > 0 && hardwareValue < 10000)
   {
     Console.WriteLine("Quote will be available");
   }
   else
   {
     throw (new HardwareValueException("HardwareValueException - value too
     high"));
    }
 } // End of try block
   catch (HardwareValueException ourException)
   {
     Console.WriteLine(ourException.Message.ToString());
   } // End of  catch block

}// End of CheckIfQuoteCanBeMade method

  } // End of ExceptionHandling class
```

65. Amend the code, as in Listing 17-17, to call the new method,
     which contains the new exception handler.

Listing 17-17. New method inside the ExceptionHandling class outside Main()

```
static void Main(string[] args)
{
  CheckIfQuoteCanBeMade();

  try
  {
    int hardwareTypeValue = 10;
    double premium = 100 / hardwareTypeValue;
    Console.WriteLine(premium);
```

66. Click the File menu.

67. Choose Save All.

68. Click the Debug menu.

69. Choose Start Without Debugging.

70. Enter a value greater than 10000, for example, 20000.

We will see that the console window, as shown in Figure 17-15, displays the message
from our custom exception.

```
What is the value of the hardware to be insured?
20000                           message from the throw a HardwareValueException
HardwareValueException - value too high
10
```

Figure 17-15. *Message from custom HardwareValueException*

rethrow

The throw keyword allows us to rethrow an exception and this is useful if we wish to
pass an exception to the caller that will then use the exception for its own purposes. In
this example

- We will call a method that will ask the user to input the value of the hardware that is to be insured.

- The method call is within a try block.

- The corresponding catch block will display the exception if there is one.

- The exception to be displayed is the exception received from the catch block of the method being called.

The method passes back the exception to the calling try catch block; it is a hierarchical structure, and this is where we use the **throw** statement without anything else. Within the catch block of the exception, we could decide to perform some operations like writing the exception details to a log file or the console, and then we can rethrow the exception, which simply means calling the throw statement without anything else, no object. The rethrow can only be used within a catch block.

When we throw an exception, we can do it in one of two ways:

- throw – Using throw on its own means the stack trace is "preserved."

- throw ex – Using the throw with the ex means the stack trace is lost.

Think about when the exceptions move up through what is the "call stack." As we go through the call stack, it would be great if the stack trace was maintained and the exception details were accumulated. Well, this is where the throw on its own works perfectly. In the same scenario, if we used the throw ex, then only the last exception stack trace would be available.

We will now create a method called GetHardwareValue()and call it from within the Main() method. We will also comment out the previous call to the CheckIfQuoteCanBeMade() method.

1. Amend the code, as in Listing 17-18, to call the method within a try and comment out the other method call.

Listing 17-18. Call the method from within a try catch block

```
static void Main(string[] args)
{
  try
  {
```

```
      GetHardwareValue();
    }
    catch (Exception ex)
    {
      /*
      Do something here that is specific to our business logic.
      */
      Console.WriteLine(ex.Message);
    }
    //CheckIfQuoteCanBeMade();

    try
    {
```

We will now create the new method that will ask the user to input a value for the hardware and it will convert the string input to a double. The conversion is within a try block and the catch block uses the throw statement to pass the exception back to the calling method.

2. Amend the code, as in Listing 17-19, to create the method that reads the user value and tries to convert it within a try block.

Listing 17-19. Create the method that converts the input from within a try catch block

```
    } // End of  catch block
}// End of CheckIfQuoteCanBeMade method

 public static void GetHardwareValue()
 {
   double hardwareValue;

    try
    {
     Console.WriteLine("What is the hardware replacement value?");
     hardwareValue = Convert.ToDouble(Console.ReadLine());
    }
```

```
  catch (Exception)
  {
    throw;
  }
} // End of GetHardwareValue() method
  } // End of ExceptionHandling class
```

Notice the throw statement; this is the rethrow that will pass the exception that has been found back to the catch block belonging to the calling method. For simplicity we will comment out the code for the while iteration that reads the text file, as in Listing 17-20.

Listing 17-20. Commenting out the code for the while iteration

```
    try
    {
      int hardwareTypeValue = 10;
      double premium = 100 / hardwareTypeValue;
      Console.WriteLine(premium);

      //StreamReader myStreamReader = new
      //              StreamReader("policydetailsXXX.txt");

      //while (myStreamReader.Peek() > 0)
      //{
      //  Console.Write(myStreamReader.Read() + "\t");
      //}
      //myStreamReader.Close();

    } // End of try block
    catch (DivideByZeroException)
```

3. Click the File menu.

4. Choose Save All.

5. Click the Debug menu.

6. Choose Start Without Debugging.

7. Enter a string value instead of a numeric value for the replacement value, for example, Two Thousand.

We will see that the console window, as shown in Figure 17-16, displays the exception, which was passed up from the exception in the method that was called.

```
What is the hardware replacement value?
Two Thousand
Input string was not in a correct format.
10
Try catch blocks ended, tidying up

C:\CoreCSharp\CoreCSharp\Chapter17\bin\Debug\net6.0\Chapter17.exe
Press any key to close this window . . .
```

Figure 17-16. *Throw the exception up the hierarchy, rethrow.*

8. Press the Enter key to close the console window.

Another way to code the multiple exceptions we have would be to enclose the exceptions within a switch construct, which we looked at in Chapter 9 on selection. The example we will now code uses the switch construct to handle one of three exception types.

9. Right-click the Chapter17 project in the Solution Explorer window.

10. Choose Add

11. Choose New.

12. Choose Class

13. Change the name to ExceptionHandlingWithSwitch.cs.

14. Press the Enter key.

The ExceptionHandlingWithSwitch class code will appear in the editor window, and we will now add

- A Main() method

- A try block with no code for now

- A catch block for a FileNotFoundException

- A catch block for a DivideByZeroException

- A catch block for a OverflowException

- A finally block

15. Amend the code, as in Listing 17-21, to include a Main() method with the try block and the three catch blocks.

Listing 17-21. Switch statement to encompass different exceptions

```
namespace Chapter17
{
internal class ExceptionHandlingWithSwitch
{
  static void Main(string[] args)
  {
    try
    {
    } // End of try block
    catch (Exception ex)
    {
      switch (ex)
      {
        case FileNotFoundException:
          Console.WriteLine("File not found Exception");
          break;
        case DivideByZeroException:
          Console.WriteLine("Divide By Zero Exception");
          break;
        case OverflowException:
          Console.WriteLine("Overflow Exception");
          break;
      } // End of switch block
    } // End of catch block
    finally
    {
      Console.WriteLine("Try catch blocks ended, tidying up");
    } // End of finally block
```

```
} // End of Main() method
} // End of ExceptionHandlingWithSwitch class
} // End of Chapter17 namespace
```

16. Amend the code, as in Listing 17-22, to include code within the try block, which will attempt to open a file that does not exist.

Listing 17-22. Try to read a file that does not exist

```
internal class ExceptionHandlingWithSwitch
  {
    static void Main(string[] args)
    {
 try
    {
      // Testing FileNotFoundException
      using (var fileStream = new FileStream(@"NoFileExists.txt",
      FileMode.Open))
      {
        // Logic for reading file would go here
      }
    } // End of try block
    catch (Exception ex)
    {
      switch (ex)
```

17. Right-click the Chapter17 project in the Solution Explorer panel.

18. Choose Properties.

19. Set the Startup object to be the ExceptionHandlingWithSwitch in the drop-down list.

20. Close the Properties window.

21. Click the File menu.

22. Choose Save All.

23. Click the Debug menu.

24.   Choose Start Without Debugging.

We will see that the console window, as shown in Figure 17-17, displays the relevant exception, which is FileNotFoundException.

```
File not found Exception!
Try catch blocks ended, tidying up

C:\CoreCSharp\CoreCSharp\Chapter17\bin\Debug\net6.0\Chapter17.exe
Press any key to close this window . . .
```

Figure 17-17. *FileNotFoundException*

25.   Press the Enter key to close the console window.

We will now comment the code we have just entered for reading the file so we can add code that will cause a DivideByZeroException.

26.   Amend the code, as in Listing 17-23, to comment the first piece of code and then include code within the try block that will attempt to perform a division by zero.

Listing 17-23. Try to perform a division by zero

```
internal class ExceptionHandlingWithSwitch
  {
    static void Main(string[] args)
    {
      try
      {
        // Testing FileNotFoundException
        //using (var fileStream = new FileStream(@"NoFileExists.txt",
        FileMode.Open))
        //{
        //   // Logic for reading file would go here
        //}

        // Testing DivideByZeroException
        int hardwareTypeValue = 0;
        double premium = 100 / hardwareTypeValue;

      } // End of try block
```

27. Click the File menu.

28. Choose Save All.

29. Click the Debug menu.

30. Choose Start Without Debugging.

We will see that the console window, as shown in Figure 17-18, displays the relevant exception, which is DivideByZeroException.

```
Divide By Zero Exception
Try catch blocks ended, tidying up

C:\CoreCSharp\CoreCSharp\Chapter17\bin\Debug\net6.0\Chapter17.exe
Press any key to close this window . . .
```

***Figure 17-18.** DivideByZeroException*

31. Press the Enter key to close the console window.

We will comment the code we entered for the division by zero. Then we can add code within the try block to ask the user for a byte value input, and this will cause an exception when the user enters a value greater than 255.

32. Remove the code from the previous steps, as in Listing 17-24.

***Listing 17-24.** Try to enter a number greater than 255*

```
try
{
    // Testing FileNotFoundException
    //using (var fileStream =
    //new FileStream(@"NoFileExists.txt", FileMode.Open))
    //{
    //  // Logic for reading file would go here
    //}

    // Testing DivideByZeroException
    //int hardwareTypeValue = 0;
    //double premium = 100 / hardwareTypeValue;
```

```
// Testing OverflowException
Console.WriteLine("How many claims are being made?");
int claimValue = Convert.ToByte(Console.ReadLine());
} // End of try block
```

33.   Click the File menu.

34.   Choose Save All.

35.   Click the Debug menu.

36.   Choose Start Without Debugging.

We will see that the console window, as shown in Figure 17-19, displays the question, and when we enter 300 and press the Enter key, the OverflowException is displayed.

```
How many claims are being made?
300
Overflow Exception
Try catch blocks ended, tidying up

C:\CoreCSharp\CoreCSharp\Chapter17\bin\Debug\net6.0\Chapter17.exe
Press any key to close this window . . .
```

Figure 17-19. *OverflowException*

This example should help us see how we can build our code using the constructs we have learned from the start of the chapters. It is important we think differently to make our code "cleaner" and easier to maintain.

Chapter Summary

So, finishing this chapter on exceptions, we have learned that

- An exception is derived from the System.Exception class.

- With a try block, we must have at least a matching catch or finally block.

- We can have multiple catch blocks.

- With multiple catch blocks, there is a hierarchy, and we should code them from the specific to the general.

- We can have a simple catch that accepts no arguments and it will handle any exception.

- We can have a catch that accepts an instance of the Exception and use its properties such as Message and StackTrace to get more details about the exception.

- We can have a finally block, which is always executed.

- We can throw an exception.

- We can create our own user-defined exception.

- We can rethrow an exception.

We are now really beginning to think like professional developers, we are considering that exceptions can occur, and we know one technique to handle the exceptions.

We are making fantastic progress in programming our C# applications and we should be very proud of our achievements. In finishing this chapter, we have increased our knowledge further and we are advancing to our target.

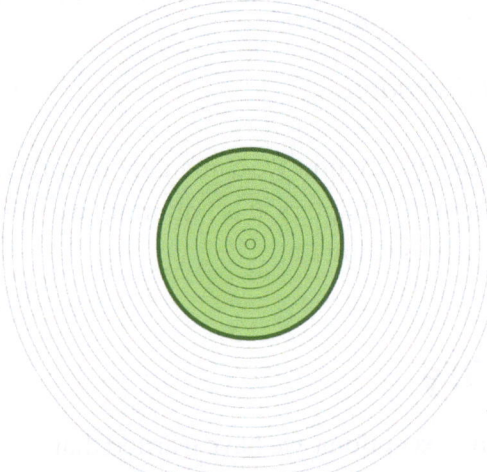

Our target is getting closer

CHAPTER 18

Serialization

Serialization and Deserialization

In Chapter 13 we gained knowledge of classes and objects. This chapter will extend our knowledge and explain how we can save an object so it can be recreated when required. The processes we will investigate are called serialization and deserialization. **By serializing we are saving the state of the object.** We will also require some of the knowledge we gained in Chapter 16 on file handling as we will write binary data, XML data, and JSON data to a file as part of the serialization process.

Serialization is a process to convert an object into a stream of bytes so that the bytes can be written into a file. We will normally do this so the serialized data can be stored in a database or sent across a network, for example, to a message queue to form part of a transaction process. The byte stream created for XML and JSON is platform independent; it is an object serialized on one platform that can be deserialized on a different platform. All fields of type private, public, and internal will be serialized.

In an enterprise we may wish to send the serialized data from one domain to another, to a Rest API web service that could then store it in a database or deserialize it and use the details in some business logic. To ensure the serialization process works without an error, there are a number of things we need to ensure:

- The class being serialized must have the [Serializable] attribute above the class. In this example the class will be called Customer, so the code will look like Listing 18-1.

© Gerard Byrne 2022
G. Byrne, *Target C#*, https://doi.org/10.1007/978-1-4842-8619-7_18

Listing 18-1. Serializable class

```
[Serializable]
public class Customer
{
}
```

- The class will have fields or properties that will have get and set accessors, but it is the fields that are serialized, and each of the three formats will be treated differently. Binary serialization will use the public and private fields including readonly members, XML will use the public fields and properties, and JSON will use the public properties.

- The class with the Main() method will instantiate the class.

- The formatter class is used to serialize the object to the required format, for example, binary, XML, or JSON.

- A file stream object is created to hold the bytes that are created after a named file has been created and opened for writing.

- The Serialize() method is then used to serialize to a stream, and we are using the FileStream class for this, as we discussed in a previous chapter.

- Finally, the stream must be closed.

Deserialization

Deserialization is the process of taking the serialized data, which is a stream, and returning it to an object as defined by the class. We will use FileStream to read it from the disk.

Attribute [NonSerialized]

When we serialize, there may be some values we do not want to save to the file. These values may contain sensitive data or data that can be calculated again. Adding the attribute **[NonSerialized]** means that during the serialization process, the relevant member, property, will not be serialized, and as such no data will be written for the nonserialized field. Listing 18-2 shows code where the [NonSerialized] attribute is used.

Listing 18-2. Serializable class with a NonSerialized field

```
[Serializable]
public class CustomerBinary
{
    private int customerAccountNumber;
    [NonSerialized] private int customerAge;
    private String customerName;
    private String customerAddress;
    private int customerYearsWithCompany;
}
```

Important Note   *From March 2022 the Microsoft documentation notifies us that*

Due to security vulnerabilities in BinaryFormatter, the following methods are now obsolete and produce a compile-time warning with ID SYSLIB0011:

```
Formatter.Serialize(Stream, Object)
```

```
Formatter.Deserialize(Stream)
```

```
IFormatter.Serialize(Stream, Object)
```

```
IFormatter.Deserialize(Stream)
```

⚠ Warning

The BinaryFormatter type is dangerous and is ***not*** recommended for data processing. Applications should stop using BinaryFormatter as soon as possible, even if they believe the data they're processing to be trustworthy. BinaryFormatter is insecure and can't be made secure.

We will look at serialization and deserialization using the BinaryFormatter not because we can still use it but because we will see existing application code that still uses the BinaryFormatter. As the Microsoft documentation also states

These methods are marked obsolete as part of an effort to wind down usage of BinaryFormatter within the .NET ecosystem.

So, while we code using the BinaryFormatter, we will also look at an alternative solution as suggested by the Microsoft documentation:

Stop using BinaryFormatter in your code. Instead, consider using JsonSerializer *or* XmlSerializer.

Let's code some C# and build our programming muscle.

Serialization is about objects, and an object as we know is an instance of a class. So let's create the class first, with its types, properties, methods, constructor, getters, and setters. The class will be called **CustomerBinary**.

Add a new project to hold the code for this chapter.

1. Right-click the solution CoreCSharp.

2. Choose Add.

3. Choose New Project.

4. Choose Console App from the listed templates that appear.

5. Click the Next button.

6. Name the project Chapter18 and leave it in the same location.

7. Click the Next button.

8. Choose the framework to be used, which in our projects will be .NET 6.0 or higher.

9. Click the Create button.

Now we should see the Chapter18 project within the solution called CoreCSharp.

10. Right-click the project Chapter18 in the Solution Explorer panel.

11. Click the Set as Startup Project option.

Notice how the Chapter18 project name has been made to have bold text, indicating that it is the new startup project and that it is the Program.cs file within it that will be executed when we run the debugging.

12. Right-click the Program.cs file in the Solution Explorer window.

13. Choose Rename.

14. Change the name to CustomerBinary.cs.

15. Press the Enter key.

16. Double-click the CustomerBinary.cs file to open it in the editor window.

17. Amend the code, as in Listing 18-3, with the namespace and class.

Listing 18-3. Serializable class – CustomerBinary

```
namespace Chapter18
{
    [Serializable]
    internal class CustomerBinary
    {
    } // End of CustomerBinary class
} // End of Chapter18 namespace
```

As we are creating a CustomerBinary class that will be instantiated and become a CustomerBinary object, which we will serialize and deserialize, we do not need a Main() method. The CustomerBinary class, or more correctly the instance of the class that we will create, will be accessed from another class, which will contain a Main() method. We should be familiar with a class having fields from our previous study of classes and objects, but in this class, we will use the special attributes [Serializable] and [NonSerializable].

18. Amend the code, as in Listing 18-4, to add the class fields.

Listing 18-4. Serializable class with fields

```
namespace Chapter18
{
  [Serializable]
  internal class CustomerBinary
  {
    /*********************************************************
    The [NonSeriazable] attribute is a 'modifier' which can be
    used in serialization. When we serialize there may be some
    values we do not want to save to the file.
```

These values may contain sensitive data or data that can be calculated again.
Adding the attribute [NonSerialized] means that during the serialization process the relevant member (type) will not be serialized and no data at all will be written for the member.

The [NonSeriazable] attribute assists us with the important role of meeting security constraints e.g. when we do not want to expose private data when we serialize.
```
**************************************************************/
    private int customerAccountNumber;
    private int customerAge;
    private string customerName;
    private string customerAddress;
    private int customerYearsWithCompany;
  } // End of Customer class
} // End of Chapter18 namespace
```

We will add a constructor for the class using parameter names of our choosing, which are not the same names as the fields. We will read shortly an explanation of why we are doing this for our learning.

19.   Amend the code, as in Listing 18-5, to add the constructor.

Listing 18-5. Adding our own constructor

```
private int customerYearsWithCompany;

/*********************************************************
Create a constructor for the Customer class.
The constructor will over-write the default constructor.
The constructor is used to accept the value passed into it
from the code used to instantiate the class.
The values passed into the constructor are used to
initialise the values of fields (members, variables!).
The keyword this is used in front of the field names.
*********************************************************/
```

```
public CustomerBinary(int accountNumberPassedIn, int agePassedIn, string
namePassedIn, string addressPassedIn, int yearsPassedIn)
  {
    customerAccountNumber = accountNumberPassedIn;
    customerAge = agePassedIn;
    customerName = namePassedIn;
    customerAddress = addressPassedIn;
    customerYearsWithCompany = yearsPassedIn;
  } // End of Customer constructor

} // End of CustomerBinary class
} // End of Chapter18 namespace
```

Info

We are now going to create getters and setters for the private members of the CustomerBinary class. As we saw in Chapter 13, private members are not accessible directly from outside the class. To make them available for reading, we use a getter method, and to make them available for changing, we use a setter method.

When using C# there is the concept of a **property** when we talk about getters and setters, and this property offers us a way to get or set the private fields. In other words, the property gives us the ability to read and write the private fields. The property can have what are called **accessors**, which are code blocks for the get accessor and the set accessor. Figure 18-1 shows the concept of a property, with its getter and setter for the private field. When creating the property for the member, we can have

- A get and a set, where we can read the member value and change the member value

- A get, where we can only read the member value but not change its value

- A set, where we can only change the member's value but not read it

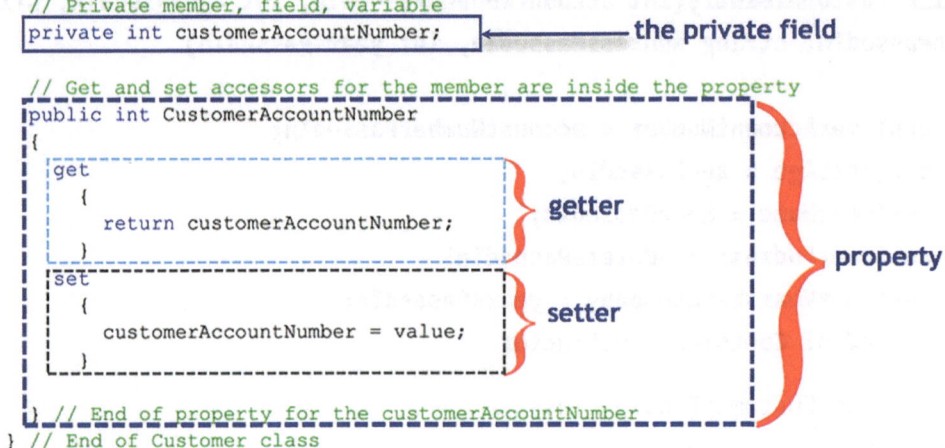

Figure 18-1. *Property containing a getter and a setter*

Remember, we do not always need to have a get and a set for every member; it will depend on what we need. If we have a lot of members, then it would take us a little time to code each getter and setter, so remember we could use the built-in functionality of Visual Studio 2022. When we create the getter and setter for each member, we should ask ourselves, "Where do we want them to be located in our code?" The Visual Studio 2022 "shortcut" might add them as a block where we have our cursor, it might add them as a block at the end of the code after the constructor, it might add them as a block after the members, or indeed it might add them individually under the corresponding members.

With C# there are a number of different approaches that have evolved to create the getters and setters for the members we have created. The different approaches are shown in Listings 18-6, 18-7, 18-8, and 18-9.

Approach 1: Probably the More "Dated"

Listing 18-6. Get by returning the variable or assign the new value

```
class CustomerBinary
{
  // Private member, field, variable
  private int customerAccountNumber;

  // Get and set accessors for the member are inside the property
  public int CustomerAccountNumber
```

```
{
  get
    {
      return customerAccountNumber;
    }
  set
    {
      customerAccountNumber = value;
    }
} // End of property for the customerAccountNumber
} // End of CustomerBinary class
```

Approach 2: Available from C# 2

Listing 18-7. Use get; and set; in the auto-implemented properties

```
class CustomerBinary
{
  /*
    A Private member, field, variable with the get and set
    being written beside the member.
    We will now have a member and its corresponding
    getter and setter.
  */
  public int CustomerAccountNumber
    {
      get;
      set;
    }
} // End of CustomerBinary class
```

Or if we only wanted a getter so that the member is readable from outside the class but only settable from within the class using the setter, we could code it as in Listing 18-8.

Listing 18-8. Use get; and a private set;

```
class CustomerBinary
{
  /*
   Private member, field, variable with the get and set
   being written beside the member.
   We will now have a getter but the setter is private.
  */
  public int CustomerAccountNumber
  {
    get;
    private set;
  }
} // End of CustomerBinary class
```

We could also have a private get and public set, and we can also have properties marked as public, private, protected, internal, protected internal, or private protected.

Approach 3: Available from C# 7

In C# 7 we were introduced to the concept of **expression-bodied members**, which were aimed at providing a quicker or shorter way to define properties and methods. The fat arrow, =>, can therefore be used with properties that consists of only one expression. As we know

- A get accessor does one thing: it gets the value of the member.

- A set accessor does one thing: it sets the value of the member.

Therefore, the fat arrow, =>, can be used within our get and set accessors and it also allows us to remove the curly braces and the return.

Listing 18-9. Use get and set with the fat arrow =>

```
class Customer
{
  /*
   Private member, field, variable with the get and set
   being written beside the member.
   We will now have a member and its corresponding
```

```
    getter and setter.
  */
  private int customerAccountNumber;

  public int CustomerAccountNumber
  {
    get => customerAccountNumber;
    set => customerAccountNumber = value;
  }
} // End of Customer class
```

Yes, we might be thinking, *That sounds good.* It is indeed good; it might even be awesome. But we are learning to program, and it might just be a little too much for us to understand now. Either way, we will keep the declaring of get and set accessors straightforward, and when we understand the concepts, we can start using the shorter expression-bodied member style.

20. Amend the code, as in Listing 18-10, to add a getter and setter for each of the private properties of the CustomerBinary class.

Listing 18-10. Getters and setters for the private properties

```
  } // End of CustomerBinary constructor

  // Property for each member/field
  public int CustomerAccountNumber
  {
    get { return customerAccountNumber; }
    set { customerAccountNumber = value; }
  }// End of CustomerAccountNumber property
  public int CustomerAge
  {
    get { return customerAge; }
    set { customerAge = value; }
  }// End of CustomerAge property
  public string CustomerName
```

```
    {
      get { return customerName; }
      set { customerName = value; }
    }// End of CustomerName property
    public string CustomerAddress
    {
      get { return customerAddress; }
      set { customerAddress = value; }
    }// End of CustomerAddress property
    public int CustomerYearsWithCompany
    {
      get { return customerYearsWithCompany; }
      set { customerYearsWithCompany = value; }
    }// End of CustomerYearsWithCompany property
  } // End of Customer class
} // End of Chapter18 namespace
```

Serializing the Object

Now that we have the class that is to be serialized, we will create a class that will perform the serialization on the instance of the class, the object. So let's create the class called SerializedCustomer and add the required code.

1. Right-click the Chapter18 project in the editor window.

2. Choose Add.

3. Choose Class

4. Change the name to SerializedCustomer.cs.

5. Click the Add button.

6. The SerializedCustomer class code will appear in the editor window. Amend the code to add the Main() method, as in Listing 18-11.

Listing 18-11. Class template code with a Main() method

```
namespace Chapter18
{
  internal class SerializedCustomer
  {
    static void Main(string[] args)
    {
    }//End of Main() method
  } //End of SerializedCustomer class
} //End of Chapter18 namespace
```

7. Amend the code, as in Listing 18-12, to add some comments about serialization. You may choose to leave these out and go to the next step.

Listing 18-12. Add comments

```
namespace Chapter18
{
  internal class SerializedCustomer
  {
  /*
  Serialization is a process to convert an object into a stream
  of bytes so that the bytes can be written into a file or
  elsewhere.
  We will normally do this so the serialized data can be used to
  store the data in a database or for sending it across a network
  e.g. to a message queue to form part of a transaction process.
  The byte stream created for XML and JSON is platform independent, it is
  an object serialized on one platform that can be de serialized on a
  different platform.
  */

    static void Main(string[] args)
    {
    }//End of Main() method
```

We will now create an instance of the CustomerBinary class, the object, passing to the constructor the initial values for the properties. We will create this code inside the Main() method.

8.   Amend the code, as in Listing 18-13.

Listing 18-13. Instantiate the class, passing it values

```
static void Main(string[] args)
{
    /********************************************************
    Create an instance of the Customer class passing in the
    initial values that will be used to set the values of the
    members (fields) in the Customer object being created.
    As a matter of good practice we will use a .ser extension
    for the file name.
    ********************************************************/
    CustomerBinary myCustomerObject = new CustomerBinary(123456, 45,
    "Gerry", "1 Any Street, Belfast, BT1 ANY", 10);
```

We will now create an instance of the BinaryFormatter class. We will see that this formatter is used to give us the method we need when we wish to serialize the object.

9.   Amend the code, as in Listing 18-14.

Listing 18-14. Instantiate the BinaryFormatter class, which we will use

```
Customer myCustomerObject = new Customer(123456, 45, "Gerry", "1 Any
Street, Belfast, BT1 ANY", 10);

    IFormatter formatterForTheClass = new BinaryFormatter();
}//End of Main() method
```

10.   Add the code in Listing 18-15, to import the required namespaces for the BinaryFormatter and IFormatter.

Listing 18-15. Add the required imports

```
using System.Runtime.Serialization;
using System.Runtime.Serialization.Formatters.Binary;
```

When we studied file handling in Chapter 16, we saw that the FileStream class could be used to read a file or write to a file. In instantiating the FileStream class, the created object can have four parameters:

- **filename**, the name, path, and extension of the file that will hold the data

  For example, CustomerSerializedData.ser

- **file mode**, the mode in which to open the file

  For example, Open, Create, Append

- **file access**, the access given to this file

  For example, Read, Write, ReadWrite

Now we will create a file stream, which will be used to create the file, so we will be using the property Create and we will use the property Write so we can write to the newly created file.

11. Amend the code, as in Listing 18-16.

Listing 18-16. Use FileStream to create the file that will hold the serialized data

```
IFormatter formatterForTheClass = new BinaryFormatter();

Stream streamToHoldTheData = new FileStream("CustomerSerializedData.
ser", FileMode.Create, FileAccess.Write);
}//End of Main() method
```

Now we will call the Serialize() method of the formatter class, passing it the stream that will hold the data and the object to be serialized. We will then close the file stream.

12. Amend the code, as in Listing 18-17.

Listing 18-17. Call the Serialize() method of the FileStream class

```
Stream streamToHoldTheData =
  new FileStream("CustomerSerializedData.ser",
  FileMode.Create, FileAccess.Write);
```

```
formatterForTheClass.Serialize(streamToHoldTheData, myCustomerObject);

streamToHoldTheData.Close();

}//End of Main() method
```

13. Click the File menu.

14. Choose Save All.

15. Click the Debug menu.

16. Choose Start Without Debugging.

17. Press any key to close the console window that appears.

18. In the Solution Explorer, click the Chapter18 project.

19. Click the Show All Files icon, as shown in Figure 18-2.

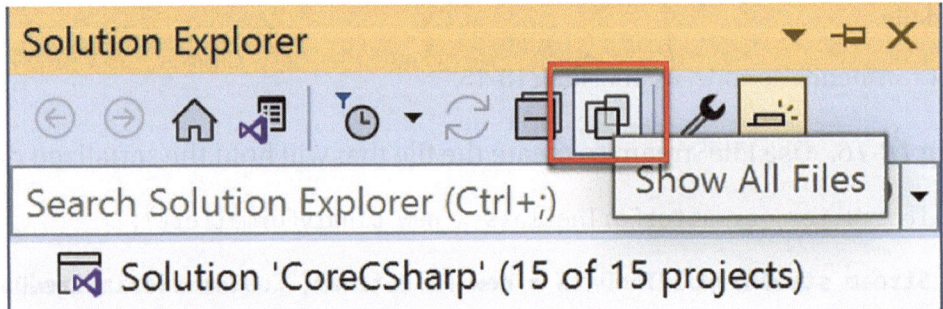

Figure 18-2. *Show All Files*

20. Click the Refresh button, as shown in Figure 18-3.

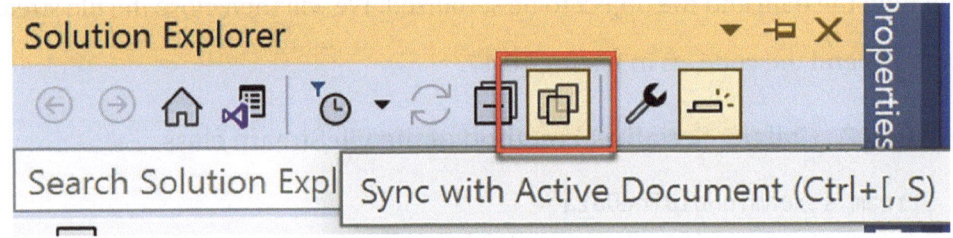

Figure 18-3. *Refresh or sync*

The serialized file should be displayed in the net6.0 folder, which is in the Debug folder, which is inside the bin folder, as shown in Figure 18-4.

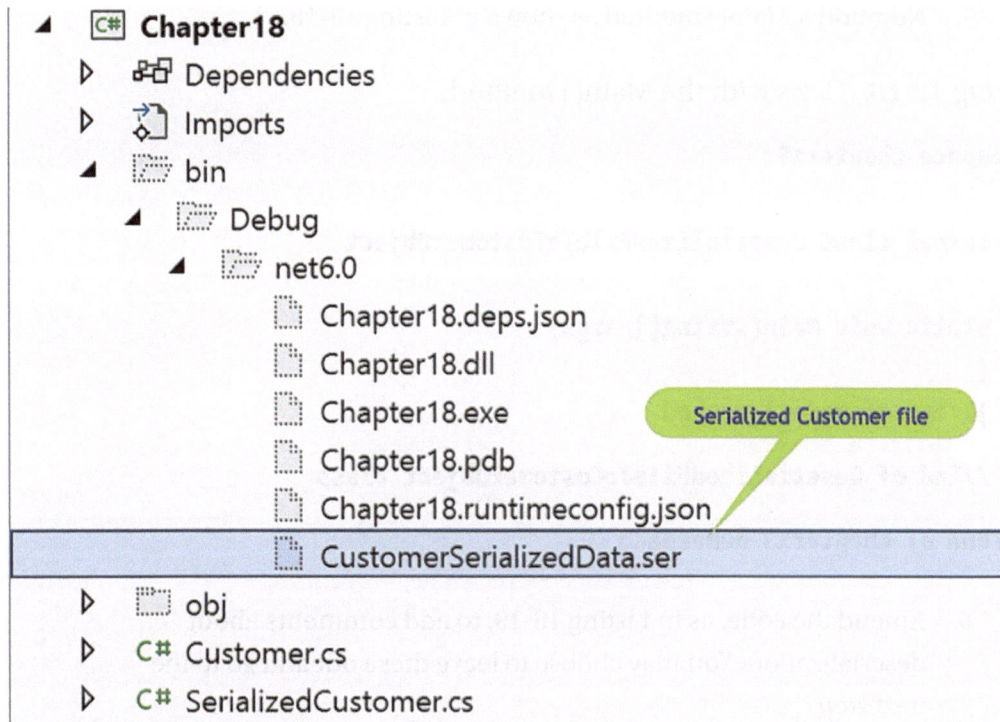

Figure 18-4. *Serialized file has been written*

Brilliant! We have a serialized file. The serialized file contains the state of the instance class; in other words, it has the customer details that we supplied when we used the constructor.

Deserializing the Serialized File to a Class

1. Right-click the Chapter18 project in the Solution Explorer window.

2. Choose Add.

3. Choose Class

4. Change the name to DeserializedFileToCustomerObject.cs.

5. Click the Add button.

6. The DeserializedFileToCustomerObject class code will appear in the editor window.

7. Now add a Main() method as shown in Listing 18-18.

Listing 18-18. Class with the Main() method

```
namespace Chapter18
{
  internal class DeserializedFileToCustomerObject
  {
    static void Main(string[] args)
    {
    }//End of Main() method

  } //End of DeserializedFileToCustomerObject class

} //End of Chapter18 namespace
```

8. Amend the code, as in Listing 18-19, to add comments about deserialization. You may choose to leave these out and go to the next step.

Listing 18-19. Comments about deserialization

```
internal class DeserializedFileToCustomerObject
{
/*
De-serialization is the process of taking the serialized data
(file) and returning it to an object as defined by the class.

When we serialized, there may be some values we do not want to
  save to the file. These values may contain sensitive data or
  data that can be calculated again. Adding the attribute
  [NonSerialized] means that during the serialization process
  the relevant member (field) will not be  serialized and as
  such the data will be ignored and no data for the field
  will be written.
*/

  static void Main(string[] args)
```

9.   Amend the code, as in Listing 18-20, to create an instance of the CustomerBinary class, the object, and set it null.

Listing 18-20. Create an instance of the CustomerBinary class

```
static void Main(string[] args)
{
  CustomerBinary myCustomer = null;

}//End of Main() method
```

In the serialization code, we created an instance for the BinaryFormatter and based it on the interface IFormatter. Remember we said program to an interface. In this example however, we will create an instance of the BinaryFormatter that is based on the BinaryFormatter class, just to show a different approach. Both approaches are perfectly acceptable.

We will now create an instance of the BinaryFormatter so that later we can use the method that allows us to deserialize the object.

10.   Amend the code, as in Listing 18-21.

Listing 18-21. Create an instance of the BinaryFormatter

```
static void Main(string[] args)
{
  CustomerBinary myCustomer = null;

  BinaryFormatter binaryFormatterForTheClass = new BinaryFormatter();

}//End of Main() method
```

11.   Add the code in Listing 18-22, to import the required namespace for the BinaryFormatter.

Listing 18-22. Add the required import

using System.Runtime.Serialization.Formatters.Binary;

namespace Chapter18

We will now create an instance of the FileStream, giving it the serialized filename and the Open and Read properties for its parameters.

12.   Amend the code, as in Listing 18-23.

Listing 18-23. Create a FileStream to allow file opening and reading

```
BinaryFormatter binaryFormatterForTheClass =
  new BinaryFormatter();

FileStream fileStreamToHoldTheData = new FileStream("CustomerSerializ
edData.ser",FileMode.Open, FileAccess.Read);

}//End of Main() method
```

In the serialization code, we did not use a try catch block, which could have been a problem if there was an error. We should always use a try catch block when working with files, and we saw this when we looked at exception handling. In the code in Listing 18-24, we will use a try catch block while we attempt to read the serialized file we created during the serialization process.

13.   Amend the code, as in Listing 18-24.

Listing 18-24. Try catch block while reading the serialized file

```
FileStream fileStreamToHoldTheData =
  new FileStream("CustomerSerializedData.ser",
  FileMode.Open, FileAccess.Read);

try
{
 using (fileStreamToHoldTheData)
 {
 myCustomer =  (CustomerBinary)binaryFormatterForTheClass.Deserializ
 e(fileStreamToHoldTheData);

 } // End of the using block
} // End of the try block
catch
{
}// End of the catch block

}//End of Main() method
```

Now that we have the deserialized data in a CustomerBinary object, we can display it using the property method of each member. In reality we will only use the get accessor to get the value and then display it along with a relevant message. The format for using the get accessor is to simply call the property of the member, for example:

- CustomerName calls the CustomerName property that will return the customerName private field.

- CustomerAge uses the get accessor of the customerAge member.

The format for using the set accessor, if we were to use it, is to simply assign the property of the member to a value, for example:

- CustomerName = "WHO" would use the set accessor of the customerName member.

- CustomerAge = 21 would use the set accessor of the customerAge member.

So let us now display the details obtained from the deserialized file. We will display each member of the deserialized CustomerBinary class to ensure that it contains the data that was written to the file during the serialization process.

14.   Amend the code, as in Listing 18-25.

Listing 18-25. Display the details of the deserialized CustomerBinary class

```
try
{
 using (fileStreamToHoldTheData)
 {
  myCustomer =
(Customer)binaryFormatterForTheClass.Deserialize(fileStreamToHoldTheData);

Console.WriteLine("Customer Details");
Console.WriteLine("Customer Name: " + myCustomer.CustomerName);
Console.WriteLine("Customer Age: " + myCustomer.CustomerAge);
Console.WriteLine("Customer Account No: " + myCustomer.
CustomerAccountNumber);
Console.WriteLine("Customer Address: " + myCustomer.CustomerAddress);
```

```
Console.WriteLine("Customer Years a Customer: " + myCustomer.
CustomerYearsWithCompany);
```

```
    } // End of the using block
  } // End of the try block
  catch
  {
  }// End of the catch block
```

15. Amend the code, as in Listing 18-26, to add a message in the catch block.

Listing 18-26. Catch block message

```
  catch
  {
      Console.WriteLine("Error creating the Customer from the
      serialized file");
  }// End of the catch block
```

16. Right-click the Chapter18 project in the Solution Explorer panel.

17. Choose Properties.

18. Set the Startup object to be the Chapter18.
    DeserializedFileToCustomerObject in the drop-down list, as
    shown in Figure 18-5.

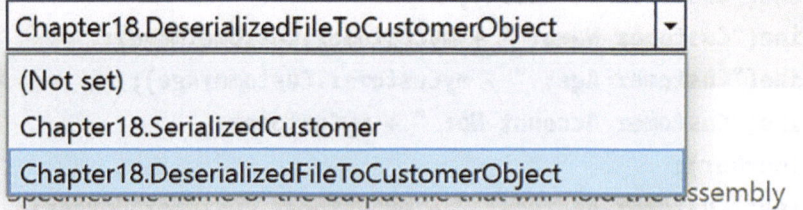

Startup object

Defines the entry point to be called when the application loads.
Generally this is set either to the main form in your application or to
the 'Main' procedure that should run when the application starts.
Class libraries do not define an entry point.

| Chapter18.DeserializedFileToCustomerObject | ▾ |

(Not set)

Chapter18.SerializedCustomer

Chapter18.DeserializedFileToCustomerObject

Figure 18-5. Set the startup program

19.   Close the Properties window.

20.   Click the File menu.

21.   Choose Save All.

22.   Click the Debug menu.

23.   Choose Start Without Debugging.

The console window will appear, as shown in Figure 18-6, and display the CustomerBinary object details, confirming that the deserialization has been successful.

```
Customer Details
Customer Name: Gerry
Customer Age: 45                    deserialized Customer data - Customer
Customer Account No:123456
Customer Address:1 Any Street, Belfast, BT1 ANY
Customer Years a Customer:  10


C:\CoreCSharp\CoreCSharp\Chapter18\bin\Debug\net6.0\Chapter18.exe
Press any key to close this window . . .
```

Figure 18-6.   *Details from the deserialized file*

24.   Press any key to close the console window that appears.

Access Modifier [NonSerialized]

At the start of the chapter, we read that when we serialize, there may be some values we do not want to save to the file because the values may contain sensitive data or data that can be calculated again. We read that by adding the **[NonSerialized]** attribute to a field, the data will not be serialized. Now we will code using the **[NonSerialized]** attribute on the customerAge field, which has been designated as "secret," and confirm that the data is not written to the serialized file.

25.   Open the CustomerBinary.cs class.

26.   Amend the code, as in Listing 18-27.

Listing 18-27. NonSerializable member

```
private int customerAccountNumber;
[NonSerialized] private int customerAge;
private String customerName;
private String customerAddress;
private int customerYearsWithCompany;
```

27. Click the File menu.

28. Choose Save All.

Now set the SerializedCustomer.cs file as the Startup object and run the code again to create the new version of the CustomerSerializedData.ser file with the default value being written.

Now set the Startup object back to the DeserializedFileToCustomerObject.

29. Click the Debug menu.

30. Choose Start Without Debugging.

The console window will appear and display the CustomerBinary object details, as shown in Figure 18-7, confirming that the deserialization has been successful and that age has the default value.

```
Customer Details
Customer Name: Gerry                          [NonSerialized] private int CustomerAge;
Customer Age: 0 ─────────────  default value
Customer Account No:123456
Customer Address:1 Any Street, Belfast, BT1 ANY
Customer Years a Customer:  10

C:\CoreCSharp\CoreCSharp\Chapter18\bin\Debug\net6.0\Chapter18.exe
Press any key to close this window . . .
```

Figure 18-7. *Details from the deserialized file with age nonserialized*

Brilliant! We can serialize and deserialize a class, or strictly speaking the instance of the class. But, as we were cautioned at the start of the chapter, due to security vulnerabilities in BinaryFormatter, the methods are now obsolete, so we will now look at serialization in a different way, using XML.

750

Serialization Using XML

When we perform XML serialization, the serialization only applies to public fields and property values of an object, and the serialization does not include any type information – no methods or private fields will be serialized. If we need to serialize all private fields, public fields, and properties of an object, then we can use the DataContractSerializer rather than XML serialization, but this will not be covered in this book.

When serializing an object to XML, certain rules apply:

- The class needs to have a default constructor. In the CustomerBinary class that we created earlier, we coded our own constructor, thereby overwriting the default constructor. This means that we will need to add a default constructor, a constructor that is parameterless.

- Only the appropriate public fields and properties of the class will be serialized.

1. Right-click the CustomerBinary.cs file in the Solution Explorer panel.

2. Choose Copy.

3. Right-click the Chapter18 project in the Solution Explorer panel.

4. Choose Paste.

5. Right-click the new CustomerBinary – Copy.cs file.

6. Choose Rename and rename the file as CustomerXML.cs.

Now we must ensure that the class name and constructor name are the same, CustomerXML, and that the class has an access modifier of public.

7. Amend the CustomerXML file as in Listing 18-28, which has had the comments removed for ease of reading.

Listing 18-28. Change class name and constructor name to CustomerXML

```
using System;

namespace Chapter18
{
  [Serializable]
```

```
public class CustomerXML
{
 private int customerAccountNumber;
 [NonSerialized] private int customerAge;
 private string customerName;
 private string customerAddress;
 private int customerYearsWithCompany;

 public CustomerXML(int accountNumberPassedIn, int agePassedIn,
 String namePassedIn, String addressPassedIn, int yearsPassedIn)
   {
```

8. Amend the file to include a default constructor, as in Listing 18-29.

Listing 18-29. Added a default constructor

```
public class CustomerXML
{
 private int customerAccountNumber;
 [NonSerialized] private int customerAge;
 private string customerName;
 private string customerAddress;
 private int customerYearsWithCompany;

 public CustomerXML()
 {

 }

 public CustomerXML(int accountNumberPassedIn, int agePassedIn,
 String namePassedIn, String addressPassedIn, int yearsPassedIn)
 {
```

Now we will make all fields public and remove the accessors.

9. Amend the customerAge field to remove the [NonSerializable] and make all the fields public, as in Listing 18-30.

Listing 18-30. Make all fields public

```
public int customerAccountNumber;
public int customerAge;
public string customerName;
public string customerAddress;
public int customerYearsWithCompany;

public CustomerXML()
{

}
```

In Listing 18-31 that follows, the comment has been changed to make the code more relevant to XML serialization, but we do not need to change the comment in our copied file if we do not wish to do so.

10.   Amend the code to remove the unnecessary accessors, as in Listing 18-31.

Listing 18-31. Class with getters and setters removed

```
using System;

namespace Chapter18
{
    [Serializable]
    public class CustomerXML
    {

    /********************************************************
    The fields are public because in XML serialization only the
    public fields and properties will be serialized
    ********************************************************/
    public int customerAccountNumber;
    public int customerAge;
    public string customerName;
    public string customerAddress;
    public int customerYearsWithCompany;
```

```
public CustomerXML()
{

}

/***********************************************************
Create a constructor for the Customer class.
The constructor will over-write the default constructor.
The constructor is used to accept the value passed into it
from the code used to instantiate the class.
The values passed into the constructor are used to
initialise the values of fields (members, variables!).
The keyword this is used in front of the field names.
***********************************************************/
public CustomerXML(int accountNumberPassedIn, int agePassedIn, string
namePassedIn, string addressPassedIn, int yearsPassedIn)
{
   customerAccountNumber = accountNumberPassedIn;
   customerAge = agePassedIn;
   customerName = namePassedIn;
   customerAddress = addressPassedIn;
   customerYearsWithCompany = yearsPassedIn;
} // End of Customer constructor

} // End of CustomerXML class
} // End of Chapter18 namespace
```

Now that the class being serialized to XML has the required elements, a default constructor, and public fields, we can create the serialize and deserialize code, which we will do in a similar way to binary serialization, using two separate classes.

Creating the Serialization Code

Before writing any code, we will look at the steps to be followed in order to create the code required to serialize the class object. These steps will be similar to the code we used in binary serialization:

- Create an instance of the CustomerXML class using our custom constructor to pass values to the fields in the class:

```
CustomerXML myCustomerObject =
new CustomerXML(123456, 45, "Gerry", "1 Any Street, " +
"Belfast, BT1 ANY", 10);
```

- Create an instance of the XmlSerializer informing it that we are using a class of type CustomerXML. This is like binary serialization when we used the BinaryFormatter or IFormatter:

```
XmlSerializer myXMLSerialiser = new XmlSerializer(typeof(
CustomerXML));
```

- Create an instance of StreamWriter and pass it the name of the file we wish to add the XML to, in our case CustomerSerialisedData.xml:

```
StreamWriter myStreamWriter = new StreamWriter("Customer
SerialisedData.xml");
```

- Call the serialize method of the XmlSerializer, passing it the StreamWriter name and the instance of the object to be serialized:

```
myXMLSerialiser.Serialize(myStreamWriter, myCustomerObject);
```

- Close the StreamWriter instance:

```
myStreamWriter.Close();
```

Now we can code the steps.

11. Right-click the Chapter18 project in the Solution Explorer.

12. Choose Add.

13. Choose Class.

14. Name the class XMLSerialisation.cs.

15. Click the Add button.

16. Amend the code, as in Listing 18-32, to add a Main() method and code the steps needed to serialize to XML.

Listing 18-32. Adding the code to serialize the CustomerXML object

```
using System.Xml.Serialization;

namespace Chapter18
{
  public class XMLSerialisation
  {
    static void Main(string[] args)
    {
      /*********************************************************
      Create an instance of the Customer class passing in the
      initial values that will be used to set the values of the
      members (fields) in the Customer object being created.
      As a matter of good practice we will use a .ser extension
      for the file name.
      *********************************************************/
      CustomerXML myCustomerObject =
          new CustomerXML(123456, 45, "Gerry", "1 Any Street, " +
          "Belfast, BT1 ANY", 10);

      // Create an instance of the XmlSerializer
      XmlSerializer myXMLSerialiser = new
                  XmlSerializer(typeof(CustomerXML));

      //Create an instance of the StreamWriter using the xml file
      StreamWriter myStreamWriter = new
                  StreamWriter("CustomerSerialisedData.xml");

      // Serialize the object using the StreamWriter
     myXMLSerialiser.Serialize(myStreamWriter, myCustomerObject);

      // Close the StreamWriter
      myStreamWriter.Close();

    } // End of Main() method

  } // End of XMLSerialisation class
} // End of Chapter18 namespace
```

17. Right-click the Chapter18 project in the Solution Explorer panel.

18. Choose Properties.

19. Set the Startup object to be the XMLSerialisation in the drop-down list.

20. Exit the Properties window.

21. Click the File menu.

22. Choose Save All.

23. Click the Debug menu.

24. Choose Start Without Debugging.

25. Press the Enter key to close the console window.

The serialized file should be displayed in the net6.0 folder, which is in the Debug folder, which is inside the bin folder, as shown in Figure 18-8.

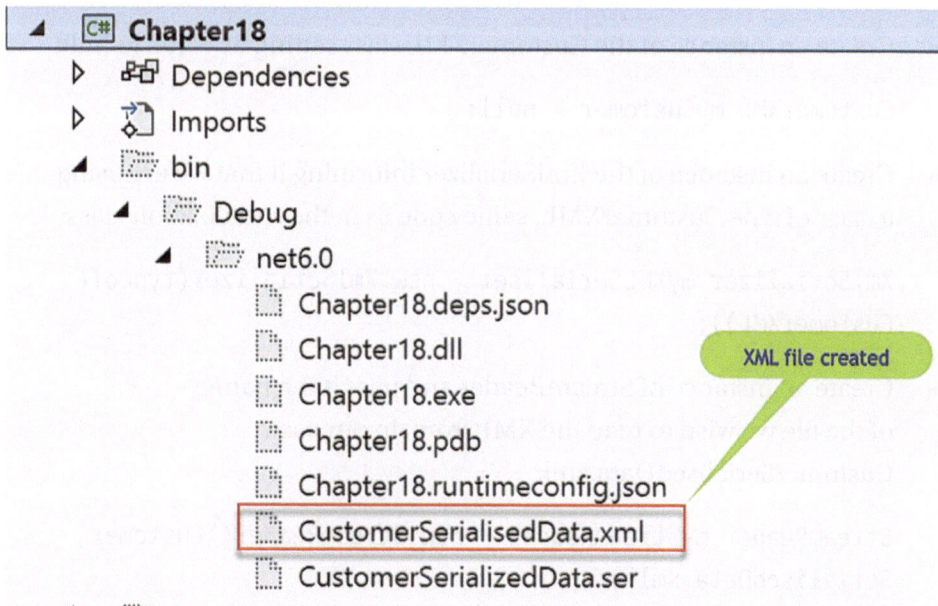

Figure 18-8. *XML serialized file*

Brilliant! We have a serialized file containing XML, as shown in Listing 18-33. The XML file contains the state of the instance class; in other words, it has the CustomerXML details that we supplied when we used the constructor.

Listing 18-33. The XML data from the CustomerSerialisedData.xml file execution

```
<?xml version="1.0" encoding="UTF-8"?>
<CustomerXML xmlns:xsd="http://www.w3.org/2001/XMLSchema"
xmlns:xsi="http://www.w3.org/2001/XMLSchema-instance">
<customerAccountNumber>123456</customerAccountNumber> <customerAge>45
</customerAge>
<customerName>Gerry</customerName>
<customerAddress>1 Any Street, Belfast, BT1 ANY</customerAddress>
<customerYearsWithCompany>10</customerYearsWithCompany>
</CustomerXML>
```

Creating the Deserialization Code

Before writing any code, we will look at the steps to be followed in order to create the code required to deserialize, convert the XML to a class object. These steps will be similar to the code we used in binary deserialization:

- Create an instance of the CustomerXML class setting its value to null:

  ```
  CustomerXML myCustomer = null;
  ```

- Create an instance of the XmlSerializer informing it that we are using a class of type CustomerXML, same code as in the serialization class:

  ```
  XmlSerializer myXMLSerialiser = new XmlSerializer(typeof(
  CustomerXML));
  ```

- Create an instance of StreamReader and pass it the name of the file we wish to read the XML from, in our case CustomerSerialisedData.xml:

  ```
  StreamReader myStreamReader = new StreamReader("Customer
  SerialisedData.xml");
  ```

- Call the deserialize method of the XmlSerializer, passing it the StreamReader name, then cast the returned value to a CustomerXML object, and assign this to the myCustomer instance of the CustomerXML object we created in the first step:

```
try
{
myCustomer = (CustomerXML)mySerialser.Deserialize(myStreamReader);
} // End of the try block
catch
{
Console.WriteLine("Error creating the Customer" +
    " from the serialised file");
}// End of the catch block
```

- As the deserialization may cause an exception, we will add the code within a try catch block.

- Now we will display the details of the object created from the XML file by calling the accessor from the myCustomer instance of the CustomerXML class, for example, customer name would be displayed using the code

```
Console.WriteLine("Customer Name: " +
    myCustomer.customerName);
```

We are not using accessors, so be careful with the field name – it has no capital letter.

- Close the StreamReader instance:

```
myStreamReader.Close();
```

Now we can code the steps.

26. Right-click the Chapter18 project in the Solution Explorer panel.

27. Choose Add.

28. Choose Class.

29. Name the class XMLDeserialisation.cs.

30. Click the Add button.

31. Amend the code, as in Listing 18-34, to add a Main() method and code the steps needed to deserialize to a CustomerXML object and then display the details of the customer.

Listing 18-34. Adding the code to deserialize XML to a CustomerXML object

```
using System.Xml.Serialization;

namespace Chapter18
{
  internal class XMLDeserialisation
  {
    static void Main(string[] args)
    {
    /*
    De-serialisation is the process of taking the serialized data
    (file) and returning it to an object as defined by the class.
    */

      // Create an instance of the Customer class
      CustomerXML myCustomer = null;

      // Create an instance of the XmlSerializer
XmlSerializer mySerialser = new XmlSerializer(typeof(CustomerXML));

      // Create an instance of the StreamReader using the xml file
      StreamReader myStreamReader = new StreamReader("CustomerSerialisedD
      ata.xml");

  try
  {
    myCustomer = (CustomerXML)mySerialser.Deserialize(myStreamReader);

    Console.WriteLine("Deserialize completed"); ;

    Console.WriteLine("Customer Details");
    Console.WriteLine("Customer Name: " + myCustomer.customerName);
    Console.WriteLine("Customer Age: " + myCustomer.customerAge);
    Console.WriteLine("Customer Account No: " +
            myCustomer.customerAccountNumber);
    Console.WriteLine("Customer Address: " +
            myCustomer.customerAddress);
    Console.WriteLine("Customer Years a Customer: " +
            myCustomer.customerYearsWithCompany);
```

```
} // End of the try block
catch
 {
    Console.WriteLine("Error creating the Customer" +
      " from the serialised file");
 }// End of the catch block
  myStreamReader.Close();
} // End of Main() method

  } // End of XMLDeserialisation class
} // End of Chapter18 namespace
```

32. Right-click the Chapter18 project in the Solution Explorer panel.

33. Choose Properties.

34. Set the Startup object to be the XMLDeserialisation in the drop-down list.

35. Exit the Properties window.

36. Click the File menu.

37. Choose Save All.

38. Click the Debug menu.

39. Choose Start Without Debugging.

The deserialized object should be displayed as shown in Figure 18-9.

```
Deserialize completed
Customer Details                    XML data deserialised to a CustomerXML object
Customer Name: Gerry
Customer Age: 45
Customer Account No:123456
Customer Address:1 Any Street, Belfast, BT1 ANY
Customer Years a Customer:  10

C:\CoreCSharp\CoreCSharp\Chapter18\bin\Debug\net6.0\Chapter18.exe
Press any key to close this window . . .
```

Figure 18-9. *XML file returned as a CustomerXML object*

40. Press the Enter key to close the console window.

Brilliant! We can now serialize and deserialize C# objects in two different ways. XML is widely used in the commercial environment, but there is also another widely used format called JSON, and we will now complete our chapter by looking at how we can serialize and deserialize using the JSON format.

Serialization Using JSON

JSON is an acronym for JavaScript Object Notation and it is a widely used format to represent information. JSON can represent our data in a very easy-to-read format. Many applications in the commercial world will use JSON to represent data and transfer it as part of Hypertext Transfer Protocol (HTTP) requests and responses. But remember the important note at the start of the chapter where we saw the quote from the Microsoft site:

> *Stop using BinaryFormatter in your code. Instead, consider using JsonSerializer or XmlSerializer.*

So now we will look at the JSON option. There are different "tools" we can use to serialize with JSON, but we will use the System.Text.Json namespace since it was specially created by Microsoft to be included as a built-in library from .NET Core 3.0. By using this library, we will not need to use external libraries, and we will have access to methods such as Serialize(), Deserialize(), SerializeAsync(), and DeserializeAsync(). All this is all we need.

1. Right-click the Chapter18 project in the Solution Explorer panel.

2. Choose Add.

3. Choose Class.

4. Name the class JSONSerialisation.cs.

5. Click the Add button.

6. Right-click the Chapter18 project in the Solution Explorer panel.

7. Choose Add.

8. Choose Class.

9. Name the class CustomerJSON.cs.

10. Click the Add button.

We will amend the CustomerJSON class to add the members with a get and set attached and a constructor to set the member values. We will also use the attribute [JsonIgnore] so that the customerAge field is not serialized. [JsonIgnore] therefore is the JSON equivalent of the [NonSerialized] attribute, which we used in a previous example.

11. Double-click the CustomerJSON file to open it in the editor window.

12. Amend the code as shown in Listing 18-35 to create the class and use a different way to get and set the member values.

Listing 18-35. Class that has auto-implemented properties and [JsonIgnore]

```
using System.Text.Json.Serialization;

namespace Chapter18
{
  public class CustomerJSON
  {
    /*********************************************************
    The [JsonIgnore] attribute is a 'modifier' which can be
    used in JSON serialization to ensure the member (type) will
    not be serialized.
    *********************************************************/
    public int CustomerAccountNumber { get; set; }

    [JsonIgnore]
    public int CustomerAge { get; set; }

    public String CustomerName { get; set; }
    public String CustomerAddress { get; set; }
    public int CustomerYearsWithCompany { get; set; }

    /*********************************************************
    Create a constructor for the Customer class.
    The constructor will over-write the default constructor.
    The constructor is used to accept the value passed into it
    from the code used to instantiate the class.
    The values passed into the constructor are used to
```

```
initialise the values of fields (members, variables!).
The keyword this is used in front of the field names.
*********************************************************/
public CustomerJSON(int customerAccountNumber,
   int customerAge, String customerName,
   String customerAddress, int customerYearsWithCompany)
{
   this.CustomerAccountNumber = customerAccountNumber;
   this.CustomerAge = customerAge;
   this.CustomerName = customerName;
   this.CustomerAddress = customerAddress;
   this.CustomerYearsWithCompany = customerYearsWithCompany;
} // End of Customer constructor

} // End of CustomerJSON class
} // End of Chapter18 namespace
```

We will amend the JSONSerialisation class:

- Add a Main() method

- Inside the Main() method, we will create an instance of the class CustomerJSON by passing values to the constructor.

- Call the JSON Serialize() method, passing it the instance of our CustomerJSON and assigning the returned JSON to a string variable called jsonString.

- Display the returned JSON to the console.

Let's code these steps as shown in Listing 18-36.

13. Amend the code, as in Listing 18-36, to add the Main() method and the class instantiation and perform the assignment.

Listing 18-36. Adding a Main() method and other code

```
using System.Text.Json;

namespace Chapter18
{
  internal class JSONSerialisation
  {
    public static  void Main()
    {

      CustomerJSON myCustomer =
        new CustomerJSON(123456, 45, "Gerry",
        "1 Any Street, Belfast, BT1 ANY", 10);

      //Serialize
      string jsonString =
        JsonSerializer.Serialize<CustomerJSON>(myCustomer);

      Console.WriteLine(jsonString);

    } // End of Main() method

  } // End of JSONSerialisation class
} // End of Chapter18 namespace
```

14. Click the File menu.

15. Choose Save All.

16. Right-click the Chapter18 project in the Solution Explorer panel.

17. Choose Properties.

18. Set the Startup object to be the JSONSerialisation in the drop-down list.

19. Exit the Properties window.

20. Click the Debug menu.

21. Choose Start Without Debugging.

The console window will appear and display the object details in JSON format, as shown in Figure 18-10, confirming that the serialization has been successful with the customer age not included.

```
{"customerAccountNumber":123456,"customerName":"Gerry","customerAddress":"1 Any Street, Belfast, BT1 ANY","customerYears
WithCompany":10}

C:\CoreCSharp\CoreCSharp\Chapter18\bin\Debug   t6.0\Chapter18.exe (process 5740) exited with code 0.
Press any key to close this wind     JSON serialisation with no customer age
```

Figure 18-10. *JSON format from the serialization displayed*

22.   Press the Enter key to close the console window.

Great, but we haven't written the JSON to a file. Obviously, we could have created the code for that within the code shown in Listing 18-36, but we will achieve it through a new method that we will create, and this will allow us to look at serializing using an asynchronous approach.

We will amend the class to

- Add an async method called CreateJSON(), which will accept a CustomerJSON object.

- Declare a string, assigning it the name of the file to be used.

- Use an instance of the FileStream class to create the file – this is our stream.

- Call the SerializeAsync() method, passing it the stream and the instance of our CustomerJSON object.

- Dispose of the unmanaged resource of the stream.

- Display the contents of the JSON file to the console.

23.   Amend the code, as in Listing 18-37, to add the new method outside the Main() method but inside the namespace.

Listing 18-37. Adding a CreateJSON() method

```
} // End of Main() method

public static async Task CreateJSON(CustomerJSON myCustomer)
{
  string fileName = "Customer.json";
```

```
    using FileStream createStream = File.Create(fileName);
    await JsonSerializer.SerializeAsync(createStream, myCustomer);
    await createStream.DisposeAsync();

    Console.WriteLine(File.ReadAllText(fileName));
  } // End of CreateJSON() method

} // End of JSONSerialisation class
} // End of Chapter18 namespace
```

24. Amend the code, as in Listing 18-38, to call the CreateJSON()
    method from within the Main() method, passing it the
    myCustomer object. The Main() method will need to be async so
    that we can await properly.

Listing 18-38. Adding a call to the CreateJSON() method

```
public static async Task Main()
{

    CustomerJSON myCustomer = new CustomerJSON(123456, 45, "Gerry", "1
    Any Street, Belfast, BT1 ANY", 10);

    //Serialize
    string jsonString = JsonSerializer.Serialize<CustomerJSON>(my
    Customer);

    Console.WriteLine(jsonString);

    await CreateJSON(myCustomer);

} // End of Main() method

public static async Task CreateJSON(CustomerJSON myCustomer)
{
```

25. Click the File menu.

26. Choose Save All.

27. Click the Debug menu.

28.   Choose Start Without Debugging.

The console window will appear and display the object details in JSON format, as shown in Figure 18-10.

29.   Press the Enter key to close the console window.

We also wrote the code so that a file was created, so we should also look in the net6.0 folder, inside the Debug folder, inside the bin folder, and see that the Customer.json file has been created.

30.   Double-click the Customer.json file to open it in the editor window.

A raw form as displayed in Visual Studio 2022 is shown in Listing 18-39, while a "pretty" form of the Customer.json is shown in Listing 18-40.

Listing 18-39. JSON file contents as shown in Visual Studio 2022

```
{"customerAccountNumber":123456,"customerName":"Gerry","customerAddress":"1
Any Street, Belfast, BT1 ANY","customerYearsWithCompany":10}
```

Listing 18-40. JSON file contents in "pretty" format

```
{
  "CustomerAccountNumber": 123456,
  "CustomerName": "Gerry",
  "CustomerAddress": "1 Any Street, Belfast, BT1 ANY",
  "CustomerYearsWithCompany": 10
}
```

Notice CustomerAge was a [JsonIgnore] field so it does not appear. We will amend the class to

- Add a method called ReadJSON().

- Declare a string, assigning it the name of the file to be used.

- Use an instance of the FileStream class to open and read the file – this is our stream.

- Call the DeSerialize() method, passing it the stream.

- Display the contents of the JSON file to the console.

31. Amend the code, as in Listing 18-41, to add the new method outside the Main() method but inside the namespace.

Listing 18-41. Adding a ReadJSON() method

```
} // End of CreateJSON() method

public static void ReadJSON()
{
 string fileName = "Customer.json";
 using FileStream myStream = File.OpenRead(fileName);
 CustomerJSON myCustomer = JsonSerializer.Deserialize<CustomerJSON>(
 myStream);

Console.WriteLine("Customer Details");
Console.WriteLine("Customer Name: " + myCustomer.CustomerName);
Console.WriteLine("Customer Age: " + myCustomer.CustomerAge);
Console.WriteLine("Customer Account No: " + myCustomer.
CustomerAccountNumber);
Console.WriteLine("Customer Address: " + myCustomer.CustomerAddress);
Console.WriteLine("Customer Years a Customer: " +
myCustomer.CustomerYearsWithCompany);

 } // End of ReadJSON() method

   } // End of JSONSerialisation class
} // End of Chapter18 namespace
```

32. Amend the code, as in Listing 18-42, to call the ReadJSON() method.

Listing 18-42. Call the ReadJSON() method

```
    await CreateJSON(myCustomer);

    ReadJSON();
} // End of Main() method
```

33. Click the File menu.

34. Choose Save All.

35. Click the Debug menu.

36. Choose Start Without Debugging.

The console window will appear and display the object details, as shown in Figure 18-11.

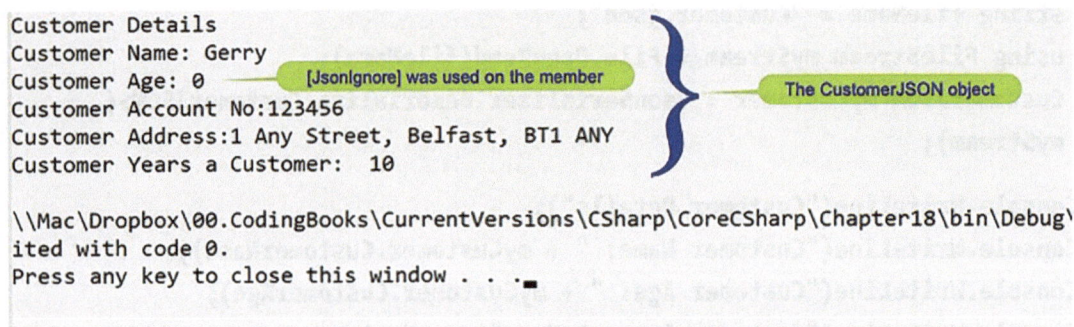

```
Customer Details
Customer Name: Gerry
Customer Age: 0        [JsonIgnore] was used on the member            The CustomerJSON object
Customer Account No:123456
Customer Address:1 Any Street, Belfast, BT1 ANY
Customer Years a Customer:  10

\\Mac\Dropbox\00.CodingBooks\CurrentVersions\CSharp\CoreCSharp\Chapter18\bin\Debug\
ited with code 0.
Press any key to close this window . . .
```

Figure 18-11. *Deserialized object showing the [JsonIgnore] attributed worked*

37. Press the Enter key to close the console window.

Chapter Summary

So, finishing this chapter on object serialization and deserialization, we should be familiar with the use of a class and the instantiation of the class to create an object. We realize that our object, instantiated class, will be treated like all the other objects we have in our code when the application is closed. When we close our application, our object and every other object will not be accessible. We saw in Chapter 16 that we could persist data by writing it to a text file, which is accessible to us after the application stops. So we can now think of serialization as a method to write the object with its real data to a file so we can reuse it at a later stage. We may want to transfer the object, with its state, to another computer over the network or Internet, and through serialization we can use different formats such as binary data, XML data, and JSON data. We also saw that deserialization allows us to reverse the process carried out by serialization, which means converting our serialized byte stream back to our object.

Wow, what an achievement. This is not basic coding. We are doing some wonderful things with our C# code. We should be immensely proud of the learning to date. In finishing this chapter, we have increased our knowledge further and we are advancing to our target.

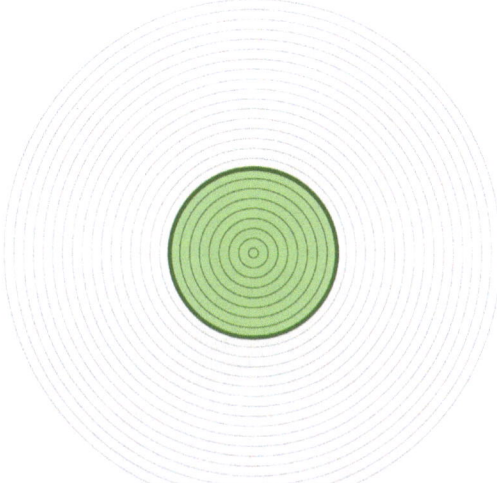

Our target is getting closer

CHAPTER 19

Structs

Concept of a Struct as a Structure Type

In the previous chapter, we looked at serialization, which allows us to store the state of an object, where an object is an instance of a specific class. We looked at different ways to serialize and store the data, and two such formats were XML and JSON. We also learned how to deserialize the serialized data, which is usually stored in a file, and therefore convert it to the same class structure it was in originally. The reason we serialize an object or objects is to allow it to be transferred across a network or shared with other people. Serialization also works across programming languages. In Chapter 13 we gained knowledge of classes and objects, which formed the foundations for the serialization and deserialization processes. Classes are a structure, and in this chapter we will extend our knowledge of structures by looking at the C# struct.

In C# a struct is a lightweight alternative to a class, but it is not a class. The struct can have members and methods, or put another way, we say it can have data and functionality. A struct in C# is defined using the keyword **struct**. Interestingly, we have, without thinking, used simple structs already when coding our applications, since all the value types we have used – for example, int, float, double, bool, char, etc. – are structs. Before we begin, let us take a look at the difference between value types and reference types in relation to structs and classes.

Value and Reference Types

Structs are value types, whereas a class is a reference type, and they are dealt with by the runtime in different ways:

- When a value type instance is made, there is one single space allocated in memory to store the value. We have discussed primitive data types such as int and float and these are value types like a struct. When the runtime deals with the value type, it is dealing directly with the data.

© Gerard Byrne 2022
G. Byrne, *Target C#*, https://doi.org/10.1007/978-1-4842-8619-7_19

- On the other hand, with reference types, an object is created in memory and dealt with through a pointer.

  Example for a Struct

  ```
  CustomerStruct myCustomerStruct = new CustomerStruct();
  ```

  Here one single space is allocated in memory to store the myCustomerStruct, and if we were to copy the struct object to a new variable as

  ```
  CustomerStruct myCustomer2Struct = myCustomerStruct;
  ```

  then myCustomer2Struct would be completely independent of myCustomerStruct and have its own fields.

  Example for a Class

  ```
  CustomerClass myCustomerClass= new CustomerClass();
  ```

  Here two spaces are allocated in memory. One stores the CustomerClass object, and the other stores its reference myCustomerClass. So we could show the example code like this:

  ```
  CustomerClass myCustomerClass;
  myCustomerClass = new CustomerClass();
  ```

  Now if we were to copy the class object to a new variable as

  ```
  CustomerClass myCustomer2Class = myCustomerClass;
  ```

  then myCustomer2Class would be simply a copy of the reference CustomerClass, and therefore myCustomerClass and myCustomer2Class point to the same object.

Difference Between Struct and Class

Some ways in which structs differ from classes are as follows:

- Structs are value types, and we use the actual struct. On the other hand, a class is a reference type, and we point to the actual class.

- Structs cannot be coded by us to have a constructor that has no parameters, a default constructor, since the default constructor is automatically defined and not available to change.

- Structs cannot inherit from other structs or classes, whereas a class can inherit from other classes.

- Structs can implement one or more interfaces.

- Structs cannot declare a finalizer, which is a destructor used to garbage collect.

- If we use the new keyword to create an object of the struct, the default constructor is called and the object is created. A struct can be instantiated without using the new keyword, whereas a class cannot be instantiated without using the new keyword.

- If the struct is used without the new keyword, the members of the struct will remain unassigned and we cannot use the struct object until we have initialized all the members.

- Members, fields, cannot be initialized, for example, public int policy_ number = 0; causes an error in C# 10 or lower.

In writing our code, there may be times when we wish to access an object directly, in the same way that value types are accessed. To address these concerns, C# offers the structure as described previously and, in our programming, we would use structs to represent more simple data structures. The format of the struct declaration is

```
struct name
{
  member declarations

  constructor if required
}
```

Let's code some C# and build our programming muscle.

We will create a Customer struct in a similar manner to the Customer class we created when we completed Chapter 13 on classes and objects.

Add a new project to hold the code for this chapter.

1. Right-click the solution CoreCSharp.

2. Choose Add.

3. Choose New Project.

4. Choose Console App from the listed templates that appear.

5. Click the Next button.

6. Name the project Chapter19 and leave it in the same location.

7. Click the Next button.

8. Choose the framework to be used, which in our projects will be .NET 6.0 or higher.

9. Click the Create button.

Now we should see the Chapter19 project within the solution called CoreCSharp.

10. Right-click the Chapter19 project in the Solution Explorer panel.

11. Click the Set as Startup Project option.

Notice how the Chapter19 project name has been made to have bold text, indicating that it is the new startup project and that it is the Program.cs file within it that will be executed when we run the debugging.

12. Right-click the Program.cs file in the Solution Explorer window.

13. Choose Rename.

14. Change the name to CustomerExample.cs.

15. Press the Enter key

16. Double-click the CustomerExample.cs file to open it in the editor window.

Struct with a Default Constructor Only

We will now add a Main() method. Then we will add a struct called Customer, which is outside the class but inside the namespace and will hold the variables we require. In the code in Listing 19-1, the Customer struct has been created above the Main() method, but it could also have been created below the Main() method. The Customer struct will not be given a constructor in our code, but the default constructor still exists.

17.   Amend the code, as in Listing 19-1.

Listing 19-1. Customer struct inside namespace

```
namespace Chapter19
{
  struct Customer
  {
    public int AccountNo;
    public int Age;
    public string Name;
    public string Address;
    public int LoyaltyYears;
  } // End of Customer struct

  internal class CustomerExample
  {
    static void Main(string[] args)
    {
    } // End of Main() method

  } // End of CustomerExample class

} // End of Chapter19 namespace
```

We will now add code inside the Main() method to create an instance of the Customer struct, then assign values to the Customer struct fields, and then display the Customer struct values in a formatted display. This should all look familiar to us as we have coded applications using classes and objects.

18.   Amend the code, as in Listing 19-2.

Listing 19-2. Assign values to the Customer struct fields and display the data

```
internal class CustomerExample
{
  static void Main(string[] args)
  {
    // Create an object, myCustomer, of type struct Customer
    Customer myCustomer;
```

```
        // Assign values to the myCustomer properties
        myCustomer.AccountNo = 123456;
        myCustomer.Age = 30;
        myCustomer.Name = "Gerry Byrne";
        myCustomer.Address = "1 Any Street";
        myCustomer.LoyaltyYears = 10;

        // Display the myCustomer struct details
        Console.WriteLine($"{"Customer account number is",-30} {myCustomer.
        AccountNo,15}");
        Console.WriteLine($"{"Customer age is",-30} {myCustomer.Age,15}");
        Console.WriteLine($"{"Customer name is",-30} {myCustomer.Name,15}");
        Console.WriteLine($"{"Customer address is",-30} {myCustomer.
        Address,15}");
        Console.WriteLine($"{"Customer loyalty years",-30} {myCustomer.
        LoyaltyYears,9} years");
    } // End of Main() method
} // End of CustomerExample class
```

19.   Click the File menu.

20.   Choose Save All.

21.   Click the Debug menu.

22.   Choose Start Without Debugging.

The console window will appear, as shown in Figure 19-1, and show details of this Customer instance.

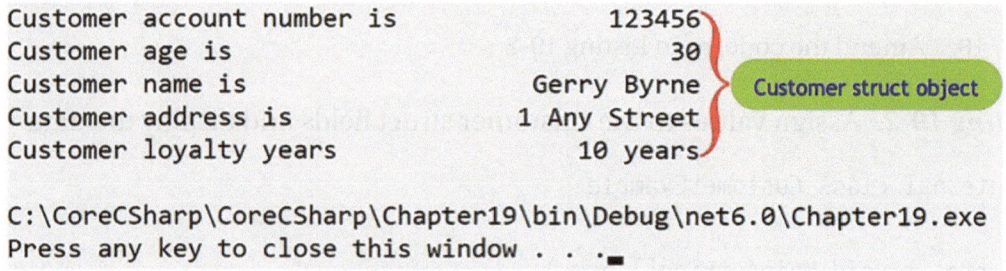

Figure 19-1. *Struct details displayed for the instance*

23.   Press the Enter key to close the console window.

Struct with a User Constructor

As we have seen, a C# struct is a value type. This means that when we create an instance of the struct, we must pass to it values for each of its members. This can be achieved by

- Using the default constructor method to give default values of the members

- Having a user-defined constructor method to assign values to the members

We will code an example of an insurance policy that we might have for our home building insurance, home contents insurance, car insurance, travel insurance, etc. All these policy types will have common data that needs to be stored for the specific customer policy, the policy object. We will create a sample C# policy struct and include a constructor, which we did not use in the last example.

24. Right-click the Chapter19 project in the Solution Explorer window.

25. Choose Add.

26. Choose Class.

27. Name the class PolicyExample.cs.

28. Open the PolicyExample.cs file in the editor window.

29. Amend the code, as in Listing 19-3, to create a Policy struct outside the class and inside the namespace.

Listing 19-3. Create a struct called Policy

```
namespace Chapter19
{
  struct Policy
  {
    public int policyNumber;
    public string policyType;
    public double monthlyPremium;
    public string policyEndDate;
  } // End of Policy struct
```

```
internal class PolicyExample
{
} // End of PolicyExample class

} // End of Chapter19 namespace
```

Struct Instantiation Without the New Keyword

We will now create a Main() method inside the class and instantiate the struct WITHOUT using the new keyword, and then we will display the four struct values in the console.

30.   Amend the code as in Listing 19-4.

Listing 19-4. Instantiate the Policy struct without using the new keyword

```
internal class PolicyExample
{
  static void Main(string[] args)
  {
    /*
    Using an instance without the new keyword
    if the struct is used without the new keyword the members
      of the struct will remain unassigned, no values, and
      we cannot use the struct object until we have
      initialised all the members
    Using the code below we will see that
       - myPolicy is an instance of Policy
       - myPolicy.PolicyNumber is unassigned but
       - doing myPolicy.PolicyNumber = 123456 means it exists
       - same applies for all members
    */
    Policy myPolicy;

    Console.WriteLine(myPolicy.policyNumber);
    Console.WriteLine(myPolicy.policyType);
    Console.WriteLine(myPolicy.monthlyPremium);
```

```
    Console.WriteLine(myPolicy.policyEndDate);
  } // End of Main() method

} // End of PolicyExample class
```

Now if we look at the code, we will see that under the four struct member names, we will have a red underline indicating there are errors.

31. Hover over the policyNumber code that has the red underline and look at the error message, as shown in Figure 19-2.

```
Console.WriteLine(myPolicy.policyNumber);
Console.WriteLine(myPo
Console.WriteLine(myPo   [◈] (local variable) Policy myPolicy
Console.WriteLine(myPo
// End of Main() metho   CS0170: Use of possibly unassigned field 'policyNumber'
```

Figure 19-2. *Errors because of unassigned values*

The message tells us what we already know from reading the earlier sections of this chapter:

If the struct is used without the new keyword, the members of the struct will remain unassigned and we cannot use the struct object until we have initialized all the members.

Struct Instantiation with the New Keyword

We will now instantiate the struct WITH the new keyword and then display the four struct values to the console.

32. Amend the code, as in Listing 19-5. Only one line of code needs amended.

Listing 19-5. Instantiate the Policy struct using the new keyword

```
Policy myPolicy = new Policy();

Console.WriteLine(myPolicy.policyNumber);
Console.WriteLine(myPolicy.policyType);
Console.WriteLine(myPolicy.monthlyPremium);
Console.WriteLine(myPolicy.policyEndDate);
} // End of Main() method
```

As we will see, the four struct member names are error-free. We read earlier that if we use the new keyword to create an object of the struct, the default constructor is called and the object is created, and the members will be assigned the default value for their specific data type. The default values for our struct members will be 0 for an int and null for a string, which will therefore display nothing. Let us see if this is the case by running the code.

33. Right-click the Chapter19 project in the Solution Explorer panel.

34. Choose Properties from the pop-up menu.

35. Choose the Chapter19.PolicyExample class in the Startup object drop-down list.

36. Close the Properties window.

37. Click the File menu.

38. Choose Save All.

39. Click the Debug menu.

40. Choose Start Without Debugging.

The console window will appear, as shown in Figure 19-3, and show details of the policy. The display shows the default values of 0 for the int and double and null for the two strings.

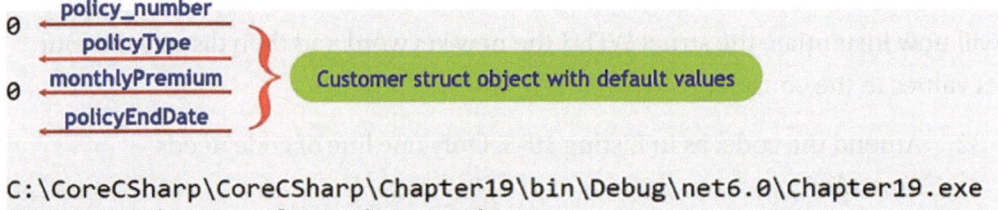

```
C:\CoreCSharp\CoreCSharp\Chapter19\bin\Debug\net6.0\Chapter19.exe
Press any key to close this window . . .
```

Figure 19-3. *Struct default values 0 and null by using the default constructor*

41. Press the Enter key to close the console window.

Creating a Constructor

The default constructor is automatically defined and not available for change. Remember, a default constructor is parameterless; it accepts no values. However, a struct allows a constructor to be added that contains parameters.

We will now add a custom constructor to the struct and this constructor will accept values for all the struct members. The constructor will therefore have four parameters, which will accept the values passed to it when a new instance of the struct is created.

42.   Amend the code, as in Listing 19-6.

Listing 19-6. Add a constructor to the struct

```
struct Policy
{
  public int policyNumber;
  public string policyType;
  public double monthlyPremium;
  public string policyEndDate;

  public Policy(int policyNumber, string policyType,
    double monthlyPremium, string policyEndDate)
  {
    this.policyNumber = policyNumber;
    this.policyType = policyType;
    this.monthlyPremium = monthlyPremium;
    this.policyEndDate = policyEndDate;
  } // End of user constructor

} // End of Policy struct
```

We should note that the existing code we have, where we are creating an instance of the Policy, `Policy myPolicyNew = new Policy();`, still works because the default constructor still exists. However, we will amend this code line to pass the new constructor four values for this new policy.

43.   Amend the code to add the four values to be passed to the constructor of the struct. Only the one line of code needs amended, as Listing 19-7:

Listing 19-7. Instantiate using the custom constructor

```
Policy myPolicy = new Policy(123456, "Computer Hardware", 9.99,
"31/12/2021");

Console.WriteLine(myPolicy.policyNumber);
Console.WriteLine(myPolicy.policyType);
Console.WriteLine(myPolicy.monthlyPremium);
Console.WriteLine(myPolicy.policyEndDate);
} // End of Main() method

} // End of PolicyExample class
```

44.   Click the File menu.

45.   Choose Save All.

46.   Click the Debug menu.

47.   Choose Start Without Debugging.

The console window will appear, as shown in Figure 19-4, and show details of the policy with the new initialized values passed to the constructor from the instance.

```
123456
Computer Hardware          Customer struct object with values set by the custom constructor
9.99
31/12/2021

C:\CoreCSharp\CoreCSharp\Chapter19\bin\Debug\net6.0\Chapter19.exe
Press any key to close this window . . ._
```

Figure 19-4. *Struct values as set by the instance using the custom constructor*

48.   Press the Enter key to close the console window.

Creating Member Properties (Get and Set Accessors)

Members of a struct can, like members of a class, have a property, which is used to get and set the value of the member. We saw this being used in Chapter 13 on classes, so now we will see it in action with structs. We also saw in the last chapter that there can be several flavors of properties.

49. Amend the code, as in Listing 19-8, to make the members of the struct have access modifiers of private.

Listing 19-8. Make members private

```
struct Policy
{
    private int policyNumber;
    private string policyType;
    private double monthlyPremium;
    private string policyEndDate;
```

Look at the display lines of the code where we have used the dot notation to access the struct members, and we will see that we have errors. Hovering over one of the errors, as shown in Figure 19-5, tells us what we should realize the member is not accessible as it is private to the struct.

```
Console.WriteLine(myPolicy.PolicyNumber);
Console.WriteLine(myPolicy.PolicyTy
Console.WriteLine(myPolicy.MonthlyP        readonly struct System.Int32
Console.WriteLine(myPolicy.PolicyEr        Represents a 32-bit signed integer.
// End of Main() method
                                           CS0122: Policy.PolicyNumber' is inaccessible due to its protection level
/ End of PolicyExample class
```

Figure 19-5. Inaccessible members due to access modifier

We will now create the property for each member, and because we are more experienced in our understanding of C# code, we will use the Visual Studio 2020 help, in the form of Quick Actions and Refactorings, which we discussed in Chapter 6.

50. Highlight the four members of the struct.

51. Right-click in the highlighted code.

52. Choose Quick Actions and Refactorings as shown in Figure 19-6.

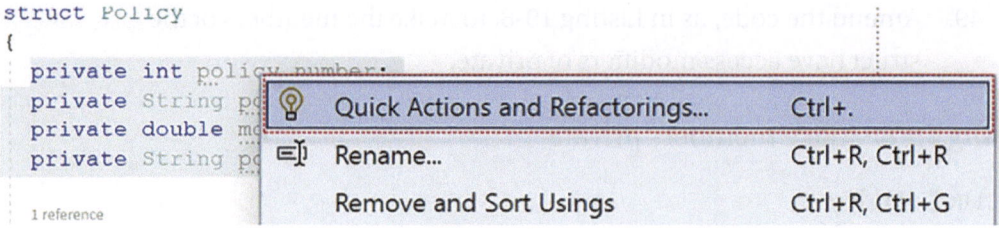

Figure 19-6. *Quick Actions and Refactorings to add properties*

53.   Choose Encapsulate field (but still use field).

The property for each member will appear either above or below the constructor. Either is fine, as shown in Listing 19-9. The struct will now have the members, the constructor, and the properties, just like a class can have these.

Listing 19-9. Member properties created, the get and the set

```
struct Policy
  {
    private int policyNumber;
    private string policyType;
    private double monthlyPremium;
    private string policyEndDate;

    public Policy(int policyNumber, string policyType,
      double monthlyPremium, string policyEndDate)
    {
      this.policyNumber = policyNumber;
      this.policyType = policyType;
      this.monthlyPremium = monthlyPremium;
      this.policyEndDate = policyEndDate;
    } // End of user constructor

    public int PolicyNumber
    {
      get => policyNumber;
      set => policyNumber = value;
    }
```

```
    public string PolicyType
    {
      get => policyType;
      set => policyType = value;
    }
    public double MonthlyPremium
    {
      get => monthlyPremium;
      set => monthlyPremium = value;
    }
    public string PolicyEndDate
    {
      get => policyEndDate;
      set => policyEndDate = value;
    }
  } // End of Policy struct
```

Now we need to change the dot notation in the WriteLine() code lines that refer to the members directly and refer them instead to the property of the member. The property uses the capitalized form of the member.

54.   Amend the code, as in Listing 19-10, to refer to the property.

Listing 19-10. Call the property, not the member, with a capital letter

```
    Console.WriteLine(myPolicy.PolicyNumber);
    Console.WriteLine(myPolicy.PolicyType);
    Console.WriteLine(myPolicy.MonthlyPremium);
    Console.WriteLine(myPolicy.PolicyEndDate);
    } // End of Main() method
  } // End of PolicyExample class
} // End of Chapter19 namespace
```

55.   Click the File menu.

56.   Choose Save All.

57.   Click the Debug menu.

58.   Choose Start Without Debugging.

The console window will appear, as shown in Figure 19-7, and details of the policy will be displayed.

```
123456
Computer Hardware
9.99
31/12/2021
```
Customer values retrieved using getters and setters

```
C:\CoreCSharp\CoreCSharp\Chapter19\bin\Debug\net6.0\Chapter19.exe
Press any key to close this window . . .
```

Figure 19-7. *Values retrieved using property accessors*

59.   Press the Enter key to close the console window.

Encapsulation

The code we have just run produced the same result as the previous example, but we have made use of the properties, get and set, for the private variables. This has therefore given us a little exposure to encapsulation, where we refer to encapsulation as hiding the variables of a class or struct so that they can only be accessed from outside the class or struct by special methods called properties. We achieve encapsulation, as we have just seen, by making the access modifier of the fields private and then generating a property for each member. We do not need to have a property for every member if we do not want to, and we do not have to have a get and a set in each property. This will depend on what we wish for the given situation.

A struct can include concrete methods just like classes can include concrete methods. We have not included methods in our examples, but it would be easy to do so, in the same way we did when we coded the applications in Chapter 13 on classes and objects.

Readonly Struct

When we want to limit access to the struct data, we can make the struct **readonly**. The keyword readonly is therefore a modifier indicating that something cannot be changed. With structs we can use the readonly modifier with the

- struct – In which case the whole struct is readonly. We could therefore say that the structure is **immutable**; it is "final." In this case all the members are readonly, and consequently every member property does not require a set accessor, a setter – remember YAGNI. The only way to change the member values is at the time of creating the instance object, which calls the constructor whose purpose is to set the initial values of the members. The members of the readonly struct are readonly, and therefore no method in the struct can change its value, which essentially means that we will not see a statement like myPolicy.PolicyType = "Jewellery".

- Member of the struct – From C# 8, a member can be set to readonly, in which case the value of the member cannot be changed. If the member is readonly, then its property does not require a set accessor, a setter. Allowing readonly members means we do not need to make the whole struct readonly.

Creating a Readonly Struct

We will use the PolicyExample as our starting point for this exercise on readonly structs.

60. Open the PolicyExample.cs file in the Chapter19 project.

61. Amend the code, as in Listing 19-11, to make the Policy struct readonly.

Listing 19-11. Readonly struct

```
readonly struct Policy
{
   private int policyNumber;
   private String policyType;
   private double monthlyPremium;
   private String policyEndDate;
```

Now we will see that there are errors indicated under the struct members because they will need to be made readonly as well. Hovering over the error will display the error message, as shown in Figure 19-8.

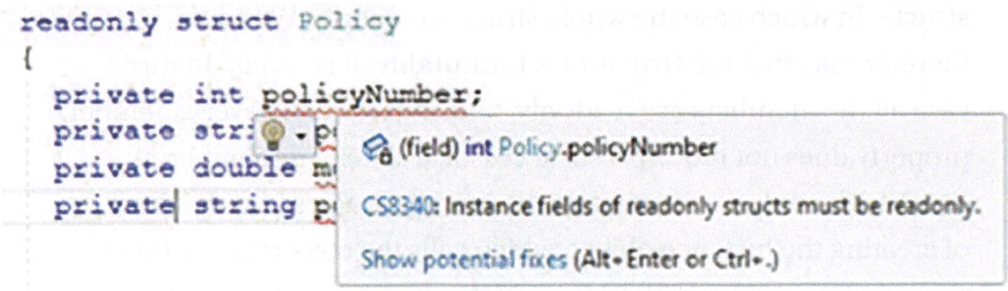

Figure 19-8. *Readonly struct needs readonly fields*

62. Amend the code, as in Listing 19-12, to make the member fields readonly.

Listing 19-12. Readonly fields

```
readonly struct Policy
{
    readonly int policyNumber;
    readonly String policyType;
    readonly double monthlyPremium;
    readonly String policyEndDate;
```

Now we will see that the errors for the members are removed. However, we will also see errors in the set accessor of each member property. We will now correct the set errors by commenting the code. This is not a normal programming practice (YAGNI), but we will keep the code for reference.

63. Amend the code, as in Listing 19-13, to comment the setters.

Listing 19-13. Setters are not required; comment them

```
public int PolicyNumber
{
    get => policyNumber;
    //set => policyNumber = value;
}
public string PolicyType
```

```
  {
    get => policyType;
    //set => policyType = value;
  }
  public double MonthlyPremium
  {
    get => monthlyPremium;
    //set => monthlyPremium = value;
  }
  public string PolicyEndDate
  {
    get => policyEndDate;
    //set => policyEndDate = value;
  }
} // End of Policy struct
```

Within the Main() method, the code that uses the members is accessing them through the property of the member, really the get accessor of the property, so this will still work because we do have the getters but not the setters as the struct is readonly. Perfect! Our code should work well.

64. Click the File menu.

65. Choose Save All.

66. Click the Debug menu.

67. Choose Start Without Debugging.

The console window will appear displaying details of the policy, as shown in Figure 19-9.

```
123456
Computer Hardware    }  Struct is readonly, we have used the getters to read the values
9.99
31/12/2021


C:\CoreCSharp\CoreCSharp\Chapter19\bin\Debug\net6.0\Chapter19.exe
Press any key to close this window . . .
```

Figure 19-9. Readonly struct, readonly fields with no setters – code works

68. Press the Enter key to close the console window.

We have achieved the same result, but we have seen the use of a readonly struct, with readonly members and member properties that only require a get accessor since the member values cannot be changed, unless it is done through the constructor. Now we will try and assign a new value to a readonly struct member.

69. Amend the code in the Main() method to attempt to assign a new value to the policyNumber as shown in Listing 19-14.

Listing 19-14. Attempt to assign a value to a readonly struct

```
        Console.WriteLine(myPolicy.PolicyEndDate);

        myPolicy.PolicyNumber =
      } // End of Main() method

  } // End of PolicyExample class


} // End of Chapter19 namespace
```

Even before we have completed the line of code, we will see that the compiler is complaining, and this is indicated in Visual Studio 2022 by the red underline. On hovering over the red underline, a pop-up window with a message appears, and we should note that we are being told it is not possible to assign a value, because we are dealing with a readonly struct member.

70. Hover over the red underline of PolicyNumber as shown in Figure 19-10.

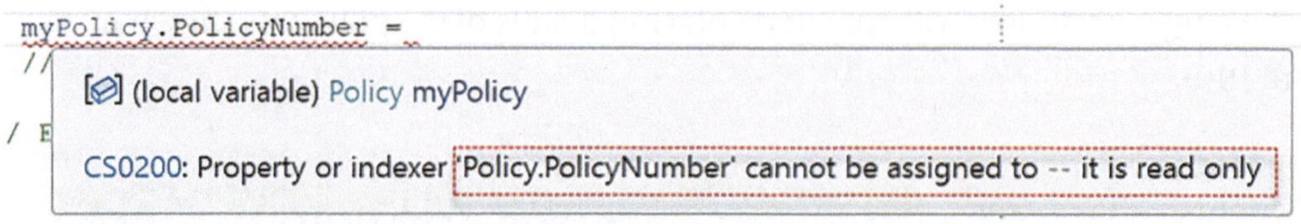

```
myPolicy.PolicyNumber =
//
/ E
```
    (local variable) Policy myPolicy

    CS0200: Property or indexer 'Policy.PolicyNumber' cannot be assigned to -- it is read only

Figure 19-10. *Cannot change readonly struct member*

71. Remove the partial line of code.

72. Click the File menu.

73. Choose Save All.

C# 8 readonly Members

Prior to C# 8 we could have a readonly struct and all the fields had to be readonly, as we have just seen in the example we coded. From C# 8 we were introduced to a new feature for the struct, which allows us to declare members of the struct as readonly without the struct being readonly. This has the advantage of making the code more specific and more granular, because we target those fields that need to be readonly rather than having to make all the fields readonly.

We will now use the same Policy struct code we used earlier, to illustrate the use of the readonly field without the struct being readonly. As we already have a Policy struct in the namespace, we will have to rename the struct from Policy, so we will call it PolicyReadOnlyMembers.

74. Right-click the Chapter19 project in the Solution Explorer window.

75. Choose Add.

76. Choose Class.

77. Name the class PolicyExampleReadOnlyMember.cs.

We will now amend the code to add a struct, which will have two readonly fields, two private fields, and a property for each field with a get for all fields and a set for the non-readonly fields.

78. Amend the PolicyExampleReadOnlyMember class code, as shown in Listing 19-15.

Listing 19-15. Creating the struct with readonly fields

```
namespace Chapter19
{
  struct PolicyReadOnlyMembers
  {
    private readonly int policy_number;
    private string policyType;
    private double monthlyPremium;
    private readonly string policyEndDate;
```

```csharp
    public PolicyReadOnlyMembers(int policy_number,
    string policyType, double monthlyPremium,
            string policyEndDate)
    {
      this.policy_number = policy_number;
      this.policyType = policyType;
      this.monthlyPremium = monthlyPremium;
      this.policyEndDate = policyEndDate;
    } // End of user constructor

    // Properties used to get and set the members
    public int Policy_number
    {
      get => policy_number;
    } // End of Policy_number property

    public string PolicyType
    {
      get => policyType;
      set => policyType = value;
    } // End of PolicyType property

    public double MonthlyPremium
    {
      get => monthlyPremium;
      set => monthlyPremium = value;
    } // End of MonthlyPremium property

    public string PolicyEndDate
    {
      get => policyEndDate;
    } // End of PolicyEndDate property
  } // End of PolicyReadOnlyMembers struct

  internal class PolicyExampleReadOnlyMember
  {

  } // End of PolicyExampleReadOnlyMember class
} // End of Chapter19 namespace
```

We will now add a Main() method that will contain the code to instantiate the struct and have two lines of code to set the values of the two readonly fields.

79.   Amend the class code, as in Listing 19-16.

Listing 19-16. Instantiate the struct and try to assign values to readonly fields

```
internal class PolicyExampleReadOnlyMember
{
  static void Main(string[] args)
  {
    PolicyReadOnlyMembers PolicyReadOnlyMember =
      new PolicyReadOnlyMembers(123456, "Computer Hardware",
                                9.99, "31/12/2021");

    Console.WriteLine(PolicyReadOnlyMember.Policy_number);
    Console.WriteLine(PolicyReadOnlyMember.PolicyType);
    Console.WriteLine(PolicyReadOnlyMember.MonthlyPremium);
    Console.WriteLine(PolicyReadOnlyMember.PolicyEndDate);

    PolicyReadOnlyMember.Policy_number = 567890;
    PolicyReadOnlyMember.PolicyType = "Monitor";
    PolicyReadOnlyMember.MonthlyPremium = 5.99;
    PolicyReadOnlyMember.PolicyEndDate = "01/01/2099";

  } // End of Main() method
} // End of PolicyExampleReadOnlyMember class
} // End of Chapter19 namespace
```

Now look at the assignment lines that are trying to set the values of the readonly fields; they have a red underline indicating a problem. If we hover over the red underline of any of the assignments, we will see a message telling us we cannot assign a value to a readonly field.

80.   Hover of the red underline of any of the assignment lines, and note the message, as shown in Figure 19-11.

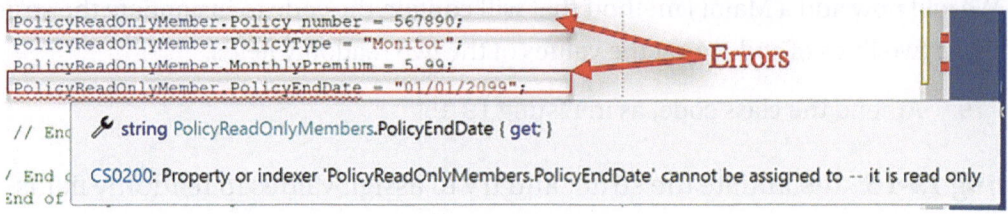

Figure 19-11. *Readonly error message only on readonly fields*

This is the C# 8 readonly field of a struct in action. The struct is not readonly, but the fields marked with the readonly keyword are, and as we know, we cannot change the value of a readonly member.

81.   Comment the two lines that are causing the error, as in Listing 19-17.

Listing 19-17. Comment the lines causing the error (or delete them)

```
    //PolicyReadOnlyMember.Policy_number = 567890;
    PolicyReadOnlyMember.PolicyType = "Monitor";
    PolicyReadOnlyMember.MonthlyPremium = 5.99;
    //PolicyReadOnlyMember.PolicyEndDate = "01/01/2099";
  } // End of Main() method
 } // End of PolicyExampleReadOnlyMember class
} // End of Chapter19 namespace
```

82.   Right-click the Chapter19 project in the Solution Explorer panel.

83.   Choose Properties from the pop-up menu.

84.   Choose the PolicyExampleReadOnlyMember class in the Startup object drop-down list.

85.   Close the Properties window.

86.   Click the File menu.

87.   Choose Save All.

88.   Click the Debug menu.

89.   Choose Start Without Debugging.

Figure 19-12 shows the console window displaying the details of the policy.

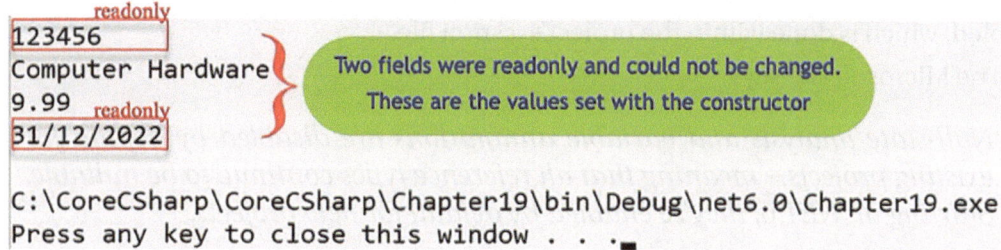

Figure 19-12. *Using readonly fields*

So we have shown that readonly members cannot be assigned new values. The values are set through the custom constructor, if there is one, or the parameterless default constructor.

C# 8 Nullable Reference Types

In Chapter 6 on data types, we looked at conversion and parsing, and we read about the C# 8 nullable reference type. We read how we could use the ? to ensure that a null value was acceptable, given that from C# 8, reference types are non-nullable by default. In our reading we used two code examples using strings, one using the ? and the other not using it:

Example 1 was

```
/*
This will cause a warning as all reference types are
non-nullable by default. The warning will be similar to:
Converting null literal or possible null value to
non-nullable reference type.
*/
string policyId = null;
```

Example 2 was

```
/*
This will not cause a warning as null is acceptable
*/
string? policyId = null;
```

For some reinforcement, we will apply the nullable reference type to the struct example we have just completed, but this will require the project to have Nullable enabled, which is done within the project's .csproj file.

The Microsoft site says

> *Null-state analysis and variable annotations are disabled by default for existing projects – meaning that all reference types continue to be nullable. Starting in .NET 6, they're enabled by default for new projects.*

The line of code, `<Nullable>enable</Nullable>`, would need to be added to the .csproj file, but as we have been using .NET 6, we will not need to make this change, as Nullable is enabled by default. Listing 19-18 shows the contents of our Chapter19.csproj file, and we can see that Nullable is indeed enabled.

Listing 19-18. Enable Nullable in the .csproj file

```
<Project Sdk="Microsoft.NET.Sdk">

  <PropertyGroup>
    <OutputType>Exe</OutputType>
    <TargetFramework>net6.0</TargetFramework>
    <ImplicitUsings>enable</ImplicitUsings>
    <Nullable>enable</Nullable>
    <StartupObject>Chapter19.PolicyExampleReadOnlyMember</StartupObject>
  </PropertyGroup>

</Project>
```

We can also enable or disable the nullable reference type within the code of a .cs file. This is achieved by using the code line `#nullable enable` above any line where the action is required or `#nullable disable` above any line where the action is not required. This can be seen in this code snippet where the nullable reference type has been disabled for the policyId field because it was enabled at the project level:

```
#nullable disable
string policyId = null;
```

The Microsoft site also says

The nullable annotation context and nullable warning context can be set for a project using the <Nullable> *element in your .csproj file. This element configures how the compiler interprets the nullability of types and what warnings are emitted.*

Note:

Deference warnings occur when the application deferences (tries to obtain the address of something held in a location from a pointer) and expects it to be valid but is returned a null.

An assignment warning is issued when we try to assign incorrectly, for example, in an if construct, we might try to do if(amount = amountLimit) but we would get an assignment warning as it should be if(amount == amountLimit).

The Microsoft site also gives us details about the contexts we can use:

If we use disable, then

- All reference types are nullable.

- We do not need to use the ? suffix.

- Deference warnings are disabled.

- Assignment warnings are disabled.

If we use enable, then

- All reference types are non-nullable unless declared using the ?.

- We can use the ? suffix.

- Deference warnings are enabled.

- Assignment warnings are enabled.

If we use warnings, then

- All reference types are nullable but members are considered not null at the opening brace of methods.

- We can use the ? suffix but it produces a warning.

- Deference warnings are enabled.

- Assignment warnings are not applicable.

If we use annotations, then

- All reference types are non-nullable unless declared using the ?.

- We can use the ? suffix and it declares the nullable type.

- Deference warnings are disabled.

- Assignment warnings are disabled.

90. Amend the PolicyReadOnlyMembers struct so that the policyType is assigned a null value within the constructor, as in Listing 19-19.

Listing 19-19. Assign a null value to the policyType field

```
public PolicyReadOnlyMembers(int policy_number,
    string policyType, double monthlyPremium,
          string policyEndDate)
{
    this.policy_number = policy_number;
    //this.policyType = policyType;
    this.policyType = null;
    this.monthlyPremium = monthlyPremium;
    this.policyEndDate = policyEndDate;
} // End of user constructor
```

Hovering over the word null will show a pop-up window with a message, and reading this message tells us that we cannot have a nullable – the string field policyType cannot be assigned a null value.

91. Hover over the word null, as in Figure 19-13, and read the warning message.

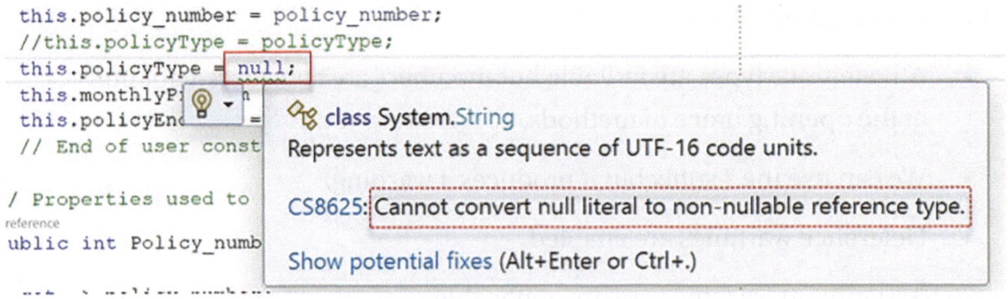

Figure 19-13. *Null literal error message*

We will now amend the declaration of the policyType within the struct, so that the type string is marked with the ?:

```
private string? policyType;
```

This will enable the policyType to accept a null value.

92.   Amend the code, as in Listing 19-20.

Listing 19-20. Using the ? to permit a null value

```
struct PolicyReadOnlyMembers
{
    readonly private int policy_number;
    private string? policyType;
    private double monthlyPremium;
    readonly private String policyEndDate;
```

Notice the warning under the null in the code has disappeared.

93.   Click the File menu.

94.   Choose Save All.

95.   Click the Debug menu.

96.   Choose Start Without Debugging.

The console window will appear displaying details of the policy, as shown in Figure 19-14. We can see that the nullable value has been accepted, and this is where the second line is displaying as "empty."

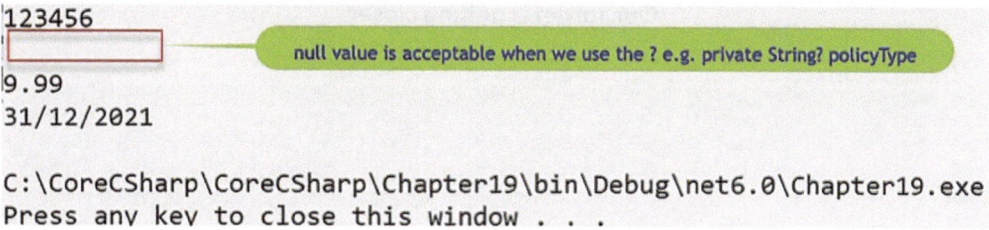

Figure 19-14. *Null value used for policyType field*

Chapter Summary

So, finishing this chapter on structs, we can see the similarity with classes and objects. A struct is a value type, which must have a default parameterless constructor, but they can also have custom constructors. The fields can be set to private and we can use properties, getters and setters, to access them. The whole struct can be set to readonly and this means all fields must also be readonly, but from C# 8 we can have readonly fields without the struct being readonly. Finally, we looked at nullable references and the use of the ? to permit null values.

Wow, what an achievement. This is not basic coding. We are doing some wonderful things with our C# code. We should be immensely proud of the learning to date. In finishing this chapter, we have increased our knowledge further and we are advancing to our target.

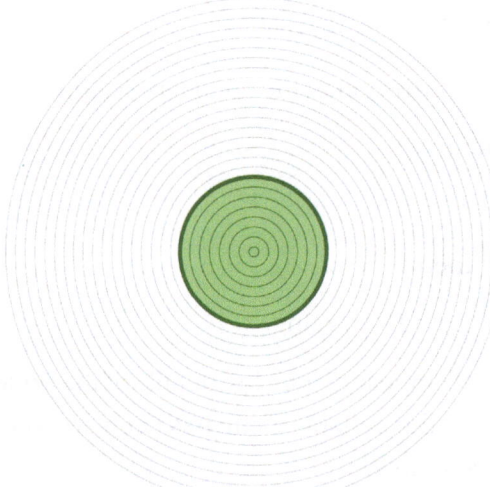

Our target is getting closer

CHAPTER 20

Enumerations

Concept of Enumerations

In the last chapter, we learned about the struct, which is a C# type and is similar to a class, encapsulating data and functionality, that is, variables and methods. We saw that a struct can have a custom constructor, but will always have a default parameterless constructor, and the struct can contain properties for accessing the private members. In terms of accessibility, we saw that the struct could be made readonly, which means all fields automatically become set as readonly. However, we learned that from C# 8 individual fields could be set to have the readonly access, thereby leaving other fields to remain readable and writeable. Finally, we learned that structs are value types, whereas a class is a reference type.

We will now look at another structure called the enumeration, or enum as it is also called. Enumerations are essentially a group of integer values, which have been assigned names with the aim of making the code more readable. In Chapter 10 on iteration, we talked about magic numbers and how they are not acceptable when we wish to have clean code. Well, the enumeration helps us avoid the use of "magic numbers" by assigning names to them.

We use the keyword **enum** to identify the enumeration, which is used to hold a set of named integer **constants.** In C# an enumeration is a value data type, which means it will not inherit and has its own values. As we know from constants, the values do not change, so when we declare the constants in an enumeration, they cannot be changed in the code. As we said earlier, the "nice thing" about using an enumeration to declare constants is that we use descriptive names for the constants, thereby making them more user-friendly and helping the code to be more readable. We could say that they fit in well with the concept of clean code.

© Gerard Byrne 2022
G. Byrne, *Target C#*, https://doi.org/10.1007/978-1-4842-8619-7_20

Defining an Enumeration

In its basic form, the simplest way to declare an enumeration is to give the enumeration a name and then list all the possible names in a set of braces after the enumeration's name. We use the enum keyword as a prefix to the enumeration name, so that the compiler understands that the definition is an enumeration. By default, an enumeration list makes the first item in the curly braces have a value of 0 with each remaining value being incremented by 1.

Enumeration Examples

Example 1

A declaration defining a constant for every day of the week, which means 0 is Sunday, 1 is Monday, etc. as shown in the following:

```
//
// Summary:
//      Specifies the day of the week.
public enum DayOfWeek
{
  //
  // Summary:
  //      Indicates Sunday.
  Sunday = 0,
  //
  // Summary:
  //      Indicates Monday.
  Monday = 1,
  //
  // Summary:
  //      Indicates Tuesday.
  Tuesday = 2,
  //
  // Summary:
  //      Indicates Wednesday.
  Wednesday = 3,
  //
```

```
// Summary:
//      Indicates Thursday.
Thursday = 4,
//
// Summary:
//      Indicates Friday.
Friday = 5,
//
// Summary:
//      Indicates Saturday.
Saturday = 6
}
```

Now we will see that this enumeration called DayOfWeek can be used in a C# application as shown in the code snippet:

```
// Create a Policy renewal date
DateTime dt = new DateTime(2018, 7, 04);
Console.WriteLine("Policy is due for renewal on {0:d}", dt);

/*
Use the DayOfWeek enumeration to find the day of the
Day of the week
*/
Console.WriteLine("This date is a is {0}",  dt.DayOfWeek);
```

We will use this example in our code later, but what we might be surprised to hear is that the DayOfWeek enumeration is part of .NET. So enumerations exist in the real world.

Example 2

A declaration defining a constant for every month of the year, which means 0 is Jan, 1 is Feb, etc.:

```
enum Month
{
  Jan, Feb, Mar, Apr, May, Jun, Jul, Aug, Sep, Oct, Nov, Dec
}
```

Example 3

A declaration defining a constant for every suit in a deck of cards, which means 0 is Diamonds, 1 is Hearts, etc.:

```
enum Suit
{
  Diamonds, Hearts, Spades, Clubs
}
```

Example 4

A declaration defining a constant for every examination possibility, which means 0 is Pass, 1 is Fail, etc.:

```
enum Result
{
  Pass, Fail, Resit
}
```

Example 5

A declaration defining a constant for insurance types, which means 0 is Home, 1 is Auto, etc.:

```
enum InsuranceType
{
  Home, Auto, Travel, Computing, Jewellery
}
```

Enumerated Values: Use and Scope

In C# we declare an enumeration anywhere and, like other items declared within a class, the methods of the class are able to use the values of the enumeration list. Our application code simply needs to use the name of the enumeration and the value of the item within the list.

Let's code some C# and build our programming muscle.

Add a new project to hold the code for this chapter.

1. Right-click the solution CoreCSharp.

2. Choose Add.

3. Choose New Project.

4. Choose Console App from the listed templates that appear.

5. Click the Next button.

6. Name the project Chapter20 and leave it in the same location.

7. Click the Next button.

8. Choose the framework to be used, which in our projects will be .NET 6.0 or higher.

9. Click the Create button.

Now we should see the Chapter20 project within the solution called CoreCSharp.

10. Right-click the Chapter20 project in the Solution Explorer panel.

11. Click the Set as Startup Project option.

Notice how the Chapter20 project name has been made to have bold text, indicating that it is the new startup project and that it is the Program.cs file within it that will be executed when we run the debugging.

12. Right-click the Chapter20 project.

13. Choose Add.

14. Choose Item.

15. Choose Class.

16. Name the class Enumerations.cs.

17. Amend the code to have a different namespace and have the Month enumeration within this namespace, as shown in Listing 20-1.

Listing 20-1. Declaring the enumeration in a different namespace

```
namespace Enumerations
{
  public enum Month
  {
    Jan, Feb, Mar, Apr, May, Jun, Jul, Aug, Sep, Oct, Nov, Dec
  } // End of enum

} // End of namespace
```

18. Right-click the Program.cs file in the Solution Explorer window.

19. Choose Rename.

20. Change the name to MonthExample.cs.

21. Press the Enter key.

22. Double-click the MonthExample.cs file to open it in the editor window.

23. Amend the code, as in Listing 20-2, to use the Enumerations namespace through the using statement on the first line, add the namespace for this class, and add the Main() method.

Listing 20-2. Declaring the enumeration and Main() method

```
using Enumerations;

namespace Chapter20
{
  internal class MonthExample
  {
    static void Main(string[] args)
    {
    } //End of Main() method

  } // End of MonthExample class
} // End of Chapter20 namespace
```

Now we will investigate some of the methods from the System.Enum abstract class that we can use when working with enumerations.

Enumeration Methods

Three of the methods we can use with an enumeration are

- The GetNames(Type) method of the Enum class, which is used to return a String array with the names of the constants in the enumeration.

- The GetName(Type, value) method of the Enum class, which is used to return the name of the constant in the enumeration with the specified value.

- The ToString() method, which will convert the value of the enum instance to its equivalent string representation. This method may be an easier option than the GetName().

We will now set the starting point of our enumeration to be Jan, which is constant value 0, and then we will iterate the enumeration displaying each value of the enumeration to the console.

24. Amend the code, as in Listing 20-3.

Listing 20-3. Set starting value of the enumeration, iterate, and display items

```
static void Main(string[] args)
{
  Month month = Month.Jan;

  Console.WriteLine("Using iteration with hard coded value");
  for (int counter = 0; counter < 12; counter++)
  {
    Console.Write($" {month++} \t");
  } //End of iteration

} //End of Main() method
```

In the code in Listing 20-3, we are iterating through our enumeration and displaying the items in the enumeration to the console. We use the name of the enumeration instance, in this case month, and increment it. In the console output, as shown in Figure 20-1, we see the names of the items of the enumeration, converted to string. In a later example, we will use the "index" of the item.

25.   Click the File menu.

26.   Choose Save All.

27.   Click the Debug menu.

28.   Choose Start Without Debugging.

```
Using iteration with hard coded value
  Jan     Feb     Mar     Apr     May     Jun     Jul     Aug     Sep     Oct     Nov     Dec
C:\CoreCSharp\CoreCSharp\Chapter20\bin\Debug\net6.0\Chapter20.exe (process 5944) exited with code 0.
Press any key to close this window . . ._
```

Figure 20-1. *Iterated items*

29.   Press the Enter key to close the console window.

This works fine, but what about our discussion in a previous chapter about the **"magic number"**? The iteration of the enumeration is hard-coded to stop at less than 12, but 12 just appears. We know that 12 is the number of items in the Month enumeration, the length, so can we use the length in the iteration, in a similar manner to when we discussed arrays? Yes, indeed we can, but it is not just as easy as using Length. We effectively need to look at the enumeration as an array and then get the length of the array. We can do this using the Enum class, which has a static method called GetNames(), which will return an array object to us. Finally, we can easily get the length of the array using the Length property. Our line of code to get the enumeration length, the number of names in the enumeration, is

```
int enumMonthLength = Enum.GetNames(typeof(Month)).Length;
```

Now we will add this line to our code and amend the iteration so that it refers to the enumeration length variable we will create.

30.   Amend the code, as in Listing 20-4.

Listing 20-4. Using the enum length

```
static void Main(string[] args)
{
  Month month = Month.Jan;

  Console.WriteLine("Using an iteration based on the enum Length from
  GetNames");
```

```
int enumMonthLength = Enum.GetNames(typeof(Month)).Length;

for (int counter = 0; counter < enumMonthLength; counter++)
{
    Console.Write($" {month++} \t");
} //End of iteration

Console.WriteLine();

} //End of Main() method
```

31. Click the File menu.

32. Choose Save All.

33. Click the Debug menu.

34. Choose Start Without Debugging.

Figure 20-2 shows we have the same output as before but we have cleaner code.

```
Using an iteration based on the enum Length from GetNames
 Jan    Feb    Mar    Apr    May    Jun    Jul    Aug    Sep    Oct    Nov    Dec
C:\CoreCSharp\CoreCSharp\Chapter20\bin\Debug\net6.0\Chapter20.exe (process 4440) exited with code 0.
Press any key to close this window . . .
```

Figure 20-2. *Iterated items using Enum.GetNames(typeof(Month)).Length*

35. Press the Enter key to close the console window.

Using the foreach Iteration

We have used a for iteration in our code application, but we could also have used the foreach iteration, both of which we read about and used in Chapter 10 on iteration. In Listing 20-4 we used the GetNames() method to return a string array and then we used the Length property. If we use the foreach iteration, we remove the need to know the enumeration length.

36. Amend the code, as in Listing 20-5.

Listing 20-5. Foreach iteration

```
int enumMonthLength = Enum.GetNames(typeof(Month)).Length;

for (int counter = 0; counter < enumMonthLength; counter++)
{
  Console.Write($" {month++} \t");
} //End of iteration

Console.WriteLine();

Console.WriteLine("Using a foreach iteration which" +
                  " handles the length for us");

// Returns a String[] array so type is String
foreach (String valueFound in Enum.GetNames(typeof(Month)))
{
  Console.Write($" {valueFound} \t");
} //End of foreach

Console.WriteLine();

} //End of Main() method
```

37. Click the File menu.

38. Choose Save All.

39. Click the Debug menu.

40. Choose Start Without Debugging.

Once again, we will see from Figure 20-3 that we have the same output, but in our code we did not need the length to be known, as the foreach construct handles this for us, but we might also suggest that we have cleaner code.

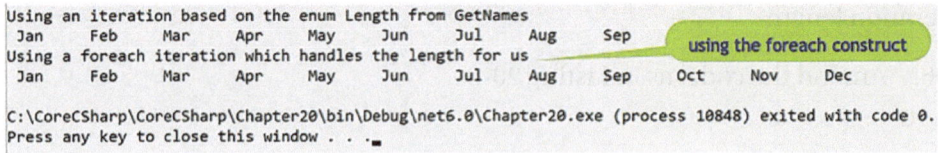

Figure 20-3. *Iterated items using the foreach construct*

41.   Press the Enter key to close the console window.

We will now use the GetName() method where we pass the enum object and the value, which in this example will be the counter value, and we will be given the constant name in the enumeration at that position.

42.   Amend the code, as in Listing 20-6, to add a new iteration that uses the GetName() method.

Listing 20-6. Use the GetName() to find the constant name at a specific position

```
// Returns a String[] array so type is String
foreach (String valueFound in Enum.GetNames(typeof(Month)))
{
  Console.Write($" {valueFound} \t");
}

Console.WriteLine();

// Using GetName() to find name of the value
for (int counter = 0; counter < enumMonthLength; counter++)
{
  Console.WriteLine(Enum.GetName(typeof(Month), counter));
} //End of iteration

Console.WriteLine();

  } //End of Main() method

 } // End of MonthExample class
} // End of Chapter20 namespace
```

43.   Click the File menu.

44.   Choose Save All.

45.   Click the Debug menu.

46.   Choose Start Without Debugging.

Figure 20-4 shows the names that were assigned to the constants are displayed.

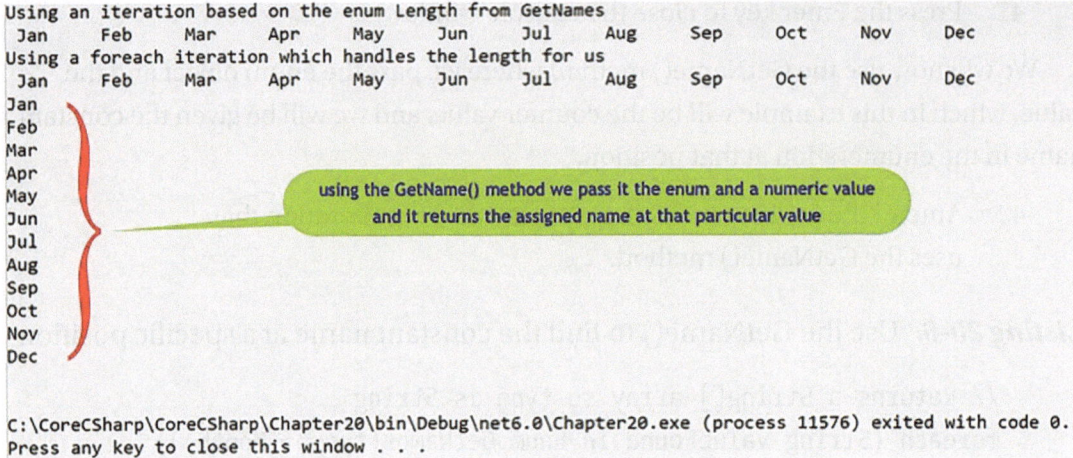

```
Using an iteration based on the enum Length from GetNames
 Jan     Feb     Mar     Apr     May     Jun     Jul     Aug     Sep     Oct     Nov     Dec
Using a foreach iteration which handles the length for us
 Jan     Feb     Mar     Apr     May     Jun     Jul     Aug     Sep     Oct     Nov     Dec
Jan
Feb
Mar
Apr
May
Jun
Jul
Aug
Sep
Oct
Nov
Dec
```

using the GetName() method we pass it the enum and a numeric value
and it returns the assigned name at that particular value

```
C:\CoreCSharp\CoreCSharp\Chapter20\bin\Debug\net6.0\Chapter20.exe (process 11576) exited with code 0.
Press any key to close this window . . .
```

Figure 20-4. *GetName() returns the name of the constant at a particular value*

47.   Press the Enter key to close the console window.

Enumeration Values: GetValues()

We will now use the GetValues(Type) method of the Enum class to return an array of the values in the enumeration, and then we can iterate the array to display the values. We will code a new iteration that uses the GetValues() method of the Enum class to get the integer values rather than the names.

48.   Amend the code, as in Listing 20-7.

Listing 20-7. Use the GetValues() to find the constant values

```
// Using GetName() to fund name of the value
for (int counter = 0; counter < enumMonthLength; counter++)
{
  Console.WriteLine(Enum.GetName(typeof(Month), counter));
} //End of iteration

Console.WriteLine();

Console.WriteLine("Using a foreach iteration to display the Month
values");
```

```
    foreach (int integerFound in Enum.GetValues(typeof(Month)))
    {
      Console.Write($" {integerFound} \t");
    }

    Console.WriteLine();

  } //End of Main() method
 } // End of MonthExample class
} // End of Chapter20 namespace
```

49. Click the File menu.

50. Choose Save All.

51. Click the Debug menu.

52. Choose Start Without Debugging.

Figure 20-5 shows that the constant values are displayed using the GetValues() method.

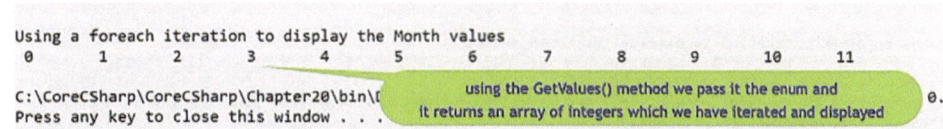

Figure 20-5. *GetValues() gives us the value of the constant*

53. Press the Enter key to close the console window.

Assigning Our Own Values to the Enumeration

It is possible for us to assign different values to the months, for example, we may wish April to be month 0 as it might be the first month of a tax year. We will now amend the existing enumeration to assign a value to the Apr name, and then on executing our code, we will see the effect this has on the other names in the enumeration. We will see that the default values for the names after Apr have been automatically amended.

54. Amend the code, as in Listing 20-8.

Listing 20-8. In the Enumerations namespace, change the Apr constant

```
internal class MonthExample
{
  enum Month
  {
  Jan, Feb, Mar, Apr = 4, May, Jun, Jul, Aug, Sep, Oct, Nov, Dec
  };
```

55. Click the File menu.

56. Choose Save All.

57. Click the Debug menu.

58. Choose Start Without Debugging.

We see from the output, as shown in Figure 20-6, that the months are displayed as their integer value starting with 0, then 1, then 2, and then 4, as we assigned the integer 4 to April. From this point on, all the values are altered to their new consecutive value, 5, 6, 7, 8, 9, 10, 11, and 12.

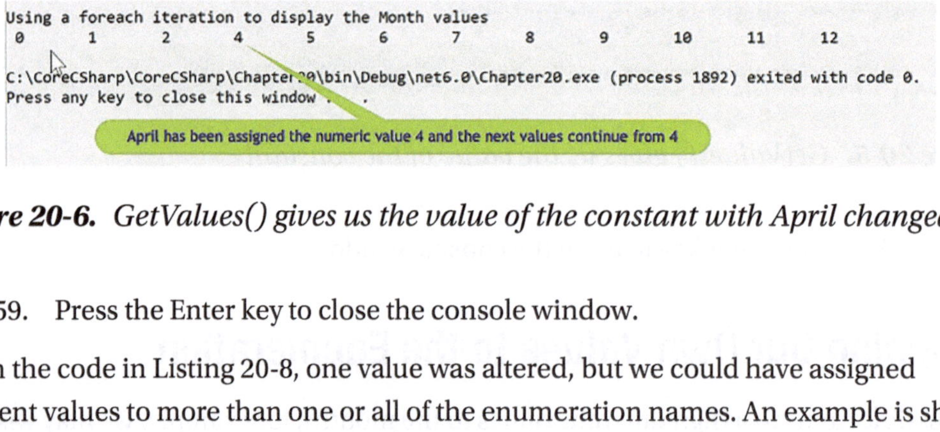

Figure 20-6. *GetValues() gives us the value of the constant with April changed*

59. Press the Enter key to close the console window.

In the code in Listing 20-8, one value was altered, but we could have assigned different values to more than one or all of the enumeration names. An example is shown in Listing 20-9.

Listing 20-9. Change the values for all constants

```
enum Suit { Diamonds = 1, Hearts = 2, Spades = 4, Clubs = 8 };
```

Use the GetName() and GetValues() Methods

If we know the integer value of an item in the enumeration, we can get the name that is associated with it. Remember what we said earlier, the GetNames() method returns a string array of the names in the enumeration and the GetName() method is passed a value and uses the value to get the assigned name. The GetValues() method returns an array of the values in the enumeration.

60. Amend the code, as in Listing 20-10, to use the GetValues() and GetName() methods.

Listing 20-10. GetName() and GetValues() methods

```
Console.WriteLine("Using a foreach iteration to display the Month
values");

 foreach (int integerFound in Enum.GetValues(typeof(Month)))
 {
   Console.Write($" {integerFound} \t");
 }

Console.WriteLine();

Console.WriteLine("Get the enumeration name from the value");
foreach (int integerFound in Enum.GetValues(typeof(Month)))
{
  Console.WriteLine($"The integer value of {integerFound} is the value
  {Enum.GetName(typeof(Month), integerFound)}");
 }
 Console.WriteLine();

 } //End of Main() method

 } // End of MonthExample class
} // End of Chapter20 namespace
```

61. Click the File menu.

62. Choose Save All.

63.   Click the Debug menu.

64.   Choose Start Without Debugging.

```
Get the enumeration name from the value         GetValues(typeOf(Month)) returns an integer array which we iterate
The integer value of 0 is the value Jan
The integer value of 1 is the value Feb
The integer value of 2 is the value Mar
The integer value of 3 is the value Apr
The integer value of 4 is the value Apr
The integer value of 5 is the value May
The integer value of 6 is the value Jun
The integer value of 7 is the value Jul
The integer value of 8 is the value Aug
The integer value of 9 is the value Sep
The integer value of 10 is the value Oct
The integer value of 11 is the value Nov
The integer value of 12 is the value Dec
                                                GetName(typeOf(Month), value) returns the name at the integer value
C:\CoreCSharp\CoreCSharp\Chapter20\bin\Debug\net6.0\Chapter20.exe (process 5660) exited with code 0.
Press any key to close this window . . .
```

Figure 20-7. *GetName() and GetValues() methods*

Figure 20-7 shows the output displaying the integer value in the enumeration alongside its equivalent assigned name. The value is coming from the GetValues() method, while the name is coming from the GetName() method.

65.   Press the Enter key to close the console window.

Sample Application Using Enumerations

We will now code an application that will have three enumerations to hold data for

- Five types of computer hardware

- Three types of policy offered for computer hardware

- Five factors required to calculate a quote (essentially 0, 1, 2, 3, 4, 5)

The enumerations are the constants that we will use in our code.
The application will also ask the user to input the

- Hardware type

- Policy type

- Hardware value

The application will then calculate the monthly premium based on the formula
hardwareTypeFactor * policyTypeFactor * hardwareValueFactor;

- where the hardwareTypeFactor is obtained from the logic

    Laptop is 5, Large_Screen is 5, Desktop is 4, Printer is 3, Small_
    Screen is 2

- where the policyTypeFactor is obtained from the logic

    Gold is 5, Silver is 3, Bronze is 2

- where the hardwareValueFactor is obtained from the logic

    Hardware value divided by 5000

Note

This is just an example to reinforce some of the features of C# enumerations.
The code has not been written with attention being made to clean code. It is about
reading the code as we enter it and understanding what is happening in terms of the
enumeration concepts we have looked at.

1. Right-click the Chapter20 project.

2. Choose Add.

3. Choose Class.

4. Name the class ComputerInsurance.cs.

5. Click the Add button.

6. Amend the code, as in Listing 20-11, to create a Main() method
   within the class and import the Enumerations namespace.

Listing 20-11. Three enumerations and a Main() method

```
using Enumerations;

namespace Chapter20
{
    internal class ComputerInsurance
    {
        static void Main(string[] args)
        {
```

```
} //End of Main() method

} // End of ComputerInsurance class
} // End of Chapter20
```

7. Amend the Enumerations.cs code, as in Listing 20-12, to create the additional enumerations we will be using.

Listing 20-12. Three additional enumerations

```
namespace Enumerations
{
  public enum Month
  {
   Jan, Feb, Mar, Apr = 4, May, Jun, Jul, Aug, Sep, Oct, Nov, Dec
  } // End of enum

  enum HardwareType
  {
    Laptop, Large_Screen, Desktop, Printer, Small_Screen
  }

  enum PolicyType
  {
    Gold, Silver, Bronze
  }

  enum Factors
  {
    Zero, One, Two, Three, Four, Five
  }
} // End of namespace
```

8. Amend the ComputerInsurance class code to add the class-level variables as in Listing 20-13.

Listing 20-13. Add the required class-level variables

```
internal class ComputerInsurance
{
    static double hardwareValue, monthlyPremiumAmount;
    static int hardwareType, policyType;

    static void Main(string[] args)
    {
    } //End of Main() method
```

9. Amend the class, as in Listing 20-14, to add the method, outside the Main() but inside the namespace, that will ask for user input.

Listing 20-14. Method that accepts user input

```
} //End of Main() method

public static void AcceptUserInput()
{
Console.WriteLine("0. Laptop");
Console.WriteLine("1. Large_Screen");
Console.WriteLine("2. Desktop ");
Console.WriteLine("3. Printer ");
Console.WriteLine("4. Small_Screen");
Console.WriteLine("What is the int value of the hardware type?");
hardwareType = Convert.ToInt32(Console.ReadLine());

Console.WriteLine("0. Gold");
Console.WriteLine("1. Silver");
Console.WriteLine("2. Bronze");
Console.WriteLine("What policy type is required?");
policyType = Convert.ToInt32(Console.ReadLine());

Console.WriteLine("What is the estimated value of the hardware?");
 hardwareValue = Convert.ToDouble(Console.ReadLine());

 }   // End of AcceptUserInput method

} // End of ComputerInsurance class
} // End of Chapter20 namespace
```

10.   Amend the class, as in Listing 20-15, to add the method that will
calculate the hardware type factor.

Listing 20-15. Method that calculates the hardware type factor

```
}  // End of AcceptUserInput method

public static int CalculateHardwareTypeFactor()
{
  switch (hardwareType)
  {
    case 0:
      return (int)Factors.Five;
    case 1:
      return (int)Factors.Five;
    case 2:
      return (int)Factors.Four;
    case 3:
      return (int)Factors.Three;
    case 4:
      return (int)Factors.Two;
    default:
      return (int)Factors.Zero;
  } // End of switch statement
}// End of CalculateHardwareTypeFactor method

} // End of ComputerInsurance class
} // End of Chapter20 namespace
```

11.   Amend the class, as in Listing 20-16, to add the method that will
calculate the policy type factor.

Listing 20-16. Method that calculates the policy type factor

```
}// End of calculateHardwareTypeFactor method

public static int CalculatePolicyTypeFactor()
{
```

```
    switch (policyType)
    {
      case 0:
        return (int)Factors.Five;
      case 1:
        return (int)Factors.Three;
      case 2:
        return (int)Factors.Two;
      default:
        return (int)Factors.Zero;
    } // End of switch statement
  }// End of CalculatePolicyTypeFactor method

  } // End of ComputerInsurance class
} // End of Chapter20 namespace
```

12. Amend the class, as in Listing 20-17, to add the method that will calculate the hardware value factor.

Listing 20-17. Method that calculates the hardware value factor

```
  }// End of CalculatePolicyTypeFactor method

  public static double CalculateValueFactor()
  {
    return hardwareValue / 5000;
  }// End of CalculatePolicyTypeFactor method

  } // End of ComputerInsurance class
} // End of Chapter20 namespace
```

13. Amend the class, as in Listing 20-18, to add the method that will calculate the monthly premium.

Listing 20-18. Method that calculates the monthly premium

```
}// End of CalculatePolicyTypeFactor method

public static void CalculateMonthlyPremium(int hardwareTypeFactor, int
policyTypeFactor, double hardwareValueFactor)
{
  if (hardwareTypeFactor == 0 || policyTypeFactor == 0)
  {
    Console.WriteLine("Hardware or policy type incorrect");
  }
  else
  {
    monthlyPremiumAmount = hardwareTypeFactor * policyTypeFactor *
    hardwareValueFactor;

    Console.WriteLine($"Monthly premium for a {Enum.
    GetName(typeof(HardwareType), hardwareType)}({hardwareType}) {Enum.
    GetName(typeof(PolicyType), policyType)} ({policyType}) policy is
    ${monthlyPremiumAmount: 0.00}");

    Console.WriteLine($"HardwareType enumeration at position
    {hardwareType} is {Enum.GetName(typeof(HardwareType),
    hardwareType)}");

    Console.WriteLine($"PolicyType enumeration at position {policyType}
    is {Enum.GetName(typeof(PolicyType), policyType)}");
  }
}// End of CalculateMonthlyPremium method

} // End of ComputerInsurance class
} // End of Chapter20 namespace
```

14. Amend the code, as in Listing 20-19, to add the calls to the methods from within the Main() method and assign them to method-level variables.

Listing 20-19. Call the methods

```
static void Main(string[] args)
{
  int hardwareTypeFactor, policyTypeFactor;
  double hardwareValueFactor;

  AcceptUserInput();

  hardwareTypeFactor = CalculateHardwareTypeFactor();
  policyTypeFactor = CalculatePolicyTypeFactor();
  hardwareValueFactor = CalculateValueFactor();

  CalculateMonthlyPremium(hardwareTypeFactor, policyTypeFactor,hardware
  ValueFactor);

} //End of Main() method
```

15.   Right-click the Chapter20 project in the Solution Explorer panel.

16.   Choose Properties from the pop-up menu.

17.   Choose the ComputerInsurance class in the Startup object drop-down list.

18.   Close the Properties window.

19.   Click the File menu.

20.   Choose Save All.

21.   Click the Debug menu.

22.   Choose Start Without Debugging.

We will see in Figure 20-8 that the console has the request for information.

23.   Type 0, representing a Laptop, for the hardware type, as in Figure 20-8.

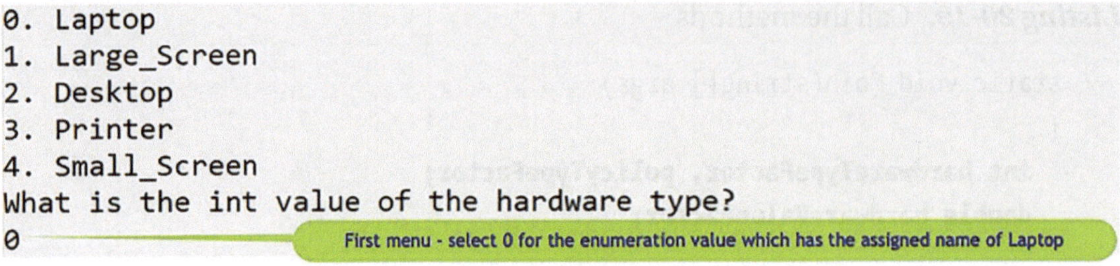

```
0. Laptop
1. Large_Screen
2. Desktop
3. Printer
4. Small_Screen
What is the int value of the hardware type?
0                          First menu - select 0 for the enumeration value which has the assigned name of Laptop
```

Figure 20-8. *First menu – select Laptop by typing 0 as the enumeration value*

24. Press the Enter key to move to the next menu.

25. Type 0, representing a Gold policy, for the policy type, as in
     Figure 20-9.

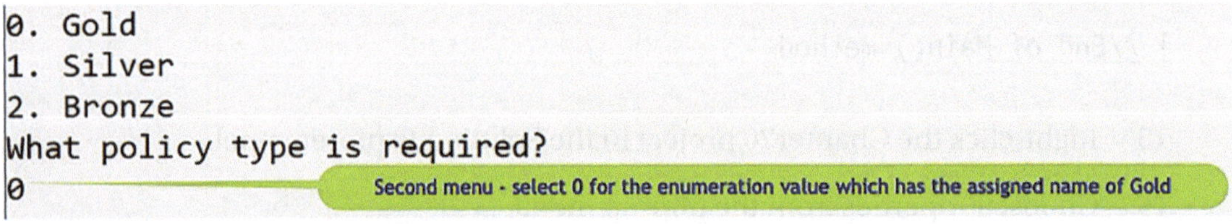

```
0. Gold
1. Silver
2. Bronze
What policy type is required?
0                          Second menu - select 0 for the enumeration value which has the assigned name of Gold
```

Figure 20-9. *Second menu – select Gold by typing 0 as the enumeration value*

26. Press the Enter key to move to the next input request.

27. Type 1000 for the laptop value, as Figure 20-10, and press the
     Enter key.

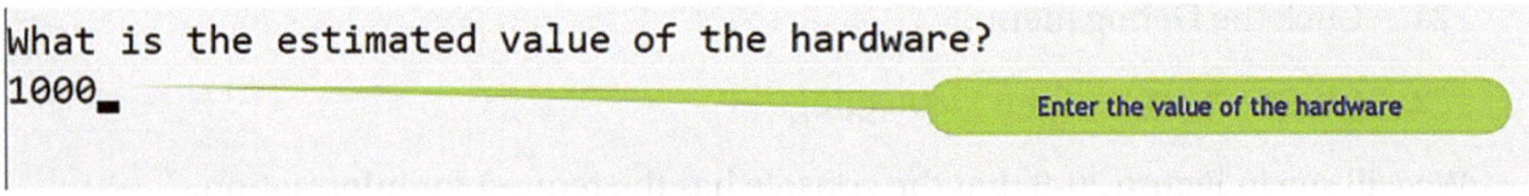

```
What is the estimated value of the hardware?
1000_
                                           Enter the value of the hardware
```

Figure 20-10. *Third entry for the hardware value*

Figure 20-11 shows the console window displaying the monthly premium for our
chosen hardware type, policy type, and the estimated value.

```
Monthly premium for a Laptop(0) Gold(0) policy is $ 5.00
HardwareType enumeration at position 0 is Laptop
PolicyType enumeration at position 0 is Gold

C:\CoreCSharp\CoreCSharp\Chapter20\bin\Debug\net6.0\Chapter20.exe
Press any key to close this window . . .
```

Figure 20-11. *Output from sample application that uses three enumerations*

28. Press the Enter key to close the console window.

Are we sure this is the correct premium amount?

Laptop   has a factor of 5.

Gold   has a factor of 5.

1000   has a factor of 1000/5000   =   0.2.

MonthlyPremium is   5 X 5 x 0.2   =   5.00.

Figure 20-11 therefore does show the correct answer, so our code looks great. Let's try different options.

29. Click the File menu.

30. Choose Save All.

31. Click the Debug menu.

32. Choose Start Without Debugging.

We will see in Figure 20-12 that the console has the request for information.

33. Type 4, representing a Small_Screen, for the hardware type

34. Press the Enter key.

35. Type 2, representing a Bronze policy, for the policy type .

36. Press the Enter key.

37. Type 100 for the screen value.

38. Press the Enter key.

```
0. Laptop
1. Large_Screen
2. Desktop
3. Printer
4. Small_Screen
What is the int value of the hardware type?
4
0. Gold
1. Silver
2. Bronze
What policy type is required?
2
What is the estimated value of the hardware?
100
Monthly premium for a Small_Screen(4) Bronze(2) policy is $ 0.08
HardwareType enumeration at position 4 is Small_Screen
PolicyType enumeration at position 2 is Bronze

C:\CoreCSharp\CoreCSharp\Chapter20\bin\Debug\net6.0\Chapter20.exe (process 9456)
Press any key to close this window . . .
```

Figure 20-12. *Output from sample application that uses three enumerations*

Figure 20-12 shows the console window displaying the monthly premium for our chosen hardware type, policy type, and the estimated value.

Are we sure this is the correct premium amount?

Small_Screen   has a factor of 2.

Bronze   has a factor of 2.

100 has a factor of   100/5000   =   .02.

MonthlyPremium is   2 X 2 x 0.02   =   0.08.

Figure 20-12 therefore does show the correct answer, so our code looks great.

Now let's try to use a different way to "convert" an integer value to the corresponding name in an enumeration. This is just another option, so rather than using the

```
Enum.GetName(typeof(HardwareType), hardwareType)
```

we will use

```
(Enumeration Name)integer value
```

39. Amend the monthly premium method to add the new casting
        style to the display lines, as in Listing 20-20.

Listing 20-20. Casting style for conversion

```
Console.WriteLine($"PolicyType enumeration at " +
   $"position {policyType} is " +
   $"{Enum.GetName(typeof(PolicyType), policyType)}");

Console.WriteLine("*****Casting the enumeration VALUE to the enumeration
NAME*****");

Console.WriteLine($"HardwareType enumeration at position {hardwareType} is
{(HardwareType)hardwareType}");

Console.WriteLine($"PolicyType enumeration at position {policyType} is
{(PolicyType)policyType}");   }
}// End of calculateMonthlyPremium method

} // End of ComputerInsurance class
} // End of Chapter20 namespace
```

40. Click the File menu.

41. Choose Save All.

42. Click the Debug menu.

43. Choose Start Without Debugging.

We will see in Figure 20-13 that the console has the request for information.

44. Type 4, representing a Small_Screen, for the hardware type.

45. Type 2, representing a Bronze policy, for the policy type.

46. Type 100 for the screen value.

```
Monthly premium for a Small_Screen(4) Bronze(2) policy is $ 0.08
HardwareType enumeration at position 4 is Small_Screen
PolicyType enumeration at position 2 is Bronze
*****Casting the enumeration VALUE to the enumeration NAME
HardwareType enumeration at position 4 is Small_Screen
PolicyType enumeration at position 2 is Bronze                  Conversion using casting

C:\CoreCSharp\CoreCSharp\Chapter20\bin\Debug\net6.0\Chapter20.exe (process 10996)
Press any key to close this window . . .
```

Figure 20-13. *Output from the casting-style conversion*

Figure 20-13 shows the console window displaying the monthly premium for our chosen hardware type, policy type, and the estimated value. It also confirms that the casting, (HardwareType)hardwareType and (PolicyType)policyType, has been successful.

Chapter Summary

So, finishing this chapter on enumerations, we can see that an enumeration is a value data type. We use an enumeration to declare constants with a descriptive name for the constants. In its basic form, an enumeration has a name, followed by a set of braces, which will contain a list of all the possible names. We use the enum keyword as a prefix to the enumeration name so that the compiler understands that the definition is an enumeration. By default, an enumeration will make the first item within the curly braces have a value 0, with each remaining value being incremented by 1. We can use the methods of the Enum abstract class to get the names and values of the constants, and we use GetName(), GetNames(), and GetValues() as well as the Length property.

Once again, another dive into an advanced feature of programming, which can be applied to our C# code helping make it more readable and easier to maintain. We should be immensely proud of our learning to date. In finishing this chapter, we have increased our knowledge further and we are advancing to our target.

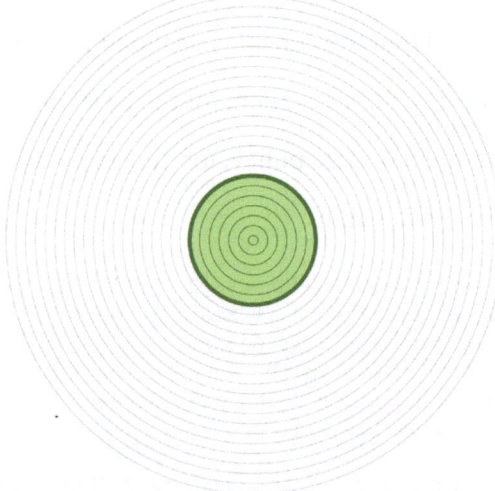

Our target is getting closer

CHAPTER 21

Delegates

Concept of Delegates

In the last chapter, we learned about enumerations and saw how they allow us to assign meaningful names to constants. In their basic form, the first name will represent the value 0 and each subsequent name will have a value of one more, but it is possible to assign different values to the names and thereby change the default values. Enumerations, we learned, help make code more readable, and we can use methods of the Enum class to get the name or value of an item or items in the enumeration. Finally, we also saw that an enumeration is a "special" data type, which is defined by the developer.

In this chapter we will look at delegates, which are also a type, but they are a reference type that holds a reference to a method.

The Microsoft site explains delegates as follows:

A delegate is a type that represents references to methods with a particular parameter list and return type. When you instantiate a delegate, you can associate its instance with any method with a compatible signature and return type. You can invoke (or call) the method through the delegate instance.

Put in more simple terms, we should think of a delegate as being a **type** that is used to represent a method with a **return type** and **method signature**. We read in Chapter 14 with interface methods, we wrote them as a line of code showing the return type followed by the method signature. Examples of method signatures we looked at are

- VatCalculation(double itemPrice)
- CalculateTax(double itemPrice, int quantity)
- CalculateTax(int quantity, double itemPrice)

© Gerard Byrne 2022
G. Byrne, *Target C#*, https://doi.org/10.1007/978-1-4842-8619-7_21

When we added the **return type** in front of the method signature, we had the interface method:

- **double** VatCalculation(double itemPrice)

- **void** CalculateTax(double itemPrice, int quantity)

- **double** CalculateTax(int quantity, double itemPrice)

Now, also thinking back Chapter 12, we saw that we could pass arguments to a method, and the method accepted the arguments as its parameters. The arguments and parameters are types, for example, an int or a string or a float. **However, we never read about passing a method as an argument to another method, which would accept the method as its parameter.** Well, this is where we could use a delegate, to pass a method to another method. The Microsoft site also says

Delegates are used to pass methods as arguments to other methods.

The ability to pass methods as arguments makes the delegate a perfect candidate when defining what are referred to as callback methods, as we will see throughout the examples we code. When we develop code that needs to work with a delegate, we will use three stages to achieve this:

- Declare the delegate with its return type and method signature.

- Then set a target method for the delegate, having created the instance of the delegate.

- Then invoke the delegate because it has been defined and points to a method.

When we declare a delegate, it will have a similar format to declaring an abstract method, a return type followed by the method signature. Some examples of delegate declarations are

- public delegate int VATCalculation(double itemPrice);

- private delegate int CalculationTax(double itemPrice, int quantity);

- internal delegate int CalculateTax(int quantity, double itemPrice);

Even just on what we have read so far, we can think of delegates as

- Having an access modifier of public, private, or internal

- Allowing methods to be passed as arguments to a method that accepts them as parameters

- Being used when we wish to use callback methods

But they can also

- Be joined, chained, so that multiple methods can be called from a single delegate, and this is referred to as **multicast delegates**

- Be assigned to any method that matches the delegate's signature, for example, if the delegate declaration is

```
delegate double Calculation(int valueOne, double
valueTwo);
```

then either or both of these methods can be assigned to an instance of Calculation

```
public static double CalculateTax(int quantity, double
itemPrice)
{
    return quantity * itemPrice * 0.20;
}
```

```
public static double CalculateTotalBeforeVAT(int quantity,
double itemPrice)
{
   return quantity * itemPrice;
}
```

since both methods match the delegate signature.
On the other hand, the method shown in the following cannot be assigned to the Calculation delegate as the method signature is different; it has a double followed by an int rather than an int followed by a double:

```
public static double calculateTotalBeforeVAT(double
itemPrice, int quantity)
    {
        return quantity * itemPrice;
    }
```

Let's code some C# and build our programming muscle.
Add a new project to hold the code for this chapter.

1. Right-click the solution CoreCSharp.

2. Choose Add.

3. Choose New Project.

4. Choose Console App from the listed templates that appear.

5. Click the Next button.

6. Name the project Chapter21 and leave it in the same location.

7. Click the Next button.

8. Choose the framework to be used, which in our projects will be .NET 6.0 or higher.

9. Click the Create button.

Now we should see the Chapter21 project within the solution called CoreCSharp.

10. Right-click the Chapter21 project in the Solution Explorer panel.

11. Click the Set as Startup Project option.

Notice how the Chapter21 project name has been made to have bold text, indicating that it is the new startup project and that it is the Program.cs file within it that will be executed when we run the debugging.

Amend the name of the Program.cs file, remembering the coding principle of "self-documenting" code.

12. Right-click the Program.cs file in the Solution Explorer window.

13. Choose Rename.

14. Change the name to Delegates.cs.

15. Press the Enter key.

Single Delegate

Looking back to Chapter 13 on classes, we had two methods as shown in the following:

```
/****************** METHOD TWELVE ******************/
 public double AccumulateClaimAmount(double
 claimAmountPassedIn, double totalOfAllClaims)
 {
   totalOfAllClaims += claimAmountPassedIn;
   return totalOfAllClaims;
 }// End of method AccumulateClaimAmount()

/****************** METHOD THIRTEEN ******************/
 public double DetermineVATAmount(double totalValueOfClaimsPassedIn, double
 vatAmount)
 {
   vatAmount = totalValueOfClaimsPassedIn -
                      (totalValueOfClaimsPassedIn / 1.20);
   return vatAmount;
 } // End of method DetermineVATAmount()
}  // End of Chapter13 namespace
```

We will now use these two methods, in a modified form, to work with delegates.

Declare the Delegate with Its Return Type and Method Signature

We will now declare a delegate, outside the class but inside the namespace, and create a Main() method.

16. Amend the code as in Listing 21-1.

Listing 21-1. Declare a delegate

```
namespace Chapter21
{
  /*
  A delegate is a type used to represent a method with a
  return type and method signature.
  Here the delegate is called Calculation and the return type
```

```
is double and the two parameters are double
*/
delegate double Calculation(double itemPrice, double vatAmount);

internal class Delegates
{
    static void Main(string[] args)
    {

    } // End of Main() method

} // End of Delegates class
} // End of Chapter21 namespace
```

Instantiate the Delegate and Set Its Target Method

We will now add the "old" method 13 code with amendments, outside the Main() but inside the class, that will become the target for the delegate.

17.   Amend the code, as in Listing 21-2.

Listing 21-2.   Add the method that will be the target for the delegate

```
    } // End of Main() method

    /****************** METHOD THIRTEEN ******************/
    public static double DetermineVATAmount(double
    totalValueOfClaimsPassedIn, double vatAmount)
    {
        vatAmount = totalValueOfClaimsPassedIn - (totalValueOfClaimsPassedIn
        / 1.20);

        Console.WriteLine($"The DetermineVATAmount method is executing using
        the parameter {totalValueOfClaimsPassedIn} \nand the output produced
        is ${vatAmount} which represents the VAT amount\n");

        return vatAmount;
    } // End of method DetermineVATAmount()

} // End of Delegates class
} // End of Chapter21 namespace
```

We will now instantiate the delegate and then set the target method for the delegate instance to be the method we have just added, DetermineVATAmount(), but without using the ().

18.   Amend the code as in Listing 21-3.

Listing 21-3. Instantiate the delegate and set the target method

```
static void Main(string[] args)
 {
   // Instantiate the delegate
   Calculation myCalculationDelegate;

   /*
   Point the delegate object myCalculationDelegate to
   the method DetermineVATAmount
   We are making a reference to the method
   */
   myCalculationDelegate = DetermineVATAmount;

 } // End of Main() method
```

Invoke the Delegate

We will now invoke the delegate using our delegate instance. The call will be made and the returned value will be assigned to a local variable. We will then display the returned value from within a WriteLine method.

19.   Amend the code, as in Listing 21-4.

Listing 21-4. Invoke the delegate

```
myCalculationDelegate = DetermineVATAmount;

/*
Invoke the delegate - in other words the delegate
points to the method that accepts a double data type,
performs its business logic and then returns a double.
So here we invoke our myCalculationDelegate delegate
passing it the value 120.00
```

```
*/
Console.WriteLine("Invoking myCalculationDelegate \n");
double vatAmount = myCalculationDelegate(120.00, 0.00);

Console.WriteLine($"Invoked delegate returned VAT of ${vatAmount}");
```

} // End of Main() method

20. Click the File menu.

21. Choose Save All.

22. Click the Debug menu.

23. Choose Start Without Debugging.

The console output will be as shown in Figure 21-1, and we can see that the method, DetermineVATAmount(), has taken the 120 and the 0.00 and calculated that 20 of this 120 is VAT so the 0.00 was the VAT amount going in and it comes out of the method as 20.

```
Invoking myCalculationDelegate

The DetermineVATAmount method is executing using the parameter 120    Delegate is invoked and passes 120
and the output produced is $20 which represents the VAT amount          to the method which then displays
                                                                                    these details
Invoked delegate returned VAT of $20
```

Figure 21-1. *Output from the casting-style conversion*

24. Press the Enter key to close the console window.

Very good, we might be thinking. But couldn't we just have called the method directly as we did in Chapter 12 and as we do with methods like the WriteLine()? Yes, we could. So why use a delegate then? Simply put, because we can use a delegate to pass a method to another method, and we will see this later when we code an example related to filtering policies. This example was just used to get us started with delegates.

Multicast Delegates

At the start of the chapter, we read that delegates can be joined or chained, so that multiple methods can be called from a single delegate, and this is also referred to as

multicast delegates. If we think of it another way, we could say a multicast delegate is a delegate that has references to more than one method. This means that when we invoke a multicast delegate, all the methods it is pointing to will be invoked in the order they have been declared.

25. Amend the code, as in Listing 21-5, to add a local variable that the method will use.

Listing 21-5. Add a local level variable to be used by the new method

```
static void Main(string[] args)
{
  // Create the variables we need
  double totalOfAllClaims;
```

26. Amend the code, as in Listing 21-6, to add another method that will become the target for the delegate – this was the "old" method 12.

Listing 21-6. Add a second method that will become a target for the delegate

```
} // End of method DetermineVATAmount()

/*
Create the method that will be the target of the
delegate, this was Method 12
*/
public static double AccumulateClaimAmount(double claimAmountPassedIn,
double totalOfAllClaims)
{
  totalOfAllClaims += claimAmountPassedIn;

  Console.WriteLine($"The AccumulateClaimAmount method is executing
  using the parameter {claimAmountPassedIn} \nand the output produced
  is ${totalOfAllClaims} which represents the total claims\n");

  return totalOfAllClaims;
} // End of AccumulateClaimAmount method
} // End of Delegates class
} // End of Chapter21 namespace
```

Instantiate the Delegate Again and Set the New Instances' Target Method

27. Amend the code, as in Listing 21-7, to instantiate the delegate again for two more instances calling them myAccumulateDelegate and myMulticastDelegate:

Listing 21-7. Instantiate the delegate twice more

```
static void Main(string[] args)
{
  // Instantiate the delegates
  Calculation myCalculationDelegate, myAccumulateDelegate,
  myMulticastDelegate;
```

28. Amend the code, as in Listing 21-8, to set the target method for the new myAccumulateDelegate instance, that is, point it to the target method.

Listing 21-8. Point the myAccumulateDelegate to the new method

```
/*
Point the delegate object myCalculationDelegate to
the method DetermineVATAmount
We are making a reference to the method
*/
myCalculationDelegate = DetermineVATAmount;

/*
Point the delegate object myAccumulateDelegate to the
method AccumulateClaimAmount
We are making a reference to the method
*/
myAccumulateDelegate = AccumulateClaimAmount;
```

Chain the Delegates

We will now chain the delegates, which effectively means we join the delegates to "compound" the action. The chaining creates a multicast delegate.

    29.   Amend the code, as in Listing 21-9.

Listing 21-9. Chain the delegates

```
/*
Point the delegate object myAccumulateDelegate to the
method AccumulateClaimAmount
We are making a reference to the method
*/
myAccumulateDelegate = AccumulateClaimAmount;

/*
The two delegates, myCalculationDelegate and myAccumulateDelegate, are
combined into form myMultipleDelegate
*/
myMulticastDelegate = myCalculationDelegate + myAccumulateDelegate;
```

Invoke the Multicast Delegate

    30.   Amend the code, as in Listing 21-10, to invoke the multicast delegate through our delegate instance, passing it the value 1500, which is the claim amount, and the value 0.00, which will be used in the first method as the vatAmount and in the second method as the totalOfAllClaims.

Listing 21-10. Invoke the multicast delegate

```
Console.WriteLine("Invoking myCalculationDelegate \n");
double vatAmount = myCalculationDelegate(120.00, 0.00);

Console.WriteLine($"Invoked delegate returned VAT of ${vatAmount}");
```

```
        Console.WriteLine("------------------------------");
        Console.WriteLine("Invoking myMulticastDelegate:");
        myMulticastDelegate(1500, 0.00);

} // End of Main() method
```

31. Click the File menu.

32. Choose Save All.

33. Click the Debug menu.

34. Choose Start Without Debugging.

The console output will be as shown in Figure 21-2.

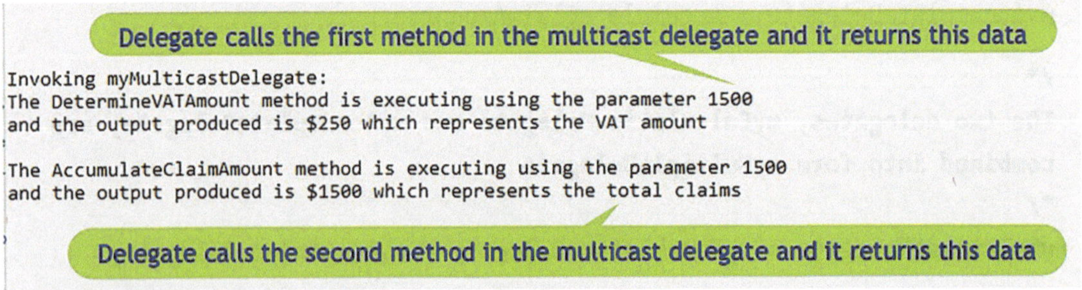

Delegate calls the first method in the multicast delegate and it returns this data

```
Invoking myMulticastDelegate:
The DetermineVATAmount method is executing using the parameter 1500
and the output produced is $250 which represents the VAT amount

The AccumulateClaimAmount method is executing using the parameter 1500
and the output produced is $1500 which represents the total claims
```

Delegate calls the second method in the multicast delegate and it returns this data

Figure 21-2. *Multicast delegate invoked*

35. Press the Enter key to close the console window.

Great, we have an understanding on what a delegate is, how to declare a delegate, how to set the target for the delegate instance, and how to invoke the delegate. We have also coded a multicast delegate that invokes multiple methods. Yes, this example could be improved, but it has helped us understand the concept of multicast delegates.

More Complex Example

Now we will look at a more complex example, which

- Uses a Policy class.

- Creates six instances of the Policy class, each of which passes different values to the constructor.

- Adds the six instances to a list that holds objects of type Policy.

- Creates a delegate that accepts a Policy.

- Creates a method that accepts the delegate as one of its parameters and assigns it to a method. The first time we use the method, we pass it the HardwareType method. The second time, it will be the PolicyDueForRenewal method, and lastly it will be the PremiumGreaterThanTwenty method:

- Inside the method the delegate is invoked and therefore calls the HardwareType() method or the PolicyDueForRenewal() method or the PremiumGreaterThanTwenty() method.

- When any of the three methods are called, they are passed a Policy.

- The HardwareType method returns those items in the list that contain the string Laptop, as their PolicyType, while the other methods check for a date or a value.

So, when we asked the question, "Why use a delegate?", this example will show that it allows us to pass a method to a method.

Create a Policy class.

1. Right-click the Chapter21 project in the Solution Explorer panel.

2. Choose Add.

3. Choose Class.

4. Name the class Policy.cs.

5. Amend the Policy.cs class to have members, a constructor, and a property for each member containing a get and a set accessor for the private members, as in Listing 21-11.

Listing 21-11. Policy class with constructor, members, and property accessors

```
namespace Chapter21
{
  internal class Policy
  {
    private int policyNumber;
```

```csharp
    private String policyType;
    private double monthlyPremium;
    private String policyEndDate;

    public Policy(int policyNumber, string policyType,
      double monthlyPremium, string policyEndDate)
    {
      this.PolicyNumber = policyNumber;
      this.PolicyType = policyType;
      this.MonthlyPremium = monthlyPremium;
      this.PolicyEndDate = policyEndDate;
    } // End of user constructor

    public int PolicyNumber
    {
      get => policyNumber;
      set => policyNumber = value;
    }
    public string PolicyType
    { get => policyType;
      set => policyType = value;
    }
    public double MonthlyPremium
    { get => monthlyPremium;
      set => monthlyPremium = value;
    }
    public string PolicyEndDate
    { get => policyEndDate;
      set => policyEndDate = value;
    }
  } // End of Policy class
} // End of Chapter21 namespace
```

6. Right-click the Chapter21 project in the Solution Explorer panel.

7. Choose Add.

8. Choose Class.

9. Name the class DelegatePolicy.cs.

10. Amend the DelegatePolicy.cs class to have a Main() method and the imports, as in Listing 21-12.

Listing 21-12. DelegatePolicy class with the Main() method

```
using System.Collections.Generic;

namespace Chapter21
{
  internal class DelegatePolicy
  {
    static void Main(string[] args)
    {
    } // End of Main() method

  } // End of DelegatePolicy class
} // End of Chapter21 namespace
```

We will now, at the class level, declare a delegate with the return type bool, which accepts a Policy as its parameter in the method signature.

11. Amend the DelegatePolicy.cs class, as in Listing 21-13.

Listing 21-13. Declare a delegate that accepts a Policy object

```
internal class DelegatePolicy
{
  /*
  Declare the delegate we will use.
  In this case we have a return type of bool and the method
  signature states that the method must accept a Policy object
  */
  internal delegate bool FindByDelegate(Policy policy);

  static void Main(string[] args)
```

We will now, within the Main() method, create six instances of the Policy class.

12.   Amend the class, as in Listing 21-14.

Listing 21-14. Create six instances of the Policy class

```
static void Main(string[] args)
{
  /*
  Create 6 objects of type Policy - Policy is a separate class
  The Policy class has 4 members - policy_number, policyType
  monthlyPremium and the policyEndDate;
  */

  // Laptops
  Policy myPolicyOne = new Policy(123456, "Laptop", 19.99, "31/12/2021");
  Policy myPolicyFive = new Policy(156790, "Laptop", 18.99,
  "30/12/2021");
  Policy myPolicySix = new Policy(123456, "Laptop", 15.99, "15/12/2021");

  // Need renewed
  Policy myPolicyTwo = new Policy(267890, "Printer", 15.99,
  "01/11/2021");
  Policy myPolicyThree = new Policy(345908, "Small_Screen", 9.99,
  "01/10/2021");

  // Monthly premium greater than $20
  Policy myPolicyFour = new Policy(455666, "Large_Screen", 29.99,
  "01/12/2021");
} // End of Main() method
```

We will now continue adding code within the Main() method to declare and create a list that will hold the six instances of the Policy class. The list can be thought of as a collection of a specific type.

13.   Amend the class, as in Listing 21-15.

Listing 21-15. Create a list to hold the six Policy instances

```
// Monthly premium greater than $20
Policy myPolicyFour = new Policy(455666, "Large_Screen", 29.99,
"01/12/2021");

/*
Create a strongly typed List to hold the six Policy objects.
The List of policies will be iterated later
*/
List<Policy> policies = new List<Policy>()
{ myPolicyOne, myPolicyTwo, myPolicyThree,
  myPolicyFour, myPolicyFive, myPolicySix
};
```

```
} // End of Main() method
```

We will now create a method that will find the list of policies based on the delegate passed to the method. First, as we are inside the Main() method, we will call the method we will be creating, three times, passing in different delegates in each call.

14. Amend the class, as in Listing 21-16, to call the not-yet-created method.

Listing 21-16. Call a method, passing it the Policy list and delegate

```
List<Policy> policies = new List<Policy>()
{ myPolicyOne, myPolicyTwo, myPolicyThree,
  myPolicyFour, myPolicyFive, myPolicySix
};

/*
Call the FindPolicesByGivenDelegate method passing
it the delegate to be used
*/
FindPolicesByGivenDelegate("The list of Laptops policies are", policies,
HardwareType);

FindPolicesByGivenDelegate("The list of policies due for renewal are",
policies, PolicyIsDueForRenewal);
```

```
FindPolicesByGivenDelegate("The list of policies with a premium greater
than $20.00 are", policies, PremiumGreaterThanTwenty);
```

`} // End of Main() method`

Now we need to create the method that will

- Accept a string value to be used as a heading.

- Accept the list of policies that will be used

- Accept the delegate that is to be used. This will be in the form of
  an instantiation – FindByDelegate filterMethodToBeUsed – so the
  filterMethodToBeUsed will be one of the methods. It will be the
  method HardwareType() or the method PolicyIsDueForRenewal() or
  the method PremiumGreaterThanTwenty().

- Iterate the list of policies, six policies in our example.

- Invoke the method referred to by the delegate, which will pass back a
  true or false, and this calling method then displays the details for the
  policy if the returned value was true.

- Use a "divider" at the end of the method before the next call is made.

15. Amend the class, as in Listing 21-17, to create the method, outside
    the Main() method but inside the class.

Listing 21-17. Create the method that accepts the Policy list and delegate

```
} // End of Main() method

/*
In this method we use the delegate, FindByDelegate to
invoke the method it is pointing to.
The delegate method name is passed to this method.
*/
static void FindPolicesByGivenDelegate(string title,
  List<Policy> policies, FindByDelegate filterMethodToBeUsed)
{
  Console.WriteLine(title);

  foreach (Policy policy in policies)
```

```
    {
      if (filterMethodToBeUsed(policy))
      {
        Console.WriteLine($"\t{policy.PolicyType} policy " +
          $"number {policy.PolicyNumber} is due for renewal " +
          $"on {policy.PolicyEndDate} and the current " +
          $"premium is {policy.MonthlyPremium}");
      } // End of if construct

    } // End of foreach iteration

    // Separate the three filters for display purposes
    Console.WriteLine("----------------------------");
  } // End of FindPolicesByGivenDelegate

  } // End of DelegatePolicy class
} // End of Chapter21 namespace
```

Now we need to create the method to find those policies that are Laptops when the delegate passed in is HardwareType. Remember the delegate is pointing to a method; it refers to a method.

16. Amend the class to create this method called HardwareType, outside the Main() method, as in Listing 21-18.

Listing 21-18. Create the HardwareType method

```
  } // End of FindPolicesByGivenDelegate

/**********************************************************
 *    Methods that will be pointed to by the delegate     *
 **********************************************************/
//Check if the policy type is a laptop and return true or false
  static bool HardwareType(Policy policyPassedIn)
  {
    return policyPassedIn.PolicyType.Equals("Laptop");
  } // End of HardwareType method

  } // End of DelegatePolicy class
} // End of Chapter21 namespace
```

Now we need to create the method to find those policies whose renewal date is less than or equal to a given date. In this case we have hard-coded the data as 30/11/2021, when the delegate passed in is PolicyIsDueForRenewal.

17. Amend the class to create this method called PolicyIsDueForRenewal, outside the Main() method, as in Listing 21-19.

Listing 21-19. Create the PolicyIsDueForRenewal method

```
} // End of HardwareType method

/*
Check if policy is due for renewal and return true or false
Here we have, for simplicity hard coded a date
*/
static bool PolicyIsDueForRenewal(Policy policyPassedIn)
{
  string today = "30/11/2021";
  return DateTime.Parse(policyPassedIn.PolicyEndDate)<= DateTime.
  Parse(today);
} // End of PolicyIsDueForRenewal method

  } // End of DelegatePolicy class
} // End of Chapter21 namespace
```

Now we need to create the method to find those policies whose monthly premium is greater than 20.00.

18. Amend the class, as in Listing 21-20, to create this method called PremiumGreaterThanTwenty, outside the Main() method.

Listing 21-20. Create the PremiumGreaterThanTwenty method

```
} // End of PolicyIsDueForRenewal method

/*
Check if the monthly premium is greater than $20
and return true or false
*/
```

```
static bool PremiumGreaterThanTwenty(Policy policyPassedIn)
{
    return policyPassedIn.MonthlyPremium > 20.00;
} // End of PremiumGreaterThanTwenty method
```

```
} // End of DelegatePolicy class
} // End of Chapter21 namespace
```

19. Right-click the Chapter21 project in the Solution Explorer panel.

20. Choose Properties from the pop-up menu.

21. Choose the DelegatePolicy class in the Startup object drop-down list.

22. Close the Properties window.

23. Click the File menu.

24. Choose Save All.

25. Click the Debug menu.

26. Choose Start Without Debugging.

The console window will appear, as shown in Figure 21-3, displaying the details from the invoked methods as referred to by the delegate.

```
The list of Laptops policies are
    Laptop policy r   Hardware delegate invoked and the method searches for Laptop   mium is 19.99
    Laptop policy n                                                                   emium is 18.99
    Laptop policy number 123456 is due for renewal on 15/12/2021 and the current premium is 15.99
----------------------------       PolicyIsDueForRenewal delegate invoked and searches by the date < 30/11/2022
The list of policies due for renewal are
    Printer policy number 267890 is due for renewal on 01/11/2021 and the current premium is 15.99
    Small_Screen policy number 345908 is due for renewal on 01/10/2021 and the current premium is 9.99
----------------------------
The list of policies with a premium greater than $20.00 are
    Large_Screen policy number 455666 is due for renewal on 01/12/2021 and the current premium is 29.99
----------------------------
                        PremiumGreaterThanTwenty delegate invoked and searches by the amount > 20.00
C:\CoreCSharp\CoreCSharp\Chapter21\bin\Debug\net6.0\Chapter21.exe (process 9492) exited with code 0.
Press any key to close this window . . .
```

Figure 21-3. *Multicast delegate invoked – complex example*

27. Press the Enter key to close the console window.

Now that really was a complex application using delegates, so we will probably need to read the code carefully, several times, to fully appreciate what is going on.

Chapter Summary

So, finishing this chapter on delegates, we should see that we have extended our knowledge of methods and that we can use delegates to pass methods to methods. We have seen that when we declare a delegate, it has a similar format to declaring an abstract method, a return type followed by the method signature. We also learned how delegates could be chained, so that multiple methods could be called from a single delegate. This is referred to as multicast delegates.

Wow, what an achievement. This is definitely not basic coding. We are seriously doing some elaborate things with our C# code. We should be immensely proud of the learning to date. In finishing this chapter, we have increased our knowledge further. We are getting very close to our target, which once seemed so far away.

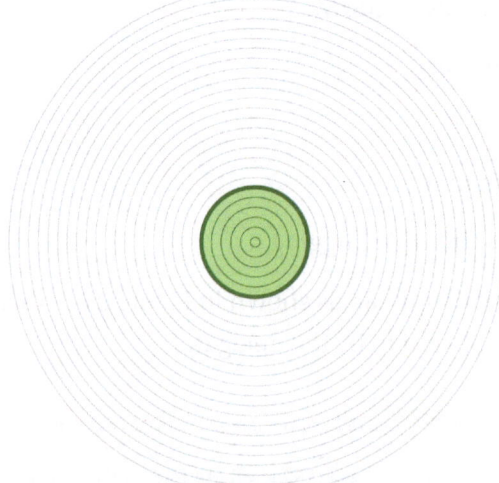

Our target is getting closer

CHAPTER 22

Events

Concept of Events

Publisher and Subscriber

In the last chapter, we learned about delegates, which when created allow us to pass a method as a parameter to other methods. A delegate is really a class that encapsulates a method signature. We saw how to create a delegate, reference it to a method, and then invoke the delegate, which therefore calls the method. We saw that we could chain delegates so we could call multiple methods and this has the name multicast delegates. In this chapter we will look at events, and delegates are intrinsically linked to events.

Let us think about some everyday situations we may be familiar with and relate them to events:

- Think about watching television and then deciding to increase the volume. We pick up the television remote control and press the button that is programmed to control the volume. We press the + button and the volume increases. The **event** is pressing the button and sending a message to an electronic part in the television circuitry. The remote control + volume button is a **sender** of the message, and the electronic part in the television circuitry is the **receiver**. We can take this terminology a little further by saying that we have a **publisher** and a **subscriber.**

- Think about being on the Internet and signing up to a newsletter of a news channel, using our email address. As new material becomes available from the publisher, it will be pushed to us as the subscriber at our email address. The event is triggered at the publisher end when a new newsletter is published.

© Gerard Byrne 2022
G. Byrne, *Target C#*, https://doi.org/10.1007/978-1-4842-8619-7_22

- What about the Internet of Things (IoT)? We have our phone and we can switch on and off a connected plug or thermostat, we can open and close our curtains, and we can activate our indoor security camera. With the Internet of Things, we have events with senders and receivers.

So, when we think of events in C#, we can think of activities we might undertake, like moving our mouse, clicking a button, or pressing a key. And we can also think about events that happen within the system we use, like an icon of a battery with a red bar generated by the phone software when the battery is in need of recharging. When we do something like clicking a button, we are raising an event, which will be managed in the application code by an event handler. When the operating system on the phone checks the battery level and it is below a specified level, it raises an event, which is handled by an event handler, a method, that acts upon it.

In our real-life examples, and any other we can think about, we will see a trend where there is an action that will be delegated when the event takes place. We could even have our phone that is connected to our Internet of Things devices, switch on all the connected lights, and turn on the heating. This is the concept of multicast delegates that we looked at in the previous chapter on delegates.

Now using C# programming terminology, we can say that an object raises an event, while another object or multiple objects handle the event. The object that raises the event is called the publisher, while the object(s) that handles the event is called the subscriber(s). The publisher does not know who the subscribers are or even if there are any subscribers; it simply knows that there is a method it must notify about the raised event. The subscribers do not need to worry about the published event; they simply know that the event has occurred and they need to act on it. This concept of "not knowing or caring about the other part" is ideal when we wish to develop **loosely coupled** applications. By acting on the event, the subscriber might do nothing, because that is what has been coded, or it might do something. Either way, the subscriber is notified and it takes an appropriate action. The way that we connect the publisher and the subscriber is by using a "contract," which in reality means we use a **delegate**. As we saw and coded in Chapter 21, a delegate is a reference, a pointer, to a method, and remember that a single delegate can point to more than one method, which is called a multicast delegate. Great, so now we know that the publisher is an object and the publisher talks to the delegate, which knows the specific method or methods to work with. When the delegate and method are in a class, we say that it is the subscriber class.

Considering all that we have read about events so far and thinking back to Chapter 21, we can see that methods are a common feature. Delegates reference a method, and events are handled by an event handler, so it will be no surprise to us when we realize that delegates and events are interlinked.

An event is a special kind of multicast delegate that can only be invoked from within the class (or derived classes) or struct where it is declared (the publisher class). If other classes or structs subscribe to the event, their event handler methods will be called when the publisher class raises the event. The event can be made static so it is available to any caller and there is no need to instantiate the class. An event can also be a virtual event by using the virtual keyword, and this enables any derived class to override the event behavior by using the override keyword. An event overriding a virtual event can also be sealed, which specifies that for derived classes it is no longer virtual.

If an event is declared abstract, this will mean that the compiler will not generate the add and remove event accessor blocks, which means the derived classes must provide their own implementation.

When we used a delegate, we declared it outside the class, but with an event it must be part of the class, a member, which ensures that the event will only be invoked by some part of the class it is a member of, the publisher class.

Think about a publisher and subscriber in relation to a customer changing their bank details with their utility company. The customer logs on to the company website and completes a form to change their bank details. The company system that accepts the change notifies the accounts department of the change. So the initial class that accepts the change is the publisher, and the accounts department class will be the subscriber. There may be other subscribers who have been registered and they will pick up that the publisher has raised an event. A sample flow of the Publisher, Event, and Subscriber is shown in Figure 22-1.

Figure 22-1. *Publisher, Event, and Subscriber flow*

Declare an Event

When dealing with events, we have an event listener that listens for a specific event and then notifies an event handler, which is a method containing code written by the developer that will be executed in response to the event that occurs in the application.

The event is connected to its event handler by using an event delegate, and we looked at delegates in the last chapter. To make the event and the response work correctly, we need the delegate that links the event to the handler method, and we need the class that holds the event data. We will see how we add the delegate instance to the event object using the += operator, and this means the event handler is called when the event happens. The event handler delegate will have two parameters representing the object instance that raised the event and the object that holds the event data. The signature of the delegate and event handler methods must match.

In declaring an event we can use different syntax:

<access modifier> event keyword <delegate type> event name

- **Example**

  ```
  public event EventHandler CollectPolicyData
  ```

  Here the delegate type is an EventHandler.

- **Example**

  ```
  public event Action CollectPolicyData
  ```

  Here the delegate type is an Action that accepts no arguments.

- **Example**

  ```
  public event Action<int> CollectPolicyData
  ```

  Here the delegate type is an Action that accepts one argument.

- **Example**

  ```
  public event Func<int, int>  CollectPolicyData
  ```

  Here the delegate type is an Func and it accepts two arguments.

In the preceding examples, we have seen the use of two different delegate types, the EventHandler that we also read handled an event and the Action, but we can use any delegate type within C#. We can also use Func instead of Action since a Func is a delegate that points to a method that accepts one or more arguments and returns a value, whereas Action is a delegate that points to a method that in turn accepts one or more arguments but returns no value. In other words, we can **use Action when our delegate points to a method that returns void**.

Table 22-1 shows where we declare a delegate called Calculation and then we use this delegate as the event using the event keyword.

Table 22-1. *Delegate declaration and event using the delegate*

Example	
The delegate declaration	public delegate void Calculation();
The event declaration	public event Calculation CalculateEvent

Raise an Event

Using multicasting we can have multiple event handlers attached to an event, which is a great concept, having a single delegate that invokes more than one method. The downside is that we do not have any control over the order in which the events get executed.

Now, as we should know, when we have our event, we will want to raise it at some stage. To raise the event we need to **invoke** the event delegate, for example, `CalculateEvent.Invoke();`, and then subscribe using the += operator. The += operator has nothing to do with arithmetic operators. Unsubscribing from the event involves using the -= operator.

Handle an Event

When an event is raised, it will need to be handled, and this is where we need an event handler. The event handler will have the code required to respond to the event. In the application code we will enter shortly, the following will occur:

- The Main() method creates a new Customer, passing relevant details to the Customer constructor.

- The Customer constructor sets the initial values of the Customer members, fields.

- The Customer class declares a delegate called **ActivatePolicyEventHandler.**

- The Customer class links an event called **AccountStatusToggled** to the delegate.

- In the Policy class, we will associate the event with the method called ChangeAccountStatus().

- The Customer class has a ToString() method that will display details about the Customer.

- The Main() method creates a new Policy, passing it the Customer we have created.

- The Policy class then associates an event handler with the event we created.

- The method we have associated with the event is then created and in essence it changes the status to true.

- Finally in the Main() method, we call the ToggleAccountStatus() method of the Customer class, which has code to raise the event, which then causes any event handler attached to the event to be called. In this scenario we will have only one event handler associated with the event, ChangeAccountStatus(). When executed we see a message displayed that confirms the change in status.

Let's code some C# and build our programming muscle.

Add a new project to hold the code for this chapter.

1. Right-click the solution CoreCSharp.

2. Choose Add.

3. Choose New Project.

4. Choose Console App from the listed templates that appear.

5. Click the Next button.

6. Name the project Chapter22 and leave it in the same location.

7. Click the Next button.

8. Choose the framework to be used, which in our projects will be .NET 6.0 or higher.

9.   Click the Create button.

Now we should see the Chapter22 project within the solution called CoreCSharp.

10.   Right-click the project Chapter22 in the Solution Explorer panel.

11.   Click the Set as Startup Project option.

Notice how the Chapter22 project name has been made to have bold text, indicating that it is the new startup project and that it is the Program.cs file within it that will be executed when we run the debugging.

12.   Right-click the Program.cs file in the Solution Explorer window.

13.   Choose Rename.

14.   Change the name to EventsExample.cs.

15.   Press the Enter key.

16.   Double-click the EventsExample.cs file to open it in the editor window.

We will be creating a Customer class and a Policy class as we code this example, but first we will add the namespace and the Main() method and will instantiate the Customer and Policy classes.

17.   Amend the code, as in Listing 22-1.

Listing 22-1. Create the Main() method; instantiate the Customer and Policy classes

```
namespace Chapter22
{
  class EventsExample
  {
    static void Main(string[] args)
    {
      /*
      Create a new instance of the Customer class
      i.e we have a new Customer.
      */
      Customer myNewCustomer = new Customer(123456, "Gerry Byrne", false);
```

```
        /*
        Create a new instance of the Policy class
        i.e. a new Policy for the new Customer.
        */
        Policy myNewPolicy = new Policy(myNewCustomer);

        /*
        Call the Customer method that will change the
        status of the Customer account
        */
        myNewCustomer.ToggleAccountStatus();
    } // End of Main() method

  } // End of EventsExample class
} // End of Chapter22 namespace
```

Now we will create the Customer class, which will be created outside the
EventsExample class but within the namespace. We will also add the member
declarations and a constructor.

    18.   Amend the code, as in Listing 22-2.

Listing 22-2. Create the Customer class with members and constructor

```
    } // End of Main() method

    // Customer class - the Publisher class
    class Customer
    {
      // Declare the members, fields
      public int accountNo;
      public string name;
      public bool status = false;

      // Create a constructor used to initialise all the members
      public Customer(int accountNo, string name, bool status)
      {
        this.accountNo = accountNo;
        this.name = name;
```

```
        this.status = status;
    }  // End of Customer constructor

  } // End of Customer class
} // End of Chapter22 namespace
```

In terms of the ToString() method, the Microsoft documentation says

Object.ToString is the major formatting method in the .NET Framework. It converts an object to its string representation so that it is suitable for display. Default implementations of the Object.ToString method return the fully qualified name of the object's type.

We would prefer to see more than the fully qualified name of our object so we will override the ToString() method.

19.   Amend the Customer class to have a ToString() method that overrides the default ToString(), as in Listing 22-3.

Listing 22-3. Create a ToString() method in the Customer class

```
    }  // End of Customer constructor

    /*
    Override the ToString() method of the class to
    display details of the customer
    */
    public override string ToString()
    {
      return ($"The customer details are:\n\tAccount number\t{this.
      accountNo}\n\tCustomer name\t{this.name}\n\tAccount status\t{this.
      status}\n");
    } // End of ToString() method

  } // End of Customer class
} // End of Chapter22 namespace
```

20.   Amend the Customer class, as in Listing 22-4, to declare the delegate we will use.

Listing 22-4. Declare the delegate

```
} // End of ToString() method

/*
Define the delegate. We name the delegate using the name
of our event and add the phrase EventHandler. So here we
are saying the event will be called ActivatePolicy.
*/
public delegate void ActivatePolicyEventHandler();

} // End of Customer class
} // End of Chapter22 namespace
```

21. Amend the Customer class, as in Listing 22-5, to declare the event
     we will use and associate it with the delegate we have just created.

Listing 22-5. Declare the event to be associated with the delegate

```
public delegate void ActivatePolicyEventHandler();

/*
Think of the event as being a restricted delegate and
classes can choose to subscribe or unsubscribe from
the event. The event is a member of the class.
*/
public event ActivatePolicyEventHandler AccountStatusToggled;

} // End of Customer class
} // End of Chapter22 namespace
```

22. Amend the Customer class, as in Listing 22-6, to create the
     method that will be called when the event is raised.

Listing 22-6. Create the method to be called when the event is raised

```
public event ActivatePolicyEventHandler AccountStatusToggled;

// Create the method to be called when the event is raised.
public void ToggleAccountStatus()
```

```
  {
    this.status = true;
    AccountStatusToggled();
  } // End of ToggleAccountStatus()

 } // End of Customer class
} // End of Chapter22 namespace
```

Create the Policy class.

We will now create the Policy class, which will have a constructor that accepts a Customer object. The class will be created outside the Customer class but within the namespace.

23.   Amend the code, as in Listing 22-7.

Listing 22-7. Create the Policy class

```
  } // End of Customer class

  class Policy
  {
    // Store the Customer instance
    Customer myCustomer;

    public Policy(Customer customer)
    {
      /*
      Inject a Customer object into the Policy
      i.e. the Policy can reference the instance of Customer
      */
      myCustomer = customer;

    } // End of Policy constructor

  } // End of Policy class
} // End of Chapter22 namespace
```

Add a Method to an Event Using +=

In the Policy constructor, we will now add a reference to the method called ChangeAccountStatus, which will be created and will be used when the event is raised. We are actually chaining the method to the event. The += is used to add the reference, or we could say it subscribes to the event. The method on the right-hand side of our += will be added to the list of delegates, and ultimately when the event is executed, all the delegates in the internal list will be called.

24.   Amend the code, as in Listing 22-8.

Listing 22-8. Add a reference to the method ChangeAccountStatus

```
myCustomer = customer;

/*
We have the event and we will now add a reference to
the method that will be used when the event is raised.
So, we are chaining the new method onto the event,
even though presently there is only one method
associated with the event.
*/
myCustomer.AccountStatusToggled += ChangeAccountStatus;

    } // End of Policy constructor
} // End of Policy class
```

We will now create the ChangeAccountStatus() method in the Policy class. This method contains business logic that changes the status to true and displays a message and the details of the new Customer object.

25.   Amend the code, as in Listing 22-9.

Listing 22-9. Create the ChangeAccountStatus method to be called by the event

```
    } // End of Policy constructor

/*
Create the method that is referred to by the event when
it is raised. Here we change the Customer field to true
```

```
indicating that the account has been set up.
*/
public void ChangeAccountStatus()
{
   Console.WriteLine($"The account status was updated to {myCustomer.
   status}\n");
   Console.WriteLine(myCustomer.ToString());
} // End of changeAccountStatus() method
} // End of Policy class
```

26.   Click the File menu.

27.   Choose Save All.

28.   Click the Debug menu.

29.   Choose Start Without Debugging.

The console window will appear, as Figure 22-2, and display the details from the invoked method as referred to by the delegate.

```
The account status was updated to True

The customer details are :
        Account Number   123456
        Customer name    Gerry Byrne
        Account status   True


C:\CoreCSharp\CoreCSharp\Chapter22\bin\Debug\net6.0\Chapter22.exe
Press any key to close this window . . .
```

Figure 22-2. *Delegate invoked the method*

30.   Press the Enter key to close the console window.

Refer the Event to a Second Method Using +=

In the Policy class, we will create a second method called EmailNotification(), which will "simulate" the process of sending an email notification. The EmailNotification() will be added to the event and will therefore be called when the event is fired.

31.   Amend the code, as in Listing 22-10.

Listing 22-10. Create the EmailNotification() method to be called by the event

```
} // End of changeAccountStatus() method

/*
Create a second method that is referred to by the event
when it is raised. Here we 'emulate' an email being sent,
we write a message to the console.
*/
public void EmailNotification()
{
  Console.WriteLine("Email sent to accounts department");
} // End of EmailNotification() method

} // End of Policy class
} // End of Chapter22 namespace
```

32.   Amend the code, as in Listing 22-11, to add the EmailNotification() method to the event within the Policy constructor.

Listing 22-11. Add the EmailNotification() method to the event

```
myCustomer.AccountStatusToggled += ChangeAccountStatus;
myCustomer.AccountStatusToggled += EmailNotification;

} // End of Policy constructor
```

33.   Click the File menu.

34.   Choose Save All.

35.   Click the Debug menu.

36.   Choose Start Without Debugging.

Figure 22-3 shows the console window displaying the details from the invoked methods as referred to by the delegate. The additional method shows the email notification.

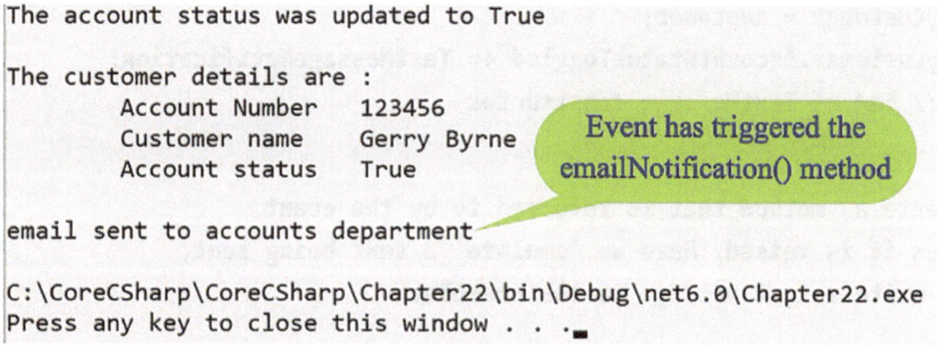

```
The account status was updated to True

The customer details are :
        Account Number    123456
        Customer name     Gerry Byrne
        Account status    True

email sent to accounts department

C:\CoreCSharp\CoreCSharp\Chapter22\bin\Debug\net6.0\Chapter22.exe
Press any key to close this window . . .
```

Event has triggered the emailNotification() method

Figure 22-3. *Delegate invoked both methods*

37.   Press the Enter key to close the console window.

Refer the Event to a Third Method Using +=

We will now send the customer a text message so we will create a TextMessage class where we will create a method called TextMessageNotification(), which will "simulate" the process of sending a text notification. The TextMessageNotification() will be added to the event and will therefore be called when the event is fired.

38.   Amend the code, as in Listing 22-12, to add the new TextMessage class.

Listing 22-12. Add a TextMessage class and use += to attach the TextMessageNotification() method

```
} // End of Policy class

class TextMessage
{
  // Store the Customer instance
  Customer myCustomer;

  public TextMessage(Customer customer)
  {
    /*
    Inject a Customer object into the TextMessage
    i.e. the TextMessage can reference the instance of Customer
      */
```

867

```
  myCustomer = customer;
  myCustomer.AccountStatusToggled += TextMessageNotification;
} // End of TextMessage constructor

/*
Create a  method that is referred to by the event
when it is raised. Here we 'emulate' a text being sent,
we write a text message to the console.
*/
public void TextMessageNotification()
{
  Console.WriteLine("Text message sent to customer");
} // End of TextMessageNotification() method
} // End of TextMessage class
} // End of Chapter22 namespace
```

39. Amend the code, as in Listing 22-13, to instantiate the
    TextMessage class passing it the Customer object.

Listing 22-13. Instantiate the TextMessage class

```
/*
Create a new instance of the Policy class
i.e. a new Policy for the new Customer.
*/
Policy myNewPolicy = new Policy(myNewCustomer);

/*
Create a new instance of the TextMessage class
i.e. a new TextMessage for the new Customer.
*/
TextMessage myNewEmailer = new TextMessage(myNewCustomer);

  /*
  Call the Customer method that will change the
  status of the Customer account
  */
  myNewCustomer.ToggleAccountStatus();
} // End of Main() method
```

40.   Click the File menu.

41.   Choose Save All.

42.   Click the Debug menu.

43.   Choose Start Without Debugging.

Figure 22-4 shows the console window displaying the details from the invoked methods as referred to by the delegate. The additional method shows the text notification.

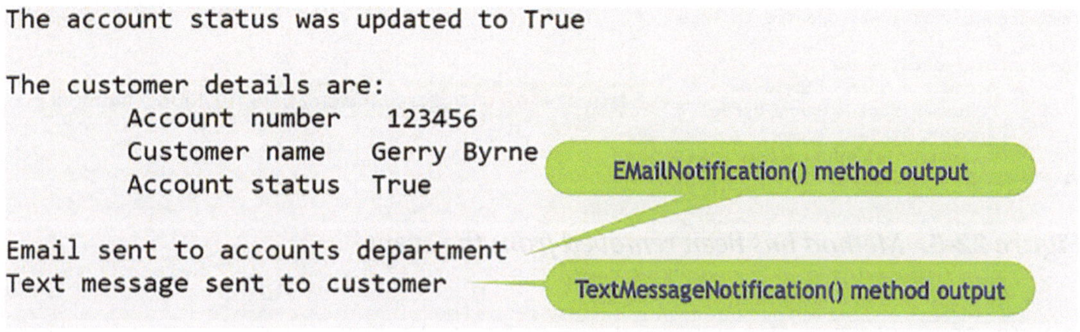

```
The account status was updated to True

The customer details are:
        Account number    123456
        Customer name     Gerry Byrne
        Account status    True                    EMailNotification() method output


Email sent to accounts department
Text message sent to customer              TextMessageNotification() method output
```

Figure 22-4. *Multicast delegate invoked method from new class*

Remove a Method from an Event Using -=

We will now remove the EmailNotification() method from the event.

44.   Amend the code, as in Listing 22-14.

Listing 22-14. Remove a method from an event

```
myCustomer.AccountStatusToggled += ChangeAccountStatus;
myCustomer.AccountStatusToggled += EmailNotification;

// Remove an event using -= followed by the method name
myCustomer.AccountStatusToggled -= EmailNotification;

} // End of Policy constructor
```

45.   Click the File menu.

46.   Choose Save All.

47.   Click the Debug menu.

48.   Choose Start Without Debugging.

The console window will appear and display the details from the invoked methods as referred to by the delegate, and as we have removed the EmailNotification() method, the message will not appear, as shown in Figure 22-5.

Figure 22-5. *Method has been removed from the event*

49.   Press the Enter key to close the console window.

Chapter Summary

So, finishing this chapter on events, we should see the relationship between events and delegates and indeed with methods as well. The event is used to trigger a method or multiple methods. We saw that in C# programming terminology, we can say that an object raises an event, while another object or multiple objects handle the event. We also learned about the publish and subscribe concept where the object that raises the event is called the publisher and the object that handles the event is called the subscriber. We saw that in the publish and subscribe architecture, the publisher does not know who the subscribers are; it simply knows that there is a method it must notify about the raised event. The subscriber does not worry about the publisher of the event; it simply knows that the event has occurred and it needs to act on it.

Wow, what an achievement. This is really good. We are touching on some very intricate topics and applying them in C# code. We should be immensely proud of the learning to date. In finishing this chapter, we have increased our knowledge further. We are getting very close to our target, which once seemed so far away.

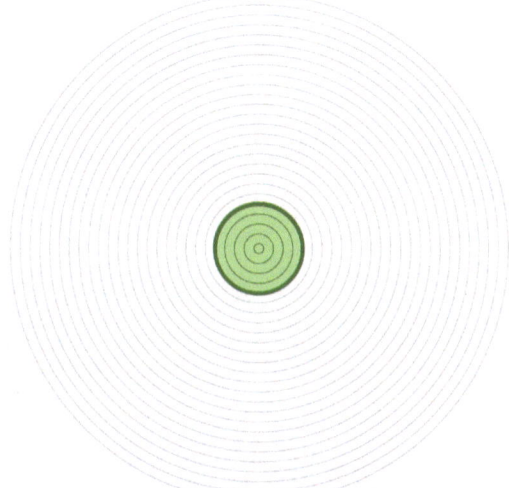

Our target is getting closer

CHAPTER 23

Generics

Concept of Generics

In the last chapter, we learned about events and how there is a relationship between events and delegates, which themselves have a strong relationship with methods. We learned that events trigger event handlers, so the action of the event is to trigger a method. We also learned that we have a publish and subscribe relationship where the object that raises the event is the publisher, while the object that handles the event is the subscriber. Now in this chapter, we will look at a very useful concept called generics.

When we see the word *generics* in C#, we should think of the word general. So, in C# when we define a data type specification that uses generic parameters, we should look on them as substitute parameter types. The real parameter type will replace these generic parameters when we need to use the data type in our code. The C# language allows us to define generic interfaces, generic abstract classes, generic classes, generic events, generic delegates, generic fields, generic methods, etc. The generic type will appear in a set of open and close angle brackets, < >, so we could have something like this in our code:

```
public class PolicyClass<T>
```

where T is the parameter type.

Let us now consider a PolicyMatcher class based on a policy matching routine where

- The PolicyMatcher class has one method called checkIfTheSame().

- The method only accepts integer values.

- The method is used to check if the policy numbers passed in are equal.

- It uses a selection construct to display an appropriate message.

873

© Gerard Byrne 2022
G. Byrne, *Target C#*, https://doi.org/10.1007/978-1-4842-8619-7_23

The PolicyMatcher class can be instantiated from within the Main() method and we can then call the checkIfTheSame() method, passing it our two integer values. Now let us code this example.

Let's code some C# and build our programming muscle.

Add a new project to hold the code for this chapter.

1. Right-click the solution CoreCSharp.

2. Choose Add.

3. Choose New Project.

4. Choose Console App from the listed templates that appear.

5. Click the Next button.

6. Name the project Chapter23 and leave it in the same location.

7. Click the Next button.

8. Choose the framework to be used, which in our projects will be .NET 6.0 or higher.

9. Click the Create button.

Now we should see the Chapter23 project within the solution called CoreCSharp.

10. Right-click the project Chapter23 in the Solution Explorer panel.

11. Click the Set as Startup Project option.

Notice how the Chapter23 project name has been made to have bold text, indicating that it is the new startup project and that it is the Program.cs file within it that will be executed when we run the debugging.

12. Right-click the Program.cs file in the Solution Explorer window.

13. Choose Rename.

14. Change the name to Generics1.cs.

15. Press the Enter key.

16. Double-click the Generics1.cs file to open it in the editor window.

We will now create the namespace, the class, and the Main() method within the Generics1 class. We will also create a PolicyMatcher class outside the Generics1 class, and it will contain the method to check if the values are the same. The code is commented to explain what is being done in each line or block of code.

17.   Amend the Generics1.cs, as in Listing 23-1.

Listing 23-1. Class with the Main() method and try block

```
namespace Chapter23
{
  class Generics1
  {
    static void Main(string[] args)
    {
    } // End of Main() method

  } // End of Generics1 class

    class PolicyMatcher
    {
      /*
      A method which is not generic because it has specified
      the parameter data types. The method cannot be used
      when passing floats etc. It is specific not generic.
      */
      public string checkIfTheSame(int itemOne, int itemTwo)
      {
        if (itemOne.Equals(itemTwo))
        {
          return ($"The {itemOne.GetType()} values {itemOne} and {itemTwo}
          are equal");
        }
        else
        {
          return ($"The {itemOne.GetType()} values {itemOne} and {itemTwo}
          are not equal");
        }
```

```
    }// End of checkIfTheSame() method
  } // End of PolicyMatcher class
} // End of Chapter23 namespace
```

We will now amend the code to create an instance of the PolicyMatcher class and then call the checkIfTheSame() method, passing it two integer values.

18.   Amend the class as in Listing 23-2.

Listing 23-2. Create instance of PolicyMatcher class and call checkIfTheSame()

```
static void Main(string[] args)
{
// Instantiate the PolicyMatcher class
PolicyMatcher myPolicyMatcher = new PolicyMatcher();

/*
Call the add method passing it the two policy values
with the correct data type
*/
Console.WriteLine(myPolicyMatcher.checkIfTheSame(10000, 20000));

} // End of Main() method
```

19.   Click the File menu.

20.   Choose Save All.

21.   Click the Debug menu.

22.   Choose Start Without Debugging.

Figure 23-1 shows the console window displaying the details returned from the method.

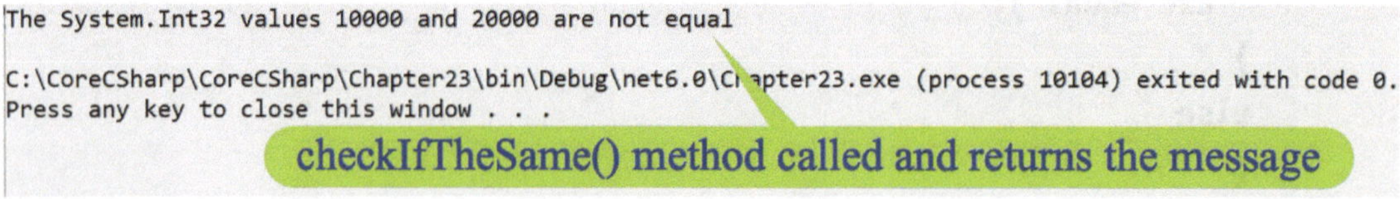

```
The System.Int32 values 10000 and 20000 are not equal

C:\CoreCSharp\CoreCSharp\Chapter23\bin\Debug\net6.0\Chapter23.exe (process 10104) exited with code 0.
Press any key to close this window . . .
```
              checkIfTheSame() method called and returns the message

Figure 23-1. *Method returns its message*

23.   Press the Enter key to close the console window.

We have just shown that this application code works well because it gives us the correct output as shown in Figure 23-1. However, this is a method that is specific in its parameter data types and, while this might be fine for now, because we are only checking integer values, we have a **tightly coupled** method. Tight coupling in programming is not good, and it would be better if we could make the method generic, so that it could accept different data types. If we could achieve this, we would have **loosely coupled** code. Thankfully, when we wish to have similar logic for similar types, this is where generics come to the rescue.

Generic Class, Generic Method, Generic Parameters

24.   Right-click the Generics1 filename in the Solution Explorer panel.

25.   Choose Copy.

26.   Right-click the Chapter23 project name.

27.   Choose Paste.

28.   Right-click the Generics1 – Copy file.

29.   Choose Rename.

30.   Name the class Generics2.cs and leave it in the same location.

31.   Open the Generics2.cs file in the editor window.

We will now amend the copied file.

32.   Amend the class name in the file to be Generics2 as in Listing 23-3.

Listing 23-3. Amended Generics1 class name

```
namespace Chapter23
{
  class Generics2
  {
```

33. Amend the PolicyMatcher class name to be PolicyMatcherGeneric as shown in Listing 23-4.

Listing 23-4. Amended PolicyMatcher class name

```
Console.WriteLine(myPolicyMatcher.checkIfTheSame(10000, 20000));

    } // End of Main() method

  } // End of Generics2 class

  class PolicyMatcherGeneric
  {
```

34. Amend the instantiation to reference PolicyMatcherGeneric, as shown in Listing 23-5.

Listing 23-5. Amended instantiation to PolicyMatcherGeneric

```
    static void Main(string[] args)
    {
      // Instantiate the PolicyMatcher class
      PolicyMatcherGeneric myPolicyMatcher = new PolicyMatcherGeneric();
```

We will now amend the code so that the class accepts the type <OurGenericType>. OurGenericType is a made-up name, a generic name, and it is used so we can replace it with a specific data type when required. The amended code is shown in Listing 23-6.

Listing 23-6. Class accepts <OurGenericType> type

```
    } // End of Main() method

  } // End of Generics2 class

  class PolicyMatcherGeneric<OurGenericType>
  {
```

Now we will amend the method code, so that the two parameters are of the type <OurGenericType>.

35. Amend the code as shown in Listing 23-7.

Listing 23-7. Amended method to accept the type <OurGenericType>

```
class PolicyMatcherGeneric<OurGenericType>
  {
    /*
    A method which is not generic because it has specified
    the parameter data types. The method cannot be used
    when passing floats etc. It is specific not generic.
    */
    public string checkIfTheSame(OurGenericType itemOne, OurGenericType
    itemTwo)
```

Now that we have amended our class, we must change the way we have instantiated it. Here we will be using integer values so we will have the data type shown as <int>, but remember we are dealing with generics so we should be able to use any data type. We will also call the checkIfTheSame() method of the instance, displaying the returned value to the console.

    36.   Amend the code, as in Listing 23-8.

Listing 23-8. Instantiate the class using the int type

```
    static void Main(string[] args)
    {
      // Instantiate the PolicyMatcher class
      PolicyMatcherGeneric<int> myPolicyMatcher =
      new PolicyMatcherGeneric<int>();

  /*
  Call the add method passing it the two policy values
  with the correct data type
  */
Console.WriteLine(myPolicyMatcherString.checkIfTheSame( 10000, 20000));

    } // End of Main() method
```

Here we have passed in an int type. If we wished to pass in a string or a double, could we do this? Yes, we have made the class generic by using the <OurGenericType>, and therefore we can instantiate the class using <int>, <string>, <double>, etc.

Now we will instantiate the class again, but this time we will have string types rather than int types. We will then call the checkIfTheSame() method of the instance, displaying the returned value to the console.

37.   Amend the code in the Main() method, as in Listing 23-9.

Listing 23-9. Instantiate the class a second time to accept string type

```
Console.WriteLine(myPolicyMatcher.checkIfTheSame(10000, 20000));

// Instantiate the PolicyMatcher class for strings
  PolicyMatcherGeneric<string> myPolicyMatcherString =
    new PolicyMatcherGeneric<string>();

  /*
  Call the add method passing it the two policy values
  with the correct data type
  */
Console.WriteLine(myPolicyMatcherString.checkIfTheSame( "PL123456",
"PL123456"));
    } // End of Main() method
```

When we hover over either of the two method calls, we will see that the parameter types have adapted to those specified in our instantiation. Figures 23-2 and 23-3 show this adaptation in action. Amazing!

```
/*
Call the add method passing it the two policy values
with the correct data type
*/
Console.WriteLine(myPolicyMatcher.checkIfTheSame(10000, 20000));

// Instantiate the PolicyMatcher c
PolicyMatcherGeneric<string> myPoli
```

[string PolicyMatcherGeneric<int>.checkIfTheSame(int itemOne, int itemTwo) (+ 1 overload)]

checkIfTheSame() has adapted to accept int followed by int

Figure 23-2. *Method can accept an int followed by an int*

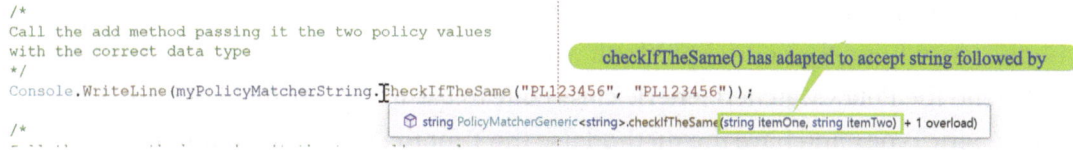

```
/*
Call the add method passing it the two policy values
with the correct data type
*/
Console.WriteLine(myPolicyMatcherString.CheckIfTheSame("PL123456", "PL123456"));

/*
```

checkIfTheSame() has adapted to accept string followed by

string PolicyMatcherGeneric<string>.checkIfTheSame(string itemOne, string itemTwo) + 1 overload)

Figure 23-3. *Method can accept a string followed by a string*

The generic class and its generic method have served us well since we can now pass in a policy numeric value or a policy string value and so on and the method still works. No need for separate methods to suit all the different data types. Loosely coupled indeed.

38. Click the File menu.

39. Choose Save All.

40. Right-click the Chapter23 project in the Solution Explorer panel.

41. Choose Properties from the pop-up menu.

42. Choose the Generics2 class in the Startup object drop-down list.

43. Close the Properties window.

44. Click the Debug menu.

45. Choose Start Without Debugging.

The console window will appear, as shown in Figure 23-4, and display the details returned from both method calls.

```
The System.Int32 values 10000 and 20000 are not equal
The System.String values PL123456 and PL123456 are equal

C:\CoreCSharp\CoreCSharp\Chapter23\bin\Debug\net6.0\Chapter23.exe (process 9116) exited with code 0.
Press any key to close this window . . .
```

Figure 23-4. *Method returns the two messages, one for each call to it*

46. Press the Enter key to close the console window.

Brilliant.

Now that we have an understanding of generics, let us look at what we might see when we look at generics example code on the Microsoft or another website. We will see that often the letter T is used to represent the type. The T is a generic type parameter; T is not a C# reserved keyword. In our Listing 23-7 example, we used the name

OurGenericType rather than T. So in our code we could replace the OurGenericType with the letter T and the code should still work fine.

Amend the PolicyMatcherGeneric class code to use the <T> instead of the existing <OurGenericType> and have the method use the T for the type of the parameters as shown in Listing 23-10.

Listing 23-10. Class with <T> and method using generic T

```
class PolicyMatcherGeneric<T>
{
  /*
  A method which is not generic because it has specified
  the parameter data types. The method cannot be used
  when passing floats etc. It is specific not generic.
  */
  public string checkIfTheSame(T itemOne, T itemTwo)
  {
    if (itemOne.Equals(itemTwo))
    {
      return ($"The {itemOne.GetType()} values {itemOne} " +
        $"and {itemTwo} are equal");
    }
    else
    {
      return ($"The {itemOne.GetType()} values {itemOne}" +
        $" and {itemTwo} are not equal");
    }
  }// End of checkIfTheSame() method
```

In this example our class is generic, `PolicyMatcherGeneric<T>`. The T allows any type. T is just a placeholder for a type, and therefore our class can represent a collection of objects, the type of which will be dictated when we create the class. An example is shown for reference in Listings 23-11 and 23-12.

Listing 23-11. Type is int

```
The specific type being defined as int:
PolicyMatcherGeneric<int> myPolicyMatcher = new
                              PolicyMatcherGeneric<int>();
```

Listing 23-12. Type is string

```
The specific type being defined as string:
PolicyMatcherGeneric<string> myPolicyMatcher = new
                              PolicyMatcherGeneric<string>();
```

Generic Class, Generic Method, Mixed Parameter Types

We will now create another method called checkIfTheSame(), but it will have a specified parameter type, followed by a generic parameter type, followed by a specified data type parameter. This is an example of method overloading.

47. Amend the PolicyMatcherGeneric class to add the new method, as in Listing 23-13.

Listing 23-13. New overloaded method called checkIfTheSame()

```
  }// End of checkIfTheSame() method

/*
A method which is generic because one parameter is of type T.
This specifies that the parameter data types could be used
when passing floats, strings etc. as the second argument.
It is generic.
*/
public string checkIfTheSame(string itemOne, T itemTwo, double premium)
{
  /*
  The contains method returns true if the itemTwo is
  contained in itemOne otherwise it returns false
  */
```

```
if (itemOne.Contains(itemTwo.ToString()))
{
  return ($"The policy value {itemOne} corresponds with the value
  {itemTwo} and the premium is {premium}");
}
else
{
  return ($"The policy {itemOne} does not correspond with the value
  {itemTwo} and the premium is {premium}");
}
}// End of second checkIfTheSame() method
```

We will now call the new overloaded method from within the Main() method. As we are using the int type, we will use the <int> version of the instantiation, which we named as myPolicyMatcher.

48.   Amend the Main() method as in Listing 23-14.

Listing 23-14. Call the overloaded checkIfTheSame()

```
/*
Call the add method passing it the two policy values
with the correct data type
*/
Console.WriteLine(myPolicyMatcherString.checkIfTheSame("PL123456",
"PL123456"));

/*
Call the new method passing it the two policy values
with the correct data type
*/
Console.WriteLine(myPolicyMatcher.checkIfTheSame("PL123456",
123456, 9.99));
    } // End of Main() method
  } // End of Generics2 class
```

49.   Click the File menu.

50.   Choose Save All.

51.   Click the Debug menu.

52.   Choose Start Without Debugging.

The console window will appear, as shown in Figure 23-5, and display the details returned from the overloaded method call, which was passed an int to replace the generic T.

```
The System.Int32 values 10000 and 20000 are not equal
The System.String values PL123456 and PL123456 are equal
The policy value PL123456 corresponds with the value 123456 and the premium is 9.99

C:\CoreCs   checkIfTheSame() overloaded method has executed, the T was replaced with an int   code 0.
Press any key to close this window . . .
```

Figure 23-5. *Overloaded method returns its message*

53.   Press the Enter key to close the console window.

Generic Method Only

Think about a RenewalMatcher class that will have a method that can

- Check if the first parameter is a string.

- Convert the string to a date to see if it contains the current month:

  - If it does have this month, then the policy is due for renewal and a renewal message will be displayed.

  - Otherwise, a message stating the month of renewal will be displayed.

- If it is not a date, it must be a double.

- The first parameter is converted to a double.

- The second parameter represents the percentage increase, for example, 10 means 10%.

- The new monthly premium is calculated.

The class is not defined as generic, but the method is made generic and has two generic parameters.

54. Amend the code, as in Listing 23-15, to add the RenewalMatcher class, inside the namespace of the Generics2 class. The class has one method, which is called checkIfRenewalDateOrPremiumIncrease().

Listing 23-15. RenewalMatcher class added

```
} // End of PolicyMatcherGeneric  class

// Declare the class
class RenewalMatcher
{
  /*
  A method which is generic because of the <T>
  The method has parameters of type T.
  The method can be used when passing floats, strings etc.
  It is generic.
  */
  public string checkIfRenewalDateOrPremiumIncrease<T>(T
    itemOne, T itemTwo)
  {
    /*
    The is operator checks if the result of an expression
    is compatible with a given type
    */
    if (itemOne is string)
    {
      DateTime renewalDate = Convert.ToDateTime(itemOne);
      if (renewalDate.Month == DateTime.Now.Month)
      {
        return ($"The customers {itemTwo} " +
          $"policy is due for renewal this month ");
      }
      else
```

```
    {
        return ($"The customers {itemTwo} policy is not " +
            $"due for renewal until month {renewalDate.Month}");
    }
}
else
{
double monthlyPremium = Convert.ToDouble(itemOne.ToString());
double premiumIncrease = Convert.ToDouble(itemTwo.ToString());
double newMonthlyPremium = monthlyPremium
        + (monthlyPremium * premiumIncrease / 100);

return ($"The new monthly premium is {newMonthlyPremium:0.00}");
    }

    }// End of checkIfRenewalDateOrPremiumIncrease() method
} // End of RenewalMatcher class
} // End of Chapter23 namespace
```

Now we will make three calls, from the Main() method, to the method in our new class:

- The first call passes a string followed by a string with the month being 05, **but we should change the month in this string to match the current month on our computer.**

- The second call passes a string followed by a string with the month being 06, **but we should change the month in this string so it does not match the current month on our computer.**

- The third call passes a double followed by an int.

55. Amend the Main() method to instantiate the new class, as in Listing 23-16.

Listing 23-16. Instantiate the RenewalMatcher class added

```
/*
Call the new method passing it the two policy values
with the correct data type
```

```
*/
Console.WriteLine(myPolicyMatcher.checkIfTheSame("PL123456",
123456, 9.99));
```

// Instantiate the RenewalMatcher class
RenewalMatcher myRenewalMatcher = new RenewalMatcher();

```
} // End of Main() method
```

56. Amend the Main() method to call the new class method three
    times, as in Listing 23-17.

Listing 23-17. Call the new method three times

```
Console.WriteLine(myPolicyMatcher.checkIfTheSame("PL123456",
123456, 9.99));

// Instantiate the RenewalMatcher class
RenewalMatcher myRenewalMatcher = new RenewalMatcher();
```

// Call the checkIfRenewalDateOrPremiumIncrease three times
Console.WriteLine(myRenewalMatcher.
checkIfRenewalDateOrPremiumIncrease("01/02/2021", "Life Insurance"));
    Console.WriteLine(myRenewalMatcher.
    checkIfRenewalDateOrPremiumIncrease("01/06/2021", "Home Insurance"));
    Console.WriteLine(myRenewalMatcher.
    checkIfRenewalDateOrPremiumIncrease(9.99, 10));
```
    } // End of Main() method
```

57. Click the File menu.

58. Choose Save All.

59. Click the Debug menu.

60. Choose Start Without Debugging.

The console window will appear, as in Figure 23-6, and display the details returned
from the three method calls.

```
The System.Int32 values 10000 and 20000 are not equal
The System.String values PL123456 and PL123456 are equa
The policy value PL123456 corresponds with the value 123
The customers Life Insurance policy is due for renewal this month
The customers Home Insurance policy is not due for renewal until month 6
The new monthly premium is 10.99

C:\c  Call three - first parameter is a double, monthly premium is calculated  3.exe (pro
Press any key to close this window . . .
```

Call one - first parameter is a string, the month is the current month, so renewal is required

Call two - first parameter is a string, the month is not the current month, so renewal not required yet

Figure 23-6. *Method with two generic parameters executed*

So we have just used a generic method within a normal class, but we should look at the code of this method and see that it could and should be divided into two overloaded methods because what we are passing is a string followed by a string or double followed by an int. This method should not be doing different things depending on the types. At the start of the chapter, we said this, "Thankfully, when we wish to **have similar logic for similar types**, this is where generics come to the rescue."

So let us create overloaded methods to split out the business logic in the current method.

61. Amend the RenewalMatcher class so it now contains the two overloaded methods, as in Listing 23-18.

Listing 23-18. Overloaded methods to separate the business logic

```
} // End of PolicyMatcherGeneric class

class RenewalMatcher
  {
    /*
    Method overloading
    */
    public string checkIfRenewalDateOrPremiumIncrease<T>(string itemOne,
    T itemTwo)
    {
      /*
      The is operator checks if the result of an expression
      is compatible with a given type
      */
      DateTime renewalDate = Convert.ToDateTime(itemOne);
```

889

```
    if (renewalDate.Month == DateTime.Now.Month)
    {
      return ($"The customers {itemTwo} policy is due for renewal this
      month");
    }
    else
    {
      return ($"The customers {itemTwo} policy is not due for renewal
      until month {renewalDate.Month}");
    }

  }// End of checkIfRenewalDateOrPremiumIncrease() method

  /*
  Method overloading
  */
  public string checkIfRenewalDateOrPremiumIncrease<T>(double itemOne,
  T itemTwo)
  {
    double monthlyPremium = Convert.ToDouble(itemOne.ToString());
    double premiumIncrease = Convert.ToDouble(itemTwo.ToString());
    double newMonthlyPremium = monthlyPremium + (monthlyPremium *
    premiumIncrease / 100);

    return ($"The new monthly premium is {newMonthlyPremium:0.00}");

  }// End of checkIfRenewalDateOrPremiumIncrease() method

} // End of RenewalMatcher class
} // End of Chapter 23 namespace
```

62. Click the File menu.

63. Choose Save All.

64. Click the Debug menu.

65. Choose Start Without Debugging.

The console window will appear, as in Figure 23-7, and display the same details returned from the three method calls, but we have used overloaded methods.

```
The System.Int32 values 10000 and 20000 are not equal
The System.String values PL123456 and PL123456 are equal
The policy value PL123456 corresponds with the value 123456 and the premium
The customers Life Insurance policy is due for renewal this month
The customers Home Insurance policy is not due for renewal until month 6
The new monthly premium is 10.99

C:\CoreCSharp\CoreC                          hapter23.exe (process 1
Press any key to c
```

Call one - first parameter is a string, the month is the current month, so renewal is required

Call two - first parameter is a string, the month is not the current month, so renewal not required yet

Call three - first parameter is a double, monthly premium is calculated

Figure 23-7. *Overloaded methods used*

Chapter Summary

So, finishing this short chapter on generics, we should have seen much of what we have covered in the previous chapters on methods and classes and objects. We have seen a class that is generic and a method that is generic, and the methods we looked at could have fully generic parameters or a mixture of generic parameters and non-generic parameters. We have seen that generics give us great flexibility when we program an application, so instead of having different methods that accept different types, we can make one method that accepts different types through the use of generic types.

Wow, seriously, what an achievement. This really is elaborate programming with advanced C# features and concepts. We should be immensely proud of the learning to date. In finishing this chapter, we have increased our knowledge further. We are getting incredibly close to our target, which once seemed so far away.

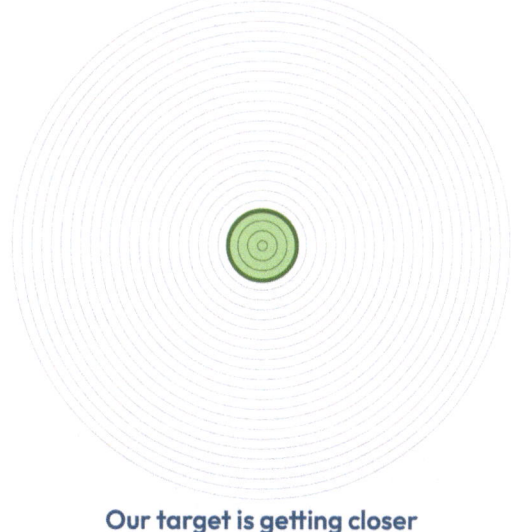

Our target is getting closer

CHAPTER 24

Common Routines

Common Programming Routines with C#

Now as we come to the end of our book and we reach our learning target, we have the core skills required to write applications in C#. We will now turn our attention to using the skills we have learned and apply them to search and sort routines that developers may commonly use when programming commercial applications. Firstly, we will look at two common search routines, linear search and binary search, and then we will look at two common sorting algorithms, bubble sort and insertion sort.

Linear Search

A linear search is used to search a series of elements in a data structure for a specified element. While a linear search can be used successfully, it will generally be slower than a binary search, which we will also look at. The linear search can be thought of as a "brute-force" algorithm since it simply compares each item in the data structure with the element being searched for. It does not need to have the state of the data structure changed before it begins, for example, it does not need to have a sorted set of elements in a chronological or alphabetical order.

If we were to see an academic or technical interview question based on a linear search, it might be in the form of a scenario like this:

> Starting with an array of n integers and having a value to find,
> decide if the value to be found exists within the given array using
> the linear search algorithm. If the target exists in the array, display
> the array index of the required value.

The algorithm to solve this problem using a linear search is as follows:

© Gerard Byrne 2022
G. Byrne, *Target C#*, https://doi.org/10.1007/978-1-4842-8619-7_24

1. Start at the first array element.

2. Check if the value being searched for matches this current value of the data structure.

3. If there is a match, the value has been found, and we return the index of the current data structure value and display it.

4. If there is no match, the value has not been found, and –1 is returned.

5. Move to the next array value.

6. Repeat from step 2 to step 5 until the end of the array has been met.

Let's code some C# and build our programming muscle.

Create an Application That Will Implement a Linear Search

Add a new project to hold the code for this chapter.

1. Right-click the solution CoreCSharp.

2. Choose Add.

3. Choose New Project.

4. Choose Console App from the listed templates that appear.

5. Click the Next button.

6. Name the project Chapter24 and leave it in the same location.

7. Click the Next button.

8. Choose the framework to be used, which in our projects will be .NET 6.0 or higher.

9. Click the Create button.

Now we should see the Chapter24 project within the solution called CoreCSharp.

10. Right-click the Chapter24 project in the Solution Explorer panel.

11. Click the Set as Startup Project option.

Notice how the Chapter24 project name has been made to have bold text, indicating that it is the new startup project and that it is the Program.cs file within it that will be executed when we run the debugging.

12. Right-click the Program.cs file in the Solution Explorer window.

13. Choose Rename.

14. Change the name to LinearSearch.cs.

15. Press the Enter key.

16. Double-click the LinearSearch.cs file to open it in the editor window.

We will now create the namespace, the class, and the Main() method.

17. Amend the code as shown in Listing 24-1.

Listing 24-1. Namespace with class and Main() method

```
namespace Chapter24
{
  internal class LinearSearch
  {
    static void Main(string[] args)
    {
    } // End of Main() method

  } // End of Customer class
} // End of Chapter24 namespace
```

We will now add a comment block, create an array, and initialize the values.

18. Amend the code as in Listing 24-2.

Listing 24-2. Comment added and array declared and initialized

```
namespace Chapter24
{
  /*
  A Linear search is a simple searching algorithm that searches
  for an element in a list in sequential order. The linear
```

```
search starts at the start of the list and checks each
element until the desired element is not found.
*/
internal class LinearSearch
{
  static void Main(string[] args)
  {
    // Declare and create the array of claim values
    int[] claimValues = { 6000, 9000, 3000, 4000, 8000, 1000, 2000,
    5000, 7000 };
  } // End of Main() method

} // End of Customer class
} // End of Chapter24 namespace
```

19. Amend the code, as in Listing 24-3, to create the variable that will
     hold the value to be found, the key.

Listing 24-3. Declare a variable and assign it the value to be found

```
static void Main(string[] args)
{
  // Declare and create the array of claim values
  int[] claimValues = { 6000, 9000, 3000, 4000, 8000, 1000, 2000,
  5000, 7000 };

  // Value to be located using linear search
  int valueToBeLocated = 1000;
} // End of Main() method
```

20. Amend the code, as in Listing 24-4, to call a method that will
     display the elements of the array.

Listing 24-4. Call a method that will display the array elements

```
  // Value to be located using linear search
  int valueToBeLocated = 1000;

  // Display the elements of the array
```

```
    DisplayArrayElements(claimValues);
  } // End of Main() method

 } // End of Customer class
} // End of Chapter24 namespace
```

We will now call a method that will perform a linear search of the array looking for a specified value and then assign the returned value to a variable.

21.   Amend the code as in Listing 24-5.

Listing 24-5. Call a method that will perform a linear search

```
// Display the elements of the array
DisplayArrayElements(claimValues);

/*
Call the linear search method passing it the array and the
value to be located and store the returned value in a variable
called returnedValue
*/
int returnedValue = SearchForTheValue(claimValues, valueToBeLocated);
  } // End of Main() method

 } // End of Customer class
} // End of Chapter24 namespace
```

We will now display one message if the returned value is –1 and another message if the returned value is not –1. The –1 value means no match was found.

22.   Amend the code as in Listing 24-6.

Listing 24-6. Display an appropriate message based on the returned value

```
int returnedValue = SearchForTheValue(claimValues, valueToBeLocated);

// Display the appropriate message (located or not)
if (returnedValue == -1)
{
  Console.WriteLine("The value is not present in array");
}
```

```
    else
    {
      // Using an interpolated string
      Console.WriteLine($"The value was located at index {returnedValue}
      (position {returnedValue + 1})");
    } // End of if else construct
} // End of Main() method

  } // End of Customer class
} // End of Chapter24 namespace
```

We will now create the method that will search the array for the required value. The method will have the array passed to it, as well as the value that is to be searched for. It is a parameter method, and it will return an integer value. The method will be created outside the Main() method.

23.   Amend the code as in Listing 24-7.

Listing 24-7. Create the method that will search the array

```
} // End of Main() method


    /*
    This value method takes in an array of integers and the
    int value of the item to be found
    */
public static int SearchForTheValue(int[] claimValuesPassedIn, int
valueToBeLocatedPassedIn)
  {
    for (int counter = 0; counter < claimValuesPassedIn.Length;
    counter++)
    {
      /*
      This line is used to display the values being
      compared, remove when completed
      */
      Console.WriteLine($"Comparing {claimValuesPassedIn[counter]} and
      {valueToBeLocatedPassedIn}");
```

```
    if(claimValuesPassedIn[counter] == valueToBeLocatedPassedIn)
    {
        return counter;
     } // End of if block
     } // End of for block

    return -1;
    } // End of SearchForTheValue() method

  } // End of Customer class
} // End of Chapter24 namespace
```

Great, that will have one of the red underlined messages in the Main() method satisfied, because the method being called now exists. So we will now create the second method that will display the array values, and this will clear the red underlined message we still have.

24.   Amend the code as in Listing 24-8.

Listing 24-8. Create the method that will display the array values

```
    return -1;
    } // End of SearchForTheValue() method

    /* Prints the array */
    static void DisplayArrayElements(int[] claimValuesPassedIn)
    {
      for (int counter = 0; counter < claimValuesPassedIn.Length;
      ++counter)
      {
        Console.WriteLine($"{claimValuesPassedIn[counter]}");
      }
    } // End of DisplayArrayElements

  } // End of Customer class
} // End of Chapter24 namespace
```

25.   Click the File menu.

26.   Choose Save All.

27. Click the Debug menu.

28. Choose Start Without Debugging.

Figure 24-1 shows the console window, and we can see that the first method to display all array elements has worked and that the second method has compared the value 1000 with the array elements and then stopped when it has found the first occurrence, which is at position 6, index 5.

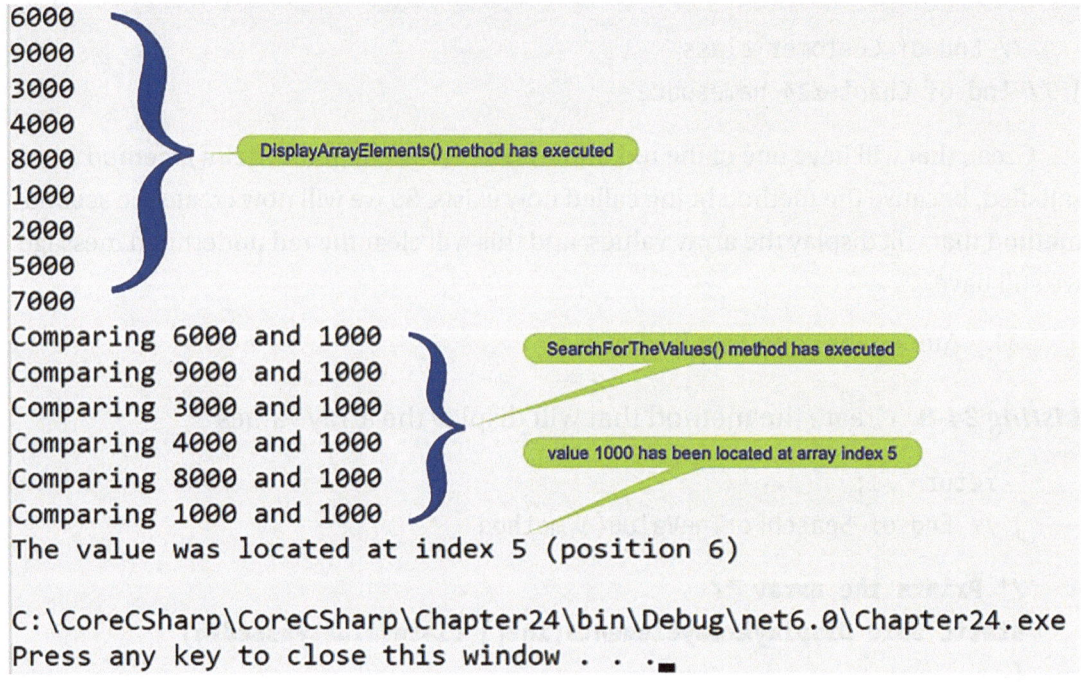

Figure 24-1. *Array elements shown; comparisons find 1000 at index 5*

29. Press the Enter key to close the console window.

Binary Search (Iterative Binary Search)

A binary search is used to search a series of elements in a data structure for a specified value, sometimes called the key. Unlike the linear search, the binary search only works when the array is sorted. The binary search starts with the full sorted array and checks if the search value is less than the item in the middle of the array:

- If it is, the search is narrowed to the lower half of the array, the left side.

- If it is not, then we use the upper half, the right side, and we repeat the process, until the value is found or there are no elements to halve.

The binary search represents a divide-and-conquer algorithm, and the algorithm will discard one half of the array in each iteration.

If we were to see an academic or technical interview question based on a binary search, it might be in the form of a scenario like this:

> Starting with a sorted array of n integers and having a value to find, decide if the value to be found exists within the given array using the binary search algorithm. If the target exists in the array, display the array index of the value.

The algorithm to solve this problem using a binary search is as follows:

- If the value to be found = array[middle value], return the middle value.

- If the value to be found < array[middle value], then discard the elements of the array to the right of the middle value including the middle value.

- If the value to be found > array[middle value], then discard the elements of the array to the left of the middle value including the middle value.

Let's code some C# and build our programming muscle.

1. Right-click the Chapter24 project.

2. Choose Add.

3. Choose Class.

4. Name the class BinarySearch.cs.

5. Click the Add button.

The BinarySearch class code will appear in the editor window and will be similar to Listing 24-9.

Listing 24-9. Namespace with BinarySearch class

```
namespace Chapter24
{
  internal class BinarySearch
  {
  } // End of BinarySearch class
} // End of Chapter24 namespace
```

6. Create a Main() method within the class, as in Listing 24-10, since this was not produced automatically, and delete the unwanted imports.

Listing 24-10. Main() method added to class

```
namespace Chapter24
{
  internal class BinarySearch
  {
    static void Main(string[] args)
    {
    } // End of Main() method
  } // End of BinarySearch class
} // End of Chapter24 namespace
```

7. Amend the code, as in Listing 24-11, to add a comment block, create an array, and initialize the values.

Listing 24-11. Comment block added, array created with initial values

```
namespace Chapter24
{
  /*
  With a binary search we must first ensure the array is sorted.
  The binary search starts with the whole array and checks if
  the value of our search key is less than the item in the
  middle of the array.
```

If it is, the search is narrowed to the lower
(left) half of the array.
If it is not, then we use the upper (right) half.
We repeat the process until the value is found or there
are elements left to half.
*/

```
internal class BinarySearch
{
  static void Main(string[] args)
  {
    // Declare and create the array of claim values
    int[] claimValues = {6000, 9000, 3000, 4000, 8000, 1000, 2000,
    5000, 7000};
  } // End of Main() method
} // End of BinarySearch class
```

8. Amend the code, as in Listing 24-12, to create the variable that will
   hold the value to be found, the key.

Listing 24-12. Declare a variable and assign it the value to be found

```
static void Main(string[] args)
{
  // Declare and create the array of claim values
  int[] claimValues = {6000, 9000, 3000, 4000, 8000, 1000, 2000,
  5000, 7000};

  // Value to be located using binary search
  int valueToBeLocated = 6000;
} // End of Main() method
} // End of BinarySearch class
```

We will now sort the array since a binary search requires a sorted array to perform a
search correctly.

9. Amend the code to sort the array as in Listing 24-13.

Listing 24-13. Sort the array prior to doing a binary search

```
// Value to be located using binary search
int valueToBeLocated = 6000;

// Sort the array as this is essential for a Binary search
Array.Sort(claimValues);
} // End of Main() method
```

10. Amend the code, as in Listing 24-14, to call a method that will display the array.

Listing 24-14. Call the method that will display the elements of the array

```
// Sort the array as this is essential for a Binary search
Array.Sort(claimValues);

// Display the elements of the array
DisplayArrayElements(claimValues);

} // End of Main() method
} // End of BinarySearch class
```

We will now call the method that will perform a binary search of the array looking for a specified value and then assign the returned value to a variable.

11. Amend the code as in Listing 24-15.

Listing 24-15. Call the method that will do the binary search

```
// Display the elements of the array
DisplayArrayElements(claimValues);

/*
Call the binary search method passing it the array and the
value to be located and store the returned value in a
variable called returnedValue
*/
int returnedValue = PerformBinarySearch(claimValues,
valueToBeLocated);
```

```
    } // End of Main() method
  } // End of BinarySearch class
```

We will perform a selection that will display one message if the returned value is –1 and a different message if the returned value is not –1. A –1 value means no match has been found.

12. Amend the code as in Listing 24-16.

Listing 24-16. Perform a selection and display an appropriate message

```
int returnedValue = PerformBinarySearch(claimValues,
valueToBeLocated);

// Display the appropriate message (located or not)
if (returnedValue == -1)
{
  Console.WriteLine("The value is not present in array");
}
else
{
  // Using an interpolated string
  Console.WriteLine($"The value was located at index {returnedValue}
  (position { returnedValue + 1})");
 } // End of if else construct
```
```
    } // End of Main() method
  } // End of BinarySearch class
```

We will now create the method that will binary search the array for the required value. In this example we are using an iterative method to perform the binary search, but there is an alternative recursive method that will work. The method will be created outside the Main() method.

13. Amend the code as in Listing 24-17.

Listing 24-17. Create the method to perform a search and return a value

```
/*
This value method takes in an array of integers and the
int value of the item to be found
*/
public static int PerformBinarySearch(int[] claimValuesPassedIn,
int valueToBeLocatedPassedIn)
{
  int firstPosition = 0;
  int lastPosition = claimValuesPassedIn.Length - 1;
  int middlePosition = (firstPosition + lastPosition) / 2;

  while (firstPosition <= lastPosition)
  {
    if (claimValuesPassedIn[middlePosition] < valueToBeLocatedPassedIn)
    {
      firstPosition = middlePosition + 1;
    }
    else if (claimValuesPassedIn[middlePosition] ==
    valueToBeLocatedPassedIn)
    {
      break;
    }
    else
    {
      lastPosition = middlePosition - 1;
    }
    middlePosition = (firstPosition + lastPosition) / 2;
  } // End of while iteration

  if (firstPosition > lastPosition)
  {
    middlePosition = -1;
  }
```

```
   return middlePosition;
 } // End of PerformBinarySearch() method
} // End of BinarySearch class
```

Great, that will have one of the red underlined messages satisfied in the Main()
method because the method being called now exists. So let us now create the second
method that will display the array values, and this will clear the red underlined message
we still have. The method will be created outside the Main() method.

14.   Amend the code as in Listing 24-18.

Listing 24-18. Create the method to display the array values

```
   return middlePosition;
 } // End of PerformBinarySearch() method

 /* Prints the array */
 static void DisplayArrayElements(int[] claimValuesPassedIn)
 {
   for (int counter = 0; counter < claimValuesPassedIn.Length;
   ++counter)
   {
     Console.WriteLine($"{claimValuesPassedIn[counter]}");
   }
 } // End of DisplayArrayElements
} // End of BinarySearch class
```

Now that we have all the code we require, we can run the application to ensure it
works as expected.

15.   Right-click the Chapter24 project in the Solution Explorer panel.

16.   Choose Properties from the pop-up menu.

17.   Choose the BinarySearch class in the Startup object drop-
      down list.

18.   Close the Properties window.

19.   Click the File menu.

20.   Choose Save All.

21.   Click the Debug menu.

22.   Choose Start Without Debugging.

Figure 24-2 shows the console, and we can see that 6000 was correctly identified as being at array index 5, which is position 6.

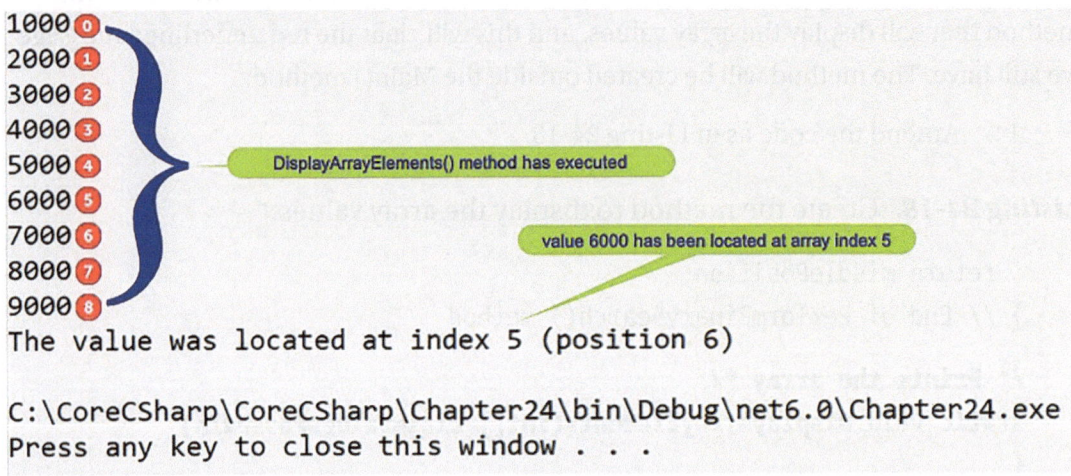

Figure 24-2.   *Array elements shown and 6000 found at index 5*

23.   Press the Enter key to close the console window.

Bubble Sort

A bubble sort is a simple sorting algorithm that works by comparing two adjacent elements of an array, and if the first element is numerically greater than the next one, the elements are swapped. The process is then repeated to move across all the elements of the array. In Chapter 11 on arrays, we saw the sort method being used through code as `Array.Sort()`. Now we are going to look at how such a sort method might work "under the hood."

If we were to see an academic or technical interview question based on a bubble sort, it might be in the form of a scenario like this:

> Starting with an array of n integers, use a bubble sort to arrange the array values in ascending order.

The algorithm to solve this problem using a bubble sort is as follows:

1. Pick the first value in the array.

2. Compare this current value with the next value.

3. If the next value is smaller than the current value, swap the two values; otherwise, leave the values as they are.

4. Move to the next number in the array.

5. Repeat steps 2–4 until we reach the last value in the array.

Let's code some C# and build our programming muscle.

1. Right-click the Chapter24 project.

2. Choose Add.

3. Choose Class.

4. Name the class BubbleSort.cs.

5. Click the Add button.

The BubbleSort class code will appear in the editor window and will be similar to Listing 24-19.

Listing 24-19. Namespace with BubbleSort class

```
namespace Chapter24
{
  internal class BubbleSort
  {
  } // End of BubbleSort class

} // End of Chapter24 namespace
```

6. Create a Main() method within the class, as in Listing 24-20, since this was not produced automatically, and delete the unwanted imports.

Listing 24-20. BubbleSort class with Main() method

```
namespace Chapter24
{
  internal class BubbleSort
  {
    static void Main(string[] args)
    {
    }// End of Main() method
  } // End of BubbleSort class
} // End of Chapter24 namespace
```

7. Amend the code, as in Listing 24-21, to add a comment block, create an array, and initialize the values.

Listing 24-21. Create the array and add a comment block

```
namespace Chapter24
{
  /*
  A Bubble sort is a simple algorithm which compares
  two adjacent elements of the array. If the first element
  is numerically greater than the next one, the elements
  are swapped. The process is then repeated to move across
  all the elements of the array.
  */
  internal class BubbleSort
  {
    static void Main(string[] args)
    {
      // Declare and create the array of claim values
      int[] claimValues = {6000, 9000, 3000, 4000, 8000, 1000, 2000,
      5000, 7000 };

    }// End of Main() method
  } // End of BubbleSort class

} // End of Chapter24 namespace
```

We will now call the method that will perform a bubble sort of the array.

8.   Amend the code, as in Listing 24-22.

Listing 24-22. Call the bubble sort method

```
static void Main(string[] args)
{
  // Declare and create the array of claim values
  int[] claimValues = {6000, 9000, 3000, 4000, 8000, 1000, 2000,
  5000, 7000 };

  /*
  Pass the array of claim values to the
  method BubbleSortTheArray()
  */
  BubbleSortOfTheArray(claimValues);

}// End of Main() method
} // End of BubbleSort class
```

9.   Amend the code, as in Listing 24-23, to call a method that will display the array.

Listing 24-23. Call the method that displays the array items

```
  BubbleSortOfTheArray(claimValues);

  Console.WriteLine("The sorted array is");

  //Pass the array to the method DisplayArrayElements()
  DisplayArrayElements(claimValues);

}// End of Main() method
} // End of BubbleSort class
} // End of Chapter24 namespace
```

We will now create the method that will bubble sort the array. The method will be created outside the Main() method.

10. Amend the code, as in Listing 24-24.

Listing 24-24. Create the method to perform a bubble sort

```
}// End of Main() method

    static void BubbleSortOfTheArray(int[] claimValuesPassedIn)
    {
      for (int outerCounter = 0; outerCounter < claimValuesPassedIn.
      Length - 1;outerCounter++)
      {
       for (int innerCounter = 0; innerCounter < claimValuesPassedIn.
       Length - outerCounter - 1; innerCounter++)
               {
        if (claimValuesPassedIn[innerCounter] > claimValuesPassedIn[inner
        Counter + 1])
        {
          // Swap the two values
          int temporaryValue = claimValuesPassedIn[innerCounter];
          claimValuesPassedIn[innerCounter] = claimValuesPassedIn[inner
          Counter + 1];
          claimValuesPassedIn[innerCounter + 1] = temporaryValue;
          DisplayArrayElements(claimValuesPassedIn);
        } // End of if construct
       } // End of for iteration inner iteration
      } // End of for iteration inner iteration
    } // End of BubbleSortTheArray method
} // End of BubbleSort class
} // End of Chapter24 namespace
```

Great, that will have one of the red underlined messages in the Main() method removed, because the method being called now exists. So we will now create the second method that will display the array values, and this will clear the red underlined message we still have. The method will be created outside the Main() method.

11. Amend the code, as in Listing 24-25.

Listing 24-25. Create the method to display the array items

```
    } // End of for iteration inner iteration
  } // End of BubbleSortTheArray method

    /* Prints the array */
    static void DisplayArrayElements(int[] claimValuesPassedIn)
    {
      for (int counter = 0; counter < claimValuesPassedIn.Length;
      ++counter)
      {
        Console.WriteLine($"{claimValuesPassedIn[counter]}");
      }
    } // End of DisplayArrayElements

  } // End of BubbleSort class
} // End of Chapter24 namespace
```

Now that we have all the code we require, we can run the application to ensure it works as expected.

12. Right-click the Chapter24 project in the Solution Explorer panel.

13. Choose Properties from the pop-up menu.

14. Choose the BubbleSort class in the Startup object drop-down list.

15. Close the Properties window.

16. Click the File menu.

17. Choose Save All.

18. Click the Debug menu.

19. Choose Start Without Debugging.

Figure 24-3 shows the last part of the console window, with the final version of the sorted array displayed.

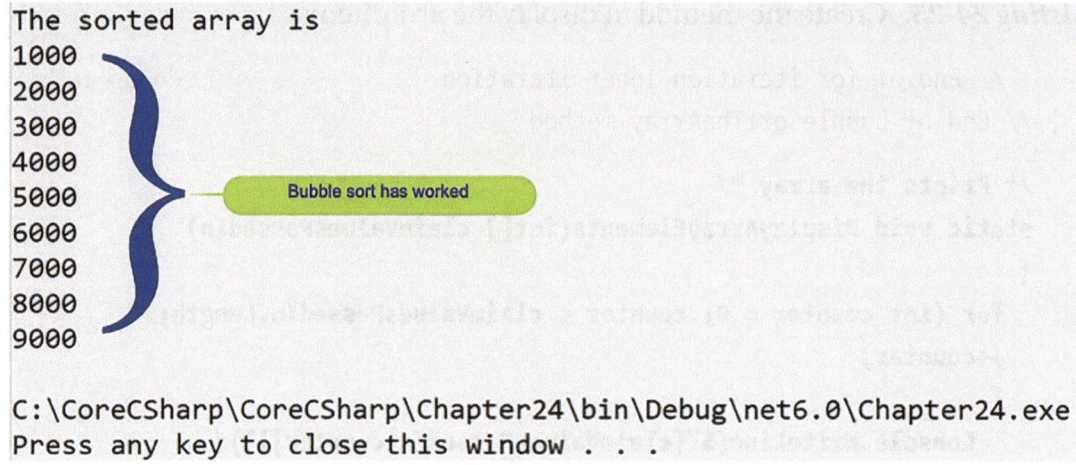

```
The sorted array is
1000
2000
3000
4000
5000          Bubble sort has worked
6000
7000
8000
9000

C:\CoreCSharp\CoreCSharp\Chapter24\bin\Debug\net6.0\Chapter24.exe
Press any key to close this window . . .
```

Figure 24-3. *Array elements sorted using a bubble sort*

20.   Press the Enter key to close the console window.

Insertion Sort

An insertion sort is similar to a bubble sort but it is a more efficient sort. We should think about using the insertion sort when we have a large number of elements to sort since larger data sets will take more time.

If we were to see an academic or technical interview question based on an insertion sort, it might be in the form of a scenario like this:

> Starting with an array of n integers, use an insertion sort to arrange the array values in ascending order.

The algorithm to solve this problem using an insertion sort is as follows:

1.   Pick the second value in the array.

2.   Compare this current value with the value to the left.

3.   If the value to the left is greater than the current value, swap the two values, repeating this comparison to the value on the left until we meet a value less than it; otherwise, leave the values as they are.

4.   Move to the next number, from the original position, in the array.

5. Repeat steps 2–4 until we reach the last value in the array.

Let's code some C# and build our programming muscle.

1. Right-click the Chapter24 project.

2. Choose Add.

3. Choose Class.

4. Name the class InsertionSort.cs.

5. Click the Add button.

The InsertionSort class code will appear in the editor window and will be similar to Listing 24-26.

Listing 24-26. Namespace with InsertionSort class

```
namespace Chapter24
{
  internal class InsertionSort
  {

  } // End of Insertion class
} // End of Chapter24 namespace
```

6. Create a Main() method within the class, as in Listing 24-27, since this was not produced automatically, and delete the unwanted imports.

Listing 24-27. InsertionSort class with Main() method

```
namespace Chapter24
{
  internal class InsertionSort
  {
    static void Main(string[] args)
    {
    } // End of Main() method
```

```
  } // End of Insertion class
} // End of Chapter24 namespace
```

7. Amend the code, as in Listing 24-28, to add a comment block, create an array, and initialize the values.

Listing 24-28. Create the array and add a comment block

```
namespace Chapter24
{
  /*
  An Insertion Sort is similar to a Bubble sort, however, it is
  a more efficient sort. We should think about using the
  Insertion sort when we have a large number of elements to sort.
  Larger data sets will take more time.
  */
  internal class InsertionSort
  {
    static void Main(string[] args)
    {
      // Declare and create the array of claim values
      int[] claimValues = {6000, 9000, 3000, 4000, 8000, 1000, 2000,
      5000, 7000 };

    } // End of Main() method

  } // End of Insertion class
} // End of Chapter24 namespace
```

We will now call the method that will perform an insertion sort of the array, and in calling the method, the array will be passed.

8. Amend the code, as in Listing 24-29.

Listing 24-29. Call the InsertionSort method, passing it the array

```
    static void Main(string[] args)
    {
      // Declare and create the array of claim values
```

```
int[] claimValues =
  {6000, 9000, 3000, 4000, 8000, 1000, 2000, 5000, 7000 };

/*
Pass the array of claim values to the
method InsertionSortTheArray()
*/
InsertionSortOfTheArray(claimValues);

} // End of Main() method
} // End of Insertion class
```

We will now call the method that will display the array elements, and in calling the method, the array will be passed.

9. Amend the code, as in Listing 24-30.

Listing 24-30. Call the method that displays the array items

```
/*
Pass the array of claim values to the
method insertionSortTheArray()
*/
InsertionSortOfTheArray(claimValues);

Console.WriteLine("The sorted array is");

// Pass the array to the method DisplayArrayElements()
DisplayArrayElements(claimValues);

} // End of Main() method
} // End of Insertion class
```

We will now create the method that will perform the insertion sort of the array. The method will be created outside the Main() method.

10. Amend the code as in Listing 24-31.

Listing 24-31. Create the method to perform the insertion sort

```
} // End of Main() method

 /* Method to sort array using an insertion sort*/
 static void InsertionSortOfTheArray(int[] claimValuesPassedIn)
 {
   for (int counter = 1; counter < claimValuesPassedIn.Length; ++counter)
 {
   int currentKeyValue = claimValuesPassedIn[counter];
   int previousValue = counter - 1;

/* Move elements that are greater than the currentArrayValue
   to one position in front of their current position */
 while (previousValue >= 0 && claimValuesPassedIn[previousValue] >
 currentKeyValue)
  {
    Console.WriteLine($"Comparing { claimValuesPassedIn[previousValue]} and
    { currentKeyValue}");

claimValuesPassedIn[previousValue + 1] = claimValuesPassedIn[previ
ousValue];
previousValue = previousValue - 1;
 }
 claimValuesPassedIn[previousValue + 1] = currentKeyValue;
     } // End of Iteration of the array
   } // End of InsertionSortOfTheArray

 } // End of Insertion class
} // End of Chapter24 namespace
```

Great, that will have one of the red underlined messages in the Main() method removed, because the method being called now exists. So we will now create the second method that will display the array values, and this will clear the red underlined message we still have. The method will be created outside the Main() method.

11.   Amend the code, as in Listing 24-32.

Listing 24-32. Create the method to display the array elements

```
} // End of insertionSortOfTheArray

/* Prints the array */
static void DisplayArrayElements(int[] claimValuesPassedIn)
{
 for (int counter = 0; counter < claimValuesPassedIn.Length; ++counter)
  {
    Console.WriteLine($"{claimValuesPassedIn[counter]}");
  }
} // End of DisplayArrayElements() method

 } // End of Insertion class
} // End of Chapter24 namespace
```

Now that we have all the code we require, we can run the application to ensure it works as expected.

12. Right-click the Chapter24 project in the Solution Explorer panel.

13. Choose Properties from the pop-up menu.

14. Choose the InsertionSort class in the Startup object drop-down list.

15. Close the Properties window.

16. Click the File menu.

17. Choose Save All.

18. Click the Debug menu.

19. Choose Start Without Debugging.

Figure 24-4 shows the last part of the console window, with the final version of the sorted array displayed.

```
1000
2000
3000
4000
5000        Insertion sort has worked
6000
7000
8000
9000
```

```
C:\CoreCSharp\CoreCSharp\Chapter24\bin\Debug\net6.0\Chapter24.exe
Press any key to close this window . . .
```

Figure 24-4. *Array elements sorted using an insertion sort*

20. Press the Enter key to close the console window.

The original array is shown in Table 24-1, and Table 24-2 shows what comparisons are made during each iteration. We will see that at the start, the following happens:

- 6000 and 9000 are compared, and as they are in the correct order, they are ignored and stay in the same positions.

- Now we swap 9000 and 3000 because 3000 is less than 9000.

- Now we check 3000 with 6000, and as 3000 is less than 6000, we swap them and so on.

Table 24-1. *Original values*

6000	9000	3000	4000	8000	1000	2000	5000	7000

Table 24-2. *Resulting iterations and the values being compared*

6000	9000	3000	4000	8000	1000	2000	5000	7000
6000	9000	3000	4000	8000	1000	2000	5000	7000
6000	3000	9000	4000	8000	1000	2000	5000	7000
3000	6000	9000	4000	8000	1000	2000	5000	7000
3000	6000	4000	9000	8000	1000	2000	5000	7000
3000	4000	6000	9000	8000	1000	2000	5000	7000
3000	4000	6000	8000	9000	1000	2000	5000	7000
3000	4000	6000	8000	1000	9000	2000	5000	7000
3000	4000	6000	1000	8000	9000	2000	5000	7000
3000	4000	1000	6000	8000	9000	2000	5000	7000
3000	1000	4000	6000	8000	9000	2000	5000	7000
1000	3000	4000	6000	8000	9000	2000	5000	7000
1000	3000	4000	6000	8000	2000	9000	5000	7000
1000	3000	4000	6000	2000	8000	9000	5000	7000
1000	3000	4000	2000	6000	8000	9000	5000	7000
1000	3000	2000	4000	6000	8000	9000	5000	7000
1000	2000	3000	4000	6000	8000	9000	5000	7000
1000	2000	3000	4000	6000	8000	5000	9000	7000
1000	2000	3000	4000	6000	5000	8000	9000	7000
1000	2000	3000	4000	5000	6000	8000	9000	7000
1000	2000	3000	4000	5000	6000	8000	7000	9000
1000	2000	3000	4000	5000	6000	7000	8000	9000

From Table 24-2 we can see what our code has produced for each iteration, and the highlighted values are the values being compared during each iteration.

Chapter Summary

In this chapter we have looked at some common search and sort algorithms in the C# programming language. The linear search, binary search, bubble sort, and insertion sort algorithms are language independent and can be used in any programming language. We simply use the same business logic, but the code will be programming language specific, for example, C#, Java, Python, JavaScript, or COBOL.

Another great achievement! This is really good. We are seeing the application of our coding skills to routines regularly used in coding. We should be immensely proud of the learning to date. In finishing this chapter, we have increased our knowledge further. We are getting very close to our target. The end is in sight.

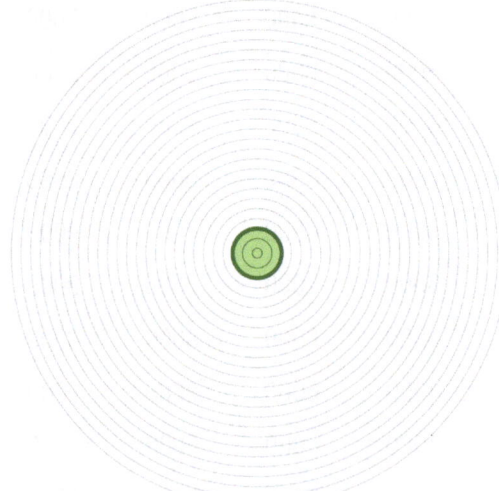

Our target is getting closer

CHAPTER 25

Programming Labs

C# Practice Exercises

The lab exercises that follow will give us an opportunity to practice what we have learned. We should complete the labs by referring to the book chapters when we are unsure about how to do something, but more importantly we should look at the previous code we have written. The code we have written should be an invaluable source of working code, and it is important not to "reinvent the wheel." Use the code - copy, paste, and amend it if required. Reuse the code – that is what the professional developer would do and is expected to do. Professional software developers are expected to create applications as fast and accurately as possible, and reusing existing code is one technique they apply, so why should we be any different?

If we really get stuck, there are sample solutions following the labs and we can refer to these, but it is important we understand any code that we copy and paste. It is also important we enjoy the challenge of developing solutions for each lab. We will apply the learning from the chapters, but more importantly we will develop our own techniques and style for coding, debugging, and problem solving.

Think about the saying

  Life begins at the edge of our comfort zone.

We will inevitably feel at the edge of our programming ability, but every new thing we learn in completing each lab should make us feel better and encourage us to learn more. While we may be "frightened" and "uncomfortable" completing the coding labs, the process will lead us to grow and develop our coding skills and build our programming muscle. We might find it "painful" at times but that is the reality of programming. We will find it exciting and challenging as we are stretched and brought to a place we have not been to before.

© Gerard Byrne 2022
G. Byrne, *Target C#*, https://doi.org/10.1007/978-1-4842-8619-7_25

Chapter 4 Labs: WriteLine()

Lab 1

Write a C# console application, using the WriteLine() command, that will display the letter E using *'s to form the shape, for example, one line could be Console. WriteLine("*******");.

Lab 2

Write a C# console application, using the WriteLine() command, that will display the letter A using *'s to form the shape, for example, one line could be Console.WriteLine (" *");.

Lab 3

Write a C# console application that will display your name and address in a format that might look like a label for an envelope – name on the first line, address line 1 on the second line, etc.

Lab 4

Using the same code that you developed for Lab 3, the name and address label, add a statement between each of the name and address lines that will require the user to press Enter on the keyboard before the display moves to the next line.

Lab 1: Possible Solution with output shown in Figure 25-1

```
namespace Labs.Chapter04
{
  internal class Lab1
  {
    static void Main(string[] args)
    {
      Console.WriteLine("*******");
      Console.WriteLine("*");
      Console.WriteLine("*");
      Console.WriteLine("*******");
```

```
        Console.WriteLine("*");
        Console.WriteLine("*");
        Console.WriteLine("*******");

    } // End of Main() method
  } // End of Lab1 class
} //End of Labs.Chapter04 namespace
```

```
*******
*
*
*******
*
*
*******
```

Figure 25-1. *Lab 1 output*

Lab 2: Possible Solution with output shown in Figure 25-2

```
namespace Labs.Chapter04
{
  internal class Lab2
  {
    static void Main(string[] args)
    {
      Console.WriteLine("      *");
      Console.WriteLine("     * *");
      Console.WriteLine("    *   *");
      Console.WriteLine("   *******");
      Console.WriteLine("  *       *");
      Console.WriteLine(" *         *");
      Console.WriteLine("*           *");

    } // End of Main() method
  } // End of Lab2 class
} //End of Labs.Chapter04 namespace
```

Figure 25-2. *Lab 2 output*

Lab 3: Possible Solution with output shown in Figure 25-3

```
namespace Labs.Chapter04
{
  internal class Lab3
  {
    static void Main(string[] args)
    {
      Console.WriteLine("Mer Gerard Byrne");
      Console.WriteLine("1 Any Street");
      Console.WriteLine("Any Road");
      Console.WriteLine("Belfast");
      Console.WriteLine("BT1 1AN");

    } // End of Main() method
  } // End of Lab3 class

} //End of Labs.Chapter04 namespace
```

```
Mr Gerard Byrne
1 Any Street
Any Road
Belfast
BT1 1AN
```

Figure 25-3. *Lab 3 output*

Lab 4: Possible Solution with output shown in Figure 25-4

```
namespace Labs.Chapter04
{
  internal class Lab4
  {
    static void Main(string[] args)
    {
      Console.WriteLine("Mr Gerard Byrne");
      Console.WriteLine("Press the enter key to continue");
      Console.ReadLine();
      Console.WriteLine("1 Any Street");
      Console.WriteLine("Press the enter key to continue");
      Console.ReadLine();
      Console.WriteLine("Any Road");
      Console.WriteLine("Press the enter key to continue");
      Console.ReadLine();
      Console.WriteLine("Belfast");
      Console.WriteLine("Press the enter key to continue");
      Console.ReadLine();
      Console.WriteLine("BT1 1AN");
    } // End of Main() method
  } // End of Lab4 class

} //End of Labs.Chapter04 namespace
```

```
Mr Gerard Byrne
Press any key to continue
1 Any Street
Press any key to continue
Any Road
Press any key to continue
Belfast
Press any key to continue
BT1 1AN
```

Figure 25-4. *Lab 4 output*

Chapter 6 Labs: Data Types

Lab 1

Write a C# console application that will calculate and display the area of a rectangle using a length of 20 and a breadth of 10, which should be hard-coded in the code. The formula for the area of a rectangle is length multiplied by breadth.

Lab 2

Write a C# console application that will calculate and display the area of a rectangle using the length and breadth that are input at the console by the user. The formula for the area of a rectangle is length multiplied by breadth.

Lab 3

Using the code from Lab 2, write a C# console application that will calculate and display the volume of a cuboid using the length, breadth, and height that are input at the console by the user. The formula for the volume of a cuboid is length multiplied by breadth multiplied by height.

Lab 4

Write a C# console application that will accept user input regarding the credit card details required for making an online purchase. The details required are

- Credit card number – Contains 16 digits and hyphens between each 4 digits

- Card expiry month – A number from 1 to 12 (Jan to Dec)

- Card expiry year – A two-digit number for the year, for example, 23

- Card issue number – A single-digit number

- Three-digit security code – A three-digit number

- Card holder name on card – A string

Display to the console the details read from the user.

Lab 1: Possible Solution with output shown in Figure 25-5

```
namespace Labs.Chapter06
{
  internal class Lab1
  {
    static void Main(string[] args)
    {
      int length;
      int breadth;
      int area;

      length = 20;
      breadth = 10;

      area = length * breadth;

      Console.WriteLine();
      Console.WriteLine($"The area of the rectangle is {area}
      square centimetres");
      Console.WriteLine();

    } // End of Main() method
  } // End of Lab1 class
} //End of Labs.Chapter06 namespace
```

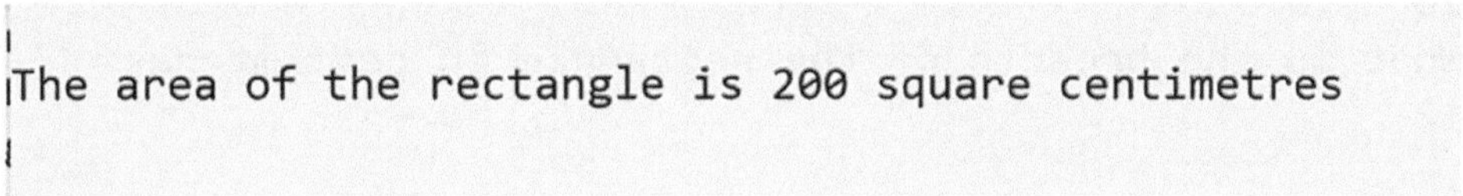

```
The area of the rectangle is 200 square centimetres
```

Figure 25-5. *Lab 1 output*

Lab 2: Possible Solution with output shown in Figure 25-6

```
namespace Labs.Chapter06
{
  internal class Lab2
  {
```

```
  static void Main(string[] args)
  {
    int length;
    int breadth;
    int area;

    Console.WriteLine("What is the length of the rectangle in
    centimetres");
    length = Convert.ToInt32(Console.ReadLine());

    Console.WriteLine("What is the breadth of the rectangle in
    centimetres");
    breadth = Convert.ToInt32(Console.ReadLine());

    area = length * breadth;

    Console.WriteLine();
    Console.WriteLine($"The area of the rectangle is {area }
    square centimetres");
    Console.WriteLine();
  } // End of Main() method
} // End of Lab2 class

} //End of Labs.Chapter06 namespace
```

```
What is the length of the rectangle in centimteres
20
What is the breadth of the rectangle in centimteres
10

The area of the rectangle is 200 square centimetres
```

Figure 25-6. Lab 2 output

Lab 3: Possible Solution with output shown in Figure 25-7

```
namespace Labs.Chapter06
{
  internal class Lab3
  {
```

```csharp
    static void Main(string[] args)
    {
      int length;
      int breadth;
      int height;
      int volume;

      Console.WriteLine("What is the length of the rectangle in
      centimetres");
      length = Convert.ToInt32(Console.ReadLine());

      Console.WriteLine("What is the breadth of the rectangle in
      centimetres");
      breadth = Convert.ToInt32(Console.ReadLine());

      Console.WriteLine("What is the height of the cuboid in
      centimetres");
      height = Convert.ToInt32(Console.ReadLine());

      volume = length * breadth * height;

      Console.WriteLine();
      Console.WriteLine($"The volume of the cuboid is {volume}
      cubic centimetres");
      Console.WriteLine();
    } // End of Main() method
  } // End of Lab3 class
} //End of Labs.Chapter06 namespace
```

```
What is the length of the rectangle in centimteres
30
What is the breadth of the rectangle in centimteres
20
What is the height of the cuboid in centimteres
10

The volume of the cuboid is 6000 cubic centimetres
```

Figure 25-7. *Lab 3 output*

Lab 4: Possible Solution with output shown in Figure 25-8

```
namespace Labs.Chapter06
{
  /*
  The class holds members (fields) and methods.
  In this example there will only be a main method.
  This is where the application will start running.
  */

  internal class Lab4
  {
    /*
    The Main method is where we will add all our variables and
    write our code. This is only suitable as we are learning to
    program but as we develop our skills we will modularise our
    code i.e. we will break the code up into small methods each
    having only one role. We might not want to declare all our
    variables in the Main method, we may want them to be
    declared inside the smaller methods (chapters). This is where
    we will begin to understand about the scope of variables.
    */
    static void Main(string[] args)
    {
    /*
    A credit card will have a 16-digit number on the front. We
    may wish to include hyphens or spaces between each set of 4
    digits. For this reason, we are making the data type string.
    */
      string creditCardNumber;

    /*
    The month in which the credit card will expire will be
    entered as a number which will be from 0 -12 based on the
    calendar months. This means we can use a byte or sbyte data
    type as it is a small value. The sbyte data type has a
    minimum value of -128 and a maximum value of 127. The byte
```

```
type has a minimum value of 0 and a maximum value of 255.
A month cannot be a negative, so we use a byte data type.
*/
  byte expiryMonth;

/*
The year of expiry only requires the last two digits of the
year, it will not require the two digits of the century.
We should use a byte data type as 0 - 255 will be an
acceptable range for the year.
*/
  byte expiryYear;

/*
The card issue number is a one or two digit number on the
front of the card. Some credit cards will not have an issue
number. For this example we should expect the user to enter
a 0 if there is no issue number.
*/
  byte issueNumber;

/*
A card verification code (CVC) is also known as the card
verification value (CVV) and is a security feature used when
the user is not present to make the payment and present the
card. It is aimed at reducing fraud.
*/
  int threeDigitCode;

/*
A credit card will have a name imprinted on it. This must be
the exact name used when making a transaction. The name will
be treated as a string input.
*/
  string nameOnCard;

//Enter the card holder name as it appears on the card
  Console.WriteLine("Enter your name as it appears " +
```

```
      "on your Credit Card");
    nameOnCard = Console.ReadLine();
```

```
  /*
```
Ask the user to enter the 16-digit credit card number as it
appears on the credit card and insert hyphens (-) between
each set of 4 digits. Then use the ReadLine() method to read
the data input at the console. The input data will be a
string, so no conversion is necessary as we are assigning
the value to a variable we declared as data type string.
```
  */
    Console.WriteLine("Enter the 16 digit credit card number");
    Console.WriteLine("Use hyphens as shown in this " +
      "example to separate each ");
    Console.WriteLine("set of 4 digits  1234-5678-1234-7890");
    creditCardNumber = Console.ReadLine();
```

```
  /*
```
Ask the user to enter the value of the expiry month. Then use
the ReadLine() method to read the data input at the console.
The input data will be a string, so a conversion is necessary
as we are assigning the value to a variable declared as data
type byte. We therefore have to use the Convert class and the
ToByte() method to convert the data read from the console.
```
  */
    Console.WriteLine("Enter the expiry month number");
    expiryMonth = Convert.ToByte(Console.ReadLine());
```

```
  /*
```
Ask the user to enter the value of the expiry year. Then use
the ReadLine() method to read the data input at the console.
```
  */
    Console.WriteLine("Enter the expiry year number");
    expiryYear = Convert.ToByte(Console.ReadLine());
```

```
  /*
```
Ask the user to enter the value for the issue number.

Then use the ReadLine() method to read the data input at the
console. The input data will be a string so a conversion is
necessary as we are assigning the value to a variable we
declared as data type byte. We therefore have to use the
Convert class and the ToByte() method to convert the data
read from the console.
*/
```
  Console.WriteLine("Enter the value for the issue number " +
    "\n(enter 0 if there is no issue number on our card)");
  issueNumber = Convert.ToByte(Console.ReadLine());
```

```
/*
```
Ask the user to enter the value of the 3-digit security code
that appears on the back of the card. Then use the ReadLine()
method to read the data input at the console. The input data
will be a string so a conversion is necessary to assign the
value to a variable we declared as data type int. We
therefore have to use the Convert class and the ToInt32()
method to convert the data read from the console.
*/
```
 Console.WriteLine("Enter the 3 digit security number " +
   "from the back of the card");
threeDigitCode = Convert.ToInt32(Console.ReadLine());
```

```
/*
```
Now we will display the data we have accepted from the user.
We use the WriteLine() method from the Console class to
display the data. The information we have between the
brackets () of the WriteLine() is a concatenation of a string
of text between the double quotes "" and a variable. We
have also used the escape sequence \n (new line) and the
\t (tab) in an attempt to format the display.
*/
```
Console.WriteLine("We have entered the following details\n");
Console.WriteLine("************************************\n");
Console.WriteLine($"Cardholder name:\t {nameOnCard}");
```

```
    Console.WriteLine($"Card number:\t\t {creditCardNumber}");
    Console.WriteLine($"Card expiry month:\t {expiryMonth}");
    Console.WriteLine($"Card expiry year:\t {expiryYear}");
    Console.WriteLine($"Card issue number:\t {issueNumber}");
    Console.WriteLine($"Card security code:\t {threeDigitCode}");
    Console.WriteLine("************************************\n");

    } // End of Main() method
  } // End of Lab4 class
} //End of Labs.Chapter06 namespace
```

```
We have entered the following details

************************************

Cardholder name:           Mr G Byrne
Card number:               1111-2222-3333-4444
Card expiry month:         6
Card expiry year:          24
Card issue number:         0
Card security code:        890
************************************
```

Figure 25-8. *Lab 4 output*

Chapter 7 Labs: Data Conversion and Arithmetic

Lab 1

Write a C# console application that will calculate the number of points accumulated by a sports team during their season. The program should ask the user to input the number of games won, the number of games drawn, and the number of games lost. The program should total the number of games played and calculate the number of points won based on the facts that 3 points are given for a win, 1 point is given for a draw, and 0 points are given for a lost game. Display the number of games played and the number of points accumulated.

Lab 2

Write a C# console application that will calculate and display

- The total score for two examinations that a student undertakes

- The average of the two scores

The two scores will be input by the user at the console and will be accepted as string values by the program code, so conversion will be needed.

Lab 1: Possible Solution with output shown in Figure 25-9

```
namespace Labs.Chapter07
{
  internal class Lab1
  {
   static void Main(string[] args)
   {
    // Declare the variables
    int numberOfGamesWon, numberOfGamesDrawn, numberOfGamesLost;
    int numberOfGamesPlayed, numberOfPointsAccumulated;

    // Input - accept user input
    Console.WriteLine("How many games were won this season?");
    numberOfGamesWon = Convert.ToInt32(Console.ReadLine());

    Console.WriteLine("How many games were drawn this season?");
    numberOfGamesDrawn = Convert.ToInt32(Console.ReadLine());

    Console.WriteLine("How many games were lost this season?");
    numberOfGamesLost = Convert.ToInt32(Console.ReadLine());

    // Process - total the number of games played
    numberOfGamesPlayed = numberOfGamesWon +
        numberOfGamesDrawn + numberOfGamesLost;

   /*
   Calculate the number of points based on 3 points for a win
   1 point for a draw and 0 points for a lost game
   */
```

```
    numberOfPointsAccumulated = (3 * numberOfGamesWon)
        + numberOfGamesDrawn;

    // Output the details
    Console.WriteLine();
    Console.WriteLine($"The number of games this season was
    {numberOfGamesPlayed}\n");
    Console.WriteLine($"The number of points achieved was
    {numberOfPointsAccumulated}");

    } // End of Main() method
  } // End of Lab1 class
} //End of Labs.Chapter07 namespace
```

```
How many games were won this season?
12
How many games were drawn this season?
10
How many games were lost this season?
8

The number of games this season was 30

The number of points achieved was 46

C:\CoreCSharp\CoreCSharp\Labs\bin\Debug\net6.0\Labs.exe
Press any key to close this window . . .
```

Figure 25-9. *Lab 1 output*

Lab 2: Possible Solution with output shown in Figure 25-10

```
namespace Labs.Chapter07
{
  internal class Lab2
  {
    static void Main(string[] args)
    {
      int scoreInTestOne, scoreInTestTwo, totalScoreForTwoTests;
      double averageOfTheTwoScores;
```

```csharp
        // Input - accept user input for test score one
        Console.WriteLine("What was the score for test one?");
        scoreInTestOne = Convert.ToInt32(Console.ReadLine());

        Console.WriteLine("What was the score for test two?");
        scoreInTestTwo = Convert.ToInt32(Console.ReadLine());

        // Process - calculate the total the number of games played
        totalScoreForTwoTests = scoreInTestOne + scoreInTestTwo;

        // Process - calculate the average the two scores
        averageOfTheTwoScores = totalScoreForTwoTests / 2.0;

        // Output the details
        Console.WriteLine("");
        Console.WriteLine($"\nThe total of the two scores is
        {totalScoreForTwoTests}");
        Console.WriteLine("\n\n");
        Console.WriteLine($"\nThe average mark for the two tests is {
        averageOfTheTwoScores}");

    } // End of Main() method
  } // End of Lab2 class
} //End of Labs.Chapter07 namespace
```

```
    What was the score for test one?
    80
    What was the score for test two?
    40

    The total of the two scores is 120
    The average mark for the two tests is 60

    C:\CoreCSharp\CoreCSharp\Labs\bin\Debug\net6.0\Labs.exe
    Press any key to close this window . . .▄
```

Figure 25-10. *Lab 2 output*

Chapter 8 Labs: Arithmetic

Lab 1

Write a C# console application that will simulate a simple payroll program. The program should

- Allow a user to input the number of hours worked by an employee.

- Allow a user to input the rate per hour, which the employee is paid.

- Calculate the gross wage, which is the hours worked multiplied by the rate per hour.

- Calculate the amount of national insurance to be deducted, where the rate of national insurance is 5% of the gross wage.

- Calculate the amount of income tax to be deducted, where the formula to be used is 20% of the gross wage after the national insurance has been deducted from the gross wage.

- Display a simplified wage slip showing, for example, the gross wage, the deductions, and the net pay.

Sample Output Using Test Data

- How many hours were worked? 40

- What was the rate per hour? £10.00

- **Payslip**

  - Hours – 40

  - Rate – £10.00

  - Gross – £400.00

  - National insurance deductions – £20.00

  - Tax deductions – £76.00

  - Net pay – £304.00

Lab 1: Possible Solution with output shown in Figure 25-11

```
namespace Labs.Chapter08
{
  internal class Lab1
  {
    static void Main(string[] args)
    {
     // Declare variables required
     int hoursWorked;
     double hourlyRate, nettPay, grossPay;
     double nationalInsuranceDeductions, incomeTaxDeductions;
     double nationalInsuranceRate = 0.05, incomeTaxRate = 0.2;

     // Input Hours Worked
     Console.WriteLine("Enter the number of hours worked: ");
     hoursWorked = Convert.ToInt32(Console.ReadLine());

     // Input Hourly Rate
     Console.WriteLine("Enter Hourly Rate: ");
     hourlyRate = Convert.ToDouble(Console.ReadLine());

     // Process - calculate the net pay
     grossPay = hoursWorked * hourlyRate;

     nationalInsuranceDeductions =
           grossPay * nationalInsuranceRate;

     incomeTaxDeductions =
       (grossPay - nationalInsuranceDeductions) * incomeTaxRate;

   nettPay = grossPay - nationalInsuranceDeductions
         - incomeTaxDeductions;

 // Output simple payslip
 Console.WriteLine($"{"PAYSLIP",22}");
 Console.WriteLine($"=================================");
 Console.WriteLine($"{"Hours Worked",-20} {hoursWorked,10}");
 Console.WriteLine($"{"Hourly Rate",-20} {hourlyRate,10:0.00}");
```

```
Console.WriteLine($"{"Gross Pay",-20} {grossPay,10:0.00}");
Console.WriteLine($"{"National
Insurance",-20}  {nationalInsuranceDeductions,10:0.00}");
Console.WriteLine($"{"Income Tax",-20}
    {incomeTaxDeductions,10:0.00}");
Console.WriteLine($"{"=======",31} \n");
Console.WriteLine($"{"Nett Pay",-20} {nettPay,10:0.00}");
Console.WriteLine($"{"=======",31} \n");

    } // End of Main() method
   } // End of Lab1 class
 } //End of Labs.Chapter08 namespace
```

```
Enter the number of hours worked:
40
Enter Hourly Rate:
10
                PAYSLIP
================================
Hours Worked                   40
Hourly Rate                 10.00
Gross Pay                  400.00
National Insurance          20.00
Income Tax                  76.00
                          =======

Nett Pay                   304.00
                          =======
```

Figure 25-11. Lab 1 output

Chapter 9 Labs: Selection

Lab 1

Write a C# console application that will ask the user to input a numeric value
representing the month of the year, 12, and the number of days in that month will be
displayed. Use a switch construct.

Lab 2

Write a C# console application that will ask the user to input the mark achieved by a student in an examination, the maximum mark being 100, and the grade achieved will be displayed. The grade will be determined using the following business logic:

- Marks greater than or equal to 90 receive Distinction.

- Marks greater than or equal to 75 receive Pass.

- Marks lesser less than 75 receive Unsuccessful.

    Use an if-else construct.

Lab 3

Write a C# console application that will ask the user to input the name of one of the programming languages – C#, Python, or Java – and a short description of the language will be displayed.

    Use an if-else construct and be careful when comparing the String values.

Lab 1: Possible Solution with output shown in Figure 25-12

```
namespace Labs.Chapter09{
  internal class Lab1{
    static void Main(string[] args){
      int month, daysInMonth = 0;
      Console.WriteLine("Enter the numeric number of the month");
      month = Convert.ToInt32(Console.ReadLine());
      switch (month)
      {
        case 1:
        case 3:
        case 5:
        case 7:
        case 8:
        case 10:
        case 12:
          daysInMonth = 31;
```

```
          break;
      case 4:
      case 6:
      case 9:
      case 11:
        daysInMonth = 30;
        break;
      case 2:
        daysInMonth = 28;
        break;
      default:
        Console.WriteLine("Invalid month!");
        break;
    }
    Console.WriteLine($"Month {month} has {daysInMonth} days");
  } // End of Main() method
} // End of Lab1 class
} //End of Labs.Chapter09 namespace
```

```
Enter the numeric number of the month
6
Month 6 has 30 days
```

Figure 25-12. *Lab 1 output*

Lab 2: Possible Solution with output shown in Figure 25-13

```
namespace Labs.Chapter09
{
  internal class Lab2
  {
    static void Main(string[] args)
    {
      String grade = null;
      Console.WriteLine("Enter the examination mark: ");
      int mark = Convert.ToInt32(Console.ReadLine());
```

```
    if (mark > 0 && mark <= 100)
    {
      if (mark >= 90)
      {
        grade = "Distinction";
      }
      else if (mark >= 75)
      {
        grade = "Pass";
      }
      else
      {
        grade = "Unsuccessful";
      }
      Console.WriteLine($"{mark} marks is a {grade} grade ");
    }
    else
    {
      Console.WriteLine("Mark must be between 1 and 100");
    }
  } // End of Main() method
 } // End of Lab2 class
} //End of Labs.Chapter09 namespace
```

```
Enter the examination mark:
78
78 marks is a Pass grade
```

Figure 25-13. *Lab 2 output*

Lab 3: Possible Solution with output shown in Figure 25-14

```
namespace Labs.Chapter09
{
  internal class Lab3
  {
```

```csharp
    static void Main(string[] args)
    {
      String userInputLanguage = null;

      Console.WriteLine("Enter the programming language: ");
      userInputLanguage = Console.ReadLine();

      if (userInputLanguage.Equals("C#"))
      {
        Console.WriteLine("C# is a modern, object-oriented, and"
        + "\n" + "type-safe programming language. C# enables "
        + "\n" + "developers to build many types of application"
        + "\n" + "that run in the .NET ecosystem.");
      }
      else if (userInputLanguage.Equals("Java"))
      {
        Console.WriteLine("Java is a programming language"
                + "\n" + "released by Sun Microsystems in 1995."
                + "\n" + "There are lots of applications and "
                + "\n" + "websites that will not work unless"
                + "\n" + "Java is installed");

      }
      else if (userInputLanguage.Equals("Python"))
      {
        Console.WriteLine("Python is an interpreted and "
                + "\n" + "object-oriented programming language");
      }
      else
      {
    Console.WriteLine("Sorry, this is not one of our languages");
      }
    } // End of Main() method
  } // End of Lab3 class
} //End of Labs.Chapter09 namespace
```

```
Enter the programming language:
C#
C# is a modern, object-oriented, and
type-safe programming language. C# enables
developers to build many types of application
that run in the .NET ecosystem.
```

Figure 25-14. *Lab 3 output*

Chapter 10 Labs: Iteration

Lab 1

Write a C# console application that will display a table showing a column with pound sterling values (£) and a second column showing the equivalent amount in US dollars ($). The pound amounts should be from £1 to £10, and the exchange rate to be used is $1.25 for each £1.00.

Sample Output

```
Pound Sterling United States Dollars
1               1.25
2               2.50
3               3.75
4               5.00
```

Lab 2

Write a C# console application that will display a table showing a column with pound sterling values (£) and a second column showing the equivalent amount in US dollars ($). Remember, reuse code. Lab 1 code might be a great starting point.

The application will ask the user to enter the number of pounds they wish to start their conversion table at and then ask them to enter the number of pounds they wish to stop their conversion table at. The application will display a table showing a column with pound values (£), starting at the user's start value and ending at the user's end value, and a second column showing the equivalent amount in US dollars ($). The exchange rate to be used is $1.25 for each £1.00.

Sample Output

```
Pound Sterling United States Dollars
5                6.25
6                7.50
7                8.75
8                10.00
```

Lab 3

Write a C# console application that will continually ask the user to input the name of a programming language, and the message "There are many programming languages including (the language input by the user)" will be displayed. The question will stop being asked when the user inputs X as the language. The message should not be displayed when X has been entered. The program will just exit.

Example Output

There are many programming languages including C#.

There are many programming languages including JavaScript.

Lab 4

Write a C# console application that will ask the user to input how many new vehicle registration numbers they wish to input. The application will continually ask the user to input a vehicle registration number until the required number of registrations have been entered. When the vehicle registration number has been entered, a message will display the number of entries that have been made.

Lab 1: Possible Solution with output shown in Figure 25-15

```
namespace Labs.Chapter10
{
  internal class Lab1
  {
    static void Main(string[] args)
    {
      // Create a variable to hold the dollar amount
      double dollarAmount;
```

```
    // Create a constant to hold the exchange rate
    const double dollarsPerPoundRate = 1.25;

    // Display a heading for the columns
    Console.WriteLine($"{"Pounds Sterling",-20} {"United States
    Dollar",-10}");

    // Iterate 10 times to convert the pounds to dollars
    for (int poundAmount = 1; poundAmount < 11; poundAmount++)
    {
      // Convert pounds to dollars at the rate assigned
      dollarAmount = poundAmount * dollarsPerPoundRate;
      Console.WriteLine($"{poundAmount,-20} {dollarAmount,-10:0.00}");
    }

  } // End of Main() method
 } // End of Lab1 class
} //End of Labs.Chapter10 namespace
```

```
Pounds Sterling          United States Dollar
1                        1.25
2                        2.50
3                        3.75
4                        5.00
5                        6.25
6                        7.50
7                        8.75
8                        10.00
9                        11.25
10                       12.50
```

Figure 25-15. *Lab 1 output*

Lab 2: Possible Solution with output shown in Figure 25-16

```
namespace Labs.Chapter10
{
  internal class Lab2
  {
```

```csharp
    static void Main(string[] args)
    {
        // Create a variable to hold the dollar amount
        double dollarAmount;

        // Create variables for the start and end values
        int startValue, endValue;

        // Create a constant to hold the exchange rate
        const double dollarsPerPoundRate = 1.25;

        // Ask the user to input the start value
        Console.WriteLine("What value do you wish to start at?");
        startValue = Convert.ToInt32(Console.ReadLine());

        // Ask the user to input the end value
        Console.WriteLine("What value do you wish to end at?");
        endValue = Convert.ToInt32(Console.ReadLine());

        // Display a heading for the columns
        Console.WriteLine($"{"Pound Sterling",-20} {"United States
        Dollar",-10}");

        /*
        Iterate starting at the users start value and
        stopping at the users end value
        */
        for (int poundAmount = startValue; poundAmount <= endValue;
        poundAmount++)
        {
            // Convert pounds to dollars at the rate assigned
            dollarAmount = poundAmount * dollarsPerPoundRate;

            Console.WriteLine($"{poundAmount,-20} {dollarAmount,-10:0.00}");
        } // End of for block

    } // End of Main() method
  } // End of Lab2 class
} //End of Labs.Chapter10 namespace
```

```
What value do you wish to start at?
5
What value do you wish to end at?
8
Pound Sterling        United States Dollar
5                     6.25
6                     7.50
7                     8.75
8                     10.00
```

Figure 25-16. *Lab 2 output*

Lab 3: Possible Solution with output shown in Figure 25-17

```csharp
using System;

namespace Labs.Chapter10{
  internal class Lab3{
    static void Main(string[] args){
      // Create a variable to hold the user input
      String programmingLanguageInput = null;
      do{
        // Ask the user to input the programming language
        Console.WriteLine("What is the programming language?");
        programmingLanguageInput = Console.ReadLine().ToUpper();

        if (programmingLanguageInput.Equals("X"))
        {
          // Display an end message
          Console.WriteLine("Goodbye");
        }
        else
        {
          // Display a heading for the columns
          Console.WriteLine($"There are many programming " +
            $"languages including {programmingLanguageInput}\n");
        }
```

```
      } while (!"X".Equals(programmingLanguageInput));
    } // End of Main() method
  } // End of Lab3 class
} //End of Labs.Chapter10 namespace
```

```
What is the programming language?
C#
There are many programming languages including C#

What is the programming language?
JavaScript
There are many programming languages including JAVASCRIPT

What is the programming language?
X
Goodbye
```

Figure 25-17. *Lab 3 output*

Lab 4: Possible Solution with output shown in Figure 25-18

```
namespace Labs.Chapter10
{
  internal class Lab4
  {
    static void Main(string[] args)
    {
      // Create a variable to hold the number of entries
      int numberOfEntriesBeingMade, numberOfEntriesCompleted = 0;

      // Ask the user to input the number of entries being made
      Console.WriteLine("How many new vehicle registrations are you
      entering?");
      numberOfEntriesBeingMade = Convert.ToInt32(Convert.ToInt32(Console.
      ReadLine()));

      while (numberOfEntriesBeingMade > numberOfEntriesCompleted)
      {
```

```
        // Ask the user to input the vehicle registration number
        Console.WriteLine("What is the vehicle registration number?");
        String vehicleRegistrationNumber = Console.ReadLine();

        // Display a message
        Console.WriteLine($"You have entered {numberOfEntriesCompleted + 1}
        vehicle registration number which was {vehicleRegistrationNumber}\n");
      numberOfEntriesCompleted++;
      }
      Console.WriteLine("Goodbye");
    } // End of Main() method
  } // End of Lab4 class
} //End of Labs.Chapter10 namespace
```

```
How many new vehicle registrations are you entering?
2
What is the vehicle registration number?
FHZ 1122
You have entered 1 vehicle registration number which was FHZ 1122

What is the vehicle registration number?
SHX 3434
You have entered 2 vehicle registration number which was SHX 3434

Goodbye
```

Figure 25-18. *Lab 4 output*

Chapter 11 Labs: Arrays

Lab 1

Write a C# console application that will use an array with the claim values: 1000.00, 4000.00, 3000.00, 2000.00. The application should calculate and display the total, average, minimum, and maximum value of the claims.

Lab 2

Write a C# console application that will ask the user to enter four employee names, store them in an array, and then iterate the array to display the names.

Lab 3

Write a C# console application that will read an array that contains a list of staff names alongside their salary and then increase the salary by 10% (1.10), and write the new details to a new array. The application should then iterate the new array and display the employee's name in column 1 and their new salary in column 1.

The original array should be

```
{"Gerry Byrne", "20000.00", "Peter Johnston", "30000.00", "Ryan Jones",
"50000.00"}
```

The new array will be

```
{"Gerry Byrne", "22000.00", "Peter Johnston", "33000.00", "Ryan Jones",
"55000.00"}
```

Lab 1: Possible Solution with output shown in Figure 25-19

```csharp
using System;

namespace Labs.Chapter11
{
 internal class Lab1
 {
  static void Main(string[] args)
  {
   // Declare the variables to be used
   double maximumValueOfClaims, minimumValueOfClaims;
   double totalValueOfClaims, averageValueOfClaims;

   // Declare and initialise the array of claim values
   double[] claimValues = {1000.00, 4000.00, 3000.00, 2000.00};

   /* Set up a variable for the total of the claim values
      and initialise its value to 0; */
    totalValueOfClaims = 0;

   // Iterate the array and accumulate the claim values
   for (int counter = 0; counter < claimValues.Length; counter++)
   {
```

```
totalValueOfClaims = totalValueOfClaims + claimValues[counter];
 } // End of for block

// Calculate the average using real arithmetic
averageValueOfClaims = totalValueOfClaims / claimValues.Length;

// Display the total and average
Console.WriteLine($"The total of the claims is " +
  $"£{totalValueOfClaims:0.00}\n");

Console.WriteLine($"The average claim value is" +
  $" £{averageValueOfClaims:0.00}\n");

// Find the maximum value - we assume first value
// is the maximum value
maximumValueOfClaims = claimValues[0];

// Compare all the other numbers to the maximum
for (int counter = 1; counter < claimValues.Length; counter++)
{
  // If the next number is greater than the maximum,
  // update the maximum
  if (claimValues[counter] > maximumValueOfClaims)
  {
    maximumValueOfClaims = claimValues[counter];
  }
} // End of for block

// Display the maximum claim value
Console.WriteLine($"The maximum claim value is " +
  $"£{maximumValueOfClaims: 0.00}\n");

// Find the minimum value- we assume the first number
// is the minimum value
 minimumValueOfClaims = claimValues[0];

// Compare all the other numbers to the minimum
for (int counter = 1; counter < claimValues.Length; counter++)
{
```

```
    // If the next number is smaller than the minimum,
    // update the minimum
    if (claimValues[counter] < minimumValueOfClaims)
    {
      minimumValueOfClaims = claimValues[counter];
    }
  } // End of for block

  // Display the minimum claim value
  Console.WriteLine($"The minimum claim value is " +
    $"£{minimumValueOfClaims: 0.00}\n");

    } // End of Main() method
  } // End of Lab1 class
} //End of Labs.Chapter11 namespace
```

```
    The total of the claims is £10000.00

    The average claim value is £2500.00

    The maximum claim value is £4000.00

    The minimum claim value is £1000.00
```

Figure 25-19. *Lab 1 output*

Lab 2: Possible Solution with output shown in Figure 25-20

```
using System;

namespace Labs.Chapter11{
  internal class Lab2{
    static void Main(string[] args){
      String[] EmployeeNames = new string[4];

      for (int employeenumber = 0; employeenumber < 4; employeenumber++)
      {
```

```
        // Ask the user to input the employee name
        Console.WriteLine($"What is the name of employee" +
          $" {employeenumber + 1}? ");

        EmployeeNames[employeenumber] = Console.ReadLine();
      }

      foreach (String name in EmployeeNames)
      {
        Console.WriteLine(name);
      }
    } // End of Main() method
  } // End of Lab2 class
} //End of Labs.Chapter11 namespace
```

```
What is the name of employee 1?
Gerry Byrne
What is the name of employee 2?
Peter Johnston
What is the name of employee 3?
Ryan Jones
What is the name of employee 4?
May Anderson
Gerry Byrne
Peter Johnston
Ryan Jones
May Anderson
```

Figure 25-20. *Lab 2 output*

Lab 3: Possible Solution with output shown in Figure 25-21

```
namespace Labs.Chapter11
{
  internal class Lab3
  {
    static void Main(string[] args)
    {
```

```
// Declare and initialise the array of employees and salary
String[] employeeAndSalary = { "Gerry Byrne", "20000.00",
  "Peter Johnston", "30000.00", "Ryan Jones", "50000.00" };

// Declare an array of employees and their new salary
String[] employeeAndSalaryWithIncrease = new
String[employeeAndSalary.Length];

// Iterate the array and find every 2nd value, the salary
for (int counter = 0; counter < employeeAndSalary.Length;
counter += 2)
{
  employeeAndSalaryWithIncrease[counter] =  employeeAndSalary[counter];

  // Create a variable of type Double (wrapper class)
  Double newSalary = Convert.ToDouble(employeeAndSalary[counter +
  1]) * 1.10;

  // Write the employee name to the new array
  employeeAndSalaryWithIncrease[counter] =
  employeeAndSalary[counter];

  // Write the Double to the array converting it to String
  employeeAndSalaryWithIncrease[counter + 1] = newSalary.
  ToString("#.00");
} // End of for block

Console.WriteLine($"{"Employee name",-20} " +
  $"{"New Salary",-15}\n");

// Compare all the other numbers to the maximum
for (int counter = 0; counter < employeeAndSalaryWithIncrease.Length;
counter += 2)
{
  // Display the Employee name and their new salary
  Console.WriteLine($"{employeeAndSalaryWithIncrease[counter],-15}
  {employeeAndSalaryWithIncrease[counter + 1],15}");
} // End of for block
```

```
    } // End of Main() method
  } // End of Lab3 class
} //End of Labs.Chapter11 namespace
```

```
Employee name            New Salary

Gerry Byrne              22000.00
Peter Johnston           33000.00
Ryan Jones               55000.00
```

Figure 25-21. Lab 3 output

Chapter 12 Labs: Methods

Lab 1

Write a C# console application that will use an array with the claim values: 1000.00, 4000.00, 3000.00, 2000.00. The application should use separate **VOID methods** to

- Calculate the total of the claim values (void method).

- Calculate the average of the claim values (void method).

- Calculate the minimum of the claim values (void method).

- Calculate the maximum of the claim values (void method).

- Display a message that states each of the calculated values (void method).

(Refer to Chapter 11 Lab 1 as the code is the same, but it is sequential.)

Lab 2

Use the code from Lab 1 to write a C# console application that will use an array with the claim values: 1000.00, 4000.00, 3000.00, 2000.00. The application should use separate **VALUE methods** to calculate the

- Total of the claim values (value method, returns a double)

- Average of the claim values (value method, returns a double)

959

- Minimum of the claim values (value method, returns a double)

- Maximum of the claim values (value method, returns a double)

and a **PARAMETER** method that accepts the four calculated values to display a message that states each of the calculated values. This parameter method will not return a value; it is also a void method.

The application should only use variables that are local to the methods we use. The declaration of the array can be at the class level.

Lab 1: Possible Solution with output shown in Figure 25-22

```
namespace Labs.Chapter12
{
  internal class Lab1
  {
    // Declare and initialise the array of claim
    // values at the class level
    static double[] claimValues = {1000.00,4000.00,3000.00,2000.00};

    /*
     Set up the variables at the class level.
    */
    static double maximumValueOfClaims, minimumValueOfClaims;
    static double totalValueOfClaims, averageValueOfClaims;

    static void Main(string[] args)
    {
      TotalOfClaimValues();
      AverageOfClaimValues();
      MaximumClaimValue();
      MinimumClaimValue();
      DisplayTheCalculatedValues();

    } // End of Main() method

    /****************************************************
    CREATE THE METHODS OUTSIDE THE MAIN METHOD
    BUT INSIDE THE CLASS
    ****************************************************/
```

```
public static void TotalOfClaimValues()
{
// Iterate the array and accumulate the claim values
for (int counter = 0; counter < claimValues.Length; counter++)
{
 totalValueOfClaims = totalValueOfClaims + claimValues[counter];
}
} // End of TotalOfClaimValues() method

public static void AverageOfClaimValues()
{
// Calculate the average using real arithmetic
averageValueOfClaims = totalValueOfClaims / claimValues.Length;
}

public static void MaximumClaimValue()
{
  // Find the maximum value - we assume first
  // value is the maximum value
  maximumValueOfClaims = claimValues[0];

  // Compare all the other numbers to the maximum
  for (int counter = 1; counter < claimValues.Length; counter++)
  {
    // If the next number is greater than the
    // maximum, update the maximum
    if (claimValues[counter] > maximumValueOfClaims)
    {
      maximumValueOfClaims = claimValues[counter];
    }
  }
} // End of MaximumClaimValue() method

public static void MinimumClaimValue()
{
  // Find the minimum value- we assume the
  // first number is the minimum value
```

```
    minimumValueOfClaims = claimValues[0];

    // Compare all the other numbers to the minimum
    for (int counter = 1; counter < claimValues.Length; counter++)
    {
      // If the next number is smaller than the minimum,
      // update the minimum
      if (claimValues[counter] < minimumValueOfClaims)
      {
        minimumValueOfClaims = claimValues[counter];
      }
    }
} // End of MinimumClaimValue() method

public static void DisplayTheCalculatedValues()
{
  // Display the total of the claim values
  Console.WriteLine($"The total of the claims " +
    $"is £{totalValueOfClaims:0.00}\n");

  // Display the average of the claim values
  Console.WriteLine($"The average claim value" +
    $" is £{averageValueOfClaims:0.00}\n");

  // Display the maximum claim value
  Console.WriteLine($"The maximum claim value is " +
    $"£{ maximumValueOfClaims:0.00}\n");

      // Display the minimum claim value
      Console.WriteLine($"The minimum claim value is " +
        $"£{ minimumValueOfClaims:0.00}\n");
  }   // End of DisplayTheCalculatedValues() method

} // End of Lab1 class
} //End of Labs.Chapter12 namespace
```

```
The total of the claims is £10000.00

The average claim value is £2500.00

The maximum claim value is £4000.00

The minimum claim value is £1000.00
```

Figure 25-22. *Lab 1 output*

Lab 2: Possible Solution with output shown in Figure 25-23

```
namespace Labs.Chapter12
{
  internal class Lab2
  {
    // Declare and initialise the array of claim
    // values at the class level
    static double[] claimValues = {1000.00,4000.00,3000.00,2000.00};

    /*
     Set up the variables at the class level.
    */
    static double maximumValueOfClaims, minimumValueOfClaims;
    static double totalValueOfClaims, averageValueOfClaims;

    static void Main(string[] args)
    {
      totalValueOfClaims = TotalOfClaimValues();
      averageValueOfClaims = AverageOfClaimValues();
      maximumValueOfClaims = MaximumClaimValue();
      minimumValueOfClaims = MinimumClaimValue();

      DisplayTheCalculatedValues(totalValueOfClaims,
      averageValueOfClaims,maximumValueOfClaims,
      minimumValueOfClaims);

    } // End of Main() method
```

```
/****************************************************
CREATE THE METHODS OUTSIDE THE MAIN METHOD
BUT INSIDE THE CLASS
****************************************************/
    public static double TotalOfClaimValues()
    {
      double totalOfClaims = 0.00;
      // Iterate the array and accumulate the claim values
      for (int counter = 0; counter < claimValues.Length; counter++)
      {
        totalOfClaims = totalOfClaims + claimValues[counter];
      }
      return totalOfClaims;
    } // End of TotalOfClaimValues() method

    public static double AverageOfClaimValues()
    {
      double averageOfClaims = 0.00;
      // Calculate the average using real arithmetic
      averageOfClaims = TotalOfClaimValues() / claimValues.Length;
      return averageOfClaims;
    }
    public static double MaximumClaimValue()
    {
      // Find the maximum value - we assume first
      // value is the maximum value
      double maximumOfClaims = claimValues[0];

      // Compare all the other numbers to the maximum
      for (int counter = 1; counter < claimValues.Length; counter++)
      {
        // If the next number is greater than the maximum,
        // update the maximum
        if (claimValues[counter] > maximumOfClaims)
        {
          maximumOfClaims = claimValues[counter];
```

```
    }
  }
  return maximumOfClaims;
} // End of MaximumClaimValue() method

public static double MinimumClaimValue()
{
  // Find the minimum value- we assume the first
  // number is the minimum value
  double minimumOfClaims = claimValues[0];

  // Compare all the other numbers to the minimum
  for (int counter = 1; counter < claimValues.Length; counter++)
  {
    // If the next number is smaller than the minimum,
    // update the minimum
    if (claimValues[counter] < minimumOfClaims)
    {
      minimumOfClaims = claimValues[counter];
    }
  }
  return minimumOfClaims;
} // End of MinimumClaimValue() method

public static void DisplayTheCalculatedValues(
  double totalValueOfClaimsPassedIn,
  double averageValueOfClaimsPassedIn,
  double maximumValueOfClaimsPassedIn,
  double minimumValueOfClaimsPassedIn)
{
  // Display the total of the claim values
  Console.WriteLine($"The total of the claims is £{totalValueOfClaimsPa
  ssedIn:0.00}\n");

  // Display the average of the claim values
  Console.WriteLine($"The average claim value is £{ averageValueOfClaim
  sPassedIn:0.00}\n");
```

```
    // Display the maximum claim value
    Console.WriteLine($"The maximum claim value is £{ maximumValueOfClaims
    PassedIn:0.00}\n");

    // Display the minimum claim value
    Console.WriteLine($"The minimum claim value is £{ minimumValueOfClaims
    PassedIn:0.00}\n");
    }  // End of DisplayTheCalculatedValues() method

  } // End of Lab2 class
} //End of Labs.Chapter12 namespace
```

```
The total of the claims is £10000.00

The average claim value is £2500.00

The maximum claim value is £4000.00

The minimum claim value is £1000.00
```

Figure 25-23. *Lab 2 output*

Chapter 13 Labs: Classes

Lab 1

Using the code from Chapter 12 Lab 2, write a C# console application that will have

- A class called CalculatedValues, with no Main() method, and inside it

  - Declare an array with the claim values: 1000.00, 4000.00, 3000.00, 2000.00.

  - Use separate **VALUE methods** to calculate the

    - Total of the claim values (value method, returns a double)

    - Average of the claim values (value method, returns a double)

    - Minimum of the claim values (value method, returns a double)

    - Maximum of the claim values (value method, returns a double)

- Declare a **PARAMETER** method that accepts the four calculated values to display a message that states each of the calculated values. This parameter method will not return a value; it is also a void method.

- A class called ClaimCalculator, with the Main() method, and inside it

  - Instantiate the CalculatedValues class.

  - Call each of the four value methods and assign the returned values to variables.

  - Pass the four variables to the parameter method, which will display the values.

The application should only use variables that are local to the methods we use. The declaration of the array can be at the class level.

Lab 2

Write a C# console application for an insurance quote that will have

- A class called QuoteMethodsClass and inside it

  - Create separate **methods** to ask the user to input

    - Their name

    - The age of their vehicle

    - The engine capacity of their vehicle

    Calculate the quote value based on the following formula:

    100 * (engine capacity/1000) * (10/age of vehicle)

  - Create a method to display the quote amount.

    Example Test 1

    Engine cc 1600

    Age of vehicle 2

    Quote value = 100 * (1600/1000) * (10/2) = 100 * 1.6 * 5 = 800

    Example Test 2

Engine cc 3000

Age of vehicle 10

Quote value = 100 * (3000/1000) * (10/10) = 100 * 3 * 1 = 300

- A class called QuoteCalculatorClass and inside it

  - Instantiate the QuoteMethodsDetails class.

  - Call each of the five methods.

The display should show the quote amount and the details that were input.

Lab 1: Possible Solution with output shown in Figure 25-24

ClaimCalculator

```
namespace Labs.Chapter13
{
  internal class ClaimCalculator
  {
    static void Main(string[] args)
    {
    /*
    Set up the variables at the class level.
    */
      double maximumValueOfClaims, minimumValueOfClaims;
      double totalValueOfClaims, averageValueOfClaims;

      // Instantiate the CalculatedValues class
      CalculatedValues myCalculatedValues = new CalculatedValues();

      // Call each method and assign each to a value
      totalValueOfClaims = myCalculatedValues.TotalOfClaimValues();
      averageValueOfClaims = myCalculatedValues.AverageOfClaimValues();
      maximumValueOfClaims = myCalculatedValues.MaximumClaimValue();
      minimumValueOfClaims = myCalculatedValues.MinimumClaimValue();

      // Pass each value to the display method
      myCalculatedValues.DisplayTheCalculatedValues(
      totalValueOfClaims, averageValueOfClaims,
```

```
      maximumValueOfClaims, minimumValueOfClaims);

    } // End of Main() method
  } // End of ClaimCalculator class
} //End of Labs.Chapter13 namespace
```

CalculatedValues

```
namespace Labs.Chapter13
{
  internal class CalculatedValues
  {
    // Declare and initialise the array of claim
    // values at the class level
    static double[] claimValues = {1000.00,4000.00,3000.00,2000.00};

    /**************************************************
      CREATE THE METHODS OUTSIDE THE MAIN METHOD
      BUT INSIDE THE CLASS
      **************************************************/
    public double TotalOfClaimValues()
    {
      double totalOfClaims = 0.00;
      // Iterate the array and accumulate the claim values
      for (int counter = 0; counter < claimValues.Length; counter++)
      {
        totalOfClaims = totalOfClaims + claimValues[counter];
      }
      return totalOfClaims;
    } // End of TotalOfClaimValues() method

    public double AverageOfClaimValues()
    {
      double averageOfClaims = 0.00;
      // Calculate the average using real arithmetic
      averageOfClaims = TotalOfClaimValues() / claimValues.Length;
      return averageOfClaims;
    }
```

```java
public double MaximumClaimValue()
{
  // Find the maximum value - we assume first
  // value is the maximum value
  double maximumOfClaims = claimValues[0];

  // Compare all the other numbers to the maximum
  for (int counter = 1; counter < claimValues.Length; counter++)
  {
    // If the next number is greater than the maximum,
    // update the maximum
    if (claimValues[counter] > maximumOfClaims)
    {
      maximumOfClaims = claimValues[counter];
    }
  }
  return maximumOfClaims;
} // End of MaximumClaimValue() method

public double MinimumClaimValue()
{
  // Find the minimum value- we assume the first number
  // is the minimum value
  double minimumOfClaims = claimValues[0];

  // Compare all the other numbers to the minimum
  for (int counter = 1; counter < claimValues.Length; counter++)
  {
    // If the next number is smaller than the minimum,
    // update the minimum
    if (claimValues[counter] < minimumOfClaims)
    {
      minimumOfClaims = claimValues[counter];
    }
  }
  return minimumOfClaims;
} // End of MinimumClaimValue() method
```

```
    public void DisplayTheCalculatedValues(
      double totalValueOfClaimsPassedIn,
      double averageValueOfClaimsPassedIn,
      double maximumValueOfClaimsPassedIn,
      double minimumValueOfClaimsPassedIn)
    {
      // Display the total of the claim values
      Console.WriteLine($"The total of the claims is £{totalValueOfClaimsPa
      ssedIn:0.00}\n");

      // Display the average of the claim values
      Console.WriteLine($"The average claim value is £{averageValueOfClaims
      PassedIn:0.00}\n");

      // Display the maximum claim value
      Console.WriteLine($"The maximum claim value is £{maximumValueOfClaims
      PassedIn:0.00}\n");

      // Display the minimum claim value
      Console.WriteLine($"The minimum claim value is £{minimumValueOfClaims
      PassedIn:0.00}\n");
    }  // End of DisplayTheCalculatedValues() method

  } // End of CalculatedValues class
} //End of Labs.Chapter13 namespace
```

```
The total of the claims is £10000.00

The average claim value is £2500.00

The maximum claim value is £4000.00

The minimum claim value is £1000.00
```

Figure 25-24. *Lab 1 output*

Lab 2: Possible Solution with output shown in Figure 25-25

QuoteMethodsClass

```
namespace Labs.Chapter13
{
  internal class QuoteMethodsClass
  {
    string customerName;
    int ageOfVehicle;
    double engineCapacity,quoteAmount;

    public void AcceptUserName()
    {
      Console.WriteLine("What is the name of the customer?");
      customerName = Console.ReadLine();
    } // End of AcceptUserName() method

    public void AcceptAgeOfVehicle()
    {
      Console.WriteLine("What is the age of the vehicle?");
      ageOfVehicle = Convert.ToInt32(Console.ReadLine());
    } // End of AcceptAgeOfVehicle() method

    public void AcceptEngineCapacityOfVehicle()
    {
      Console.WriteLine("What is the engine capacity?");
      engineCapacity = Convert.ToInt32(Console.ReadLine());
    } // End of AcceptEngineCapacityOfVehicle() method

    public void CalculateQuoteAmount()
    {
     quoteAmount = 100 * (engineCapacity/1000) * (10/ageOfVehicle);
    } // End of CalculateQuoteAmount() method

    public void DisplayQuote()
    {
```

```
        Console.WriteLine($"The vehicle to be insured for customer
        {customerName:0.00} is {ageOfVehicle} years old and has an engine
        capacity of {engineCapacity}");

        Console.WriteLine($"The quote estimate is £{quoteAmount:0.00}");
      } // End of DisplayQuote() method

  } //End of class QuoteMethodsClass
} // End of namespace Labs.Chapter13
```

QuoteCalculatorClass

```
namespace Labs.Chapter13
{
  internal class QuoteCalculatorClass
  {
    static void Main(string[] args)
    {
      QuoteMethodsClass myQuote = new QuoteMethodsClass();

      myQuote.AcceptUserName();
      myQuote.AcceptAgeOfVehicle();
      myQuote.AcceptEngineCapacityOfVehicle();
      myQuote.CalculateQuoteAmount();
      myQuote.DisplayQuote();
    } // End of Main() method

  } //End of class QuoteCalculatorClass
} // End of namespace Labs.Chapter13
```

```
What is the name of the customer?
Gerry Byrne
What is the age of the vehicle?
2
What is the engine capacity?
1600
The vehicle to be insured for customer Gerry Byrne is 2 years old and has an engine capacity of 1600
The quote estimate is £800.00
```

Figure 25-25. *Lab 2 output*

Chapter 14 Labs: Interfaces

Lab 1

Write a C# console application for an insurance quote that will have

- An interface called IVehicleInsuranceQuote and inside it there will be

  - An interface method that returns no value, has no parameters, and is called AskForDriverAge

  - An interface method that returns no value, has a parameter of type int to hold the age, and is called AskForVehicleValue

  - An interface method called CalculateQuote that returns no value and has two parameters, one of type int to hold the driver age and the other of type double to hold the vehicle value

- A class called VehicleInsuranceQuote that implements the IVehicleInsuranceQuote interface and the methods will

  - Ask the user to input their age at their last birthday.

  - Ask the user to input the value of the vehicle being insured.

  - Calculate the monthly premium based on the following formula:

(60/age of driver) * (vehicle value/5000) * 10

Example: 20-year-old driver with a car of value 50000

Monthly premium is (60/20) * (50000/5000) * 10, which is (3) * (10) * 10, which is 300.

  Have an additional method to display the quote details – driver age, vehicle value, and quote amount.

- A class called QuoteCalculator with a Main() method that calls the AskForDriverAge() method. The AskForDriverAge() method should call the AskForVehicleValue() method, passing it the age. The AskForVehicleValue() method should call the CalculateQuote() method, passing it the age and value. And the CalculateQuote() method should call the DisplayQuote() method, passing it the age, value, and quote amount.

Lab 1: Possible Solution with output shown in Figure 25-26

Interface - IVehicleInsuranceQuote

```
namespace Labs.Chapter14
{
  internal interface IVehicleInsuranceQuote
  {
    void AskForDriverAge();
    void AskForVehicleValue(int age);
    void CalculateQuote(int age, double value);
  } // End of interface IVehicleInsuranceQuote

} // End of namespace Labs.Chapter14
```

VehicleInsuranceQuote Class

```
namespace Labs.Chapter14
{
  internal class VehicleInsuranceQuote : IVehicleInsuranceQuote
  {
    public void AskForDriverAge()
    {
      Console.WriteLine("What is the age of the driver?");
      int ageOfDriver = Convert.ToInt32(Console.ReadLine());
      AskForVehicleValue(ageOfDriver);
    } // End of AskForDriverAge() method

    public void AskForVehicleValue(int ageOfDriver)
    {
      Console.WriteLine("What is the value of the vehicle?");
      double vehicleValue =  Convert.ToDouble(Console.ReadLine());
      CalculateQuote(ageOfDriver, vehicleValue);
    } // End of AskForVehicleValue() method

    public void CalculateQuote(int ageOfDriver, double vehicleValue)
    {
      double monthlyPremium = (60 / ageOfDriver) * (vehicleValue /
      5000) * 10;
```

```
      DisplayQuote(ageOfDriver, vehicleValue, monthlyPremium);
    } // End of CalculateQuote() method

    public static void DisplayQuote(int ageOfDriver, double vehicleValue,
    double monthlyPremium)
    {
      Console.WriteLine($"{"Driver age is:",-20} {ageOfDriver, -20}");
      Console.WriteLine($"{"Vehicle value is:",-20} {vehicleValue,-20}");
      Console.WriteLine($"{"Monthly premium is:",-20}
      {monthlyPremium,-20}");
    }
  } // End of class VehicleInsuranceQuote
} // End of namespace Labs.Chapter14
```

QuoteCalculator Class

```
namespace Labs.Chapter14
{
  internal class QuoteCalculator
  {
    public static void Main(string[] args)
    {
      IVehicleInsuranceQuote VehicleInsuranceQuote = new
      VehicleInsuranceQuote();

      VehicleInsuranceQuote.AskForDriverAge();


    }// End of Main() method
  } // End of class QuoteCalculator
} // End of namespace Labs.Chapter14
```

```
What is the age of the driver?
20
What is the value of the vehicle?
50000
Driver age is:        20
Vehicle value is:     50000
Monthly premium is:   300
```

Figure 25-26. *Lab 1 output*

Chapter 15 Labs: String Handling

Lab 1

Write a C# console application that will

- Have a class called Registrations and inside it

  - Declare an array of strings with the following vehicle registrations: ABC 1000, FEA 2222, QWA 4444, FAC 9098, FEA 3344.

  - Have a method to

    - Find all vehicle registrations beginning with an F and display them in the console window.

Lab 2

Write a C# console application that will

- Have a class called ClaimsPerState and inside it

  - Declare an array of strings with the following claim details: 1000IL, 2000FL, 1500TX, 1200CA, 2000NC, 3000FL.

- Have separate methods to

  - Display the full array of claim details in alphabetical order.

- Check whether a given string ends with the contents of another string and, if it does, write it to the console. In this example we will look for the string FL.

- Read the claim values and find the total of all the claim values given that the claim values are the first four numbers in the claim string.

Lab 1: Possible Solution with output shown in Figure 25-27

```
namespace Labs.Chapter15
{
  internal class Registrations
  {
    static void Main(string[] args)
    {
     string[] vehicleRegistrations = {"ABC 1000", "FEA 2222", "QWA
     4444","FAC 9098", "FEA 3344"};

   // Call the method that will find the registration
      AllRegistrationsBeginningWithSpecifiedLetter(vehicleRegistrations,'F');
    } // End of Main() method

    public static void AllRegistrationsBeginningWithSpecifiedLetter
    (string[] vehicleRegistrations, char letterInRegistration)
   {
   Console.WriteLine("Registrations beginning with character F");
   // Iterate the array
  for (int counter = 0; counter < vehicleRegistrations.Length; counter++)
     {
       // Check if the current element starts with the letter
       if (vehicleRegistrations[counter].StartsWith(letterInRegistration))
       {
         Console.WriteLine(vehicleRegistrations[counter]);
       }
     }
   }//End of allRegistrationsBeginningWithSpecifiedLetter() method
  } // End of Registrations class
} //End of Labs.Chapter15 namespace
```

```
Registrations beginning with F
FEA 2222
FAC 9098
FEA 3344
```

Figure 25-27. *Lab 1 output*

Lab 2: Possible Solution with output shown in Figure 25-28

Claims Per State

```
namespace Labs.Chapter15
{
  internal class ClaimsPerState
  {
    static void Main(string[] args)
    {
      string[] claimsWithStateAbbreviation = {"1000IL", "2000FL",
      "1500TX","1200CA", "2000NC", "0300FL"};

      // Call the DisplayTheSortedClaims() method
      Console.WriteLine("The sorted array elements are");

      DisplayTheSortedClaims(claimsWithStateAbbreviation);

      // Declare the state to be found
      string stateAbbreviationToFind = "FL";

      // Call the AllClaimsInASpecificState() method
      // passing it the string to be found
      Console.WriteLine($"The claims for the state of
      {stateAbbreviationToFind} are \n");
      AllClaimsInASpecificState(stateAbbreviationToFind,
      claimsWithStateAbbreviation);

      // Call the FindTheTotalOfAllClaimValues() method
      double totalOfAllClaims = FindTheTotalOfAllClaimValues
      (claimsWithStateAbbreviation);
```

```
  Console.WriteLine($"The total of the claim values is
  {totalOfAllClaims:0.00}");

} // End of Main() method

public static void AllClaimsInASpecificState(string
stateAbbreviationToFind, string[] claimsWithStateAbbreviation)
{
  // Iterate the array
  for (int counter = 0; counter < claimsWithStateAbbreviation.Length;
  counter++)
  {
    // Check if the current element of the array ends with
    // the letter passed to the method
    if (claimsWithStateAbbreviation[counter].EndsWith(stateAbbreviati
    onToFind))
    {
      Console.WriteLine(claimsWithStateAbbreviation[counter]);
    }
  }
} // End of AllClaimsInASpecificState() method
public static void DisplayTheSortedClaims(string[]
claimsWithStateAbbreviation)
{
  // Sort the claimsWithStateAbbreviation array
  Array.Sort(claimsWithStateAbbreviation);
  // Iterate the sorted array using the foreach construct
  foreach (string claim in claimsWithStateAbbreviation)
  {
    Console.WriteLine(claim);
  }
} // End of DisplayTheSortedClaims() method
public static double FindTheTotalOfAllClaimValues(string[]
claimsWithStateAbbreviation)
{
  double currentTotalValue = 0.00;
```

```
        double claimValue = 0.00;
        String firstFourCharacters;
        // Iterate the array
        for (int counter = 0; counter < claimsWithStateAbbreviation.Length;
        counter++)
        {
        /*
        Read the first four characters of the array element, parse
        (convert) it to a double and add it to the current total
        */
            firstFourCharacters = claimsWithStateAbbreviation[counter].
            Substring(0, 4);
            claimValue = Double.Parse(firstFourCharacters);
            currentTotalValue += claimValue;
        }
        return currentTotalValue;
    } // End of FindTheTotalOfAllClaimValues() method

  } // End of ClaimsPerState class
} //End of Labs.Chapter15 namespace
```

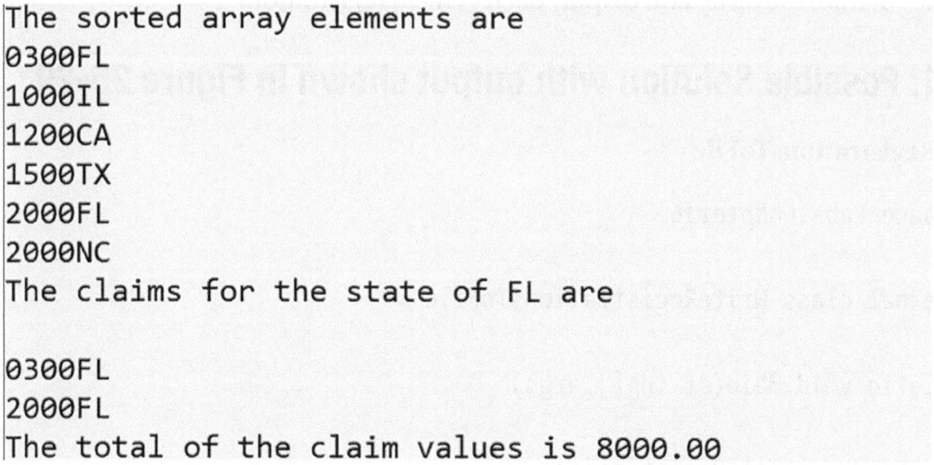

```
The sorted array elements are
0300FL
1000IL
1200CA
1500TX
2000FL
2000NC
The claims for the state of FL are

0300FL
2000FL
The total of the claim values is 8000.00
```

Figure 25-28. *Lab 2 output*

Chapter 16 Labs: File Handling

Lab 1

Write a C# console application that will

- Have a class called WriteRegistrationsToFile.

- Ask a user to input five vehicle registrations with the following format: three letters followed by a space followed by four numbers, for example, ABC 1234.

- Write each of the five vehicle registrations to a new line in a text file called vehicleregistrations.txt.

Lab 2

Write a C# console application that will

- Have a class called ReadRegistrationsFromFile.

- Declare an array of strings called vehicleRegistrations.

- Read the five lines from the vehicleregistrations.txt file created in Lab 1 and add them to the array.

- Iterate the array and display each vehicle registration.

Lab 1: Possible Solution with output shown in Figure 25-29

WriteRegistrationsToFile

```
namespace Labs.Chapter16
{
  internal class WriteRegistrationsToFile
  {
    static void Main(string[] args)
    {
      string vehicleRegistration;

      // Assign the name of the file to be used to a variable.
      string filePath = "vehicleregistrations.txt";
```

```csharp
    /*
    Create a loop to iterate 5 times asking the user
    to input a vehicle registration each time.
    */
    for (int counter = 1; counter < 6; counter++)
    {
     Console.WriteLine($"Enter registration number {counter}");
     vehicleRegistration = Console.ReadLine();

     WriteRegistrationToTextFile(vehicleRegistration, filePath);
    } // Enter of iteration

  }  // End of Main() method

  public static void WriteRegistrationToTextFile(String
  vehicleRegistration, string filePath)
  {
    // Enclose the code in a try catch to handle errors
    try
    {
      // Create a FileStream with mode CreateNew
      FileStream stream = new FileStream(filePath, FileMode.Create);

      // Create a StreamWriter from FileStream
      using (StreamWriter writer = new StreamWriter(stream))
      {
        writer.WriteLine(vehicleRegistration);
      }
    } // End of try block
    catch (Exception ex)
    {
      Console.WriteLine($"Error writing file {filePath} error was {ex}");
    } // End of the catch section of the error handling
   } // End of the writeRegistrationToTextFile() method

  } // End of WriteRegistrationsToFile class
} //End of Labs.Chapter16 namespace
```

```
Enter registration number 1
FHZ 0011
Enter registration number 2
FHZ 0012
Enter registration number 3
FHZ 0013
Enter registration number 4
SHX 1111
Enter registration number 5
SHX 1112
```

```
▲  [C#] Labs
   ▷  🖧  Dependencies
   ▷  🔊  Imports
   ▲  🗀  bin
      ▲  🗀  Debug
         ▲  🗀  net6.0
               🗋  Labs.deps.json
               🗋  Labs.dll
               🗋  Labs.exe
               🗋  Labs.pdb
               🗋  Labs.runtimeconfig.json
               🗋  vehicleregistrations.txt
```

Figure 25-29. *Lab 1 output*

Lab 2: Possible Solution with output shown in Figure 25-30

ReadRegistrationsFromFile

```
namespace Labs.Chapter16
{
  internal class ReadRegistrationsFromFile
  {
    static void Main(string[] args)
    {
      // Assign the name of the file to be used to a variable.
      string filePath = "vehicleregistrations.txt";

      // Declare and create an array to hold the 5 registrations
      string[] vehicleRegistrations = new string[5];

      ReadRegistrationFromTextFile(vehicleRegistrations, filePath);
      DisplayArrayItems(vehicleRegistrations);
    }// End of Main() method

    public static void ReadRegistrationFromTextFile(string[]
    vehicleRegistrations, string filePath)
    {
      // Set up a string variable to hold the lines read
      string line = null;
      int lineCountValue = 0;
```

```
    // Create a StreamReader from a FileStream
    using (StreamReader reader =
      new StreamReader(new FileStream(filePath,FileMode.Open)))
    {
      // Read line by line
      while ((line = reader.ReadLine()) != null)
      {
        vehicleRegistrations[lineCountValue] = line;
        lineCountValue++;
      }
    } // End of using block
  } // End of the ReadRegistrationFromTextFile() method

  public static void DisplayArrayItems(string[] vehicleRegistrations)
  {
    // Iterate the sorted array using the foreach construct
    foreach (string vehicleRegistration in vehicleRegistrations)
    {
      Console.WriteLine(vehicleRegistration);
    }
  } // End of DisplayArrayItems() method

  } // End of ReadRegistrationsFromFile class
} //End of Labs.Chapter16 namespace
```

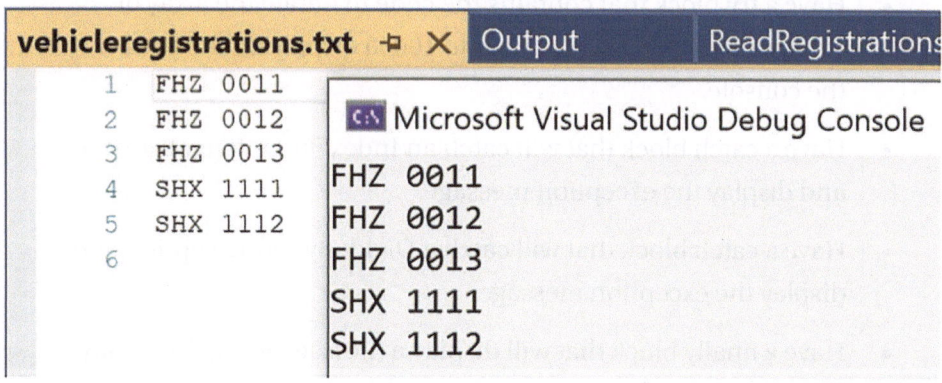

Figure 25-30. *Lab 2 output*

Chapter 17 Labs: Exceptions

Lab 1

Write a C# console application that will

- Have a class called OutOfBoundsException, which will contain a Main() method that will have code to

  - Declare an array of integers called claimValues containing the following claim values: 1000, 9000, 0, 4000, 5000.

  - Iterate the array of values and display each value to the console.

  - Have a try block that contains the code to display the sixth array item.

  - Have a catch block that will catch an IndexOutOfRangeException and display the exception message.

Lab 2

Write a C# console application that extends the code from Lab 1. The application will

- Have a class called MultipleTryCatch, which will contain a Main() method that will have code to

  - Declare an array of integers called claimValues containing the following claim values: 1000, 9000, 0, 4000, 5000.

  - Have a try block that contains the code to iterate the array of values and divide each value into 10000 displaying the answer in the console.

  - Have a catch block that will catch an IndexOutOfRangeException and display the exception message.

  - Have a catch block that will catch a DivideByZeroException and display the exception message.

  - Have a finally block that will display a message to say "In finally block tidying up".

Lab 1: Possible Solution with output shown in Figure 25-31

```
namespace Labs.Chapter17
{
 internal class OutOfBoundsException
 {
 public static void Main(string[] args)
 {
 int[] claimValues = { 1000, 9000, 0, 4000, 5000 };

 for (int i = 0; i < claimValues.Length; i++)
 {
   Console.WriteLine(claimValues[i]);
 }

 try
 {
   // Write a value which is outside the array upper limit
   Console.WriteLine(claimValues[5]);

 }
 catch (IndexOutOfRangeException ex)
 {
  // Display the exception message received
    Console.WriteLine($"Exception is - {ex.Message}");
 }
 }// End of Main() method
} // End of OutOfBoundsException class
} //End of Labs.Chapter17 namespace
```

```
1000
9000
0
4000
5000
Exception is - Index was outside the bounds of the array.
```

Figure 25-31. Lab 1 output

Lab 2: Possible Solution with output shown in Figure 25-32

```
namespace Labs.Chapter17{
  internal class MultipleTryCatch{
    public static void Main(string[] args){
      int[] claimValues = { 1000, 9000, 0, 4000, 5000 };
      try
      {
        // Divide each array vale into 10000
        for (int i = 0; i < claimValues.Length; i++)
        {
    Console.Write($"Dividing 10000 by {claimValues[i]} gives ");
          Console.WriteLine($"{10000 / claimValues[i]}");
        }
        // Write a value which is outside the array upper limit
        Console.WriteLine(claimValues[5]);
      }
      catch (IndexOutOfRangeException ex)
      {
        // Display the exception message received
        Console.WriteLine($"Exception is {ex.Message}");
      }
      // Catch block to catch the divide by zero exception
      catch (DivideByZeroException ex)
      {
      Console.WriteLine($"an exception - {ex.Message}");
      }
      // Finally block to tidy up etc, this block always runs
      finally
      {
          Console.WriteLine("\nIn finally block tidying up");
      }
    }// End of Main() method
  } // End of OutOfBoundsException class
} //End of Labs.Chapter17 namespace
```

```
Dividing 10000 by 1000 gives 10
Dividing 10000 by 9000 gives 1
Dividing 10000 by 0 gives an exception - Attempted to divide by zero.

In finally block tidying up
```

Figure 25-32. *Lab 2 output*

Chapter 18 Labs: Serialization of a Class

Lab 1

Write a C# console application that will

- Have a class called Vehicle, which implements Serializable.

- The Vehicle class will have

  - Two private string properties called vehicleManufacturer and vehicleType

  - One private nonserialized property called vehicleChassisNumber

  - A constructor using all three properties

  - Getters and setters for the properties

- Have a class called VehicleJson, which will

  - Instantiate the Vehicle class and pass details of a vehicle to the constructor, for example:

    ```
    Vehicle myVehicle = new Vehicle("Ford", "Mondeo", "VIN
    1234567890");
    ```

  - Write the serialized data to a file called vehicleserialized.ser.

  - Read the serialized data file and display the vehicle details.

Lab 2

Write a C# console application that will

- Have a class called AgentEntity, which implements Serializable

  - The AgentEntity class will have

  - The following private properties:

- agentNumber, which is of data type int

- agentYearsOfService, which is of data type int

- agentFullName, which is of data type string

- The following private nonserialized properties:

  - agentDOB, which is of data type string

  - agentCapitalInvestment, which is of data type double

- A constructor using all the properties

- Getters and setters for all the properties

- Have a class called AgentJson, which will

  - Instantiate the AgentEntity class and pass details of an agent to the constructor, for example:

    AgentEntity myAgentEntity = **new** AgentEntity(190091, 25, "Gerry Byrne", "01/01/1970", 50000.00);

  - Write the serialized data to a file called agentserialized.ser.

  - Read the serialized data file and display the agent details.

Lab 1: Possible Solution with output shown in Figure 25-33

Vehicle Class (Entity)

```
using System.Text.Json.Serialization;

namespace Labs.Chapter18
{
  [Serializable]
  internal class Vehicle
  {
    // Members of the class.
    // [JsonIgnore] members are not serialised
    private string vehicleManufacturer;
    private string vehicleType;

    // Example for [NonSerialized]
```

```csharp
    [JsonIgnore] private String vehicleChassisNumber;

    public string VehicleManufacturer
    {
      get => vehicleManufacturer; set => vehicleManufacturer = value;
    }
    public string VehicleType
    {
      get => vehicleType; set => vehicleType = value;
    }
    public string VehicleChassisNumber
    {
      get => vehicleChassisNumber; set => vehicleChassisNumber = value;
    }

    public Vehicle(string vehicleManufacturer, string vehicleType, string
    vehicleChassisNumber)
    {
      this.VehicleManufacturer = vehicleManufacturer;
      this.VehicleType = vehicleType;
      this.VehicleChassisNumber = vehicleChassisNumber;
    } // End of constructor

  } // End of Vehicle class
} // End of namespace Labs.Chapter18
```

VehicleJson Serialization and Read Class

```csharp
using System.Text.Json;

namespace Labs.Chapter18
{
  internal class VehicleJson
  {
    public static async Task Main()
    {
      string filePath = "vehicleserialized.ser";

      Vehicle myVehicle = new Vehicle("Ford", "Mondeo", "VIN 1234567890");
```

```
    //Serialize
    string jsonString = JsonSerializer.Serialize<Vehicle>(myVehicle);

    Console.WriteLine(jsonString);

    await CreateJSON(myVehicle, filePath);

    ReadJSON(filePath);
} // End of Main() method

public static async Task CreateJSON(Vehicle myVehicle, string filePath)
{
    using FileStream createStream = File.Create(filePath);
    await JsonSerializer.SerializeAsync(createStream, myVehicle);
    createStream.Close();
    await createStream.DisposeAsync();

    Console.WriteLine(File.ReadAllText(filePath));
} // End of CreateJSON() method

public static void ReadJSON(string filePath)

    using FileStream myStream = File.OpenRead(fileName);
    Vehicle myVehicle = JsonSerializer.Deserialize<Vehicle>(myStream);

    Console.WriteLine("Vehicle Details");
    Console.WriteLine("Vehicle Name: " + myVehicle.VehicleManufacturer);
    Console.WriteLine("VehicleVehicle Age: " + myVehicle.VehicleType);
    Console.WriteLine("Customer Account No: " + myVehicle.
    VehicleChassisNumber);

    } // End of ReadJSON() method
  } // End of class VehicleJson
} // End of namespace
```

```
{ ⊟
    "VehicleManufacturer":"Ford",
    "VehicleType":"Mondeo",
    "VehicleChassisNumber":"VIN 1234567890"
}
```

Labs.pub
Labs.runtimeconfig.json
Vehicle.json
vehicleregistrations.txt
VehicleSerialisedData.ser
vehicleserialized.ser
anter04

Figure 25-33. *Lab 1 output*

Lab 2: Possible Solution with output shown in Figure 25-34

AgentEntity Class

```
using System.Text.Json.Serialization;

namespace Labs.Chapter18
{
  [Serializable]
  internal class AgentEntity
  {
  /*
  Members of the class are private as we have getters and
  setters and we have two [NonSerialized] members as we do
  not want them to be serialised
  */
    private int agentNumber;
    private int agentYearsOfService;
    private string agentFullName;
    [JsonIgnore] private String agentDOB;
    [JsonIgnore] private double agentCapitalInvestment;

    public AgentEntity(int agentNumber, int agentYearsOfService,
      string agentFullName, string agentDOB,
      double agentCapitalInvestment)
    {
      this.agentNumber = agentNumber;
      this.agentYearsOfService = agentYearsOfService;
      this.agentFullName = agentFullName;
      this.agentDOB = agentDOB;
      this.agentCapitalInvestment = agentCapitalInvestment;
    } // End of AgentEntity constructor

    public int AgentNumber
    {
      get => agentNumber;
      set => agentNumber = value;
    }
```

```
    public int AgentYearsOfService
    {
      get => agentYearsOfService;
      set => agentYearsOfService = value;
    } // End of AgentYearsOfService property
    public string AgentFullName
    {
      get => agentFullName;
      set => agentFullName = value;
    } // End of AgentFullName property
    public string AgentDOB
    {
      get => agentDOB;
      set => agentDOB = value;
    } // End of AgentDOB property
    public double AgentCapitalInvestment
    {
      get => agentCapitalInvestment;
      set => agentCapitalInvestment = value;
    } // End of AgentCapitalInvestment property

  }// End of class AgentEntity
} // End of namespace Labs.Chapter18
```

AgentJson Serialization and Read Class

```
using System.Text.Json;

namespace Labs.Chapter18
{
  internal class AgentJson
  {
    public static async Task Main()
    {
      string filePath = "agentserialized.ser";

      AgentEntity myAgent = new AgentEntity(190091, 25, "Gerry Byrne",
      "01/01/1970", 50000.00);
```

```csharp
    //Serialize
    string jsonString = JsonSerializer.Serialize<AgentEntity>(myAgent);

    Console.WriteLine(jsonString);

    await CreateJSON(myAgent, filePath);

    ReadJSON(filePath);
  } // End of Main() method

  public static async Task CreateJSON(AgentEntity myAgent, string
  filePath)
  {
    using FileStream createStream = File.Create(filePath);
    await JsonSerializer.SerializeAsync(createStream, myAgent);
    createStream.Close();
    await createStream.DisposeAsync();

    Console.WriteLine(File.ReadAllText(filePath));
  } // End of CreateJSON() method

  public static void ReadJSON(string filePath)
  {
    using FileStream myStream = File.OpenRead(filePath);
    AgentEntity myAgent = JsonSerializer.Deserialize<AgentEntity>(myStream);

    Console.WriteLine("Agent Details");
    Console.WriteLine("Agent Number: " + myAgent.AgentNumber);
    Console.WriteLine("Years of service: " + myAgent.
    AgentYearsOfService);
    Console.WriteLine("Full Name: " + myAgent.AgentFullName);
    Console.WriteLine("Date of birth: " + myAgent.AgentDOB);
    Console.WriteLine("Investment: " + myAgent.AgentCapitalInvestment);

  } // End of ReadJSON() method
 } // End of class VehicleJson
} // End of namespace
```

```
{"AgentNumber":190091,"AgentYearsOfService":25,"AgentFullName":"
Gerry Byrne","AgentDOB":"01/01/1970","AgentCapitalInvestment":50
000}
Agent Details
Agent Number: 190091
Years of service: 25
Full Name: Gerry Byrne
Date of birth: 01/01/1970
Investment: 50000
```

Figure 25-34. *Lab 2 output*

Chapter 19 Labs: Structs

Lab 1

Write a C# console application that will

- Have a class called AutoInsurance, which will have

    - A struct called Vehicle, which will have

        - Variables to hold the vehicle manufacturer, chassis number, color, and engine capacity

        - A constructor that accepts values for all four variables

        - Getters and setters for the variables

        - A method to display the manufacturer name

        - A method to display the engine capacity

- Have a Main() method that will have code to

    - Instantiate the Vehicle struct and pass details of a vehicle to the constructor, for example:

        Vehicle myVehicle = **new** Vehicle("Ford", "VIN 1234567890", "Blue",1600);

    - Call the method that displays the manufacturer name.

    - Call the method that displays the engine capacity.

Lab 2

Write a C# console application that will

- Have a class called PropertyInsurance, which will have

  - A struct called Apartment, which will have

    - Variables to hold the number of rooms, area of the floor, and the estimated value

    - A constructor that accepts values for all three variables

    - A constructor that accepts values for the number of rooms variable and the area of the floor variable and sets the estimated value to be 1000000

    - A method to display a message stating the values of the three struct members

- Have a Main() method that will have code to

  - Instantiate an Apartment struct and pass details of an apartment with all three values to the constructor, for example:

    ```
    Apartment studioOne= new Apartment(2, 50, 120000);
    ```

  - Instantiate an Apartment struct and pass details of an apartment with only two values to the constructor, for example:

    ```
    Apartment studioTwo= new Apartment(3, 60);
    ```

  - Call the method that displays the apartment details for studioOne.

  - Call the method that displays the apartment details for studioTwo.

Lab 1: Possible Solution with output shown in Figure 25-35

```
namespace Labs.Chapter19
{
  internal class AutoInsurance
  {
```

```csharp
struct Vehicle
{
  //Variables
  string vehicleManufacturer;
  string vehicleChassisNumber;
  string vehicleColor;
  int vehicleEngineCapacity;

  // Custom constructor
  public Vehicle(string vehicleManufacturer,
    string vehicleChassisNumber, string vehicleColor,
    int vehicleEngineCapacity)
  {
    this.vehicleManufacturer = vehicleManufacturer;
    this.vehicleChassisNumber = vehicleChassisNumber;
    this.vehicleColor = vehicleColor;
    this.vehicleEngineCapacity = vehicleEngineCapacity;
  }

  //Properties for the struct variable - getters and setters
  public string VehicleManufacturer
  {
    get => vehicleManufacturer;
    set => vehicleManufacturer = value;
  }
  public string VehicleChasisNumber
  {
    get => vehicleChassisNumber;
    set => vehicleChassisNumber = value;
  }
  public string VehicleColor
  {
    get => vehicleColor;
    set => vehicleColor = value;
  }
  public int VehicleEngineCapacity
```

```
    {
      get => vehicleEngineCapacity;
      set => vehicleEngineCapacity = value;
    }

    // Methods of the struct
    public void DisplayManufacturerName()
    {
      Console.WriteLine($"The vehicle manufacturer is
      {vehicleManufacturer}");
    } // End of DisplayManufacturerName() method

    public void DisplayEngineCapacity()
    {
      Console.WriteLine($"The engine capacity is
      {vehicleEngineCapacity}");
    } // End of DisplayEngineCapacity() method

  } // End of the Vehicle struct

  // Main method code for the AutoInsurance class
  static void Main(string[] args)
  {
    Vehicle myVehicle = new Vehicle("Ford", "VIN 1234567890",
    "Blue", 1600);

    myVehicle.DisplayManufacturerName();
    myVehicle.DisplayEngineCapacity();
  } // End of Main() method

  } // End of class AutoInsurance
} // End of namespace Labs.Chapter19
```

```
The vehicle manufacturer is Ford
The engine capacity is 1600
```

Figure 25-35. *Lab 1 output*

Lab 2: Possible Solution with output shown in Figure 25-36

```
namespace Labs.Chapter19
{
  internal class PropertyInsurance
  {
    public struct Apartment
    {
      int numberOfRooms;
      int floorArea;
      double estimatedValue;

      // Members are initialized using the constructor
      public Apartment(int numberOfRooms, int floorArea,
        double estimatedValue)
      {
        this.numberOfRooms = numberOfRooms;
        this.floorArea = floorArea;
        this.estimatedValue = estimatedValue;
      } // End of the first constructor

      // A second constructor to initialize 1 member that has not
      // been given a value in this form of the constructor
      public Apartment(int numberOfRooms, int floorArea)
      {
        this.numberOfRooms = numberOfRooms;
        this.floorArea = floorArea;
        this.estimatedValue = 1000000.00;
      } // End of the second constructor

      public void DisplayValues()
      {
        Console.WriteLine($"The apartment has {this.numberOfRooms.
        ToString()} rooms");

        Console.WriteLine($"The floor area of the apartment is {this.
        floorArea.ToString()} square metres");
```

```
        Console.WriteLine($"The estimated value of the apartment is {this.
        estimatedValue.ToString()}");

        Console.WriteLine();
      } // End of the DisplayValues() method

    } // End of the struct Apartment

    static void Main(string[] args)
    {
      Apartment studioOne = new Apartment(2, 50, 120000.00);
      Apartment studioTwo = new Apartment(3, 60 );

      studioOne.DisplayValues();

      Console.WriteLine();
      Console.WriteLine("This apartment was not been given an estimated
      value\nso the constructor that has been used has set the value as
      1000000");
      Console.WriteLine();
      studioTwo.DisplayValues();
    }  // End of the Main() method

  } // End of the class PropertyInsurance
} // End of the namespace Labs.Chapter19
```

```
The apartment has 2 rooms
The floor area of the apartment is 50 square metres
The estimated value of the apartment is 120000


This apartment was not been given an estimated value
so the constructor that has been used has set the
value as 1000000

The apartment has 3 rooms
The floor area of the apartment is 60 square metres
The estimated value of the apartment is 1000000
```

Figure 25-36. Lab 2 output

Chapter 20 Labs: Enumerations
Lab 1

Write a C# console application that will

- Have a class called AutoInsurance, which will have

    - An enumeration called **Manufacturer**, which will have the values Ford, Chevrolet, Jeep, and Honda

    - An enumeration called **Color**, which will have the values Red, Blue, and Green

    - A struct called Vehicle, which will have

        - Variables to hold the vehicle manufacturer of enum type **Manufacturer** and the vehicle color of enum type **Color**

        - A constructor that accepts values for the two variables of enum type **Manufacturer** and enum type **Color**

        - A method to display the manufacturer name and the vehicle color

- Have a Main() method that will have code to

    - Instantiate a Vehicle struct and pass details of a vehicle to the constructor, for example:

      ```
      Vehicle myVehicleOne = new Vehicle(Manufacture.Ford,
      Color.Blue);
      ```

    - Call the method that displays the vehicle details.

    - Instantiate a Vehicle struct and pass details of a vehicle to the constructor, for example:

      ```
      Vehicle myVehicleTwo = new Vehicle(Manufacture.Jeep,
      Color.Green);
      ```

- Call the method that displays the vehicle details.

Lab 2

Write a C# console application that will

- Have a class called PropertyInsurance, which will have

    - An enumeration called **InsuranceRiskEnum**, which will have the values Low = 1, Medium = 10, and High = 20

    - An enumeration called **LocationFactorEnum**, which will have the values NotNearRiver, NearRiver

    - An enumeration called **PropertyTypeEnum**, which will have the values Bungalow, House, and Apartment

    - Have a Main() method that will have code to

    - Call an AskForPropertyType() method that returns an int and assign it to a variable of type int called propertyType.

    The method will display a menu and return the integer value entered:

    ```
    Console.WriteLine("What is the property type, 1 2 or 3?");
    Console.WriteLine("1. Bungalow ");
    Console.WriteLine("2. House");
    Console.WriteLine("3. Apartment");
    int  propertyType = Convert.ToInt32(Console.ReadLine());

    return propertyType;
    ```

    - Call an AskForPropertyLocation() method that returns a string and assign it to a variable of type string called isNearARiver.

    The method will ask if the property is within 50 meters of a river and returns the value entered, either Y or N:

    ```
    Console.WriteLine("Is the property within 50 metres " +
    "of a river?");

    string nearARiver = Console.ReadLine();
    return nearARiver;
    ```

- Call an AskForPropertyValue() method that returns a double and assign it to a variable of type double called estimatedValue.

  The method will ask for the property value and return the estimated value:

  ```
  Console.WriteLine("What is the estimated value of " +
  "the property?");
  ```

  ```
  double estimatedValue = Convert.ToDouble(Console.ReadLine());
  return estimatedValue;
  ```

- Call the method QuoteAmount(), passing it the values for the propertyType, isNearARiver, and estimatedValue.

  Calculate the quote amount based on the following formula:

  ```
  double quoteAmount = (propertyTypeRiskFactor *
  (propertyValue / 10000) * locationFactor
  ```

  The propertyTypeRiskFactor is based on the property type in the enum InsuranceRiskEnum – Bungalow is High, House is Medium, and Apartment is Low.

  The locationFactor is whether the property is located near a river and uses the enum LocationFactorEnum – Y (Yes) is 10, N (No) is 1.

- Call the method that displays the quote details.

Lab 1: Possible Solution with output shown in Figure 25-37

```
using System;

namespace Labs.Chapter20
{
  internal class AutoInsurance
  {
    public enum Manufacturer
    {
      Ford,
      Chevrolet,
```

```csharp
    Jeep,
    Honda
}

public enum Color
{
    Red,
    Blue,
    Green
}

struct Vehicle
{
    //Variables
    Manufacturer vehicleManufacturer;
    Color vehicleColor;

    // Custom constructor
    public Vehicle(Manufacturer vehicleManufacturer, Color vehicleColor)
    {
        this.vehicleManufacturer = vehicleManufacturer;
        this.vehicleColor = vehicleColor;
    }
    // Methods of the struct
    public void DisplayVehiclerDetails()
    {
        Console.WriteLine($"The vehicle manufacturer is
        {vehicleManufacturer}");
        Console.WriteLine($"The vehicle color is {vehicleColor}");
    } // End of DisplayVehiclerDetails() method

} // End of the Vehicle struct

// Main method code for the AutoInsurance class
static void Main(string[] args)
{
```

```
        Vehicle myVehicleOne =
          new Vehicle(Manufacturer.Ford,Color.Blue);

        myVehicleOne.DisplayVehiclerDetails();

        Console.WriteLine();
        Vehicle myVehicleTwo =
          new Vehicle(Manufacturer.Jeep, Color.Green);

        myVehicleTwo.DisplayVehiclerDetails();
      } // End of Main() method

    } // End of class AutoInsurance
} // End of namespace Labs.Chapter20
```

```
The vehicle manufacturer is Ford
The vehicle color is Blue

The vehicle manufacturer is Jeep
The vehicle color is Green
```

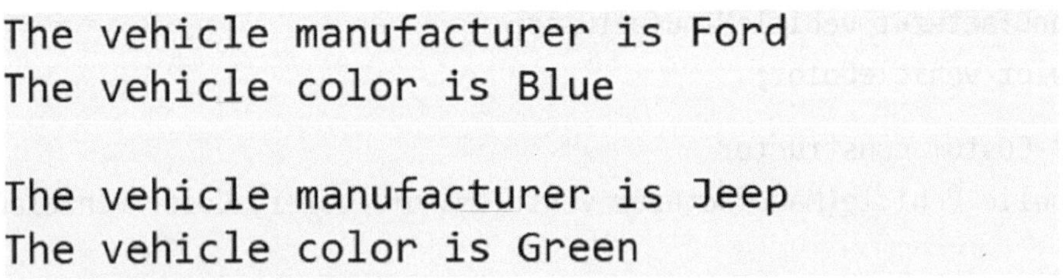

Figure 25-37. *Lab 1 output*

Lab 2: Possible Solution with output shown in Figure 25-38

```
using System;

namespace Labs.Chapter20
{
  internal class PropertyInsurance
  {
    public enum InsuranceRiskEnum
    {
      Low = 1,
      Medium = 10,
      High = 20,
    }
```

```
public enum LocationFactorEnum
{
  NotNearRiver = 1,
  NearRiver = 10,
}

public enum PropertyTypeEnum
{
  Bungalow,
  House,
  Apartment
}
static void Main(string[] args)
{
  int propertyType = AskForPropertyType();
  string isNearARiver = AskForPropertyLocation();
  double estimatedValue = AskForPropertyValue();

  QuoteAmount(propertyType, isNearARiver, estimatedValue);
} // End of Main() method

public static int AskForPropertyType()
{
  Console.WriteLine("What is the property type, 1 2 or 3?");
  Console.WriteLine("1. Bungalow ");
  Console.WriteLine("2. House");
  Console.WriteLine("3. Apartment");
  int  propertyType = Convert.ToInt32(Console.ReadLine());
  return propertyType;
} // End of PropertyType() method

public static string AskForPropertyLocation()
{
  Console.WriteLine("Is the property within 50 metres " +
    "of a river?");
```

```csharp
      string nearARiver = Console.ReadLine();
      return nearARiver;
    } // End of PropertyLocation() method

    public static double AskForPropertyValue()
    {
      Console.WriteLine("What is the estimated value of " +
        "the property?");

    double estimatedValue = Convert.ToDouble(Console.ReadLine());
      return estimatedValue;
    } // End of PropertyValue() method

  public static int PropertyLocationRiskFactor(string nearRiver)
    {
      int locationFactor;
      if (nearRiver.Equals("Y"))
      {
       locationFactor = (int)LocationFactorEnum.NearRiver;
      }
      else
      {
        locationFactor = (int)LocationFactorEnum.NotNearRiver;
      }
      return locationFactor;
    } // End of PropertyRiskFactor() method

    public static void QuoteAmount(int propertyType,
      string isPropertyNearARiver, double propertyValue)
    {
      int propertyTypeRiskFactor;
      switch (propertyType)
      {
        case 1:
          propertyTypeRiskFactor = (int)InsuranceRiskEnum.High;
          break;
```

```
      case 2:
        propertyTypeRiskFactor = (int)InsuranceRiskEnum.Medium;
        break;
      case 3:
        propertyTypeRiskFactor = (int)InsuranceRiskEnum.Low;
        break;
      default:
        propertyTypeRiskFactor = 9999;
        break;
    }

    double quoteAmount = (propertyTypeRiskFactor
        * (propertyValue / 10000)
        * PropertyLocationRiskFactor(isPropertyNearARiver));

    DisplayQuote(propertyType, isPropertyNearARiver,
      propertyValue, quoteAmount);
} // End of QuoteAmount() method

public static void DisplayQuote(int propertyType,
  string isPropertyNearARiver, double propertyValue,
  double quoteAmount)
{
  if (isPropertyNearARiver.Equals("Y"))
  {
    isPropertyNearARiver = "Yes";
  }
  else
  {
    isPropertyNearARiver = "No";
  }
  Console.WriteLine("Quote Details");
  Console.WriteLine($"{"Property Type is:", -30} " +
    $"{Enum.GetName(typeof(PropertyTypeEnum),
    propertyType-1), -20}");
```

```
    Console.WriteLine($"{"Property Near River:",-30} " +
        $"{isPropertyNearARiver,-20}");

    Console.WriteLine($"{"Property Value is:",-30} " +
        $"{propertyValue,-20}");

    Console.WriteLine();
    Console.WriteLine($"{"Quote amount is:",-30} " +
        $"{quoteAmount,-20}");

    } // End of DisplayQuote() method


  } // End of class PropertyInsurance
} // End of namespace Labs.Chapter20
```

```
What is the property type, 1 2 or 3?
1. Bungalow
2. House
3. Apartment
1
Is the property within 50 metres of a river?
Y
What is the estimated value of the property?
100000
Quote Details
Property Type is:              Bungalow
Property Near River:           Yes
Property Value is:             100000

Quote amount is:               2000
```

Figure 25-38. *Lab 2 output*

Chapter 21 Labs: Delegates

Lab 1

Write a C# console application that will allow for funds to be added to or withdrawn from a bank account. The application will

- Have a class called CustomerAccount and inside it

  - Declare a static variable `double currentBalance`.

    - Declare a method called **AddFunds**. The method is a value method that returns a value of type double, accepts a value of type double, adds the value passed in to the current balance, and returns the new balance.

  - Define the delegate at the namespace level (**this is step 1 of 3**):

    `public delegate double AmendFundsDelegate(double amount);`

- Have a Main() method that will

  - Instantiate the CustomerAccount class as

    `CustomerAccount myCustomer = new CustomerAccount();`

  - Instantiate the delegate `AmendFundsDelegate amendBalance;` and then create the new object, passing it the AddFunds method (**this is step 2 of 3**):

    `amendBalance = new AmendFundsDelegate(myCustomer.AddFunds);`

  - Have a variable of type double called transactionAmount, assigning it a value of 100.00.

  - Invoke the delegate, passing it the transactionAmount (**this is step 3 of 3**).

  - Display the new account balance.

Lab 2

Write a C# console application that will act as a simple calculator to add numbers. The application will

- Define the delegate at the namespace level (**this is step 1 of 3**):

  ```
  public delegate void CalculatorDelegate(int firstNumber, int
  secondNumber);
  ```

- Have a class called **Calculator** and inside it

  - Declare a method called **Add.** The method is a void method that accepts two values of type int and displays the sum of the two values.

  - Declare a method called **Subtract.** The method is a void method that accepts two values of type int and displays the difference between the two values.

- Have a class called **CalculatorApplication** and inside it

  - Have a Main() method that will

    - Instantiate the Calculator class as

      ```
      Calculator my Calculator = new Calculator();
      ```

    - Instantiate the delegate (**this is step 2 of 3**):

      ```
      CalculatorDelegate myDelegate1 = new CalculatorDelegate
      (myCalculator.Add);
      ```

    - Invoke the delegate, passing it the two required values 8 and 2 (**this is step 3 of 3**):

      ```
      myDelegate1.Invoke(8, 2);
      ```

Repeat steps 2 and 3 for the Subtract method, passing in 8 and 2.

Lab 1: Possible Solution with output shown in Figure 25-39

```
namespace Labs.Chapter21
{
  internal class CustomerAccount
  {
    static double currentBalance;

    /*
    Define the methods we will use. Here we will use one
    non static methods
    */
    public double AddFunds(double amountIn)
    {
      return currentBalance += amountIn;
    } // End of AddFunds() method

    public double WithdrawFunds(double amountOut )
    {
      return currentBalance -= amountOut;
    } // End of WithdrawFunds() method

    /*
    Define the delegates
    We have an access modifier, a return type and the
    parameters of the delegate. This essentially defines the
    methods that can be associated with the delegate, the methods
    must have the same attributes

    A delegate can be declared in the class and therefore
    it is available only to that class's members
    It can be declared in the namespace and therefore it is
    available to all namespace classes and outside the namespace
    */

    /*
    This is step 1. define the delegate, of 3 steps
    */
    public delegate double AmendFundsDelegate(double amount);
```

```csharp
    static void Main(string[] args)
    {
      /*
      The steps to use when dealing with delegates are
      1. define the delegate
      2. instantiate the delegate
      3. invoke the delegate
      */
      // Instantiate the CustomerAccount class
      CustomerAccount myCustomer = new CustomerAccount();

      /*
      Instantiate delegate by passing the name of the
      target function as its argument. In this case we will use
      the non static methods so we use the instance name
      This is step 2. instantiate the delegate, of 3 steps
      */
      AmendFundsDelegate amendBalance;
      amendBalance = new AmendFundsDelegate(myCustomer.AddFunds);

      double transactionAmount = 100.00;

      /*
      Now we Invoking The Delegates
      This is step 3. invoke the delegate, of 3 steps
      we could also just use amendBalance(100);
      */
      amendBalance.Invoke(transactionAmount);

      Console.WriteLine($"The new balance is : {currentBalance}");

     // Console.WriteLine(amendBalance.Invoke(transactionAmount + 1000));
    } // End of Main() method
  } // End of class CustomerAccount

} // End of namespace Labs.Chapter21
```

```
The new balance is : 100
```

Figure 25-39. *Lab 1 output*

Lab 2: Possible Solution with output shown in Figure 25-40

```
namespace Labs.Chapter21
{
  /*
  Define the delegates
  We have an access modifier, a return type and the
  parameters of the delegate. This essentially defines the
  methods that can be associated with the delegate, the methods
  must have the same attributes
  This is step 1. define the delegate, of 3 steps

  A delegate can be declared in the class and therefore
  it is available only to that class's members
  It can be declared in the namespace and therefore it is
  available to all namespace classes and outside the namespace
  */
  public delegate void CalculatorDelegate(int firstNumber, int secondNumber);

  internal class Calculator
  {
    /*
    Define the methods we will use. Here we will use one
    non static and one static method
    */
    public void Add(int numberOne, int numberTwo)
    {
      Console.WriteLine($"The total of {numberOne} and {numberTwo}, is
      {numberOne + numberTwo}");
    }
```

```csharp
    public void Subtract(int numberOne, int numberTwo)
  {
    Console.WriteLine($"The difference between {numberOne} and
    {numberTwo}, is {numberOne - numberTwo}");
  }
} // End of the class Calculator

internal class CalculatorApplication
{
  static void Main(string[] args)
  {
    // Instantiate the Calculator class
    /*
     The steps to use when dealing with delegates are
      1. define the delegate
      2. instantiate the delegate
      3. invoke the delegate
    */
    Calculator myCalculator = new Calculator();

    /*
    Instantiate delegate by passing the name of the
    target function as its argument. In this case we will use
    the non static method so we use the instance name
    This is step 2. instantiate the delegate, of 3 steps
    */
    CalculatorDelegate myDelegate1 = new
    CalculatorDelegate(myCalculator.Add);
    /*
    Now we Invoking The Delegates
    This is step 3. invoke the delegate, of 3 steps
    we could also just use myAddDelegate(8, 2);
    */
    myDelegate1.Invoke(8, 2);
```

```
    /*
    Instantiate delegate by passing the name of the
    target function as its argument. In this case we will use
    the static method so we use the class name not the instance
    This is step 2. instantiate the delegate, of 3 steps
    */
    CalculatorDelegate myDelegate2 = new CalculatorDelegate(myCalculator.
    Subtract);

    /*
    Now we Invoking The Delegates
    This is step 3. invoke the delegate, of 3 steps
    we could also just use myAddDelegate(8, 2);
    */
    myDelegate2.Invoke(8, 2);
  }
 } // End of the class CalculatorApplication
} // End of namespace Labs.Chapter21
```

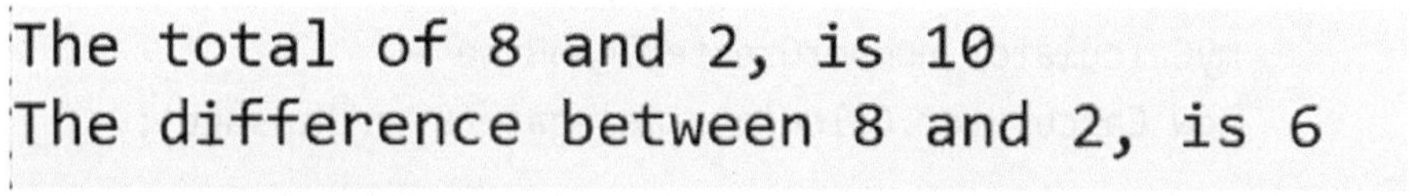

```
The total of 8 and 2, is 10
The difference between 8 and 2, is 6
```

Figure 25-40. *Lab 2 output*

Chapter 22 Labs: Events

Lab 1

Write a C# console application that will allow numbers to be added together, and when the total is greater than a specific value, an event is fired. The application will

- Have a class called Calculator and inside it
  - Define the delegate:

    `public delegate void CalculatorDelegate();`

  - Define the event that links to the delegate:

    `public event CalculatorDelegate NumberGreaterThanNine;`

- Have an Add() method that

  - Accepts two integers as its parameters.

  - Adds the two numbers and assigns the answer to a variable called answer.

  - Will have a selection construct to check if the answer is greater than 9. If it is, the event `NumberGreaterThanNine()` is called; otherwise, no action is needed.

  - Display the two numbers and the answer in the console.

- Have another class called CalculatorApplication, in the same namespace, and inside it

  - Have a Main() method that will

    - Instantiate the Calculator class as

      ```
      Calculator myCalculator = new Calculator();
      ```

    - Bind the event with the delegate and point to the EventMessage() method:

      ```
      myCalculator.numberGreaterThanNine +=
      new Calculator.CalculatorDelegate(EventMessage);
      ```

    - Call the Add() method from the Calculator class, passing it the values 8 and 2:

      ```
      myCalculator.Add(8,2);
      ```

  Outside the Main() method but inside the CalculatorApplication class

    - Create the EventMessage() method so that it outputs a message:

      ```
      static void EventMessage()
      {
      Console.WriteLine("*Number greater than 9  detected*");
      }
      ```

Lab 2

Write a C# console application that will check if any repair claim amounts are greater than a value of 5000, displaying a message if they are. The application will

- Have a class called RepairClaimCheckerLogic and inside it

    - Define the delegate:

      ```
      public delegate void RepairClaimCheckerDelegate(int
      claimNumber, double claimValue);
      ```

    - Define the event that links to the delegate:

      ```
      public event RepairClaimCheckerDelegate OverLimit;
      ```

    - Declare and create an array to hold three values of data type double:

      ```
      double[] repairClaimsAmounts = new double[3];
      ```

    - Have a GetRepairClaimData() method that

        - Accepts no parameters

        - Will have an iteration construct to iterate three times and ask the user to input the repair claim amount, storing each input value in the array of doubles

    - Have a ReadAndCheckRepairClaims() method that

        - Accepts no parameters

        - Will have an iteration construct to iterate three times and read the repair claim amount from the array of doubles and check if the value is greater than 5000. If the value is greater than 5000, then the overLimit event is called, passing it the position of the value in the array and the value that is exceeding the 5000 limit.

- Have another class called RepairClaimChecker, in the same namespace, and inside it

    - Have a Main() method that will

        - Instantiate the RepairClaimCheckerLogic class as

```
RepairClaimCheckerLogic myRepairClaimCheckerLogic
= new RepairClaimCheckerLogic();
```

- Call the GetRepairClaimData() method from the
  RepairClaimCheckerLogic class:

```
myRepairClaimCheckerLogic.GetRepairClaimData();
```

- Bind the event with the delegate and point to the
  OverLimitMessage() method:

```
myRepairClaimCheckerLogic.overLimit
+= new RepairClaimCheckerLogic.RepairClaimChecker
Delegate(OverLimitMessage);
```

Outside the Main() method but inside the
RepairClaimChecker class, create the OverLimitMessage()
method so that it outputs a message:

```
static void OverLimitMessage(int claimNumber,
double value)
{
Console.WriteLine($"*** Claim {claimNumber} for
{value} needs to be verified***");
}
```

- Call the ReadAndCheckRepairClaims () method from the
  RepairClaimCheckerLogic class:

```
myRepairClaimCheckerLogic.ReadAndCheckRepairClaims();
```

Lab 1: Possible Solution with output shown in Figure 25-41

```
namespace Labs.Chapter22
{
  // Subscriber class
  public class CalculatorApplication
  {
    static void Main(string[] args)
    {
      Calculator myCalculator = new Calculator();
```

```
    /*
    Event is bound with the delegate
    Here we are creating a delegate, a pointer, to the method
    called EventMessage and adding it to the list of
    Event Handlers
    */
    myCalculator.NumberGreaterThanNine +=
      new Calculator.CalculatorDelegate(EventMessage);

    // Call the Add method in the Calculator class
    myCalculator.Add(8,2);
  }

  /*
  Delegates call this method when the event is raised.
  This is the code that executes when NumberGreaterThanNine
  is fired
  */
  static void EventMessage()
  {
    Console.WriteLine("* Number greater than 9 detected *");
  }
} // End of the class CalculatorApplication

// Publisher class
public class Calculator
{
  /*
  Declare the delegate. This delegate can be used to point to
  any method which is a void method and accepts no parameters
  */
  public delegate void CalculatorDelegate();

  /*
  Declare the event. This event can cause any method that
  matches the CalculatorDelegate to be called
  */
  public event CalculatorDelegate NumberGreaterThanNine;
```

```
    public void Add(int numberOne, int numberTwo)
    {
      int answer = numberOne + numberTwo;
      if(answer > 9)
      {
        /*
        Here we are raising the event and this event is linked
        to the method called EventMessage() which accepts
        no values and displays a message
        */
        NumberGreaterThanNine(); // Raised event
      }
      Console.WriteLine($"The total of {numberOne} and {numberTwo}, is
      {numberOne + numberTwo} ");
    }

  } // End of the class Calculator
} // End of namespace Labs.Chapter22
```

```
* Number greater than 9 detected *
The total of 8 and 2, is 10
```

Figure 25-41. *Lab 1 output*

Lab 2: Possible Solution with output shown in Figure 25-42

```
namespace Labs.Chapter22
{
  /*
  A DELEGATE is a type which defines a method signature and
  holds a reference for a method whose signature will match the
  delegate. Therefore delegates are used to reference a method.

  An EVENT is a 'notification' which is raised by an object
  to signify the occurrence of some action. Our delegate is then
  associated with the event and holds a reference to a
  method which will be called when the event is raised.
```

An event is associated with an Event Handler using a Delegate.
When the Event is raised it sends a signal to delegates
and the delegate executes the correct matching function.

The steps to use events are:

1: Define the Delegate
2: Define the Event with same the same name as the Delegate.
3: Define the Event Handler that responds when event is raised.
*/
// Subscriber class
public class RepairClaimChecker
{
  static void Main(string[] args)
  {
    RepairClaimCheckerLogic myRepairClaimCheckerLogic =
      new RepairClaimCheckerLogic();

    myRepairClaimCheckerLogic.GetRepairClaimData();

    /*
    Event is bound with the delegate
    Here we are creating a delegate, a pointer, to the method
    called OverLimitMessage and adding it to the list of
    Event Handlers
    */
    myRepairClaimCheckerLogic.OverLimit
      += new RepairClaimCheckerLogic.RepairClaimCheckerDelegate
      (OverLimitMessage);

    myRepairClaimCheckerLogic.ReadAndCheckRepairClaims();
  }

  /*
  Delegates call this method when the event is raised.
  This is the code that executes when OverLimit is fired
  */

```csharp
    static void OverLimitMessage(int claimNumber, double value)
    {
      Console.WriteLine($"*** Claim {claimNumber} for {value} needs to be
      verified***");
    }
} // End of the class RepairClaimChecker

// Publisher class
public class RepairClaimCheckerLogic
{
  /*
  Declare the delegate. This delegate can be used to point
  to any method which is a void method and accepts an int
  followed by a double as its parameters
  */
  public delegate void RepairClaimCheckerDelegate(int claimNumber, double
  claimValue);

  /*
  Declare the event. This event can cause any method that
  matches the RepairClaimCheckerDelegate to be called
  */
  public event RepairClaimCheckerDelegate OverLimit;

  double[] repairClaimsAmounts = new double[3];

  public void GetRepairClaimData()
  {
    for (int i = 0; i < 3; i++)
    {
      Console.WriteLine("What is the repair claim amount?");

      double claimAmount = Convert.ToDouble(Console.ReadLine());
      repairClaimsAmounts[i] = claimAmount;
    } // End of the for iteration construct
```

```
  } // End of GetRepairClaimData() method

  public void ReadAndCheckRepairClaims()
  {
    for (int i = 0; i < 3; i++)
    {
      if (repairClaimsAmounts[i] > 5000)
      {
        /*
        Here we are raising the event and this event is linked
        to the method called  OverLimitMessage() which accepts
        the two values and displays a message
        */
        OverLimit(i, repairClaimsAmounts[i]); // Raised event
      } // End of the if selection construct
    } // End of the for iteration construct

  } // End of the ReadAndCheckRepairClaims() method

 } // End of the class RepairClaimCheckerLogic

} // End of namespace Labs.Chapter22
```

```
What is the repair claim amount?
9000
What is the repair claim amount?
4000
What is the repair claim amount?
6000
*** Claim 0 for 9000 needs to be verified***
*** Claim 2 for 6000 needs to be verified***
```

Figure 25-42. *Lab 2 output*

Chapter 23 Labs: Generics

Lab 1

Write a C# console application that will use a generic class and method, allowing any two value types to be passed to the method, which will add the two values and return the answer. The values can therefore be int, float, double, string, etc. The application will

- Have a class called Calculator, which accepts any type. It is generic <T> and this class will

  - Have a method called AddTwoValues(), which has two parameters. The first parameter is called valueOne of type T and the second parameter is called valueTwo of type T, and inside the method

    - There is a variable called firstValue, which is of data type dynamic, and it is assigned to valueOne.

    - There is a variable called secondValue, which is of data type dynamic, and it is assigned to valueTwo.

    - The answer variable is assigned the "sum" of firstValue and secondValue (`firstValue + secondValue`).

      The method is a value method and it returns the variable answer.

- Have a class called CalculatorApplicaton and inside it

  - A Main() method that

    - Instantiates the Calculator class with type <int>, naming the instantiation intCalculator

    - Then calls the AddTwoValues() method, passing it the values 80 and 20, and writes the returned value to the console

    - Instantiates the Calculator class with type <string>, naming the instantiation stringCalculator

- Then calls the AddTwoValues() method, passing it the values "Gerry" and "Byrne", and writes the returned value to the console

  Repeat the instantiation and method call for float and double data types.

Lab 2

Write a C# console application that will use a generic method, allowing any value type to be passed to it, and on identification of the type, a Boolean true or false will be returned. The application will use claim values and policy ids, which will be passed to the method where the total of the claims will be calculated. The application will

- Have a class called ClaimLogic and inside it

  - There will be a method to create an ArrayList with the following values:

    "POL1234", 2000.99, "POL1235", 3000.01, "POL1236", 599.99, "POL1237", 399.01, "POL1238", 9000, "POL1239"

    Then this ArrayList is passed to the next method.

  - A method is created that accepts the ArrayList and iterates the values, and for each value it passes the value to another method that is generic and accepts any value type. The generic method then returns true if the value passed to it is an int or a double and false if it is any other type.

  - When the value returned to the iteration is Boolean true, add the value to an accumulated total of the claims, and increment a number of valid claims variable by 1.

  - When the value returned to the iteration is Boolean false, increment a number of policy ids variable by 1.

  - Finally, display the total of the claims, the number of claims, and the number of policy ids.

- Have a class called CompareClaims and inside it

  • Have a Main() method that calls the method that creates the
    ArrayList.

Lab 1: Possible Solution with output shown in Figure 25-43

```
using System;

namespace Labs.Chapter23
{
  internal class CalculatorApplication
  {
    static void Main(string[] args)
    {
      Calculator<int> intCalculator = new Calculator<int>();
      Console.WriteLine($"Using integers: {intCalculator.
      AddTwoValues(80, 20)}");

      Calculator<string> stringCalculator = new Calculator<string>();
      Console.WriteLine($"Using strings: {stringCalculator.
      AddTwoValues("Gerry", "Byrne")}");

      Calculator<float> floatCalculator = new Calculator<float>();
      Console.WriteLine($"Using floats: {floatCalculator.AddTwoValues(3.5F,
      100.0F)}");

      Calculator<double> doubleCalculator = new Calculator<double>();
      Console.WriteLine($"Using doubles: {doubleCalculator.
      AddTwoValues(8.99, 1.02)}");

    } // End of Main() method
  } // End of CalculatorApplication class

  // Create a generic class
  public class Calculator<T>
  {
    public T AddTwoValues(T valueOne, T valueTwo)
    {
      /*
      In C# we have a dynamic type which is used avoid
```

```
      compile-time type checking of the variable.
      Instead the compiler gets the type at the run time and
      this suits this example well as we are using generic types.
      */
      dynamic firstValue = valueOne;
      dynamic secondValue = valueTwo;

      return firstValue + secondValue;
    } //End of AddTwoValues() method
  } // End of Calculator class

} // End of namespace Labs.Chapter23
```

```
Using integers: 100
Using strings: GerryByrne
Using floats: 103.5
Using doubles: 10.01
```

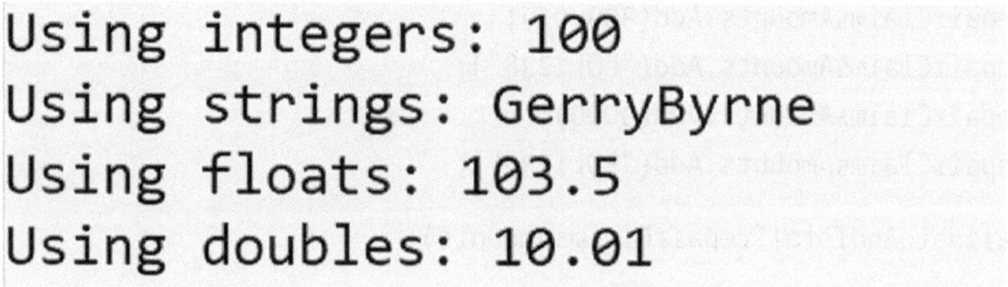

Figure 25-43. Lab 1 output

Lab 2: Possible Solution with output shown in Figure 25-44

```
using System.Collections;

namespace Labs.Chapter23
{
  internal class CompareClaims
  {
    static void Main(string[] args)
    {
      ClaimLogic myCalculatorLogic = new ClaimLogic();

      myCalculatorLogic.CreateArrayListOfValues();

    } // End of Main() method
  } // End of Calculator class
```

```
public class ClaimLogic
{
  public void CreateArrayListOfValues()
  {
    ArrayList repairClaimsAmounts = new ArrayList();
    repairClaimsAmounts.Add("POL1234");
    repairClaimsAmounts.Add(2000.99);
    repairClaimsAmounts.Add("POL1235");
    repairClaimsAmounts.Add(3000.01);
    repairClaimsAmounts.Add("POL1236");
    repairClaimsAmounts.Add(599.99);
    repairClaimsAmounts.Add("POL1237");
    repairClaimsAmounts.Add(399.01);
    repairClaimsAmounts.Add("POL1238");
    repairClaimsAmounts.Add(9000);
    repairClaimsAmounts.Add("POL1239");

    ValidateAndTotal(repairClaimsAmounts);
  }

  private void ValidateAndTotal(ArrayList repairClaimsAmounts)
  {
    double totalOfClaims = 0.00;
    int validClaims = 0, policyIds =0;

    for (int i = 0; i < repairClaimsAmounts.Count; i++)
    {
      if (Calculate(repairClaimsAmounts[i]))
      {
        totalOfClaims += Convert.ToDouble(repairClaimsAmounts[i]);
        validClaims++;
      } // End of the if selection construct
      else
      {
        policyIds++;
      }
    } // End of the for iteration construct
```

```
      Console.WriteLine($"There were {validClaims} claims");
      Console.WriteLine($"Claims total is {totalOfClaims}");
      Console.WriteLine($"There were {policyIds} policies");
    } // End of ValidateAndTotal() method

    //Now this method can accept any data type
    public static bool Calculate<T>(T value)
    {
      switch (value)
      {
        case int i:
          return true;

        case double d:
          return true;

        default:
          return false;
      }
    } // End of Calculate() method
  } // End of CalculatorLogic class
} // End of namespace Labs.Chapter23
```

```
There were 5 claims
Claims total is 15000
There were 6 policies
```

Figure 25-44. *Lab 2 output*

Chapter Summary

Well, that was a lot of coding, and hopefully we tried to use our own learnings and code style rather than just looking at the basic solutions given for the labs.

As we finish this penultimate chapter, we can say we have achieved so much. We should be immensely proud of the learning to date. We are getting so close to our target we can almost touch it, but we have just one more small step to take.

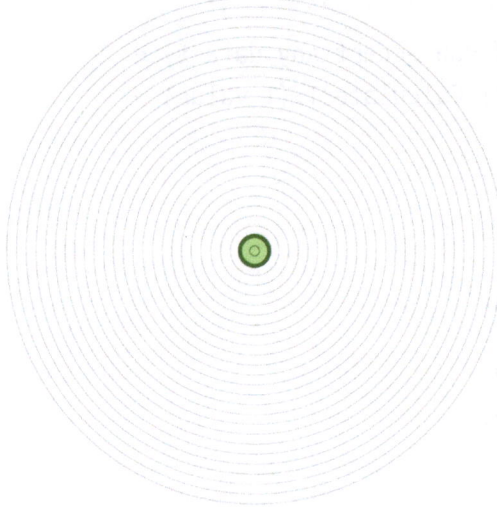

Our target is getting closer

CHAPTER 26

C# 11

C# New Features

With the latest C# release, C# 11, expected in November 2022, we will be treated to some new features to help us develop code.

We can use the features of C# 11 in their current form, prior to official release, by amending the project file, .csproj, to inform it that we wish to use the preview feature of the language. The .csproj file defines the project content, platform requirements, and, importantly for us, the language versioning information. It may also contain information about servers such as a database or web server.

To amend the .csproj file for the specific project we are working on and allow us to use the preview features, the process is as follows:

- In the Solution Explorer panel, double-click the project name.

- Amend the XML to add <LangVersion>preview</LangVersion> to the code:

```
<Project Sdk="Microsoft.NET.Sdk">
  <PropertyGroup>
    <OutputType>Exe</OutputType>
    <TargetFramework>net6.0</TargetFramework>
    <LangVersion>preview</LangVersion>
    <ImplicitUsings>enable</ImplicitUsings>
    <Nullable>enable</Nullable>
  </PropertyGroup>
</Project>
```

© Gerard Byrne 2022
G. Byrne, *Target C#*, https://doi.org/10.1007/978-1-4842-8619-7_26

Raw String Literals

When we have looked at the use of strings particularly in Chapter 15 on string handling, we have seen different modifiers used with the strings. We used the verbatim, @, and the template literal, $, and we also read that we still need to escape things like double quotes. We will code an application to apply raw string materials.

1. Right-click the solution CoreCSharp.

2. Choose Add.

3. Choose New Project.

4. Choose Console App from the listed templates that appear.

5. Click the Next button.

6. Name the project Chapter26 and leave it in the same location.

7. Click the Next button.

8. Choose the framework to be used, which in our projects will be .NET 6.0 or higher.

9. Click the Create button.

Now we should see the Chapter26 project within the solution called CoreCSharp.

10. Right-click the Chapter26 project in the Solution Explorer panel.

11. Click the Set as Startup Project option.

12. Right-click the Program.cs file in the Solution Explorer window.

13. Choose Rename.

14. Change the name to RawStringLiterals.cs.

15. Press the Enter key.

16. Double-click the RawStringLiterals.cs file to open it in the editor window.

We will start by creating a string that uses the verbatim identifier, the @ special character. When we use the @, the string literal will be interpreted verbatim, precisely as it appears. Any escape sequences such as the backslash \ will be interpreted literally.

On the other hand, the double quote escape sequence, "", is not interpreted literally and it will produce one double quotation mark.

Listing 26-1 shows an example of escaping, where we want to actually display a word or phrase with double quotes around it and we have to use "" at the start of the quoted word or phrase and at the end of the quoted word or phrase. We will add the Main() method, and inside it we will create a string literal that includes the double quotes "" at the start and end of a number of words. We will then write the string to the console.

17.   Amend the code as shown in Listing 26-1.

Listing 26-1. Escaped double quotes around a phrase using verbatim @

```
namespace Chapter26
{
  internal class RawStringLiterals
  {
    static void Main(string[] args)
    {
      string rawStringLiterals =
        @"Kathleen Dollard Principal Program Manager, .NET
        at Microsoft is quoted as saying about raw string literals
        ""If you work with strings literal that contain quotes or
        embedded language strings like JSON, XML, HTML, SQL, Regex
        and others, raw literal strings may be your favorite feature
        of C# 11.""
        and I think we may agree that this is a cool feature of C# 11.
        https://devblogs.microsoft.com/dotnet/csharp-126-preview-updates/";
      Console.WriteLine(rawStringLiterals);
    } // End of Main() method
  } // End of class RawStringLiterals
} // End of namespace Chapter26
```

18.   Click the File menu.

19.   Choose Save All.

20.   Click the Debug menu.

21.   Choose Start Without Debugging.

Figure 26-1 shows the console window and we can see that the double quote escape sequence produces a single quote.

```
Kathleen Dollard Principal Program Manager, .NET
at Microsoft is quoted as saying about raw string literals
"If you work with strings literal that contain quotes or
embedded language strings like JSON, XML, HTML, SQL, Regex
and others, raw     Double escape sequence "" produces a single
of C# 11."
and I think we may agree that this is a cool feature of C# 11.
https://devblogs.microsoft.com/dotnet/csharp-11-preview-updates/
```

Figure 26-1. *Double quote escape sequence produces a single quote*

22.   Press the Enter key to close the console window.

C# 11 introduces us to raw string literals as a new format for string literals. This new feature means string literals can now contain arbitrary text, which means we can now include embedded quotes or new lines or whitespace and other special characters, all without having to use escape sequences. The new raw string literal is depicted by starting with at least three double quote """ characters, and it must end with the same number of double quote characters.

We will now add a new raw string literal starting with three double quotes and ending with the same three double quotes and assign it to a new variable.

23.   Amend the code as in Listing 26-2, to use the new raw string literal, starting with three double quotes and ending with the same three double quotes.

Listing 26-2. New raw string literal starting and ending with three double quotes

```
and I think we may agree that this is a cool feature of C# 11.
https://devblogs.microsoft.com/dotnet/csharp-126-preview-updates/";
    Console.WriteLine(rawStringLiterals);

    Console.WriteLine($"\n*** C# 11 Raw String Literal ***");
    string rawStringLiterals11 = """
    Kathleen Dollard Principal Program Manager, .NET at
    Microsoft is quoted as saying about raw string literals
    "If you work with strings literal that contain quotes or
    embedded language strings like JSON, XML, HTML, SQL, Regex
```

```
        and others, raw literal strings may be your favorite feature
        of C# 11."
        and I think we may agree that this is a cool feature of C# 11.
        https://devblogs.microsoft.com/dotnet/csharp-126-preview-updates/"
        """;
        Console.WriteLine(rawStringLiterals11);
    } // End of Main() method
  } // End of class RawStringLiterals
} // End of namespace Chapter26
```

24.   Click the File menu.

25.   Choose Save All.

26.   Click the Debug menu.

27.   Choose Start Without Debugging.

Figure 26-2 shows the console window and we can see that the double quotes have appeared around the words of the quote even though they were only single double quotes. The use of the new raw string literal starting with the three double quotes """ and ending with the same three double quote """ characters has worked as expected.

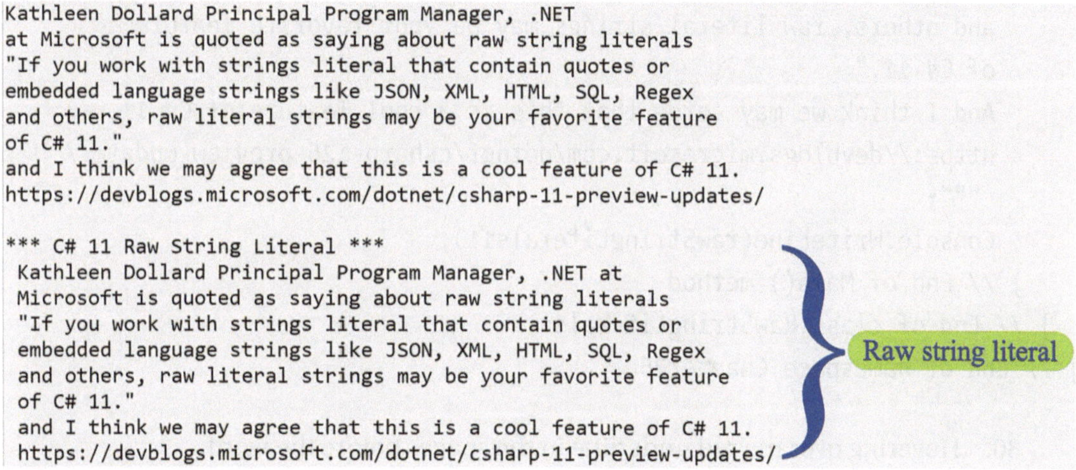

Figure 26-2. *Raw string literal using three double quotes """*

28.   Press the Enter key to close the console window.

We will now amend the raw string literal so that the last three double quote """ characters is indented. When a raw string literal is displayed, the position of the last three double quotes """ is crucial, since the first of the double quotes indicates the starting point for the text, the left margin if we wish to think of it like that. The text we have then gets displayed from this left position, and therefore none of the text can be positioned to the left of this position.

29. Amend the code as in Listing 26-3, to indent the end three double quotes by one space.

Listing 26-3. Text cannot be left of the first of the last three double quotes

```
and I think we may agree that this is a cool feature of C# 11.
https://devblogs.microsoft.com/dotnet/csharp-126-preview-updates/";
      Console.WriteLine(rawStringLiterals);

      Console.WriteLine($"\n*** C# 11 Raw String Literal ***");
      string rawStringLiterals11 = """
      Kathleen Dollard Principal Program Manager, .NET at
      Microsoft is quoted as saying about raw string literals
      "If you work with strings literal that contain quotes or
      embedded language strings like JSON, XML, HTML, SQL, Regex
      and others, raw literal strings may be your favorite feature
      of C# 11."
      And I think we may agree that this is a cool feature of C# 11.
      https://devblogs.microsoft.com/dotnet/csharp-126-preview-updates/
       """;
      Console.WriteLine(rawStringLiterals11);
    } // End of Main() method
  } // End of class RawStringLiterals
} // End of namespace Chapter26
```

30. Hovering over the red underline in the spaces before the word Kathleen will display an error message that informs us about spacing, as shown in Figure 26-3.

Kathleen Dollard Principal Program Manager, .NET at

⚙ class System.String
Represents text as a sequence of UTF-16 code units.

CS8999: Line does not start with the same whitespace as the closing line of the raw string literal.

text is past the double quote

https://   view-updates/
""";

Figure 26-3. *Text is left of three double quotes* `"""`

31. Amend the code as in Listing 26-4, to move all the text so that it is one space past the end three double quotes and ensure that the red underline disappears.

Listing 26-4. Text must be one space past the last three double quotes

```
Console.WriteLine($"\n*** C# 11 Raw String Literal ***");
string rawStringLiterals11 = """
Kathleen Dollard Principal Program Manager, .NET at
Microsoft is quoted as saying about raw string literals
"If you work with strings literal that contain quotes or
embedded language strings like JSON, XML, HTML, SQL, Regex
and others, raw literal strings may be your favorite feature
of C# 11."
and I think we may agree that this is a cool feature of C# 11.
https://devblogs.microsoft.com/dotnet/csharp-126-preview-updates/
""";
Console.WriteLine(rawStringLiterals11);
    } // End of Main() method
  } // End of class RawStringLiterals
} // End of namespace Chapter26
```

32. Click the File menu.

33. Choose Save All.

34. Click the Debug menu.

35. Choose Start Without Debugging.

Figure 26-4 shows the console window and we can see that the double quotes have marked the start of the text on the left-hand side and our text was positioned one space in from the double quotes.

```
*** C# 11 Raw String Literal ***
Kat        rd Principal Program Manager, .NET at
Mic        quoted as saying about raw string literals
"If you work with strings literal that contain quotes or
embedded language strings like JSON, XML, HTML, SQL, Regex
and others, raw literal strings may be your favorite feature
of C# 11."
and I think we may agree that this is a cool feature of C# 11.
https://devblogs.microsoft.com/dotnet/csharp-11-preview-updates/
```

Figure 26-4. *One space indented from """*

36. Press the Enter key to close the console window.

We can see that raw string literals are a nice feature, but we can go further, because raw string literals can be interpolated by preceding them with a $.

37. Amend the code as in Listing 26-5, to declare and initialize three variables, two of data type string and the other of data type int.

Listing 26-5. New WriteLine() statement and three variables declared

```
and I think we may agree that this is a cool feature of C# 11.
https://devblogs.microsoft.com/dotnet/csharp-126-preview-updates/
""";
    Console.WriteLine(rawStringLiterals11);

    Console.WriteLine($"\n*** C# 11 Interpolated Raw String Literal ***");

    string companyName = "Microsoft";
    string languageName = "C# 11";
    int version = 11;

    } // End of Main() method
  } // End of class RawStringLiterals
} // End of namespace Chapter26
```

We will now add a new interpolated raw string literal, which means we use the dollar sign, $, before the three double quotes. This new string will be called rawStringLiterals11V2. The text that we assign to it will be the same text as we have in the string variable rawStringLiterals11.

Once we paste the text, we will replace the

- Word Microsoft with the variable companyName enclosed in open and close curly braces, that is, {companyName}

- First C #11 phrase with the variable languageName enclosed in open and close curly braces, that is, {languageName}

- 11 in the second C #11 phrase with the variable version enclosed in open and close curly braces, that is, {version}

This means we have used interpolation within the raw string literal.

38. Amend the code as in Listing 26-6.

Listing 26-6. Interpolated raw string literal

```
string companyName = "Microsoft";
string languageName = "C# 11";
int version = 11;

string rawStringLiterals11V2 = $"""
Kathleen Dollard Principal Program Manager, .NET at
{companyName} is quoted as saying about raw string literals
"If you work with strings literal that contain quotes or
embedded language strings like JSON, XML, HTML, SQL, Regex
and others, raw literal strings may be your favorite feature
of {languageName}."
and I think we may agree that this is a cool feature of C# {version}.
https://devblogs.microsoft.com/dotnet/csharp-126-preview-updates/
""";

Console.WriteLine(rawStringLiterals11V2);
    } // End of Main() method
  } // End of class RawStringLiterals
} // End of namespace Chapter26
```

39. Click the File menu.

40. Choose Save All.

41. Click the Debug menu.

42. Choose Start Without Debugging.

The console window will show the final display of text, which is identical to the text shown in Figure 26-4, but this code has used interpolated values.

Nice feature. Thank you, C# 11.

New Lines in String Interpolations

Interpolation can be defined as the insertion of something of a different nature into something else. When we have looked at the use of strings, we have seen how to use string interpolation with the special character, **$**, which identifies the string literal as an interpolated string. An interpolated string is a string literal that might contain interpolation expressions. Essentially, it is a fancy word for joining our strings with other non-string variables or values, and to build a string interpolation, we will make use of the curly braces {}.

C# 11 introduces a new feature to these string interpolations, where we can now span multiple lines. The text we have between the curly braces is parsed, and we can therefore include any legal C# code including new lines. In terms of producing readable code, this feature certainly helps.

1. Right-click the Chapter26 project in the Solution Explorer panel.

2. Choose Add.

3. Choose Class

4. Change the name to NewLinesInterpolation.cs.

5. Click the Add button.

6. Amend the code to add a Main() method using the svm shortcut.

We will now create two string variables and then create an interpolated string, which uses these variables and which includes new lines in the formation of the interpolated string.

7. Amend the code as in Listing 26-7.

Listing 26-7. New line in interpolated string

```
namespace Chapter26
{
  internal class NewLinesInterpolation
  {
    static void Main(string[] args)
    {
     string policyId = "AUTO00001";
     string policyCoverage = "within the country of the policy.";

     string policyMessage = $"The policy {
         policyId
         } is limited to driving {
         policyCoverage
         }";

     Console.WriteLine(policyMessage);
    } // End of Main()
  } // End of NewLinesInterpolation class
} // End of Chapter26 namespace
```

8. Click the File menu.

9. Choose Save All.

10. Right-click the Chapter26 project in the Solution Explorer panel.

11. Choose Properties.

12. Set the Startup object to be the NewLinesInterpolation.cs in the drop-down list.

13. Close the Properties window.

14. Click the Debug menu.

15. Choose Start Without Debugging.

Figure 26-5 shows the console window and we can see that the interpolated string has executed as expected.

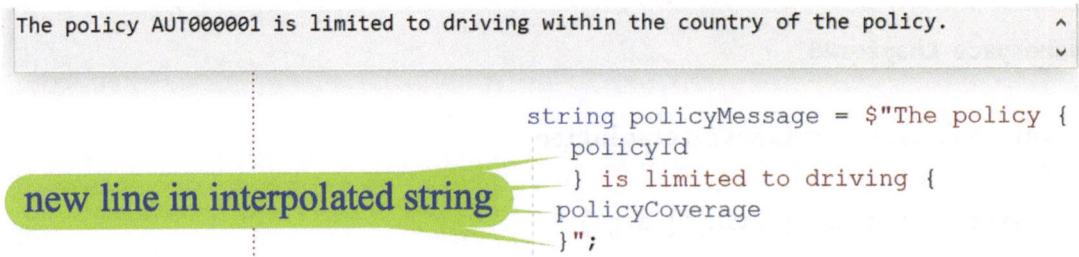

```
The policy AUT000001 is limited to driving within the country of the policy.
```

new line in interpolated string

```
string policyMessage = $"The policy {
    policyId
    } is limited to driving {
    policyCoverage
    }";
```

Figure 26-5. *New lines in interpolated string*

16. Press the Enter key to close the console window.

List Patterns

C# 11 introduces a new feature called the list pattern, which allows for matching against lists and arrays. When we use the list pattern, we can use the slice pattern, .., allowing us to match zero or more elements. The syntax used in a list pattern is values surrounded by square brackets.

When we slice an array, we are getting a range of elements from within the array. If we had an array with the elements 1,2,3,4,5,6 and we were to slice the array from index 2 to index 5 using the command `slice(2,5)`, we would get the values 3,4,5. The command `slice(2,5)` means start at index 2 and stop at index 5, which is exclusive, and therefore the element at 5 is not included.

Index	0	1	2	3	4	5	6
Array	1	2	**3**	**4**	**5**	6	
Sliced elements			↑	↑	↑		

We will now code an application where we will match the letters of a policy type against a series of patterns. We will iterate an array of policy types converting each policy type string to a character array and then pass the array to a method that will perform the matching. When a match is found, a string will be returned and is displayed to the console.

1. Right-click the Chapter26 project in the Solution Explorer window.

2. Choose Add.

3. Choose Class.

4. Name the class ListPatterns.cs.

5. Double-click the ListPatterns.cs file to open it in the editor window.

6. Amend the code as in Listing 26-8, to create the Main() method.

Listing 26-8. Namespace with class and Main() method

```
namespace Chapter26
{
  internal class ListPatterns
  {
    static void Main(string[] args)
    {
    } // End of Main() method
  } // End of class ListPatterns
} // End of namespace Chapter26
```

7. Amend the code as in Listing 26-9, to create the array of policy types.

Listing 26-9. Array of policy types added

```
namespace Chapter26
{
  internal class ListPatterns
  {
    static void Main(string[] args)
    {
      // Declare and create an array of strings
      string[] policyType = { "CONDO", "LIFE", "AUTO", "RING", "ZUNKNOWNZ" };
    } // End of Main() method
  } // End of class ListPatterns
} // End of namespace Chapter26
```

Now we will iterate the array, and in each iteration we will take the array string item, convert it to a char array, and pass it to the method we will create next. We will then write the returned value to the console.

    8.   Amend the code as in Listing 26-10.

Listing 26-10. Iterate the array

```
static void Main(string[] args)
{
  // Declare and create a array of strings
  string[] policyType = { "CONDO", "LIFE", "AUTO", "RING", "ZUNKNOWNZ" };

  /*
  Iterate the policyType array and convert the current
  item to a char array. Then pass the char array to the
  method which will check each letter against a pattern
  held in an array
  */
  foreach (string policy in policyType)
  {
    char[] charArr = policy.ToCharArray();
    Console.WriteLine(CheckPolicyType(charArr));
  } // End of foreach iteration
  } // End of Main() method
 } // End of class ListPatterns
} // End of namespace Chapter26
```

Now we will create the method that accepts the char array, which holds the letters of the policy type. The method will use a switch construct to pattern match the list of characters, and when the appropriate pattern is found, the matching string is returned to the calling statement. In the pattern we will be using the slice pattern, which is two dots, .. and means zero or more characters. The pattern we will use to match our list is Z .. Z, which means starts with Z, then has zero or more characters, and then ends with the character Z. In the switch construct, we are also using a slice pattern in the default.

    9.   Amend the code as in Listing 26-11.

Listing 26-11. Method to match the list of policy type letters and return a string

```
} // End of Main() method

/*
Create a method that accepts a char array and then checks
each letter of the char array against a pattern
held in an array
*/
public static string CheckPolicyType(char[] values)
=> values switch
{
  ['A', 'U', 'T', 'O'] => $"Auto has a factor of 1",
  ['H', 'O', 'M', 'E'] => $"Home has a factor of 2",
  ['C', 'O', 'N', 'D', 'O'] => $"Condo has a factor of 3",
  ['B', 'O', 'A', 'T'] => $"Boat has a factor of 4",
  ['L', 'I', 'F', 'E'] => $"Life has a factor of 5",
  ['Z', .. ,'Z'] => $"Specialist policy has a factor of 5",
  [..] => $"Unknown policy type has a factor of 100"
};
} // End of class ListPatterns
} // End of namespace Chapter26
```

10. Click the File menu.

11. Choose Save All.

12. Right-click the Chapter26 project in the Solution Explorer panel.

13. Choose Properties.

14. Set the Startup object to be the ListPatterns.cs in the drop-down list.

15. Close the Properties window.

16. Click the Debug menu.

17. Choose Start Without Debugging.

Figure 26-6 shows the console window and we can see that each of the policy type strings has been matched to one of the patterns.

```
Condo has a factor of 3
Life has a factor of 5
Auto has a factor of 1
Unknown policy type has a factor of 100
Specialist policy has a factor of 5
```

Splice with ['Z', .., 'Z'] has matched ZUNKNOWNZ

```
C:\CoreCSharp\CoreCSharp\Chapter25\bin\Debug\net7.0\
Press any key to close this window . . .
```

Figure 26-6. *List pattern Z..Z matches the policy ZUNKNOWNZ*

18. Press the Enter key to close the console window.

We will now add a new element, HARDWARE, to the array that does not fit the list pattern, and when we run the application, we will be given the "default" message.

19. Amend the code as in Listing 26-12, to add the additional element.

Listing 26-12. Add a new element to the array

```
static void Main(string[] args)
{
    // Declare and create an array of strings
    string[] policyType = { "CONDO", "LIFE", "AUTO", "RING", "ZUNKNOWNZ",
    "HARDWARE" };
```

20. Click the File menu.

21. Choose Save All.

22. Click the Debug menu.

23. Choose Start Without Debugging.

Figure 26-7 shows the console window and we can see that the HARDWARE policy type has been matched to the seventh pattern, [..].

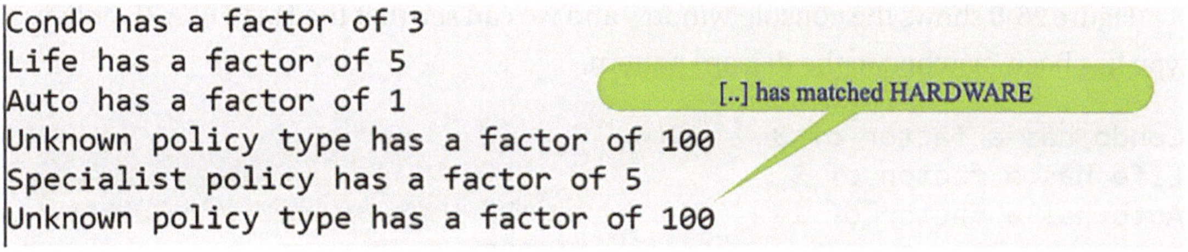

```
Condo has a factor of 3
Life has a factor of 5
Auto has a factor of 1
Unknown policy type has a factor of 100
Specialist policy has a factor of 5
Unknown policy type has a factor of 100
```

[..] has matched HARDWARE

Figure 26-7. *[..] has matched the policy type HARDWARE*

We could also have used a discard instead of the slice pattern in the switch construct. Discards, _, can be used where any value is accepted at that position. The discard pattern can be used in pattern matching with the switch expression, and every expression, including null, always matches the discard pattern.

By using the discard pattern, in the last line of the CheckPolicyType() method, our code could be as Listing 26-13, and this would mean that every other pattern not found in the first six cases would fall under this "default" case.

24. Click the File menu.

25. Choose Save All.

26. Click the Debug menu.

27. Choose Start Without Debugging.

Listing 26-13. Using the discard, _, rather than the slice pattern [..]

```
public static string CheckPolicyType(char[] values)
=> values switch
{
  ['A', 'U', 'T', 'O'] => $"Auto has a factor of 1",
  ['H', 'O', 'M', 'E'] => $"Home has a factor of 2",
  ['C', 'O', 'N', 'D', 'O'] => $"Condo has a factor of 3",
  ['B', 'O', 'A', 'T'] => $"Boat has a factor of 4",
  ['L', 'I', 'F', 'E'] => $"Life has a factor of 5",
  ['Z', .., 'Z'] => $"Specialist policy has a factor of 5",
  _ => $"Unknown policy type has a factor of 100"
};
```

Figure 26-8 shows the console window and we can see that the HARDWARE policy type has been matched to the discard pattern, _.

```
Condo has a factor of 3
Life has a factor of 5
Auto has a factor of 1                    _ discard pattern has matched HARDWARE
Unknown policy type has a factor of 100
Specialist policy has a factor of 5
Unknown policy type has a factor of 100
```

Figure 26-8. *Discard pattern _ has matched the policy type HARDWARE*

Auto Default Struct

Prior to C# 11 all fields of a struct needed to be initialized in the constructor. We saw in Chapter 19 on structs an example of a Policy struct with four fields, and the constructor was used to initialize the field values. Listing 26-14 shows code that is similar to the Chapter 19 PolicyExample.cs class, but the initialization of the monthlyPremium field does not exist in the constructor. This causes a compile error in C# 10, as we will see when we code the example. We will code this example in the Chapter19 project.

1. Right-click the **Chapter19** project, not the current Chapter26 project, in the Solution Explorer window.

2. Choose Add.

3. Choose Class.

4. Name the class StructsExample.cs.

5. Double-click the StructsExample.cs file to open it in the editor window.

We will add the code to create a struct calling it Policy10, which has two fields and a constructor for the Policy10 struct where we do not initialize the field called monthlyPremium.

6.   Amend the code as in Listing 26-14.

Listing 26-14. Policy10 struct where constructor does not initialize all fields

```
namespace Chapter19
{
    public struct Policy10
    {
        public int policy_number;
        public double monthlyPremium;

        public Policy10()
        {
            policy_number = 123456;
        } // End of user constructor

    }// End of Policy10 struct

    internal class StructsExample
    {
        static void Main(string[] args)
        {
            var myPolicy = new Policy10();

            Console.WriteLine(myPolicy.monthlyPremium);
        } // End of Main() method

    } // End of class StructsExample
} // End of namespace Chapter19
```

7.   Hover over the Policy10 word in the constructor.

Figure 26-9 shows the pop-up window that will be displayed with an error message telling us that all fields must be assigned a value. In other words, the default value of the field is not activated. We might think annoying, but alas C# 11 can help us.

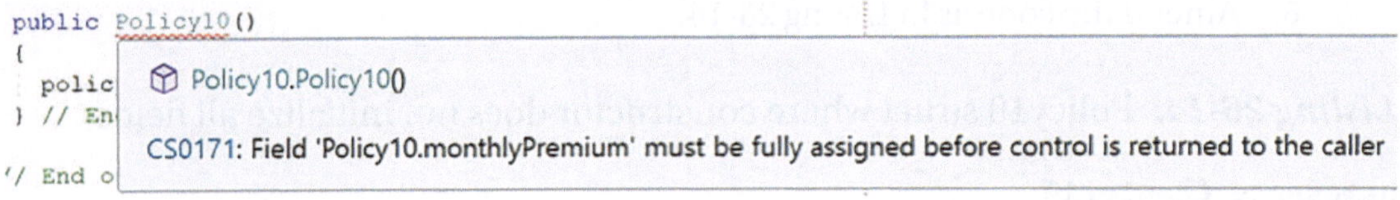

```
public Policy10()
{
  polic    🔲 Policy10.Policy10()
} // En
         CS0171: Field 'Policy10.monthlyPremium' must be fully assigned before control is returned to the caller
'/ End o
```

Figure 26-9. *Struct field must be initialized*

8.   Add the code to initialize the monthlyPremium field as in Listing 26-15.

Listing 26-15. Policy10 struct where constructor has initialized all fields

```
public struct Policy10
{
  public int policy_number;
  public double monthlyPremium;

  public Policy10()
  {
    policy_number = 123456;
    monthlyPremium = 99.00;
  } // End of user constructor
}// End of Policy10 struct
```

9.   Click the File menu.

10.   Choose Save All.

11.   Right-click the Chapter19 project in the Solution Explorer panel.

12.   Choose Set as Startup Project.

13.   Right-click the Chapter19 project in the Solution Explorer panel.

14.   Choose Properties.

15.   Set the Startup object to be the StructsExample.cs in the drop-down list.

16.   Close the Properties window.

17.   Click the Debug menu.

18.   Choose Start Without Debugging.

Figure 26-10 shows console output with the value from the one field we have chosen to display.

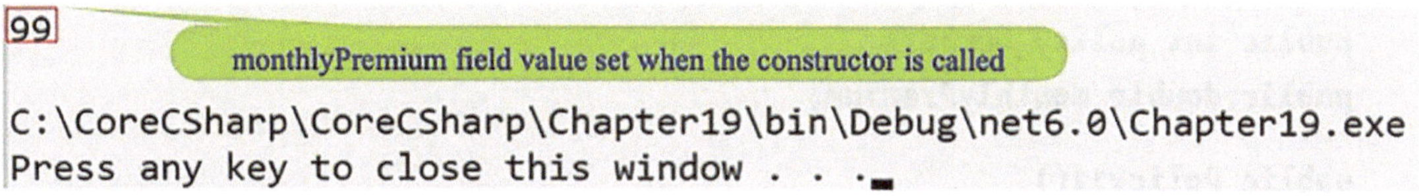

Figure 26-10.   *The field value set by the constructor call*

19.   Press the Enter key to close the console window.

Now in C# 11, this annoying feature of initialization has been changed, and the compiler ensures that all fields of a struct type are initialized to their default value as part of executing a constructor. This can be a great feature for us because any field not initialized by a constructor will automatically be initialized by the compiler. Even with the uninitialized fields, the application code will compile since those fields not explicitly initialized will be allocated the default value their type.

We will now code this example in the Chapter26 project. The code will be the same as in Listing 26-14, with the initialization of the monthlyPremium field not being coded, and we will change the struct name to be Policy11 (C# 11).

20.   Right-click the **Chapter26** project in the Solution Explorer panel.

21.   Choose Set as Startup Project.

22.   Right-click the **Chapter26** project in the Solution Explorer window.

23.   Choose Add.

24.   Choose Class.

25.   Name the class StructsExample.cs.

26.   Double-click the StructsExample.cs file to open it in the editor window.

27.   Amend the code as in Listing 26-16.

Listing 26-16. Policy11 struct where constructor has not initialized all fields

```csharp
namespace Chapter26
{
  public struct Policy11
  {
    public int policy_number;
    public double monthlyPremium;

    public Policy11()
    {
      policy_number = 123456;
    } // End of user constructor
  }// End of Policy11 struct

  internal class StructsExample
  {
    static void Main(string[] args)
    {
      var myPolicy = new Policy11();

      Console.WriteLine(myPolicy.monthlyPremium);
    } // End of Main() method
  } // End of class StructsExample
} // End of namespace Chapter26
```

28.   Click the File menu.

29.   Choose Save All.

30.   Right-click the Chapter26 project in the Solution Explorer panel.

31.   Choose Properties.

32.   Set the Startup object to be the StructsExample.cs in the drop-down list.

33.   Close the Properties window.

34.   Click the Debug menu.

35.   Choose Start Without Debugging.

Figure 26-11 shows console output with the default value from the one field we have chosen to display. This example clearly shows that the new auto default struct does indeed use the default value of a struct field if it is not initialized within the constructor.

```
0
```
monthlyPremium field value set when the constructor is called and is assigned the default type value
```
C:\CoreCSharp\CoreCSharp\Chapter26\bin\Debug\
Press any key to close this window . . .
```

Figure 26-11. *The field default value is used in C# 11.*

36.   Press the Enter key to close the console window.

Warning Wave 7

The Microsoft site `https://docs.microsoft.com/en-us/dotnet/csharp/language-reference/compiler-messages/warning-waves` tells us the following:

> *New warnings and errors may be introduced in each release of the C# compiler. When new warnings could be reported on existing code, those warnings are introduced under an opt-in system referred to as a warning wave. The opt-in system means that you shouldn't see new warnings on existing code without taking action to enable them. Warning waves are enabled using the AnalysisLevel element in your project file.*

> *When <TreatWarningsAsErrors>true</TreatWarningsAsErrors> is specified, enabled warning wave warnings generate errors. Warning wave 5 diagnostics were added in C# 9. Warning wave 6 diagnostics were added in C# 10. Warning wave 7 diagnostics were added in C# 11.*

So, if we opt in, we will see errors in our code that we may not have seen prior to opting in. C# 11 introduces a new warning wave that can produce a warning when a type is declared with all lowercase letters. According to the Microsoft documentation, any new keywords in C# will all be lowercase ASCII characters. This means that when we create our own types, for example, a class or struct, we need to be cognizant that our name may conflict with a keyword, if we use all lowercase. We can avoid this situation by

- Using at least one uppercase character or an underscore or even a digit.

- Enabling the warning waves for the project. This is an opt-in and can be enabled by double-clicking the project name and adding one line of code to the XML properties as shown:

```
<Project Sdk="Microsoft.NET.Sdk">

  <PropertyGroup>
    <OutputType>Exe</OutputType>
    <TargetFramework>net7.0</TargetFramework>
               <LangVersion>preview</LangVersion>
    <ImplicitUsings>enable</ImplicitUsings>
    <Nullable>enable</Nullable>
               <TreatWarningsAsErrors>true</
TreatWarningsAsErrors>
      <StartupObject>Chapter26.StructsExample</StartupObject>
    </PropertyGroup>

  </Project>
```

1. Right-click the Chapter26 project in the Solution Explorer window.

2. Choose Add.

3. Choose Class.

4. Name the class warningwave.cs – yes, small letters.

5. Double-click the warningwave.cs file to open it in the editor window.

6. Make sure the code looks like that shown in Listing 26-17, with the class name being small letters.

Listing 26-17. Namespace with class

```
namespace Chapter26
{
  internal class warningwave
```

```
    {
    } // End of class warningwave
} // End of namespace Chapter26
```

7. Hover over the word warningwave, the class name/

Figure 26-12 shows the pop-up window that will be displayed with a warning message.

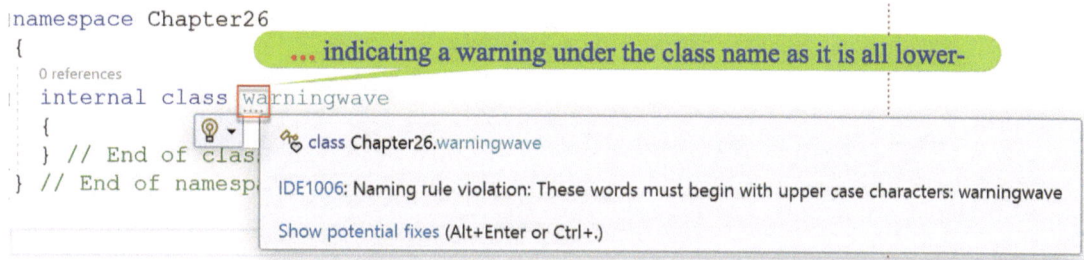

Figure 26-12. *Wave warning for class name with lowercase starting letter*

Chapter Summary

This chapter has shown us that .NET and C# are continually evolving, and as developers we need to be aware of new features, so we can make informed choices when we code our application. Not every new version will offer us features that we will want to apply in our code, but learning is a lifelong process and we need to keep track of language changes.

Having completed our final chapter, we know that we have achieved so much and have reached the target we set ourselves from the outset. We should be immensely proud of what we have achieved. We are now in a great position to look back at the applications we coded and think to ourselves, *Maybe I could have coded the examples in a different way, in a better way*. Yes, the examples in the book have helped us **Target C#** and learn the language, but we must use our knowledge to program our applications the way we feel comfortable, but within the confines of existing coding standards.

We have made the journey to **Target C#**. We should celebrate and then think about our next target, **Target ?**.

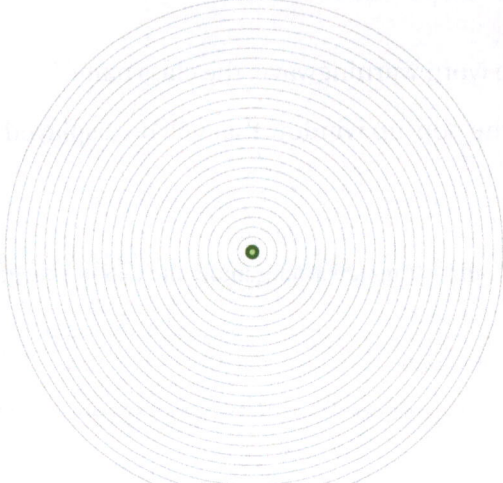

Our target has been reached

Index

A

Abstract class, *see* Interfaces/
    abstract classes
Access Modifier, 72, 74, 377–379, 383, 398,
    409, 749–750, 785
Accessors, 485, 493, 733, 737, 752,
    784–788, 792
AccountStatusToggled, 858, 862, 866
ActivatePolicyEventHandler, 857, 862
AddFunds, 1011
AddTwoValues(), 1026, 1027
AgentEntity, 989, 990, 993–994
Annotations, 800
Append versions, 664
Arguments, 407–409, 832, 857
Arithmetic operations
    AND operator
        FALSE AND TRUE testing, 253
        false section, 254
        if-else statement, 251–253
        int user input, 251
        Main() method, 250
        TRUE AND FALSE testing, 254
        TRUE AND TRUE testing, 252
        variables, 250
    BODMAS, 159
    business logic/code, 159
    clean code, 161
    comparison (*see* Comparison
        operators)
    condition, 264–273
    integer division
        CoreCSharp, 165
        division and modulus, 162

framework, 165
        modulus operator (%), 162
        naming operation, 164
        project creation, 163
        remainder, 162
        selection, 164
        solution explorer, 165
        startup project, 166
        WriteLine() method, 163
    logical (*see* Logical operators)
    mathematics, 159, 160
    NOT (!) operator, 260–264
    OR operator
        &&/||, 255
        FALSE OR FALSE testing, 259, 260
        FALSE OR TRUE testing, 257, 258
        Main() method, 255
        source code, 256, 257
        startup class, 255
        TRUE OR FALSE testing, 258, 259
        true section, 257
    PEMDAS, 160
    precedence/priority, 159
    programming labs, 940–942
    programs, 161
    selection, 195, 196
    solution explorer/project analysis
        add/subtract, 184
        code analysis, 169
        code calculation, 176
        code structure, 170
        compound assignment, 186
        CoreCSharp solution, 166
        decimal places/currency, 184

© Gerard Byrne 2022
G. Byrne, *Target C#*, https://doi.org/10.1007/978-1-4842-8619-7

Arithmetic operations (*cont.*)
discount formula, 177
divide (/=), 189
file explorer/finder, 166, 167
formatting output, 181
holding project information, 168
increment operators, 185
Main() method, 170, 171, 173
mathematical calculations, 181
message displays, 173
minus equals (-=), 188
multiply equals(*=), 188
output information, 178, 179
placeholders, 182
plus equals (+=), 187
Program.cs file, 168, 170
project file, 168
quotation output, 180
QuoteArithmetic.cs
structure, 170
solution file, 167
square root, 191–193
toolbar, 166
user input, 174–176
WriteLine() method, 181
string
case construct, 231
case statements, 233–236
class code, 232
coding technique, 239
concatenation, 243
console window, 236–239, 243–245
conversion, 233
reinforce selection, 239
startup class, 236
Switch.cs program, 231
ToUpper() method, 246
types, 245
variable type, 233
WriteLine() method, 240–242

switch construct
class template, 218
case construct code, 225
console window, 222–224
general format, 217
Main() method, 218
source code, 220, 221
stratup class, 219
string, 219, 231–239
when, 225–231
when clause
case block, 227, 228
case code, 230, 231
code completion, 229, 230
Main() method, 226
startup class, 225, 226
Arrays, 614, 647, 895, 896, 1046, 1048
data structure
collection, 329
declaration, 330
definition, 330
homogenous, 331
insurance/household
products, 329
programming concept, 329
single-dimensional arrays, 331
subscript/index, 331
types, 331
foreach loop
array items, 352
console window, 350–352, 359
declaration, 355
depiction, 360
do while loop, 357
error messages, 353, 354
foreach iteration, 358, 359
formatting method, 348
generic code, 348
IndexOutOfBounds
exception, 360–362

iterations, 348, 349, 359
Main() method, 353
variables, 353, 354, 356
labs, 953, 954, 956–961
ranges/indices
classes, 362
declaration/creation, 363
hat operator, 364, 365
index expression, 362
index from end, 365
length and index from
end, 367, 368
LINQ library, 363
Main() method, 362
output process, 364
programming statement, 363
range operator, 371, 372
Skip() and Take() methods, 370, 371
ToList()/GetRange() methods,
368, 369
traditional index/hat
operator, 367
single-/one-dimensional array
accountNumber, 333
creation, 335
data types, 332
declaration, 333
default values, 336, 337
do-while loop, 343
insurancePremiums, 334
insuranceTypes, 332
one stage, 335–338
references, 338
two stages, 334, 335
variables, 342
zero-based referencing
account number, 338
arrayPositionCounter, 344–346
claimAmount, 345
class template, 340

CoreCSharp, 339
declaration/creation, 341
details, 340
do while iteration, 348
do-while loop, 343
elements, 338
insurance type, 338, 339
integer code, 342
numberOfClaimsEntered
counter, 347
permanent, 341
project creation, 339
source code, 343, 347
startup project, 339
store declaration, 341
user input code, 346
variables, 342
vehiclePolicyNumber, 344
Array.Sort(), 908
Array values, 358, 898–900, 907, 908,
914, 918
ASCII byte values, 663
AskForVehicleValue, 974
ASP.NET web application, 40, 51
Assignment warning, 799, 800
Asynchronous processes, 678
async method, 685, 766
Attribute, 728–738
Auto default struct, 1050–1055
Auto-implemented
properties, 735, 763
AutoInsurance, 996, 1002

B

BinaryFormatter, 729, 730, 740, 745, 750
Binary search, 893, 900–908
Brute-force, 893
Bubble sort, 908–914
Byte array, 661–663, 671, 688

C

C# 8
    individual fields, 803
    nullable reference types,
        126–140, 797–801
    readonly members, 793–797
C# 11
    auto default struct, 1050–1055
    list patterns, 1044–1050
    new lines, string interpolations,
        1042–1044
    official release, 1033
    raw string literals, 1034–1042
    warning wave 7, 1055–1057
CalculatedValues, 966, 967
CalculateTax() method, 524, 831, 832
CalculateVATAmount(), 431, 432
Calculator class, 1012, 1017, 1018, 1026
Callback, 678
Call stack, 717
Casting/parsing
    boolean type, 157
    bool/string types, 153, 155
    compile error, 153
    conversion issue, 156
    CoreCSharp solution, 144
    data types, 143
    definition, 143
    error message, 150
    framework, 146
    help message, 150, 155
    initial values, 148
    integral types, 144
    int/short type, 150–152
    message displays, 149
    namespace renaming option, 148
    naming process, 145
    Parse() method, 155
    Program.cs file, 147
    project creation, 144
    quick actions/refactorings, 147
    range type, 152
    selection, 145
    solution explorer, 146
    startup project, 147
    string input and assign, 154
    ToBoolean() method, 157
    user input, 154
    variable value, 149
Catch block message, 748, 749
Chaining, delegates, 841
ChangeAccountStatus, 858, 864
CheckIfQuoteCanBeMade() method, 717
checkIfTheSame() method, 873, 874, 876,
    879, 880, 883, 884
CheckPolicyType() method, 1049
ClaimCalculator, 967–969
ClaimsPerState, 977
ClaimValues, 986
Classes, 774–776
    constructor (*see* Constructor)
    data structure
        constants, 450, 451
        data/function members, 448
        encapsulation, 448
        fields, 449, 450
        getter method, 453
        legacy languages/programs, 448
        methods, 451, 452
        properties, 453, 454
        sequential programming, 448
        setter method, 454
    labs, 966–968, 971–975
    method types, 447
    objects
        AreaOfCircle() method, 508
        AreaOfRectangle() method, 515, 517
        CircleFormulae class, 504–512
        CircumferenceOfCircle() method,
        511, 512

Main() method, 503
PerimeterOfRectangle() method, 517, 519, 520
RectangleFormulae class, 512–520
Class template, 218, 279, 300, 340, 430, 545, 653
Clean code, 63, 161, 429, 704, 819
Cleaner code, 289, 290, 811, 812
Close() method, 649, 711–713
Code commenting
  multiple-line comments, 89–91
  .NET 6 templates
    Goodbye message, 88
    keyboard input, 88
    namespace, 86
    Program.cs file, 86
    single-line comments, 87
    top-level statements, 85
    traditional code, 84
  self-documenting code, 77
  single-line (*see* Single-line comments)
  Visual Studio
    code coloring, 78
    comments, 79
    notes, 78
Code sequences, 634
Coding skills, 922, 923
Comment block, 89, 902, 903, 910, 916
Common Intermediate Language (CIL), 5, 6
Common Language Runtime (CLR), 2, 5, 377
Common routines
  binary search, 900–908
  bubble sort, 908–914
  insertion sort, 914–921
  linear search, 893–900
  programming routines, 893
Common Type System (CTS), 33–36, 94, 141
CompareTo(), 611–614

Comparison operators
  Boolean true section, 203
  else if, 216
  else if statement, 210
  if block execution, 208
  if construct, 203–208
  if-else construct, 208–210
  if-else if construct, 210–217
  if-else Statement, 198–200
  if statement, 197
  operators, 196, 197
  primary selection, 197
  switch statement, 201, 202
Compiled code, 657, 658
Compile error, 153, 587, 637, 638, 1050
Compiler, 29, 122, 356, 383, 552, 792
Composite formatting, 630
ComputerInsurance class, 819, 820
Computer program
  C# program code, 31
  ingredients/instruction, 31
  operations, 37
  overview, 27
  programming language, 27–29
  Python program code, 32
  recipe information, 29, 30
  type (*see* C# programming language)
Concat() method, 616–617
Concatenating strings, 617, 640–642
Concatenation, 113, 114, 117, 616
Conditional/ternary operator
  code analysis, 267
  error message, 268
  expression, 264
  FALSE block, 267
  if-else construct, 264
  Main() method, 265
  nested conditional operator
    console window, 270–273
    execution, 270

Conditional/ternary operator (*cont.*)
    syntax, 268
    ternary operator, 269, 270
  programming muscle, 265
  ternary operator, 266
  true section, 267
Console window, 610, 613, 616, 703,
    709, 1040
Console.WriteLine(), 58, 66, 133, 163, 627
Constants, 450–451, 463, 464, 803
Constructor, 732–734, 779, 843–845,
    1050, 1053
  DateTime parameter, 491
  default constructor, 455
  error message, 492, 498
  instantiation, 457
  overloading
    agent class, 461
    amount methods, 482
    arrays class, 462
    ClaimDetails class, 481
    class-level variable, 468
    customer class, 462
    date methods, 483
    do while construct, 480
    encapsulate field, 485
    error message, 484
    increment method, 484
    Main() method, 467
    math class, 464
    method-level variable, 483
    NumberOfClaimsEntered
      property, 485, 486
    parse method, 463
    policy number methods, 482
    quick actions/refactorings, 484
    ReadTheRepairShopId()
      method, 480
    Sqrt() method, 464
    static fields and methods, 471

    WriteRepairShopIdToTheArray()
      method, 481
  parameter method, 502
  passing data, 492
  reading method, 493
Constructor
  accessor property, 493
  arguments, 495
  code analysis, 455
  ClaimApplication class, 492, 493, 499
  ClaimDetails class, 490, 491, 496, 497
  class code, 457
  code analysis, 458
  console window, 494, 500, 502, 503
  creation, 783–785
  custom structure, 455
  definition, 454–458
  DisplayInvoiceReceipt()
    method, 497–499
  features, 456, 490
  instantiation, 457
  invoice receipt, 495, 501
  numberOfClaimsEntered, 493
  overloading
    additional fields, 472
    agent class, 461
    calling method, 487
    ClaimApplication class, 469, 479
    ClaimDetails class, 467, 472–478
    code analysis, 478, 479
    concepts, 470
    console window, 471, 488, 489
    CoreCSharp, 466
    definition, 459
    DisplayInvoiceReceipt
      methods, 487
    distinct categories/groups, 460
    encapsulate field, 484
    error message, 484
    hospital roles, 465

HowManyClaimsAreBeingMade()
    method, 470
instructions, 465
Int32 class, 463
Main() method, 460, 479
maintenance and testing, 460
math class, 464
methods, 460
MethodsV1, 459
MethodsValue.cs class, 468
MethodsValue() method, 489
objects, 471
school roles, 465
separation, 465
parameter method, 502
templates, 456
this keyword, 456
Const string interpolation, 639–644
Contains() method, 621–623
Copy a file
Copy() method, 672–674
handling processes, 671
CopyAFile(), 693
Copy() method, 672–674
CoreCSharp, 700, 730, 807, 834, 874,
        894, 1034
C# programming, 3, 4, 40, 181, 330, 854
application formats, 37
ASP.NET, 40
assigned values, 34
built-in, 33
class/classes, 36
    concepts, 48
    instances, 47
    InsuranceQuote, 47
    Main() method, 48
    naming conventions, 49, 50
    real application, 47
    valid/invalid identifiers, 50
    variables/methods, 48

common type system, 33
compilation process, 5, 6
console application, 37–39
.csproj file, 4
enumeration, 34
namespace, 46, 47
.NET MAUI, 39, 40
overwritten values, 34
reference types, 35
structure, 35
    args array, 45
    class, 44
    code analysis, 42
    CSharpNotes.docx, 43
    Main() method, 44, 45
    method, 44
    namespace, 42, 43
    syntax/format, 40
    templates, 41
    top-level statements, 41, 42
types, 32, 33
user-defined, 33
value types, 33
CreateJSON(), 766, 767
Create() method, 655
.csproj file, 4, 798, 1033
CustomerBinary class, 727, 731, 737, 745,
        747, 751
Customer class, 859–861
CustomerJSON class, 763, 764, 766
Customer.json file, 768
CustomerBinary object
        details, 749, 750
Customer struct, 775–777
CustomerXML, 751, 755, 757, 761

D

DataContractSerializer, 751
Data conversion, 936–941

Data types, 881
  common type system, 94
  conversion
    assignment, 113
    automatic conversion, 98
    blank line, 106
    brackets () method, 113
    code analysis, 111
    concatenation, 113, 114, 117
    console input/assign, 116, 118
    console output, 107, 109
    data type string, 115, 118
    debugging mode, 117
    escape sequences, 110
    framework, 101
    heading/message, 105
    implicit/explicit, 96
    Main() method, 104
    message displays, 106
    narrowing, 98
    .NET app, 100
    Program.cs file, 102
    project creation, 100
    quick actions/refactorings, 103
    ReadLine() method, 119
    refactoring option, 103
    rename option, 103
    solution folder, 101
    source code, 98, 99
    startup project, 102
    steps, 118
    string interpolation, 114–116, 120
    string variable, 104
    System.Convert class, 97
    tab indentation, 111
    type declaration, 112
    user input/assigning, 105
    variable scope, 112
    vehicleColour, 119
    vehicleManufacturer, 99, 104, 105, 108, 113
    vehicleModel variable, 116
    widening, 97
    WriteLine() method, 108
  framework types, 95, 96
  interoperability, 94
  labs, 928–935
  nullable (*see* Nullable reference types)
  primitive types, 94
  string, 96
  value/reference types, 93
  variable differences
    compiler error, 122
    convert class, 125
    code analysis, 124
    console input/assign, 121
    data type int, 120, 121
    error list window, 122
    implicit/explicit, 123
    Int32() method, 124
    Parse() method, 126
    steps, 120
    string, 121
    ToInt32() method, 125
DayOfWeek, 805
Debugging, 117, 600, 700, 923
Declaration, 112, 335, 355, 804, 806, 856, 857
Default constructor, 454, 455, 490, 492, 507, 752, 775–779
Default value, 34, 336, 337, 1055
Delegates, 854, 855
  complex example, 842–851
  concept, 831–835
  declarations, 832, 833
  labs, 1011, 1012, 1015–1019
  Microsoft site, 831–834
  signature, 833
  single (*see* Single delegate)
  stages, 832
DeleteAFile(), 693
Delete() method, 675–677

Deserialization
    code, 758, 759
    comments, 744
    file handling, 727
    serialized file, class, 743–749
Deserialize(), 762, 768
DeserializeAsync(), 762
DetermineVATAmount(), 837, 838
DivideByZeroException, 695, 697, 705, 724
Divider, 848
Double quote, 66, 113, 233, 634,
    1035–1037, 1039

E

Email address, 623, 624
EmailNotification() method, 865, 866,
    869, 870
Embedded quotes, 1036
Encapsulation, 448, 788
Enum class, 809, 810, 814
Enumerations, 1002–1010
    assigning values, 815, 816
    descriptive names, 803
    example, 804–806
    foreach iteration, 811–814
    index, 809
    instance, 809
    integer values, 803
    iterated items, 810
    length variable, 810
    methods, 809–812
    sample application, 818–830
    values, 806–808, 814, 815
Equal strings, 613
Error message, 123, 124, 150, 268, 534,
    706, 796, 800, 1051
Errors, 701, 781, 785, 789, 796
Escape sequence, 110, 111, 634, 1036
Estimated value, 826, 828, 1004

Event handler
    application code, 857, 858
    customer/policy classes, 859–864
    programming muscle, 858, 859
Events
    ChangeAccountStatus
        method, 864–865
    declaring, 856, 857
    EmailNotification() method, 865–867
    handling, 857–864
    programming labs, 1017–1026
    publisher, 853–856
    raise, 857
    remoce method, 869, 870
    subscriber, 853–856
    TextMessageNotification()
        method, 867–869
Exceptional event, 693
Exception handling
    calculation, 695
    catch block, 697–699, 702, 703
    code, 693, 694
    emergency device, 693
    FileNotFoundException, 707–710
    finally block, 699
    index out of bounds, 695
    Main() method, 700, 701
    methods and fields, 705
    multiple exceptions, 704–708
    StackTrace, 713
    theory of exceptions, 699
    tools, 696
    try block, 696
    zero exception, 695
ExceptionHandlingWithSwitch
    class, 720
Exceptions, 693, 704–707, 986–989
exNoFile.Message, 710
Expression-bodied members, 736, 737
Extra spaces, 596, 618

F

Fallback, 698

Fat arrow, 736

File access, 741

File class

    copying, 671–674

    deletion, 674–677

    file view, 657

    methods, 650, 652

    reading, 665–672

    show all files, 656

    static methods, 651

    stream, 680–685

    StreamWriter class, 679, 680

    text file, 657

    writing, 658–664

File handling, 727, 982–986

    data structure, 647

    file class, 649–658

    file path, 648

    .NET, 648

    streams, 648

File mode, 741

File name, 741

FileNotFoundException, 694, 707–710, 723

File path, 598, 648

File.ReadAllLines(), 651

FileStream class, 649, 728, 741, 745

File success message, 674

Finalizer, 775

Finally block, 696, 699, 710–713

foreach iteration, 811–814

Format() method

    code applications, 627

    formatting items, 628–630

    spacing, 633, 634

    string interpolation, 630–633

    @ Verbatim, 634–637

G

Game application, 647

Generic class, 877–885

Generic method, 877–891

Generic parameters, 877–885

Generics

    C# language, 873

    class, 877–885

    method, 877–885

    parameters, 873, 877–885

    PolicyMatcher class, 874

    programming labs, 1026–1031

    programming muscle, 874

GetBytes() method, 661

GetHardwareValue(), 717

GetName() method, 809, 813, 814, 817–818

Getters, 753, 754

GetValues() method, 814–815, 817, 818

H

HARDWARE policy type, 1048, 1050

Hardware type, 818, 826

hardwareTypeFactor, 819

HardwareType() method, 843, 849

Hardware value, 714, 815, 818, 826

HardwareValueException, 714

hardwareValueFactor, 819, 823

Hypertext Transfer Protocol (HTTP), 762

I

IFormatter, 740, 745

Immutable, 596, 597, 789

IndexOf() method, 622–624

IndexOutOfRangeException, 694, 695

Input/output operation

    black/white console, 54

    code analysis, 54–56

console app, 60

ConsoleV1 code, 62

console window, 65, 68

Console.WriteLine()/Console.
ReadLine() method, 58

context menu, 65

cubes, 57

directives, 64

dot notation, 56

event handlers, 57, 58

explorer panel, 62

framework version, 61

keyboard key, 67

language selection, 59

learning process, 53

lightning bolt symbol, 57

message displays, 69

methods/variables, 56

process, 53

project creation, 59

ReadLine() method, 65, 67, 68

solution/project details, 60, 61

spanner, 57

statements, 64

tasks, 53

traditional code, 63

unused code, 63

window preferences

    access modifier, 72, 74

    background and text, 72

    background color, 71

    console display, 69

    curly braces, 73

    Main() method, 74

    method signature, 74

    properties/methods, 72

    public keyword, 73

    text color, 70

WriteLine() method, 54, 66, 68

Insert GB, 626

Insertion sort, 914–921

Insert() method, 624–627

Instantiation, 489, 780–782

Integer values, 33, 162, 337, 407, 803, 876

Integrated Development Environment
(IDE), 4, 38, 55, 78, 166, 463, 464

Interfaces/abstract classes, 775, 974–977

abstract methods, 532

CalculateTax() method, 524

CalculateVAT() method, 533

characteristics, 529

classes, 523

class template, 531

code analysis, 533

concepts

    characteristics, 552

    coding method, 552

    console window, 562

    CountryOne class, 560

    CountryTwo/CountryThree
      classes, 561

    default methods, 552

    developer implementation, 553, 554

    developers, 555

    EcommerceApplication class, 558

    folder creation, 554

    IEcommerceBilling class, 556, 558

    manager, 553

    source code, 556

    startup object, 559

    statement, 552

    TaxCalculation() method, 556

    template code, 555

concrete class, 527, 529

CoreCSharp, 530

CRate() method, 525

default method

    compile error, 587

    concepts, 582

    console window, 586, 589

Interfaces/abstract classes (*cont.*)
    IPolicy Interface, 582
    Main() class, 585
    overridden version, 588
    PolicyApplication.cs, 584
    PolicyManager class, 583, 587
    Program class, 584
    source code, 582
    startup project, 586
    upcasting technique, 588
  definition, 524
  ecommerce application, 523
  EcommerceBilling abstract class, 528
  implementation
    card types, 563
    console window, 567, 571, 578, 581
    CountryOne class, 564
    CountryThree method, 569
    CountryTwo.cs, 576
    CountryTwoDebit class, 580
    CountryTwo methods, 567, 571
    differences, 581
    EcommerceApplication class,
      565, 570, 577
    folder creation, 572
    ICreditCardPayment.cs, 574, 575
    IEcommerceBilling.cs, 573, 574
    IEcommercePayment, 563, 572
    inheritance, 562, 564
    IPaymentMethod, 573, 574, 579
    payment method, 566
    requirement, 567
    source code, 564
    startup class, 578
    template code, 563
  instantiate
    abstract class, 533
    AbstractVATCalculations class, 535
    CalculateTotalPrice() method, 536
    CalculateVAT() method, 536

    concrete class template, 534
    console window, 537, 539
    constructor, 535
    error message, 534
    Main() method, 533
    solution explorer panel, 534
    source code, 538
    VATCalculations class, 534, 535
    VATCalculator class, 537, 539
  manager, 525
  method signatures/return types, 524, 525
  Program.cs file, 531
  project creation, 530
  RegionalRateCalculation()
    method, 525
  RegionBRate() method, 525
  sealed class, 528
  source code, 556
  static member
    AbstractVATCalculations class, 542
    CalculateDiscountedAmount()
      method, 542
    class/method abstract, 545
    class template code, 545
    concrete method, 545
    console window, 543, 550, 551
    CountryOne class, 546, 549
    CountryThree class code, 547
    CountryTwo class code, 546
    discountRate, 542
    EcommerceApplication class,
      548, 550
    Main() method, 539
    manager/instance
      characteristics, 541
    MethodsValue, 540
    VATCalculator class, 543
  static members/methods/
    fields, 590–592
  TaxCalculation() method, 524, 529

VatCalculation() method, 523
Internet of Things (IoT), 16, 854
Interpolation, 630–633, 1041
   const string, 639–644
   spacing, 633, 634
   string, 1042–1044
Interpreted verbatim, 1034
Iterations, 349, 901–909, 921
   break statement
      Boolean section, 307
      execution, 308
      if construct, 307
      maximumNumberOfClaims, 307
   concepts/constructs, 276
   construct options, 275
   continue statement
      console window, 312
      counter value, 309
      differences, 310
      implementation, 310, 311
      maximumNumberOfClaims, 309
      program execution, 313
      scenario, 309
   do (while) loop
      add variables, 315
      break/continue keywords, 313
      break statement, 321–324
      class template, 315
      code analysis, 314
      console window, 319–321
      continue statement, 324–327
      events, 318, 319
      formatting data, 314
      numberOfClaimsBeingMade, 316
      source code, 317, 318
   instructions, 275
   labs, 947–954
   for loop, 811–814
      adding option, 280
      break/continue keywords, 277

break statement, 290–294
claimAmount, 281, 282
claimDate, 282
cleaner code, 289
code construct, 277
code details, 282, 283
code execution, 283
console window, 283, 284, 290
construct, 276
continue statement, 294–298
details, 279
formatting data, 276
initial value, 288
input values, 288
Main() method, 278
maximumNumberOfClaims, 291
principle, 285
Program.cs file, 278
remove option, 286
repairShopID, 280
return keyword, 278
stages, 285, 287
variable declaration/value
   assignment, 286
variables, 279
vehiclePolicyNumber, 281
selection, 275
while loop
   break/continue keywords, 298
   code analysis, 299
   code details, 304
   comparison, 305
   console window, 305, 306
   constructs, 302
   input values, 301
   Main() method, 300
   program details, 299
   return, 298
   user input, 302, 303
   variables, 300

Iterative binary
search, 900–908
IVehicleInsuranceQuote, 974, 975

J, K

JSON, 762–770
JSONSerialisation class, 764
JSON Serialize() method, 764
Just-In-Time (JIT), 5–7

L

Language-Integrated Query (LINQ)
library, 363, 368
Legal C# code, 1042
Length property, 462, 604–605
Linear search
academic or technical
interview, 893
algorithm, 893
application, 894–900
binary search, 893
data structure, 893
parameter method, 898
returned value, 897
List patterns, 1044–1050
Logical operators
AND operator, 247
C# operators
AND, 249
OR, 249
short-circuit evaluation, 249
NOT operator, 248, 249
OR operator, 248
overview, 247
Long Term Support (LTS), 15, 16
Loosely coupled code, 877
Lower case, 620
Lowercase ASCII characters, 1055

M

Main() method, 601, 603, 655, 656, 731,
740, 764, 776, 780, 791, 845, 847,
858, 887, 895, 902, 910, 912, 1035
Matching string, 616, 1046
Member properties, 784–788
Members, 843–845
Memory usage, 597
Methods
access modifier, 377–380
CalculateCommission(), 378
concepts/functions, 375–377
general format, 378
local function, 429
application output, 434
CalculateRepairCostIncludingVAT()
method, 431, 432
CalculateVATAmount, 432
costOfRepairWithVAT, 433
Main() method, 430
message display, 433
separation of concern (SOC), 429
SOLID principles, 429
source code, 430
test-driven development
approach, 429
variables, 433
Main() method, 379
modularization, 375
null parameter checking
adding variables, 438
application output, 440, 441, 443
approaches, 441
ArgumentNullException.
ThrowIfNull() method, 442
DisplayInvoice()
method, 439, 440
holding variables, 441
Main() method, 438
overview, 437

outer method variable, 437
overloading, 425–428
parameter (*see* Parameter methods)
parentheses (), 378
procedures, 376
return type, 377
static local function, 434–437
value method, 381
    application output, 407
    assigning values, 404
    calling statement, 400, 404, 405
    code analysis, 398
    commented assignment, 402
    console window, 406
    data type, 397
    differences, 399
    instructions, 401
    method signature, 397
    MethodsVoid.cs, 399
    ordered steps, 400
    Parse() method, 399
    refactoring, 403
    return statement, 401–403, 405
    return type, 398
    source code, 398
    void methods, 397
void method, 381
    application, 387, 396
    calling, 383
    call method, 395
    class template, 385
    code analysis, 383
    console window, 395
    CoreCSharp, 384
    CurrentValueOfCounter(), 390
    declaration and
        creation, 382, 388
    DisplayAllItemsInTheArray(), 393
    Main() method, 389, 394
    MethodsVoid.cs class, 387

modularization, 397
    program code, 385–387
    Program.cs file, 384
    project creation, 384
    ReadTheAmountBeing
        Claimed(), 392
    ReadTheRepairDate(), 392
    ReadTheRepairShopId(), 390
    ReadTheVehiclePolicyNumber(), 391
    static keyword, 387, 388
    WriteClaimAmountTo
        TheArray(), 392
    WriteRepairDateToTheArray(), 393
    WriteRepairShopIdTo
        TheArray(), 391
    WriteVehiclePolicyNumber
        ToTheArray(), 391
Method signature, 74, 407, 524,
        831, 835–836
Microsoft documentation, 729, 730,
        861, 1055
Microsoft site, 798, 799, 831–834
Mixed parameter
        types, 883–885
Modifiers, 482, 785, 1034
Multicast delegates, 833, 841, 842
    chaining, 841
    invoked, 842, 843
    local level variable, 839
    references, 839
    target method, 840, 841
Multiple catch
        clauses, 705, 706
Multiple exceptions, 704–708
Multiple-line comments
    comment blocks, 89–91
    console output, 91
    Main() method, 89
    program code, 89, 90
myMixedVehicleRegistrations, 609

N

.NET programming language
  compilation process, 5, 6
  cross-platform, 3, 5, 39
  evolution/progression, 2, 3
  framework
    business, 9
    command prompt, 20
    controls, 8, 9
    current releases, 15
    formats, 13, 14
    full/maintenance, 16
    installation, 14
    inversion control, 8
    vs. library, 9
    long term support, 15
    Microsoft site, 14
    runtimes, 13, 20
    SDK version, 16–19
    verification, 19, 20
  libraries, 1
  managed/unmanaged code, 10
  MAUI, 39, 40
  Microsoft website, 40
  numerical library, 8, 9
  runtime environment, 2
  runtime errors, 7
  templates, 84–88
  time and runtime, 6, 7
  Visual Studio (*see* Visual Studio)
  WriteLine() method, 1, 2
Non-nullable, 127, 797
NonSerializable member, 750
Non-string data type, 595
Nullable reference types, 797–801
  code analysis, 130, 137
  console input/assign, 132, 134
  context, 126
  DateTime type, 135–137, 140
  decimal type, 131
  float/double data types, 130
  implicit conversion, 129, 133
  message warning, 127
  methods, 138
  non-nullable type, 127
  Parse() method, 136
  properties, 138
  structs, 139
  ToInt32() method, 129, 130
  variable, 133
  WriteLine() method, 128
Null value, 126, 440, 441,
    797, 800, 801

O

Object-oriented programming (OOP),
    447, 448
Operating system, 3, 14, 19, 854
OurGenericType, 878, 879, 882
OverflowException, 725

P

Parameterless constructor, 803
Parameter methods, 960, 967
  AccumulateClaimAmount()
    method, 420
  actual values, 407
  adding method, 419
  application output, 425
  arguments, 409, 422
  association, 410
  business logic, 408
  calling method, 423
  claimAmount() method, 415
  code analysis, 409, 410
  code declaration, 417
  code execution, 419
  console window, 424, 425
  do while construct, 420

input arguments, 408
invoice details, 423
local variables, 411
Main() method, 422
passing values, 414, 416, 418
ReadTheRepairDate() method, 417
ReadTheRepairShopId() method, 411, 412
repairShopId, 412
static keyword, 412, 414
static variable, 415, 416
test data, 424
totalOfAllClaims, 420
VAT, 419, 421
vehiclePolicyNumber, 414, 415
WriteRepairShopIdToTheArray() method, 413
Parameter types, 880, 883–885
Parsing, *see* Casting/parsing
Policy11, 1053, 1054
Policy class, 842, 843, 858, 865
PolicyDueForRenewal() method, 843
Policy instances, 847
PolicyIsDueForRenewal, 848, 850
Policy list, 848–850
PolicyMatcher class, 873–876
PolicyMatcherGeneric, 878, 882
Policy type factor, 819, 822
policyType field, 800, 801
Policy types, 800, 818, 826, 1044, 1045, 1048
Polymorphism, 426
PremiumGreaterThanTwenty() method, 843, 848, 850
Private properties, 737, 738
Programming labs, 953–959
    arithmetic, 940–942
    classes, 966–974
    coding skills, 923
    C#practice exercises, 923
    data conversion /arithmetic, 936–940
    data types, 928–936
    delegates, 1011–1017
    enumerations, 1002–1010
    events, 1017–1026
    exceptions, 986–989
    file handling, 982–986
    generics, 1026–1031
    interfaces, 974–977
    iteration, 947–953
    methods, 959–966
    selection, 942–947
    serializsation, class, 989–996
    solutions, 923–928
    string handling, 977–982
    structs, 996–1002
    WriteLine(), 924–929
Programming languages, 773
    advantages/disadvantages, 27–29
    facts, 28
Programming muscle, 730–733, 806
Property accessors, 483, 733, 734, 788, 843–845
PropertyInsurance class, 997
Publisher, 853–856

Q

QuoteMethodsClass, 967, 972–973

R

rawStringLiterals11V2, 1041
ReadAllBytes() method, 669–671
ReadAllLines() method, 667–669
ReadAllText() method, 665–667
ReadJSON(), 769, 770
Read() method, 649, 680
Readonly struct, 788
    creation, 789–792
    members, 793–798

Receiver, 853

Reference types, 93, 126–140, 773, 774, 797–801

Registrations, 977

Regular string, 599
    backslash, 599
    code, 600

RenewalMatcher class, 885–887, 889

Replace() method, 619–621

Rethrow keyboard, 716–725

Return type, 377, 383, 398, 831, 835, 836

S

Seek() method, 649, 688, 689

Selection
    labs, 942–943
    output, 944
    solutions, 943–947

Self-documenting, 704, 834

Serializable class, 728, 729, 731–733

Serialization
    access modifier, 749, 750
    attribute, 728–738
    binary data, 727
    byte stream, 727
    code, 746, 754, 755
    and deserialization, 727, 728
    JSON, 762–770
    labs, 989–996
    Main() method, 728
    nonserialized, 728–738
    object, 738–743
    refresh button, 742
    serialized file to a class, 743–749
    XML, 751–763

Serialize() method, 728, 741, 762, 764

SerializeAsync() method, 762, 766

SerializedCustomer, 738

Setters, 730, 737, 753, 754, 790, 791

Single delegate
    local variable, 837
    method signature, 835, 836
    return type, 835, 836
    target method, 836, 837

Single-line comments
    code statement, 80
    console project, 83
    CoreCSharp, 84
    forward slash symbols (//), 79
    framework, 83
    inline comment, 80
    project code, 82
    projects/solutions, 80
    rename option, 81, 82
    solution explorer, 84
    statements, 79

Software developers, 923

Software Development Kit (SDK)
    architecture options, 16–19
    download process, 17, 18
    grant permission screen, 19
    installation, 18

Solution Explorer panel, 62, 102, 1033

Space character, 608

Spacing, 633, 634

Special characters, 597, 599, 1036

Split() method, 607–610

StackTrace, 713–714

StartsWith(), 605–607

Startup program, 748

Static methods, 590–592, 651

StreamReader class, 677–679, 711
    methods, 679, 680
    Read() method, 680–682
    stream, 677, 678
    synchronous/asynchronous processes, 678

Streams, 648, 677, 678

StreamWriter class, 679, 680, 755

StreamWriter WriteLine( )
method, 682–685
String class, 246, 247, 596, 601
String.Format(), 627–637
String handling, 647
application, 595, 596
array, 614
CompareTo(), 611–615
Concat(), 616, 617
Contains(), 621–623
IndexOf() method, 622–624
Insert() method, 624–627
labs, 977–981
length property, 604, 605
literals, 597–601
manipulation, 595–597
$@ or @$, 637–644
Replace(), 619–621
replacement, 597
Split(), 607–610
StartsWith(), 605–607
String.Format(), 627–637
substring, 601–604
ToLower(), 615–617
ToUpper(), 615–617
Trim(), 617, 618
String interpolations,
630–633, 1042–1044
spacing, 633, 634
String materials
application, 1034
double quote, 1036
interpolated values, 1042
text, 1038
String variable, 99, 104, 601, 653–655
Structs, 996–1002
auto default, 1050–1055
C#, 773
C# 8, 793–801
vs. class, 774–776

coding, 773
constructor creation, 783–785
declaration, 775
default constructor, 776–778
encapsulation, 788
instantiation, 780–782
member properties, 784–788
new keyword, 780–782
readonly, 788–792
reference types, 773, 774
user constructor, 779–781
value types, 773, 774
Subscriber, 853–855
Substring() method, 601–604
Switch construct, 217–225, 720
Switch statement, 721, 722
Synchronous processes, 678
SystemException, 698
System.IO namespace, 651, 653, 672
System namespace, 595
System.Text.Json namespace, 762

T

Target method, 836, 837, 840, 841
Ternary operator, *see* Conditional/ternary
operator
Text file, 657
data written, 660
TextMessageNotification()
method, 867
TextReader class, 679, 680
Throw keyword, 699–703, 714–717
Tightly coupled method, 877
ToLower() method, 615–617
ToString() method, 809, 861
totalOfAllClaims, 410, 419, 841
ToUpper() method, 615–617
Trim() method, 617–618
Typist, 596

U

Unhandled exception, 672, 693
User constructor, 779–781
User interface (UI), 4, 38, 40
UseStreamWriterRead() method, 693

V

Value-added tax (VAT), 419, 421, 523
VALUE methods, 959
Value types, 773, 774
Variable, 734, 735, 903, 904
VatCalculation method, 523, 831, 832
VehicleInsuranceQuote class, 974
Verbatim @, 1035, 1036
@ Verbatim, 634–637
Verbatim string, 597, 1034
    backslash, 598
    line, 598
Visual Studio, 734
    community edition, 22, 38
    download page, 21
    drop-down menu, 23
    installation, 22, 23

sign in, 24
verification, 24
web page, 21

W

Warning wave 7, 799, 1055–1057
Web browser, 647
WriteAllBytes(), 661–664
WriteAllLines() method, 660, 661
WriteAllText() method, 658–660
WriteLine() method, 682, 683, 709, 787,
        837, 838, 1040
    labs, 924
    solutions, 924–927
Write() method, 649

X, Y

XmlSerializer, 755, 758
XML serialization, 751–763

Z

Zero exception, 695